KEY TO MA
QUADRO D'UNIONE
MAPA ÍNDICE
TABLEAU D'ASSEMBLAGE
KARTENÜBERSICHT

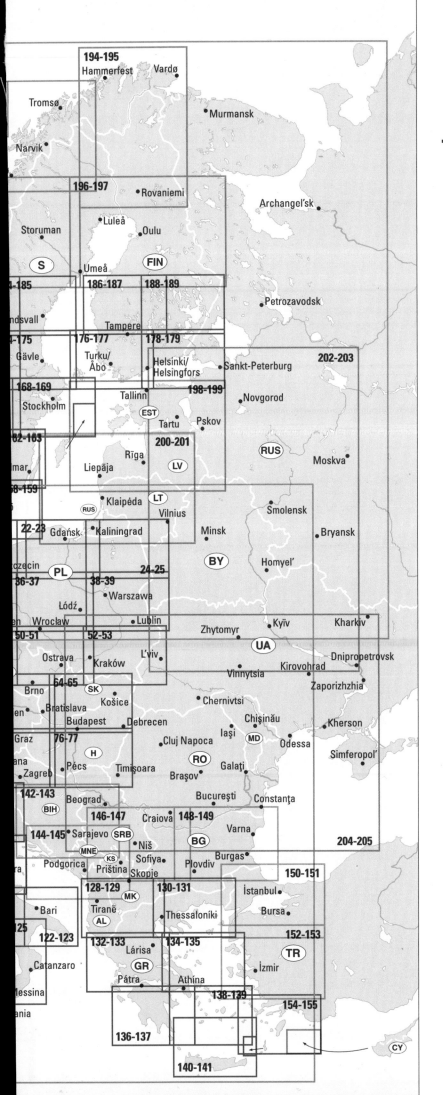

194-195
Hammerfest · Vardø
Tromsø ·
· Murmansk
Narvik ·
196-197
· Rovaniemi
· Archangel'sk
Storuman
· Luleå
· Oulu
S
Umeå ·
FIN
· Petrozavodsk
4-185
186-187
188-189
ndsvall
Tampere ·
4-175
176-177
178-179
202-203
Gävle
Turku/ Åbo
Helsinki/ Helsingfors
· Sankt-Peterburg
168-169
Tallinn ·
198-199
· Novgorod
Stockholm
EST
Tartu · · Pskov
82-183
200-201
· Rīga
RUS
· Moskva
mar
· Liepāja
LV
58-159
Klaipéda ·
LT
· Smolensk
RUS
Vilnius ·
· Bryansk
22-23
· Gdańsk · Kaliningrad
· Minsk
BY
· Homyel'
czecin
PL
24-25
36-37
38-39
· Warszawa
· Łódź
· Wrocław
· Lublin
en
Zhytomyr ·
· Kyïv
· Kharkiv
50-51
52-53
· L'viv
UA
· Dnipropetrovsk
Ostrava ·
· Kraków
Kirovohrad ·
· Vinnytsia
Brno ·
64-65
· Zaporizhzhia
SK
· Košice
· Chernivtsi
· Bratislava
· Chişinău
Budapest · · Debrecen
· Iaşi
MD
· Kherson
Graz
76-77
· Cluj Napoca
· Odessa
H
· Pécs
RO
· Simferopol'
ana
· Timişoara
· Galaţi
Zagreb ·
· Braşov
Brașov
142-143
· Beograd
· Bucureşti
· Constanţa
BIH
146-147
· Craiova
148-149
· Varna
144-145
· Sarajevo
SRB
204-205
MNE
· Niš
BG
a
Podgorica ·
KS
· Sofiya
· Burgas
· Priština
· Plovdiv
150-151
· Skopje
128-129
130-131
· İstanbul
· Bari
MK
· Bursa
· Tiranë
· Thessaloníki
AL
152-153
25
122-123
132-133
134-135
TR
· Lárisa
· İzmir
Catanzaro
GR
Messina
· Pátra
· Athína
138-139
ania
154-155
136-137
CY
140-141

Scale-Scala-Escala
Échelle-Maßstab
1 : 8 000 000

1 cm = 80 km   1 inch = 126.26 miles

0   100   200   300   400   500 km

0   50   100   150   200   250   300 miles

Scale-Scala-Escala
Échelle-Maßstab
1 : 3 000 000

1 cm = 30 km   1 inch = 47.35 miles

0   50   100   150   200 km

0   25   50   75   100 miles

Scale-Scala-Escala
Échelle-Maßstab
1 : 1 500 000
(Is. Canarias, Madeira, Açores 1 : 2 000 000)

1 cm = 15 km   1 inch = 23.67 miles

0   25   50   75   100 km

0   20   40   60 miles

Scale-Scala-Escala
Échelle-Maßstab
1 : 1 000 000

1 cm = 10 km   1 inch = 15.78 miles

0   10   20   30   40   50   60 km

0   5   10   15   20   25   30   35 miles

Scale-Scala-Escala
Échelle-Maßstab
1 : 800 000

1 cm = 8 km   1 inch = 12.63 miles

0   10   20   30   40   50 km

0   5   10   15   20   25   30 miles

LOCAL FORM / FORMA LOCALE / FORMA LOCAL / FORME LOCALE / LOKALFORM		GB	I	E	F	D
A	Österreich	Austria	Austria	Austria	Autriche	Österreich
AL	Shqipëria	Albania	Albania	Albania	Albanie	Albanien
AND	Andorra, Andorre	Andorra	Andorra	Andorra	Andorre	Andorra
B	België, Belgique	Belgium	Belgio	Bélgica	Belgique	Belgien
BG	Bălgarija	Bulgaria	Bulgaria	Bulgaria	Bulgarie	Bulgarien
BIH	Bosna i Hercegovina	Bosnia and Herzegovina	Bosnia ed Erzegovina	Bosnia-Herzegovina	Bosnie-Herzégovine	Bosnien-Herzegowina
BY	Belarus'	Belarus	Bielorussia	Bielorrusia	Biélorussie	Weißrußland
CH	Schweiz, Suisse, Svizzera	Switzerland	Svizzera	Suiza	Suisse	Schweiz
CY	Kýpros, Kıbrıs	Cyprus	Cipro	Chipre	Chypre	Zypern
CZ	Česká Republika	Czech Republic	Repubblica Ceca	República Checa	République Tchèque	Tschechische Republik
D	Deutschland	Germany	Germania	Alemania	Allemagne	Deutschland
DK	Danmark	Denmark	Danimarca	Dinamarca	Danemark	Dänemark
E	España	Spain	Spagna	España	Espagne	Spanien
EST	Eesti	Estonia	Estonia	Estonia	Estonie	Estland
F	France	France	Francia	Francia	France	Frankreich
FIN	Suomi, Finland	Finland	Finlandia	Finlandia	Finlande	Finnland
FL	Fürstentum Liechtenstein	Liechtenstein	Liechtenstein	Liechtenstein	Liechtenstein	Liechtenstein
FR	Føroyar, Færøerne	Faeroe Islands	Isole Fær Øer	Islas Feroe	Îles Féroé	Färöer
GB	Great Britain	Great Britain	Gran Bretagna	Gran Bretaña	Grande-Bretagne	Grossbritannien
GBG	Guernsey, Guernesey	Guernsey	Guernsey	Guernesey	Guernesey	Guernsey
GBJ	Jersey	Jersey	Jersey	Jersey	Jersey	Jersey
GBM	Isle of Man, Mona	Isle of Man	Isola di Man	Isla de Man	Île de Man	Insel Man
GBZ	Gibraltar	Gibraltar	Gibilterra	Gibraltar	Gibraltar	Gibraltar
GR	Hellas	Greece	Grecia	Grecia	Grèce	Griechenland
H	Magyarország	Hungary	Ungheria	Hungría	Hongrie	Ungarn
HR	Hrvatska	Croatia	Croazia	Croacia	Croatie	Kroatien
I	Italia	Italy	Italia	Italia	Italie	Italien
IRL	Ireland	Ireland	Irlanda	Irlanda	Irlande	Irland
IS	Ísland	Iceland	Islanda	Islandia	Islande	Island
KS [a]	Republika e Kosovës	Kosovo	Kosovo	Kosovo	Kosovo	Kosovo
L	Lëtzebuerg, Luxembourg	Luxembourg	Lussemburgo	Luxemburgo	Luxembourg	Luxemburg
LT	Lietuva	Lithuania	Lituania	Lituania	Lituanie	Litauen
LV	Latvija	Latvia	Lettonia	Letonia	Lettonie	Lettland
M	Malta	Malta	Malta	Malta	Malte	Malta
MC	Principauté de Monaco	Monaco	Monaco	Mónaco	Monaco	Monaco
MD	Moldova	Moldova	Moldova	Moldavia	Moldavie	Moldau
MK	Makedonija	Macedonia	Macedonia	Macedonia	Macédoine	Makedonien
MNE	Crna Gora	Montenegro	Montenegro	Montenegro	Montenegro	Montenegro
N	Norge	Norway	Norvegia	Noruega	Norvège	Norwegen
NIR	Northern Ireland	Northern Ireland	Irlanda del Nord	Irlanda del Norte	Irlande du Nord	Nordirland
NL	Nederland	Netherlands	Paesi Bassi	Países Bajos	Pays-Bas	Niederlande
P	Portugal	Portugal	Portogallo	Portugal	Portugal	Portugal
PL	Polska	Poland	Polonia	Polonia	Pologne	Polen
RO	România	Romania	Romania	Rumanía	Roumanie	Rumänien
RSM	San Marino	San Marino	San Marino	San Marino	Saint-Marin	San Marino
RUS	Rossija	Russia	Russia	Rusia	Russie	Rußland
S	Sverige	Sweden	Svezia	Suecia	Suède	Schweden
SK	Slovensko	Slovakia	Slovacchia	Eslovaquia	Slovaquie	Slowakei
SLO	Slovenija	Slovenia	Slovenia	Eslovenia	Slovénie	Slowenien
SRB	Srbija	Serbia	Serbia	Serbia	Serbie	Serbien
TR	Türkiye Cumhuriyeti	Turkey	Turchia	Turquia	Turquie	Türkei
UA	Ukraïna	Ukraine	Ucraina	Ucrania	Ukraine	Ukraine
V	Città del Vaticano	Vatican City	Città del Vaticano	Ciudad del Vaticano	Cité du Vatican	Vatikanstadt

a = unofficial

Contents

Sommario

Sumario

Sommaire

Inhaltsverzeichnis

 Legend   **Legenda**

GB Legend	I Legenda
Toll-free motorway, dual carriageway	Autostrada senza pedaggio a doppia carreggiata
Toll-free motorway, single carriageway	Autostrada senza pedaggio a singola carreggiata
Toll motorway, dual carriageway	Autostrada a pedaggio a doppia carreggiata
Toll motorway, single carriageway	Autostrada a pedaggio a singola carreggiata
Interchange; restricted interchange; service area	Svincolo; svincolo con limitazione; area di servizio
Motorway under construction (opening year)	Autostrada in costruzione (anno di apertura)
Motorway in tunnel	Autostrada in galleria
Number of motorway; european road; national road; regional or local road	Numero di autostrada; itinerario europeo; strada nazionale; strada regionale o locale
National road, dual carriageway	Strada nazionale a doppia carreggiata
National road, single carriageway	Strada nazionale a singola carreggiata
Regional road, dual carriageway	Strada regionale a doppia carreggiata
Regional road, single carriageway	Strada regionale a singola carreggiata
Local road, dual carriageway	Strada locale a doppia carreggiata
Local road, single carriageway	Strada locale a singola carreggiata
Secondary road	Strada secondaria
Road under construction (opening year)	Strada in costruzione (anno di apertura)
Road in tunnel	Strada in galleria
Motorway distances in kilometres (miles in United Kingdom and Ireland)	Distanze in chilometri (miglia nel Regno Unito e Irlanda) sulle autostrade
Road distances in kilometres (miles in United Kingdom and Ireland)	Distanze in chilometri (miglia nel Regno Unito e Irlanda) sulle strade
Gradient 14% and over; gradient 6%–13%	Pendenza maggiore del 14%; pendenza dal 6% al 13%
Panoramic routes	Percorsi panoramici
Pass with height and winter closure	Passo di montagna, quota e periodo di chiusura invernale
Toll point	Barriera di pedaggio
Railway and tunnel	Ferrovia e tunnel ferroviario
Ferry route (with car transportation) and destination	Linea di traghetto (con trasporto auto) e destinazione
Transport of cars by rail	Trasporto auto per ferrovia
National park, natural reserve	Parco nazionale, riserva naturale
International boundaries	Confini internazionali
Disputed boundary; internal boundary	Confine in contestazione; confine interno
International airport	Aeroporto internazionale
Religious building; Castle, fortress	Edificio religioso; Castello, fortezza
Isolated monument	Monumento isolato
Ruins, archaeological area; wall	Rovine, area archeologica; vallo, muraglia
Cave; natural curiosity	Grotta; curiosità naturale
Panoramic view	Punto panoramico
Other curiosities (botanical garden, zoo, amusement park etc.)	Altre curiosità (giardino botanico, zoo, parco divertimenti ecc.)
Town or place of great tourist interest	Città o luogo di grande interesse turistico
Interesting town or place	Città o luogo interessante
Other tourist town or place	Altra città o luogo turistico
Ski resort, mountain tourist resort	Stazione sciistica o di turismo montano
Area covered and page number of more detailed maps in this atlas	Area e numero di pagina delle mappe di dettaglio presenti nell'atlante

	E Leyenda	**F Légende**	**D Zeichenerklärung**
	Autopista de doble vía sin peaje	Autoroute sans péage à chaussées séparées	Zweibahnige Autobahn ohne Gebühr
	Autopista de una vía sin peaje	Autoroute sans péage à chaussée unique	Einbahnige Autobahn ohne Gebühr
	Autopista de doble vía de peaje	Autoroute à péage à chaussées séparées	Zweibahnige Autobahn mit Gebühr
	Autopista de una vía de peaje	Autoroute à péage à chaussée unique	Einbahnige Autobahn mit Gebühr
	Acceso; acceso parcial; estación de servicio	Échangeur; échangeur partiel; aire de service	Anschlussstelle; Autobahnein- und/oder -ausfahrt; Tankstelle
	Autopista en construcción (año de apertura)	Autoroute en construction (année d'ouverture)	Autobahn in Bau (Fertigstellungsjahr)
	Túnel en autopista	Tunnel autoroutier	Autobahntunnel
	Número de autopista; carretera europea; carretera nacional; carretera regional o local	Numéro d'autoroute; route européenne; route nationale; route régionale ou locale	Straßennummer: Autobahn; Europastraße; Nationalstraße; Regional- oder Lokalstraße
	Carretera nacional de doble vía	Route nationale à chaussées séparées	Zweibahnige Nationalstraße
	Carretera nacional de vía unica	Route nationale à chaussée unique	Einbahnige Nationalstraße
	Carretera regional de doble vía	Route régionale à chaussées séparées	Zweibahnige Regionalstraße
	Carretera regional de vía unica	Route régionale à chaussée unique	Einbahnige Regionalstraße
	Carretera local de doble vía	Route locale à chaussées séparées	Zweibahnige Lokalstraße
	Carretera local de vía unica	Route locale à chaussée unique	Einbahnige Lokalstraße
	Carretera secundaria	Route secondaire	Nebenstraße
	Carretera en construcción (año de apertura)	Route en construction (année d'ouverture)	Straße in Bau (Fertigstellungsjahr)
	Túnel en carretera	Tunnel routier	Straßentunnel
63	Distancias en kilómetros (millas en Gran Bretaña e Irlanda) en autopista	Distances autoroutières en kilomètres (miles en Royaume-Uni et Irlande)	Autobahnentfernungen in Kilometern (Meilen in Großbritannien und Irland)
23	Distancias en kilómetros (millas en Gran Bretaña e Irlanda) en carretera	Distances routières en kilomètres (miles en Royaume-Uni et Irlande)	Straßenentfernungen in Kilometern (Meilen in Großbritannien und Irland)
	Pendientes superiores al 14%; pendientes entre 6%–13%	Pente 14% et outre; pente 6%–13%	Steigungen über 14%; Steigungen 6%–13%
	Rutas panorámicas	Routes panoramiques	Aussichtsstraßen
Col d'Izoard 2360 10-6	Puerto de montaña con altura y cierre invernal	Col avec altitude et fermeture en hiver	Pass mit Höhe und Wintersperre
	Peaje	Barrière de péage	Gebührenstelle
	Ferrocarril y túnel	Chemin de fer et tunnel	Eisenbahn und Tunnel
Bastia	Línea marítima (con transporte de coches) y destino	Ligne de navigation (bac pour voitures) et destination	Schiffahrtslinie (Autofähre) und Ziel
	Transporte de coches por ferrocarril	Transport de voitures par chemin de fer	Autoverladung per Bahn
	Parque nacional, reserva natural	Parc national, réserve naturelle	Nationalpark, Naturschutzgebiet
	Límites internacionales	Frontières internationales	Staatsgrenzen
	Frontera en disputa; límite interno	Frontière en contestation; frontière intérieure	Strittige Grenze; Verwaltungsgrenze
	Aeropuerto internacional	Aéroport international	Internationaler Flughafen
	Edificio religioso; Castillo, fortaleza	Édifice religieux; Château, château-fort	Religiösgebäude; Schloss, Festung
	Monumento aislado	Monument isolé	Alleinstehendes Denkmal
	Ruinas, zona arqueológica; muralla	Ruines, site archéologique; vallum, muraille	Ruinen, archäologisches Ausgrabungsgebiet; Wall, Mauer
	Cueva; paraje de interés natural	Grotte; curiosité naturelle	Höhle; Natursehenswürdigkeit
	Vista panorámica	Vue panoramique	Rundblick
	Otras curiosidades (jardín botánico, zoo, parque de atracciones etc.)	Autres curiosités (jardin botanique, zoo, parc d'attractions etc.)	Andere Sehenswürdigkeiten (Botanischer Garten, Zoo, Freizeitpark usw.)
LONDON	Ciudad o lugar de gran interés turístico	Localité ou site de grand intérêt touristique	Ortschaft oder Platz von großem touristischen Interesse
RAVENNA	Ciudad o lugar interesante	Localité ou site remarquable	Sehenswerte Ortschaft oder Platz
MONTPELLIER	Otra ciudad o lugar turístico	Autre localité ou site touristique	Andere touristischen Ortschaft oder Platz
Zermatt	Estación de esquí, localidad turística de montaña	Station de ski, localité touristique de montagne	Skistation, Touristenort in den Bergen
216	Área geográfica cubierta y número de página de otros mapas más detallados en este atlas	Zone couverte et numéro de page pour des cartes plus détaillées dans cet atlas	Abgedecktes Gebiet und Seitennummer von ausführlicheren Karten in diesem Atlas

EUROPEAN ROAD NETWORK   RETE STRADALE EUROPEA
RED EUROPEA DE CARRETERAS   RÉSEAU ROUTIER EUROPÉEN
EUROPÄISCHES STRASSENNETZ

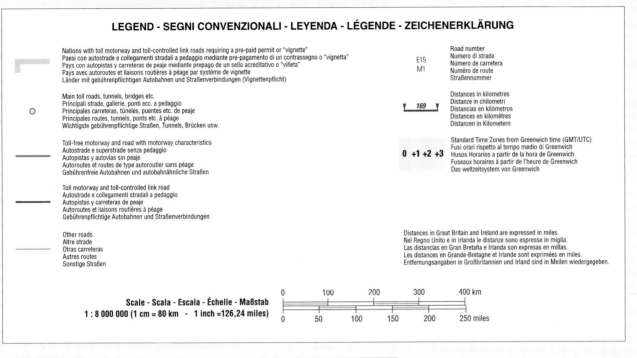

LEGEND - SEGNI CONVENZIONALI - LEYENDA - LÉGENDE - ZEICHENERKLÄRUNG

Nations with toll motorway and toll-controlled link roads requiring a pre-paid permit or "vignette"
Paesi con autostrade e collegamenti stradali a pedaggio mediante pre-pagamento di un contrassegno o "vignetta"
Pays con autopistas y carreteras de peaje mediante prepago de un sello acreditativo o "viñeta"
Pays avec autoroutes et liaisons routières à péage par système de vignette
Länder mit gebührenpflichtigen Autobahnen und Straßenverbindungen (Vignettenpflicht)

Main toll roads, tunnels, bridges etc.
Principali strade, gallerie, ponti ecc. a pedaggio
Principales carreteras, túneles, puentes etc. de peaje
Principales routes, tunnels, ponts etc. à péage
Wichtigste gebührenpflichtige Straßen, Tunnels, Brücken usw.

Toll-free motorway and road with motorway characteristics
Autostrade e superstrade senza pedaggio
Autopistas y autovías sin peaje
Autoroutes et routes de type autoroutier sans péage
Gebührenfreie Autobahnen und autobahnähnliche Straßen

Toll motorway and toll-controlled link road
Autostrade e collegamenti stradali a pedaggio
Autopistas y carreteras de peaje
Autoroutes et liaisons routières à péage
Gebührenpflichtige Autobahnen und Straßenverbindungen

Other roads
Altre strade
Otras carreteras
Autres routes
Sonstige Straßen

Road number
Numero di strada
Número de carretera
Numéro de route
Straßennummer

E15
M1

Distances in kilometres
Distanze in chilometri
Distancias en kilómetros
Distances en kilomètres
Distanzen in Kilometern

▼ 169 ▼

Standard Time Zones from Greenwich time (GMT/UTC)
Fusi orari rispetto al tempo medio di Greenwich
Husos Horarios a partir de la hora de Greenwich
Fuseaux horaires à partir de l'heure de Greenwich
Das weltzeitsystem von Greenwich

0 +1 +2 +3

Distances in Great Britain and Ireland are expressed in miles.
Nel Regno Unito e in Irlanda le distanze sono espresse in miglia.
Las distancias en Gran Bretaña e Irlanda son expresas en millas.
Les distances en Grande-Bretagne et Irlande sont exprimées en miles.
Entfernungsangaben in Großbritannien und Irland sind in Meilen wiedergegeben.

Scale - Scala - Escala - Échelle - Maßstab
1 : 8 000 000 (1 cm = 80 km   -   1 inch =126,24 miles)

| 0 | 100 | 200 | 300 | 400 km |
| 0 | 50 | 100 | 150 | 200 | 250 miles |

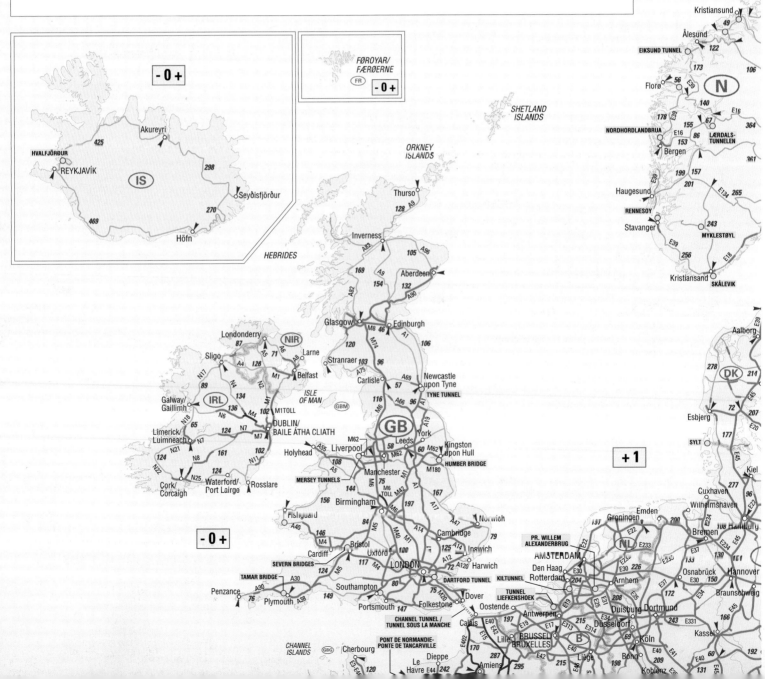

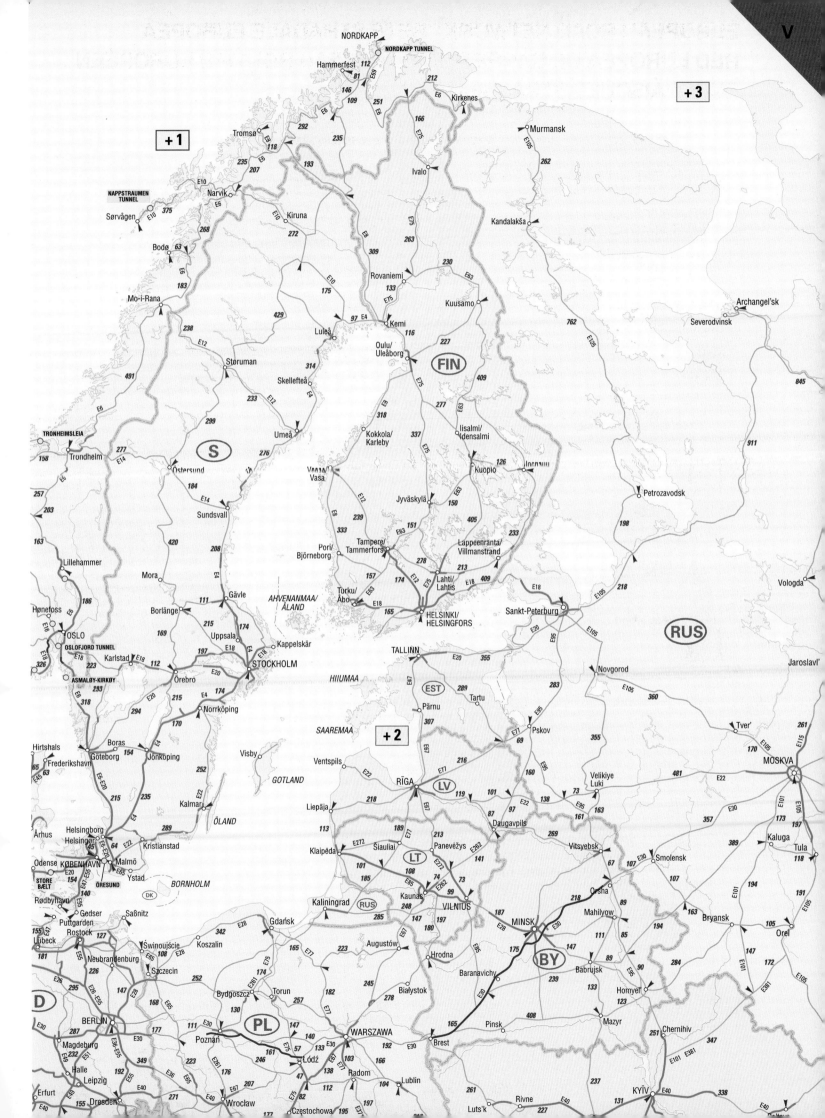

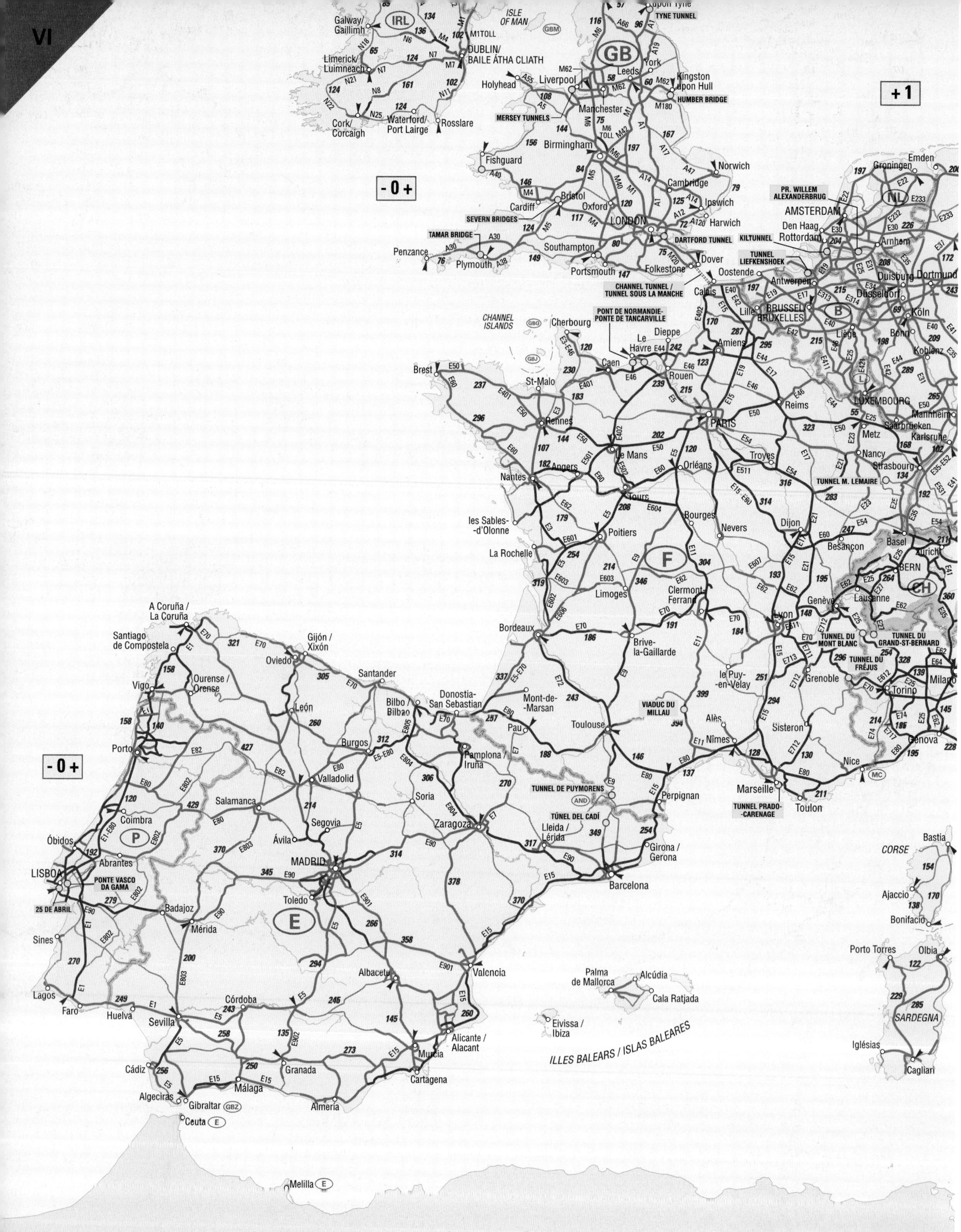

-0+

+1

-0+

ISLE OF MAN (GBM)

IRL

Galway/Gaillimh 134
136 N6 M4 102 M1TOLL
N18 65 N6 124 N7 M7 DUBLIN/BAILE ÁTHA CLIATH
Limerick/Luimneach N21 N7 161 102
N8 N11
124 N25 124 N11
Cork/Corcaigh N22 Waterford/Port Lairge Rosslare

Holyhead A55 Liverpool A5 108 Manchester M1
57 TYNE TUNNEL
116 A66 A1 96
A19 York 60 Kingston upon Hull
GB Leeds 58 M62 M62 HUMBER BRIDGE M180
MERSEY TUNNELS 144 75 M6 TOLL 167 A17
156 Birmingham 197 A14 Norwich
Fishguard A40 84 M5 M40 M1 Cambridge A47 79
146 M4 120 A1 A14 Ipswich
Cardiff Bristol Oxford 125 A12 Harwich
SEVERN BRIDGES 117 M4 A120
TAMAR BRIDGE 124 M5 London
Penzance A30 A30 Southampton 80 M20 DARTFORD TUNNEL
76 Plymouth A38 149 Portsmouth 147 Folkestone Dover
CHANNEL TUNNEL / TUNNEL SOUS LA MANCHE
Calais

CHANNEL ISLANDS (GBG)
Cherbourg PONT DE NORMANDIE-PONTE DE TANCARVILLE
Brest E50 Le Havre Dieppe Amiens
(GBJ) E50 237 120 230 Caen 123 E46 287 170 BRUSSEL/BRUXELLES
E50 E46 239 Rouen E46 295 E19
296 St-Malo 183 E401 215 E5 E15 Reims E40
E50 Rennes 144 E402 202 PARIS E50 323 55 E25
107 E50 E501 Le Mans 120 Troyes E54 Metz
182 Angers E50 E501 Orléans E511 316 TUNNEL M. LEMAIRE
Nantes 179 E62 208 Tours E604 Bourges 314 283 E23
les Sables-d'Olonne E601 Poitiers E11 304 Dijon E21 E60 Besançon
La Rochelle 254 E603 214 346 Clermont-Ferrand E62 193 E25 195
319 E603 Limoges E62 E507 Lyon E62
Bordeaux E70 186 191 184 E511 Genève Lausanne
337 E70 Brive-la-Gaillarde 399 le Puy-en-Velay 251 Grenoble
188 E72 243 VIADUC DU MILLAU 394 Alès 294 Sisteron
Mont-de-Marsan Toulouse 146 Nîmes 128 130 Nice
Pau 257 TUNNEL DE PUYMORENS 137 Marseille 211 Toulon

AMSTERDAM NL
Groningen Emden
197 E22 E233
Den Haag Rotterdam 204 Arnhem Duisburg Dortmund
Antwerpen Düsseldorf Köln
Liège Bonn
LUXEMBOURG Saarbrücken Mannheim
Nancy Karlsruhe
Strasbourg 134
Basel Zürich BERN CH
TUNNEL DU MONT BLANC TUNNEL DU GRAND-ST-BERNARD
TUNNEL DU FRÉJUS Torino Milano
Genova

P
A Coruña/La Coruña
Santiago de Compostela E70 321 E70 Gijón/Xixón
158 Ourense/Orense 305 Santander
Vigo E1 140 Oviedo Bilbo/Bilbao Donostia-San Sebastián
158 Porto E82 260 León E805 Pamplona/Iruña
120 E82 427 Burgos 312 E804 270
Óbidos E80 429 Salamanca Valladolid 306 Soria Zaragoza
192 E802 Coimbra 370 214 E804 E7
LISBOA Abrantes 345 Ávila MADRID 314 E90 317 Lleida/Lérida
PONTE VASCO DA GAMA E90 Toledo 378 349 Girona/Gerona
25 DE ABRIL 279 Badajoz E90 E901 370 Barcelona
Sines 270 Mérida 266 358 E15
E802 200 294 Albacete Valencia
Lagos 249 Córdoba 243 246 145 260 Alicante/Alacant
Faro Huelva Sevilla 258 135 273 E15 Murcia
Cádiz 256 250 Granada Cartagena
Algeciras Málaga Almería
Gibraltar (GBZ)
Ceuta (E)

Melilla (E)

CORSE
Bastia 154
Ajaccio 170 138
Bonifacio
SARDEGNA
Porto Torres Olbia 122
229 285
Iglésias Cagliari

Palma de Mallorca Alcúdia Cala Ratjada
Eivissa/Ibiza
ILLES BALEARS / ISLAS BALEARES

DRIVER INFORMATION - INFORMAZIONI UTILI - DIRECCIONES ÚTILES
INFORMATIONS UTILES - NÜTZLICHE AUSKÜNFTE

		Country	🚗📄	☎	SOS	🛣130	🛣90	🏘50	⛽%	🚗
	A	Österreich	A, C	0043	112	130	100	50	0,5 ‰	✓
	AL	Shqipëria	B, C, D/E	00355	17; 129	-	80	40	0,0 ‰	-
	AND	Andorra, Andorre	A, C	00376	110; 118	-	60-90	40	0,5 ‰	-
	B	België, Belgique	A, C	0032	112	120	90-120	50	0,5 ‰	-
	BG	Bălgarija	A, C, D/E	00359	166; 150	100	80	50	0,5 ‰	-
	BIH	Bosna i Hercegovina	A, C, D/E	00387	92; 94	130	80-100	60	0,31 ‰	-
	BY	Belarus'	B, C, D/E	00375	02; 03	110	90	60	0,49 ‰	-
	CH	Schweiz, Suisse, Svizzera	A, C	0041	112; 144	120	80-100	50	0,5 ‰	-
	CY	Kýpros, Kıbrıs	[b] A, C, E/D	00357	112	100	80	50	0,5 ‰	-
	CZ	Česká Republika	A, C	00420	112	130	90	50	0,0 ‰	[c] ✓
	D	Deutschland	A, C	0049	110	130	100	50	0,5 ‰	✓
	DK	Danmark	A, C	0045	112	130	80	50	0,5 ‰	✓
	E	España	A, C	0034	112	120	90-100	50	0,5 ‰	-
	EST	Eesti	A/B, C	00372	112	110	90	50	0,0 ‰	✓
	F	France	A, C	0033	17; 112	130	90-110	50	0,5 ‰	✓
	FIN	Suomi, Finland	A, C	00358	112	120	80-100	50	0,5 ‰	✓
	FL	Fürstentum Liechtenstein	A, C	00423	112	-	80	50	0,5 ‰	-
	GB	Great Britain and N. Ireland	A, C	0044	999; 112	112 (70 mph)	96 (60 mph)	48 (30 mph)	0,8 ‰	-
	GR	Hellas	A, C	0030	112; 171	120	90-110	50	0,5 ‰	-
	H	Magyarország	A, C	0036	112	130	90-100	50	0,0 ‰	✓
	HR	Hrvatska	A, C	00385	94; 92	130	90-110	50	0,0 ‰	✓
	I	Italia	A, C	0039	112; 118	130	90-110	50	0,5 ‰	✓
	IRL	Ireland	A, C	00353	112	120	100	50	0,8 ‰	-
	IS	Ísland	A, C	00354	112	-	80-90	50	0,5 ‰	✓
	[a] KS	Republika e Kosovës	A, C	00381	112	120	80-100	60	0,5 ‰	✓
	L	Lëtzebuerg, Luxembourg	A, C	00352	112	130	90	50	0,8 ‰	-
	LT	Lietuva	A, C	00370	112	110	90	50	0,4 ‰	✓
	LV	Latvija	A/B, C	00371	112	110	90	50	0,5 ‰	✓
	M	Malta	A, C	00356	112	-	80	50	0,8 ‰	-
	MC	Principauté de Monaco	A, C	00377	17; 9330 1945	-	80	50	0,5 ‰	-
	MD	Moldova	B, C, D	00373	902; 903	-	90	40	0,0 ‰	-
	MK	Makedonija	A, C, D	00389	112	120	80-100	50	0,5 ‰	✓
	MNE	Crna Gora	A, C, D	00382	92; 94	-	80-100	50	0,5 ‰	✓
	N	Norge	A, C	0047	112; 113	90	80	50	0,2 ‰	✓
	NL	Nederland	A, C	0031	112	120	80-100	50	0,5 ‰	-
	P	Portugal	A, C	00351	112	120	90-100	50	0,5 ‰	-
	PL	Polska	A, C	0048	112; 999	130	90-100	50	0,2 ‰	[c] ✓
	RO	România	A/B, C, D/E	0040	112	120	90	50	0,0 ‰	-
	RUS	Rossija	B, C, D/E	007	02	110	90	60	0,0 ‰	✓
	S	Sverige	A, C	0046	112	110	70-90	50	0,2 ‰	✓
	SK	Slovensko	A, C	00421	112	130	90	60	0,0 ‰	[c] ✓
	SLO	Slovenija	A, C	00386	112	130	90-100	50	0,5 ‰	✓
	SRB	Srbija	A, C, D	00381	92; 94	120	80-100	60	0,5 ‰	✓
	TR	Türkiye Cumhuriyeti	A, C, D	0090	112	120	90	50	0,5 ‰	-
	UA	Ukraïna	B, C, D	0038	02; 03	130	90-110	60	0,0 ‰	-

EU   [a] unofficial   [b] Green cards are not accepted in Northern Cyprus   [c] in winter

+1	Euro (€)	0810 101 818	www.austria.info/
+1	Lek (ALL)	4 273 281	www.albaniantourism.com/
+1	Euro (€)	875 702	www.andorra.ad/
+1	Euro (€)	(Bruxelles) 25 138 940	www.visitbelgium.com/
+2	Lev (BGN)	29 335 845	www.bulgariatravel.org/
+1	Konvertibilna Marka (BAM)	33 252 928	www.bhtourism.ba/
+2	Belarus Rouble (BYR)	172 269 900	www.belarus-misc.org/
+1	Schweizer Franken (CHF)	442 881 111	www.myswitzerland.com/
+2	ᵉ Euro (€)	22 691 100	www.cyprus.com/
+1	Koruna Česká (CZK)	221 580 111	www.czechtourism.com/
+1	Euro (€)	(0) 69 751 903	www.germany-tourism.de/
+1	Danske Krone (DKK)	70 222 442	www.visitdenmark.com/
+1	Euro (€)	913 433 500	www.spain.info/
+2	Kroon (EEK)	645 7777	www.visitestonia.com/
+1	Euro (€)	(0)142 967 000	other.franceguide.com/
+2	Euro (€)	(0)106 058 000	www.visitfinland.com/
+1	Schweizer Franken (CHF)	2 396 300	www.tourismus.li/
0	Pound Sterling (GBP)	020 8846 9000	www.visitbritain.com/
+2	Euro (€)	2 108 707 000	www.gnto.gr/
+1	Forint (HUF)	1 438 8080	www.hungary.com/
+1	Kuna (HRK)	1 469 9333	www.croatia.hr/
+1	Euro (€)	06 49711	www.enit.it/
0	Euro (€)	185 023 0330	www.ireland.ie/
0	Íslensk Króna (ISK)	5 355 500	www.visiticeland.com/
+1	Euro (€)	038 222 773	www.visitkosova.org/
+1	Euro (€)	42 82821	www.ont.lu/
+2	Litas (LTL)	52 629 660	www.travel.lt/
+2	Lats (LVL)	22 033 000	www.latviatourism.lv/
+1	Euro (€)	21 237 747	www.visitmalta.com/
+1	Euro (€)	92 166 116	www.visitmonaco.com/
+2	Leu (MDL)	22 227 620	www.turism.md/
+1	Denar (MKD)	fax: (0) 23 075 333	www.exploringmacedonia.com/
+1	Euro (€)	(0)819 797	www.visit-montenegro.com/
+1	Norsk Krone (NOK)	24 144 600	www.visitnorway.com/
+1	Euro (€)	(070) 383 1612	www.holland.com/
0	Euro (€)	848 391 818	www.visitportugal.com/
+1	Złoty (PLN)	022 536 7070	www.poland.travel/
+2	Leu (ROL)	021 314 9957	www.romaniatourism.com/
ᵈ+3	Russian Rouble (RUB)	(495) 980 8440	www.russia-travel.com
+1	Svensk Krona (SEK)	087 891 000	www.visitsweden.com/
+1	Slovenská Koruna (SKK)	48 41 36146	www.slovakiatourism.sk/
+1	Euro (€)	13 064 575	www.slovenia.info/
+1	Srpski Dinar (RSD)	11 3232 586	www.serbia-tourism.org/
+2	Türk Lirası (TRL)	212527 4503	www.tourismturkey.org/
+2	Hrivna (UAH)	(202) 223 2228	www.traveltoukraine.org/

ᵈ Moskva
ᵉ Turkish Lira is the currency in Northern Cyprus

Key to table
Legenda
Leyenda
Légende
Zeichenerklärung

Required driver's papers
Documenti di guida richiesti
Documentos requeridos para conducir
Papiers de conduire requis
Erforderliche Fahrzeugpapiere

A Driver's licence
   Patente di guida
   Carné de conducir
   Permis de conduire
   Führerschein

B International driver's licence
   Patente di guida internazionale
   Carné de conducir internacional
   Permis international de conduire
   Internationaler Führerschein

C Log-book
   Carta di circolazione
   Carné de circulación
   Permis de circulation
   Kraftfahrzeugschein

D Green card
   Carta verde
   Carta verde
   Carte verte
   Grüne Versicherungskarte

E Special insurance
   Assicurazione speciale
   Seguro especial
   Assurance spéciale
   Spezialversicherung

International code
Prefisso internazionale
Prefijo telefónico internacional
Indicatif international
Internationale Vorwahl

Emergency numbers
Numeri d'emergenza
Números de emergencia
Numéros d'urgence
Notrufnummern

Tourist office numbers
Numeri degli uffici turistici
Números de las oficinas de turismo
Numéros des bureaux de tourisme
Touristenämternummern

Tourist office websites
Siti web degli uffici turistici
Sitios web de las oficinas de turismo
Sites web des bureaux de tourisme
Touristenämterwebsites

(km/h)

Speed limit on motorway
Limite di velocità in autostrada
Límite de velocidad en autopista
Limite de vitesse sur l'autoroute
Höchstgeschwindigkeit auf der Autobahn

(km/h)

Speed limit outside the towns
Limite di velocità su strade extraurbane
Límite de velocidad en carreteras extraurbanas
Höchstgeschwindigkeit außerhalb der Städte
Limite de vitesse sur les routes extra-urbaines

(km/h)

Speed limit in towns
Limite di velocità nei centri abitati
Límite de velocidad en ciudades
Limite de vitesse dans les villes
Höchstgeschwindigkeit innerhalb der Städte

Maximum permitted alcohol level
Tasso alcolemico massimo tollerato
Límite alcohólico màximo consentido
Taux d'alcoolémie maximum admis
Höchsterlaubte Blutalkoholgehalt

Lights on during the day
Obbligo luci accese di giorno
Encender los faros durante el dia
Feux allumés obligatoires de jour
Licht-Pflicht am Tag

Time zone from Greenwich
Fuso orario da Greenwich
Huso horario de Greenwich
Fuseaux horaires de Greenwich
Zeitzone gegenüber Greenwich

Local currency
Valuta locale
Divisa local
Devise locale
Lokalwährung

Note: the table is indicative; it is advisable to check the information before leaving.
Nota: la tabella è indicativa; si consiglia di verificare le informazioni prima della partenza.
Nota: el prospecto es indicativo; se aconseja verificar las informaciones antes de partir.
Nota: le tableau est indicatif; il est conseillé de vérifier les renseignements avant de partir.
Notiz: die Informationen sind als Hinweis gedacht; es empfiehlt sich,
die Auskünfte vor der Abfahrt zu überprüfen.

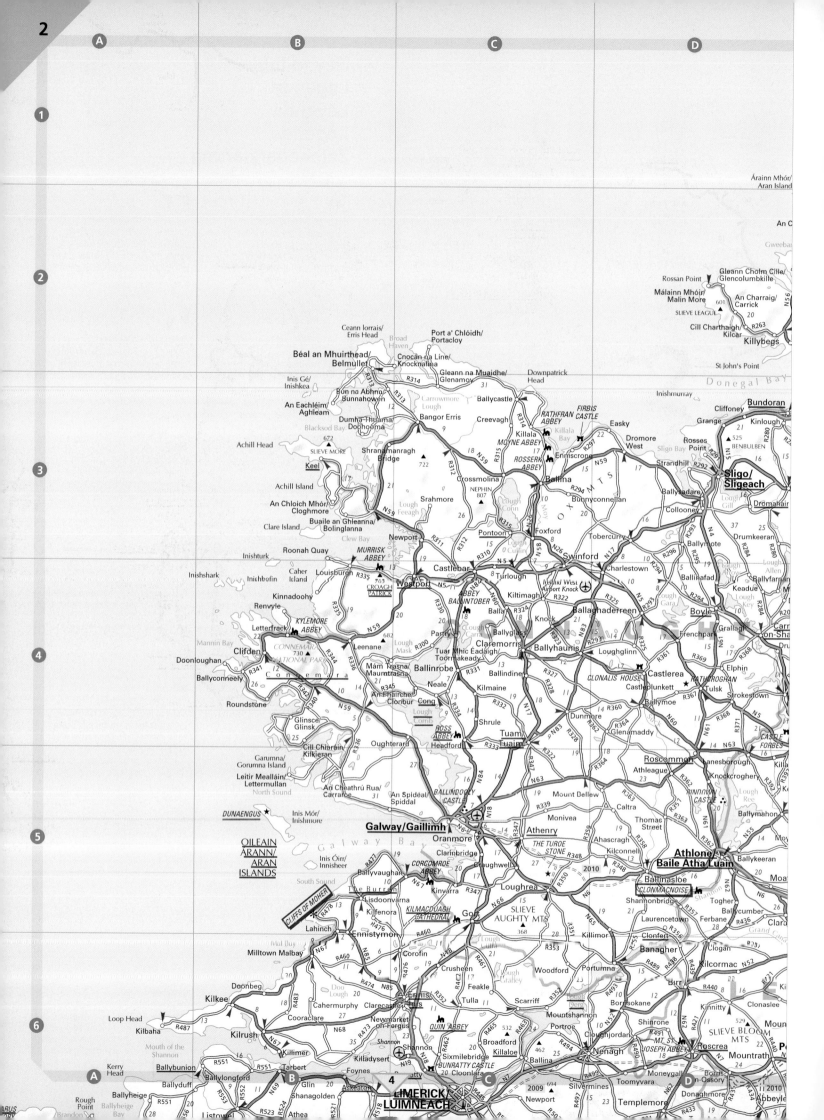

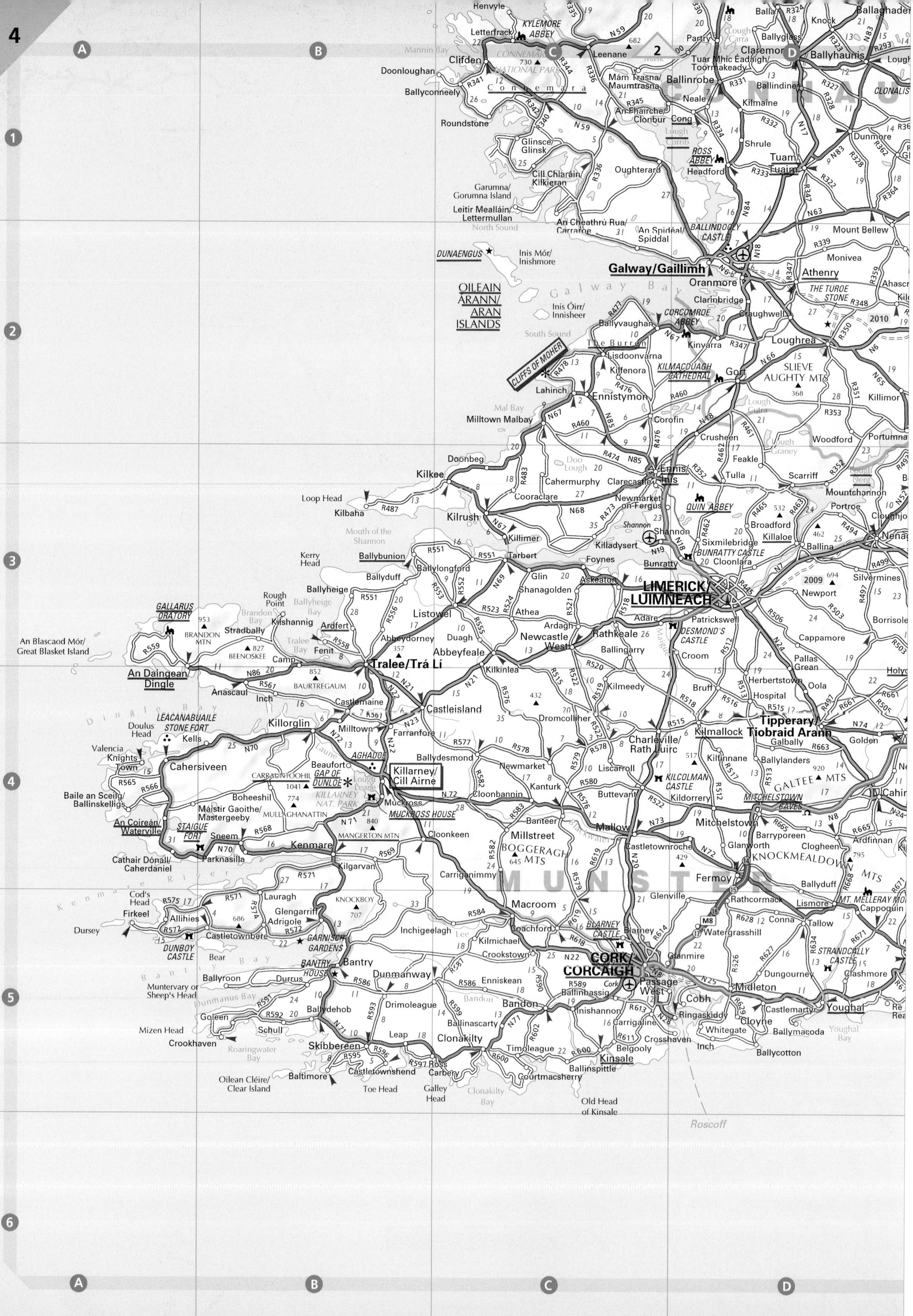

A B C D

1

2

3

4

5

6

CONNACHT

MUNSTER

Henvyle
KYLEMORE ABBEY
Letterfrack
Clifden
Leenane
Party
Claremor
Ballyhaunis
Lough
Knock
Ballyglass
CONNEMARA NATIONAL PARK
Doonloughan
Ballyconneely
Mám Trasna/Maumtrasna
An Fhairche/Clonbur
Ballinrobe
Tuar Mhic Éadaigh/Toormakeady
Ballindine
Neale
Kilmaine
Roundstone
N59
Glinsce/Glinsk
Cong
Lough Corrib
Shrule
ROSS ABBEY
Tuam/Tuaim
Dunmore
Cill Chiaráin/Kilkieran
Oughterard
Headford
Garumna/Gorumna Island
Leitir Meallain/Lettermullan
North Sound
An Cheathrú Rua/Carraroe
An Spidéal/Spiddal
BALLINDOOLY CASTLE
Mount Bellew
Monivea
DUNAENGUS
Inis Mór/Inishmore
Galway/Gaillimh
Oranmore
Athenry
OILEÁIN ARANN/ARAN ISLANDS
Inis Oírr/Innisheer
Galway Bay
Clarinbridge
THE TUROE STONE
Ahascr
South Sound
Ballyvaughan
CORCOMROE ABBEY
Craughwell
Kinvarra
Loughrea
THE BURREN
Lisdoonvarna
KILMACDUAGH CATHEDRAL
Gort
SLIEVE AUGHTY MTS
Killimor
CLIFFS OF MOHER
Kilfenora
Corofin
Woodford
Portumna
Lahinch
Ennistymon
Crusheen
Feakle
Lough Graney
Mal Bay
Milltown Malbay
Scarriff
Mountshannon
Doonbeg
Doo Lough
Cahermurphy
Clarecastle
Ennis/Inis
Tulla
Killaloe
Nenag
Kilkee
Cooraclare
Newmarket-on-Fergus
QUIN ABBEY
Ballina
Loop Head
Kilbaha
Kilrush
Killimer
Killadysert
Shannon
Sixmilebridge
Broadford
Cloughjo
Mouth of the Shannon
Foynes
Bunratty
BUNRATTY CASTLE
Cloonlara
Ballybunion
Ballylongford
Tarbert
Silvermines
Kerry Head
Ballyduff
Glin
Shanagolden
Askeaton
LIMERICK/LUIMNEACH
Newport
Borrisole
Ballyheige
Listowel
Athea
Adare
Patrickswell
Cappamore
GALLARUS ORATORY
Rough Point
BRANDON MTN
Stradbally
Kilshannig
Ardfert
Abbeydorney
Newcastle West
Rathkeale
DESMOND'S CASTLE
Croom
Pallas Green
An Blascaod Mór/Great Blasket Island
BEENOSKEE
Camp
Fenit
Tralee Bay
Abbeyfeale
Ballingarry
Herbertstown
Oola
An Daingean/Dingle
Anascaul
Inch
BAURTREGAUM
Tralee/Trá Lí
Kilmeedy
Bruff
Hospital
LEACANABUAILE STONE FORT
Castlemaine
Kilinlea
Kilmallock
Tipperary/Tiobraid Árann
Golden
Doulus Head
Killorglin
Milltown
Castleisland
Dromcolliher
Charleville/Rath Luirc
Galbally
GALTEE MTS
Valencia Knights Town
Farranfore
Kildorrery
Cahir
An Coireán/Waterville
Cahersiveen
GAP OF DUNLOE
AGHADOE
Killarney/Cill Airne
Newmarket
Liscarroll
KILCOLMAN CASTLE
MITCHELSTOWN CAVES
Baile an Sceilg/Ballinskelligs
Boheeshil
Máistir Gaoithe/Mastergeeby
KILLARNEY NAT. PARK
Muckross
MUCKROSS HOUSE
Kanturk
Buttevant
Mitchelstown
STAIGUE FORT
MULLAGHANATTIN
MANGERTON MTN
Cloonkeen
Millstreet
Mallow
Glanworth
KNOCKMEALDOWN MTS
An Coireán
Sneem
Kenmare
Kilgarvan
Carriganimmy
BOGGERAGH MTS
Castletownroche
Fermoy
Cathair Dónall/Caherdaniel
Parknasilla
Macroom
Glenville
Rathcormack
Lismore
MT MELLERAY MO
Cappoquin
Cod's Head
Firkeel
Lauragh
KNOCKBOY
Ballydesmond
Inchigeelagh
Coachford
BLARNEY CASTLE
Blarney
Watergrasshill
Conna
Tallow
Dursey
Allihies
Glengarriff
Adrigole
GARNISH GARDENS
Kilmichael
Crookstown
CORK/CORCAIGH
Glanmire
STRANDCALLY CASTLE
DUNBOY CASTLE
Castletownbere
Bear Island
BANTRY HOUSE
Bantry
Dunmanway
Enniskean
Bandon
Passage West
Midleton
Clashmore
Muntervary or Sheep's Head
Ballyroon
Durrus
Dunmanus Bay
Ballydehob
Drimoleague
Ballinascarty
Inishannon
Ringaskiddy
Cobh
Cloyne
Ballymacoda
Mizen Head
Crookhaven
Goleen
Schull
Leap
Clonakilty
Timoleague
Carrigaline
Crosshaven
Inch
Whitegate
Youghal
Roaringwater Bay
Skibbereen
Ross Carbery
Belgooly
Kinsale
Ballycotton
Oileán Cléire/Clear Island
Baltimore
Castletownshend
Toe Head
Galley Head
Ballinspittle
Courtmacsherry
Old Head of Kinsale
Youghal Bay

Roscoff

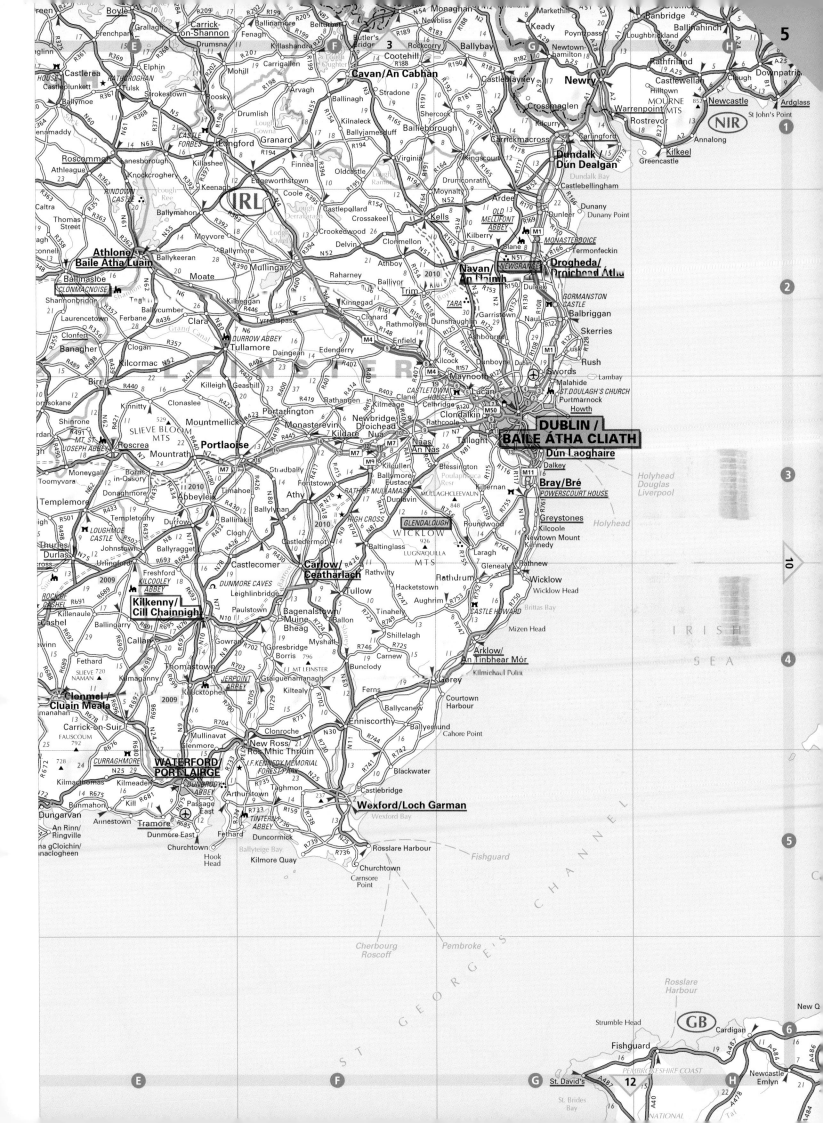

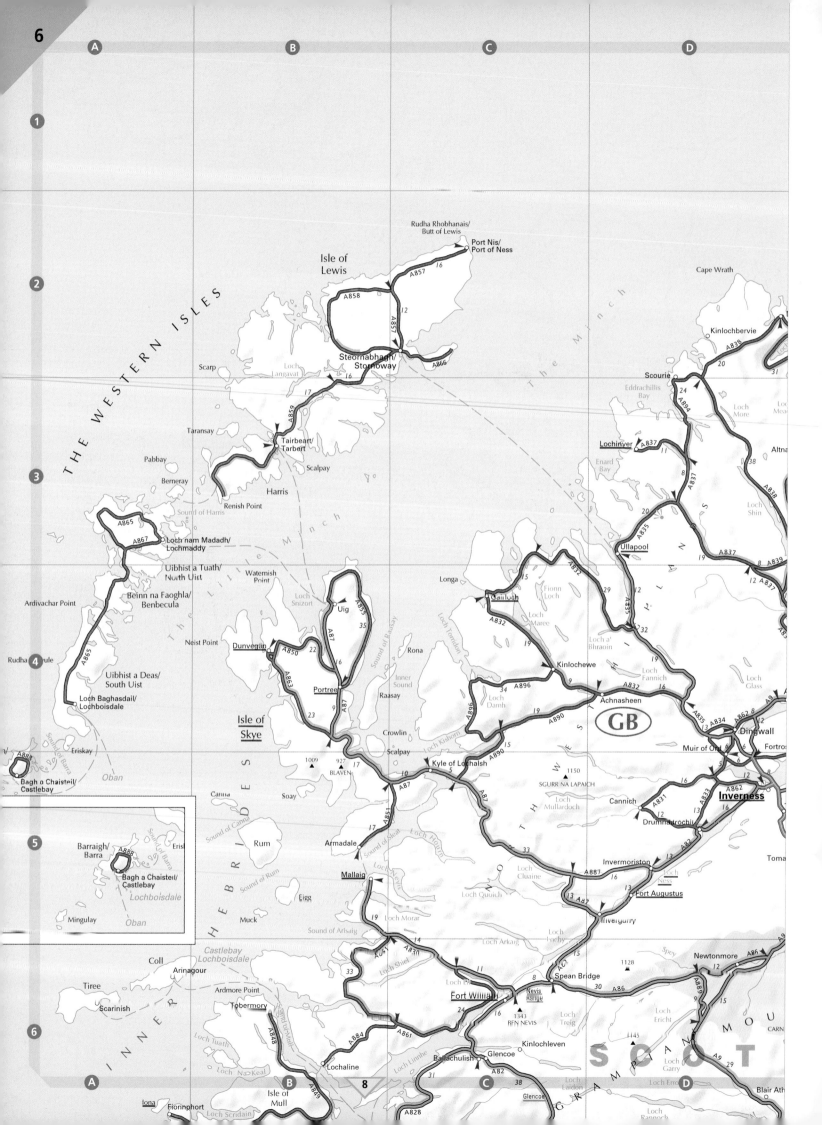

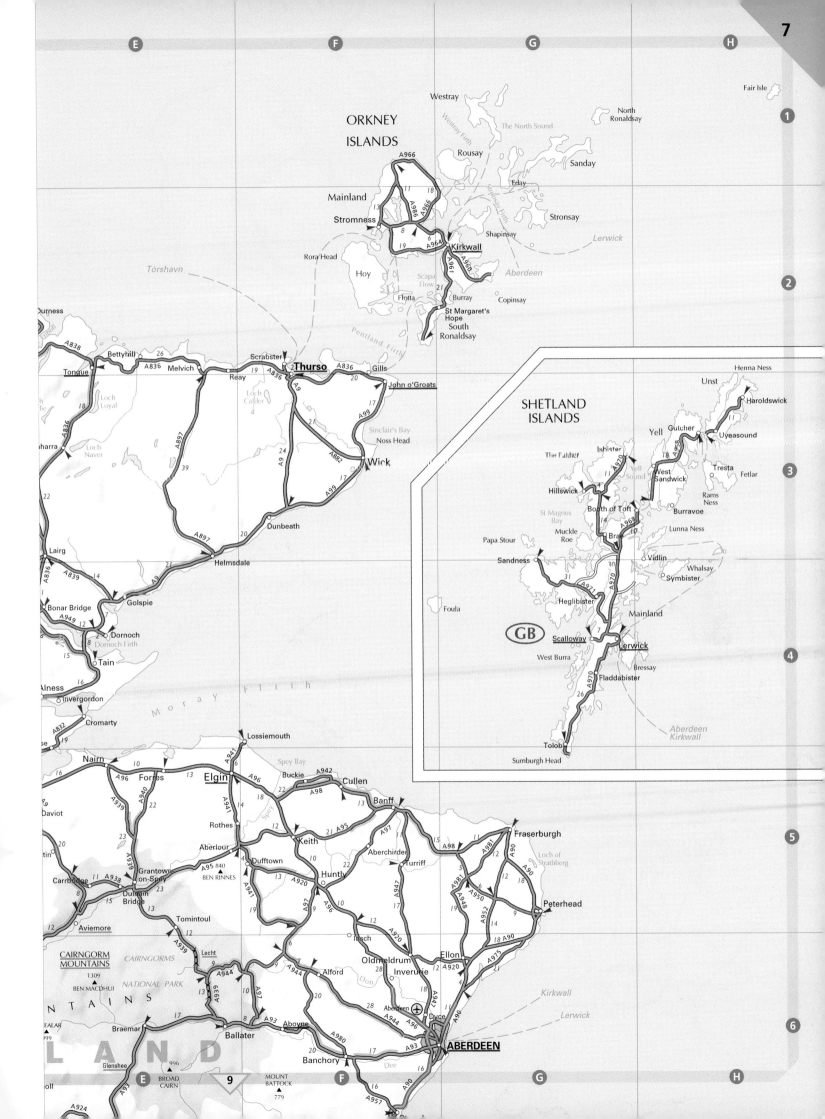

ORKNEY ISLANDS

Fair Isle

Westray

North Ronaldsay

The North Sound

Rousay

Sanday

Eday

A966

Mainland

Stronsay

Westray Firth

11 18

A966

A966

13

A986

Stromness

Shapinsay

Stronsay Firth

Lerwick

8

19

6

A964

Kirkwall

Aberdeen

A961 A960

Rora Head

Hoy

Scapa Flow

21

Burray

Copinsay

Flotta

St Margaret's Hope

South Ronaldsay

Pentland Firth

Tórshavn

SHETLAND ISLANDS

Herma Ness

Unst

Haroldswick

Yell Gutcher

11

Uyeasound

A858

A838

Durness

Bettyhill

26

Melvich

A836

Reay

19

A836

Scrabster

Thurso

A836 Gills

20

John o'Groats

The Faither

Ishister

A970

West Sandwick

18

Tresta

Fetlar

Tongue

Hillswick

Yell Sound

Rams Ness

Loch Loyal

Loch Calder

A9

A99

17

St Magnus Bay

Booth of Toft

4

A968

Burravoe

Lunna Ness

18

A836

nharra

Loch Naver

A897

24

Sinclair's Bay

Noss Head

14

Muckle Roe

10

Brae

39

A9

Papa Stour

16

Vidlin

Whalsay

22

A882

Wick

Sandness

A971

30

A970

Symbister

Lairg

A897

20

Dunbeath

Foula

Heglibister

31

Mainland

A836 A839

Helmsdale

A897

21

GB

Scalloway

7

Lerwick

1

Bonar Bridge

Golspie

A949

12

7

West Burra

A970

Bressay

Dornoch

2

Fladdabister

15

8 Dornoch Firth

Tain

26

Alness

16

West Burra

Aberdeen Kirkwall

Invergordon

A832

Cromarty

Tolob

9

19

Moray Firth

Sumburgh Head

Lossiemouth

A941

Spey Bay

Nairn

10

Forres

13

Elgin

A96

Buckie

A942

Cullen

A96

6

A940

18

22

A98

13

Banff

16

A96

A939

22

A941

14

Spey

12

21 A95

A97

Fraserburgh

Daviot

Rothes

A981

11

A98

A940

23

Aberlour

12

Keith

Aberchirder

15

5

A981

Carrbridge

11 A938

Grantown-on-Spey

A95 840

4

Dufftown

10

Huntly

22

Turriff

A947

5

A948

A90

Loch of Strathberg

12

18

8

Dulnain Bridge

23

BEN RINNES

13

A920

19

A950

Peterhead

15

13

A941

9

A96

12

17

A952

14

12

Aviemore

12

A939

Tomintoul

19

6

Insch

A920

Ellon

18 A90

CAIRNGORM MOUNTAINS

CAIRNGORMS

Lecht

9

Oldmeldrum

A975

28

1309

NATIONAL PARK

A944

A97

10

Alford

Inverurie

12 A920

BEN MACDHUI

13 A939

20

Don

A943

4

NTAINS

17

8 A93

28

Aberdeen

Kirkwall

Braemar

Ballater

Aboyne

A980

ABERDEEN

Lerwick

L A N D

996

20

17

A93

Banchory

Dee

16

A90

Glenshee

9

BROAD CAIRN

MOUNT BATTOCK

16

A924

779

A957

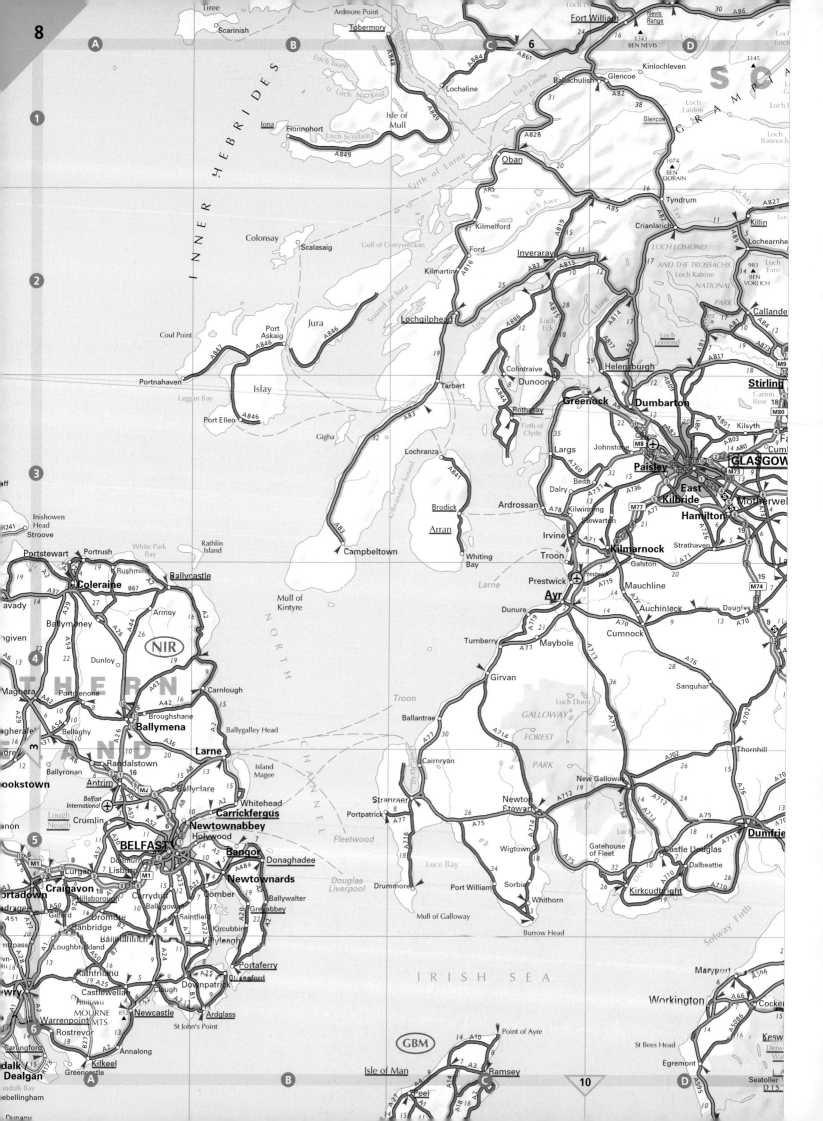

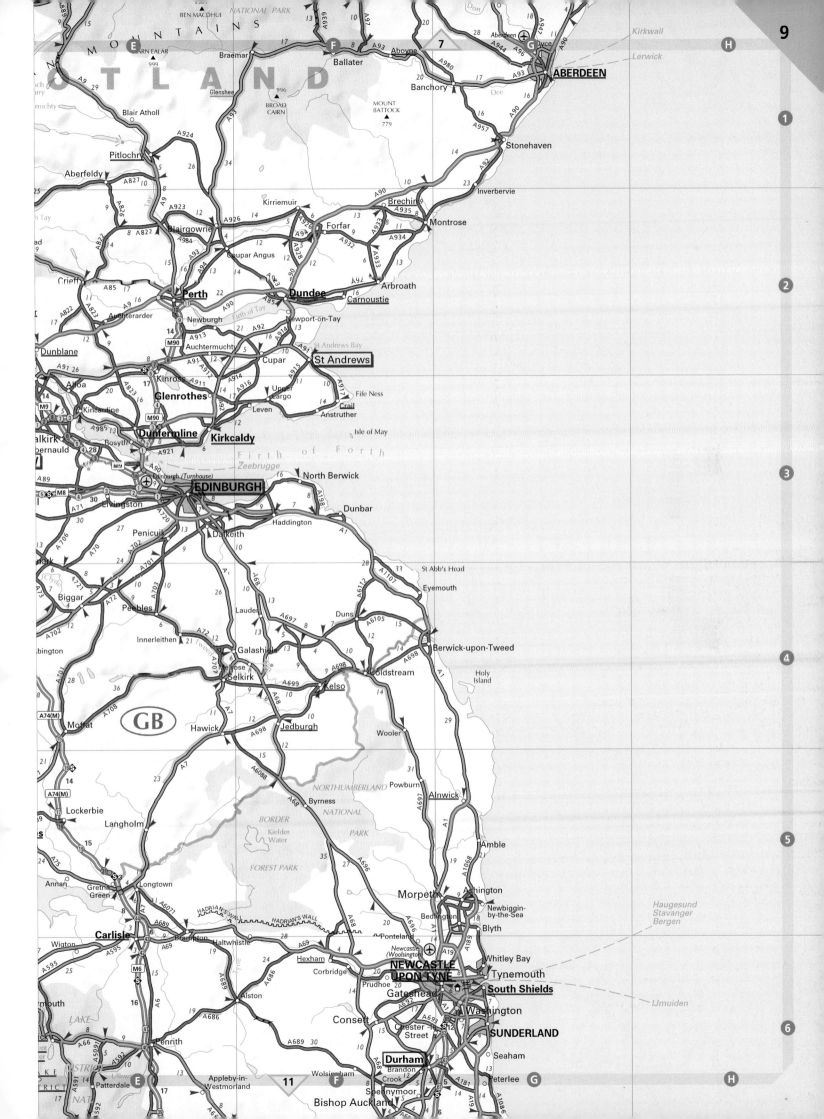

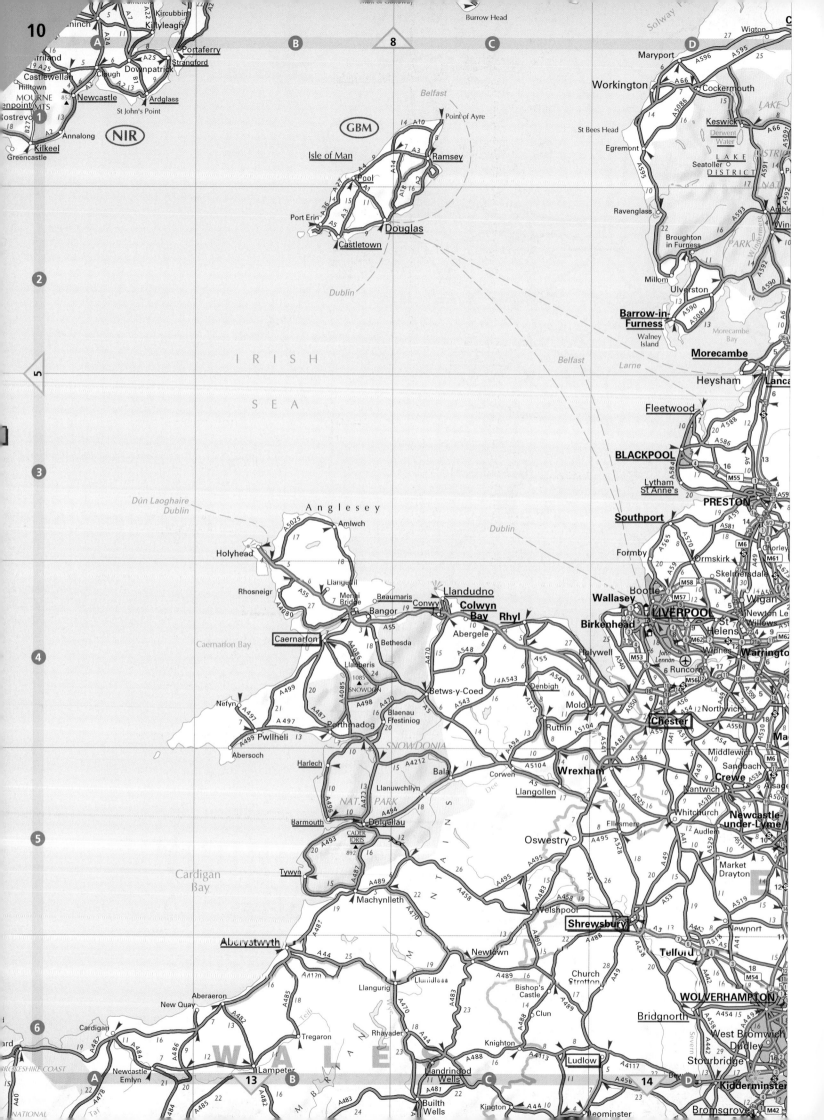

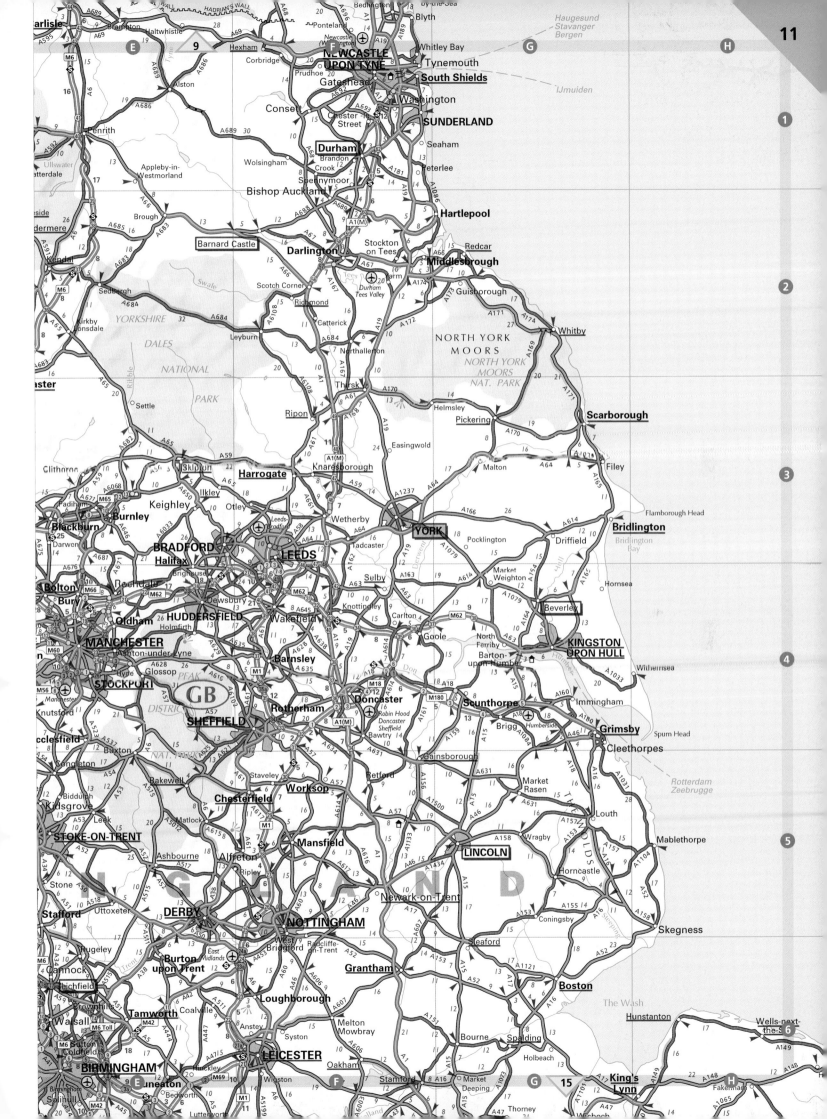

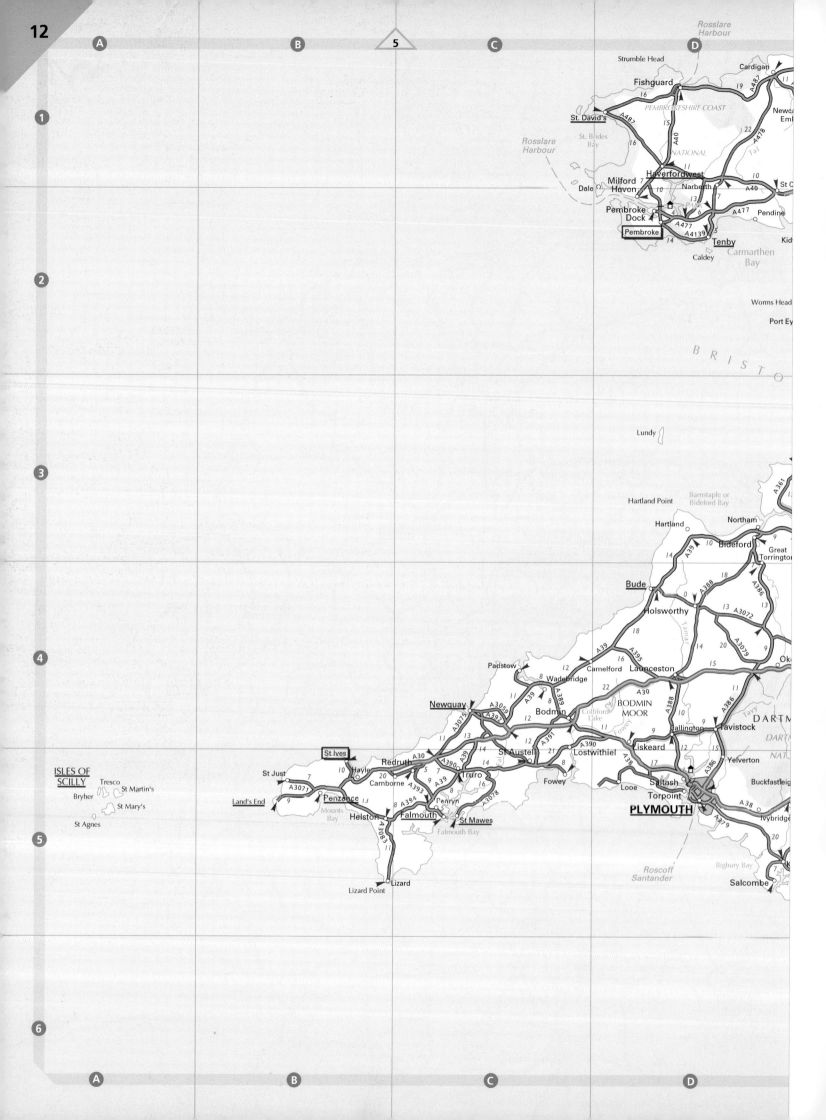

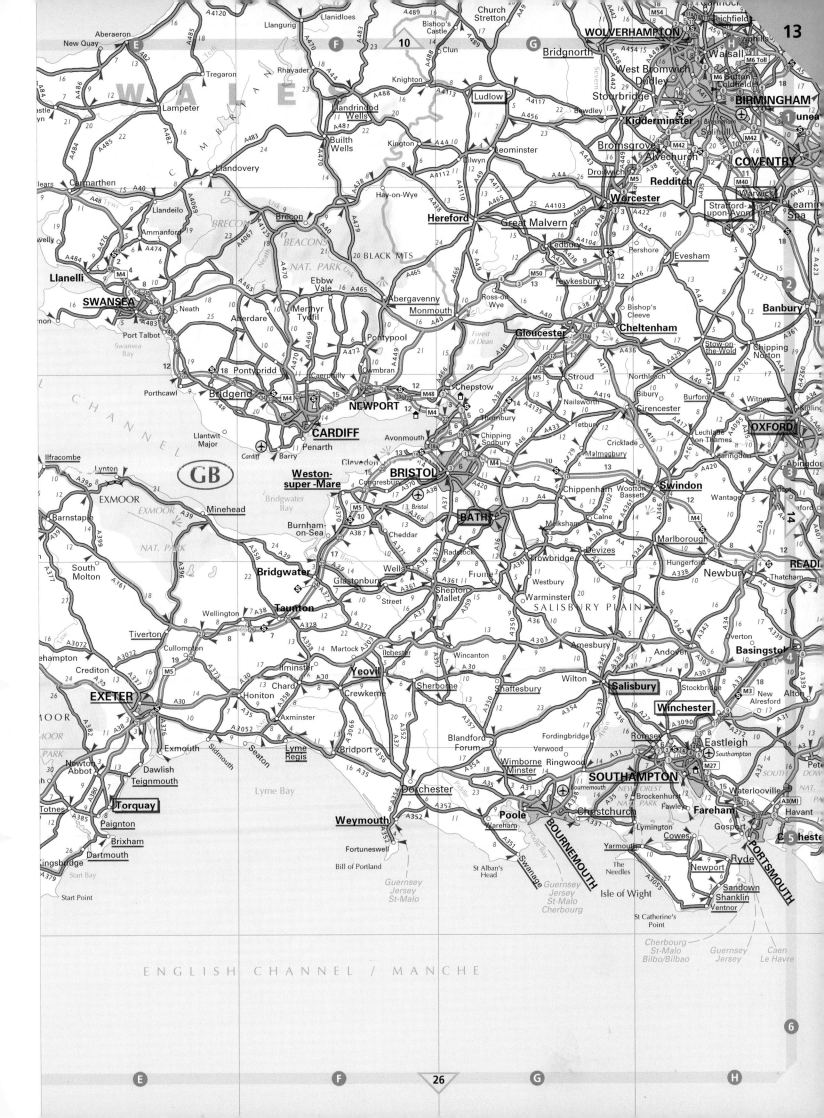

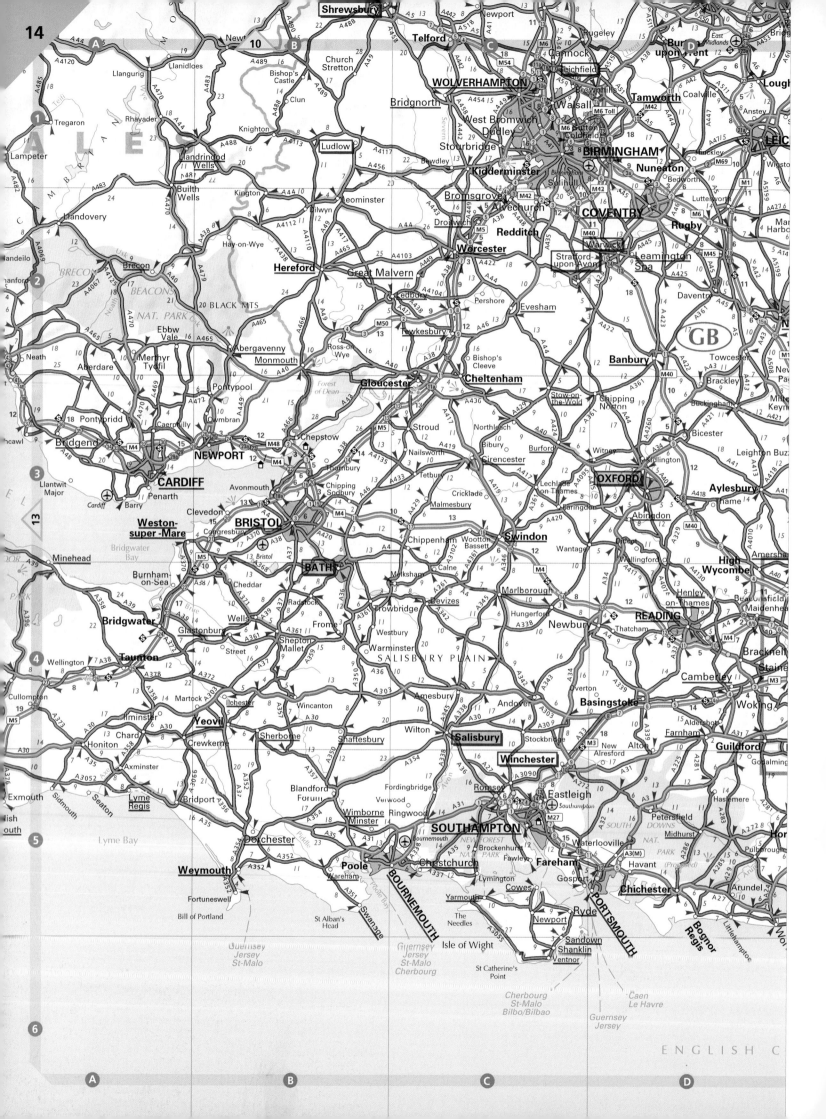

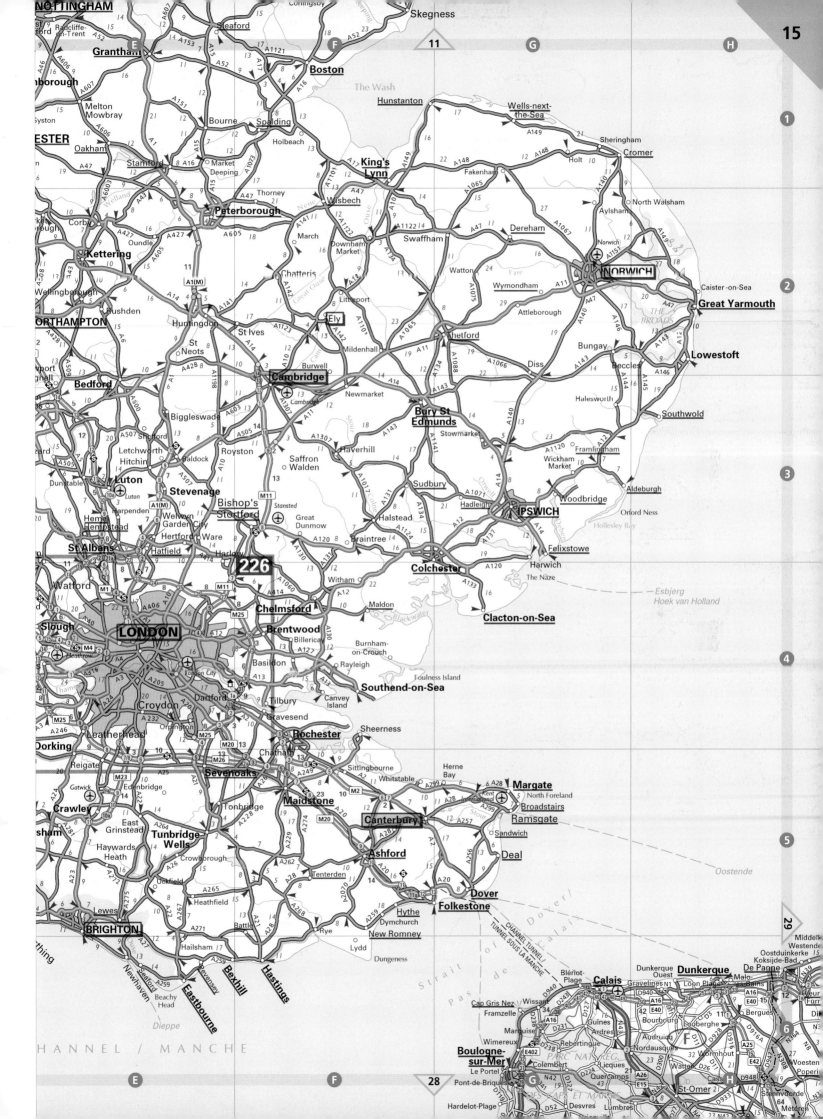

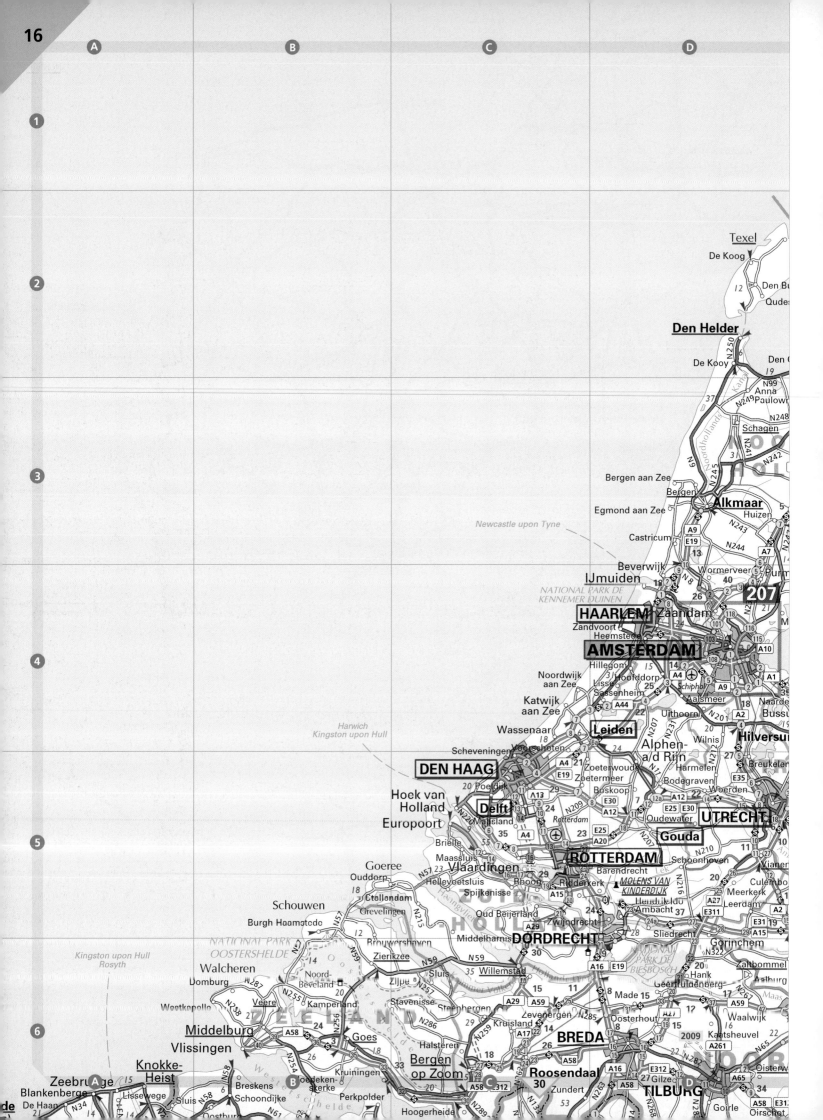

A   B   C   D

1

2

Texel
De Koog

12   Den Bu

Qudes

Den Helder

De Kooy   Den C

19

N250

N99

Anna
N249   Paulow

37   N248

Schagen

3

Bergen aan Zee

Bergen

Egmond aan Zee

Newcastle upon Tyne

Castricum

Alkmaar

Huizen

N243

A9   N244   A7

E19   13

Beverwijk   Wormerveer   Purm

IJmuiden   N8   40

NATIONAL PARK DE
KENNEMER DUINEN   26   2   **207**

HAARLEM   Zaandam   118   21

Zandvoort   24

Heemstede   101   116

AMSTERDAM   103   115   A10

4

Hillegom   15   14   A4   108   A1

Noordwijk   Hoofddorp   Schiphol   A9

aan Zee   Lisse   25

Sassenheim   S   Aalsmeer   Naarde

Katwijk   18   Bussu

aan Zee   A44   22   Uithoorn   N201   A2

Wassenaar   N207   N231   20

Voorschoten   **Leiden**   Alphen   Wilnis   N212   27   **Hilversu**

Scheveningen   Voorschoten   a/d Rijn   Harmelen   Breukele

18   A4   21   Zoeterwoude   Bodegraven   E35

DEN HAAG   E19   Zoetermeer   Boskoop   Woerden

20 Poeldijk   A13   24   A12   22   7

Hoek van   Maasland   N209   E30   A12   E25   E30   Oudewater   **UTRECHT**

Holland   **Delft**   10   Rotterdam   E25   A20   **Gouda**

Europoort   N22   44   23   N207   18

Brielle   5   A4   23   Schoonhoven   N210   11

Maassluis   12   7   5   8   **ROTTERDAM**   Barendrecht   20

5

Goeree   Vlaardingen   29   Ridderkerk   *MOLENS VAN*   N216   Meerkerk   25

Ouddorp   Hellevoetsluis   Rhoon   Ridderkerk   *KINDERDIJK*   N27   Leerdam   E31   19

18   Spijkenisse   A15   Hendrik Ido   37   E311   A2

Schouwen   Stellendam   Oud Beijerland   Ambacht   A15

Grevelingen   N213   A29   Zwijndrecht   24a   Sliedrecht   Gorinchem   N322

Burgh Haamstede   Middelharnis   **DORDRECHT**   28   *NATIONAL*   Zaltbommel

NATIONAL PARK   12   30   9   A16   E19   *PARK DE*   Hank   20   Aalburg

OOSTERSHELDE   Brouwershaven   N59   Willemstad   35   *BIESBOSCH*   Geertruidenberg   17   N261

Zierikzee   N59   N59   15   11   Made   15   12

Walcheren   14   Zijpe   N257   A29   A59   Oosterhout   A59

Domburg   Noord-   20   Stavenisse   Steenbergen   Zevenbergen   N285   Waalwijk   16

Westkapelle   Beveland   N286   29   Kruisland   N259   A17   2009   N65

Veere   N256   Halsteren   A16   **BREDA**   Kaatsheuvel   22

6

Middelburg   A58   24   Goes   18   **Bergen**   21   26   A261

Vlissingen   40   36   3   **op Zoom**   A58   27 Gilze   A65

N255   Kamperland   33   Roosendaal   E312   A58   E31

Knokke-   35   A58   E312   Zundert   N263   A58

Zeebrugge   15   Boedeken-   32   A58   30   **TILBURG**

Blankenberge   Breskens   kerke   N13

De Haan   N34   Schoondijke   Hoogerheide   Goirle

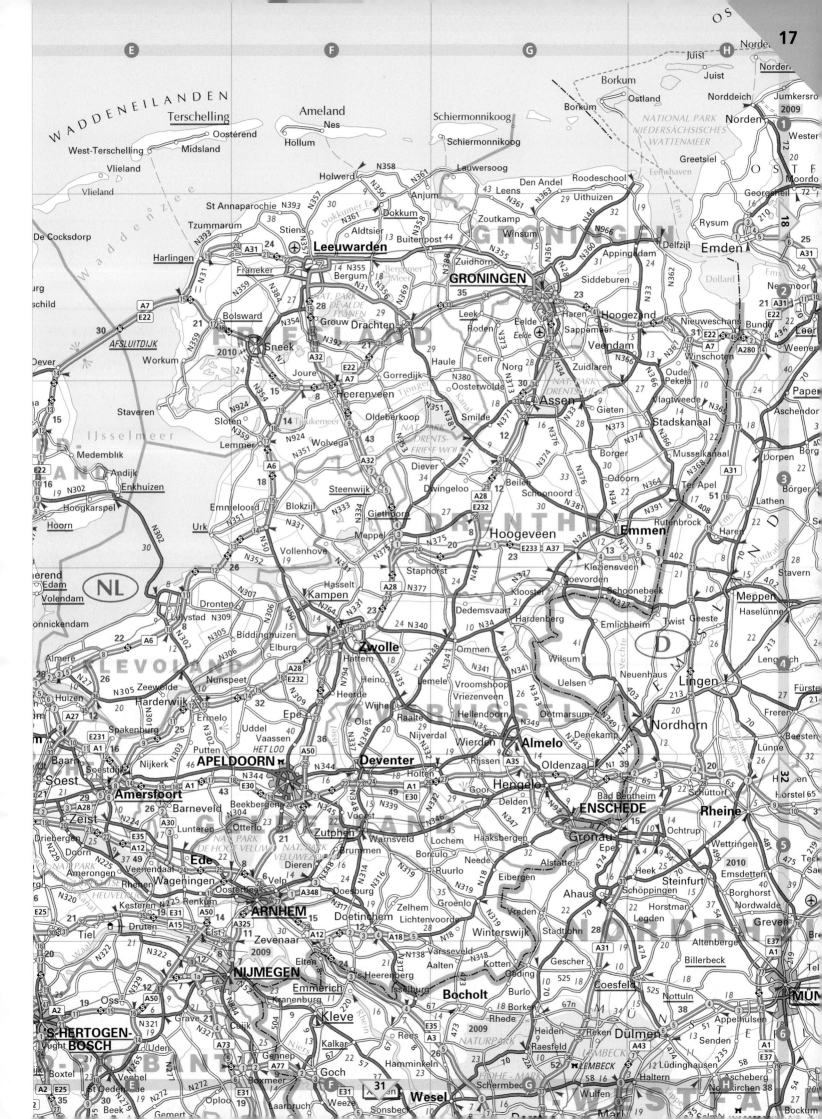

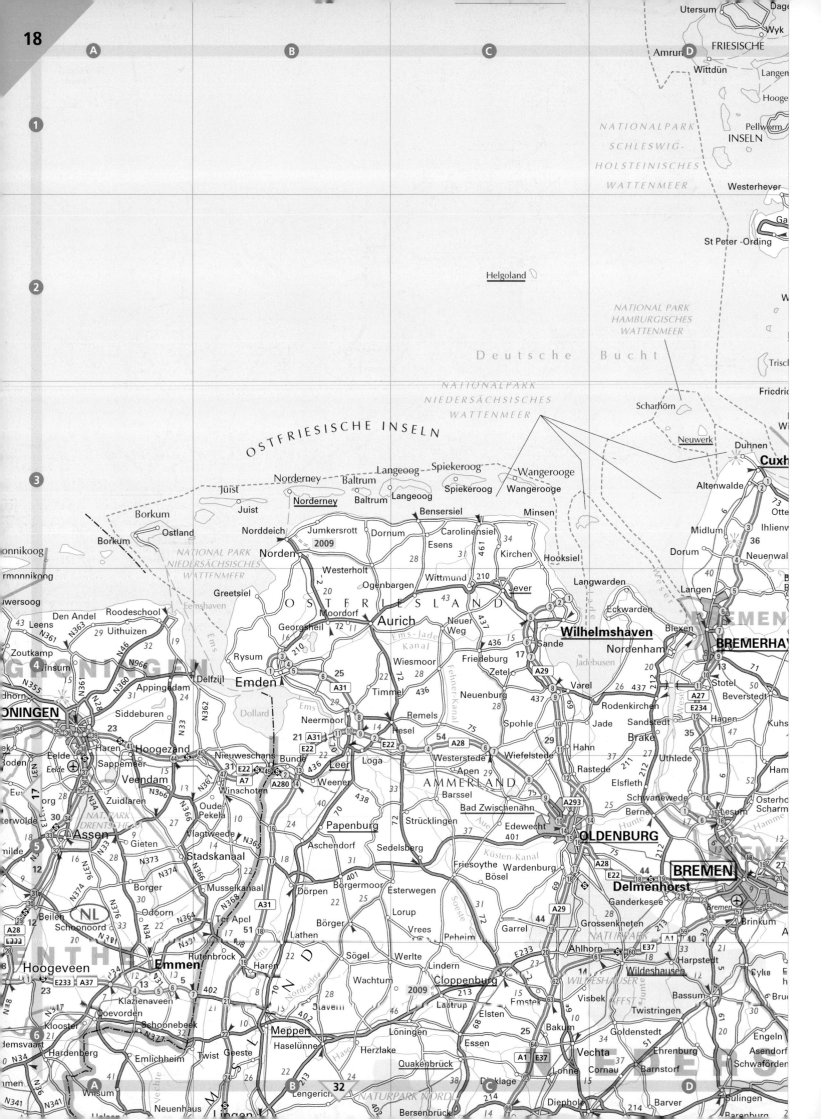

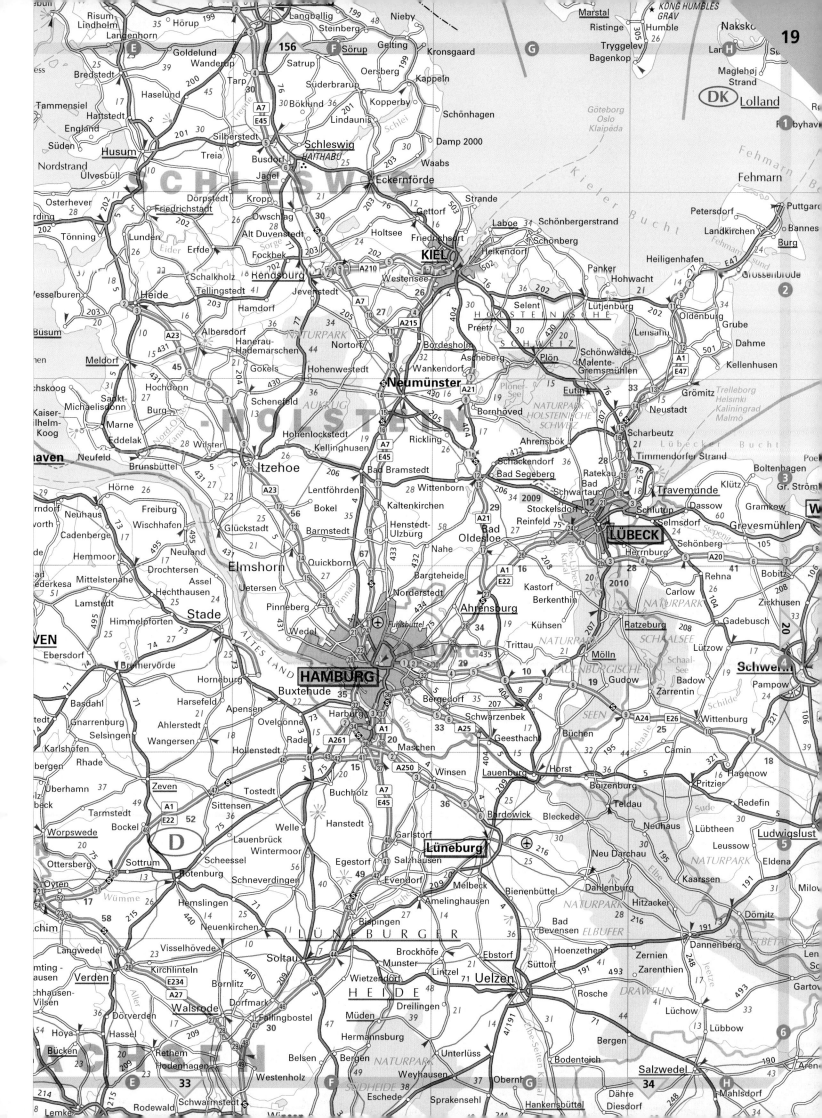

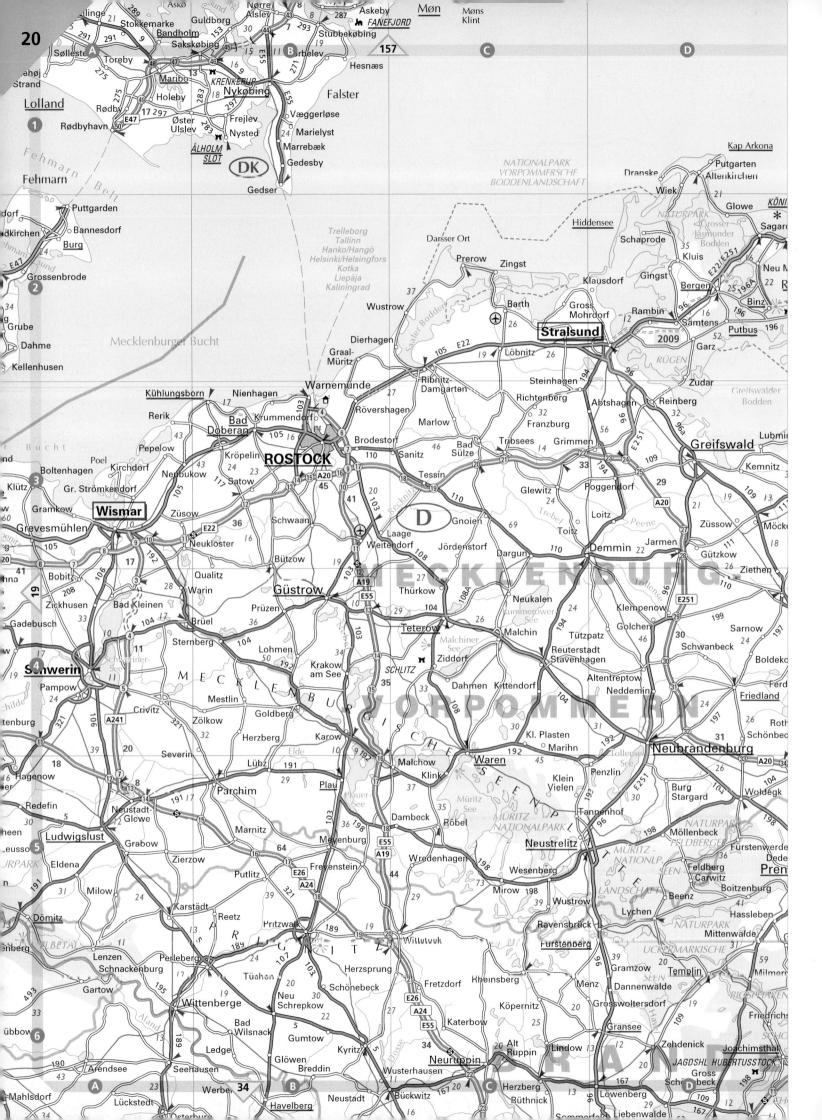

A
B
C
D
1
2
3
4
5
6
NADMORSKI PARK KRAJOBRAZOWY
Białogóra
Karwia
Jastrzębia
Władysławowo
Wierzchucino
Krokowa
Swarzewo
Puck
Celbowo
SŁOWIŃSKI PARK NARODOWY
Łeba
Ulinia
Choczewo
Jezioro Gardno
Jezioro Łebsko
Kluki
Steknica
Żelazna
Mierzyno
Wielka Piaśnica
Rowy
Wicko
Smołdzino
Zamostne
Bolszewo
Reda
Ustka
Objazda
Gąbino
Główczyce
Wejherowo
Rumia
Żelkowo
Nowa Wieś Lęborska
Godętowo
Jarosławiec
Jezioro Wicko
Lęborsk
TRÓJMIEJSKI PARK KRAJOBRAZOWY
Wicie
Lubuczewo
Damno
Postomino
Słupsk
Osowo Lęborskie
Drozdowo
Kanin
Mianowice
Koleczkowo
Darłówko
Wieprza
Rędzikowo
Łebno
Chwaszczyno
Staniewice
Lupawa
Oskowo
Dąbki
Darłowo
Warszkowo
Dębnica Kaszubska
Czarna Dąbrówka
Miszewo
Przodkowo
Rębiechowo
Bukowo Morskie
Sławno
KASZUBSKI
Kartuzy
2009
Budowo
Sierakowice
Żukowo
Łazy
Malechowo
Korzybie
Słupia
PARK KRAJOBRAZOWY
Rokity
PARK
Kolbudy Górne
Mielno
Ostrowiec
Barcino
Suchorze
DOLINA SŁUPI
Unichowo
Jasień
Klukowa Huta
arbinowo
Jezioro Jamno
Niemica
Kępice
Kołczygłowy
Sulęczyno
Egiertowo
Krąg
Pomysk Wielki
KRAJOBRAZOWY
329
Sianów
Laski
Borzysław
WIEŻYCA
Będzino
Koszalin
Mzdowo
Lubno
Bytów
Nowa Karczma
Trzepowo
Jacinki
Tuchomie
Półczno
Korne
Biesiekierz
Mostowo
Polanów
Udorpie
Kościerzyna
Godziszewo
Radew
Dretyń
POMORSK
Lipusz
Skarszewy
Niedalino
Rosnowo
Studzienice
Białogard
Piaszczyna
Wdzydze
Starogard Gdański
Głodowa
Miastko
Dziemiany
Lipnica
Byszyno
Weldkowo
Drzewiany
WDZYDZKI PARK KRAJDZRAZ.
202
Jezioro Wdzydze
Bobolice
Upiłka
ZABORSKI PARK KRAJOBRAZOWY
Zblewo
Wiele
dwilcze
Tychowo
Biały Bór
Koczała
Zielona Chocina
Bytonia
Borzechowo
orze
Nw. Ludzicko
Stare Dębno
Wierzchowo
Brusy
Osowo Leśne
Lubichowo
Parsęta
Grzmiąca
Brzezie
Konarzyny
236
Swornegacie
Męcikal
BORY
Czarna Woda
Ocypel
Kołacz
Przechlewo
PARK NAR. BORY TUCHOLSKIE
Czersk
Wda
Połczyn Zdrój
Gwda Wielka
Rzeczenica
Brda
Rytel
Osieczna
Barwice
Charzykowy
Luby
DRAWSKI PARK KRAJOBRAZOWY
Szczecinek
Legbąd
Śliwice
TUCHOLSKIE
TUCHOLSKI PARK KRAJOBRAZOWY
MORSKIE
Czarne
Człuchów
Chojnice
TUCHOLSKI PARK KRAJOBR.
Ostrowice
Jelenino
Silno
Tleń
Osie
Lotyń
Barkowo
Zamarte
Tuchola
Zarańsko
Cieszyno
Łubowo
Jezioro Pile
Borne Sulinowo
Czaplinek
Debrzno
Kamień Krajeński
Lniano
Drawsko Pomorskie
Złocieniec
Okonek
Ledyczek
Pamiętowo
Ostrowite
Machliny
Podgaje
Lipka
Gostycyn
Bisław
Laskowice
Jezioro Lubie
Radawnica
Lutowo
PL
Iłowiec
Jastrowie
Sępólno Krajeńskie
Obodowo
Sośnica
Górzna
Mąkowarsko
Tuszyny
Świecie
Byszki
Złotów
Sypniewo
KUJA
Mirosławiec
Kłębowiec
Szwecja
Więcbork
Łowinek
DOLNEJ
Chełmno
Koronowo
Pruszcz
Zbrachlin
Kalisz Pomorski
Bronikowo
Płytnica
Rudna
Wierzchucin Królewski
Wałcz
Krajenka
Gwda
Dobrcz
Łobżenica
Mrocza
Tryszczyn
E261
Unisław
Tuczno
Skórka
Wysoka
Gostomia
Ślesin
Wybcz
Piła
Kosztowo
Sadki
Rusinowo
Szydłowo
Wyrzysk
Nakło nad Notecią
Ostromecko
DRAWIEŃSKI PARK NARODOWY
Śmiłowo
Paterek
BYDGOSZCZ
Człopa
Studzienki
Trzcianka
Noteć
Smogulec
Rynarzewo
Brzoza
Solec Kujawski
Ujście
Szamocin
Radęcin
Kcynia
Szubin
Stare Osieczno
Margonin
Siedlisko
Chodzież
Łabiszyn
36
Sarbia
Ołańcz
Drawa
Krzyż Wlkp.
Wieleń
Czarnków
Budzyń
Pawłowo Żońskie
Morakowo
Murczyn
Gniewkowo

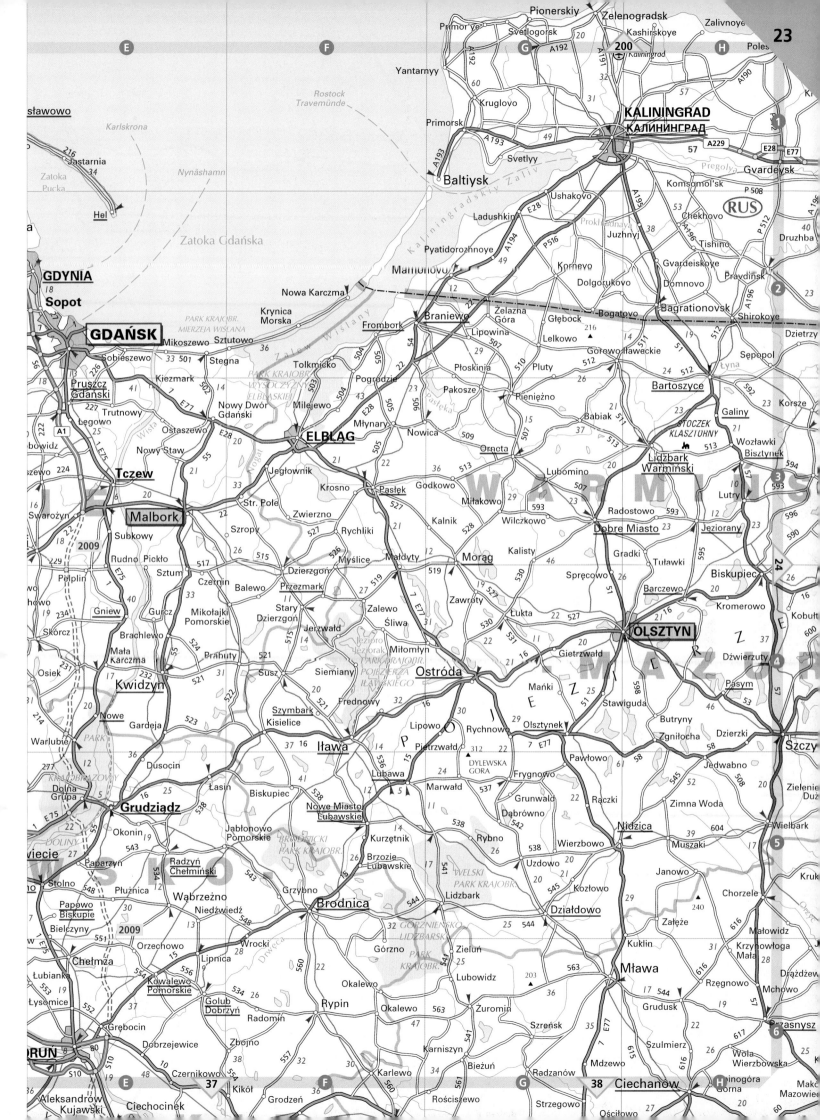

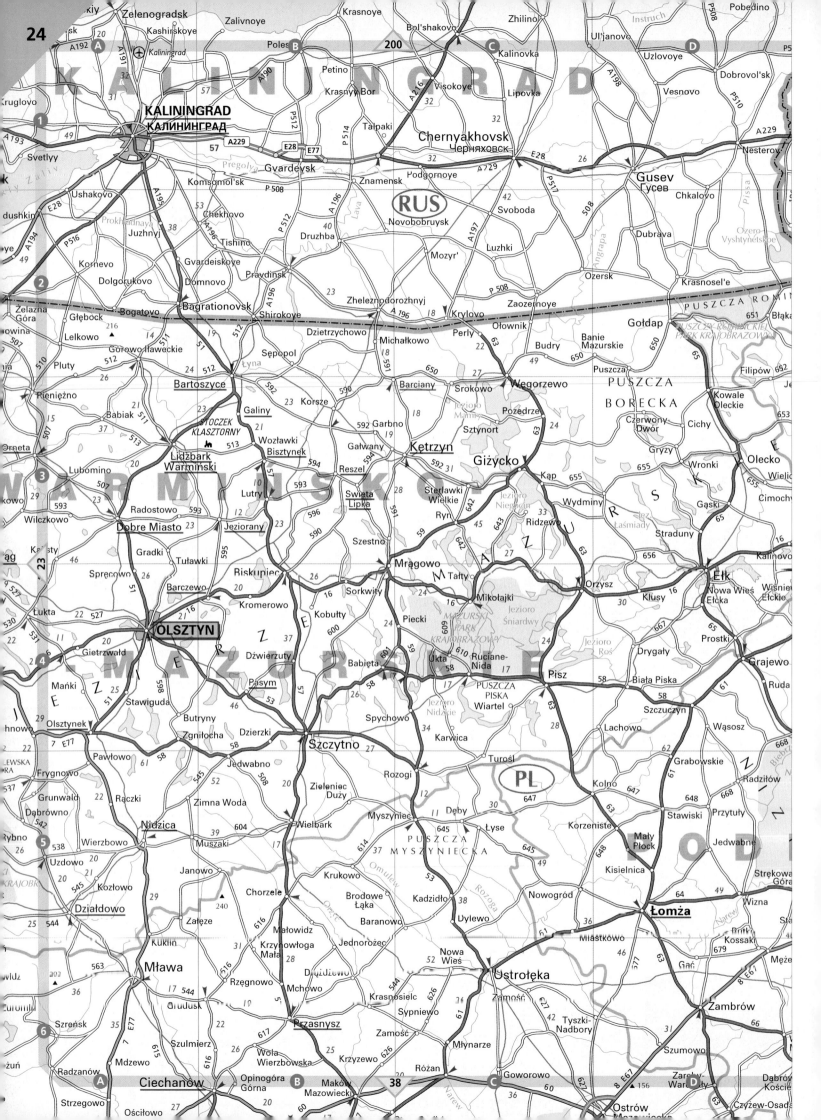

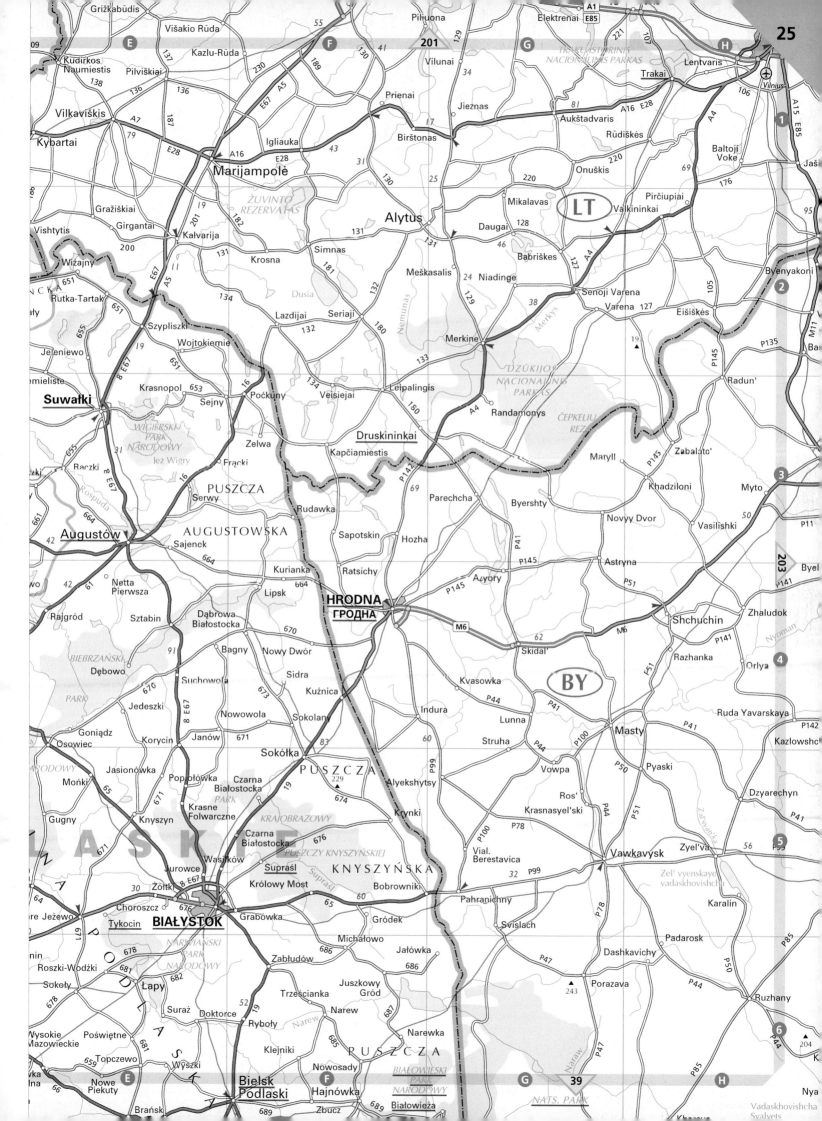

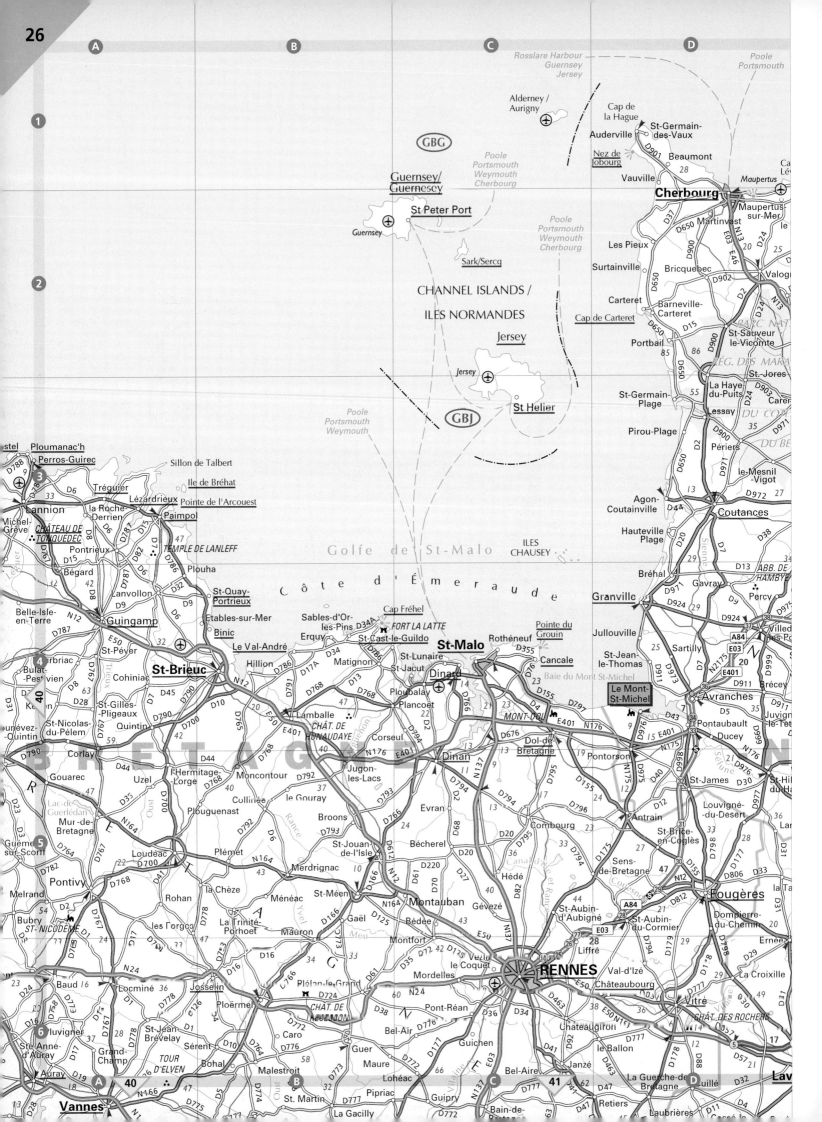

E F G H

1

ENGLISH CHANNEL/

MANCHE

2

Portsmouth

Baie de la Seine

3

4

5

6

St-Pierre-Église
Pointe de Barfleur
Barfleur
D355 D901 D902
Vast D26
Quettehou
St-Vaast-la-Hougue
D902 D14 46
Quinéville
Montebourg
D15 D421
Ste-Mère-Église
Ste-Marie-du-Mont
Grandcamp-Maisy
Isigny-sur-Mer
Vierville
St-Laurent
Port-en-Bessin
Côte du Calvados
MÉMORIAL DU OMAHA BEACH
Arromanches-les-Bains
Courseulles-sur-Mer
St-Aubin-sur-Mer
Luc-sur-Mer
Bayeux
CHÂTEAU DE FONTAINE-HENRY
Côte Fleurie
ABB. DE MONDAYE
Balleroy
Riva-Bella
Cabourg
Ouistreham
Houlgate
Dives-sur-Mer
Villers
St-Lô
Caumont
ST. CLAIR
Moon-sur-Elle
Torigni-sur-Vire
Tessy-sur-Vire
Gouvets
Vire
Villers-Bocage
Aunay-sur-Odon
Laize-la-Ville
Thury-Harcourt
Moult
Airan
Clécy
Troarn
Cambremer
Crèvecœur-en-Auge
CAEN

Cap d'Antifer
FALAISE D'AVAL
Cauville
Octeville
Cap de la Hève
LE HAVRE
Harfleur
Villerville
Honfleur
Trouville
Deauville
Beuzeville
St-Maclou
Pont-l'Évêque
Dozulé
Cormeilles
Lisieux
Thiberville
Livarot
Orbec
Bernay
Beaumont-le-Roger
Broglie
Beaumesnil
Courteilles
Landepéreuse
La Neuve-Lyre

Veulettes-sur-Mer
St-Valery-en-Caux
Varenge-sur-
Veules-les-Roses
St-Pierre-en-Port
Cany Barville
Fontaine-le-Dun
Etretat
Yport
Fécamp
Bacqueville-en-Caux
Doudeville
Yport
BAILLEUL
Goderville
Fauville
Yerville
Montivilliers
Bolbec
Yvetot
Lillebonne
Tancarville
St-Wandrille
Caudebec-en-Caux
Barentin
Duclair
POINTE DE LA ROQUE
PARC NAT. RÉG.
BOUCLES DE LA SEINE NORMANDE
Bourneville
Jumièges
Sotteville-Les-Rouen
Pont-Audemer
Bourg-Achard
Bourgtheroulde-Infreville
Elbeuf
ABB. DE BONPORT
CHÂT. DU CHAMP DU BATAILLE
Louviers
Brionne
Le Neubourg
Bosgouet

BASSE NORMANDIE
NORMANDIE

St-Sever
St-Pois
Vassy
Condé-sur-Noireau
ROCHE D'OETRE
Taillebois
Putanges-Pont-Écrepin
Falaise
Vimoutiers
Trun
Flers
Mortain
Sourdeval
St-Barthélemy
Fromental
Argentan
Exmes
Gacé
Gauville
Rugles
Damville
Barenton
Domfront
Briouze
HARAS DU PIN
Le Pin-au-Haras
Nonant-le-Pin
Ste-Gauburge-Ste-Colombe
L'Aigle
Breteuil
Conches-en-Ouche
Evreux
Le Teilleul
La Ferté-Macé
Rânes
Mortrée
Le Merlerault
Moulins-la-Marche
Verneuil-sur-Avre
Bagnoles-de-l'Orne
Carrouges
CHÂT. D'O
Sées
Courtomer
La Ferté-Vidame
Brézolles
Blévy
Couterne
Couptrain
RÉGIONAL
Bazoches-sur-Hoëne
Longny-au-Perche
Gorron
Lassay
Pré-en-Pail
MONT DES AVALOIRS
Mortagne-au-Perche
Senonches
Digny
Ambrières
Javron
Alençon
Bellême
MANOIR DE COURBOYER
La Loupe
Courville
Mayenne
Villaines-la-Juhel
NORMANDIE-MAINE
Rémalard
Chailland
Bais
Assé-le-Boisne
La Hutte
Mamers
Bellême
PARC NATUREL RÉGIONAL
Châteauneuf-en-Thymerais
CHÂT. DU ROCHER
Fresnay-sur-Sarthe
Mortsûrs
Évron
Beaumont-sur-Sarthe
Courgains
St-Cosme-en-Vairais
Nogent-le-Rotrou
Champrond-en-Gâtine
Argentré
Sillé-le-Guillaume
Ste-Suzanne
Conlie
Bonnétable
Thivars
Mamers
PERCHE
Ballon
Illiers-Combray
Luigny

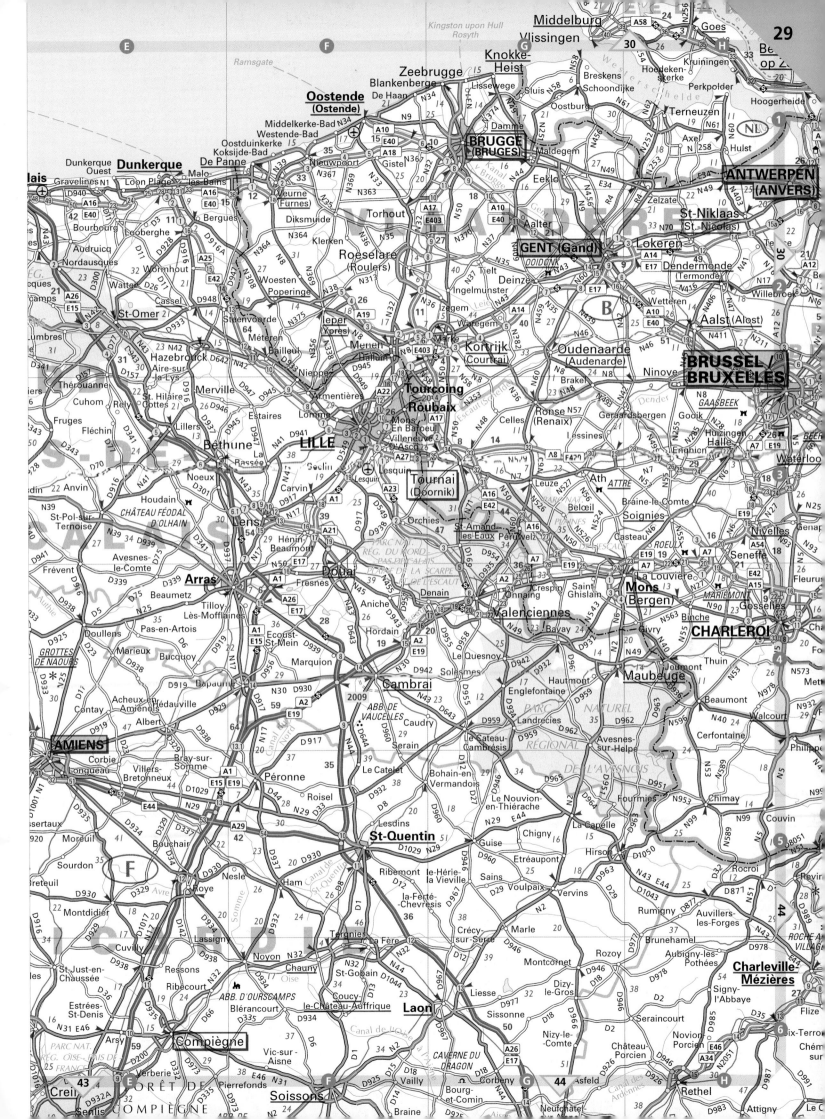

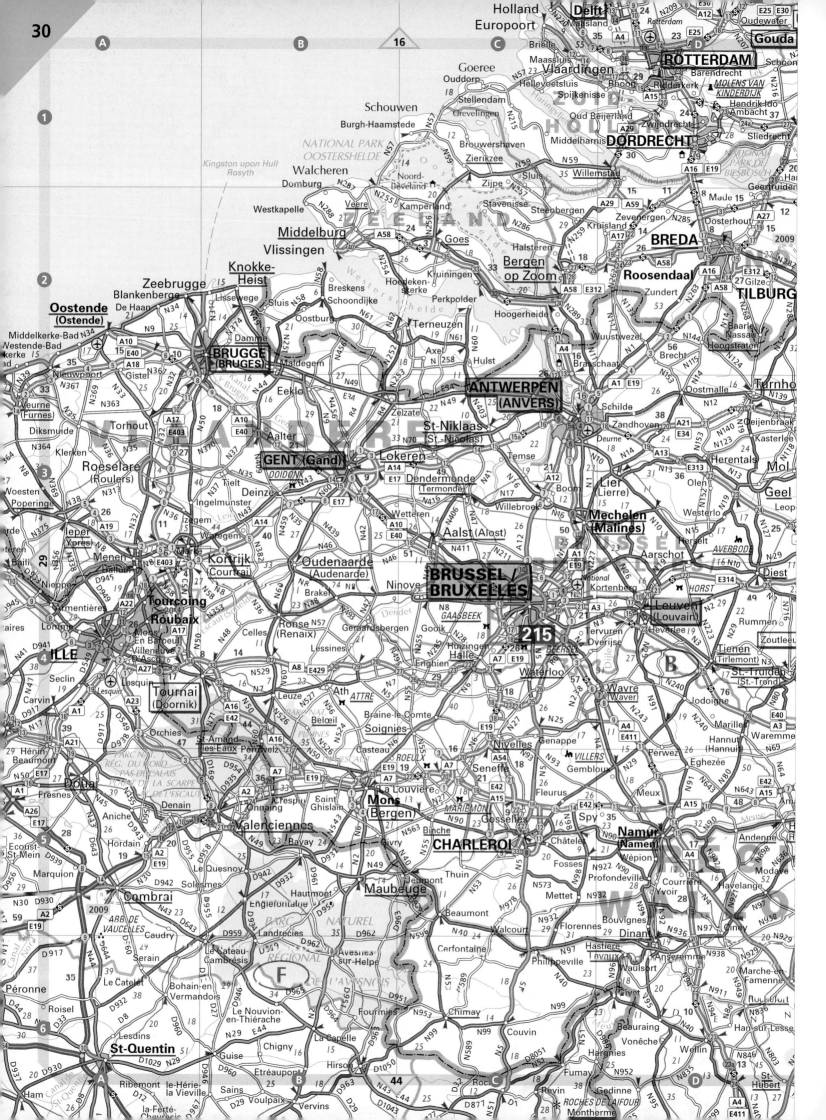

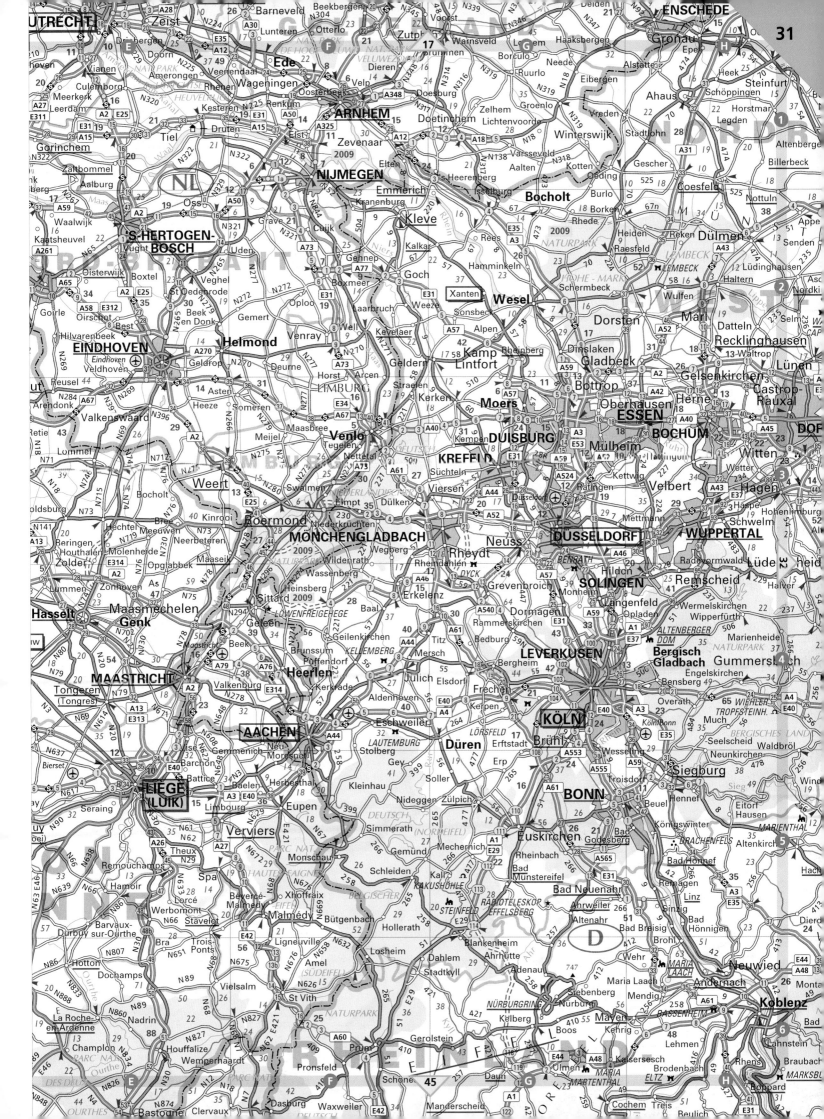

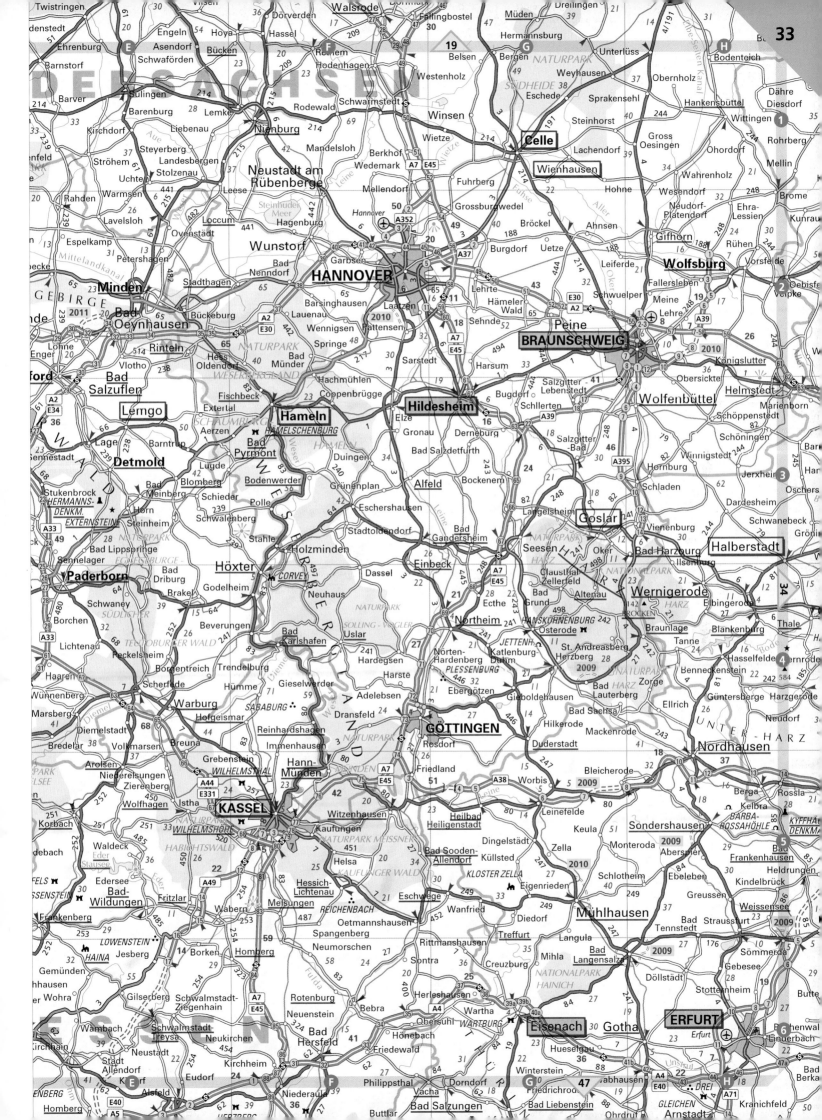

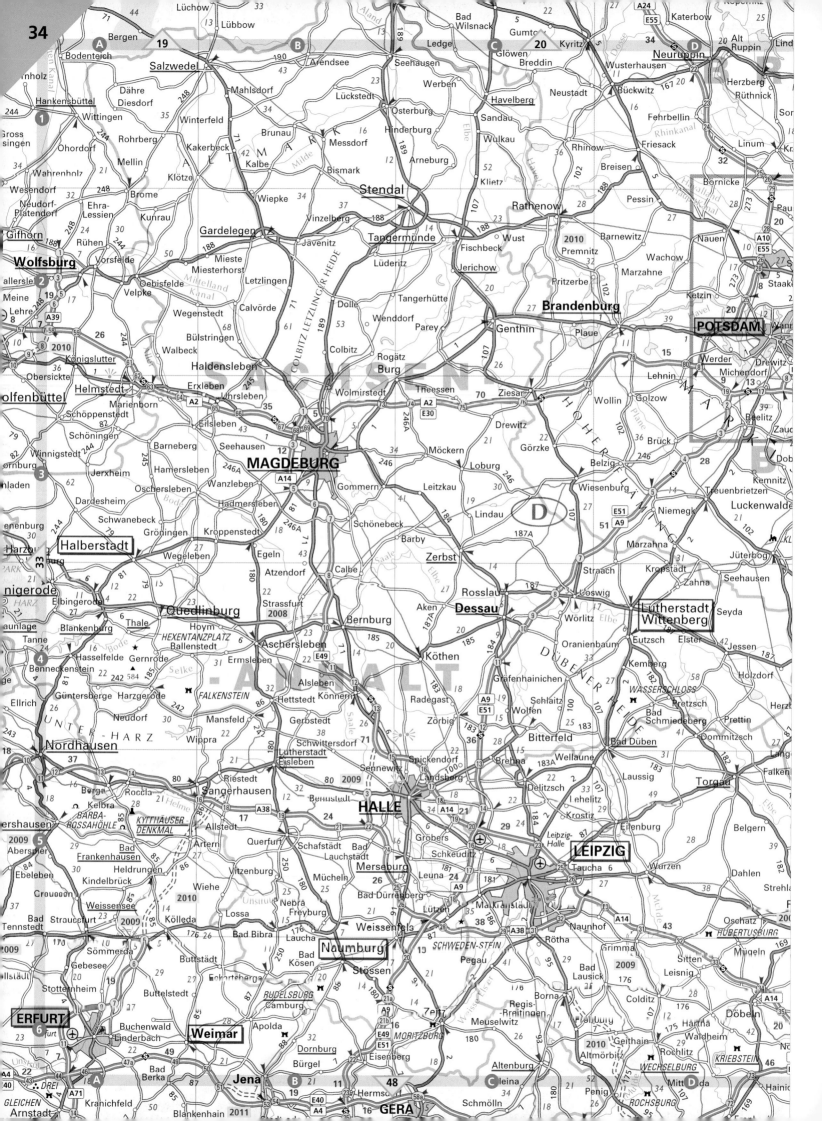

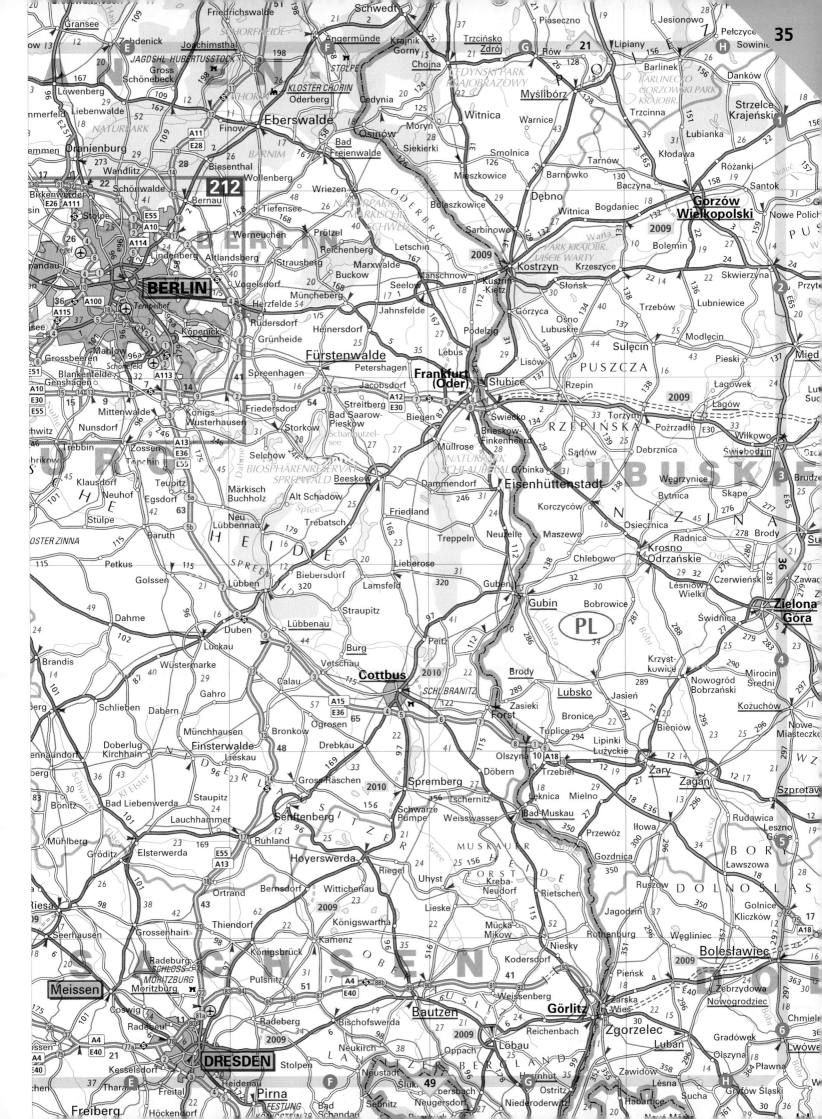

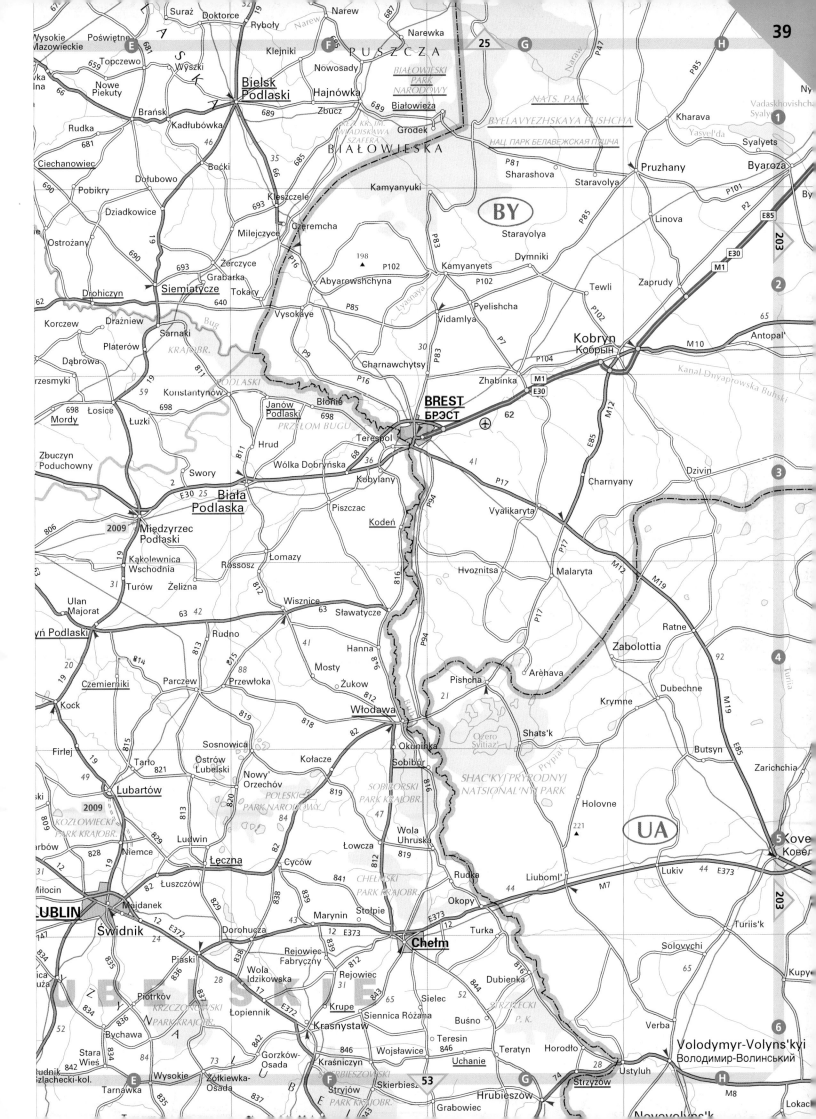

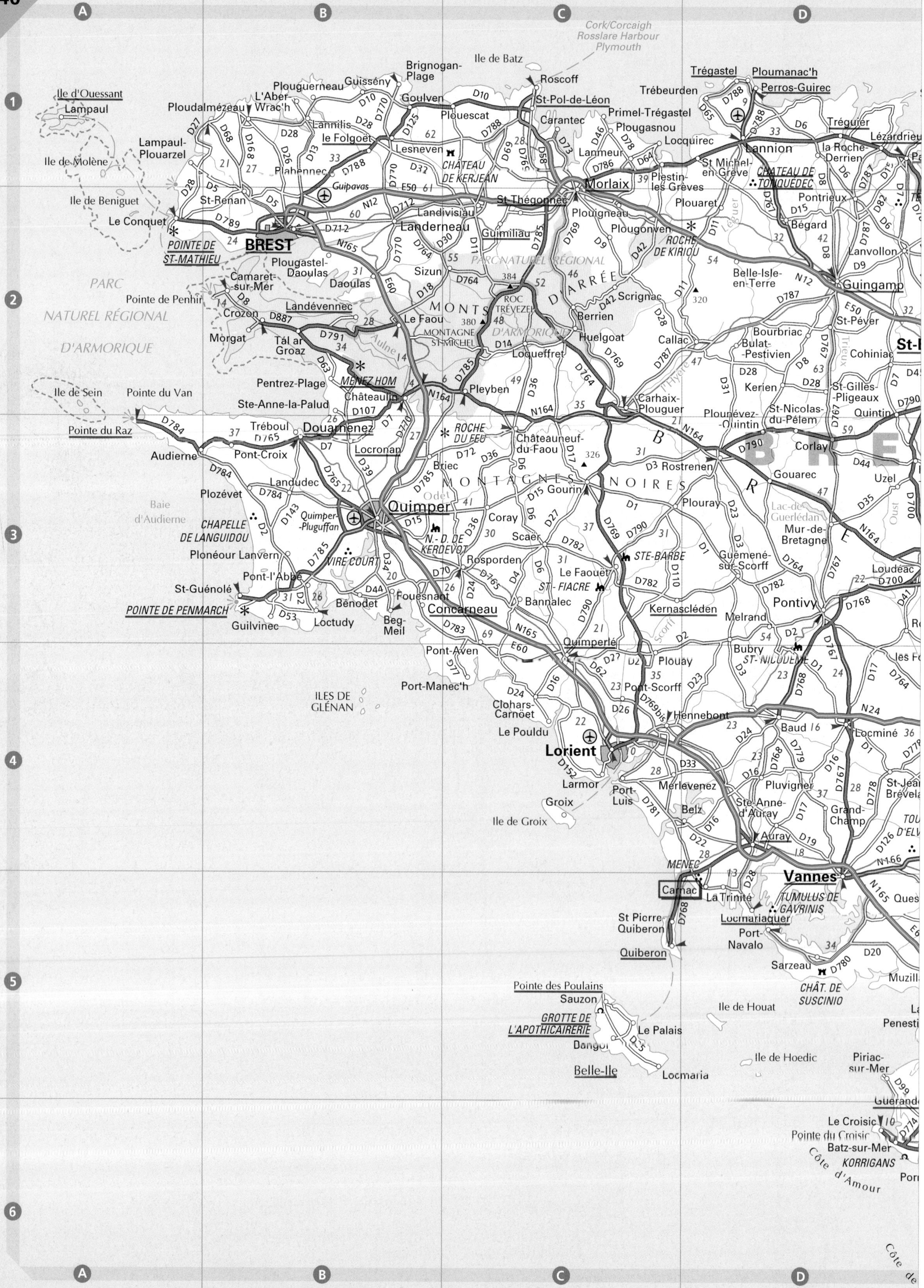

A   B   C   D

1   2   3   4   5   6

Cork/Corcaigh
Rosslare Harbour
Plymouth

Ile de Batz
Brignogan-Plage
Guissény
Roscoff
Plouguerneau
L'Aber Wrac'h
Goulven
St-Pol-de-Léon
Trégastel   Ploumanac'h
Perros-Guirec
Trébeurden
Ploudalmézeau
le Folgoët
Plouescat
Carantec
Primel-Trégastel
Plougasnou
Tréguier
Ile d'Ouessant
Lampaul
Lannilis
Lesneven
Locquirec
Lanmeur
Lannion
la Roche-Derrien
Lézardrieux
Ploudalmézeau
CHÂTEAU DE KERJEAN
St-Michel-en-Grève
CHÂTEAU DE TONQUEDEC
Lampaul-Plouarzel
Plabennec
Morlaix
Plestin-les-Grèves
Pontrieux
Bégard
Ile de Molène
Plouigneau
Guipavas
St-Thégonnec
Plouaret
Lanvollon
St-Rénan
Landivisiau
Plougonven
Belle-Isle-en-Terre
ROCHE DE KIRIOU
Guingamp
Ile de Beniguet
BREST
Landerneau
Guimiliau
ROCHE DE KIRIOU
Le Conquet
POINTE DE ST-MATHIEU
Plougastel-Daoulas
Sizun
PARC NATUREL RÉGIONAL
D'ARRÉE
St-Péver
St-
PARC
Camaret-sur-Mer
Daoulas
ROC TRÉVEZEL
Scrignac
Bourbriac
Bulat-Pestivien
Cohiniac
NATUREL RÉGIONAL
Pointe de Penhir
Le Faou
Berrien
Callac
Crozon
MONTS
MONTAGNE ST-MICHEL
Huelgoat
Kerien
St-Gilles-Pligeaux
D'ARMORIQUE
Landévennec
D'ARMORIQUE
Loqueffret
Carhaix-Plouguer
St-Nicolas-du-Pélem
Quintin
Morgat
Tál ar Groaz
Plounévez-Quintin
Ile de Sein
Pentrez-Plage
MENEZ HOM
Pleyben
Châteauneuf-du-Faou
Corlay
Pointe du Van
Ste-Anne-la-Palud
Châteaulin
ROCHE DU FEU
Rostrenen
BRE
Pointe du Raz
Tréboul
Douarnenez
MONTAGNES NOIRES
Gouarec
Uzel
Audierne
Pont-Croix
Locronan
Briec
Gourin
Lac de Guerlédan
Mur-de-Bretagne
Landudec
Coray
Plouray
Guémené-sur-Scorff
Loudéac
Plozévet
CHAPELLE DE LANGUIDOU
Quimper-Pluguffan
Quimper
Scaër
STE-BARBE
Ploméour Lanvern
N.-D. DE KERDEVOT
Rosporden
Le Faouët
ST-FIACRE
Kernascléden
Pontivy
St-Guénolé
Pont-l'Abbé
VIRE COURT
Bannalec
Melrand
POINTE DE PENMARCH
Bénodet
Fouesnant
Concarneau
Quimperlé
Bubry
ST-NICOLE
les Fo
Guilvinec
Loctudy
Beg-Meil
Plouay
Pont-Aven
Plouay
ILES DE GLÉNAN
Port-Manec'h
Pont-Scorff
Hennebont
Baud
Locminé
Clohars-Carnoët
Le Pouldu
Lorient
Larmor
Merlevenez
Pluvigner
St-Jean-Brévelai
Groix
Port-Louis
Belz
Ste-Anne-d'Auray
Grand-Champ
TOUR D'ELV
Ile de Groix
Auray
MENEC
Vannes
Carnac
La Trinité
TUMULUS DE GAVRINIS
St Pierre Quiberon
Locmariaquer
Port-Navalo
Sarzeau
Muzill
Quiberon
Pointe des Poulains
Sauzon
Ile de Houat
CHÂT. DE SUSCINIO
GROTTE DE L'APOTHICAIRERIE
Le Palais
Penesti
Dangou
Belle-Ile
Locmaria
Ile de Hoedic
Piriac-sur-Mer
Guérand
Le Croisic
Pointe du Croisic
Batz-sur-Mer
KORRIGANS
Côte d'Amour

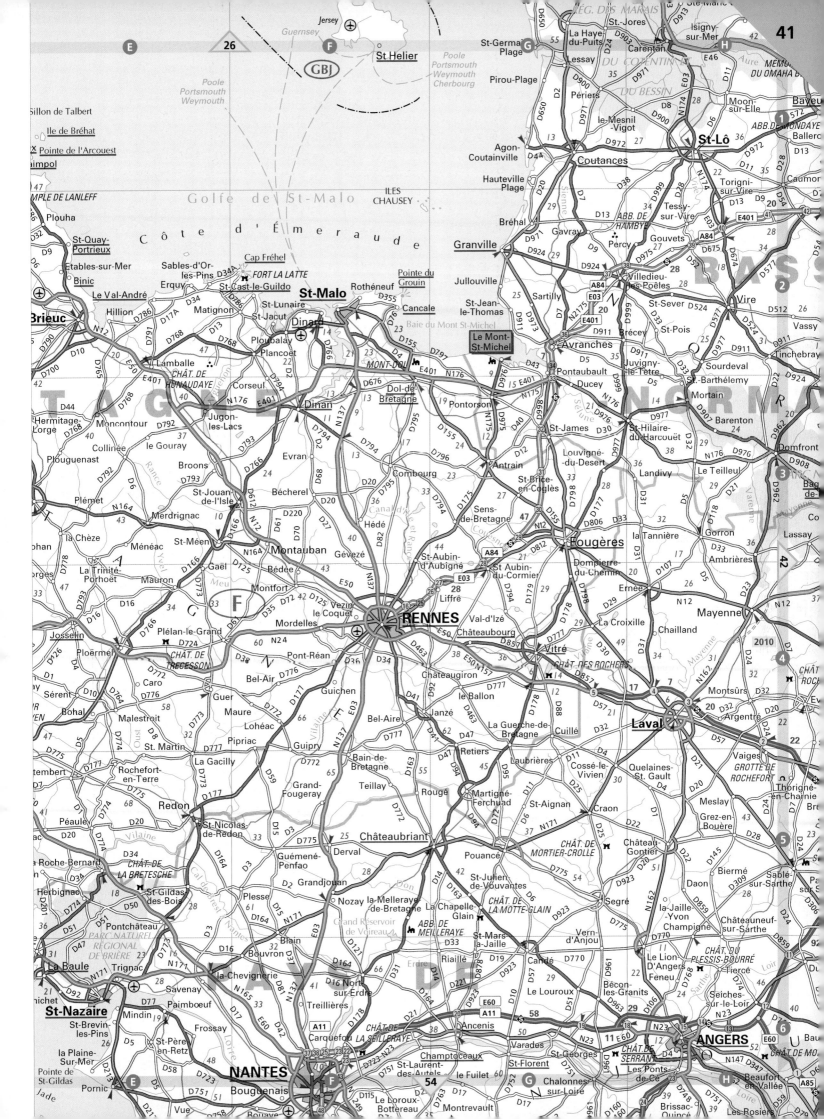

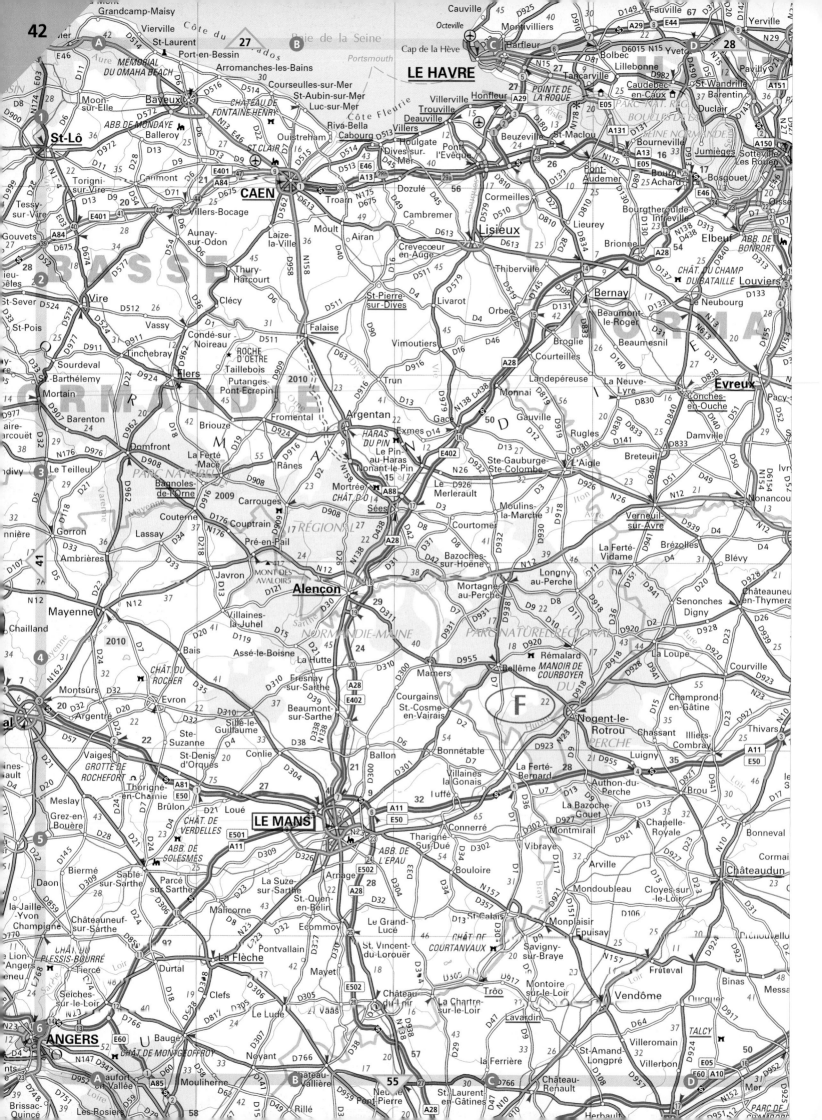

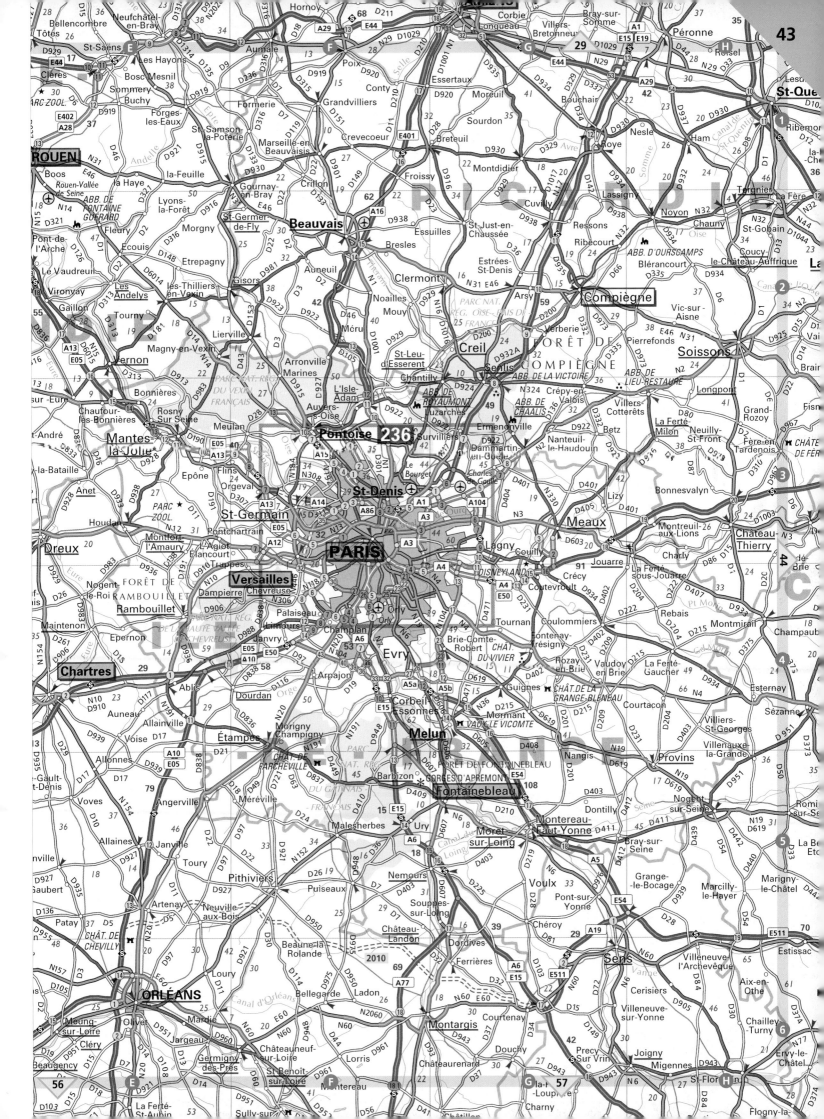

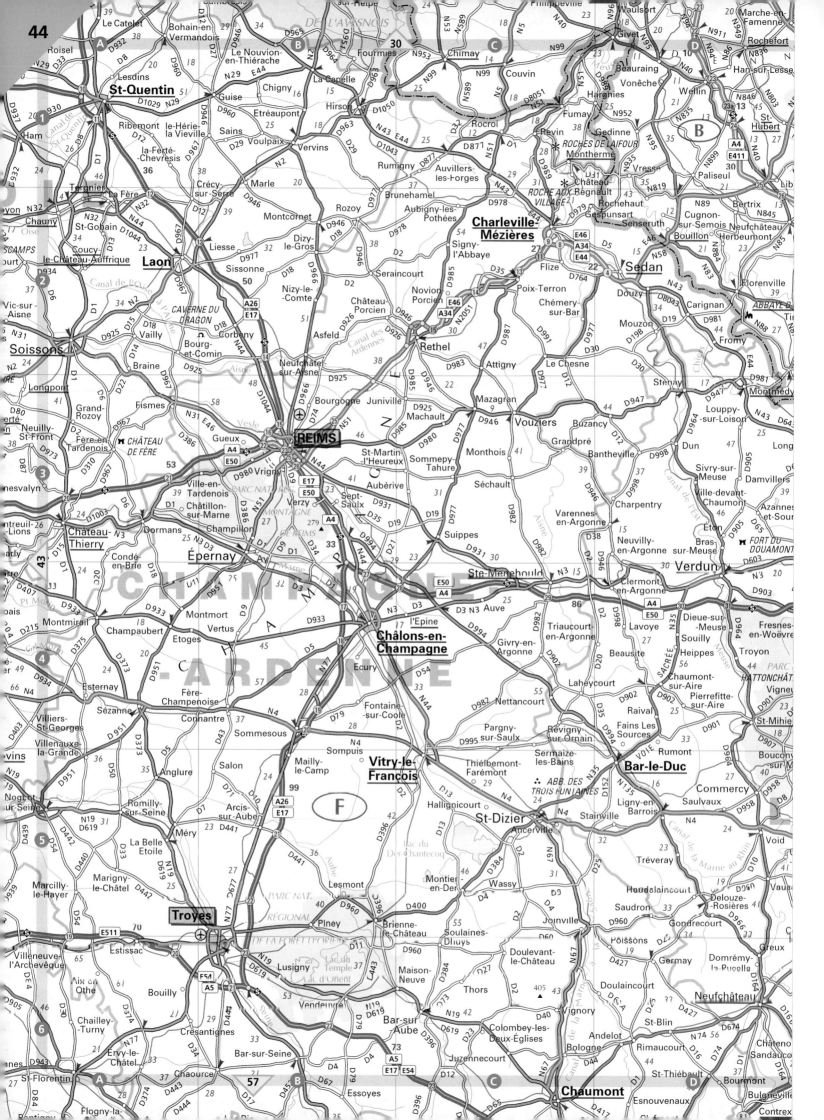

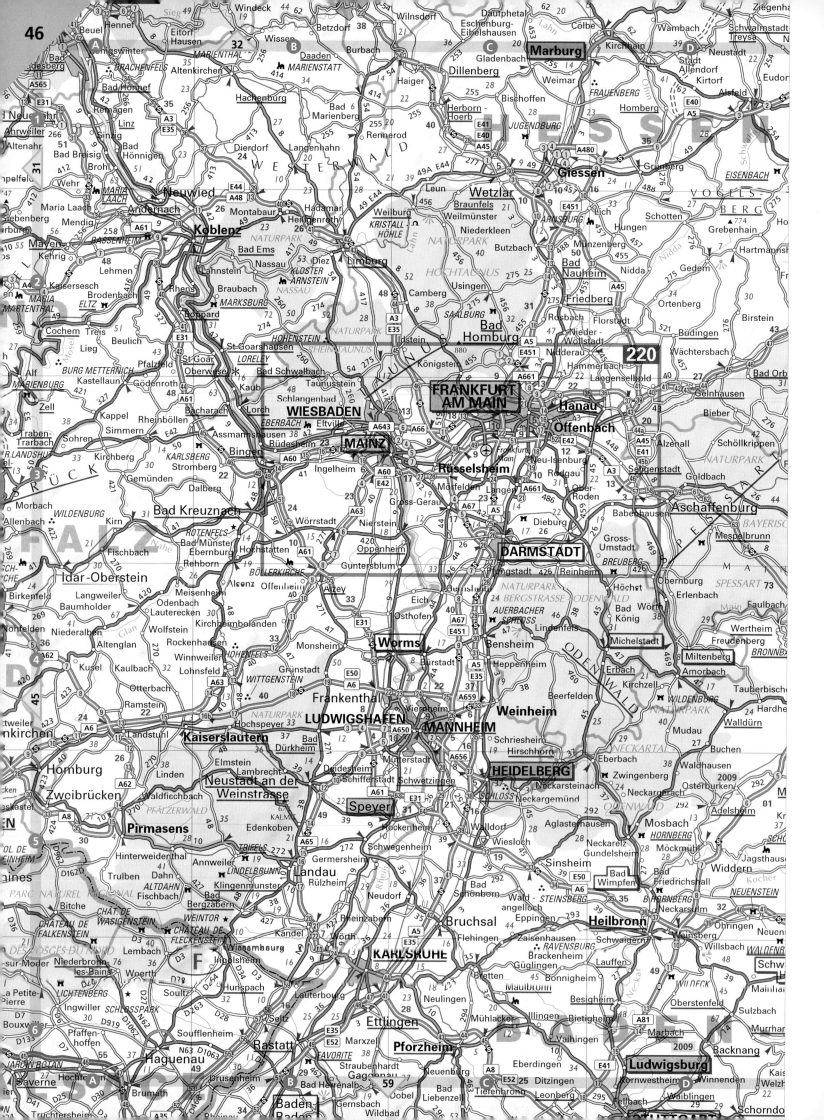

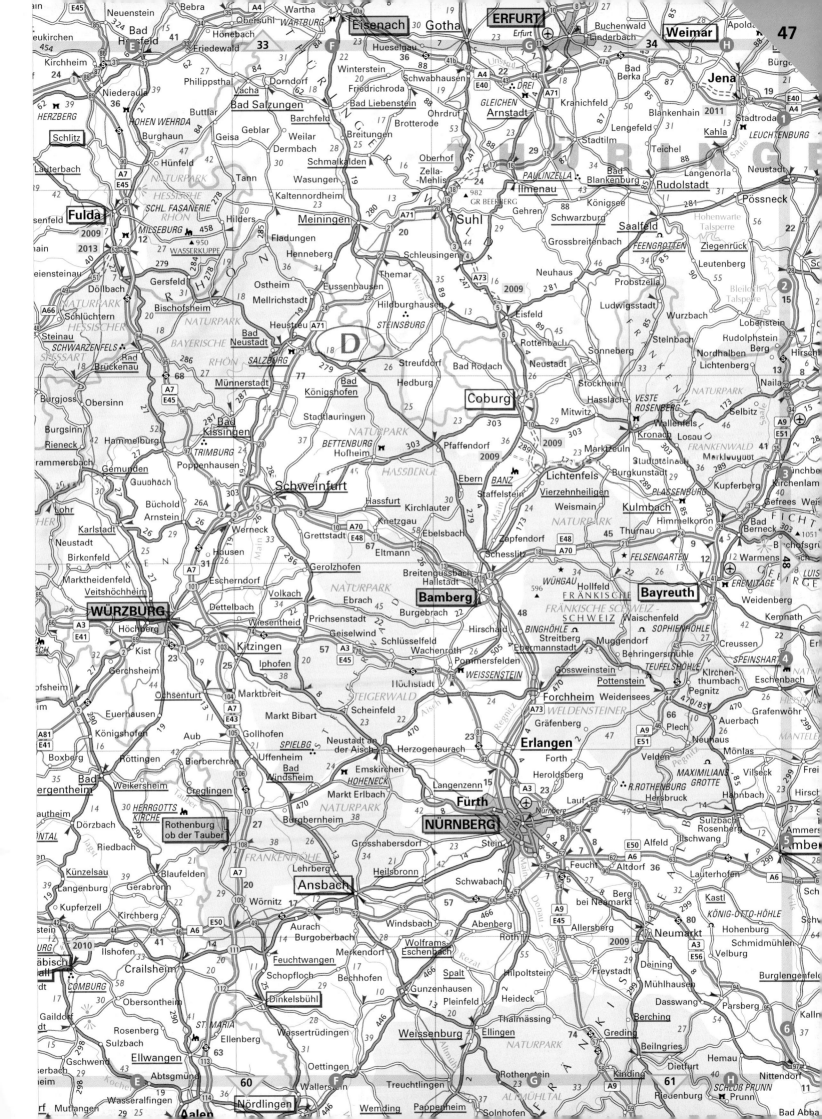

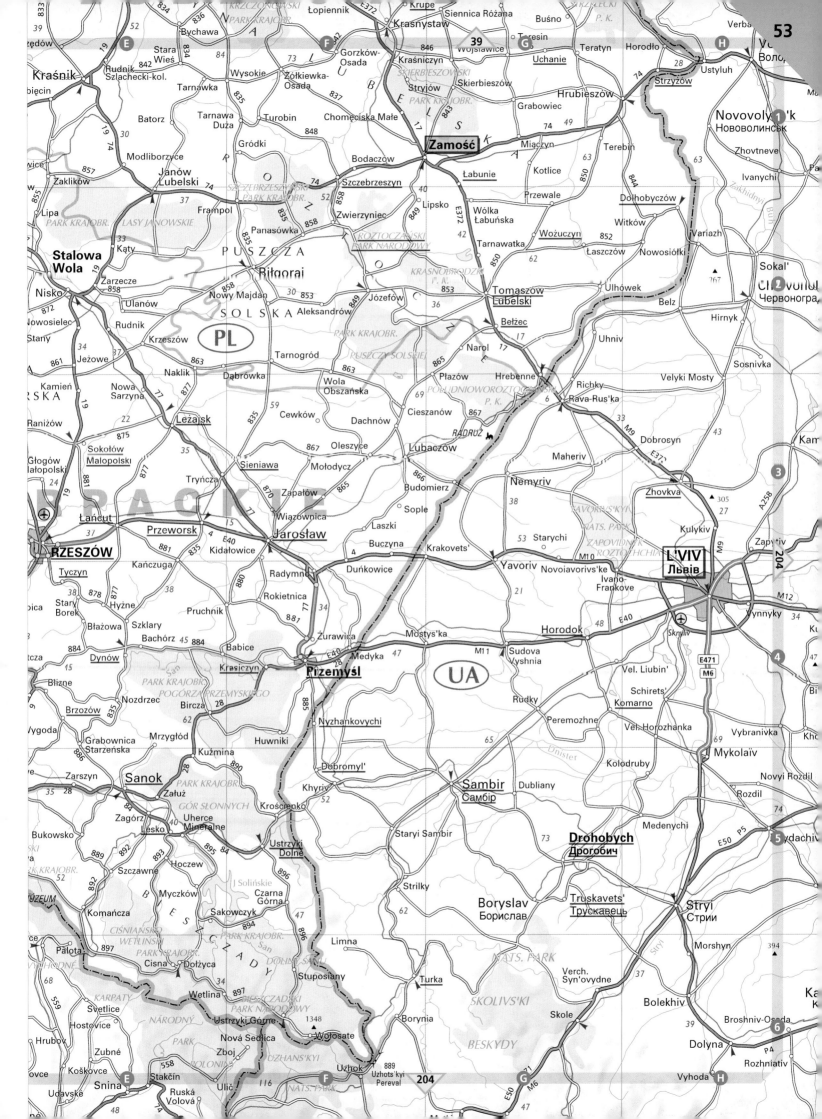

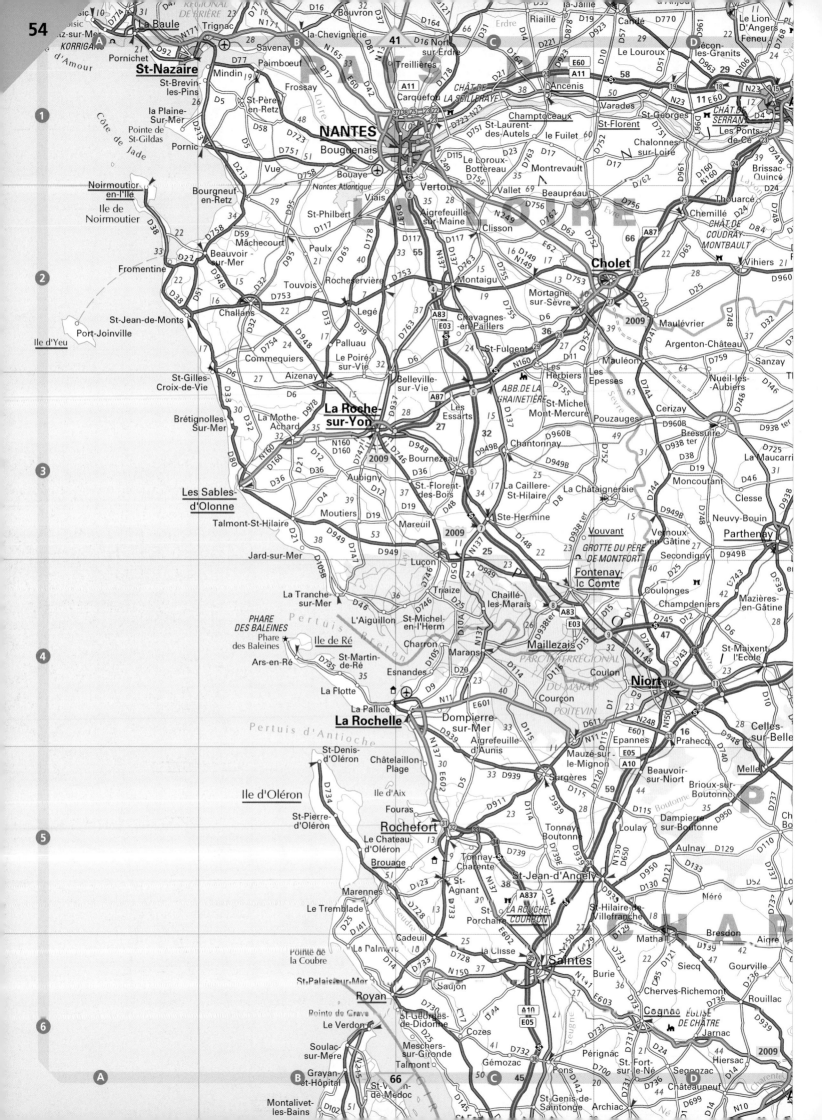

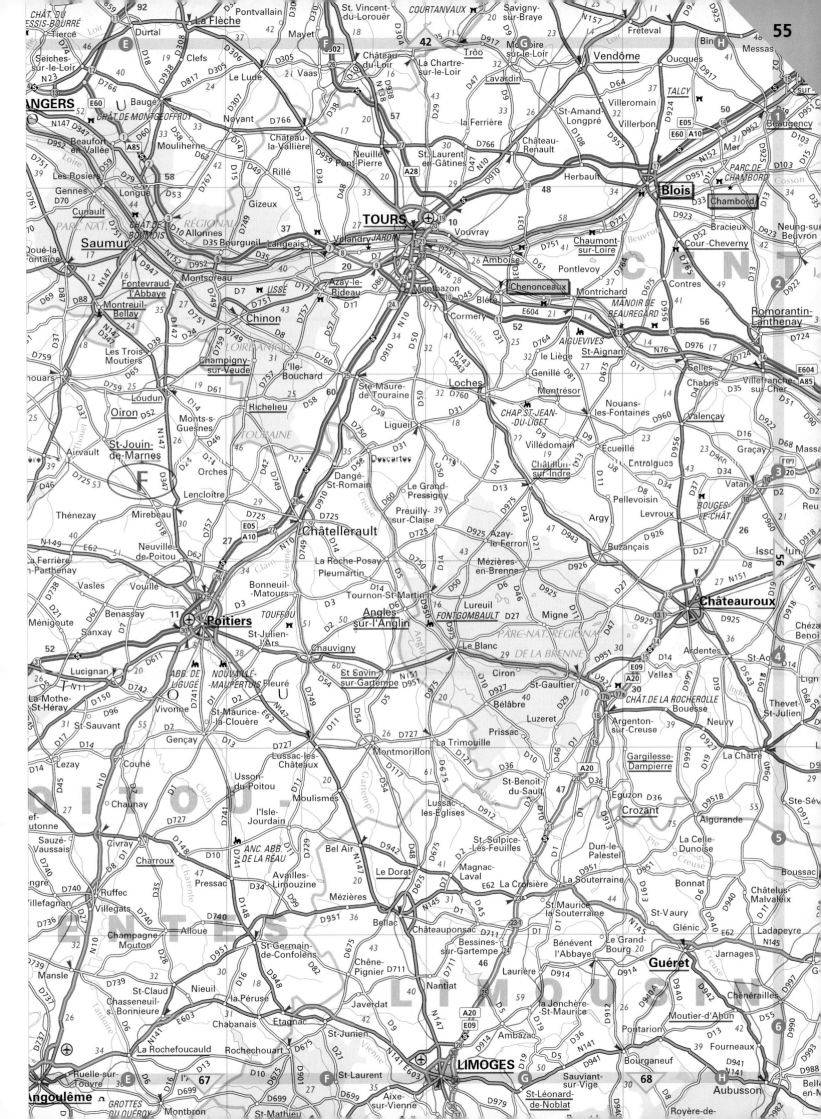

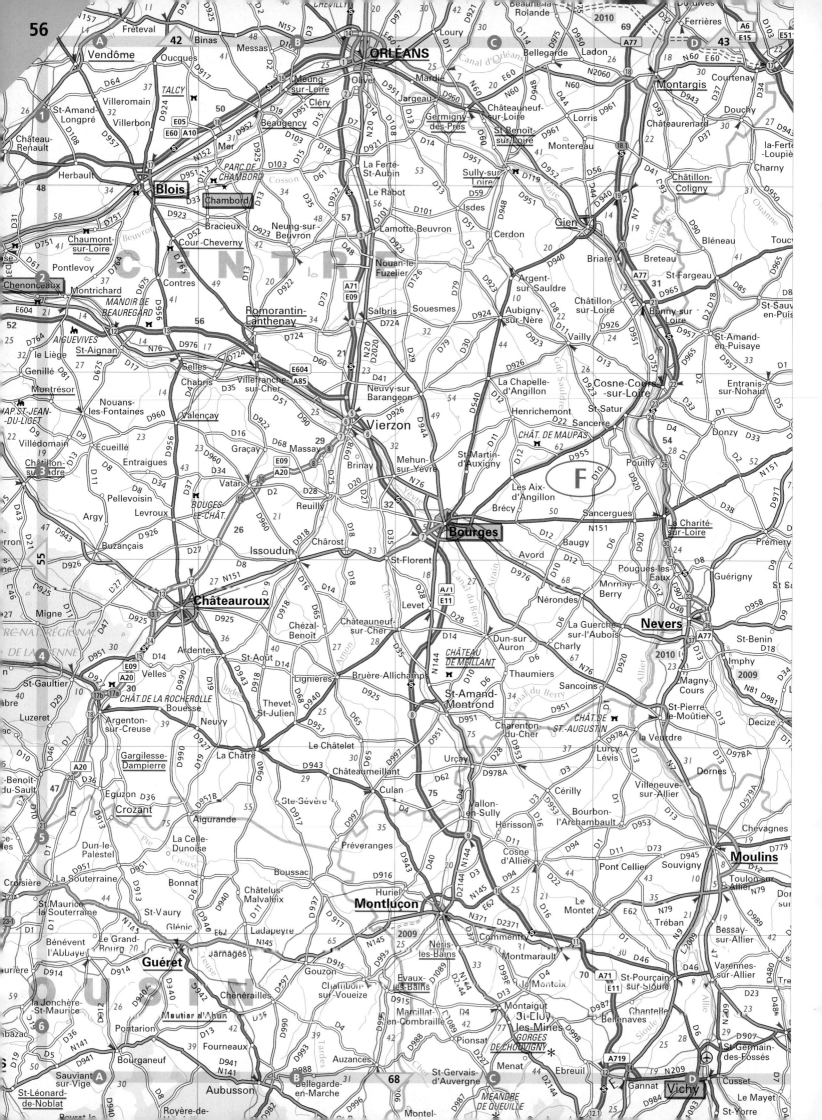

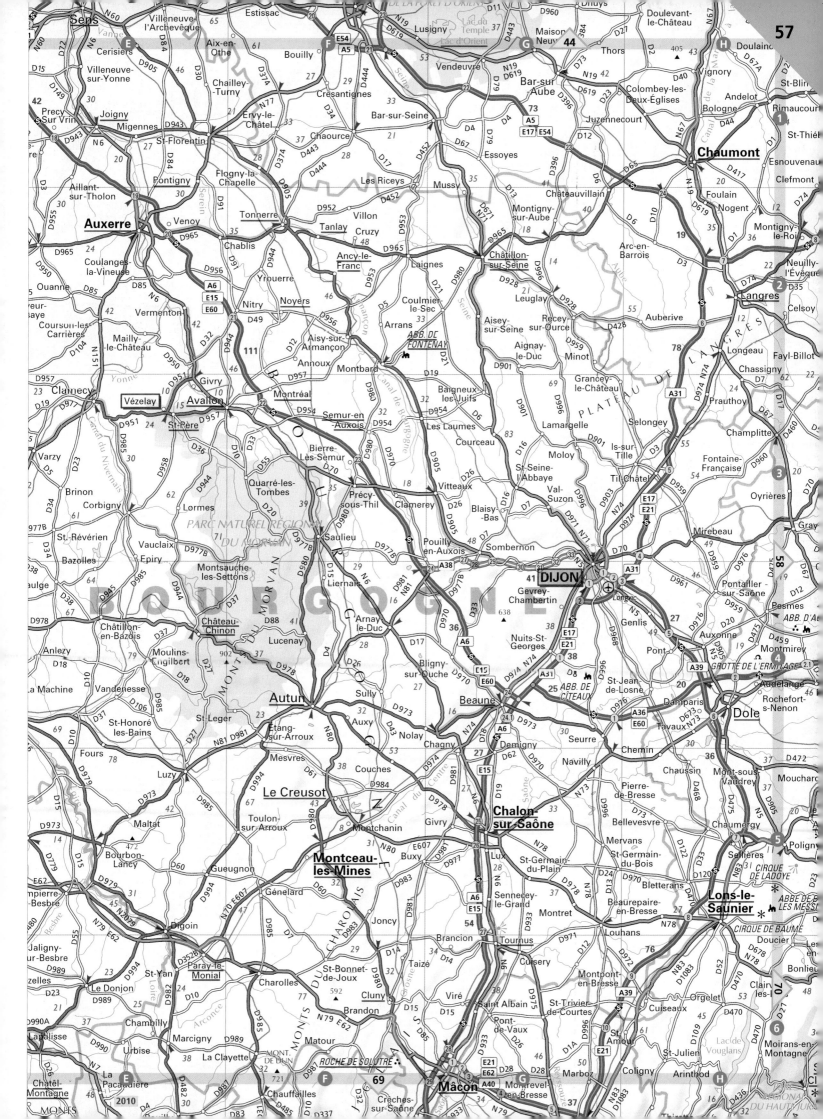

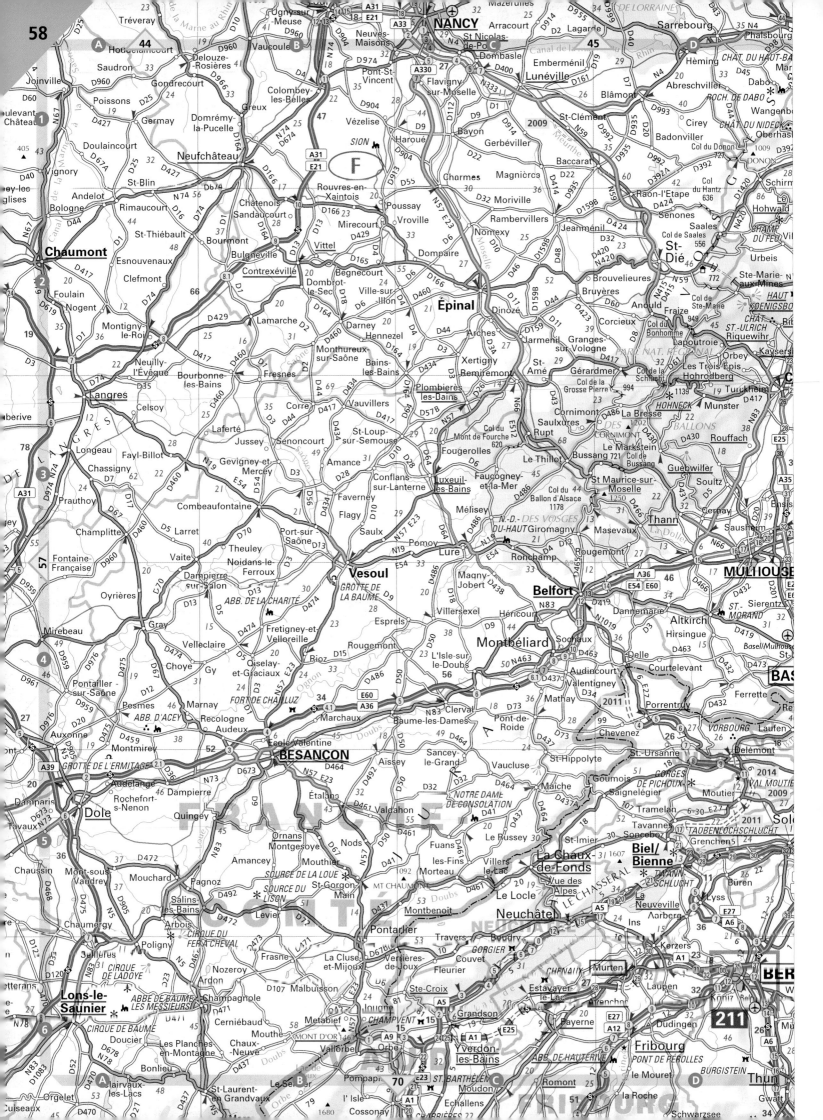

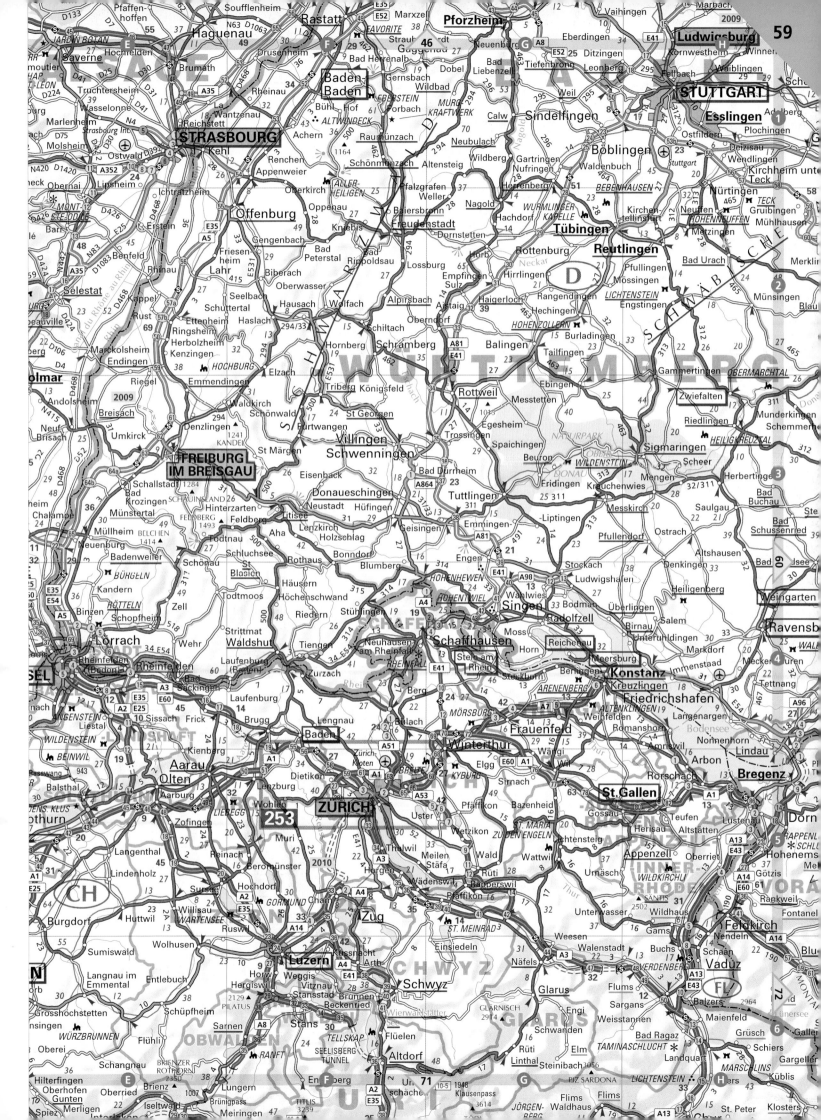

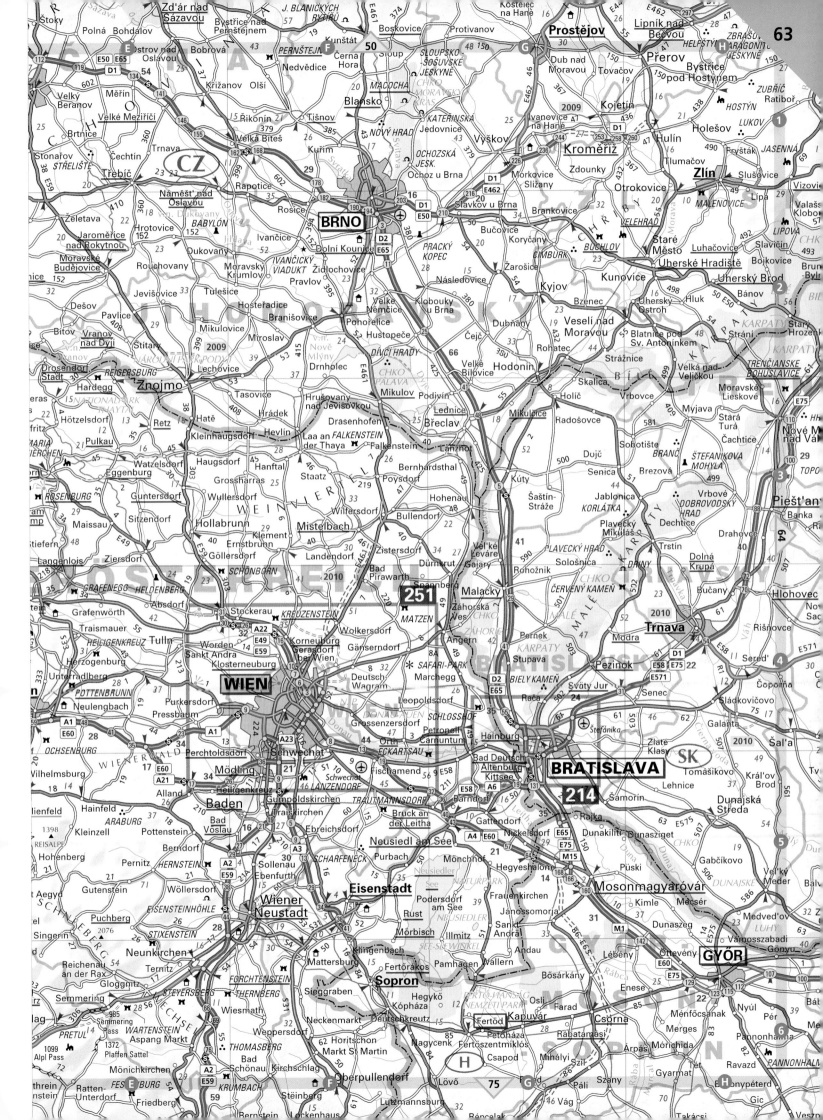

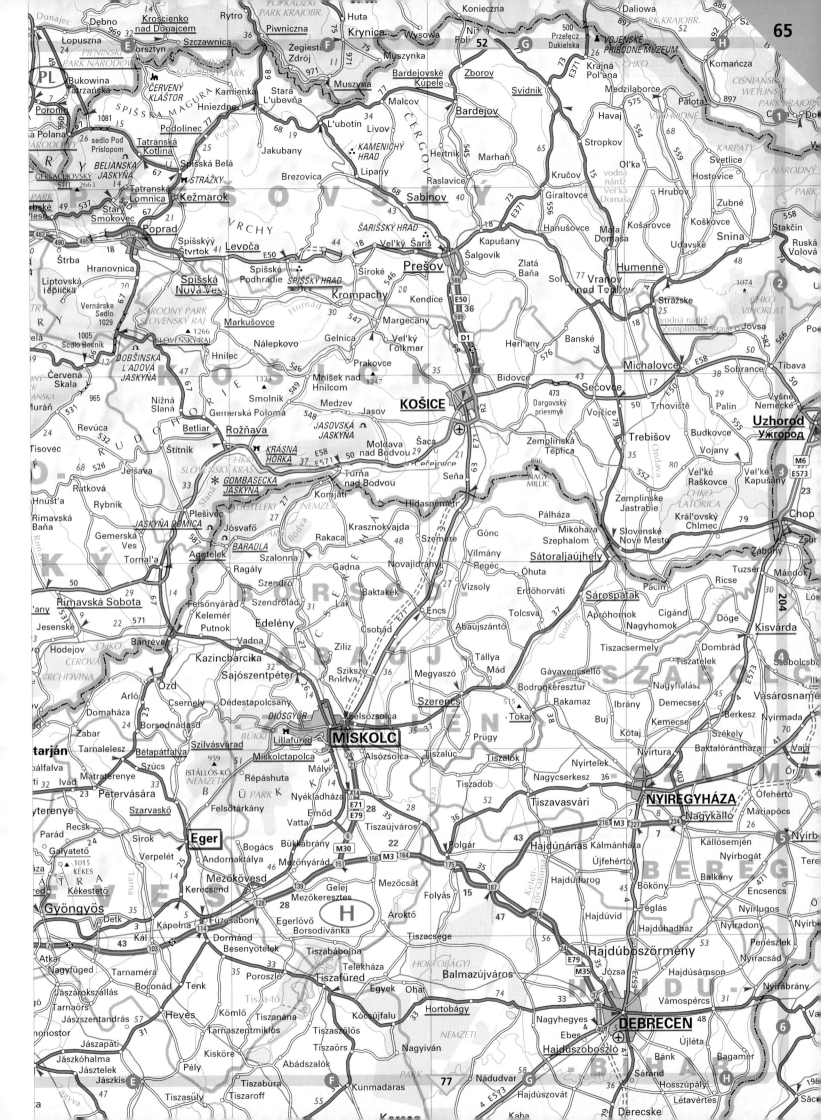

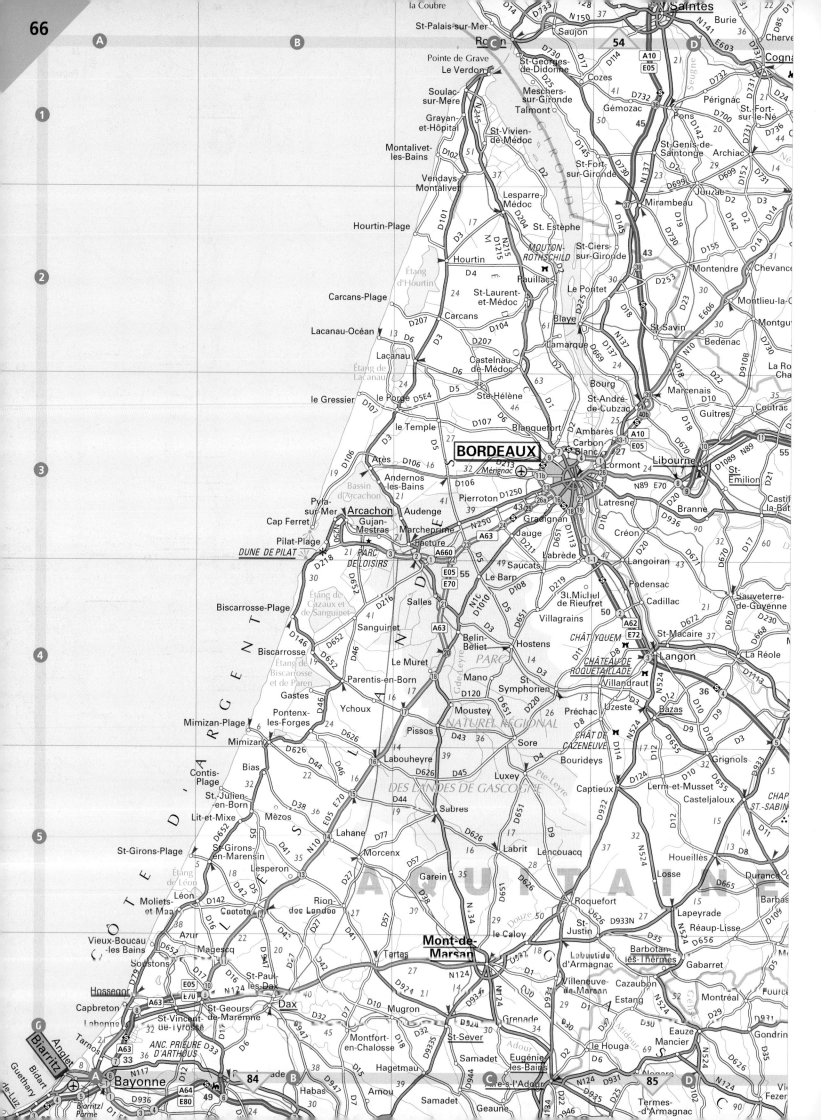

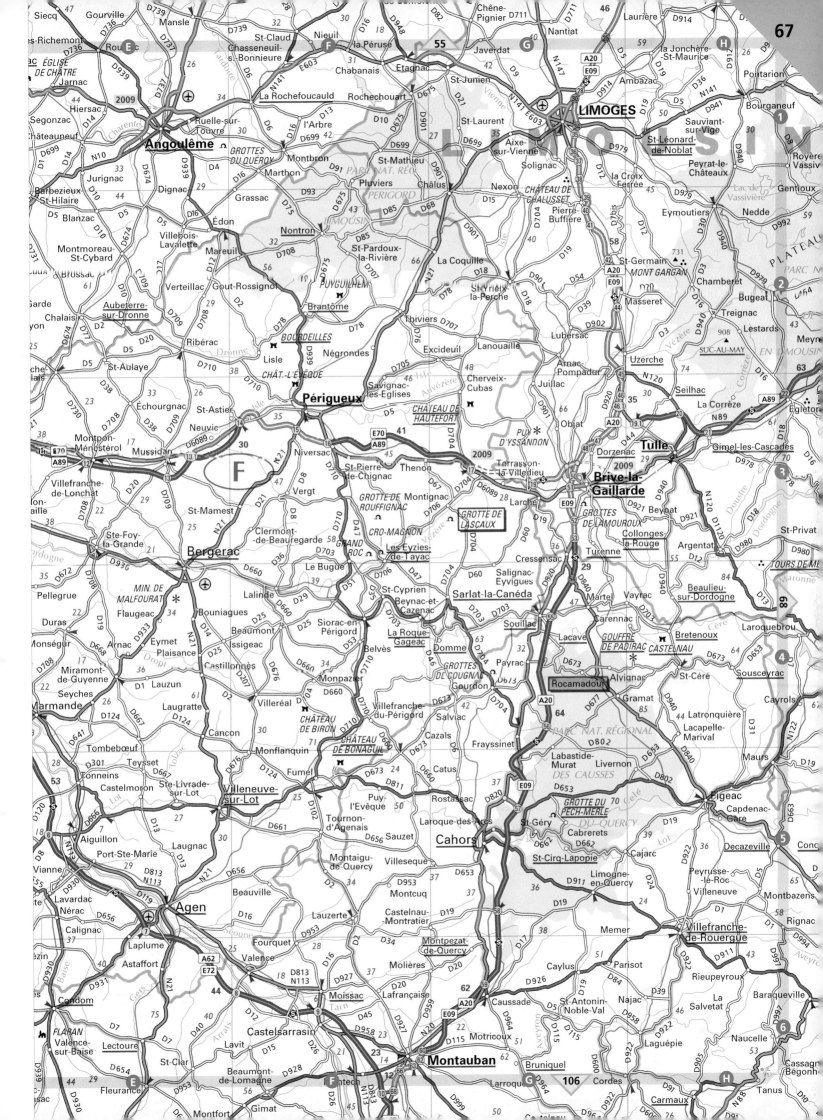

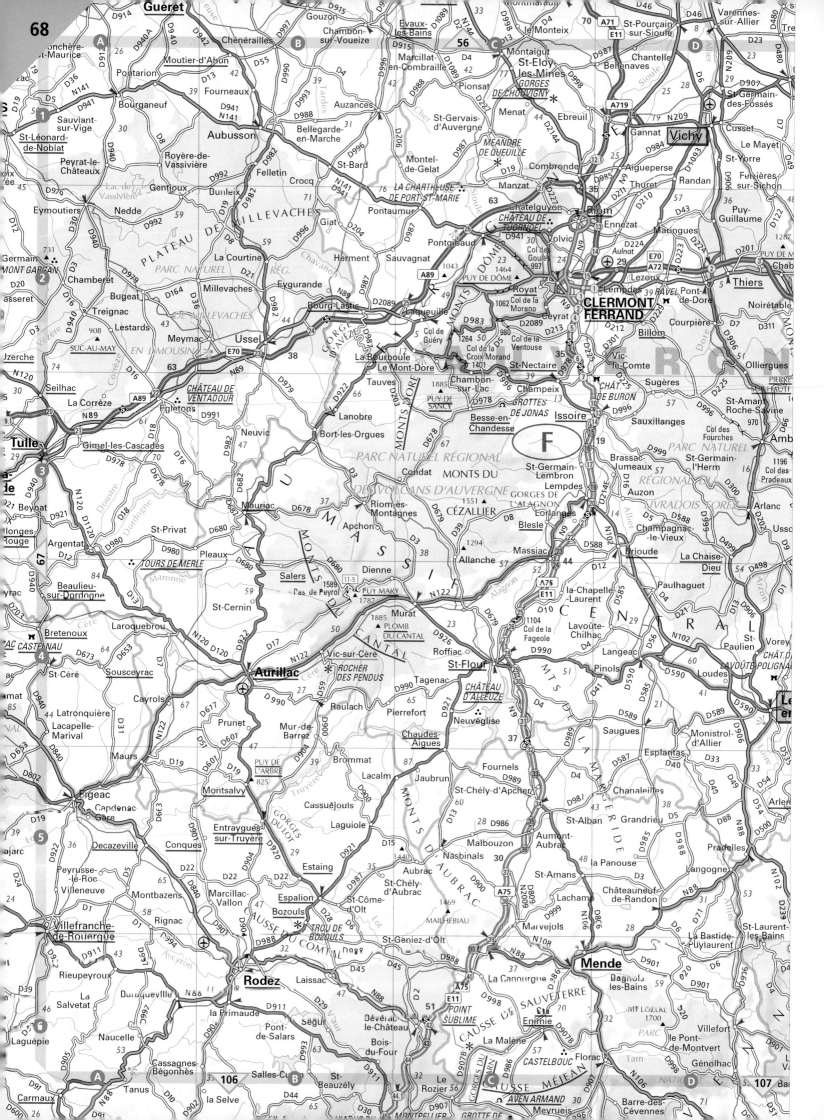

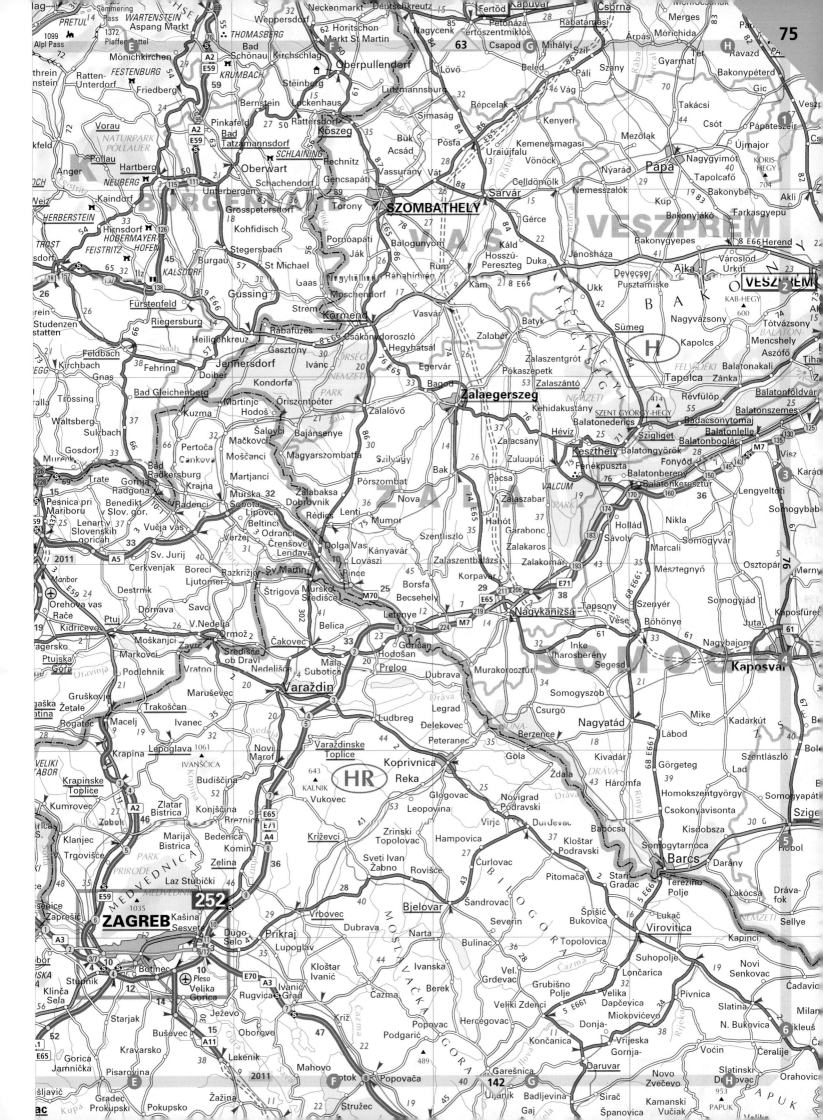

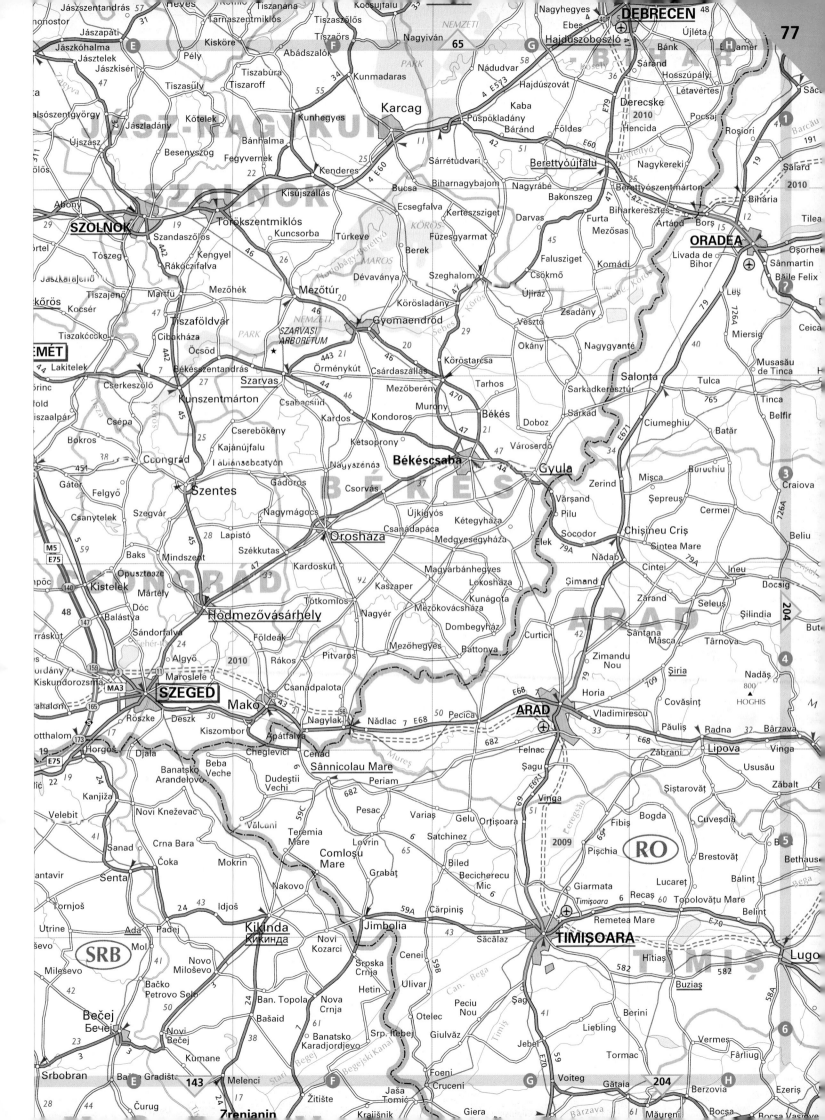

A B C D

RÍAS

1

VIXÍA HERBEIRA
Punta Candelaria
Cabo Prior
Cedeira
San Andrés
Valdoviño
AC566
AC862
2010
Mede Bo
Cabo Prioriño
Ferrol
NVI
Xubia
CASTILLO DE MOECHE
Neda
Fene
San Sadurniño
CAST. DE NARAIO
Murgados
Ares
Cabañas
AP9
MONASTERIO DE CAAVEIRO
Pontedeume
Miño
CAST. DE ANDRADE
As Pontes de García Rodrí
Puentes de García Rodrí
Monfero
Embalse de Eume
C640
Pedreira

Illas Sisargas
Cabo San Adrián
Malpica de Bergantiños
A CORUÑA / LA CORUÑA
Ria de Betanzos
Sada
Oleiros
Bergondo
Betanzos
Coirós
Irixoa
C640

Punta del Roncudo
Laxe
Ponteceso
AC422
Arteixo
A55
222
Carballo
Laracha
Cambre
Guisamo
568
AP9
E01
AC840
Curtis
Lourdes
Guitiriz
A6
E70
A8

Cabo Vilán
Camariñas
Muxía
CEREIXO
DOLMEN DE DOMBATE
CASTRO DE BORNEIRO
Baio
San Roque
Carral
Cerceda
Meson do Vento
AC413
Ordes
Lanzá
Teixeiro
Baamonde
A6

Cabo Touriñán
Vimianzo
Zás
AC552
AC2904
Silva
AC443
N550
C542
45
Ru
SOBRADO DOS MONXES
Begonte

AC445
Cee
Corcubión
Ézaro
Brandomil
AC404
AC400
Santa Comba
Bembirre
Trazo
Oroso
N634
STA. MARIA DE MEZONZO
Sobrado
Rabade

Fisterra / Finisterre
Cabo Fisterra
Ponte Oliveras
A Baña
Portomouro
Sigüeiro
Pastor
Friol
LU934

2

Pino do Val
Embalse Barrié de la Maza
Negreira
Santiago de Compostela
Labacolla
Arzúa
Lugo
El Picato

Carnota
AC550
Outes
STA. MARIA DE CONXO
N634
O Pino
N547
Melide
2009

Muros
Noia / Noya
AC543
Santiago
Fontedias
Toques
LU231

Punta Carreiros
Ria de Muros
Padrón
Teo
Ramallosa
AP53
Ponte Ulla
Embalse de Portodemouros
Palas de Rei
N547
Guntín

3

Porto do Son
CASTRO DE BAROÑA
Pobra do Caramiñal
Puebla del Caramiñal
Boiro
Catoira
Enfesta / Pontecesures
A Estrada
PAZO DE OCA
Cruces
PO840
Monterroso
Narón
Portomar

Cabo Corrubedo
Oleiros
Rianxo
Vilagarcía de Arousa
PO548
N640
Cuntis
N640
Silleda
Agolada
N640
Antas de Ulla
Paradela
LU5709

Santa Uxía de Ribeira
Illa de Arousa
Caldas de Reis
A Lagoa / Campo Lameiro
Lalín
Rodeiro
SIERRA DO FARO
Chantada
MONASTERIO DE RIBAS DO MIÑO
Escairón
LU652

Punta de Couso
O Grove
Vilanova de Arousa
Cambados
N550
Forcarei
Souteo
Dozón / Castro
STA. MARIA DA REAL
La Barrela
N540

4

Illa de Sálvora
PARQUE NACIONAL
A Toxa
VRG4.1
AP9
E01
O Convento
PO550
Poio
Combarro
Pontevedra
N541
Cerdedo
Alto de Santo Domingo
Piñor
Cea
Cambeo
Os Peares
Monforte de Lemos

Illa de Ons
DAS ILLAS
Sanxenxo
Marín
PO551
Ponte-Caldelas
PO235
Beariz
MONASTERIO DE SAN CLODIO
Maside
Punxin
Embalse dos Peares
Pantón
LU903

RÍAS
ATLÁNTICAS
Hío
Moaña
Cangas
C551
Redondela
CAST. DE SOUTOMAIOR
Berducido
Avión
O Carballiño
Leiro
Sober

BAIXAS
Illas Cíes
Ria de Vigo
VIGO
PO552
Nigrán
AG57
Mondariz-Balneario
Mondariz
OU154
OU531
OURENSE / ORENSE
MONASTERIO DE SANTO ESTEVO
Castro Caldelas
Puerto de A de Cerdeir

5

Cabo Silleiro
Panxón
Baiona
Ramallosa
Areas
Ponteareas
N120
Ribadavia
Cartelle
OU540
Esgos
OU536
Maceda
Xunqueira de Espadanedo
A Pobra Trives

Arrabal Oia
Vilameán
E01
O Porriño
PO402
Salvaterra de Miño
A Cañiza
Cortegada
Ramirás
A Merca
SANTO ESTEVO
Allariz
Xunqueira de Ambia
Paredes

A Guarda / La Guardia
PO552
Valença do Minho
Tui
Monção
N202
Melgaço
São Gregório
Padrenda
Celanova
Verea
OU531
Sandias
Vilar de Barrio
Embalse de Chandrexa
MANZANEDA
SERRA DE QU

MTE. DE STA. TEGRA
Caminha
Vila Nova de Cerveira
Lanhelas
Extremo
SERRA DA PENEDA
Bande
Xinzo de Limia / Ginzo de Limia
Trasmiras
Laza
Campohecerros

6

Moledo
Paredes de Coura
Portela
PARQUE
Arcos de Valdevez
Soajo
PARQUE NAT.
Muiños
A52
Cualedro
PAR. NAT. DO INVERNADEIRO
Villariño de Conso

Vila Praia de Âncora
Afife
A3
23
IP1
IC28
N101
Entrimo
NACIONAL
SERRA DO XURÉS
Lobios
Lindoso
Randín
Verín
N525

STA. LUZIA
Viana do Castelo
A27
IP9
N202
N203
Ponte de Lima
Ponte da Barca
Portela do Home
Baltar
A Gudiña
Oímbra
N532
Vilardevós

Darque
Deão
E01
Balugães
N204
N101
Lindoso
SERRA DE BAIXA LIMIA
Gralhos
N103
Vilarinho

Castelo do Neiva
PARQUE NATURAL DO LITORAL NORTE
A28
N101
Covide
N.S. D'ABADIA
SERRA DO GERÊS
DA PENEDA-GERÊS
Paradela
Montalegre
Ríos

Esposende
A28
Vila Verde
Caldelas
Gerês
Barragem de Paradela
Cávado
N103
A52

A B C D
Bárcelos
N205
Braga
JESUS DO MONTE
Louredo
N. SENHORA DA AZINHEIRA
Vila Verde

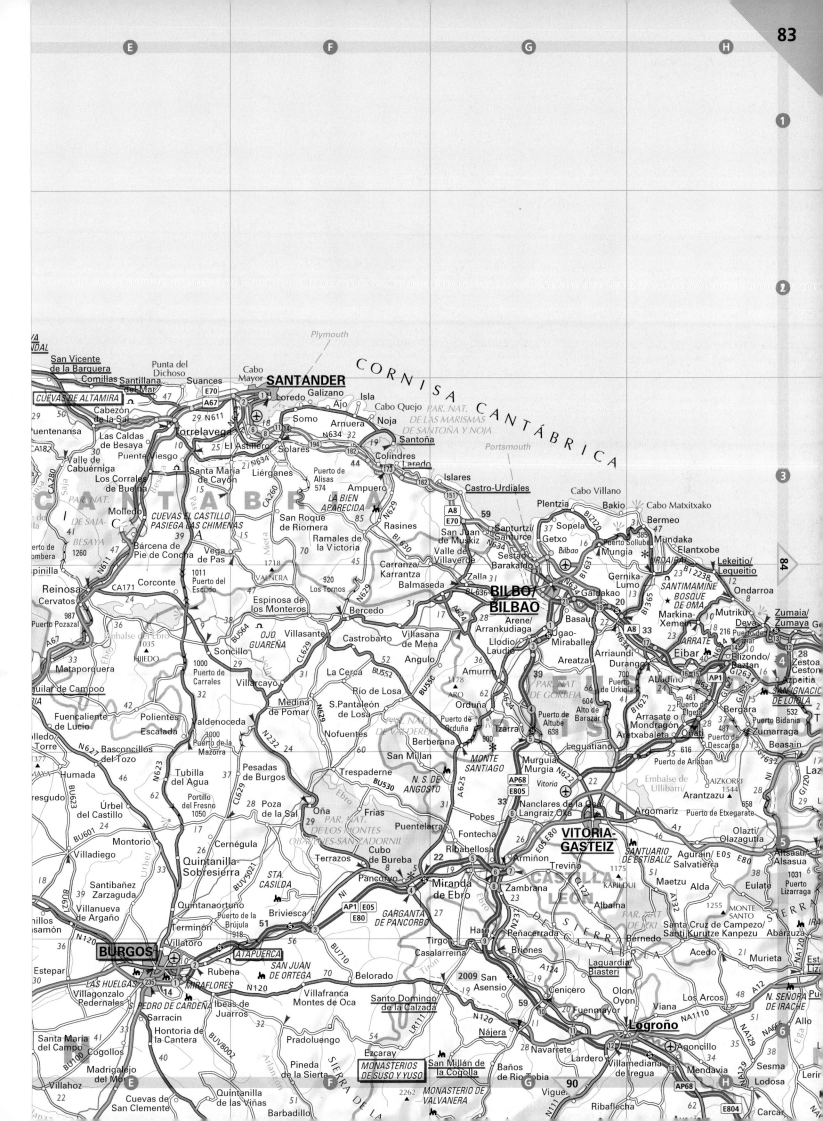

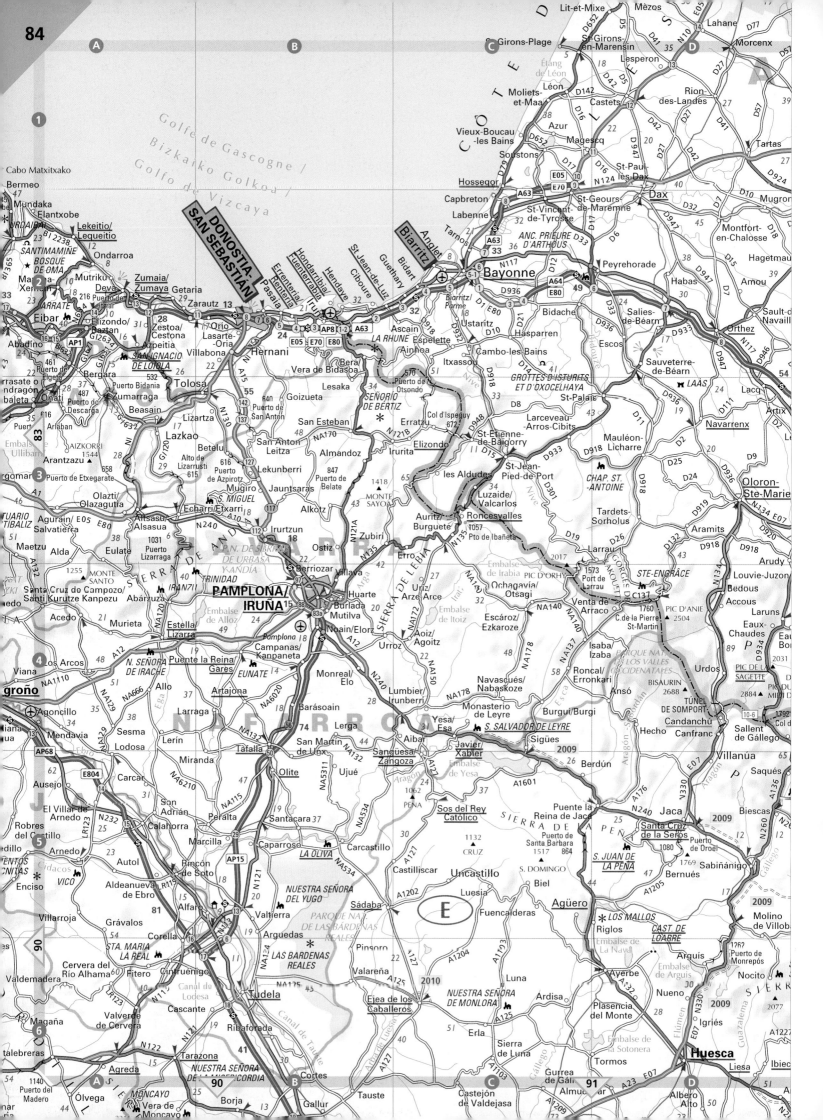

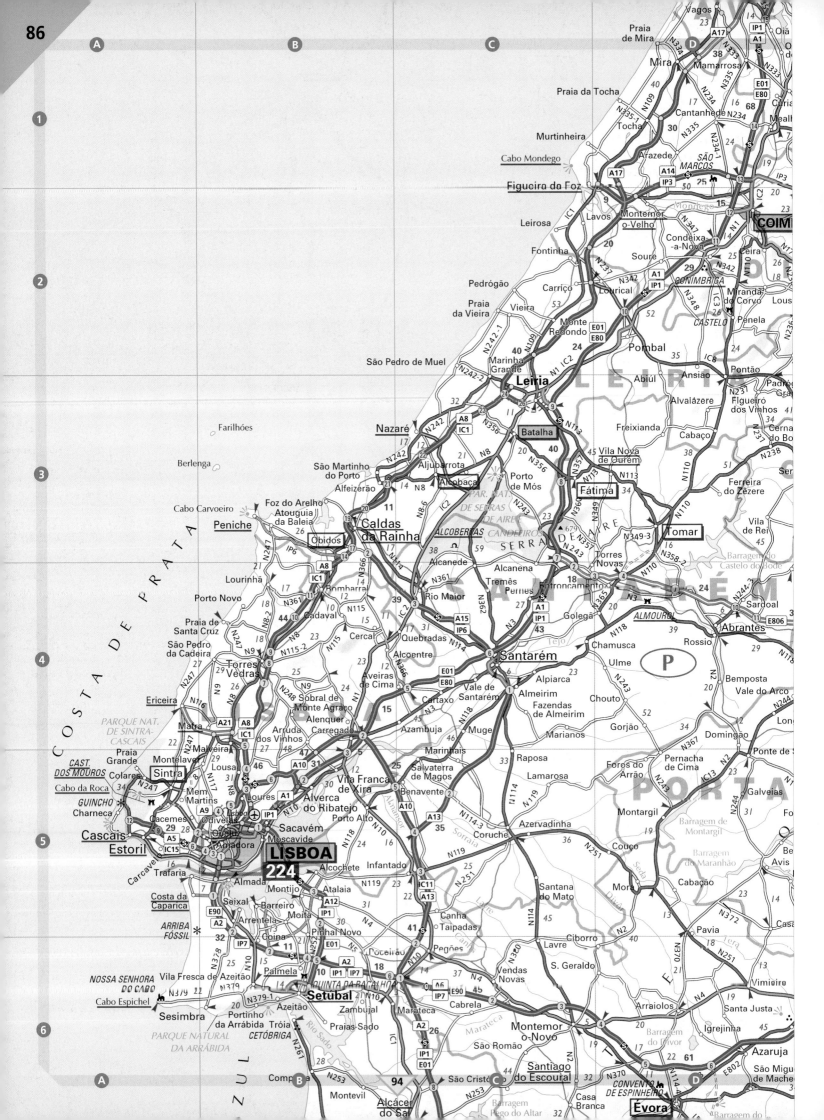

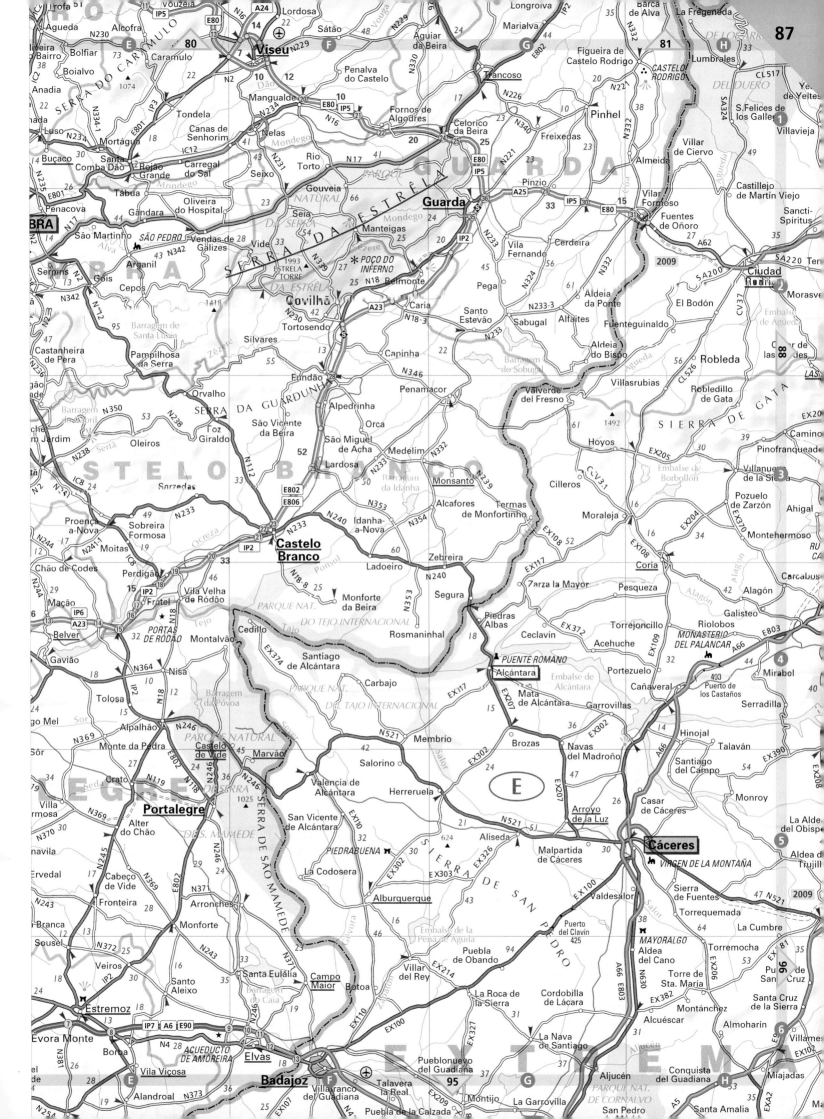

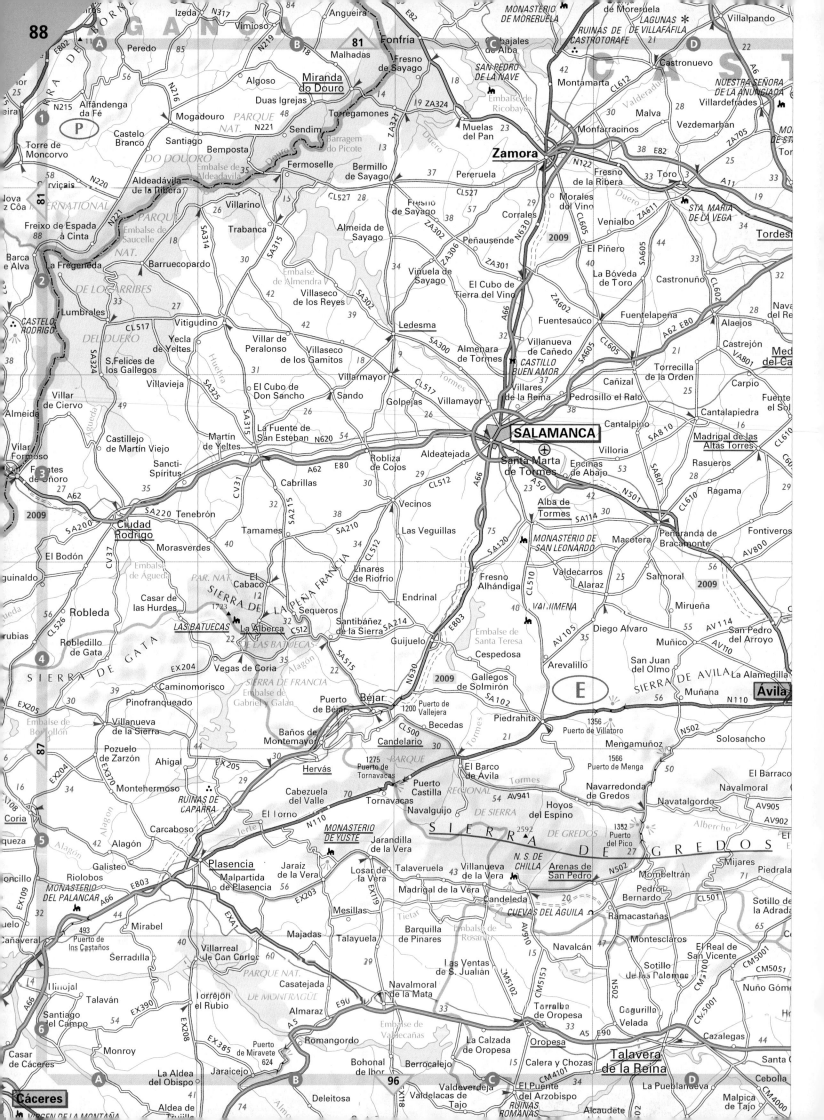

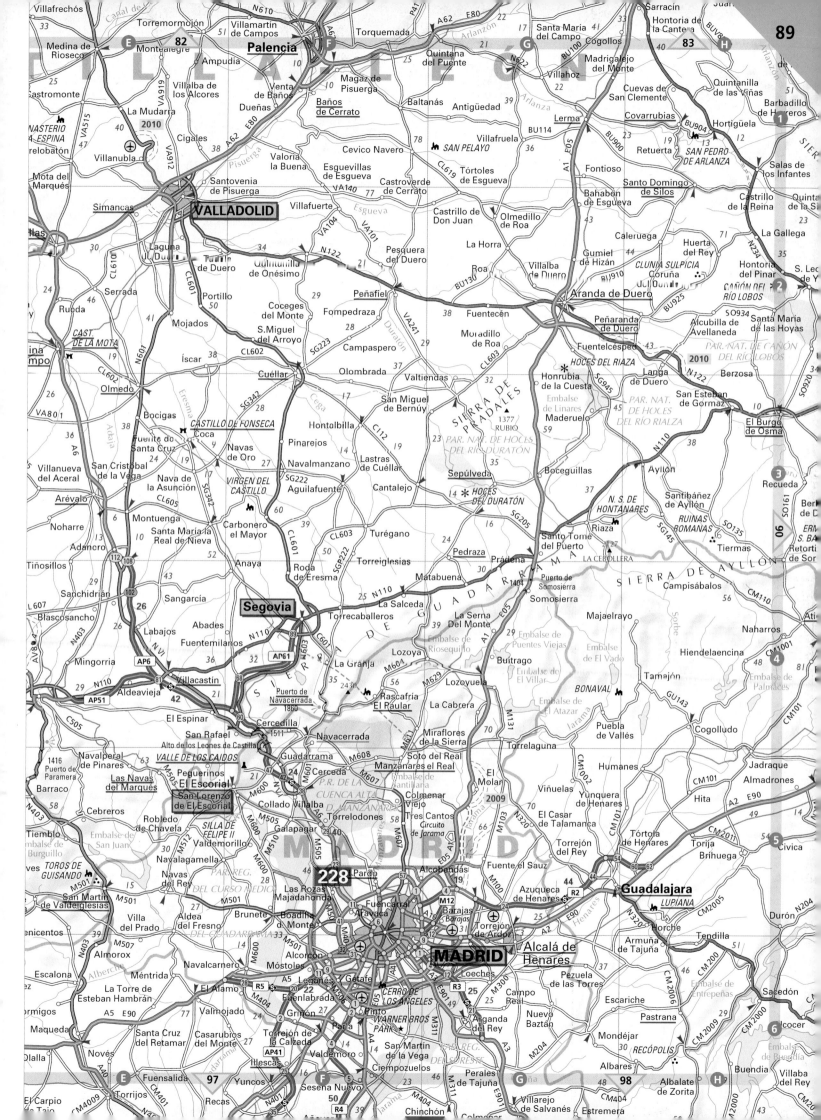

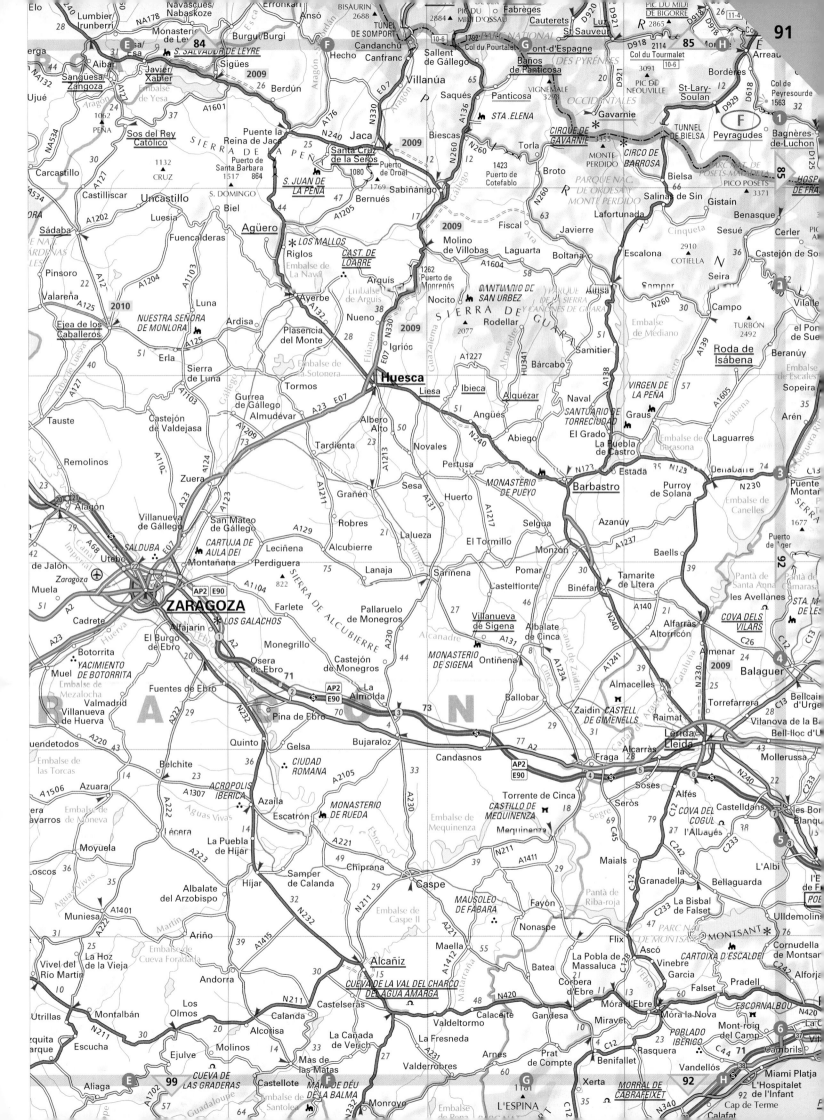

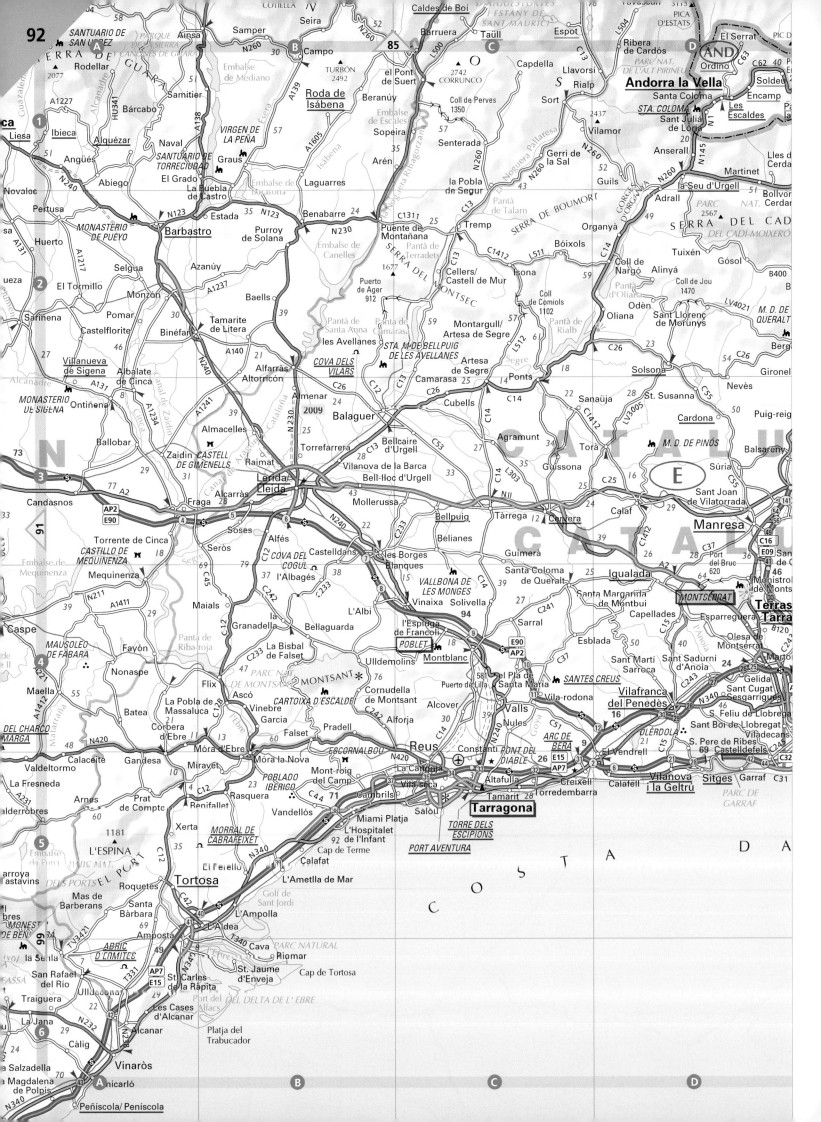

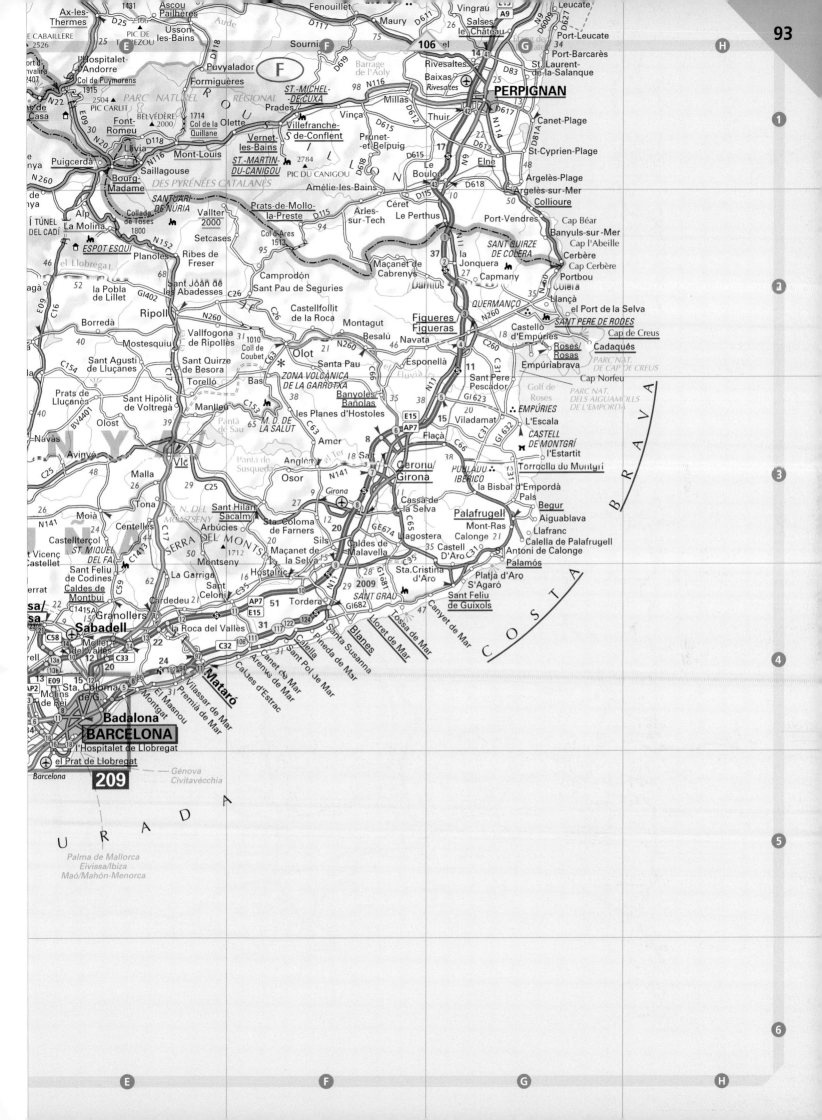

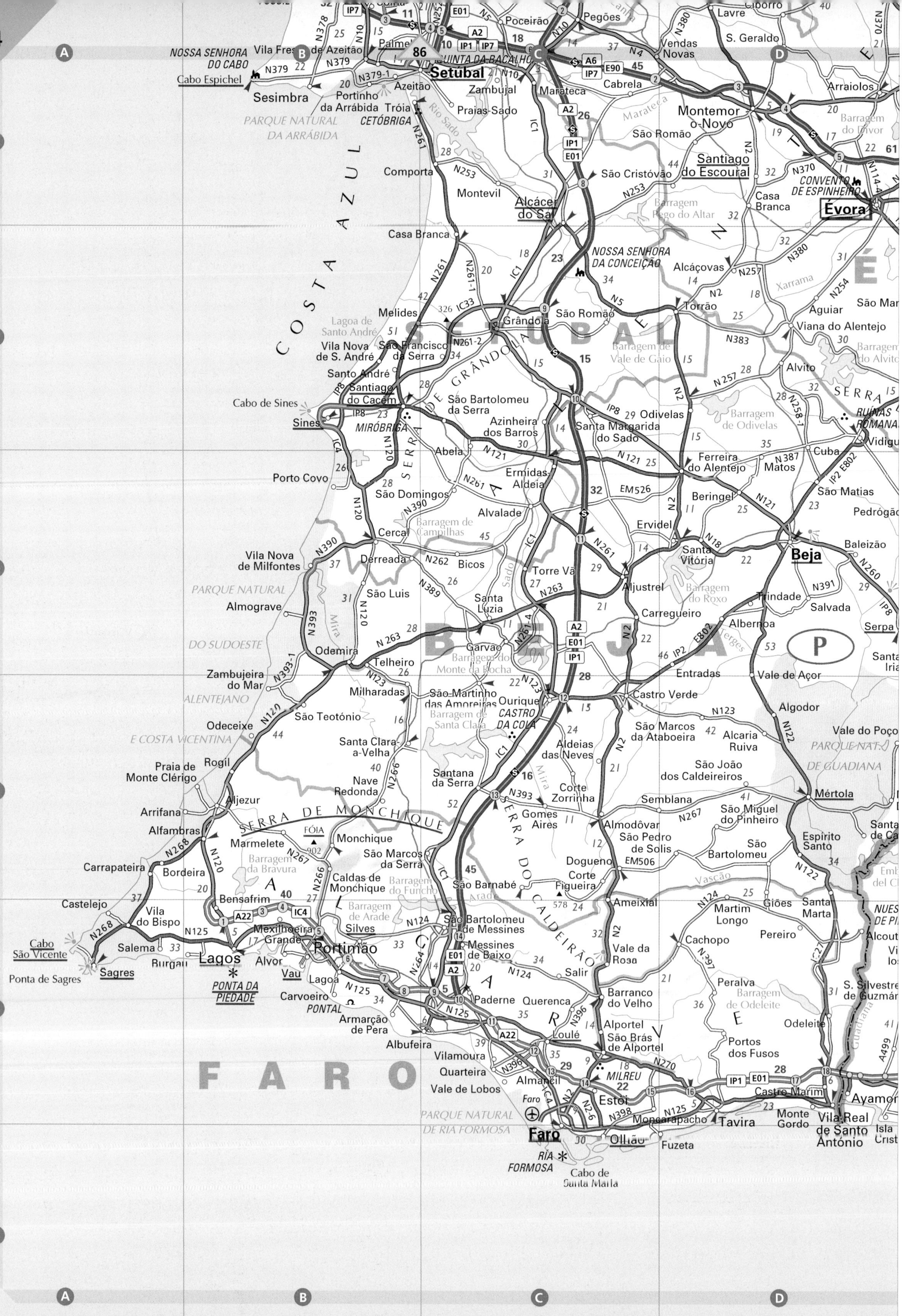

A   B   C   D

NOSSA SENHORA DO CABO
Cabo Espichel
Sesimbra

Vila Fresca de Azeitão
Azeitão
Portinho da Arrábida
Tróia
PARQUE NATURAL DA ARRÁBIDA
CETÓBRIGA

Palmela
Setubal
86
Zambujal
Praias-Sado
Quinta da Bacalhô
Marateca
Cabrela

Poceirão
Pegões
Vendas Novas
S. Geraldo
Lavre
Ciborro

Montemor-o-Novo
Arraiolos
Barragem do Divor

Comporta
Montevil
Alcácer do Sal
Casa Branca

São Romão
São Cristóvão
Santiago do Escoural
Casa Branca
CONVENTO DE ESPINHEIRO
Évora

COSTA AZUL

Melides
Lagoa de Santo André
Vila Nova de S. André
Santo André
Cabo de Sines
Sines
MIRÓBRIGA
Santiago do Cacém

São Francisco da Serra
Grândola
São Romão
SERRA DE GRÂNDOLA
São Bartolomeu da Serra
Azinheira dos Barros
Abela
Santa Margarida do Sado
Odivelas

NOSSA SENHORA DA CONCEIÇÃO
Alcáçovas
Torrão
Aguiar
Viana do Alentejo
Alvito

Barragem de Vale de Gaio
Barragem de Odivelas
Ferreira do Alentejo
Matos
Cuba
São Matias
Pedrógão
Beringel

Porto Covo
São Domingos
Alvalade
Ermidas-Aldeia

Cercal
Derreada
Bicos
Torre Vã
Aljustrel
Santa Vitória
Beja
Baleizão
Vila Nova de Milfontes
São Luis
Santa Luzia
Carregueiro
Trindade
Salvada
Serpa
Almograve
Garvão
Albernoa
Algodor

PARQUE NATURAL DO SUDOESTE ALENTEJANO E COSTA VICENTINA

Odemira
Telheiro
Barragem do Monte da Rocha
Entradas
Vale de Açor
Castro Verde

Zambujeira do Mar
Milharadas
São Martinho das Amoreiras
Ourique
CASTRO DA COLA
São Marcos da Ataboeira
Alcaria Ruiva
Vale do Poço
PARQUE NAT. DE GUADIANA

Odeceixe
São Teotónio
Santa Clara-a-Velha
Aldeias das Neves
São João dos Caldeireiros
Mértola

Praia de Monte Clérigo
Rogil
Nave Redonda
Santana da Serra
Corte Zorrinha
Semblana
São Miguel do Pinheiro
Espírito Santo
Arrifana
Aljezur
Gomes Aires
Almodôvar
São Pedro de Solis
São Bartolomeu

Alfambras
SERRA DE MONCHIQUE
FÓIA
Marmelete
Monchique
São Marcos da Serra
Dogueno
Corte Figueira
Ameixial

Carrapateira
Bordeira
Barragem da Bravura
Caldas de Monchique
São Barnabé
Martim Longo
Santa Marta

Castelejo
Vila do Bispo
Bensafrim
Mexilhoeira Grande
Barragem de Arade
Silves
São Bartolomeu de Messines
Messines de Baixo
Vale da Rosa
Salir
Cachopo
Pereiro
Giões
Alcoutim

Cabo São Vicente
Ponta de Sagres
Salema
Burgau
Lagos
Alvor
Vau
Lagoa
Portimão
Carvoeiro
Pontal
Armação de Pera
Albufeira
Vilamoura
Quarteira
Vale de Lobos
Paderne
Querença
Loulé
São Brás de Alportel
Barranco do Velho
Alportel
Peralva
Barragem de Odeleite
Odeleite
S. Silvestre de Guzmán

Sagres
PONTA DA PIEDADE

F A R O

Almancil
MILREU
Estói
Moncarapacho
Tavira
Monte Gordo
Vila Real de Santo António
Ayamonte

PARQUE NATURAL DE RIA FORMOSA
Faro
Olhão
Fuzeta
RIA FORMOSA
Cabo de Santa Maria

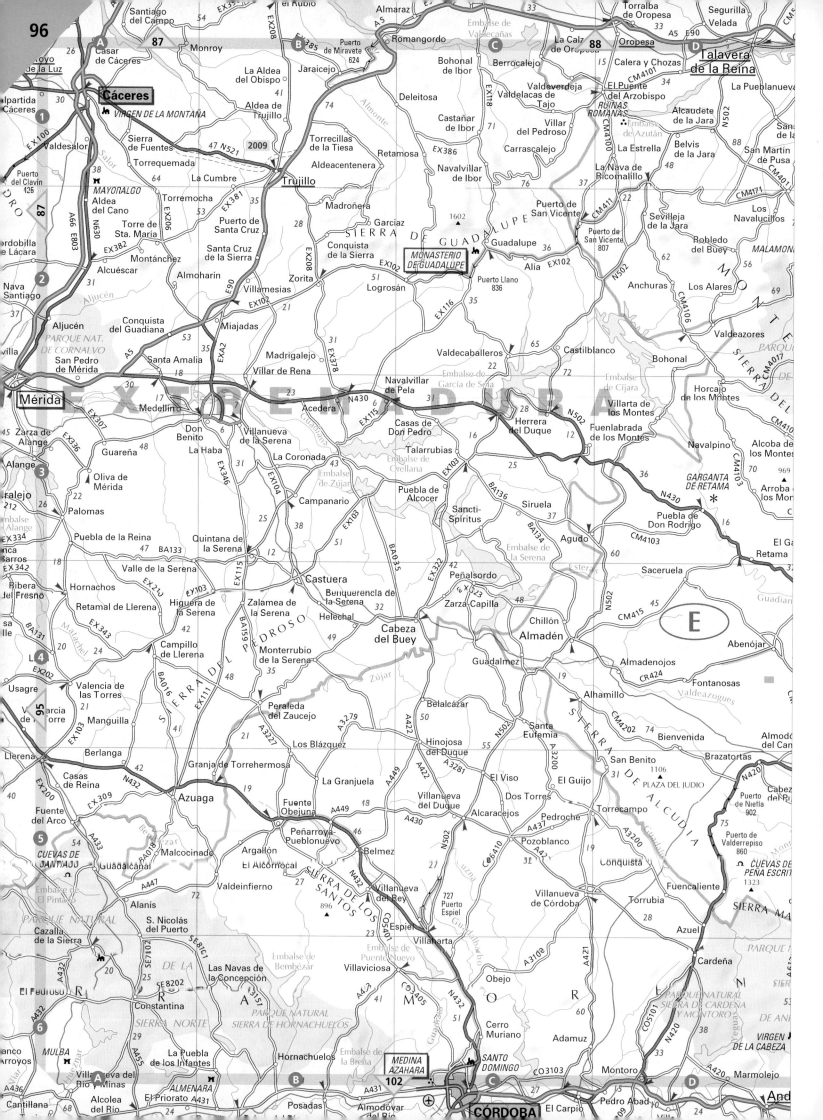

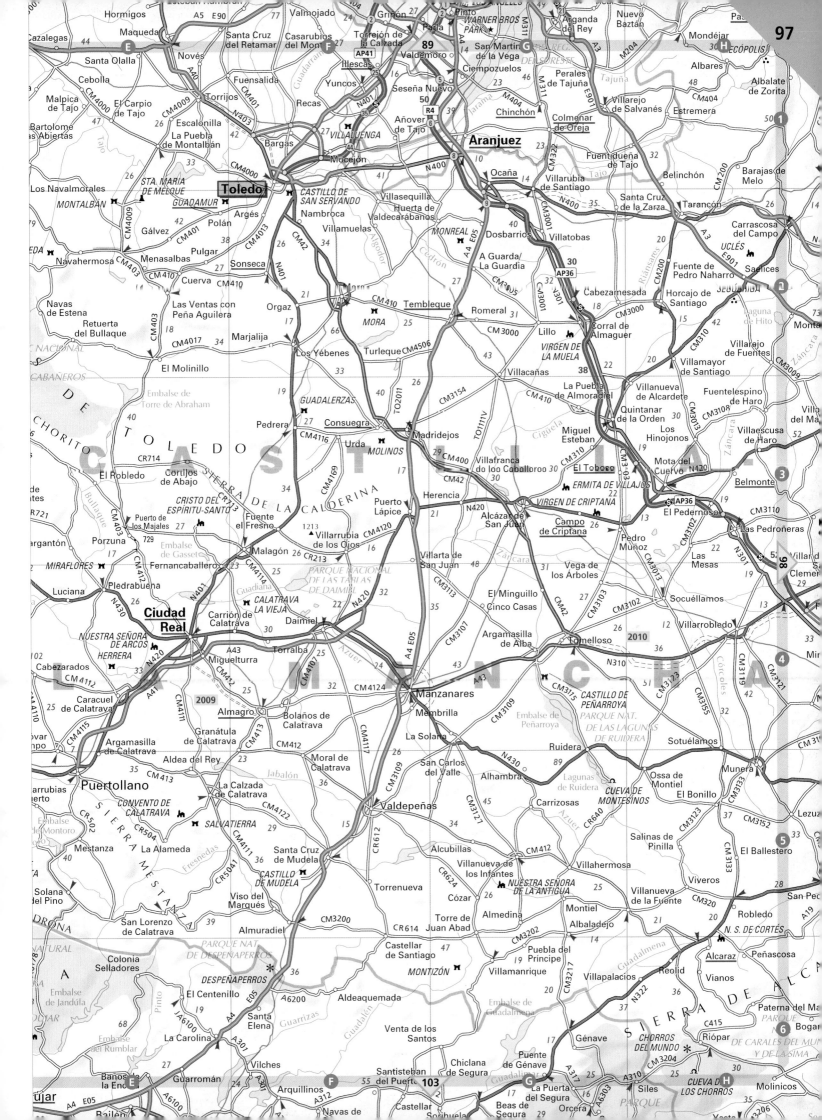

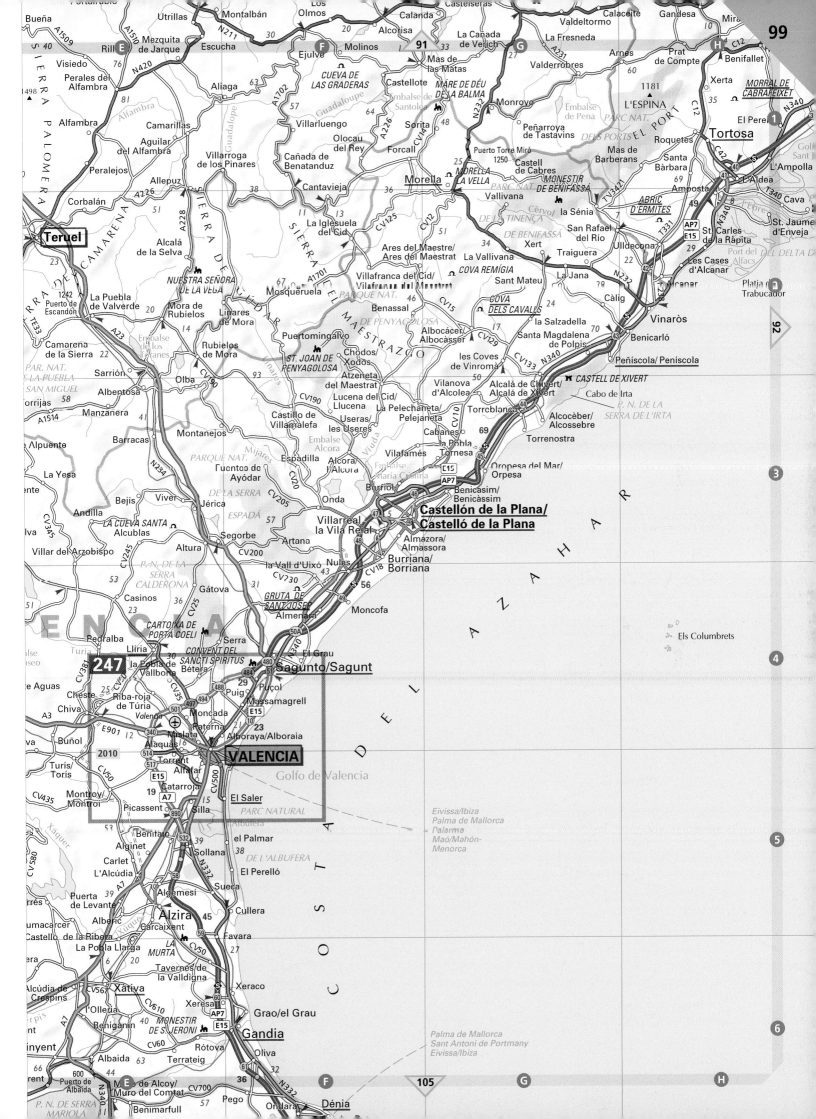

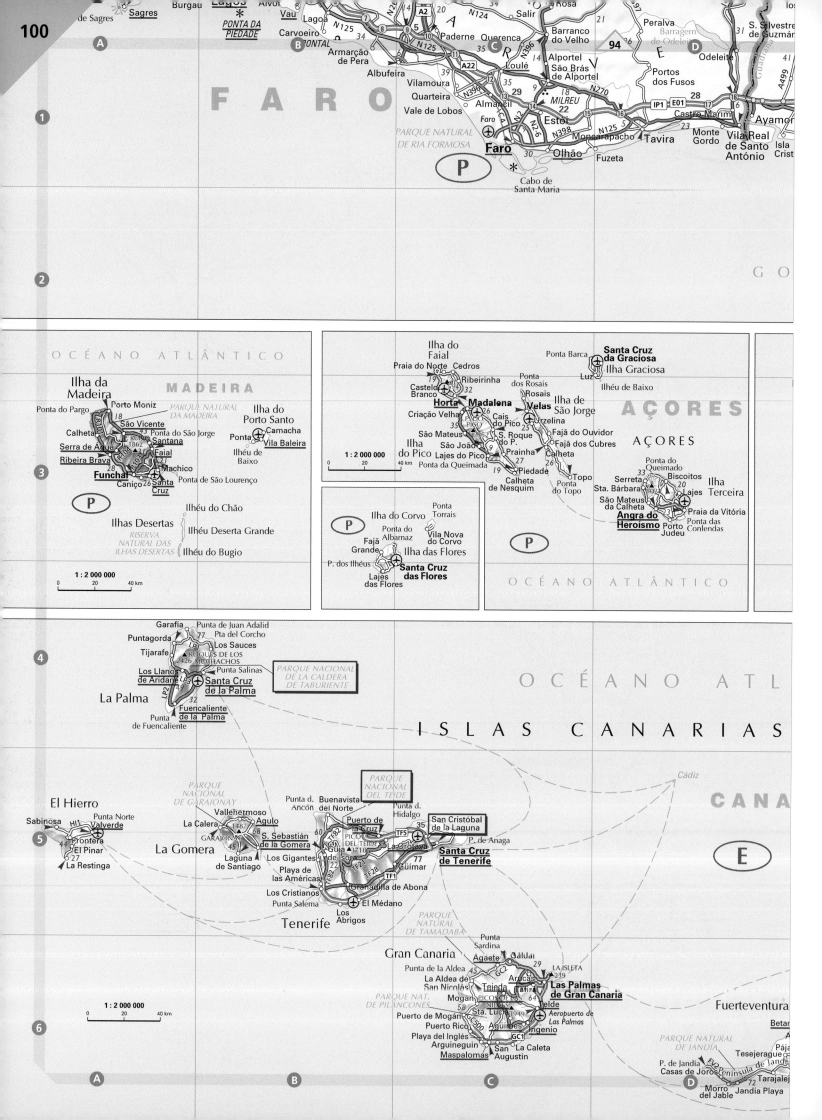

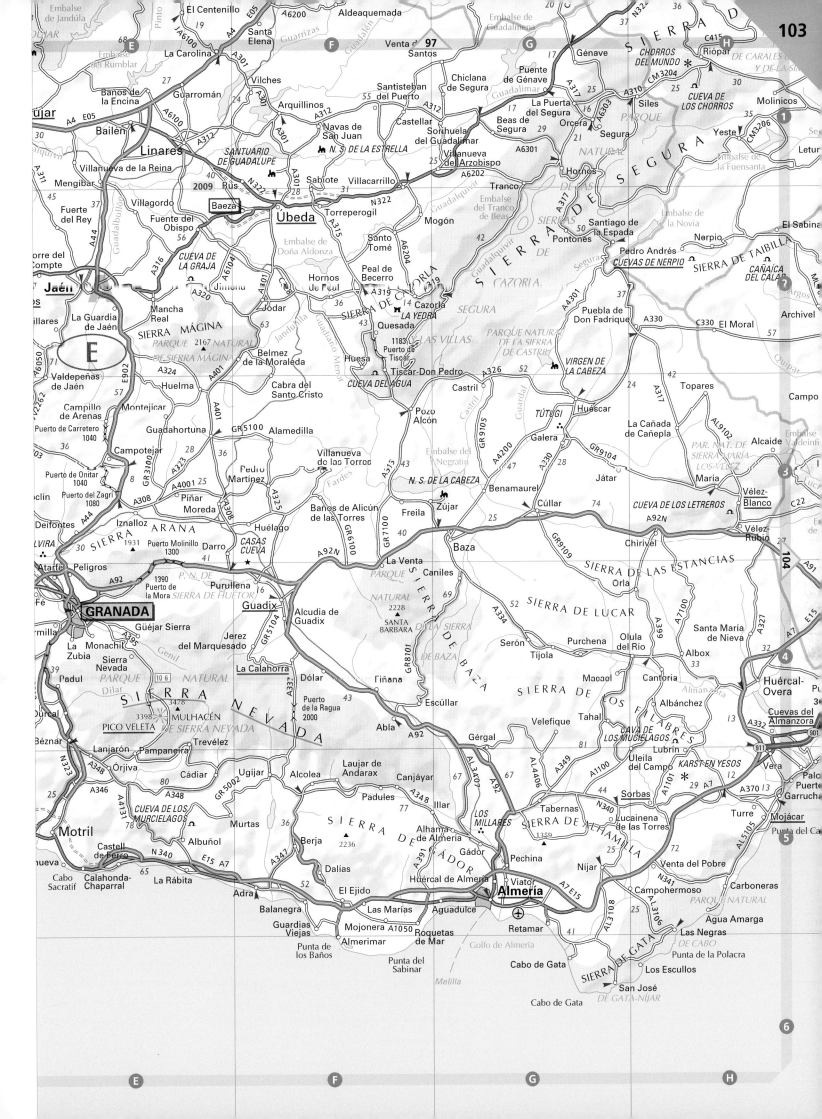

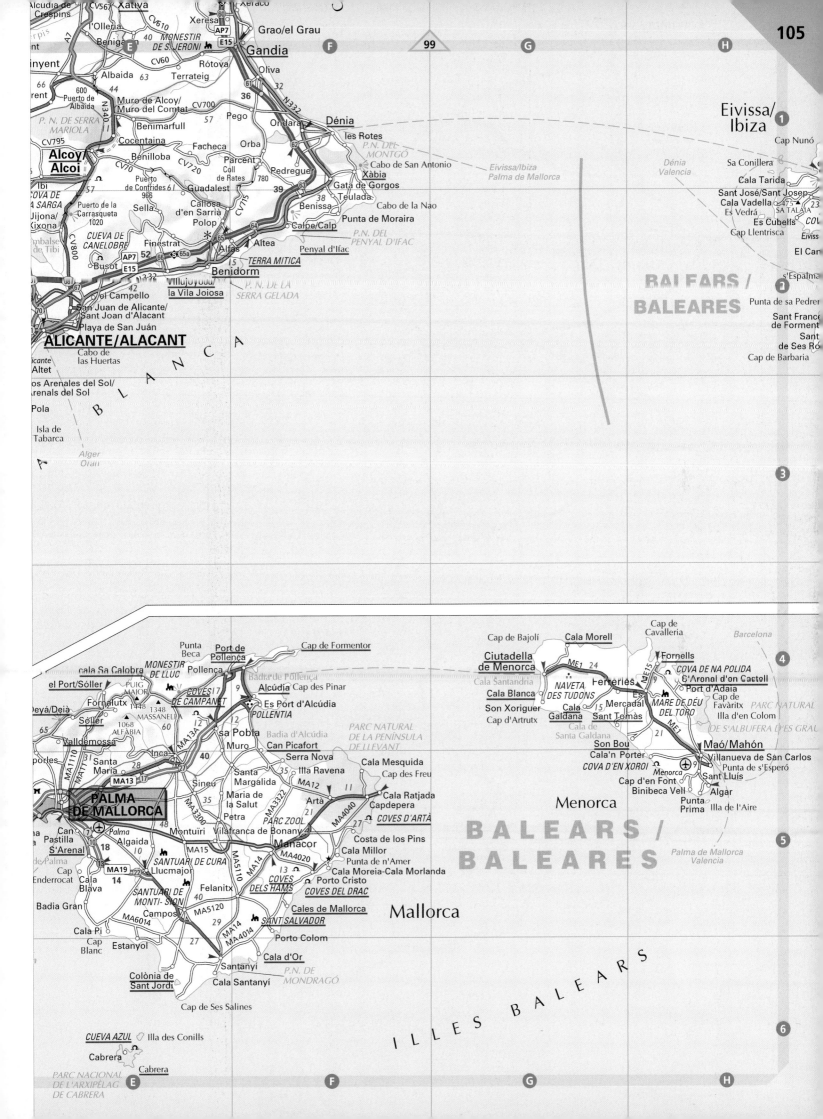

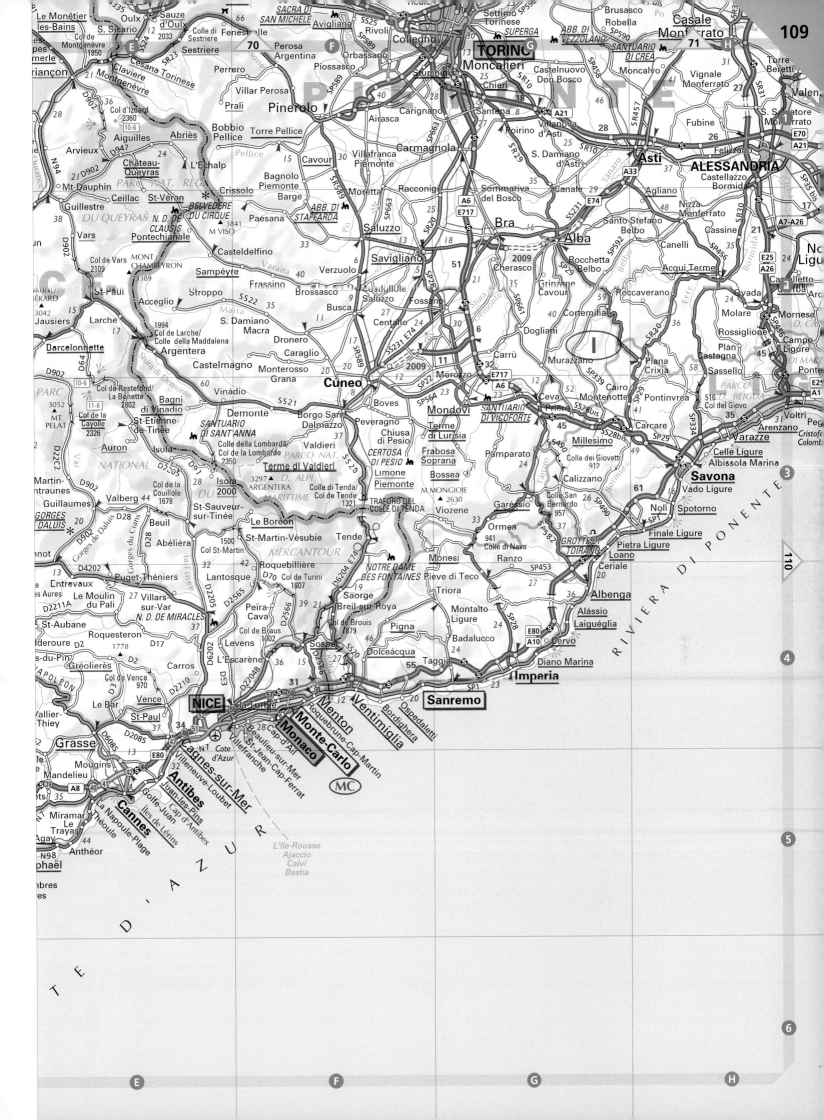

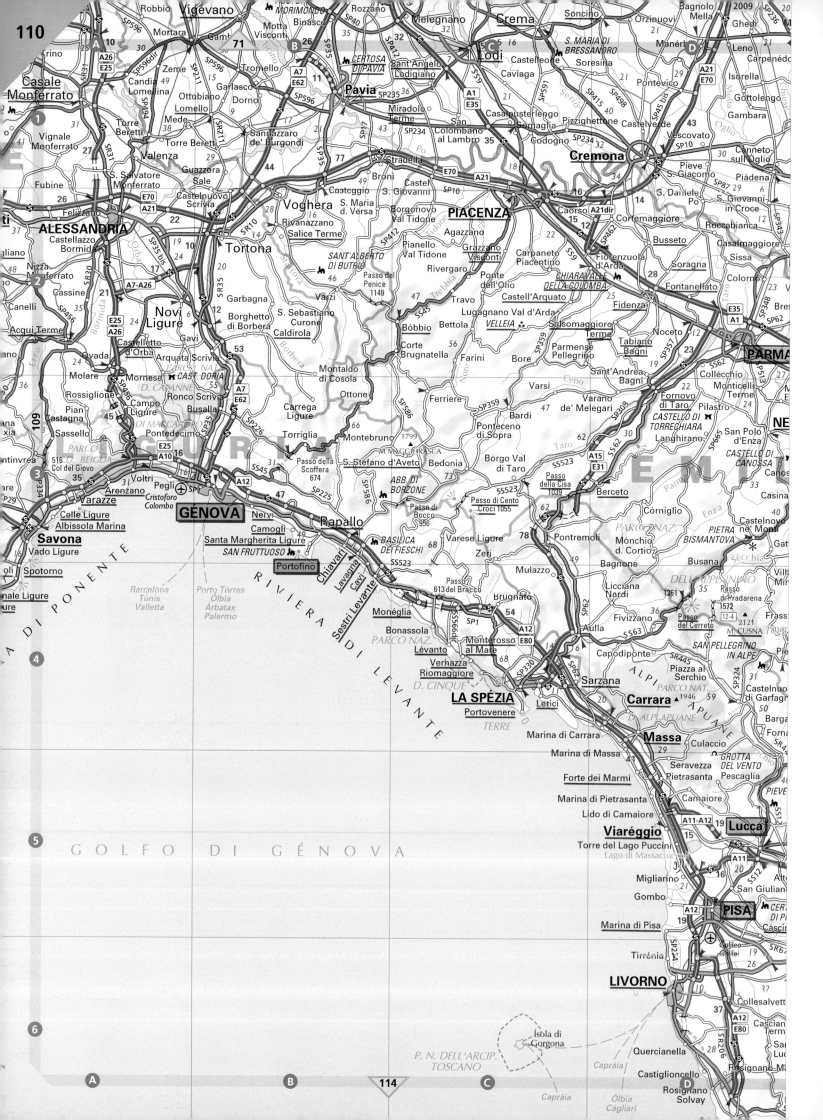

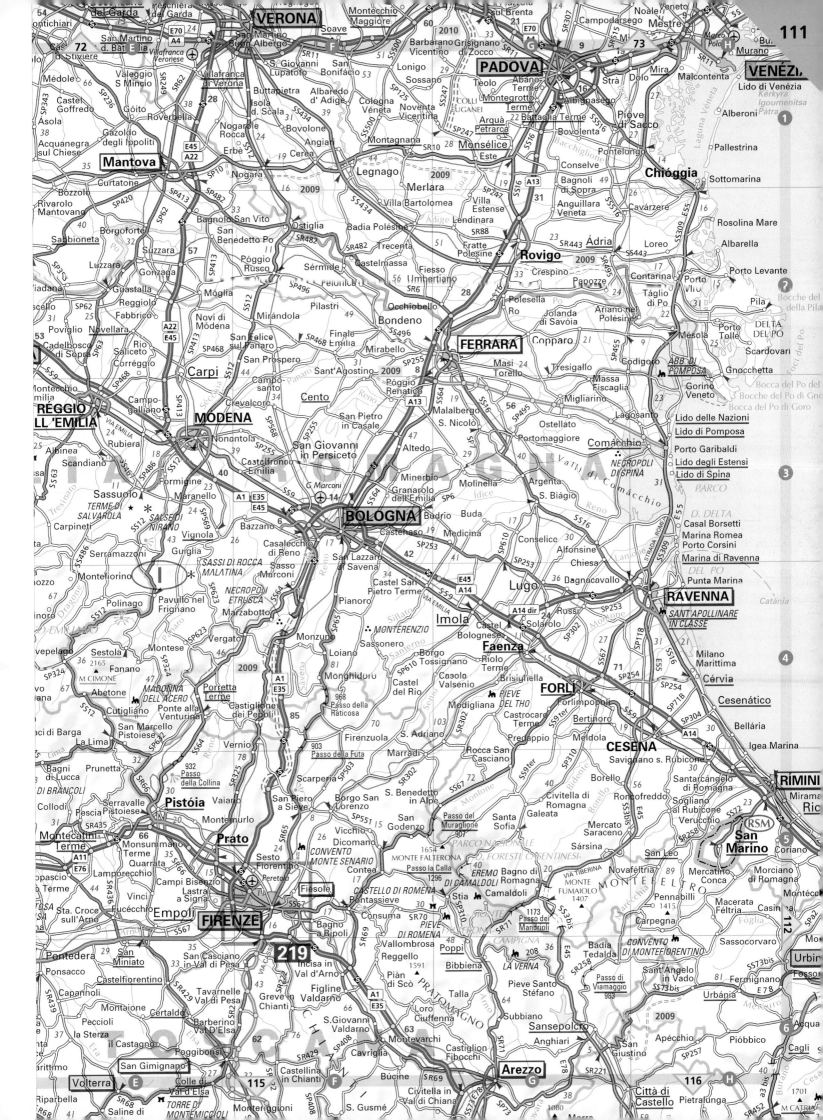

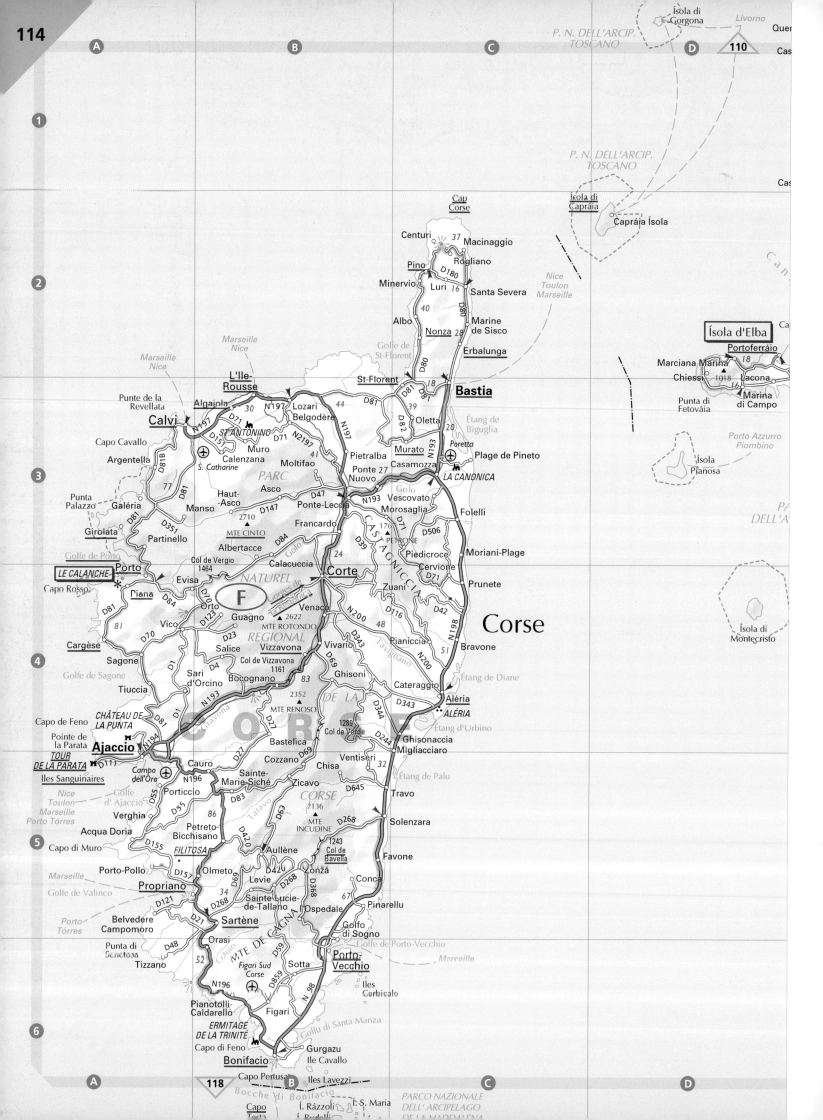

Kurba Vela

Zlarin
Brodarica

Žirje

Primošten
Prapatnica

Bristvica

Rogoznica
Seget
Split

Marina
Kaštel Stari

Rt Ploča
Trogir
Okrug

HR
Drvenik

Maslinica
Rogač

Šolta
Stomorska

E   F   G   H

1

142

Split

2

Jabuka

Komiža
Vis

Svetac
Korčula

Vis

MODRA ŠPILJA
Biševo

J

4

Palagruža

Marina

RA

ncavilla
Mare

40
Ortona

A14
45
San Vito Chietino

SP38
SAN GIOVANNI IN VENERE

iano
E55   5
Torino di Sangro Marina

SS652
Torino di Sangro

3
Punta di Penna

15
Casalbordino

SP364
54
Vasto

Atessa
Cupello
Marina di Vasto
8

Gissi
SP86
San Salvo

SS652
24   SS16
Térmoli

Colledi-
mezzo
136
Montenero
di Bisáccia
Campomarino

Villa
Santa Maria
MADONNA DI
CANNETO
SP163
97
Guglionesi
28
Marina di Chiéuti

iglione
Marino

SP168
Montefalcone
nel Sannio
A14
E55   31

Agnone
SS650
Castelmauro
SP87
S. Martino
in Pensilis
2009

otta
Guardialfiera
SP163
53
Larino
Ururi
Serracapriola

Trivento
Casacalenda
23

RUDERI ROMANI
Lucito
SP87
89
Bonefro
San Paolo
di Civitate

escolanciano
Limosano
SS647
Petrella
Tifernina
Santa Croce
di Magliano
21

Casalciprano
SP163
12
Colletorto
Torremaggiore

rpinone
E
SS647
Sant'Elia
a Pianisi
SP212
Castelnuovo
121

SP81
Carlantino

Frosolone
SS645
Lago
di Occhito
Castelnuovo
della Dáunia
22   29

Campobasso

Í Pianosa

PARCO NAZIONALE
DEL GARGANO

Í. Capráia

Í. S. Dómino
ÍSOLE TRÉMITI
Í. S. Nicola

5

Lido di
Torre Mileto
Rodi
Gargánico
Péschici

Lago di Lésina
49
Lago di
Varano
SS89
40
SP52

Lésina
SS89
Vico del
Gargano
Vieste

SS89
Carpino
SP144
SS89
SS53

Sannicandro
Gargánico
Cagnano
Varano
NAZIONALE

3
12
PROMONTORIO DEL GARGANO

Apricena
1055
SS272
SS89b
Pugnochiuso

San Marco
in Lamis
San Giovanni
Rotondo
SS272
Mattinata
59
Baia
delle Zagare

6

San
Severo
SP10   SP30
Pasta
Granata
G
Monte
Sant'Angelo
H

121
SP160
SANTA MARIA
DI SIPONTO
Manfredónia

SP2
SAN LEONARDO
Golfo di

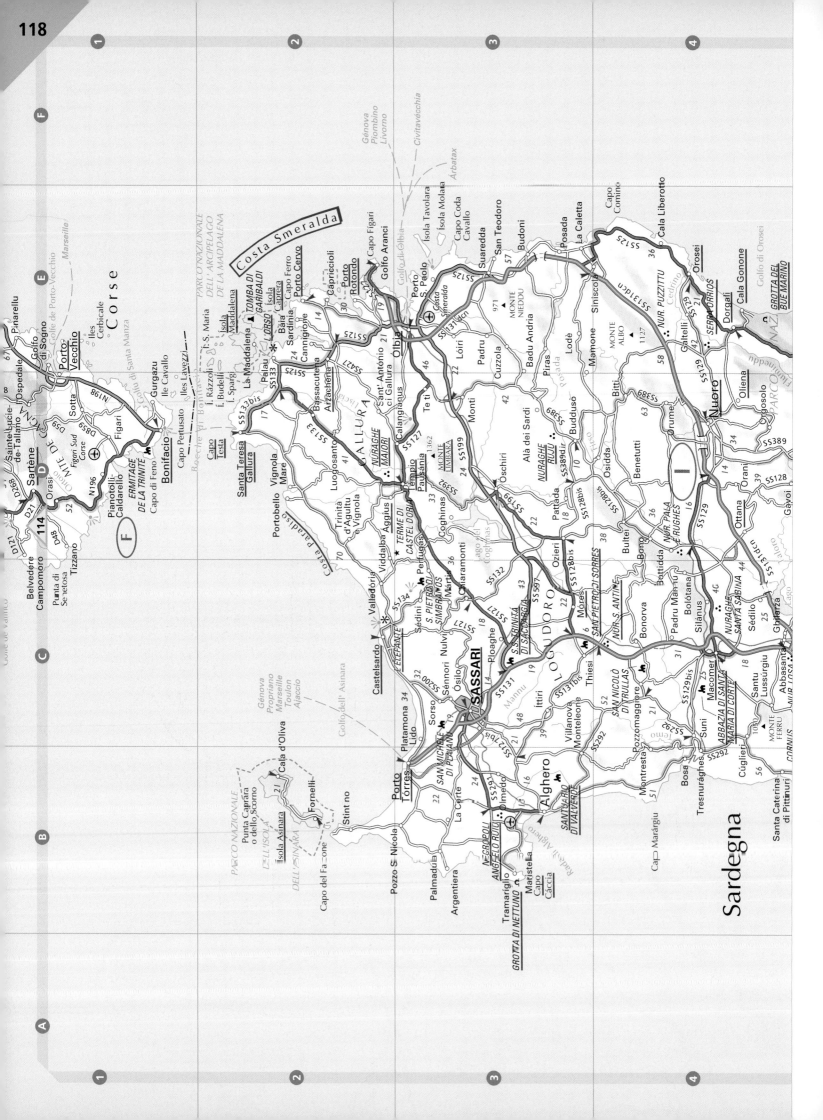

Sardegna

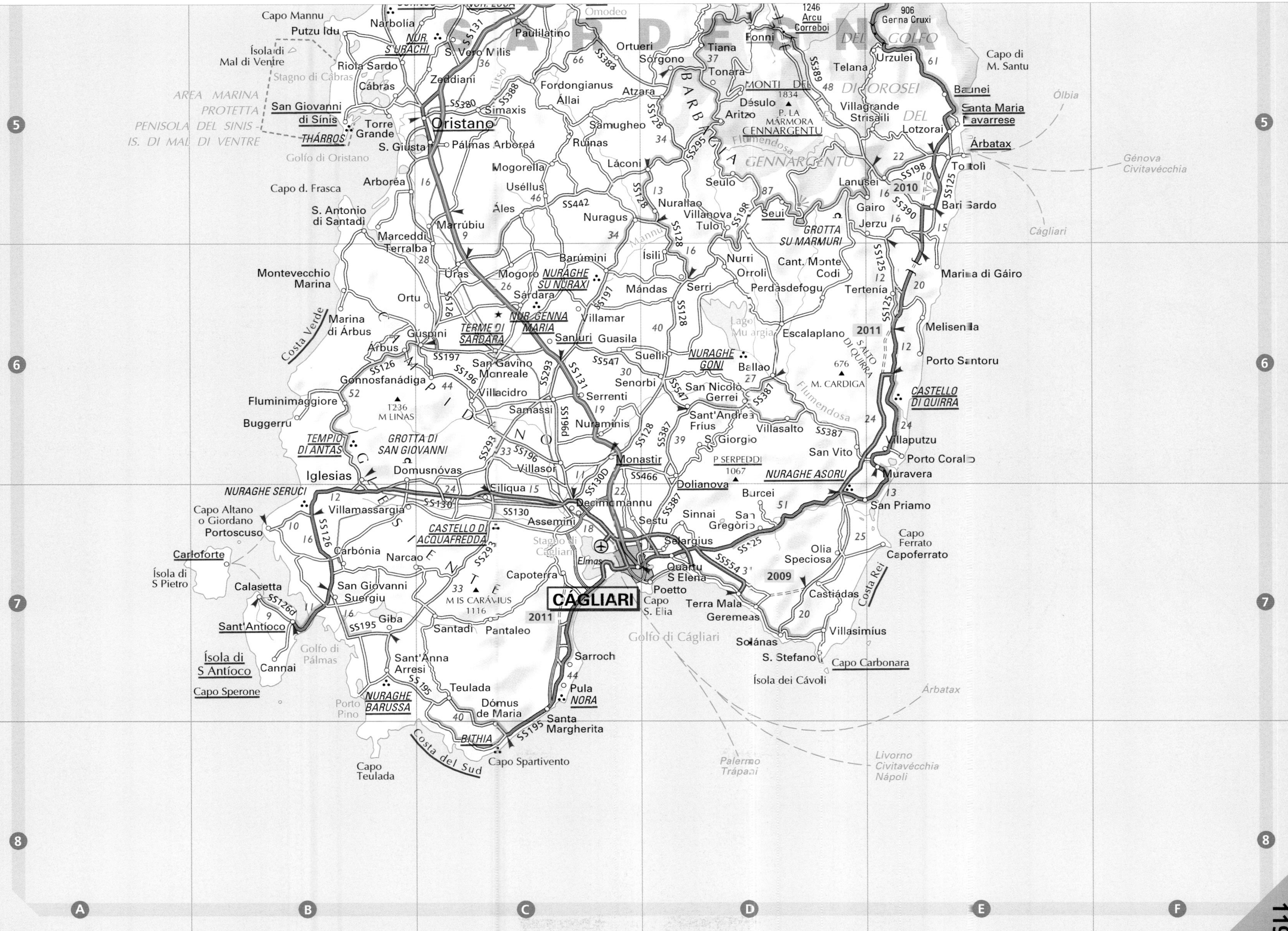

CÁGLIARI

SARDEGNA

GOLFO DI OROSEI

Capo di M. Santu
Santa Maria Navarrese
Baunei
Urzulei
Arbatax
Tortolì
Lotzorai
Bari Sardo
Marina di Gairo
Melisenda
Porto Santoru
Porto Corallo
CASTELLO DI QUIRRA
Villaputzu
Muravera
San Priamo
Capo Ferrato
Capoferrato
Arbatax
Costa Rei
Villasimius
Capo Carbonara
S. Stefano
Isola dei Cávoli

Livorno
Civitavécchia
Nápoli
Palermo
Trápani

Gerrei Cruxi
Arcu Correboi
Fonni
Tiana
Tonara
Desulo
Aritzo
MONTI DEL GENNARGENTU
P. LA MARMORA
Seui
Seulo
Nurri
Orroli
Villagrande Strisaili
Villanova Tulo
Gairo
Jerzu
Lanusei
Ussassai
Tertenia
Escalaplano
M. CARDIGA
SALTO DI QUIRRA
San Vito
M. Flumendosa
Villasalto
NURAGHE ASORU
Olia Speciosa
Castiádas

GROTTA SU MARMURI
Cant. Monte Codi
Perdasdefogu

Ortueri
Sórgono
Atzara
Sámugheo
Ruinas
Laconi
Nuragus
Isili
Mandas
Serri
Nuragus
Serri
Nurallao
NURAGHE GENNA MARIA
Villamar
Guasila
Suelli
Senorbì
Serrenti
Nuraminis
Samatzai
Monastir
Sestu
Dolianova
Burcei
Sinnai
San Gregorio
Settimo
Maracalagonis
Quartu S. Elena
Poetto
Capo S. Elia
Golfo di Cágliari
Elmas
Sarroch
Pula
NORA
Santa Margherita

Omodeo
Paulilátino
S. Vero Milis
Simaxis
Oristano
Santa Giusta
Palmas Arborea
Marrubiu
Uras
Terralba
Arborea
Mogoro
Ales
Usellus
Sárdara
TERME DI SARDARA
San Gavino Monreale
Sanluri
Villacidro
Gonnosfanádiga
M. LINAS
Arbus
Guspini
GROTTA DI SAN GIOVANNI
Domusnóvas
Iglesias
Villamassargia
Carbónia
Narcao
San Giovanni Suergiu
Giba
TEMPIO DI ANTAS
NURAGHE BARUSSA
Sant'Anna Arresi
Santadi
CASTELLO DI ACQUAFREDDA
M. IS CARAVIUS
Pantaleo
Teulada
Domus de Maria
BITHIA
Capo Teulada
Costa del Sud
Porto Pino
Golfo di Palmas

Montevecchio Marina
Marina di Arbus
Costa Verde
Fluminimaggiore
Buggerru
NURAGHE SERUCI
Portoscuso
Capo Altano o Giordano
Carloforte
Isola di S. Pietro
Calasetta
Cannai
Sant'Antioco
Isola di S. Antíoco
Capo Sperone

Capo Mannu
Putzu Idu
Napbolia
Riola Sardo
Cábras
San Giovanni di Sinis
Torre Grande
THARROS
S. Antonio di Santadi
Capo d. Frasca
AREA MARINA PROTETTA PENISOLA DEL SINIS
IS. DI MAL DI VENTRE
Capo d. Ventre

Isoladi
Mal di Ventre
Stagno di Cábras
Golfo di Oristano

Génova Civitavécchia
Óibia
Cagliari

CÁGLIARI

2011
2010
2011
2009

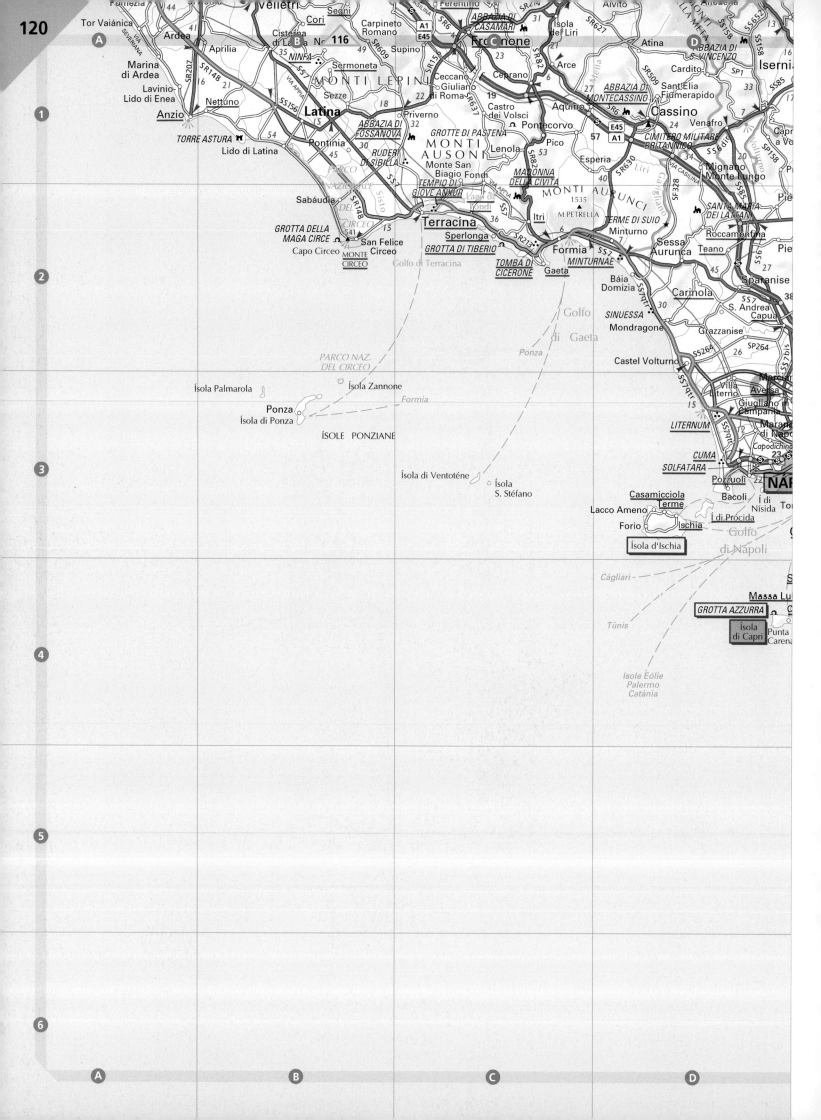

A

B

116

C

D

Isernia

1

2

3

4

5

6

Tor Vaiánica
Ardea
Aprilia
Marina
di Ardea
Lavínio
Lido di Enea
Anzio
Nettúno
TORRE ASTURA
Lido di Latina
Latina
Pontínia
Sabáudia
GROTTA DELLA
MAGA CIRCE
Capo Circeo
San Felice
Circeo
MONTE
CIRCEO

Vellétri
Segni
Cori
Cisterna
di Latina
NINFA
Sermoneta
MONTI LEPINI
Sezze
Priverno
ABBAZIA DI
FOSSANOVA
RUDERI
DI SIBILLA
PARCO
NAZIONALE
DEL
CIRCEO
Terracina
Sperlonga
GROTTA DI TIBERIO

Carpineto
Romano
Supino
Ceccano
Giuliano
di Roma
Castro
dei Volsci
Pontecorvo
Pico
GROTTE DI PASTENA
MONTI
AUSONI
Monte San
Biagio Fondi
Lenola
Lago di
Fondi
TEMPIO DI
GIOVE ANXUR
Itri
M PETRELLA
MADONNA
DELLA CIVITA
MONTI AURUNCI
TOMBA DI
CICERONE
Gaeta
Formia
MINTURNAE
TERME DI SUIO
Minturno

Ferentino
ABBAZIA DI
CASAMARI
Isola
del Liri
Frosinone
Arce
Ceprano
Aquino
ABBAZIA DI
MONTECASSINO
Esperia
Cassino
CIMITERO MILITARE
BRITANNICO
Sessa
Aurunca
Teano
Báia
Domízia
Carinola
SINUESSA
Mondragone
Castel Volturno
Grazzanise
S. Andrea
Capua
Sparanise
Roccamonfina

Alvito
Atina
ABBAZIA DI
S. VINCENZO
Cardito
Sant'Elia
Fiumerápido
Venafro
Mignano
Monte Lungo
SANTA MARIA
DEI LATTANI

Golfo di Terracina
Golfo
di Gaeta
Ponza
Formia
PARCO NAZ.
DEL CIRCEO
Ísola Palmarola
Ísola Zannone
Ponza
Ísola di Ponza
ÍSOLE PONZIANE
Ísola di Ventoténe
Ísola
S. Stéfano
Cáglïari
Tünis
Isole Èólie
Palermo
Catánia
GROTTA AZZURRA
Ísola
di Capri
Punta
Carena
Massa Lu
Casamicciola
Terme
Lacco Ameno
Forio
Ischia
Í di Prócida
Í di
Nísida
Ísola d'Ischia
Golfo
di Napoli
NÁP
Pozzuoli
Bacoli
CUMA
SOLFATARA
LITERNUM
Villa
Literno
Giugliano in
Campania
Marano
di Napo
Capodichino
Aversa

A

B

C

D

E   F   G   H

1

2

3

4

5

6

BARI

SS16 35 Mola
di Bari

Capurso

Adelfia Rutigliano

SP240 SS16 Polignano a Mare

Casamássima

Monópoli

37 Conversano

38 Turi GROTTE DI Castellana
CASTELLANA Grotte

18 SS379

SS100 SS172 Putignano Savelletri

GROTTA DI
PUTIGNANO Fasano Torre Canne

Gióia Alberobello Rosa Marina
del Colle Noci Villanova

SS172 SP16 26 SS379 52 Torre S. Sabina

SS239 37 Locorotondo Cisternino E55

A14 SS100 SS172 24 Ostuni

Martina Franca SP16 San Vito 35 SP16
dei Normanni

REGIONALE Céglie SP581 Bríndisi -
E843 28 Messápica Casale

34 Móttola SS172 San Michele GROTTA Bríndisi
Palagianello Salentino S. GIOVANNI

34 SS7 Crispiano Villa Latiano Mesagne
21 Massafra 36 Castelli 37 SS7

Palagiano Statte Grottaglie E90 15 Francavilla San Pietro 40 38
GRAVINE 22 Fontana Vernotico Casalabate

E90 18 SS7 SS603 Oria Torre Santa
Susanna San Dónaci Squinzano
Surbo

SS106 13 San Giorgio Carosino Sava San Pancrazio San
29 **TÁRANTO** Iónico 23 Salentino Dónaci San Cataldo

Marina Ísole Coradi Leporano Lizzano SS7ter SS7ter 49 Campi 12
di Ginosa o Cheradi Capo Salentina **LECCE** SP611
San Vito Mandúria 2009

METAPONTIUM Torricella Veglie Monteroni Rocca Vecchia
Lido Avetrana SP174 di Lecce 35
Silvana 47 Cavallino Sant'Andrea

Campomarino Copertino 24 SS16 Calimera
Porto 28 Martano
Cesareo

Nardò Galatina 17 SS16 Otranto
Galatone SP497 Capo d'Otranto
SP497 30 Máglie SS497 Minervino di Lecce
Gallípoli SP459 SP476 39 SS275 Santa Cesarea
13 Parábita Terme

SP459 Casarano Ruffano SP173 GROTTA ZINZULUSA
Taviano Taurisano SP474 Tricase

G O L F O   D I Ugento 50 50 Corsano
AUSENTUM Presicce

T Á R A N T O 48 SS274 Gagliano
del Capo

Marina di Capo S Maria
Léuca di Léuca

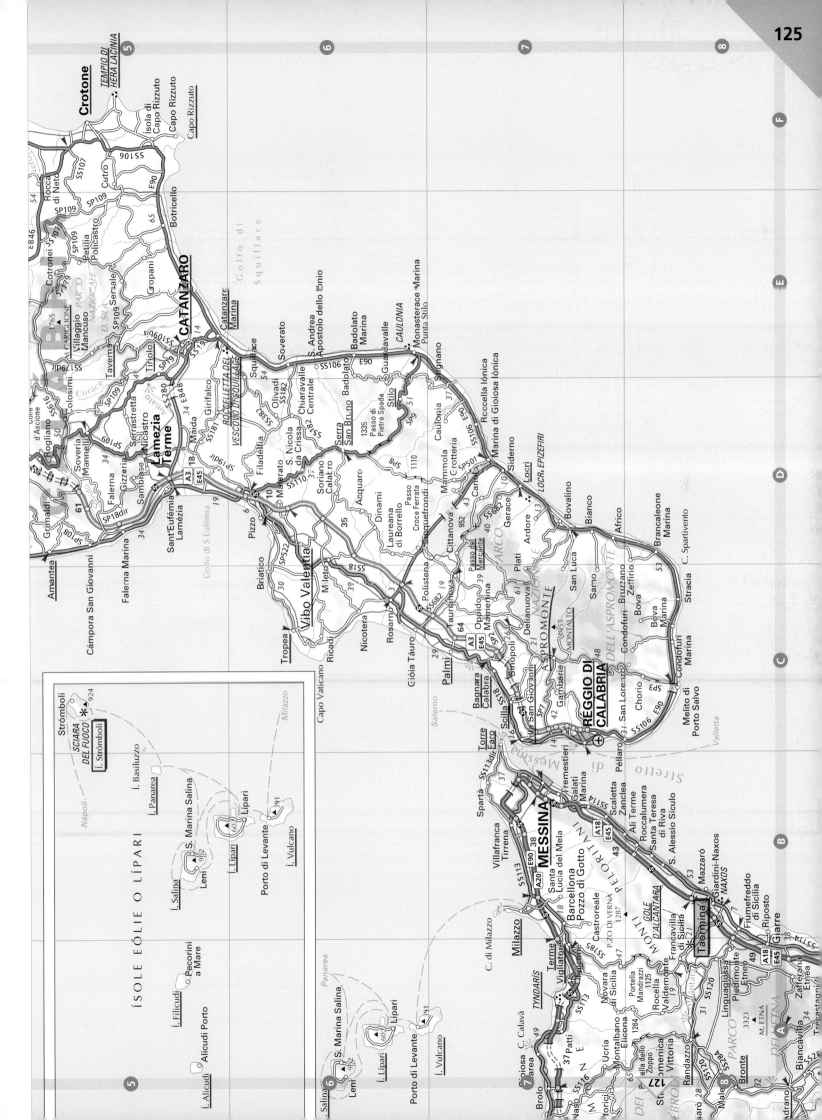

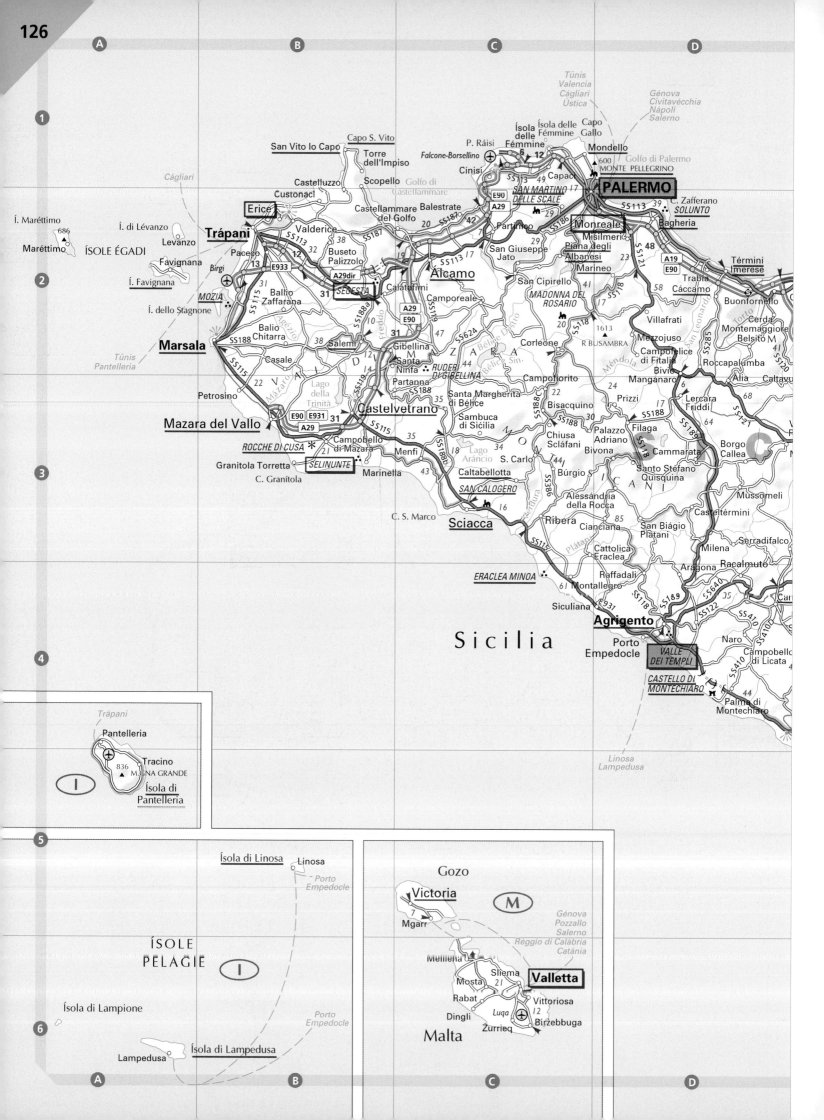

A   B   C   D

1

San Vito lo Capo
Capo S. Vito
Torre
dell'Impiso
Scopello

Castelluzzo
Custonaci

Erice

Trápani
Valderice
Paceco
Birgi

ÍSOLE ÉGADI
Í. Maréttimo
686
Maréttimo
Í. di Lévanzo
Levanzo
Í. Favignana
Favignana
Í. dello Stagnone

2

Tûnis
Pantelleria

MOZIA

Balio
Zaffarana
SS115

Marsala

Balio
Chitarra

Casale

Petrosino

3

Mazara del Vallo

Granítola Torretta
C. Granítola

Cágliari

Castellammare
del Golfo

Balestrate

Valderice
Buseto
Palizzolo

SS113
32
SS187
38
SS187

13
E933
12

31
SEGESTA

SS188.a

Calátafimi

Campobello
di Mazara
ROCCHE DI CUSA
SELINUNTE

Marinella

38 Salemi

Gibellina
M
Santa
Ninfa
Partanna

Castelvetrano

Menfi

C. S. Marco

Alcamo

Camporeale

San Giuseppe
Jato

SS113 17

Partinico

Tûnis
Valencia
Cágliari
Ústica

Ísola
delle
Fémmine
Ísola delle
Fémmine
Capo
Gallo

P. Ráisi
Falcone-Borsellino
Cínisi

SS113 49

SS113

E90
A29

SAN MARTINO
DELLE SCALE

6 12

Capaci
17
SS186
29

Monreale

Misilmeri

Piana degli
Albanesi
Marineo

San Cipirello

MADONNA DEL
ROSARIO

Corleone

1613
R. BUSAMBRA

Mondello

Golfo di Palermo
MONTE PELLEGRINO
600

PALERMO

C. Zafferano
SOLUNTO

Bagheria

SS121
48
A19
E90

Trabia
Cáccamo
58

Buonfornello

Villafrati

Mezzojuso

Campofelice
di Fitalia
Bivio

Prizzi

Lercara
Friddi

Términi
Imerese

Cerda
Montemaggiore
Belsito M
Roccapalumba
Alia

Manganaro
24
17
6
68

4

Sicilia

5

Pantelleria

Tracino
836
M.GNA GRANDE
Ísola di
Pantelleria

Trápani

ÍSOLE PELAGIE
I

Ísola di Lampione

6

Lampedusa

Ísola di Linosa
Linosa
Porto
Empedocle

Porto
Empedocle
Ísola di Lampedusa

Gozo
Victoria
Mgarr

M

Mellieħa
Mosta Sliema
Rabat
Dingli Luqa
Żurrieq

Valletta
Vittoriosa
Birżebbuġa

Malta

Génova
Pozzallo
Salerno
Réggio di Calábria
Catánia

A   B   C   D

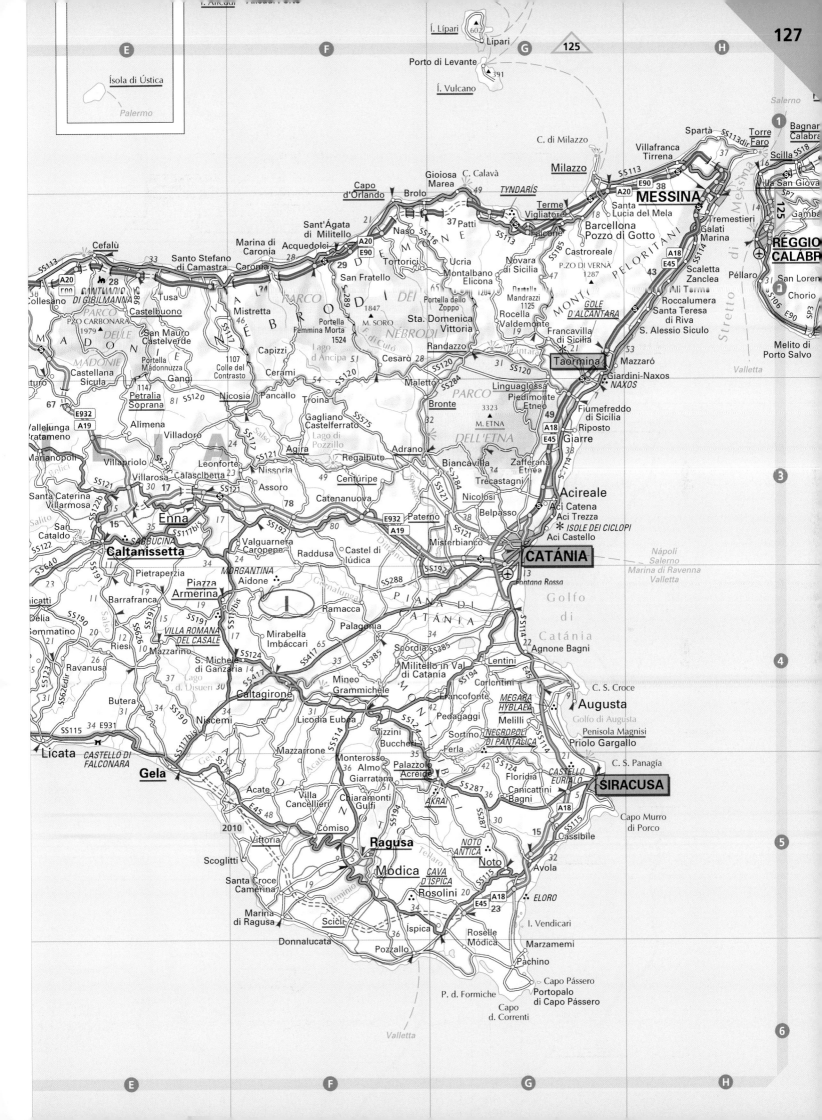

Í. Alicudi   Alicudi Porto

Í. Lípari   602

Í. Lípari
Lípari
Porto di Levante   391

G   125

Í. Vulcano

Salerno

Ísola di Ústica

Palermo

C. di Milazzo

C. Calavà

Gioiosa
Marea

Spartà   SS113dir   Torre
Faro
Villafranca   SS113   Scilla   SS518
Tirrena   37   Villa San Giova

Capo
d'Orlando   Brolo   49   Milazzo   E90   38   Scilla   16
A20   MESSINA   125

Sant'Ágata
di Militello   21   Naso   37   Patti   TYNDARÍS   Terme   Santa   14
Marina di   A20   SS116   Vigliatore   Lucia del Mela   Gamb
Caronía   Acquedolci   E90   Falcone   SS113   Barcellona
Santo Stefano   28   29   Tortorici   Castroreale   Pozzo di Gotto   REGGIO
33   di Camastra   Caronía   SS185   Tremestieri   CALÁBR
Cefalù   Ucria   Novara   Galati
SS113   San Fratello   Montalbano   di Sicilia   P.ZO DI VERNA   Marina   San Loren
Elicona   1287   A18   Chorio
Collesano   28   Mistretta   M. SORO   Rocella   1125   43   Scaletta   SP7
A20   46   1847   Sta. Domenica   Valdemonte   Mandrazzi   E45   Zanclea   SP106
SANTUARIO   Capizzi   Vittoria   19   SS114   Roccalumera   SS106   E90
DI GIBILMANNA   Randazzo   Santa Teresa   Melito di   SP3
PZO CARBONARA   Portella   1107   Lago   Alcantara   Francavilla   di Riva   Porto Salvo
1979   Femmina Morta   d'Ancipa   51   Cesarò   28   di Sicilia   S. Alessio Siculo
San Mauro   Castelbuono   1524   Colle del   54   SS289   21   GOLE
Castelverde   Contrasto   Cerami   SS120   31   D'ALCANTARA   53
PARCO   Portella   Nicosia   Troina   Malettò   SS120   Taormina   Mazzaró
DELLE   Mádonnuzza   Gangi   Pancallo   SS284   Giardini-Naxos   Valletta
MADONIE   1147   81 SS120   Linguaglossa   NAXOS
Castellana   Petralia   Piedimonte   49
67   Sícula   Soprana   Alimena   Gagliano   Lago   Etneo   A18   Fiumefreddo
Castelferrato   di Pozzillo   SS575   Bronte   M. ETNA   E45   di Sicilia
E932   Villadoro   Agira   3323   Riposto
A19   24   SS121   Adrano   DELL'ETNA   A18   Giarre
Vallelunga   Leonforte   Regalbuto   PARCO   49   E45   SS114
Pratameno   Nissoria   Centúripe   Biancavilla   Zafferana
Marianopoli   Villapriolo   Calasclbetta   49   34   Etnea   Acireale
SS121   Villarosa   Assoro   Nicolosi   Aci Catena
Santa Caterina   30   17   78   Catenanuova   SS121   Belpasso   Aci Trezza
Villarmosa   SS117bis   Paternò   38   ISOLE DEI CICLOPI
SS226   Enna   17   E932   80   Misterbianco   Aci Castello
San   15   35   SS192   A19
Cataldo   SS117bis   Valguarnera   Raddusa   CATÁNIA   Nápoli
Caltanissetta   Caropepe   Castel di   Salerno
SS640   SABBUCINA   24   lúdica   SS192   Marina di Ravenna
23   SS191   Pietraperzia   MORGANTINA   13   Fontana Rossa   Valletta
nicatti   11   Barrafranca   Aidone   SS288   Golfo
Délia   Piazza   Ramacca   PIANA DI   di
SS190   19   Armerina   CATÁNIA   Catánia
Sommatino   15   SS19   19   SS117bis   Palagonia   34   Agnone Bagni
Riesi   12   SS626   VILLA ROMANA   17   Mirabella   65   Scordia   SS385
Ravanusa   10   Mazzarino   DEL CASALE   Imbáccari   33   SS385   Carlentini
SS123   S. Michele   SS124   Militello in Val   Lentini   C. S. Croce
26   di Ganzaria   14   Mineo   di Catánia   SS194   9   Augusta
SS62dir   Lago   SS417   Grammichele   Francofonte   MEGARA
31   Butera   d. Disueri   30   42   HYBLAEA   Golfo di Augusta
SS190   Caltagirone   Pedagaggi   Melilli   Penisola Magnisi
SS62dir   31   Niscemi   34   Licodia Eubea   Sortino   NECROPOLI   Priolo Gargallo
Licata   CASTELLO DI   34   E931   SS124   Vizzini   Ferla   DI PANTALICA   21
FALCONARA   Mazzarrone   Buccheri   35   42   SS124   C. S. Panagía
Gela   36   Monterosse   Almo   Palazzolo   Floridia   SS114   CASTELLO
Acate   Villa   Giarratana   Acreide   SS287   30   EURIALO   SIRACUSA
2010   E45   48   Cancellieri   Chiaramonti   51   AKRA   Canicattini   A18
Vittoria   Cómiso   Gulfi   Bagni   15   SS115   Capo Murro
Scoglitti   7   Ragusa   NOTO   32   Cassibile   di Porco
Santa Croce   Módica   ANTICA   Avola   5
Camerina   19   CAVA   Noto   A18
Marina   D'ISPICA   I. Vendicari
di Ragusa   Scicli   Rosolini   20   A18   ELORO
Donnalucata   Íspica   34   E45   23   Roselle   Marzamemi
Pozzallo   Módica   Pachino
P. d. Formiche   Roselle   Portopalo
Módica   di Capo Pássero
Capo   Capo
d. Correnti   Pássero

Valletta

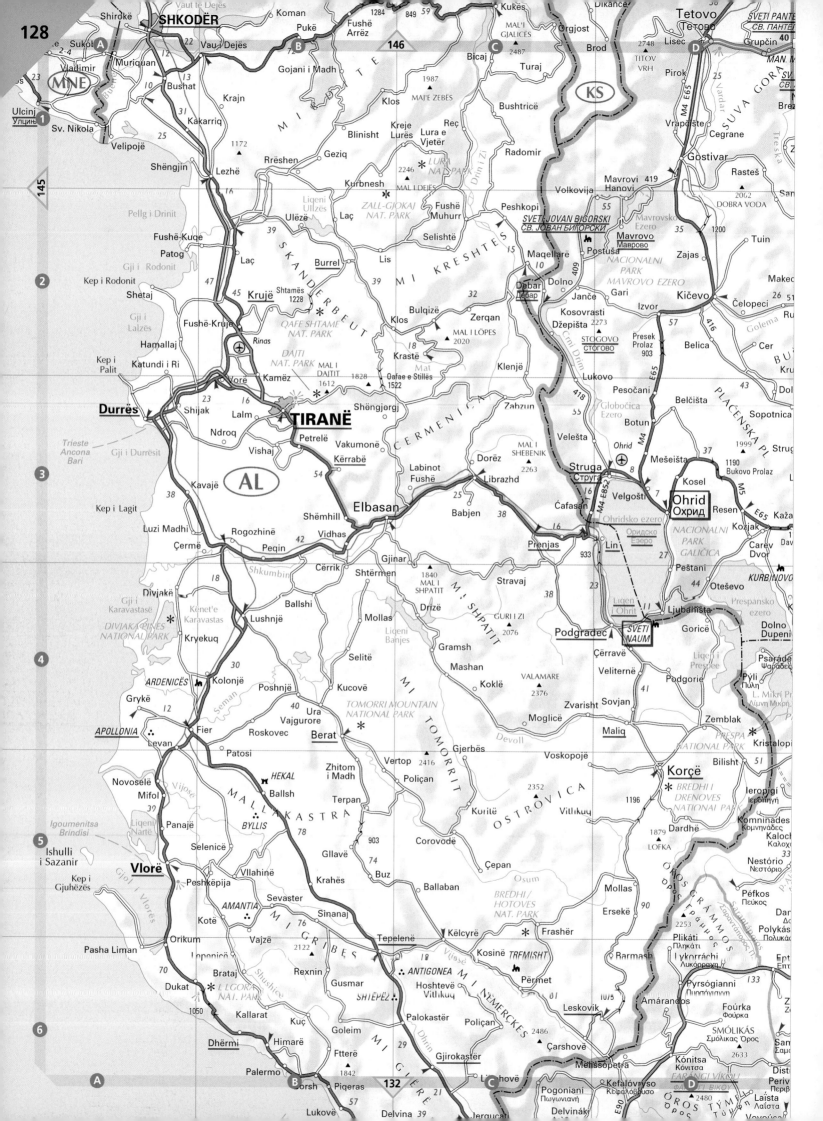

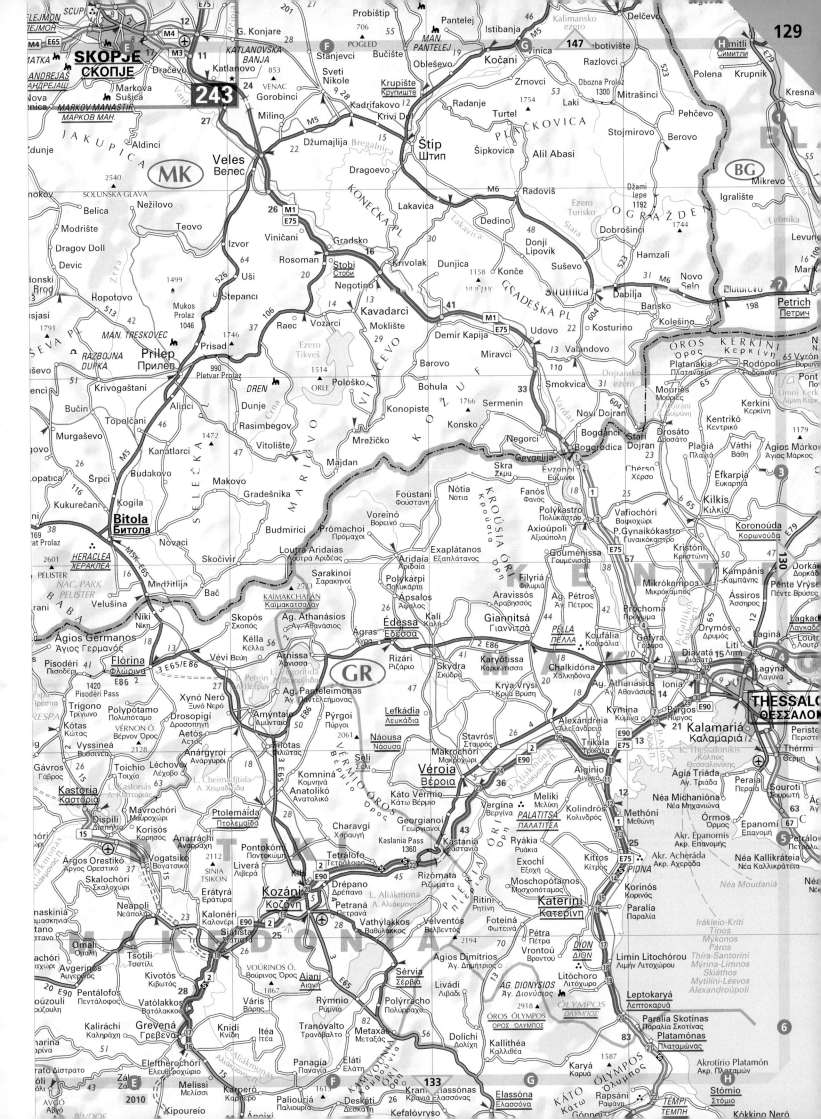

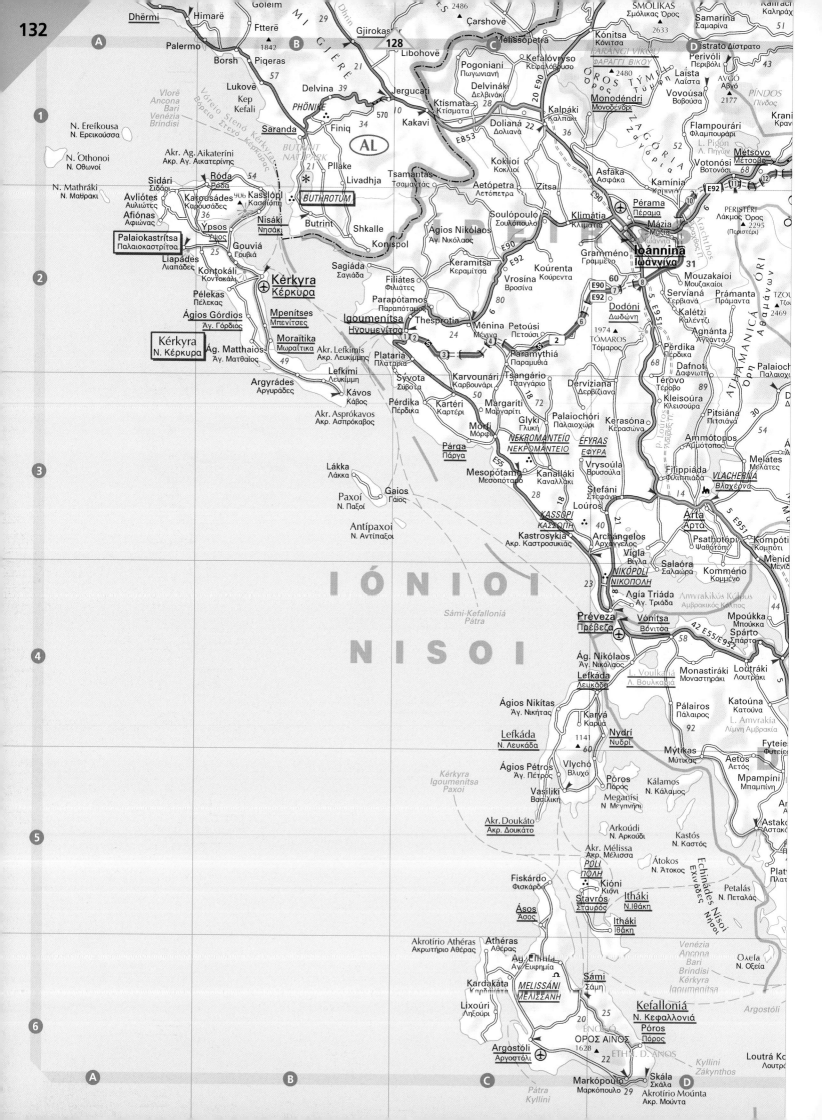

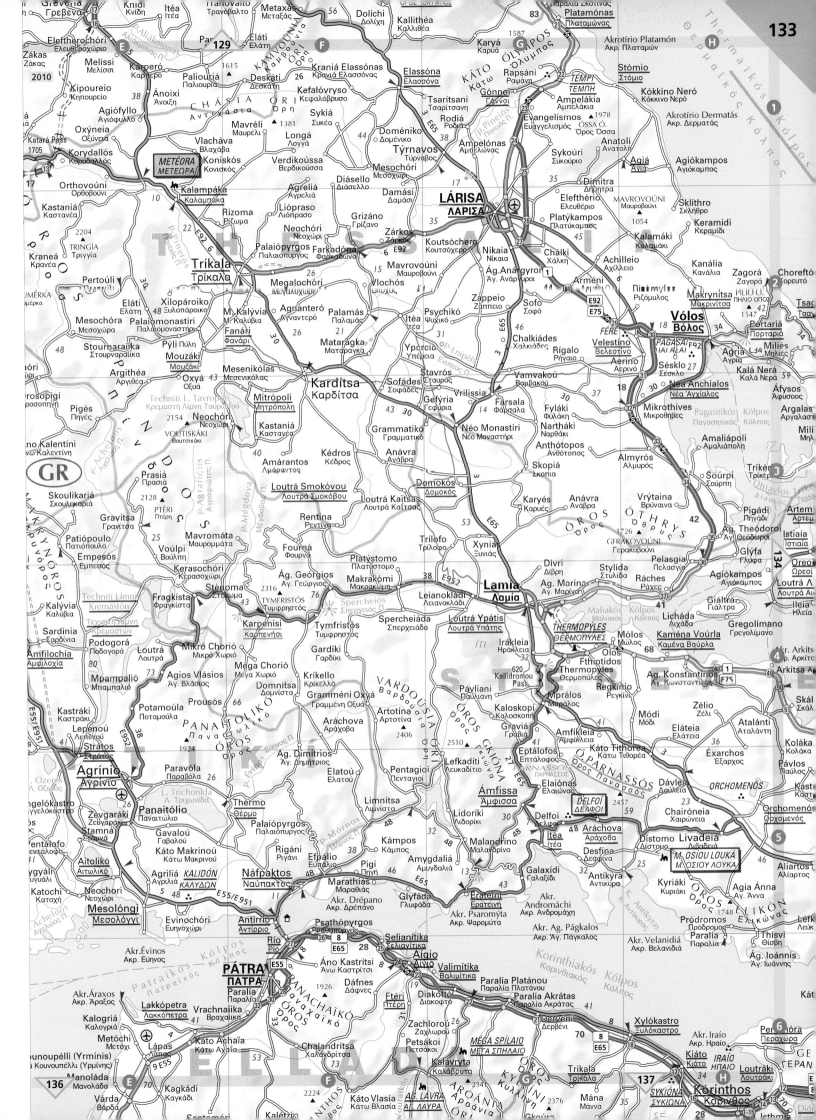

Kóntias
Κοντιάς
Mýrina
Μύρινα
Fisíni
Φισίνη

Dalyan
ALEXANDRIA TROAS — NEANDRIA

319
Skandáli
Σκανδάλι
Akr. Agía Eirínis
Ακρ. Αγ. Ειρήνης

Kösedere
Tavaklı
672
Ayvacık
Küçükkuyu
ANTANDROS

DİKİLİ TEPE
776
63
Altı.

E 131 **F** **G** 56 **H** 1
150
harlar

Mýrina-Límnos

Tuzla
Tamis
44
Kurobası
17-52 17-91

Ahmetçe

Gülpınar
Baba Burun
Bademli
Behramkale
ASSOS

Edremit Körfezi
PASSAND
Alibey
Adası

Akr. Kalamáki
Ακρ. Καλαμάκι
Mytilíni-Lésvos
Skiáthos
Thessaloníki
Mýrina-Límnos
Ágios Efstrátios
POLYMEDIUM

Ayvalık
ŞEYTAN SOFRASI
Altınova

Ó R E I O

298
Ág. Efstrátios
Άγ. Ευστράτιος
Ágios Efstrátios
Ν. Άγ. Ευστράτιος

Akr. Skamniá
Ακρ. Σκαμνιά
Sykaminéa
Συκαμινέα
Míthymna
Μήθυμνα
Mantamádos
Μανταμάδος
Pétra
Πέτρα
Stýpsi
Στύψι 21
Agía Paraskeví
Αγ. Παρασκευή
Mystegná
Μιστεγνά
Thermí
Πύργοι Θέρμης

Akrotírio Trypití
Ακρ. Τρυπητή

A I G A Í O

Mýrina-Límnos
Rafína

Sígri
Σίγρι
ÁNTISSA
Antíssa
Άντισσα
Filía
Φιλία
51
Kalloní
Καλλονή
46
36

2

Akr. Sígri
Ακρ. Σιγρίου

Eresós
Ερεσός
Vatoúsa
Βατούσα
Parákoila
Παράκοιλα
Kólpos Kallonís
Κόλπος Καλλονής
43
Kerameía
Κεραμεία
Mytilíni
Μυτιλήνη
CA

Skála Eresoú
Σκάλα Ερεσού
Skála
Σκάλα
Vasiliká
Βασιλικά
48
Ampelikó
Αμπελικό
968
Agiásos
Αγίασος
Loutrá
Λουτρά
12
Krátigos
Κράτηγος

Polychnítos
Πολιχνίτος
Vaterá
Βατερά
Skópelos
Σκόπελος
42

Lésvos
Ν. Λέσβος
Plomári
Πλωμάρι

Vólos
Chíos
Peiraiás

3

Aslan Burun
PHO

Mytilíni-Lésvos

Kara Burun
152

Hasseki
22
Karab un
Parlak
1212
ÁK DAĞ
505

Psará
Ν. Ψαρά
Agiásmata
Αγιάσματα
Kampiá
Καμπιά
Mármaro
Μάρμαρο
Küçükbahçe
Mordoğan

4

Melaniós
Μελανιός
1297
Kardámyla
Καρδάμυλα
75
Oinoússes
Ν. Οινούσσες
Balık
ç

531
Antípsara
Ν. Αντίψαρα
Psará
Ψαρά
Volissós
Βολισσός
Lagkáda
Λαγκάδα
77
Ildır
57

34
Vrontádos
Βροντάδος
300

TR

Chíos
Ν. Χίος
NÉA MONÍ
ΝΕΑ ΜΟΝΗ
Chíos
Χίος
Çeşme
Uzunkuyu

Kallimasiá
Καλλιμασιά
Thymianá
Θυμιανά
7
Alaçatı
51

Pasá Limáni
Πασά Λιμάνι
Véssa
Βέσσα
Armólia
Αρμόλια
30
61
5

Mestá
Μεστά
Kalamotí
Καλάμωτή
28
6

Pyrgío
Πυργίο
Kómi
Κώμη

Akr. Másticho
Ακρ. Μάστιχο
Emporeiós
Εμπορειός

Koraka

5

Ancona
Brindisi
Rafína
Mýkonos
Peiraiás

Sámos
Karlóvasi

afiréas
αφηρέας

Akr. Kampanós
Ακρ. Καμπανός

6

Kalivári
Καλυβάρι
Ándros
Ν. Άνδρος

Gávrio
Γαύριο
Mpatsí
Μπατσί
42 995
Apoíkia
Αποίκια

Akr. Fanári
Ακρ. Φανάρι
Ag.
Αγ.

Tínos
Me ría
Με ριά
Ándros
Άνδρος

E **F** **G** 139 **H**

Palaiópoli
Παλαιόπολη
Órmos
Όρμος

Ikaría
Ν. Ικαρία
Évdilos
Thérma
Θέρμα
Foúrnoi
Ν. Φούρνοι

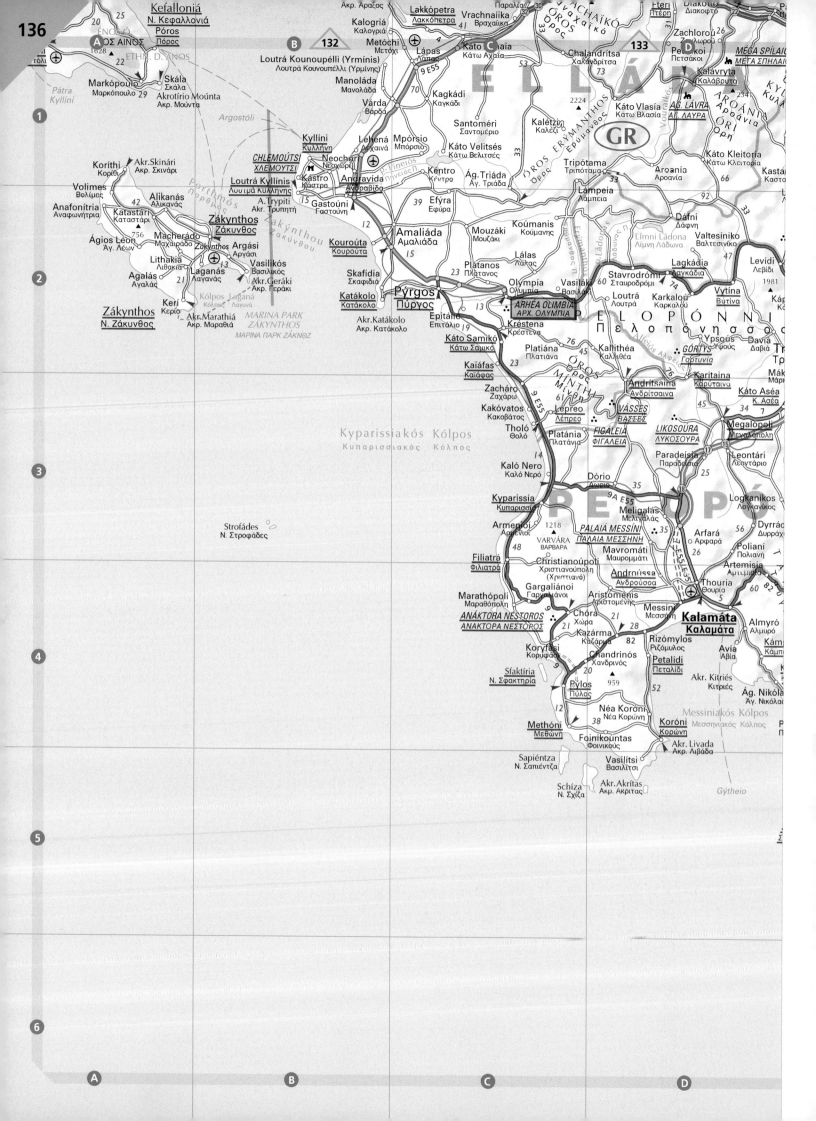

Kefalloniá
Ν. Κεφαλλονιά

ΕΝΟΣ Ο
ΑΟΣ ΑΙΝΟΣ
1628
ΕΤΗΝ. D. ΑΙΝΟΣ

Póros
Πόρος

Markópoulo 29
Μαρκόπουλο

Skála
Σκάλα

Akrotírio Moúnta
Ακρ. Μούντα

Pátra
Kyllíni

Argostóli

Korithi
Κορίθι

Akr.Skinári
Ακρ. Σκινάρι

Volimes
Βολίμες

Alikanás
Αλικανάς

Anafonítria
Αναφωνήτρια

Katastári
Καταστάρι

Ágios Léon
Αγ. Λέον

Macheádo
Μαχαιράδο

Zákynthos
Ζάκυνθος

Argási
Αργάσι

Lithakiá
Λιθακιά

Laganás
Λαγανάς

Vasilikós
Βασιλικός

Agalás
Αγαλάς

Akr.Geráki
Ακρ. Γεράκι

Zákynthos
Ν. Ζάκυνθος

Kerí
Κερίο

Kólpos Laganá
Κόλπος Λαγανά

Akr.Marathiá
Ακρ. Μαραθιά

MARINA PARK
ZAKYNTHOS
ΜΑΡΙΝΑ ΠΑΡΚ ΖΑΚΝΘΖ

Lakkópetra
Λακκόπετρα

Vrachnaíika
Βραχναίικα

Kalogriá
Καλογριά

Metóchi
Μετόχι

Lápas
Λάπας

Káto Achaïa
Κάτω Αχαΐα

Chalandrítsa
Χαλάνδριτσα

Loutrá Kounoupélli (Yrmínis)
Λουτρά Κουνουπέλλι (Υρμίνης)

Manoláda
Μανολάδα

Kagkádi
Καγκάδι

Santoméri
Σαντομέρι

GR

ELLÁDA

Varda
Βάρδα

Kalétzi
Καλέζι

Káto Vlasía
Κάτω Βλασία

AG. LÁVRA
ΑΓ. ΛΑΥΡΑ

Kyllíni
Κυλλήνη

Lehená
Λεχαινά

Mpórsio
Μπόρσιο

Káto Velitsés
Κάτω Βελιτσές

Tripótama
Τριπόταμα

Aroanía
Αροανία

Káto Kleitoría
Κάτω Κλειτορία

CHLEMOÚTSI
ΧΛΕΜΟΥΤΣΙ

Neochóri
Νεοχώρι

Kéntro
Κέντρο

Ág. Triáda
Αγ. Τριάδα

Lámpeia
Λάμπεια

Dáfni
Δάφνι

Loutrá Kyllínis
Λουτρά Κυλλήνης

Kastro
Κάστρο

Andravida
Ανδραβίδα

Efýra
Εφύρα

A. Trypití
Ακρ. Τρυπητή

Gastoúni
Γαστούνη

Koúmanis
Κούμανης

Amaliáda
Αμαλιάδα

Mouzáki
Μουζάκι

Valtesiniko
Βαλτεσίνικο

Kouroúta
Κουρούτα

Lálas
Λάλας

Lagkádia
Λαγκάδια

Levídi
Λεβίδι

Skafídia
Σκαφιδιά

Plátanos
Πλάτανος

Stavrodrómi
Σταυροδρόμι

Karkalou
Καρκαλού

Vytina
Βυτίνα

Kátakolo
Κατάκολο

Pýrgos
Πύργος

Olympía
Ολυμπία

Vasiláki
Βασιλάκι

Loutrá
Λουτρά

ELOPÓNNI
Πελοπόννησος

Akr.Katákolo
Ακρ. Κατάκολο

Epitálio
Επιτάλιο

ARHÉA OLIMBÍA
ΑΡΧ. ΟΛΥΜΠΙΑ

Kréstena
Κρέστενα

GÓRTYS
ΓΟΡΤΥΝΙΑ

Káto Samikó
Κάτω Σαμικό

Platiána
Πλατιάνα

Kallithéa
Καλλιθέα

Karitaina
Καρύταινα

Káto Aséa
Κ. Ασέα

Kaïáfas
Καϊάφας

Andritsaina
Ανδρίτσαινα

Zacháro
Ζαχάρω

Lépreo
Λέπρεο

VÁSSES
ΒΑΣΣΕΣ

Megalópoli
Μεγαλόπολη

Kakóvatos
Κακόβατος

FIGALEÍA
ΦΙΓΑΛΕΙΑ

LIKOSOÚRA
ΛΥΚΟΣΟΥΡΑ

Kyparissiakós Kólpos
Κυπαρισσιακός Κόλπος

Tholó
Θολό

Platánia
Πλατάνια

Paradeísia
Παραδείσια

Leontári
Λεοντάρι

Kaló Nero
Καλό Νερό

Dório
Δώριο

Strofádes
Ν. Στροφάδες

Kyparissía
Κυπαρισσία

Logkanikós
Λογκανικός

Armenioí
Αρμενιοί

Meligalás
Μελιγαλάς

PEL
PELOPÓN

VARVÁRA
ΒΑΡΒΑΡΑ

PALAIÁ MESSÍNI
ΠΑΛΑΙΑ ΜΕΣΣΗΝΗ

Arfará
Αρφαρά

Dyrrác
Δυρράχι

Filiatrá
Φιλιατρά

Christianoúpoli
Χριστιανούπολη (Χριστιανό)

Mavromáti
Μαυρομμάτι

Poliani
Πολιανή

Gargaliánoi
Γαργαλιάνοι

Androússa
Ανδρούσα

Artemisía
Αρτεμισία

Marathópoli
Μαραθόπολη

Aristoménis
Αριστομένης

Thouría
Θουρία

ANÁKTORA NESTOROS
ΑΝΑΚΤΟΡΑ ΝΕΣΤΟΡΟΣ

Chóra
Χώρα

Messíni
Μεσσήνη

Kalamáta
Καλαμάτα

Almyró
Αλμυρό

Kazárma
Κατζάρμα

Rizómylos
Ριζόμυλος

Avía
Αβία

Koryfási
Κορυφάσι

Chandrinós
Χανδρινός

Petalídi
Πεταλίδι

Sfaktíria
Ν. Σφακτηρία

Akr. Kitriés
Ακρ. Κιτριές

Ág. Nikóla
Αγ. Νικόλα

Pýlos
Πύλος

Néa Koróni
Νέα Κορώνη

Messiniakós Kólpos
Μεσσηνιακός Κόλπος

Methóni
Μεθώνη

Koróni
Κορώνη

Foinikoúntas
Φοινικούντας

Akr. Livada
Ακρ. Λιβάδα

Sapiéntza
Ν. Σαπιέντζα

Vasilítsi
Βασιλίτσι

Gýtheio

Schíza
Ν. Σχίζα

Akr. Akrítas
Ακρ. Ακρίτας

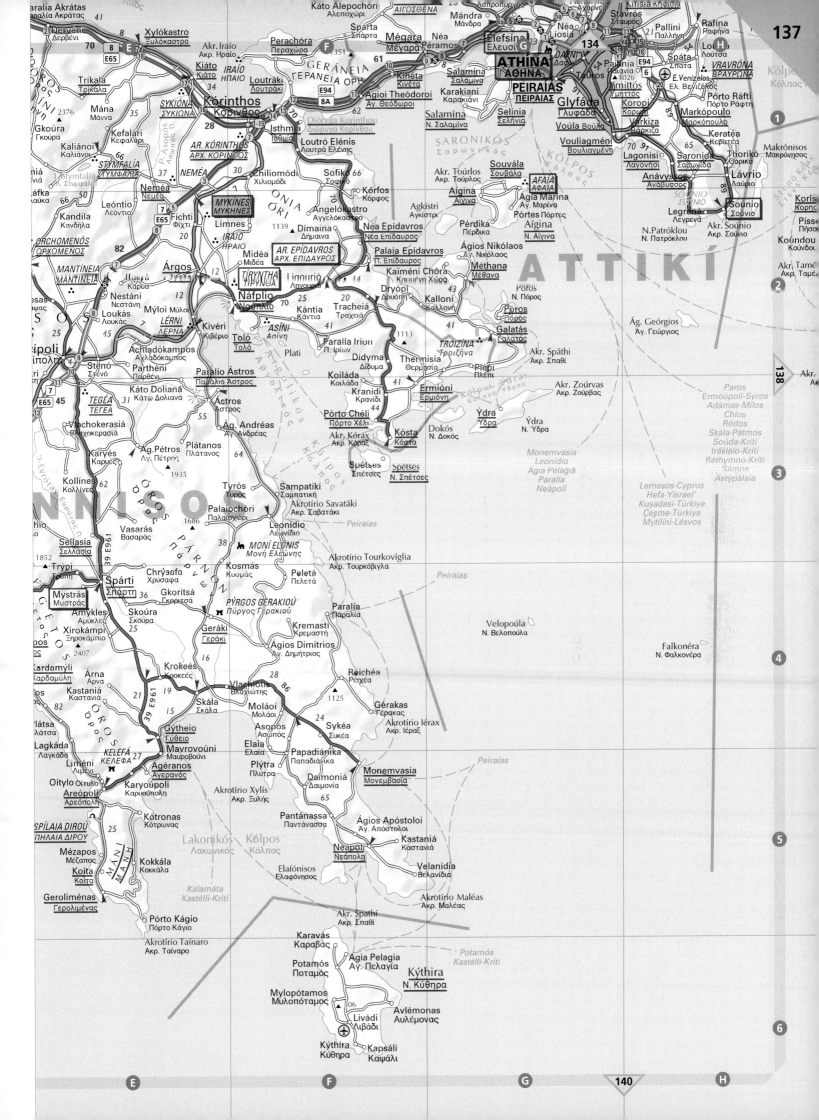

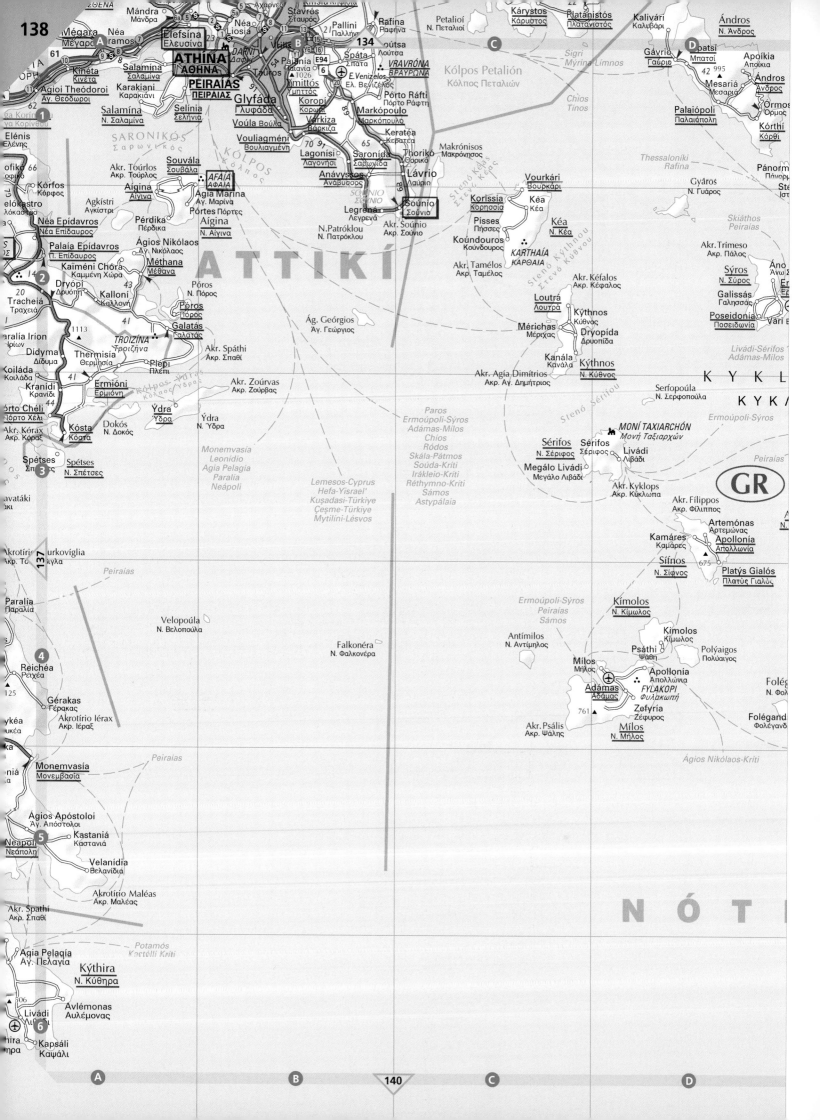

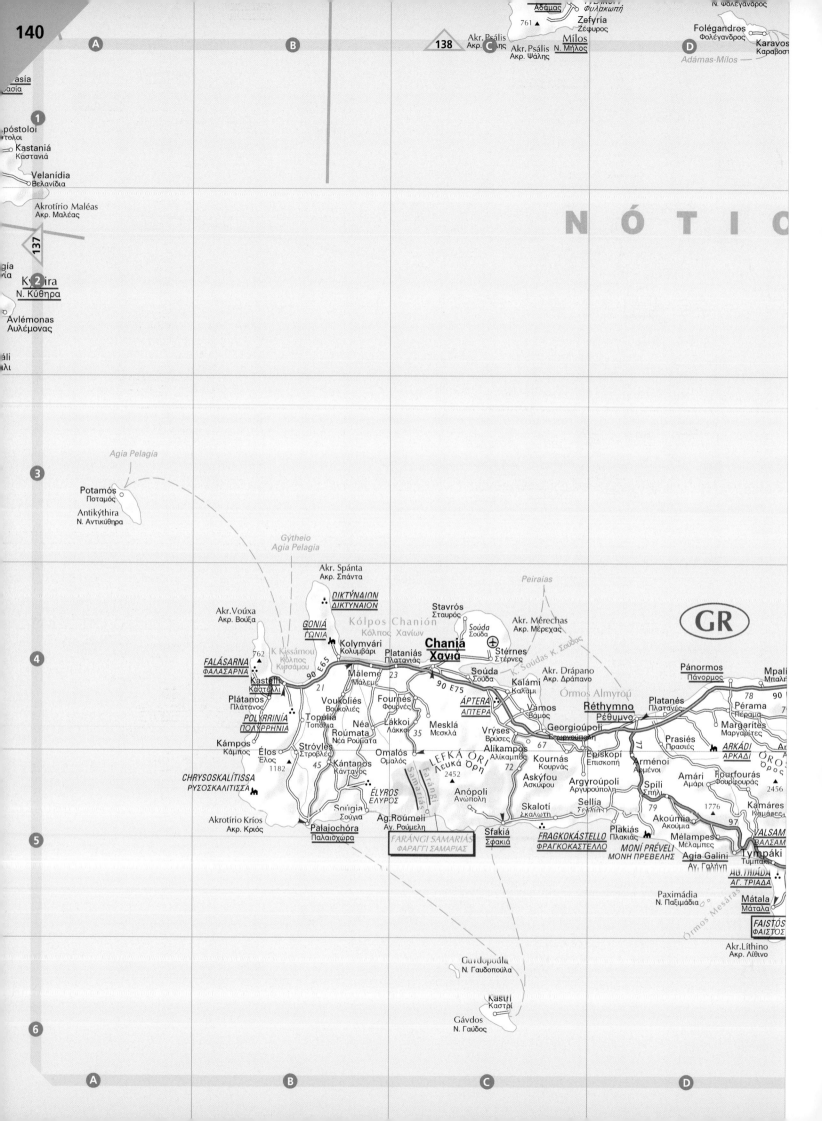

A   B   138   C   D

N Ó T I O

póstoloi
τόλοι

Kastaniá
Καστανιά

Velanídia
Βελανίδια

Akrotírio Maléas
Ακρ. Μαλέας

137

Kythira
Ν. Κύθηρα

Avlémonas
Αυλέμονας

Agia Pelagia

Potamós
Ποταμός

Antikýthira
Ν. Αντικύθηρα

Gýtheio
Agia Pelagia

Akr. Spánta
Ακρ. Σπάντα

ΔΙΚΤΥΝΔΙΟΝ
ΔΙΚΤΥΝΑΙΟΝ

Stavrós
Σταυρός

Peiraiás

Akr. Voúxa
Ακρ. Βούξα

GONIÁ
ΓΩΝΙΑ

Kólpos Chanión
Κόλπος Χανίων

Soúda
Σούδα

Akr. Mêrechas
Ακρ. Μέρεχας

GR

Kolymvári
Κολυμβάρι

Chaniá
Χανιά

FALÁSARNA
ΦΑΛΑΣΑΡΝΑ

762

K. Kissámou
Κόλπος Κισσάμου

Plataniás
Πλατανιάς

Stérnes
Στέρνες

Pánormos
Πάνορμος

Mpali
Μπαλί

Kastélli
Καστέλλι

Máleme
Μάλεμε

23

90 E75

Soúda
Σούδα

Akr. Drápano
Ακρ. Δράπανο

Órmos Almyroú

Plátanes
Πλατανές

78   90

Plátanos
Πλάτανος

21

Voukoliés
Βουκολιές

Fournés
Φουρνές

ÁPTERA
ΑΠΤΕΡΑ

Kalámi
Καλάμι

Réthymno
Ρέθυμνο

Pérama
Πέραμα

POLYRRINÍA
ΠΟΛΥΡΡΗΝΙΑ

Topólia
Τοπόλια

Néa
Νέα

Lákkoi
Λάκκοι

Mesklá
Μεσκλά

Vámos
Βάμος

Georgioúpoli
Γεωργιούπολη

Margarítes
Μαργαρίτες

Kámpos
Κάμπος

Roúmata
Νέα Ρούματα

35

Vrýses
Βρύσες

Alikampos
Αλίκαμπος

Prasiés
Πρασιές

ARKÁDI
ΑΡΚΑΔΙ

Élos
Έλος

Strovlés
Στροβλές

Omalós
Ομαλός

LEFKÁ ÓRI
Λευκά Όρη

67

Kournás
Κουρνάς

Episkopí
Επισκοπή

Arménoi
Αρμένοι

ÓRO

1182

45

Kántanos
Κάντανός

2452

72

Askýfou
Ασκύφου

Argyroúpoli
Αργυρούπολη

Spíli
Σπήλι

Amári
Αμάρι

Fourfourás
Φουρφουράς

2456

CHRYSOSKALÍTISSA
ΡΥΣΟΣΚΑΛΙΤΣΑ

ÉLYROS
ΕΛΥΡΟΣ

Anópoli
Ανώπολη

Skalotí
Σκαλωτή

Sellía
Σελλία

79

1776

Kamáres
Καμάρες

Akrotírio Kríos
Ακρ. Κριός

Soúgia
Σούγια

Ag. Roúmeli
Αγ. Ρούμελη

Skalotí

Plakiás
Πλακιάς

Akoúmia
Ακούμια

97

VALSAM

Palaiochóra
Παλαιοχώρα

FARÁNGI SAMARIÁS
ΦΑΡΑΓΓΙ ΣΑΜΑΡΙΑΣ

Sfakiá
Σφακιά

FRAGKOKÁSTELLO
ΦΡΑΓΚΟΚΑΣΤΕΛΛΟ

Mélampes
Μέλαμπες

ΒΑΛΣΑΜ

MONÍ PRÉVELI
ΜΟΝΗ ΠΡΕΒΕΛΗΣ

Agia Galíni
Αγ. Γαλήνη

Tympáki
Τυμπάκι

AΓ. ΤΡΙΑΔΑ

Paximádia
Ν. Παξιμάδια

Órmos Mesarás

Mátala
Μάταλα

FAISTÓS
ΦΑΙΣΤΟΣ

Akr. Líthino
Ακρ. Λίθινο

Gavdopoúla
Ν. Γαυδοπούλα

Kastrí
Καστρί

Gávdos
Ν. Γαύδος

A   B   C   D

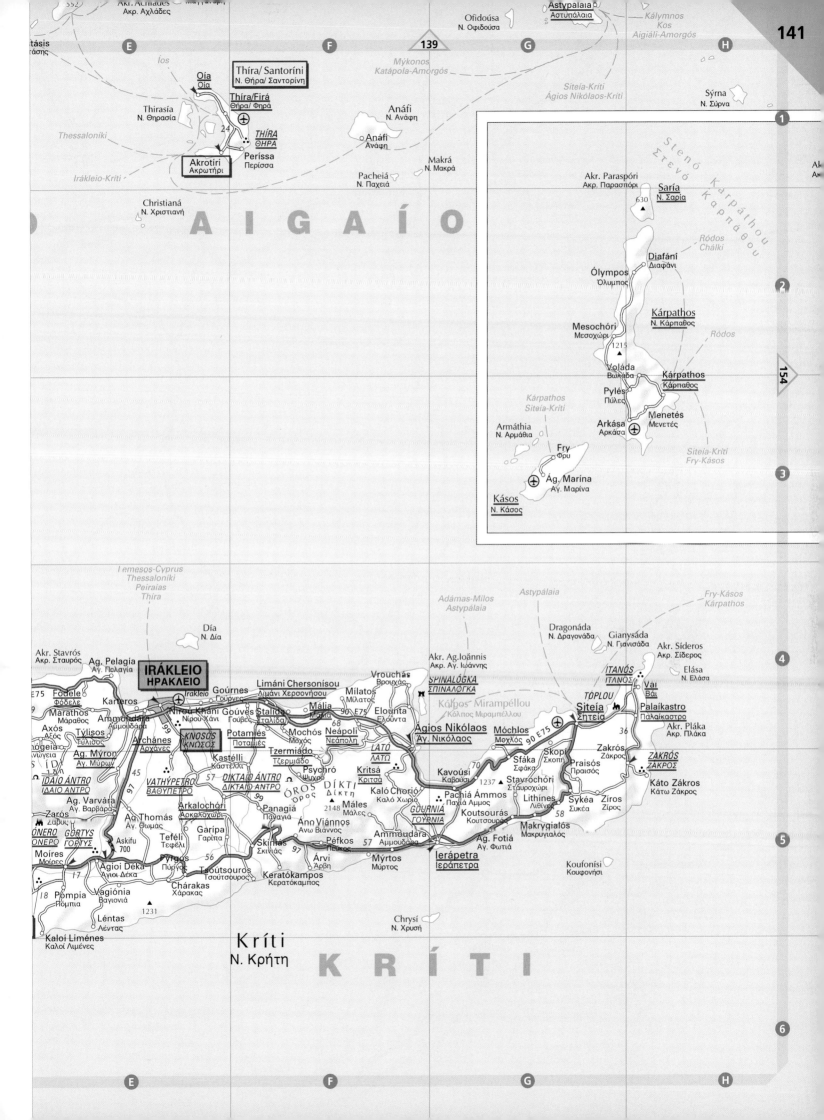

139

154

Astypálaia
Αστυπάλαια

Ofidoúsa
Ν. Οφιδούσα

Kálymnos
Kos
Aigiáli-Amorgós

Sýrna
Ν. Σύρνα

Mýkonos
Katápola-Amorgós

E   F   G   H

Oía
Οία

Thíra/Santoríni
Ν. Θήρα/ Σαντορίνη

Thirasía
Ν. Θηρασία

Thíra/Firá
Θήρα/ Φηρά

THÍRA
ΘΗΡΑ

24

Akrotíri
Ακρωτήρι

Períssa
Περίσσα

Siteía-Kríti
Ágios Nikólaos-Kríti

Anáfi
Ν. Ανάφη

Anáfi
Ανάφη

Makrá
Ν. Μακρά

Pacheiá
Ν. Παχειά

Iírakleio-Kríti

Thessaloníki

Christianá
Ν. Χριστιανή

A I G A Í O

Akr. Paraspóri
Ακρ. Παρασπόρι

Saría
Ν. Σαρία

630

Steno Karpáthou
Στενό Καρπάθου

Ródos
Chálki

Diafáni
Διαφάνι

Ólympos
Όλυμπος

Mesochóri
Μεσοχώρι

Kárpathos
Ν. Κάρπαθος

Ródos

1215

Voláda
Βωλάδα

Pylés
Πύλες

Kárpathos
Κάρπαθος

Kárpathos
Siteía-Kríti

Menetés
Μενετές

Arkása
Αρκάσα

Armáthia
Ν. Αρμάθια

Siteía-Kríti
Fry-Kásos

Fry
Φρυ

Ág. Marína
Ασ. Μαρίνα

Kásos
Ν. Κάσος

Lemesos-Cyprus
Thessaloníki
Peiraías
Thíra

Adámas-Mílos
Astypálaia

Astypálaia

Dragonáda
Ν. Δραγονάδα

Gianysáda
Ν. Γιανισάδα

Fry-Kásos
Kárpathos

Día
Ν. Δία

Akr. Stavrós
Ακρ. Σταυρός

Ag. Pelagía
Αγ. Πελαγία

IRÁKLEIO
ΗΡΑΚΛΕΙΟ

Fódele
Φόδελε

E75

Kartéros

Gournes
Γούρνες

Limáni Chersonísou
Λιμάνι Χερσονήσου

Mílatos
Μίλατος

Vrouchás
Βρουχάς

Akr. Ag.Ioánnis
Ακρ. Αγ. Ιωάννης

SPINALÓGKA
ΣΠΙΝΑΛΟΓΚΑ

Akr. Síderos
Ακρ. Σίδερος

Elása
Ν. Ελάσα

ITANÓS
ΙΤΑΝΟΣ

Vái
Βάι

Márathos
Μάραθος

Ammoudára
Αμμουδάρα

Achós
Αχός

Nírou Kháni
Νίρου Χάνι

Goúves
Γούβες

Stalida
Σταλίδα

Mália
Μάλια

90 E75

Eloúnta
Ελούντα

Kólpos Mirampéllou
Κόλπος Μιραμπέλλου

TÓPLOU

Siteía
Σητεία

Palaíkastro
Παλαίκαστρο

Tylisos
Τύλισος

KNOSÓS
ΚΝΩΣΟΣ

Nírou Khání
Νίρου Χάνι

Potamiés
Ποταμιές

Mochós
Μοχός

68

Neápoli
Νεάπολη

Ágios Nikólaos
Αγ. Νικόλαος

Móchlos
Μόχλος

90 E75

36

Akr. Pláka
Ακρ. Πλάκα

Ag. Mýron
Αγ. Μύρων

Archánes
Αρχάνες

Kastélli
Κάστελλι

Tzermiádo
Τζερμιάδο

LATÓ
ΛΑΤΩ

Skopí
Σκοπή

Zakrós
Ζάκρος

ZAKRÓS
ΖΑΚΡΟΣ

IDAÍO ÁNTRO
ΙΔΑΙΟ ΑΝΤΡΟ

VATHÝPETRO
ΒΑΘΥΠΕΤΡΟ

45

DIKTAÍO ÁNTRO
ΔΙΚΤΑΙΟ ΑΝΤΡΟ

57

Psychró
Ψυχρό

OROS DÍKTI
ΟΡΟΣ ΔΙΚΤΗ

Kritsá
Κριτσά

Kavoúsi
Καβούσι

70

Sfáka
Σφάκα

Stavrochóri
Σταυροχώρι

Praisós
Πραισός

Káto Zákros
Κάτω Ζάκρος

Zarós
Ζαρός

Aa Thomás
Αγ. Θωμάς

Arkalochóri
Αρκαλοχώρι

Panagiá
Παναγιά

99

2148

Máles
Μάλες

Kaló Chorió
Καλό Χωριό

Pachiá Ámmos
Παχιά Άμμος

1237

GOURNIÁ
ΓΟΥΡΝΙΑ

Lithínes
Λιθίνες

Sykéa
Συκέα

58

Zíros
Ζίρος

ÓNERO
ΟΝΕΡΟ

GÓRTYS
ΓΟΡΤΥΣ

Ag. Varvára
Αγ. Βαρβάρα

97

Teféli
Τεφέλι

Garípa
Γαρίπα

Áno Viánnos
Άνω Βιάννος

Árvi
Άρβη

Péfkos
Πεύκος

Koutsourás
Κουτσουράς

Ammoudára
Αμμουδάρα

Ag. Fotiá
Αγ. Φωτιά

Makrygialós
Μακρυγιαλός

Koufonísi
Κουφονήσι

Moíres
Μοίρες

Askifu
700

Pyrgos
Πύργος

56

Skiniás
Σκινιάς

97

57

Mýrtos
Μύρτος

Ierápetra
Ιεράπετρα

Agioi Déka
Αγιοι Δέκα

17

Tsoútsouros
Τσούτσουρος

Keratókampos
Κερατόκαμπος

18

Pómpia
Πόμπια

Vagiónia
Βαγιονιά

Chárakas
Χάρακας

1231

Chrysí
Ν. Χρυσή

Léntas
Λέντας

Kaloí Liménes
Καλοί Λιμένες

Kríti
Ν. Κρήτη

K R Í T I

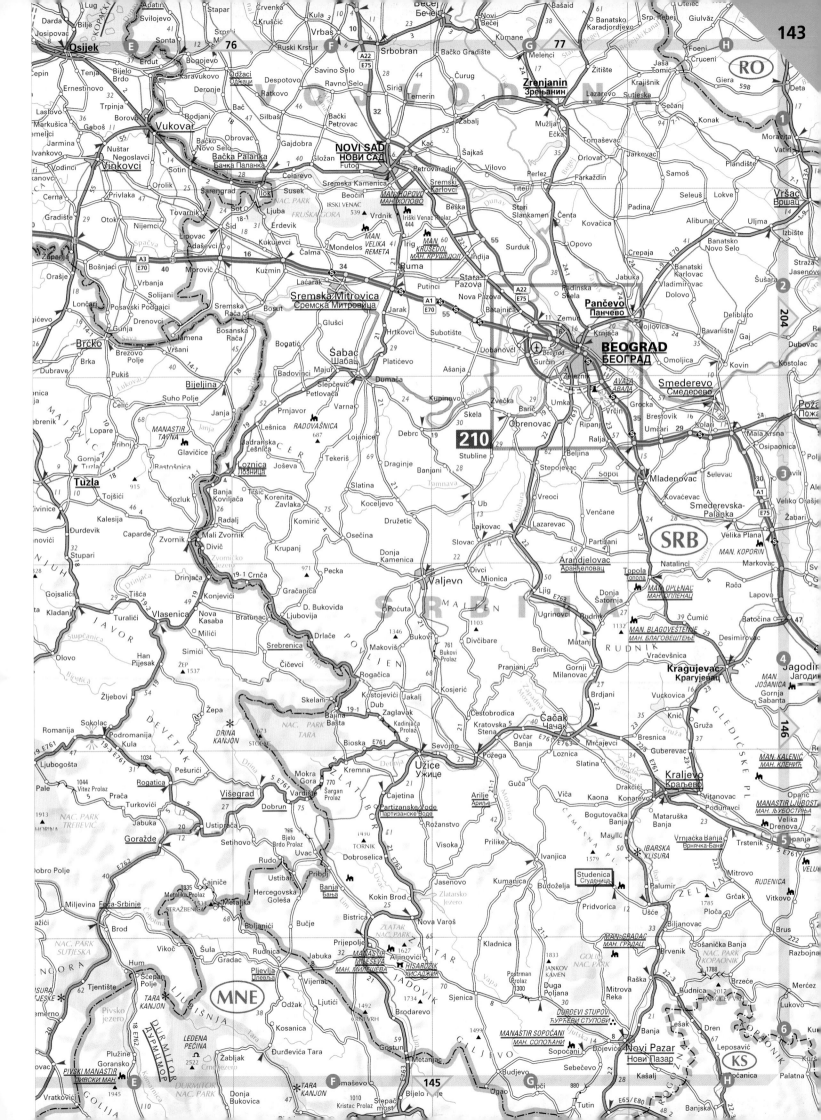

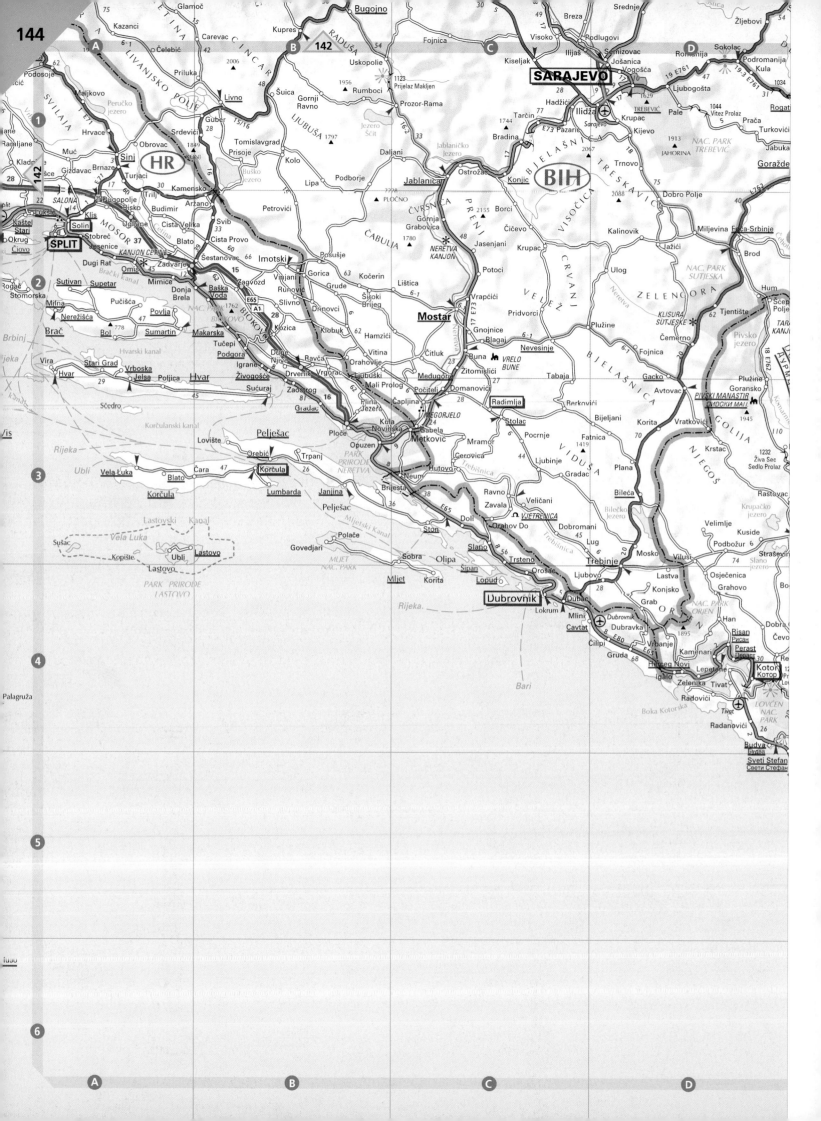

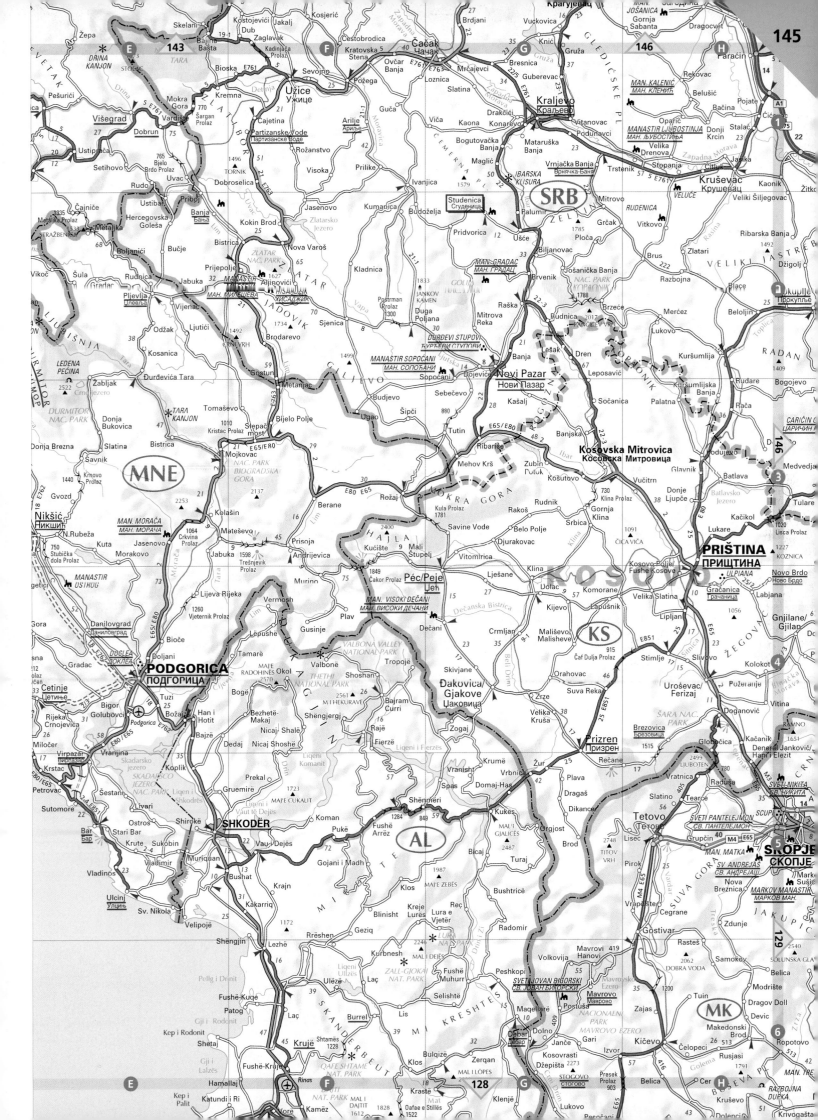

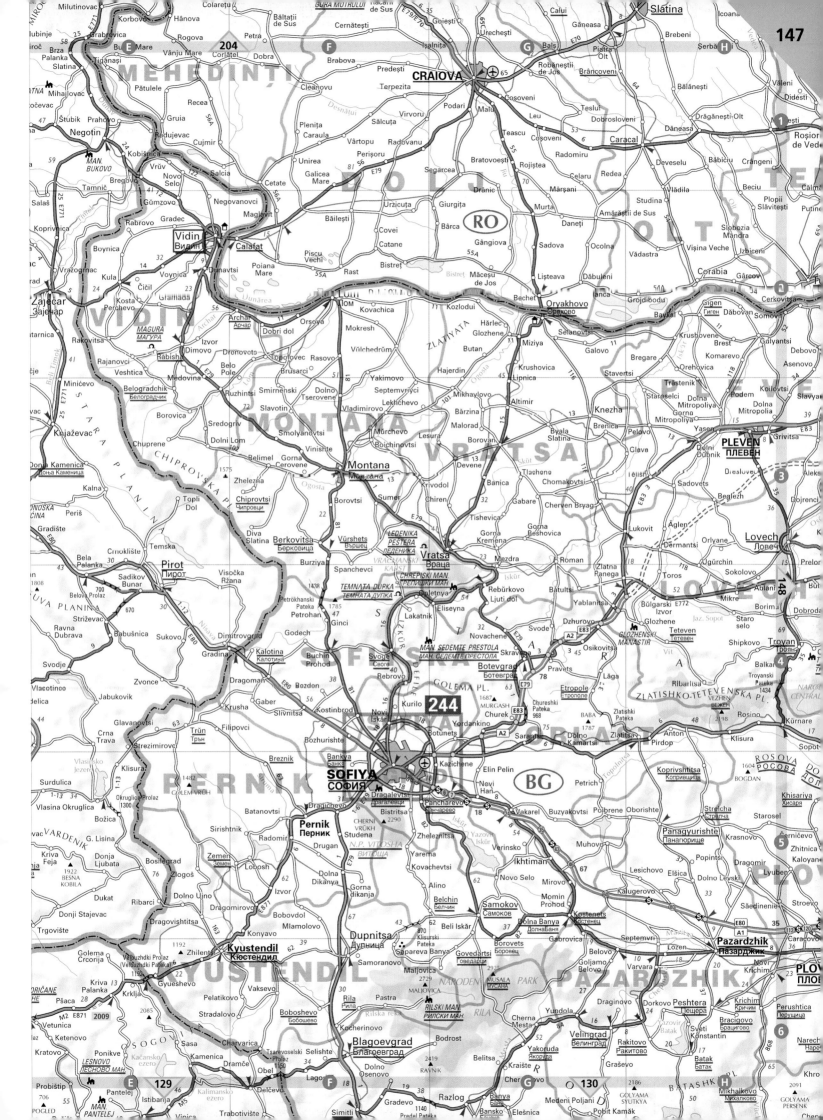

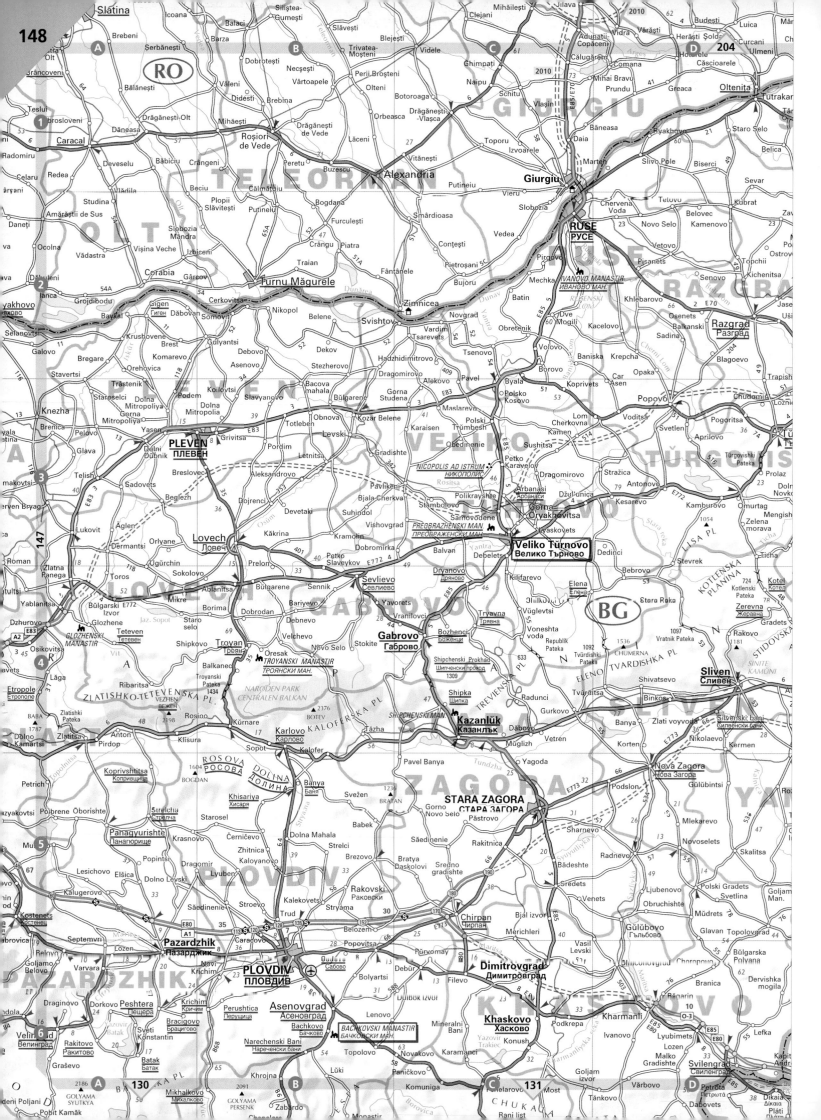

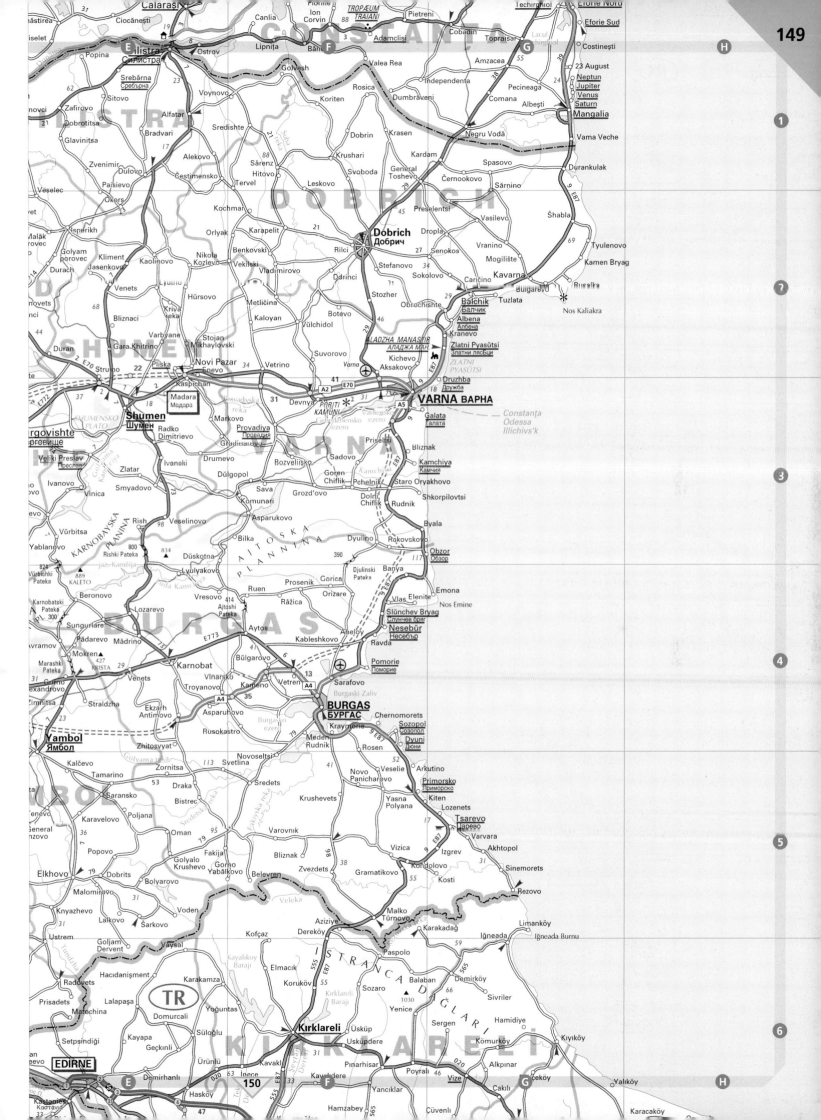

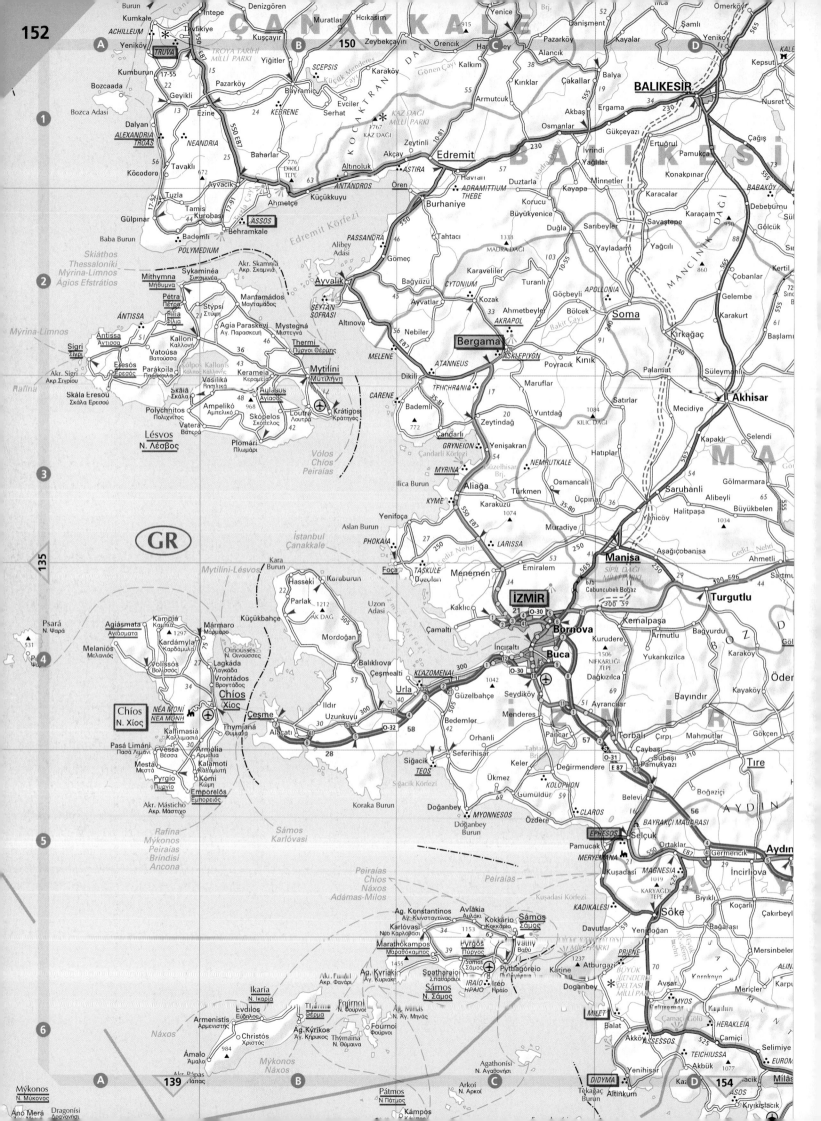

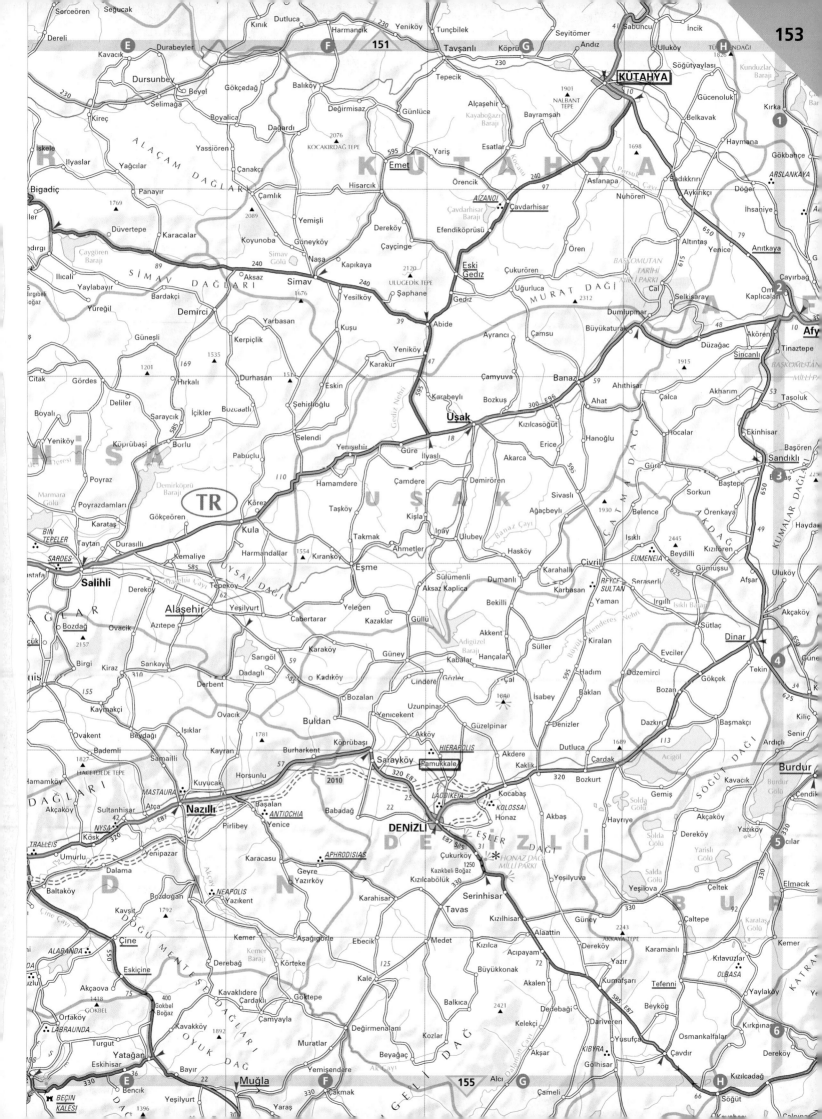

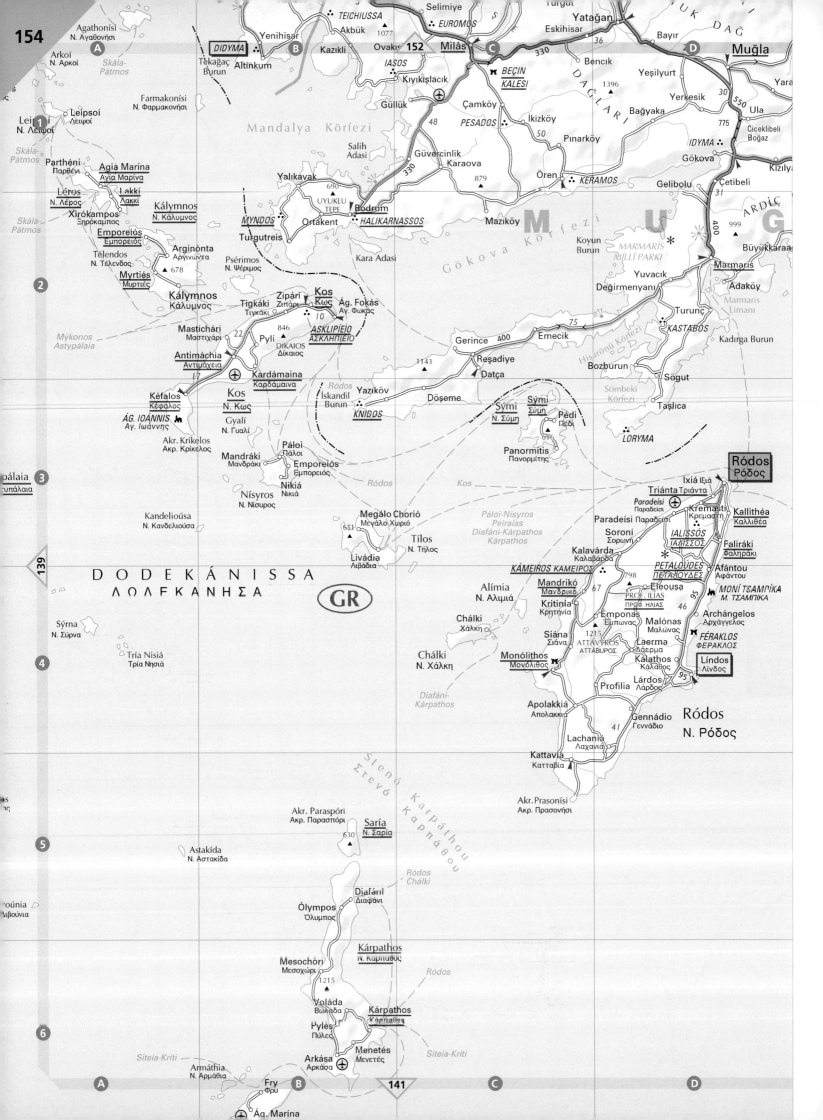

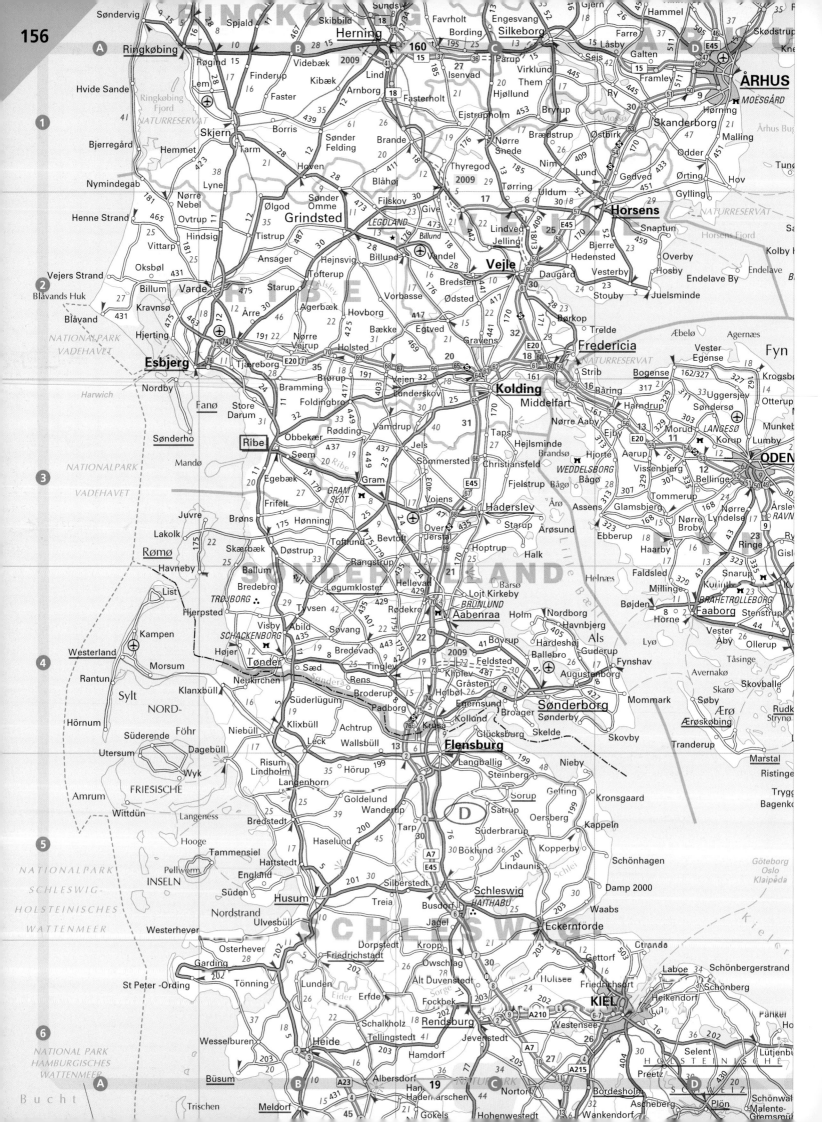

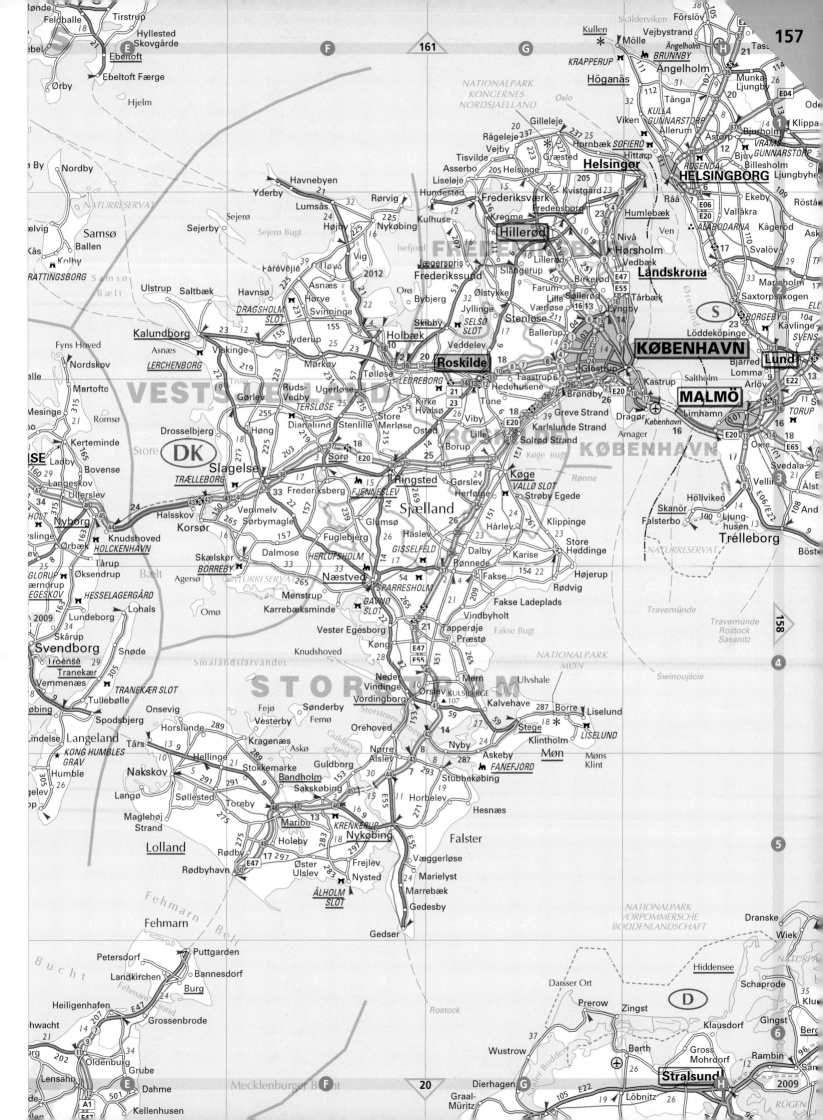

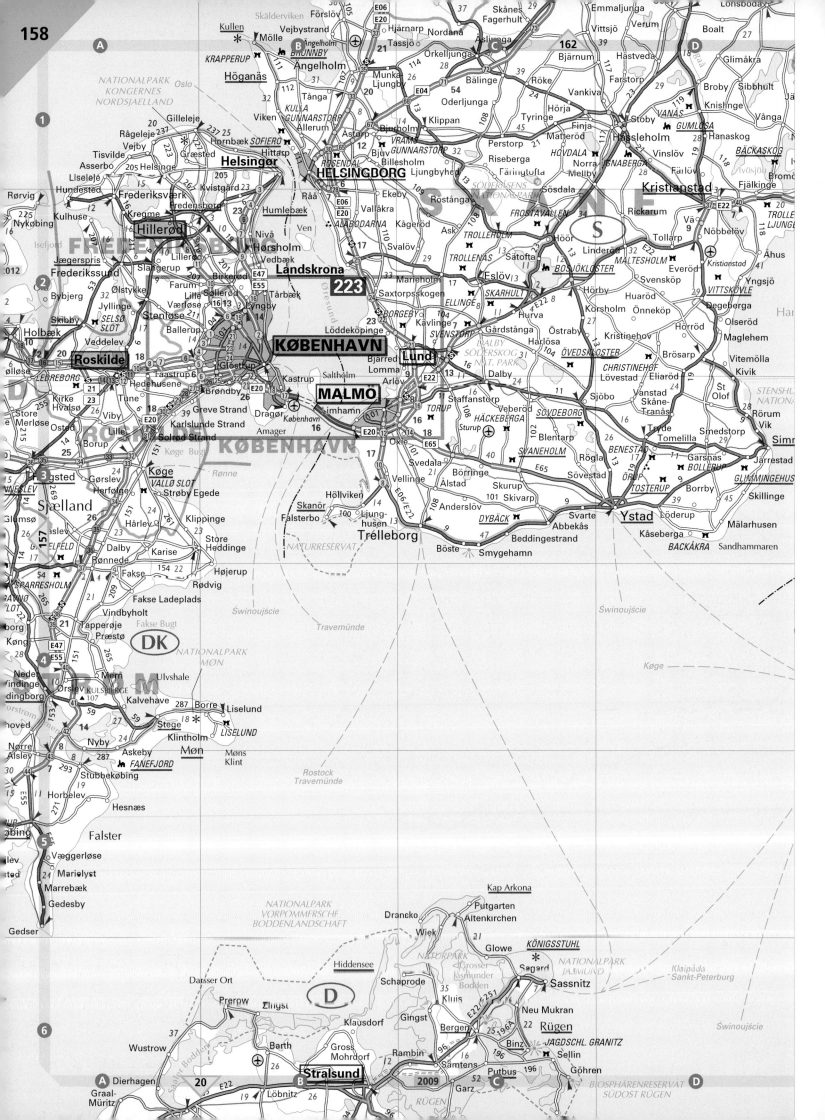

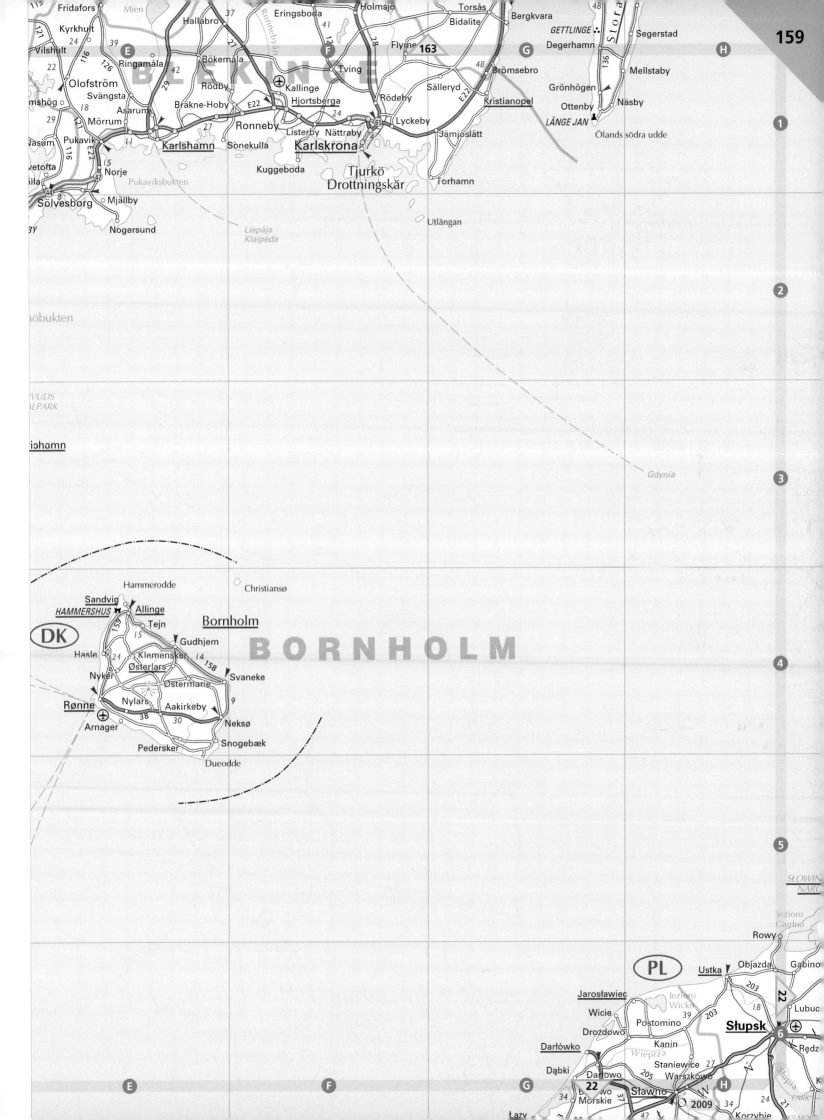

Fridafors
Mien
Eringsboda
Holmsjö
Torsås
Bergkvara
GETTLINGE
Segerstad
Kyrkhult
Hallabro
37
Bidalite
Stora
Degerhamn
Vilshult
Ringamåla
Bökemåla
41
Flyme
163
Mellstaby
BLEKINGE
42
Tving
Grönhögen
Olofström
Rödby
Kallinge
Näsby
Svängsta
Hjortsberga
Sälleryd
Brömsebro
Ottenby
Asarum
Bräkne-Hoby
E22
Rödeby
Kristianopel
LÅNGE JAN
Mörrum
Ronneby
Lyckeby
Ölands södra udde
Pukavik
Karlshamn
Listerby Nättraby
Jämjöslätt
Sonekulla
Karlskrona
Norje
Kuggeboda
Tjurkö
Torhamn
Sölvesborg
Mjällby
Drottningskär
Nogersund
Liepāja
Utlängan
Klaipėda
Gdynia
Hammerodde
Christiansø
Sandvig
Allinge
HAMMERSHUS
Tejn
DK
Gudhjem
Bornholm
BORNHOLM
Hasle
Klemensker
Østerlars
Svaneke
Nyker
Østermarie
Rønne
Nylars
Aakirkeby
Arnager
Neksø
Pedersker
Snogebæk
Dueodde
SŁOWIN
NARO
Jezioro
Gardno
Rowy
PL
Ustka
Objazda
Gabino
Jarosławiec
Słupsk
Wicie
Postomino
Lubuc
Drozdowo
Kanin
Darłówko
Wieprza
Staniewice
Dąbki
Darłowo
Rędz
Warszkowo
Morskie
Sławno
2009
Łazy

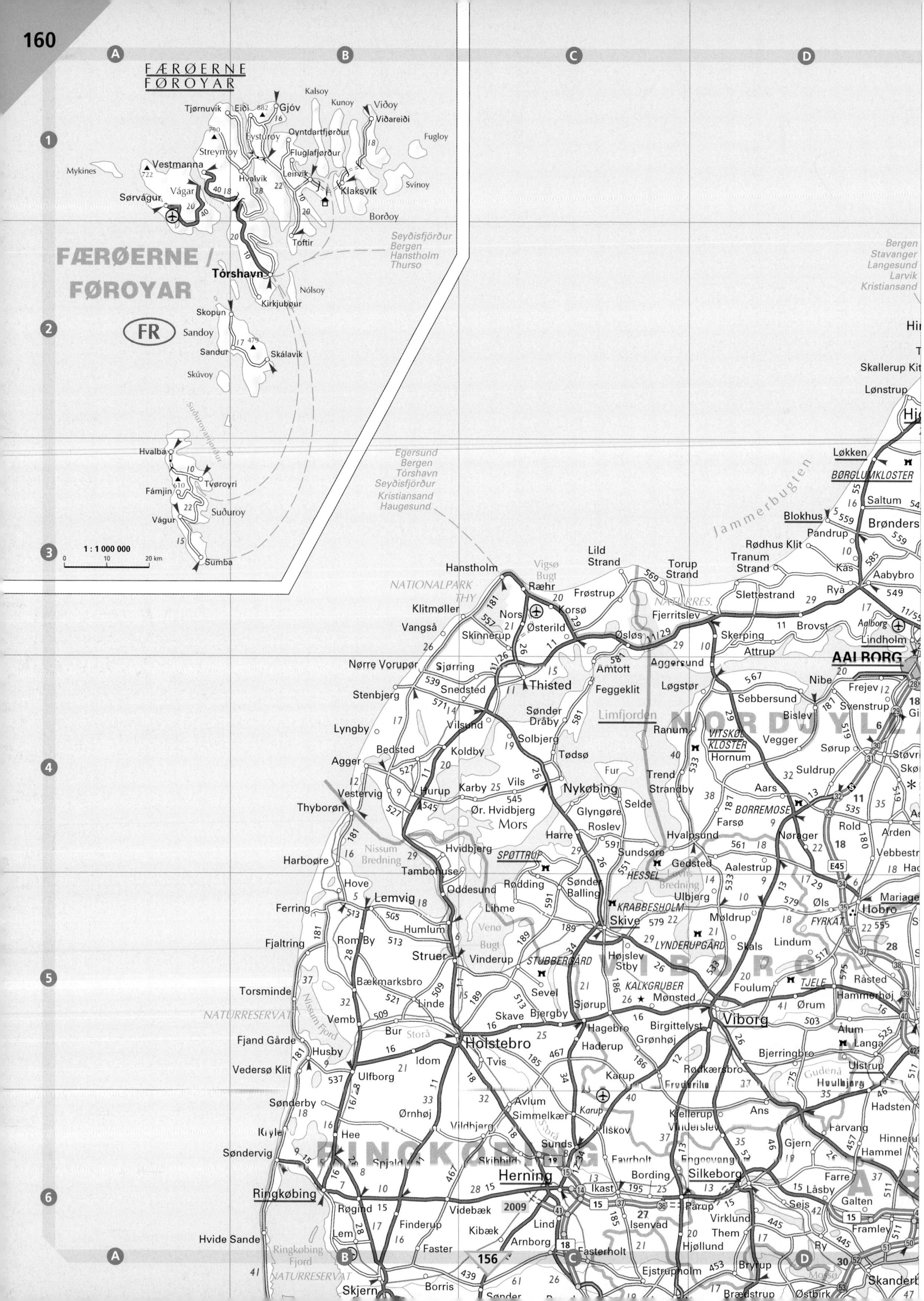

A   B   C   D

FÆRØERNE
FØROYAR

**FÆRØERNE /
FØROYAR**

(FR)

1 : 1 000 000
0   10   20 km

Mykines

Tjørnuvik   Eiði   882   Gjóv
Kalsoy   Kunoy   Viðoy
750   16   Viðareiði
Streymoy   Eysturoy   Oyntdartfjørður   Fugloy
Vestmanna   Fluglafjørður   18
722   Hvalvik   Leirvik   22
Sørvágur   Vágar   40   18   28   Klaksvík   Svínoy
20   40   20   Borðoy
20
Tóftir
Nólsoy
Tórshavn
Skopun   Kirkjubøur
Sandoy   17   479
Sandur   Skálavik
Skúvoy

Seyðisfjörður
Bergen
Hanstholm
Thurso

Hvalbá
610   10   Tvøroyri
Fámjin
Vágur   22   Suðuroy
15
Sumba

Suðuroyarfjørður

Egersund
Bergen
Tórshavn
Seyðisfjörður
Kristiansand
Haugesund

Bergen
Stavanger
Langesund
Larvik
Kristiansand

Hi...

Skallerup Kl...
Lønstrup

Hj...
Løkken
BØRGLUMKLOSTER   55
16   Saltum   54
Blokhus   5   559   Brønders...
Pandrup
Rødhus Klit   10   585   Kås...
Aabybro

Hanstholm
Vigsø Bugt   Lild Strand
Ræhr   20   Frøstrup   Torup Strand   Tranum Strand
NATIONALPARK THY   181   569   Slettestrand   29   Ryå   549
Klitmøller   557   Nors   Korsø   Fjerritslev   11   Brovst   17   11/55
Vangså   21   Østerild   29   Øsløs   1129   Skerping   **AALBORG**
Skinnerup   26   11   29   10   Attrup   Lindholm
Nørre Vorupør   Sjørring   58   Aggersund   Sebbersund   Nibe   20   Frejev   12
539   11/26   15   Amtott   Løgstør   567   Bislev   181   Svenstrup
Stenbjerg   571   14   Snedsted   11   **Thisted**   Feggeklit   Ranum   **NORDJYLL**   Vegger   Sørup   Støvri   Skø
Lyngby   17   Vilsund   Sønder Dråby   581   Limfjorden   **VITSKØL KLOSTER**   Hornum   31
Bedsted   Koldby   19   Solbjerg   Fur   40   533   32   Suldrup
Agger   527   20   Tødsø   Trend Strandby   38   Aars   187   13   32   **11**
12   Hurup   Karby   25   Vils   **Nykøbing**   Selde   **BORREMOSE**   33   535   35
Vestervig   9   545   Ør. Hvidbjerg   Glyngøre   Farsø   9   Nørager   Rold   180   Arden
Thyborøn   527   545   **Mors**   Roslev   591   Hvalpsund   561   18   **18**   Vebbestr
181   Harre   Sundsøre   Gedsted   Aalestrup   17   29   34   **E45**   18   Ha
Harboøre   Nissum Bredning   29   Hvidbjerg   **SPØTTRUP**   29   26   **HESSEL**   Løvns Bredning   14   533   13   Mariage
16   Tambohuse   Rødding   Sønder Balling   **KRABBESHOLM**   Ulbjerg   579   Øls   Hobro
Ferring   Hove   Oddesund   Lihme   591   **Skive**   579   22   Møldrup   18   **FYRKAT**
513   5   **Lemvig**   18   Veng Bugt   189   189   29   **LYNDERUPGÅRD**   Skals   Lindum   22   555
565   Humlum   6   Højslev Stby   **VIBORG**   517   28
Fjaltring   Rom By   513   Struer   Vinderup   **STUBBERGÅRD**   26   Foulum   **TJELE**   Råsted
28   Torsminde   37   Bækmarksbro   509   Sevel   21   186   **KALKGRUBER**   41   Ørum   Hammerhøj   39
32   521   Linde   Skave   Bjergby   Sjørup   26   ★ Mønsted   **Viborg**   503   Ålum   525
Vemb   509   513   Hagebro   Birgittelyst   26   Bjerringbro   Ulstrup   40
Fjand Gårde   Bur   Storå   16   467   Haderup   Grønhøj   186   Røckærsbro   75   Houlbjerg   511
537   Husby   Idom   **Holstebro**   185   34   Karup   Frederiks   26   35   46
Vedersø Klit   21   Tvis   18   25   Kjellerup   Vinderslev   Gjern   Hinner
Sønderby   Ulfborg   11   33   32   Avlum   Simmelkær   40   Ans   13   35   46   Hammel
18   Ørnhøj   Vildbjerg   Ilskov   18   Engesvang   457   Farre   37
RINGKØBING   16   Hee   Sunds   **19**   34   13   **Silkeborg**   15   Låsby   511
Søndervig   9   15   Spjald   Skibhild   **Herning**   13   Bording   36   Parup   15   Sejs   **15**   Galten
16   7   10   467   28   15   **Ikast**   195   25   445
Ringkøbing   8   **14**   **15**   185   **27**   Virklund   42   15
Røgind   15   Videbæk   **2009**   41   Isenvad   20   Them   445   Framlev
Hvide Sande   Lem   17   Kibæk   **18**   Lind   185   Hjøllund   Ry   50
28   Finderup   16   Arnborg   Easterholt   21   Bryrup   **30**   52
Ringkøbing Fjord   Faster   Ejstrupholm   Østbirk   Skanderb
NATURRESERVAT   41   Borris   61   26   Brædstrup   47
Skjern   439   Sønder   453   Mossø   Skande...

Naturreservat
Nissum Fjord

Jammerbugten

Limfjorden

NORDJYLL

VIBORG

RINGKØBING

156

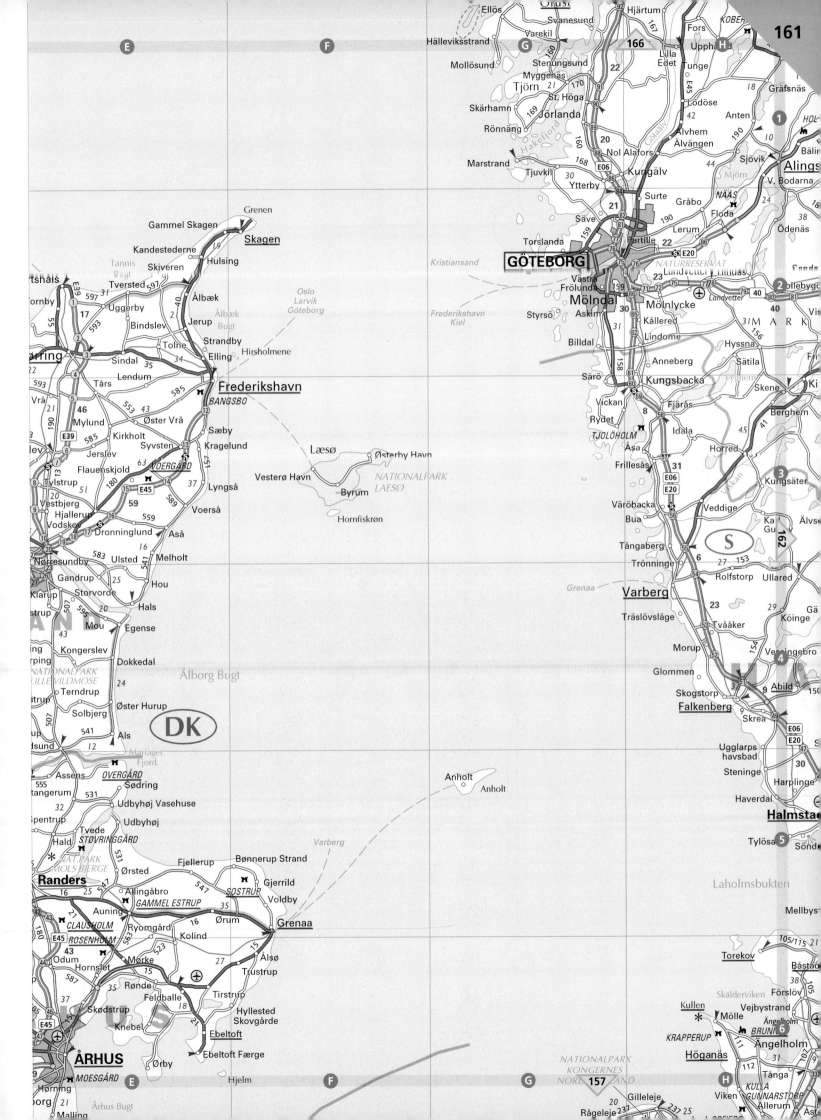

Grenen
Gammel Skagen
Skagen
Kandestederne
Hulsing
Skiveren
Tversted
Ålbæk
Uggerby
Jerup
Bindslev
Strandby
Tolne
Elling
Hirsholmene
Sindal
Frederikshavn
BANGSBO
Lendum
Øster Vrå
Sæby
Kirkholt
Kragelund
Syvsten
Jerslev
VOERGÅRD
Læsø
Østerby Havn
Flauenskjold
Vesterø Havn
NATIONALPARK
LÆSØ
Lyngså
Byrum
Vestbjerg
Voerså
Hjallerup
Hornfiskrøn
Vodskov
Dronninglund
Aså
Nørresundby
Ulsted
Melholt
Gandrup
Hou
Storvorde
Klarup
Hals
Mou
Egense
Kongerslev
Dokkedal
NATIONALPARK
LILLE VILDMOSE
Terndrup
Øster Hurup
Ålborg Bugt
Solbjerg
Als

DK

Assens
Overgård
Sødring
Udbyhøj Vasehuse
Udbyhøj
Tvede
Støvringgård
Anholt
Anholt
Fjellerup
Bønnerup Strand
Varberg
NAT.PARK
MOLS BJERGE
Randers
Ørsted
Gjerrild
Allingåbro
Gammel Estrup
Søstrup
Voldby
Auning
Ørum
Grenaa
Clausholm
Ryomgård
Rosenholm
Kolind
Odum
Hornslet
Mørke
Ålsø
Rønde
Trustrup
Feldballe
Tirstrup
Skødstrup
Hyllested
Knebel
Skovgårde
Ebeltoft
ÅRHUS
Ørby
Ebeltoft Færge
MOESGÅRD
Hjelm
Århus Bugt

Ellös
Olust
Svanesund
Hjärtum
Fors
KØBEN
Hälleviksstrand
Varekil
Upphä
Mollösund
Stenungsund
Lilla
Edet
Tunge
Gräfsnäs
Myggenäs
Tjörn
St. Höga
Skärhamn
Jörlanda
Anten
Rönnäng
Ödenäs
Alvhem
Älvängen
Marstrand
Sjövik
Bälir
Tjuvkil
Kungälv
Ytterby
Surte
Gråbo
Floda
Säve
NÄÄS
Torslanda
Lerum
Partille
Kristiansand
GÖTEBORG
Lundvetter Linnäs
Västra
Frölunda
Frederikshavn
Kiel
Styrsö
Mölndal
Mölnlycke
Askim
Kållered
Billdal
Lindome
Anneberg
Sätila
Särö
Hyssna
Kungsbacka
Vickan
Fjärås
Skene
Rydet
Berghem
Idala
Åsa
TJOLÖHOLM
Frillesås
Horred
Kungsäter
Varöbacka
Bua
Veddige
Tångaberg
S
Trönninge
Rolfstorp
Ullared
Grenaa
Varberg
Träslövsläge
Tvååker
Köinge
Morup
Veßingebro
Glommen
Skogstorp
Abild
Falkenberg
Skrea
Ugglarps
havsbad
Steninge
Harplinge
Haverdal
Halmsta
Tylösa
Laholmsbukten
Mellbys
Torekov
Båstad
Kullen
Vejbystrand
Mölle
Ängelh
KRAPPERUP
BRUNI
Ängelholm
Höganäs
NATIONALPARK
KONGERNES
NORD
157
Gilleleje
Viken
Gunnarstorp
Allerum
Rågeleje

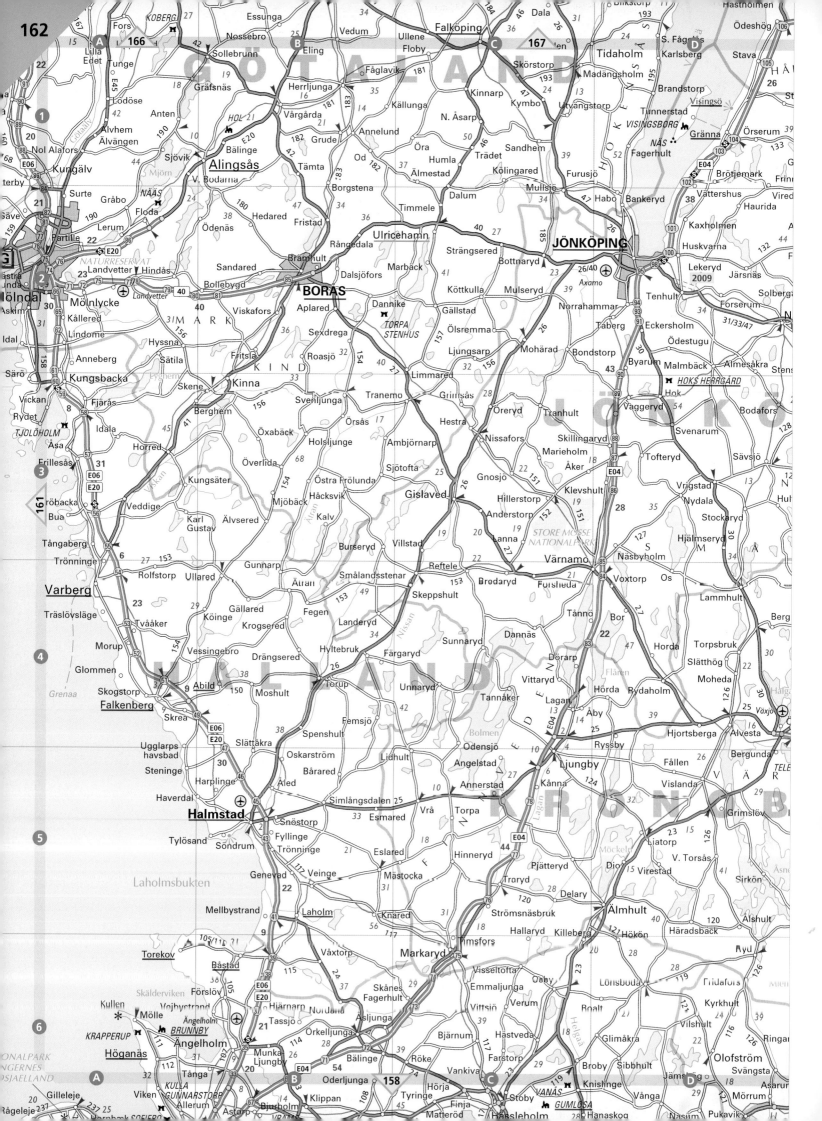

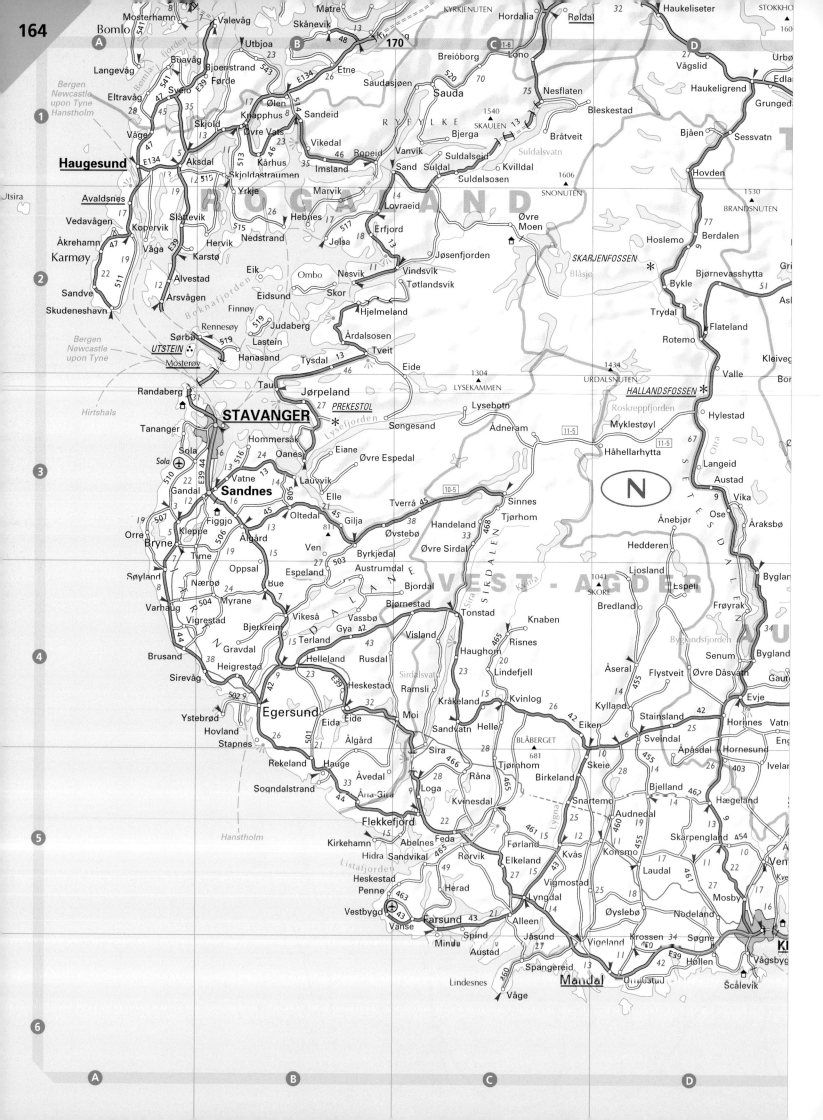

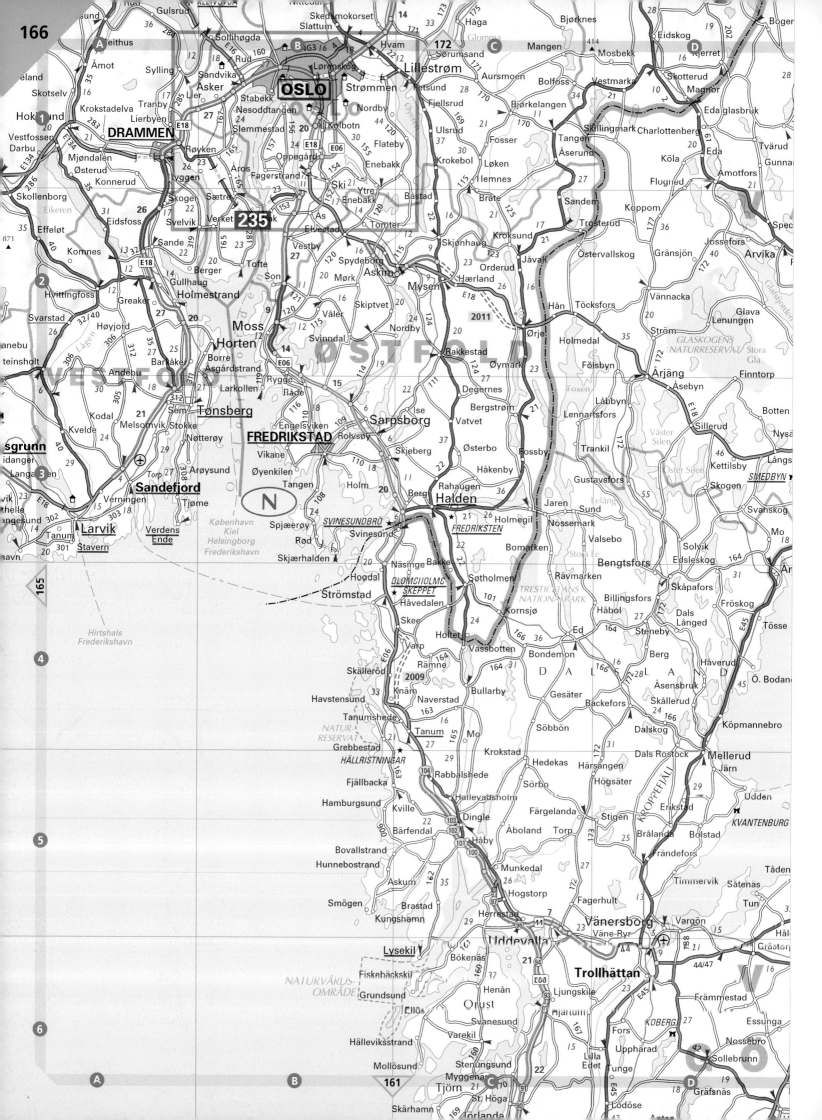

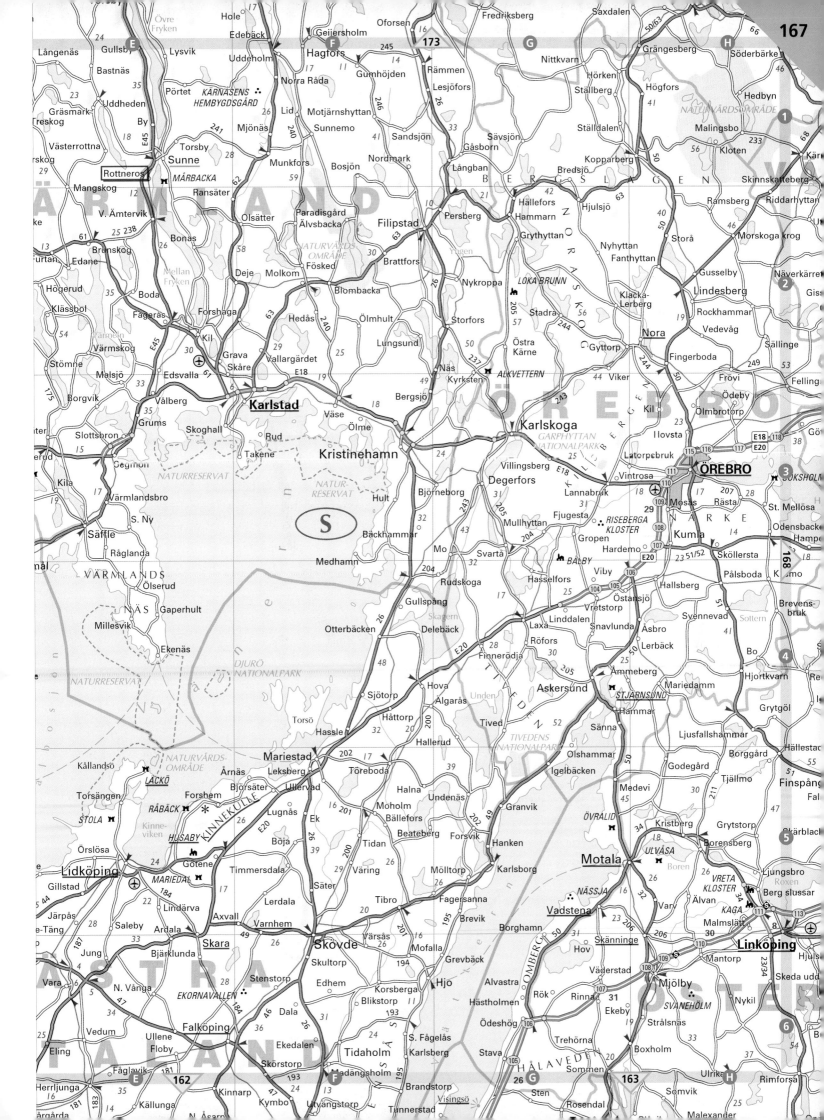

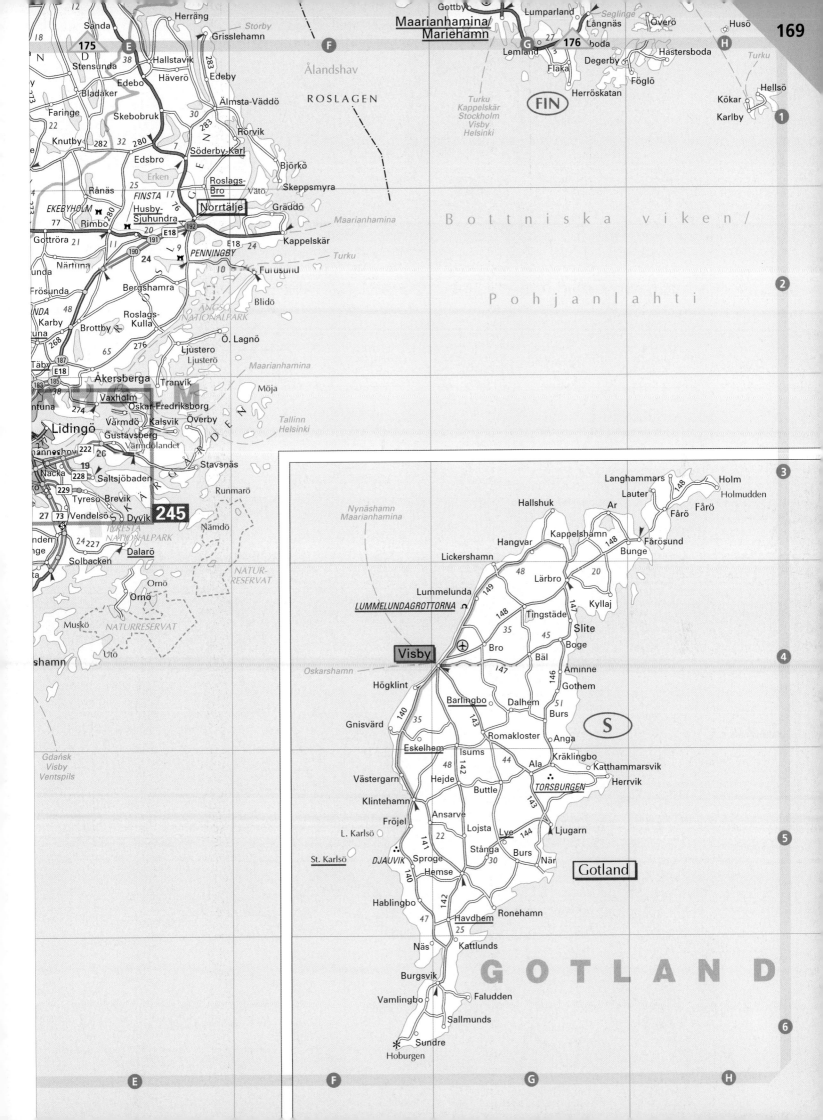

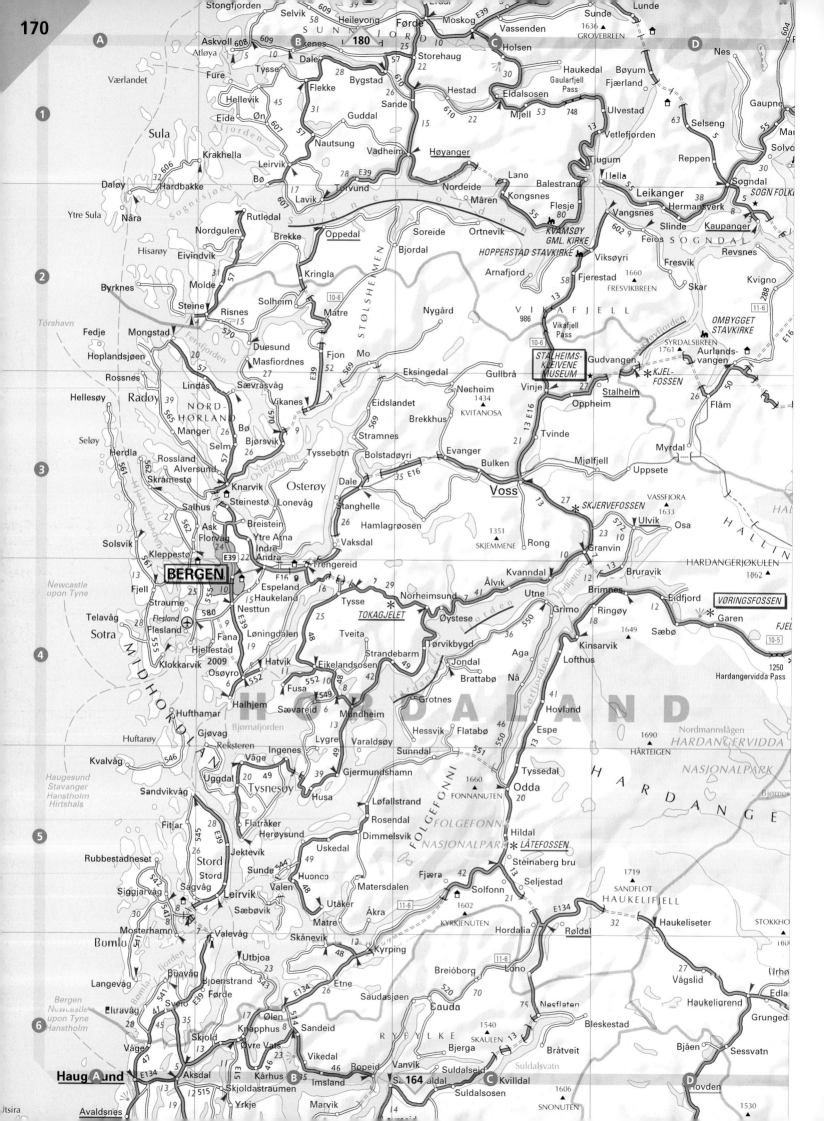

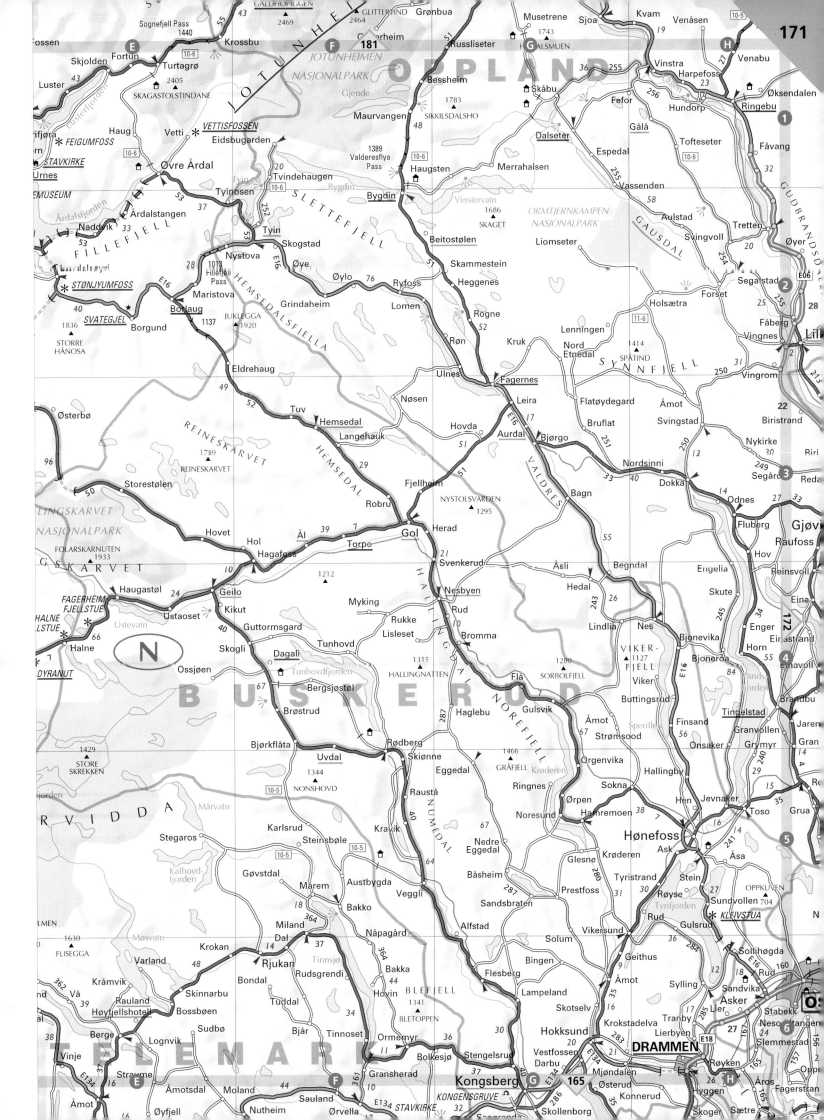

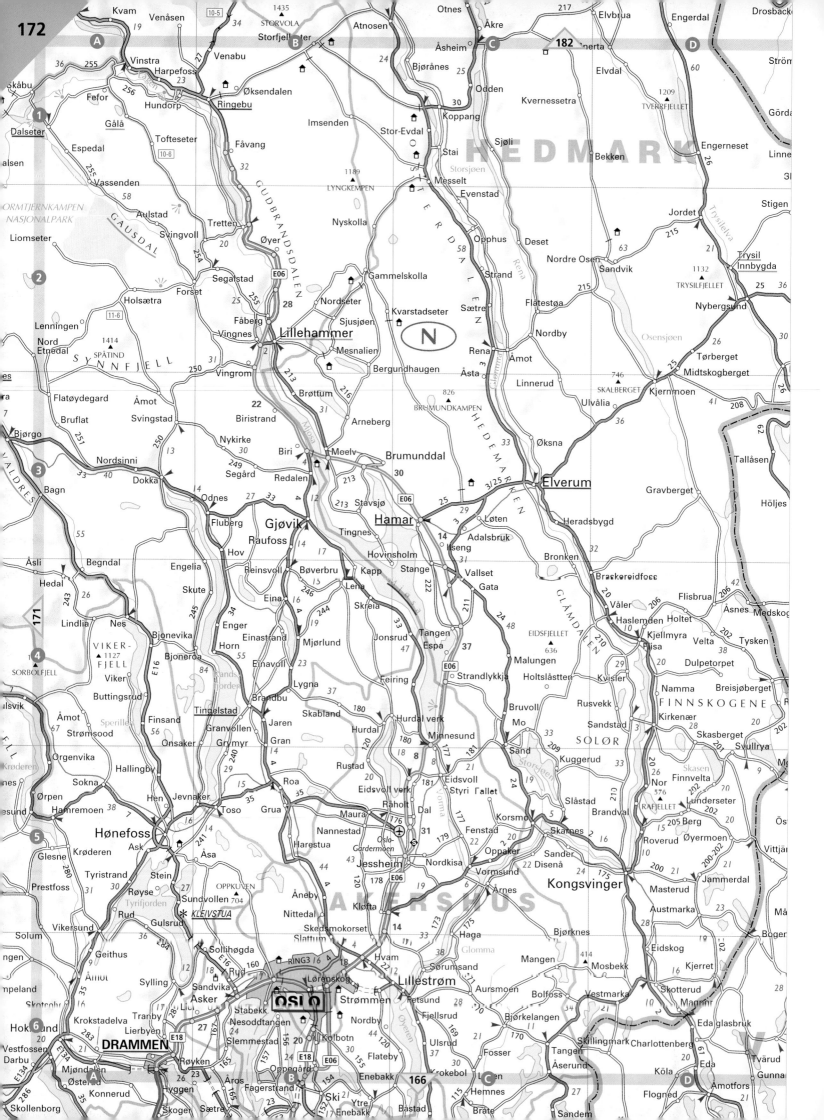

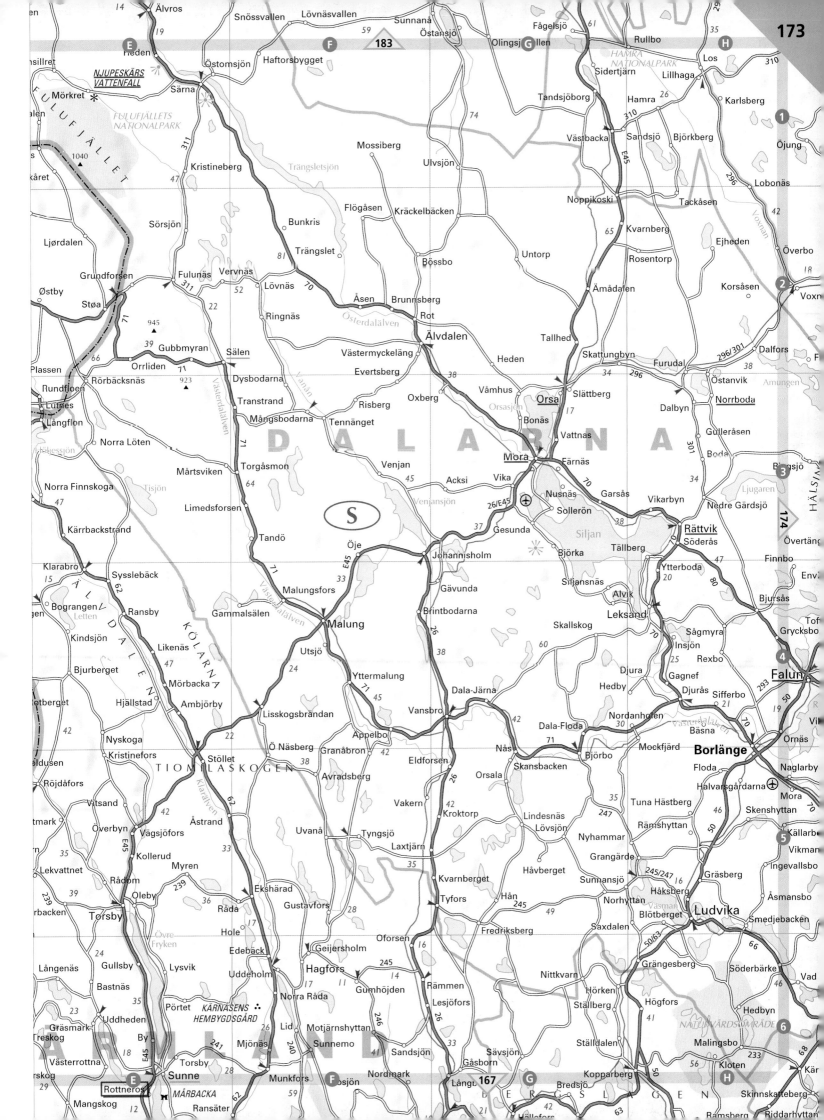

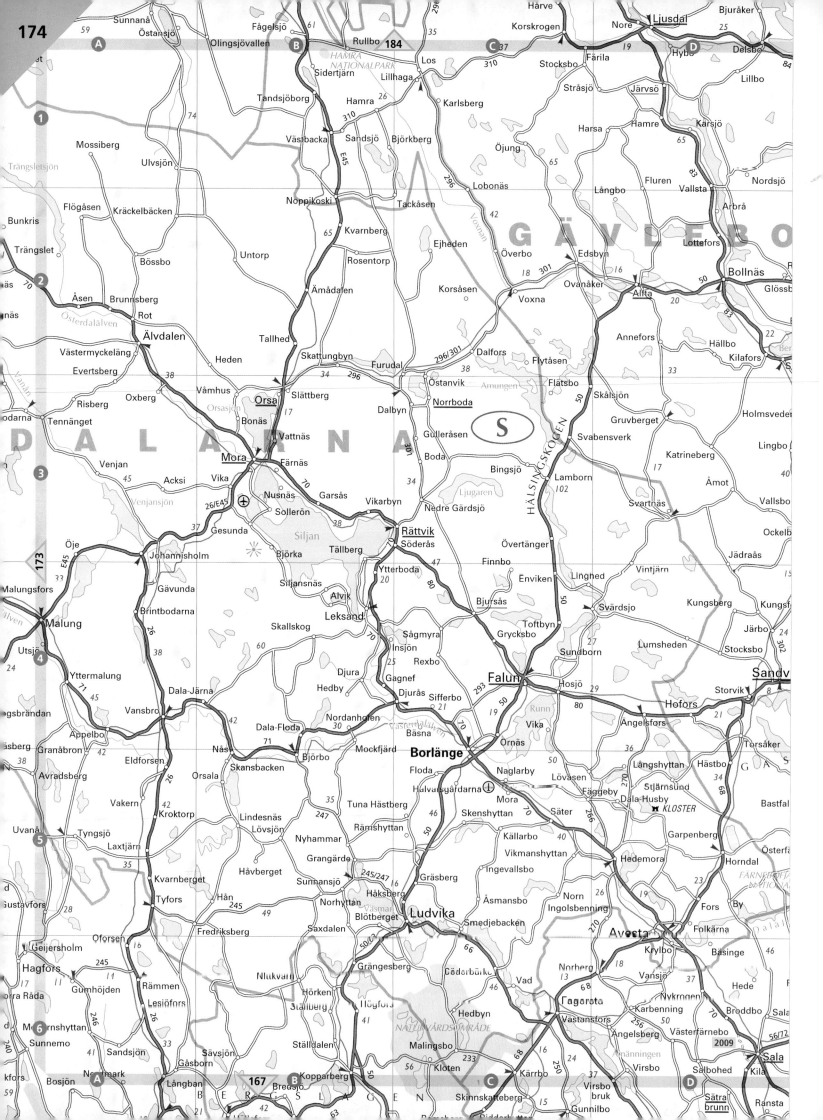

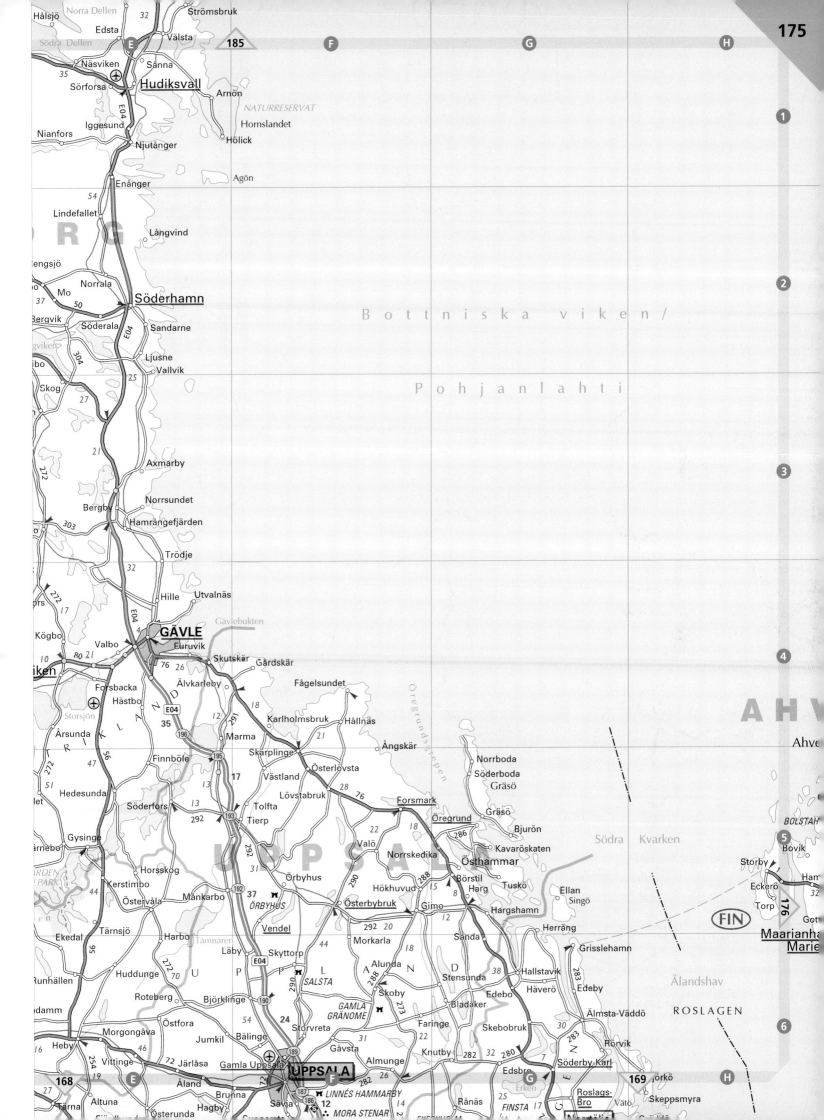

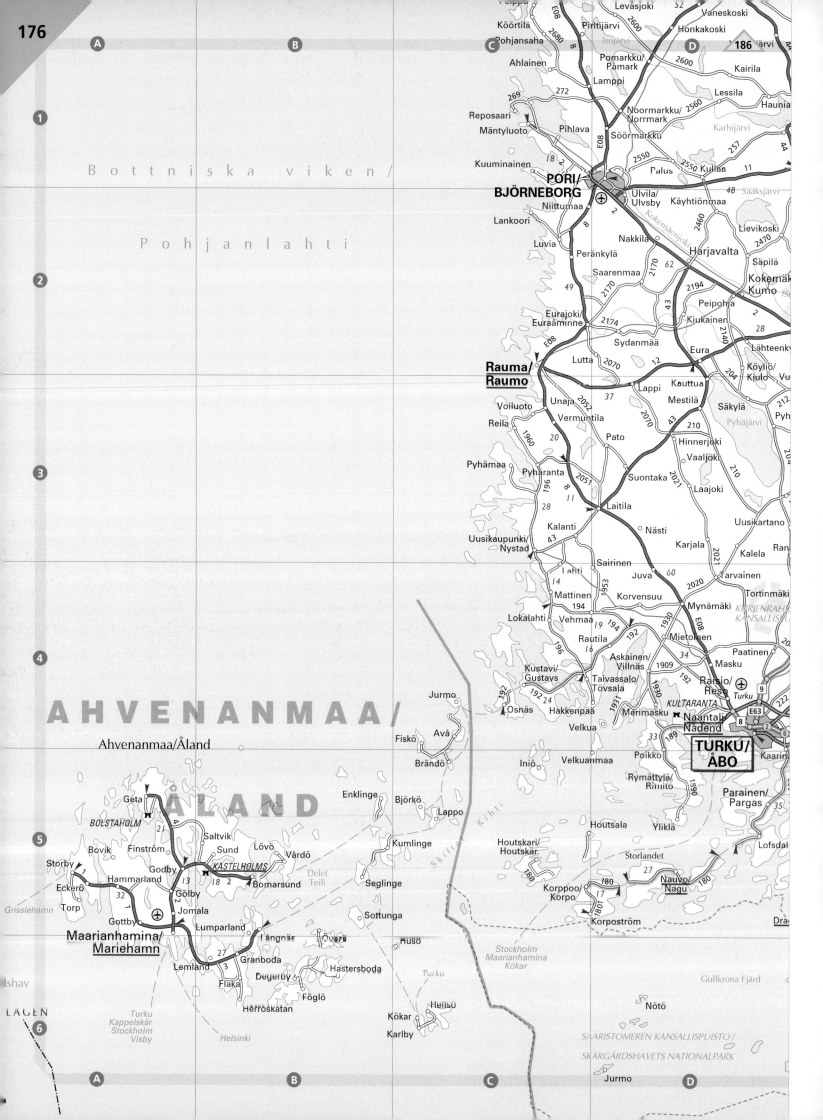

186

Bottniska viken/

Pohjanlahti

Köörtilä
Pirltijärvi
Pohjansaha
Ahlainen
Pomarkku/
Påmark
Kairila
Lessila
Haunia
Reposaari
Mäntyluoto
Noormarkku/
Norrmark
Pihlava
Söörmarkku
Karhijärvi
Kuuminainen
PORI/
BJÖRNEBORG
Ulvila/
Ulvsby
Käyhtiönmaa
Palus
Kullaa
Sääksjärvi
Niittumaa
Lankoori
Luvia
Nakkila
Lievikoski
Peränkylä
Härjavalta
Säpilä
Saarenmaa
Kokemäki/
Kumo
Eurajoki/
Euraåminne
Peipohja
Kiukainen
Lutta
Sydänmää
Eura
Köyliö/
Kjulo
Rauma/
Raumo
Lappi
Kauttua
Mestilä
Säkylä
Pyhäjärvi
Unaja
Voiluoto
Vermuntila
Pato
210
Reila
Hinnerjoki
Pyhämaa
Pyhäranta
Vaaljoki
Suontaka
Laajoki
Uusikartano
Laitila
Kalanti
Nästi
Karjala
Kalela
Uusikaupunki/
Nystad
Sairinen
Lahti
Juva
Tarvainen
Tortinmäki
Mattinen
Korvensuu
Mynämäki
Lokalahti
Vehmaa
Mietoinen
Rautila
Kustavi/
Gustavs
Askainen/
Villnäs
Masku
Taivassalo/
Tövsala
Raisio/
Reso
Turku
Merimasku
KULTARANTA
Naantali/
Nådend
Hakkenpää
Jurmo
Velkua
Osnäs
Velkuanmaa
Iniö
TURKU/
ÅBO
Avä
Fiskö
Poikko
Brändö
Rymättylä/
Rimito
Parainen/
Pargas
Enklinge
Björkö
Houtsala
Yliklä
Lappo
Lofsdal
AHVENANMAA/
Ahvenanmaa/Åland
Houtskari/
Houtskär
Storlandet
ÅLAND
Kumlinge
Nauvo
Nagu
Geta
Korppoo/
Korpo
BOLSTAHOLM
Saltvik
Seglinge
Korpoström
Bovik
Finström
Sund
Lövö
Vårdö
Storby
Godby
KASTELHOLMS
Hammarland
Delet
Teili
Eckerö
Gölby
Bomarsund
Sottunga
Grisslehamn
Torp
Jomala
Stockholm
Maarianhamina
Kökar
Gottby
Lumparland
Långnäs
Huso
Maarianhamina/
Mariehamn
Nötö
Granboda
Lemland
Gullkrona Fjärd
Flaka
Degerby
Haestersboda
Föglö
Hellsö
Turku
Kappelskär
Stockholm
Visby
Herröskatan
Kökar
SAARISTOMEREN KANSALLISPUISTO/
SKÄRGÅRDSHAVETS NATIONALPARK
Karlby
Helsinki
Jurmo

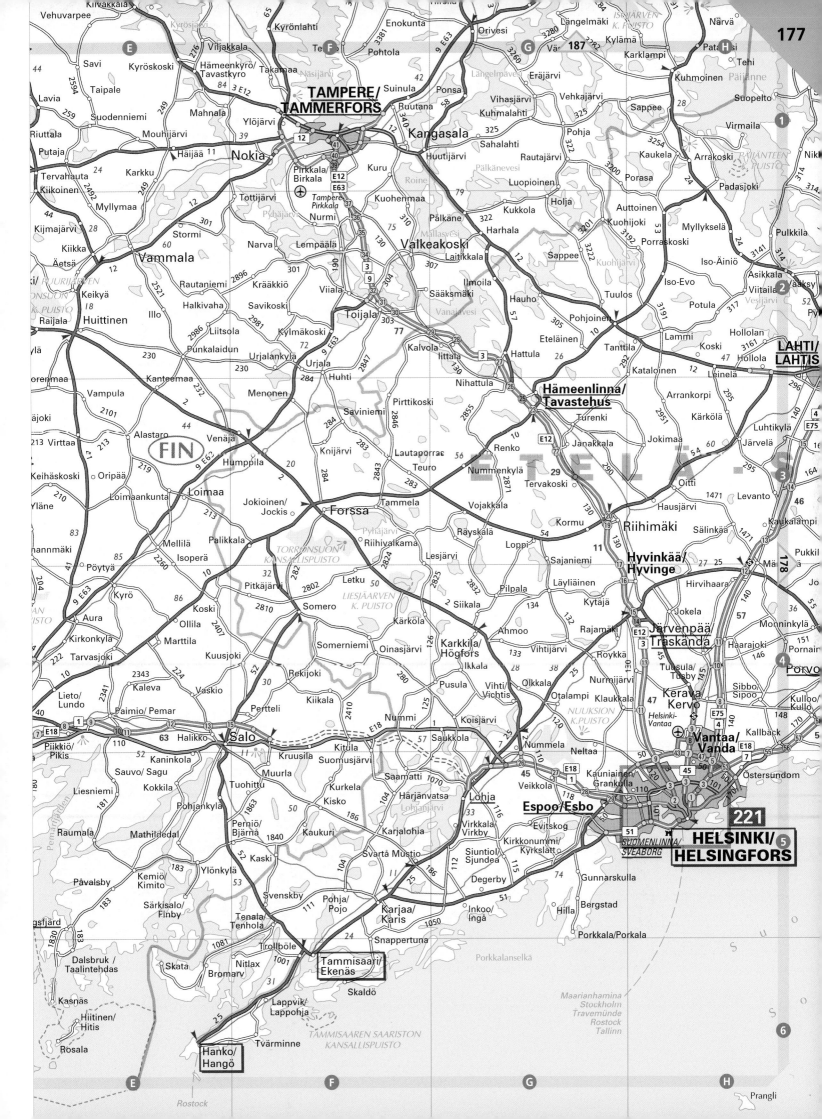

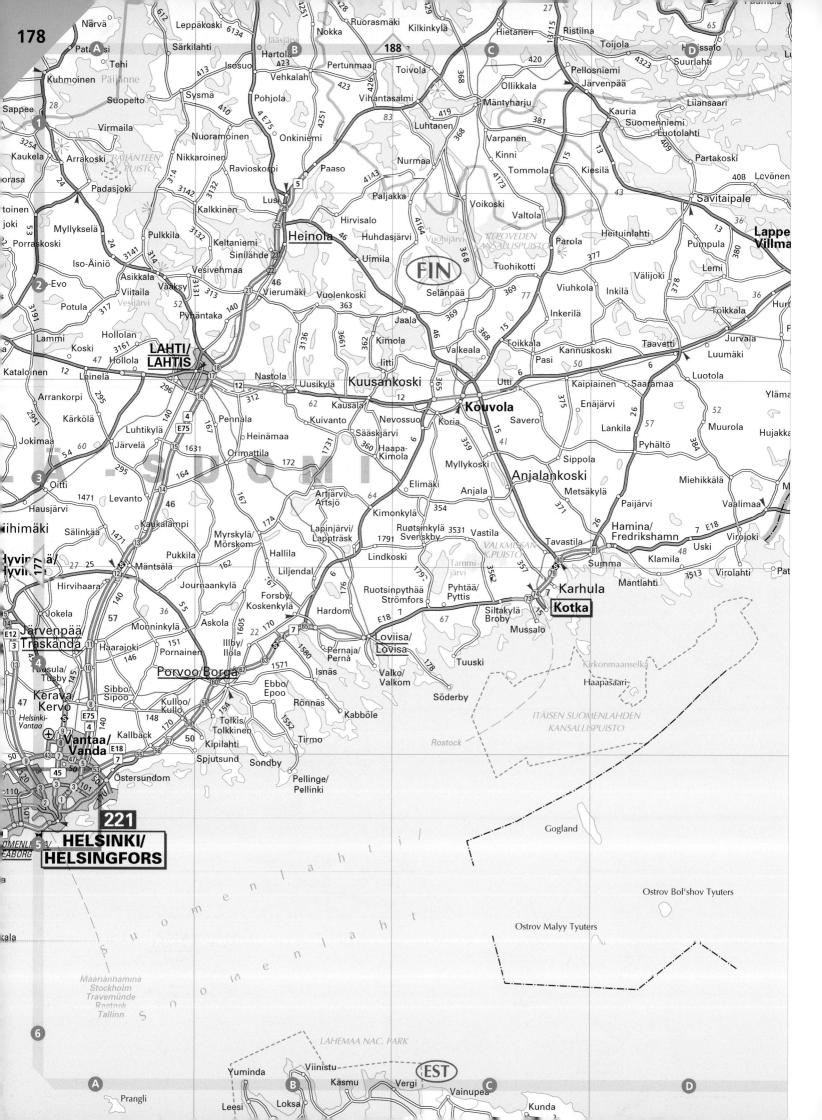

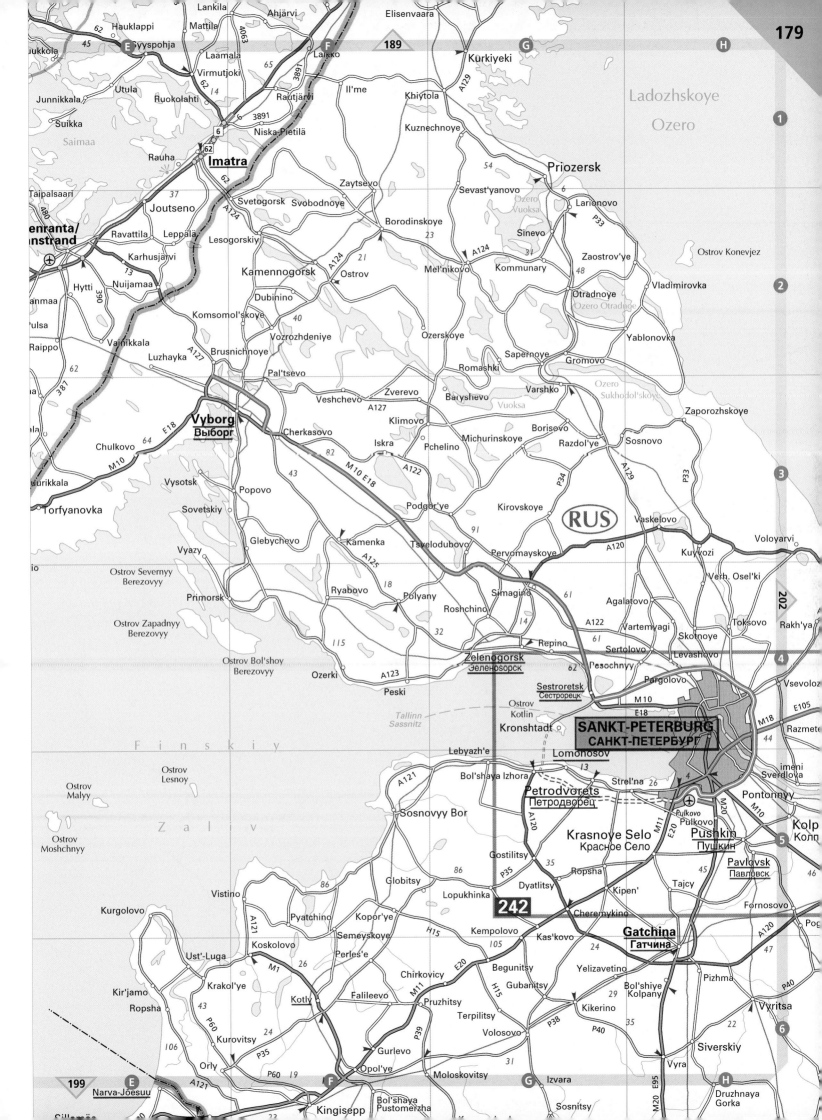

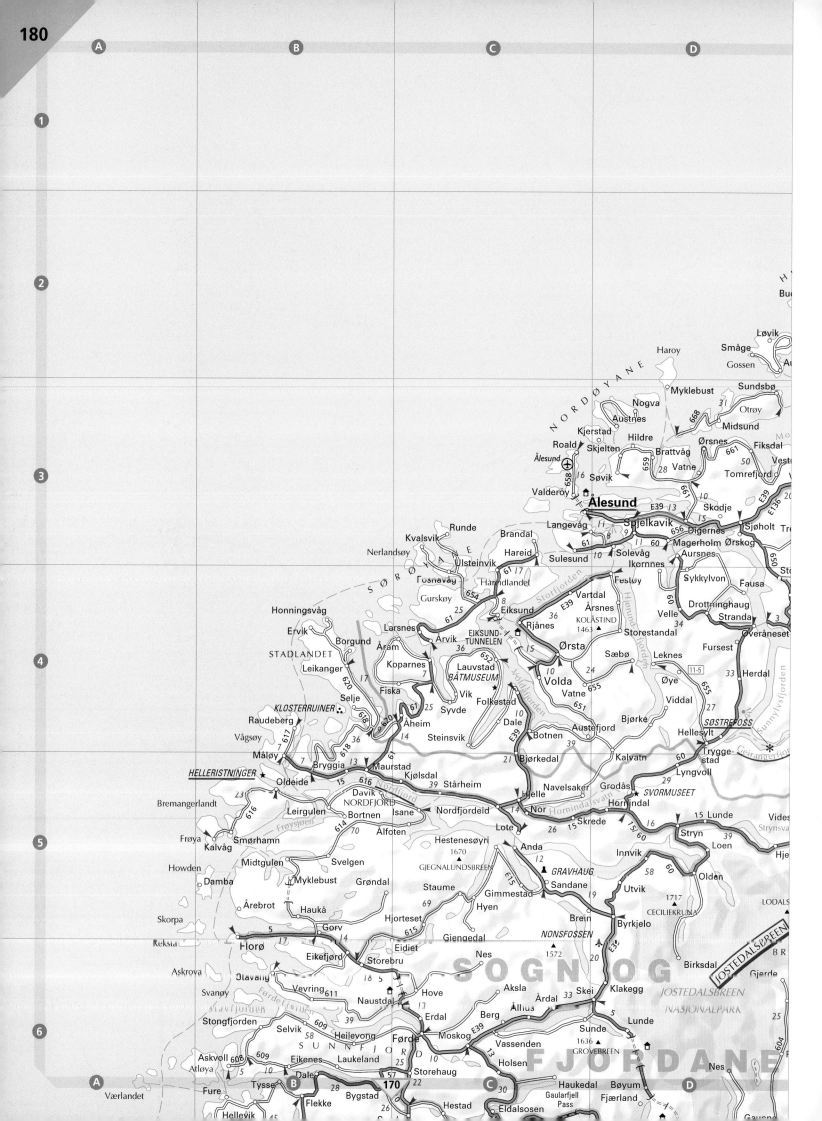

A   B   C   D

1
2
3
4
5
6

Løvik
Småge
Haroy   Gossen   Au
NORDØYANE
Myklebust   Sundsbø
Nogva   31   Otrøy
Austnes   668   Midsund
Kjerstad   Hildre   659   Ørsnes   661   Fiksdal
Roald   Skjelten   Brattvåg   50   Vesta
Ålesund   658   16   Søvik   28   Vatne   Tomrefjord
Valderøy   Skodje   E39   13   10   E39   E136   20
Ålesund   15
Langevåg   E39   13   Spjelkavik   656   Sjøholt   Tre
Runde   Brandal   11   8   Digernes
Kvalsvik   61   9   11   60   Magerholm Ørskog
Nerlandsøy   Ulsteinvik   Hareid   Sulesund   10   Solevåg   Aursnes
                    61   17   Ikornnes   Sykkylven   Fausa
Fosnavåg   654   8   Storfjorden   Festøy   60
Gurskøy   25   Eiksund   Vartdal   Drottninghaug
Honningsvåg   61   36   E39   Årsnes   Velle   Stranda
Ervik   Larsnes   Årvik   Rjånes   KOLÅSTIND   Storestandal   34   Overåneset   3
Borgund   EIKSUND-   1463   Fursest
STADLANDET   Åram   36   TUNNELEN   15   Ørsta   Sæbø   Leknes   11-5   33   Herdal
Leikanger   620   Koparnes   652   Volda   24   Øye   655
          17   7   Lauvstad   10   Vatne   655   Viddal   27
Selje   Fiska   BÅTMUSEUM   651   Bjørke   SØSTREFOSS
Raudeberg   618   Åheim   Vik   Folkestad   Austefjord   Hellesylt
KLOSTERRUINER   61   25   Syvde   Dale   E39   39   Trygge-
Vågsøy   617   36   14   Steinsvik   Botnen   Kalvatn   60   stad
Måløy   7   618   13   61   21   Bjørkedal   Lyngvoll
HELLERISTNINGER   Bryggia   616   Maurstad   Kjølsdal   29
          Oldeide   15   Stårheim   Hjelle   Navelsaker   Grodås   SVORMUSEET
Bremangerlandt   23   616   Davik   39   14   Hornindal   15   Lunde
          616   Leirgulen   NORDFJORD   Nordfjordeid   Nor   Horningdalsvatn   16   Stryn   39
Frøya   614   Bortnen   Isane   Lote   26   15   Skrede   15   60   Loen   Hje
Kalvåg   Smørhamn   70   Ålfoten   Hestenesøyri   Anda   12   Innvik
Howden   Midtgulen   Svelgen   1670   GRAVHAUG   58   Olden
Damba   Myklebust   Grøndal   GJEGNALUNDSBREEN   615   Sandane   60   1717
Skorpa   Årebrot   Hauka   Staume   Gimmestad   19   Utvik   CECILIEKRUNA   LODALS
Reksta   5   Gorv   Hyen   Brein   Byrkjelo   JOSTEDALSBREEN
          Florø   17   14   615   Gjengedal   NONSFOSSEN   20   E39   Birksdal   BR
Askrova   Eikefjord   Eidiet   Nes   1572   Skei   Klakegg   JOSTEDALSBREEN
Svanøy   Olavang   Storebru   18   5   Hove   Aksla   33   Lunde   NASJONALPARK   Gjørde
Stongfjorden   Vevring   611   Naustdal   13   Berg   Årdal   Ålhus   5
          Selvik   58   Heilevong   Erdal   Moskog   E39   Sunde   1636   GROVEBREEN   25
Askvoll   609   Eikenes   Laukeland   Førde   Vassenden   13   Holsen
Atløya   5   10   Dale   57   Storehaug   Haukedal   Bøyum   Nes
Fure   Tysse   28   170   22   30   Gaularfjell   Fjærland   604
Værlandet   Flekke   Bygstad   26   Hestad   Pass   Eldalsosen   Gaupne
Hellevik   45
SOGN OG FJORDANE
SUNNFJORD

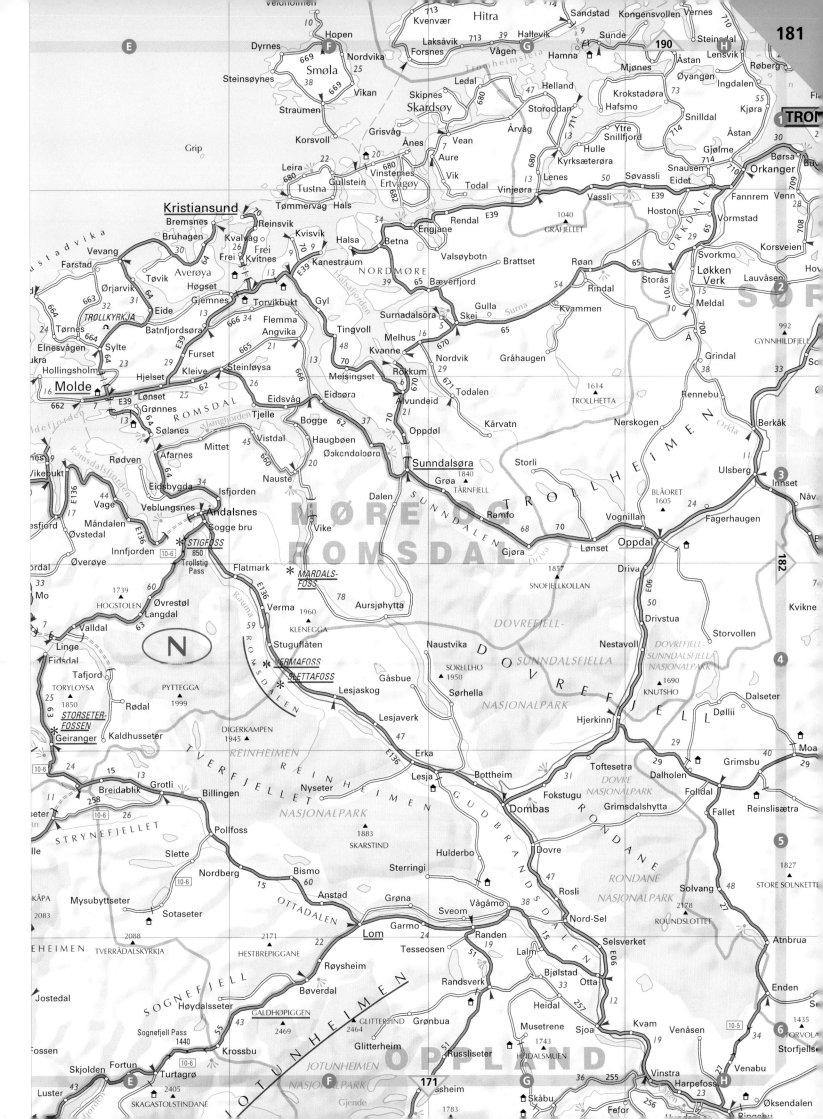

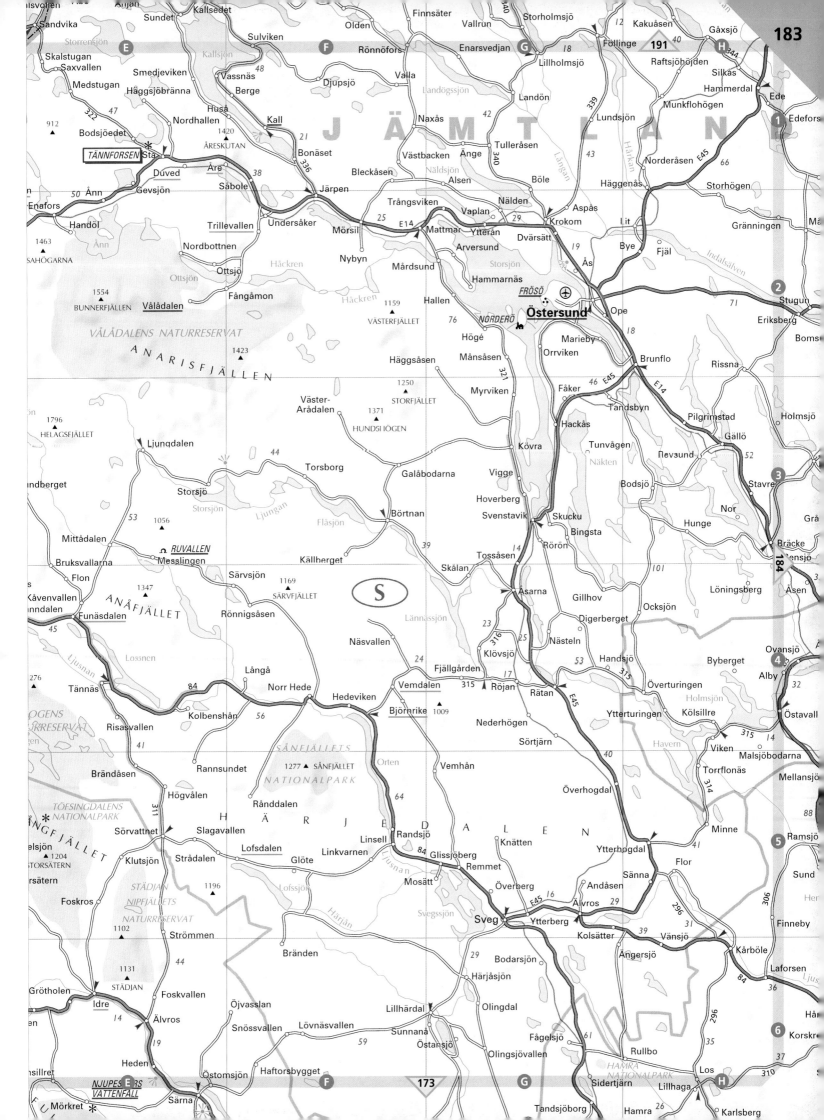

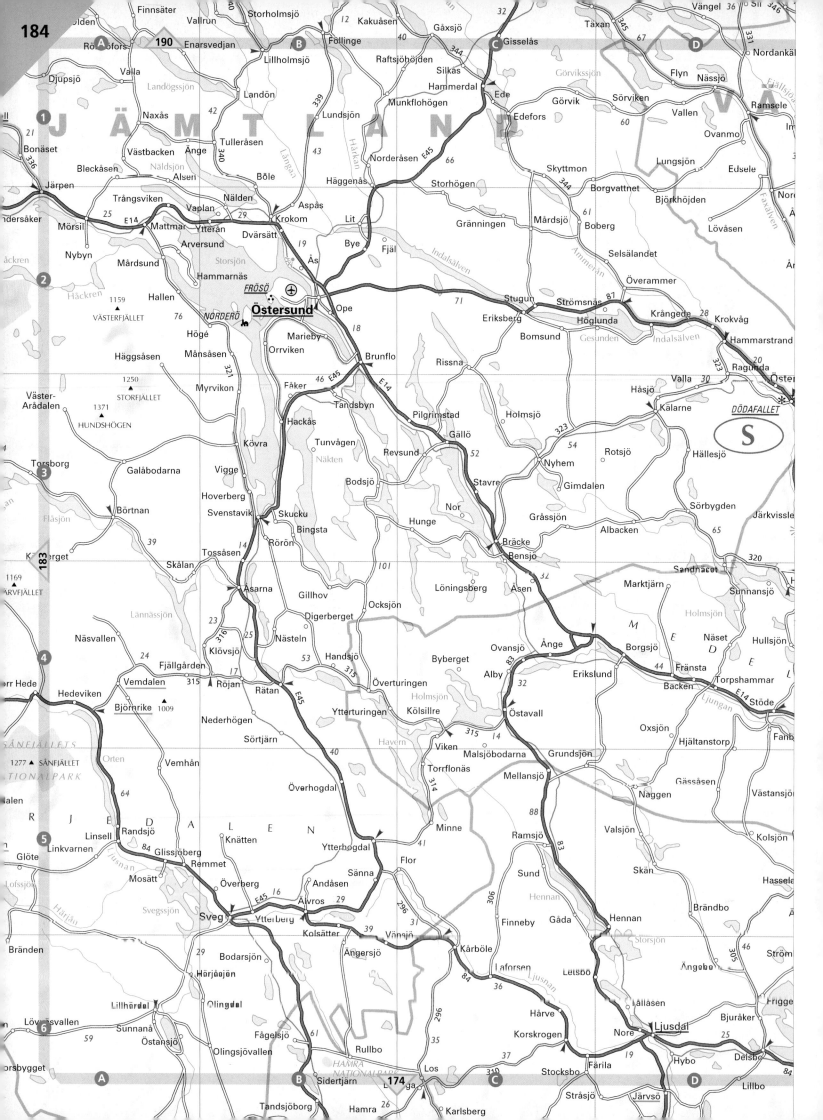

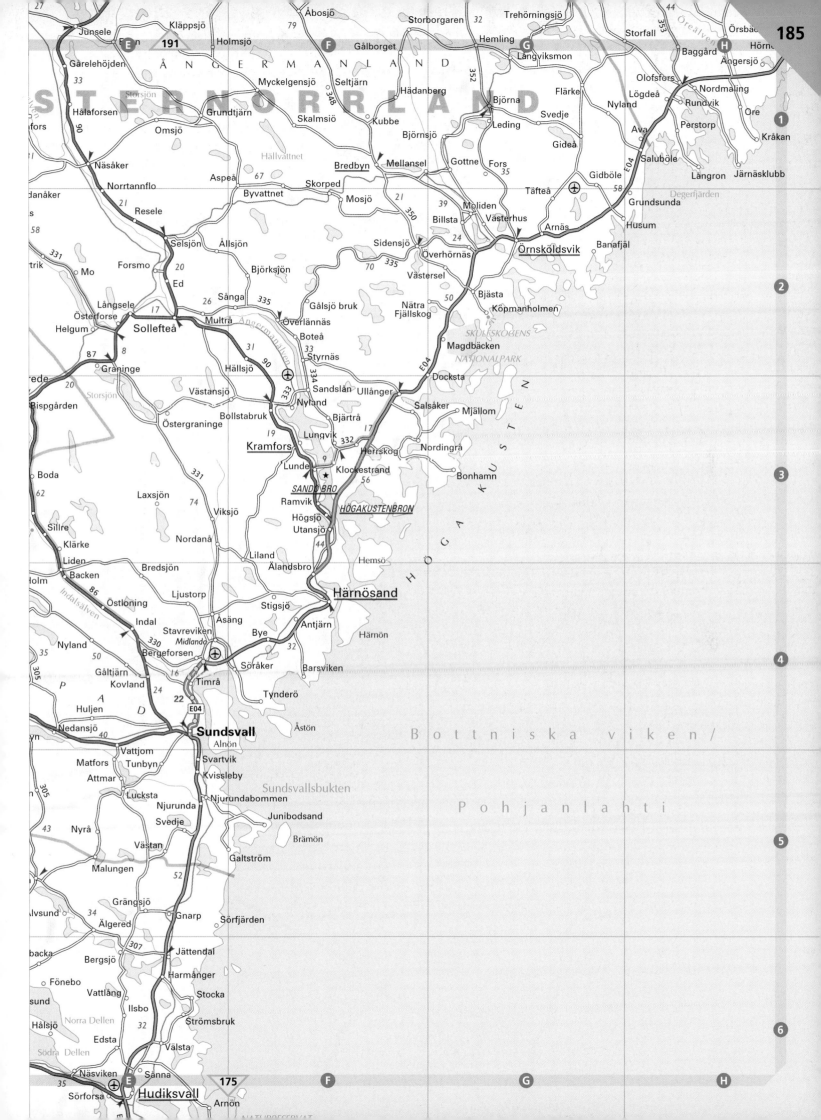

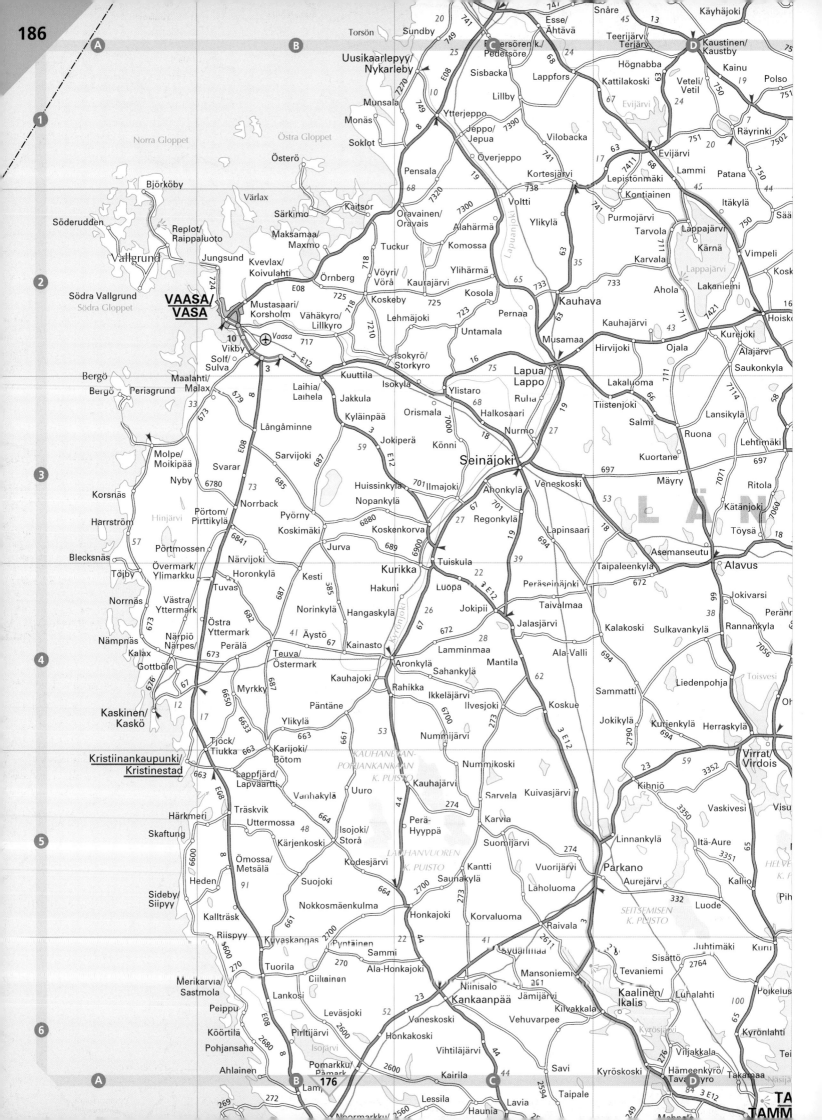

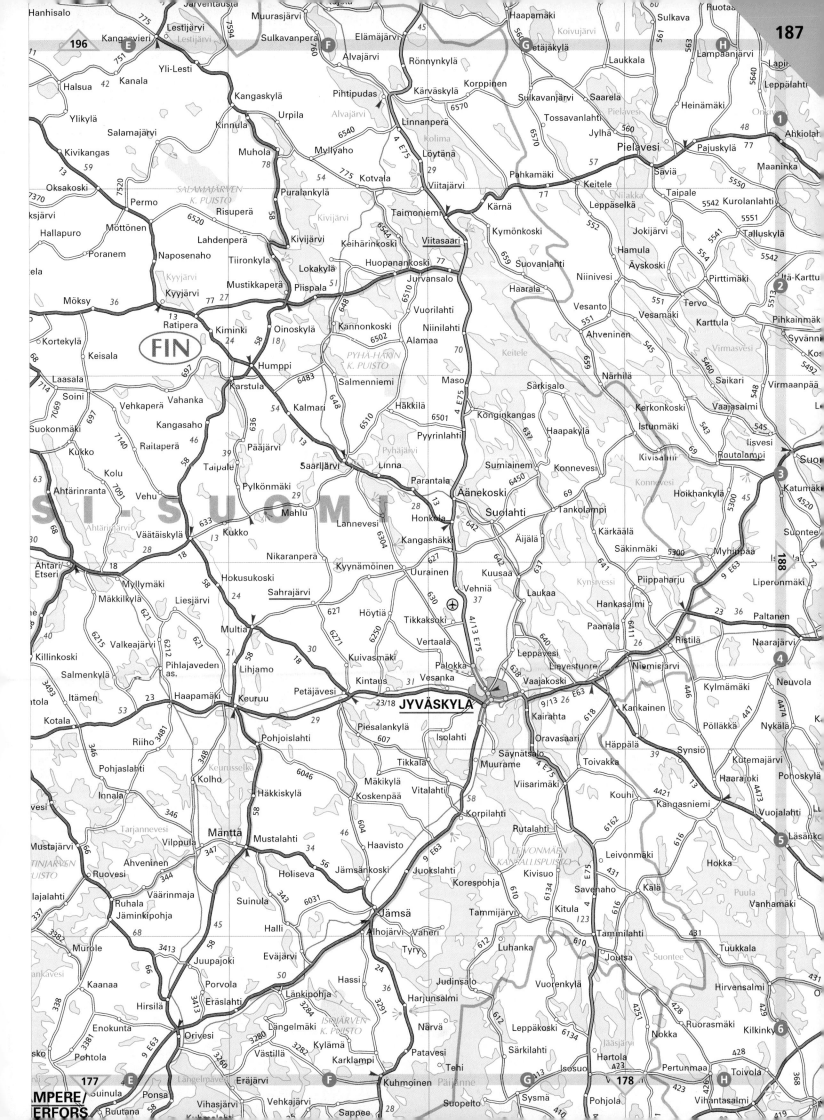

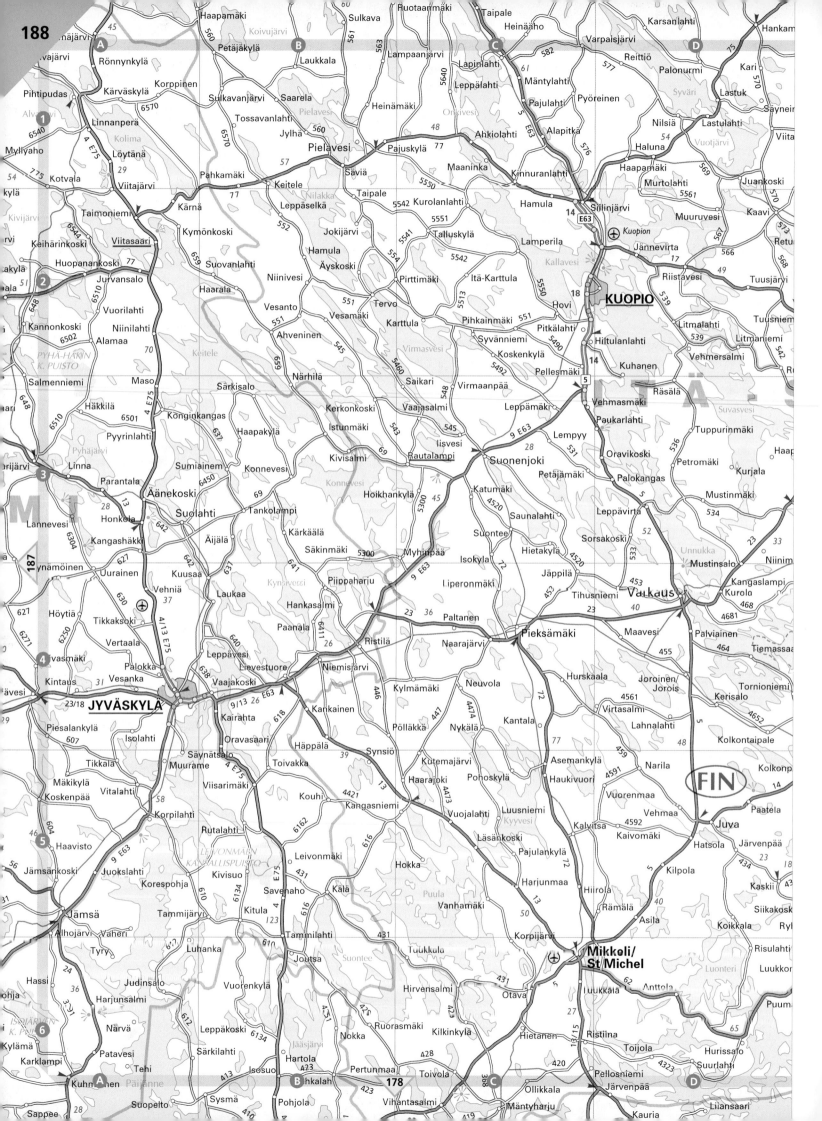

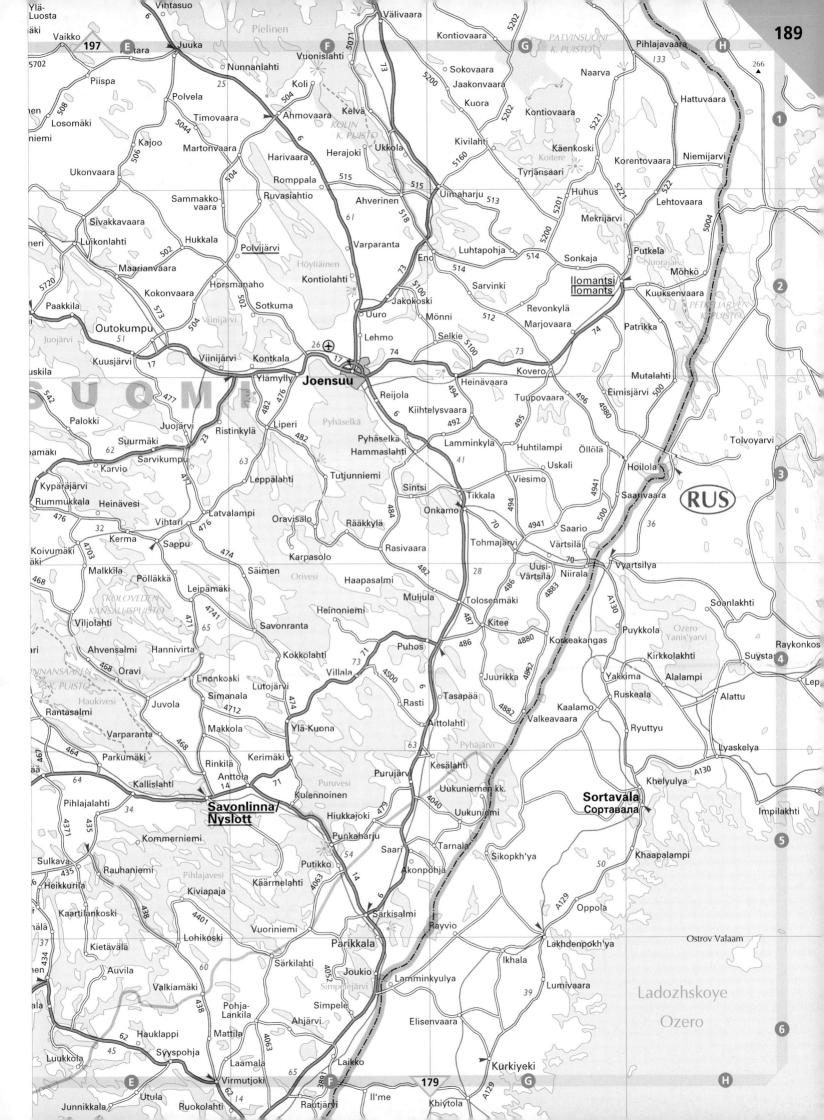

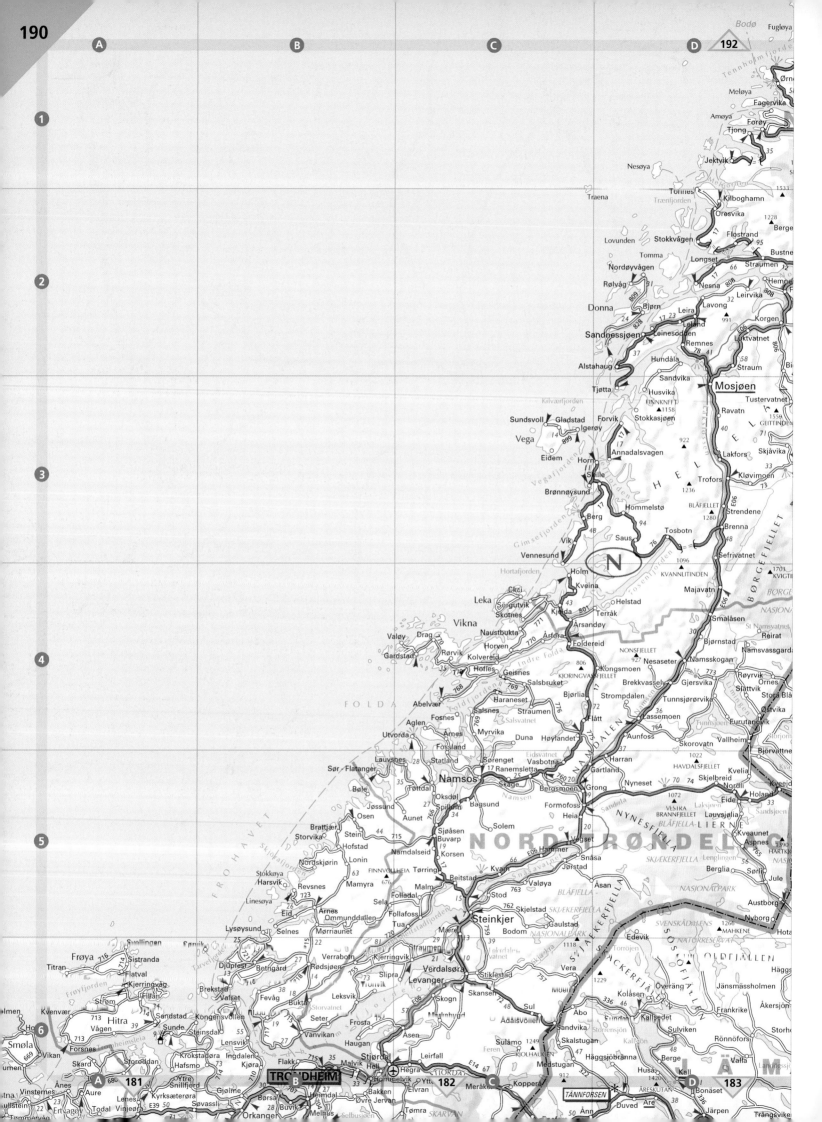

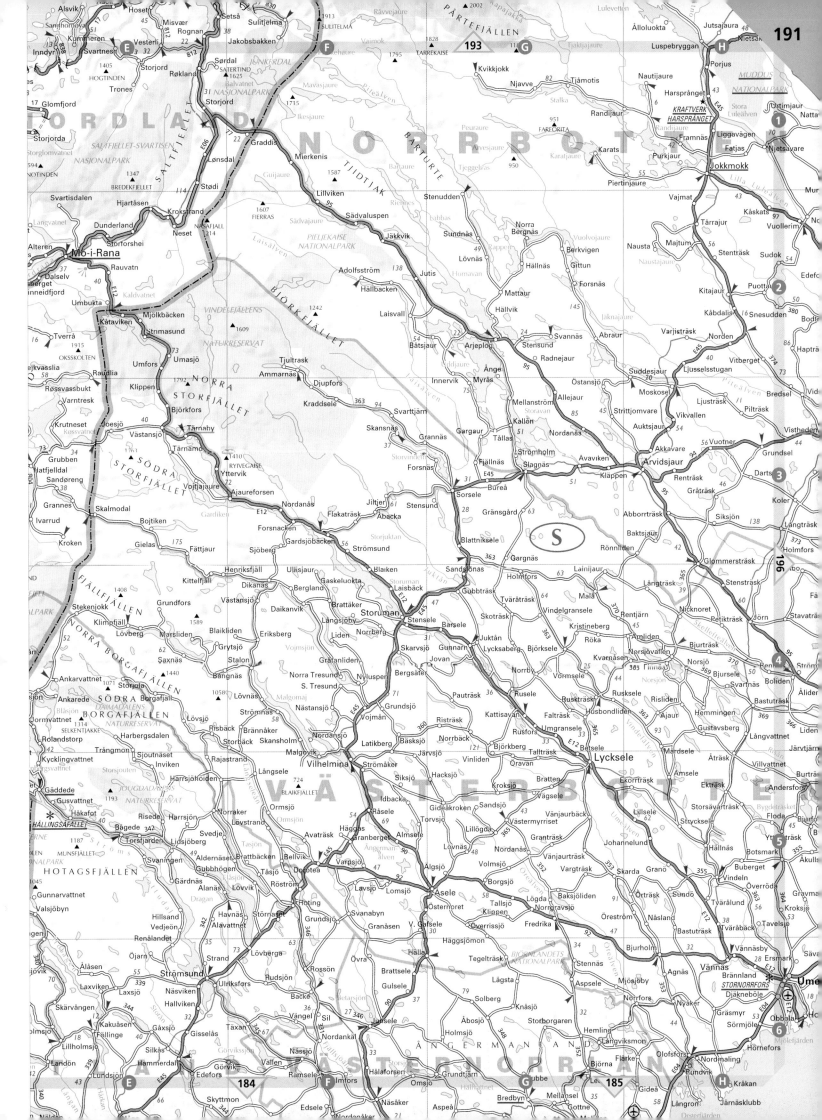

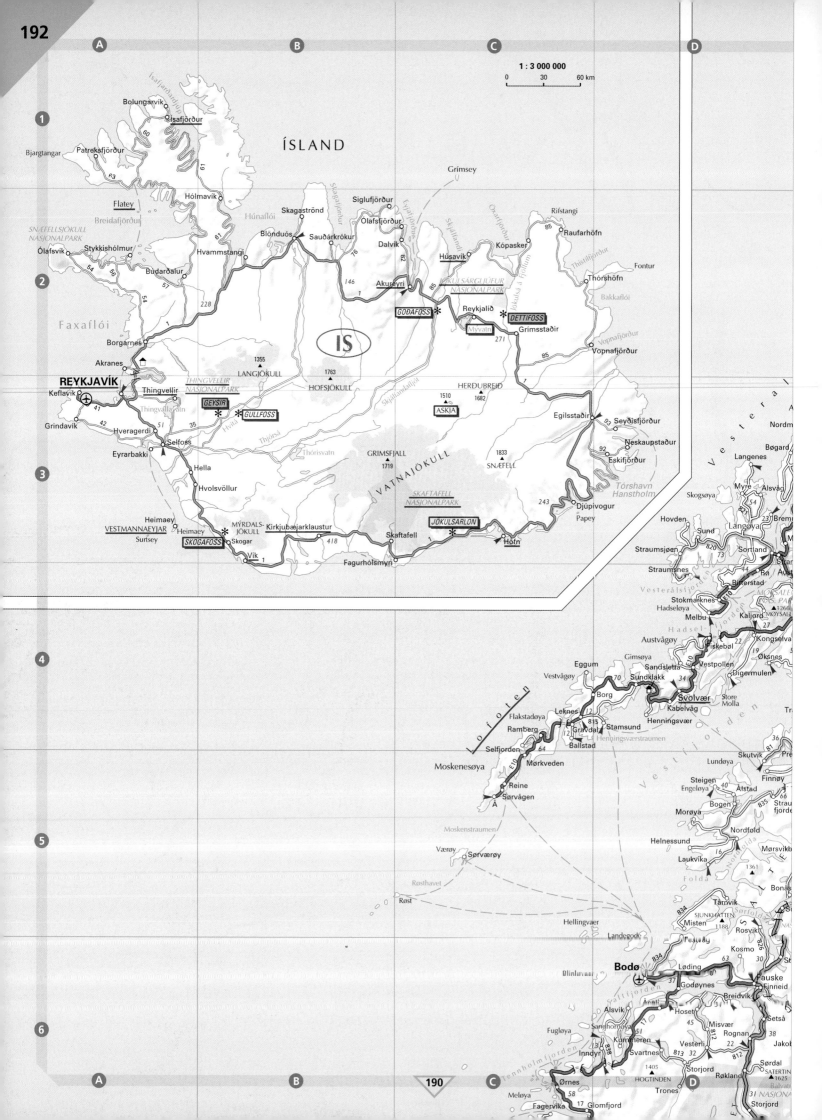

ÍSLAND

1 : 3 000 000

0   30   60 km

Bjargtangar
Bolungarvik
Ísafjörður
Patreksfjörður
60
61
R3
Hólmavík
Flatey
SNÆFELLSJÖKULL NASJONALPARK
Breidafjörður
Húnaflói
Ólafsvik
Stykkishólmur
Búdardalur
54   56
57
Hvammstangi
Blönduós
Skagaströnd
Sauðárkrókur
Siglufjörður
Ólafsfjörður
Dalvik
Húsavik
Grímsey
Rífstangi
Raufarhöfn
85
Kópasker
Þórshöfn
Fontur
228
54
78
82
146
1
Akureyri
85
Reykjalíð
JÖKULSÁRGLJÚFUR NASJONALPARK
DETTIFOSS
Grimsstaðir
271
Bakkaflói
Thistilfjörður
Faxaflói
1
GOÐAFOSS
Mývatn
85
Vopnafjörður
Vopnafjörður
Borgarnes
IS
Akranes
REYKJAVÍK
Keflavík
41
Thingvellir
THINGVELLIR NASJONALPARK
1355
LANGJÖKULL
1763
HOFSJÖKULL
Skjálfandafljót
HERÐUBREIÐ
1682
1510
ASKJA
1
Egilsstaðir
93
Seyðisfjörður
Neskaupstaður
92
Eskifjörður
Grindavík
42
Hveragerdi
51
35
GEYSIR
GULLFOSS
Thingvallavatn
Hvíta
Thjórsá
Thórisvatn
GRIMSFJALL
1719
VATNAJÖKULL
1833
SNÆFELL
Tórshavn
Hanstholm
Selfoss
Eyrarbakki
Hella
Hvolsvöllur
Heimaey
VESTMANNAEYJAR
Surtsey
Heimaey
SKOGAFOSS
Skogar
Vík
MÝRDALS-JÖKULL
Kirkjubæjarklaustur
418
Skaftafell
SKAFTAFELL NASJONALPARK
243
JÖKULSARLON
Höfn
1
Djúpivogur
Papey
Fagurhólsmyri

Skogsøya
Myre
Alsvag
Hovden
Langøya
Bremnes
54
23
Sund
820
73
Sortland
Straumsjøen
Straumsnes
44
Rø
Aust
Bitterstad
Stokmarknes
Hadseløya
1266
MØYSALE
MØYSALEN NAS. PARK
Melbu
Kaljord
27
Hadsel
Austvågøy
Fiskebøl
22
Kongselva
Øksnes
19
Svolvær
Store Molla
Eggum
Kabelvåg
Henningsvær
36
Gimsøya
Sandsletta
Vestpollen
Digermulen
Vestvågøy
70
Sundklakk
34
Skutvik
81
Borg
Lundøya
Leknes
12
Finnøy
Flakstadøya
815
Steigen
40
Åtstad
Ramberg
Grøvdal
12
Stamsund
Engeløya
Bogen
66
Strau fjorde
Selfjorden
64
Ballstad
Henningsværstraumen
835
Moskenesøya
E10
Mørkveden
Morøya
Nordføld
Reine
Helnessund
16
Mørsvikb
Sørvågen
Å
Laukvika
Folda
1361
Moskenstraumen
Tårnvik
834
SJUNKHATTEN
Misten
1188
Rosvik
Værøy
Sørværøy
Røsthavet
Bonas
Røst
Hellingvaer
Landegode
834
Festvåg
Kosmo
826
Øllinlvår
Bodø
Løding
63
30
Fauske
37
Godøynes
Breidvik
Finneid
Alsvik
Ånli
Hoset
Misvær
812
Setså
Fugløya
Sandhornøya
51
45
Rognan
38
Kummeren
813
32
22
812
Inndyr
Svartnесt
Vesterli
Storjord
Røkland
1405
SATERTIN
Ørnes
58
HOGTINDEN
1625
31 NASJONA
Trones
Meløya
Storjord
Fagervika
17
Glomfjord
Sørdal

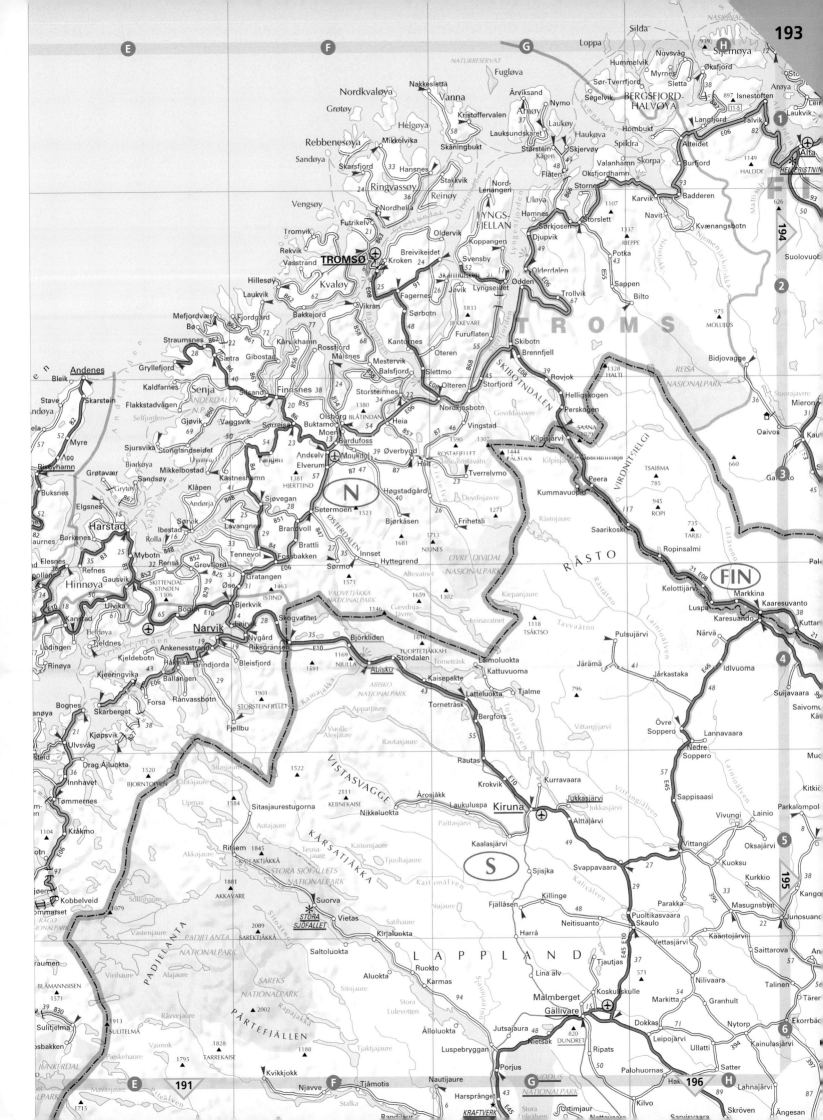

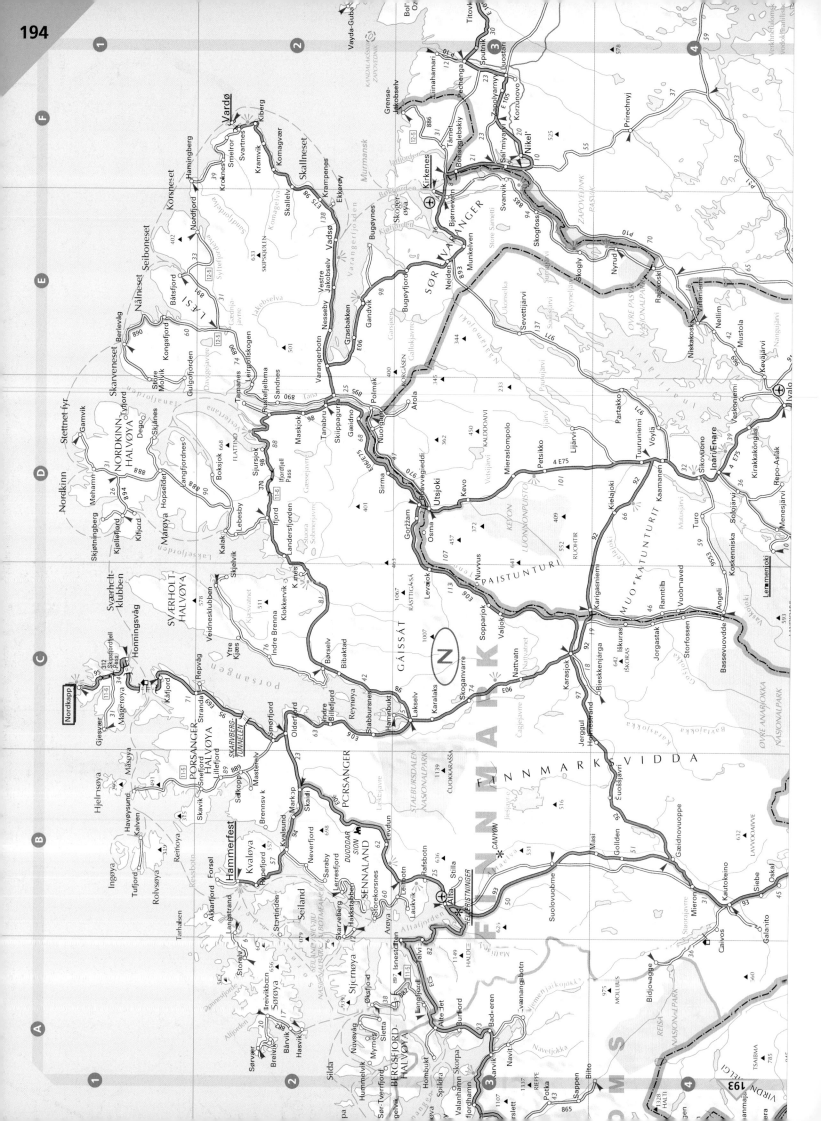

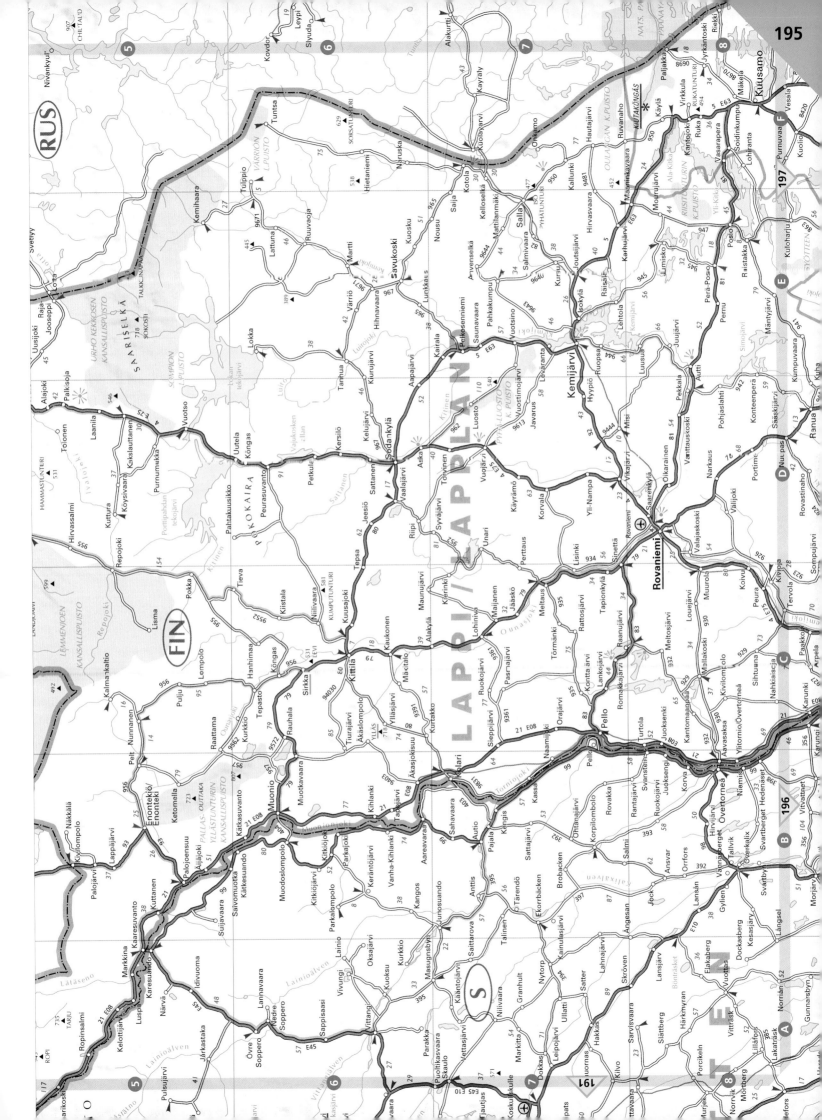

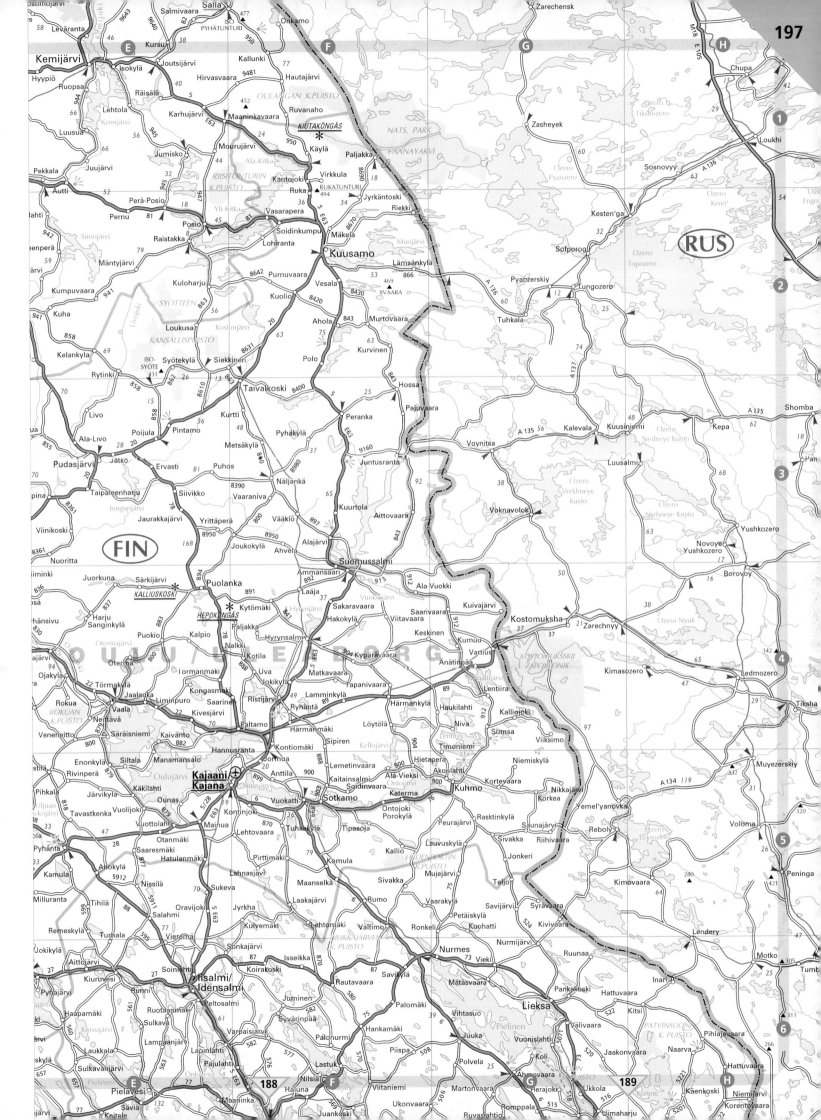

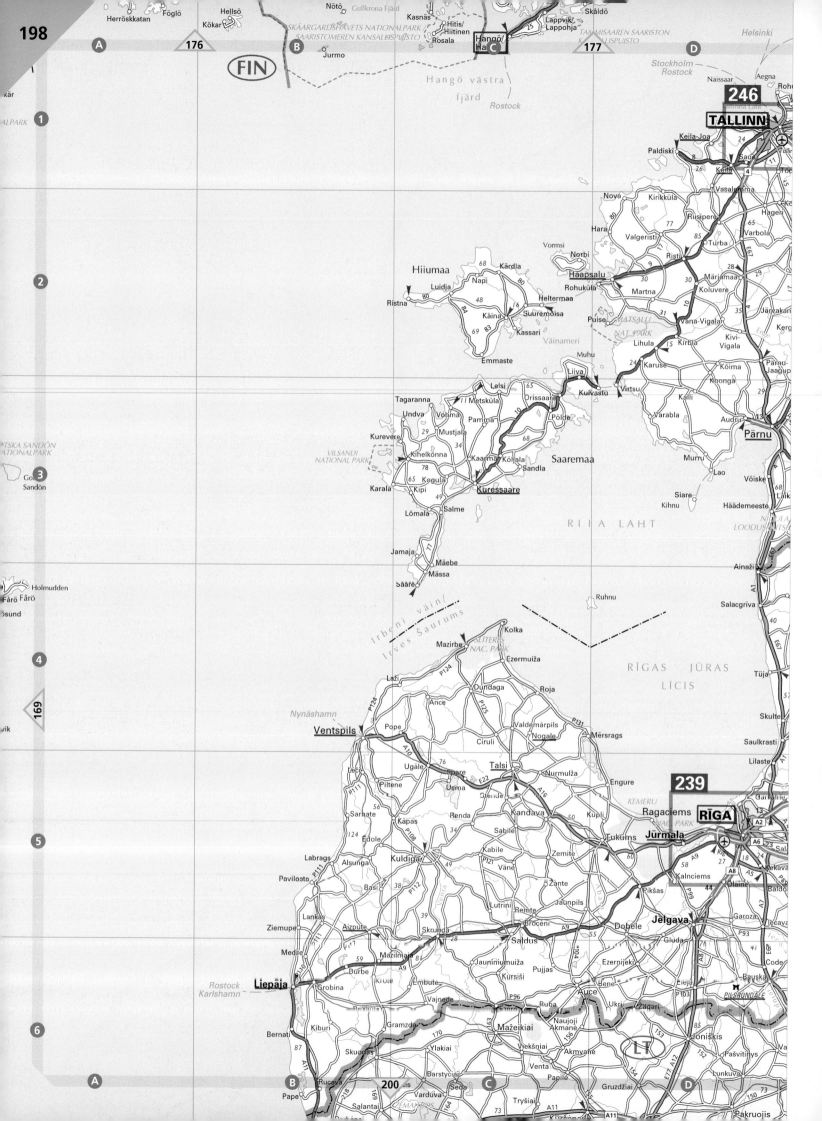

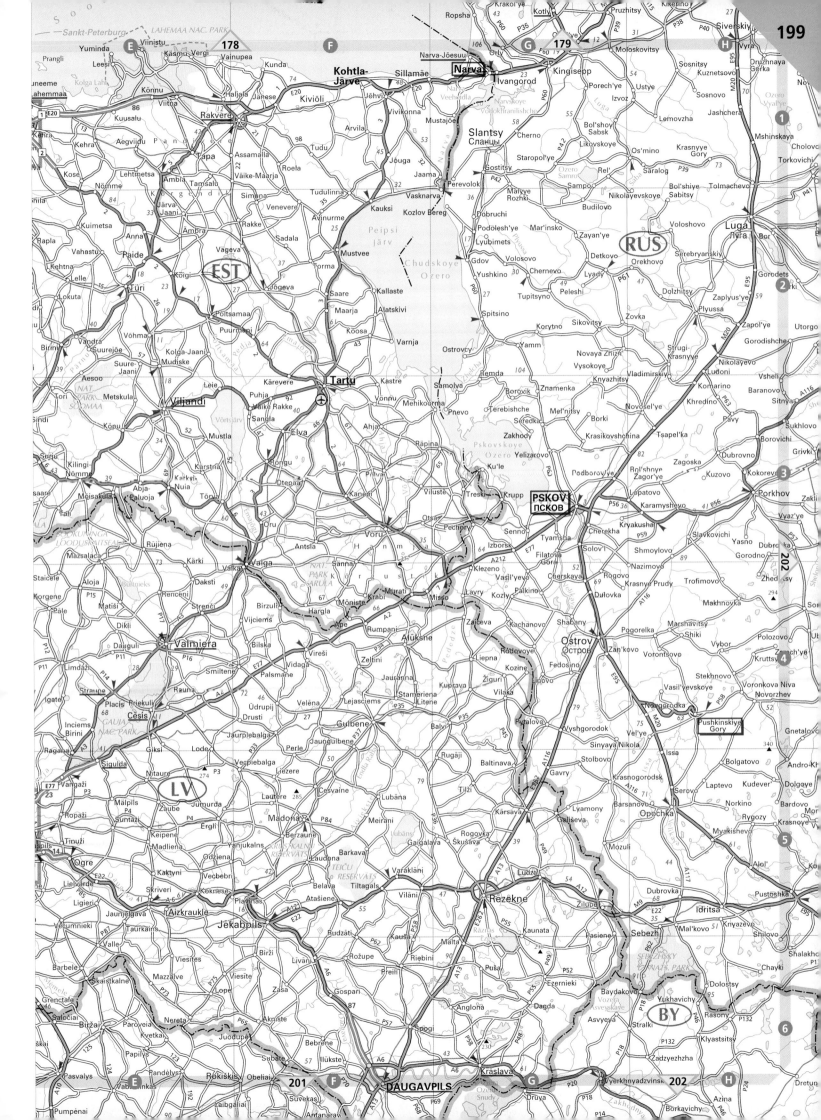

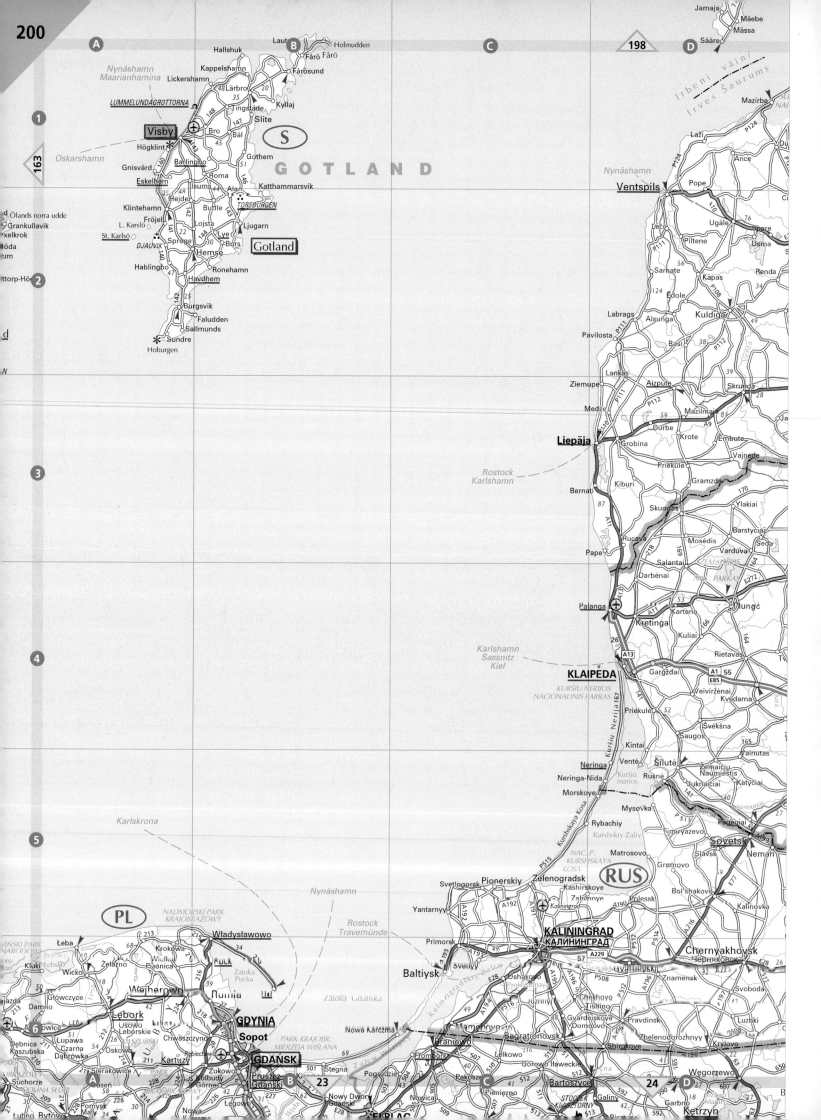

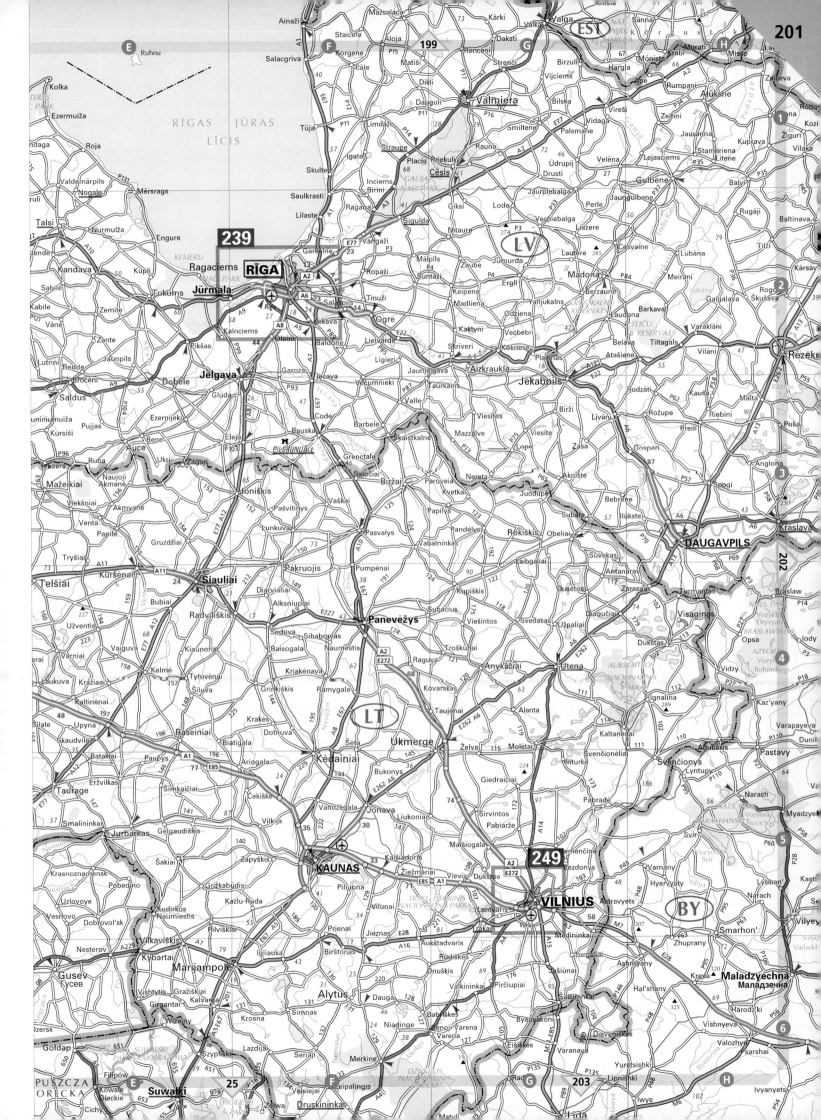

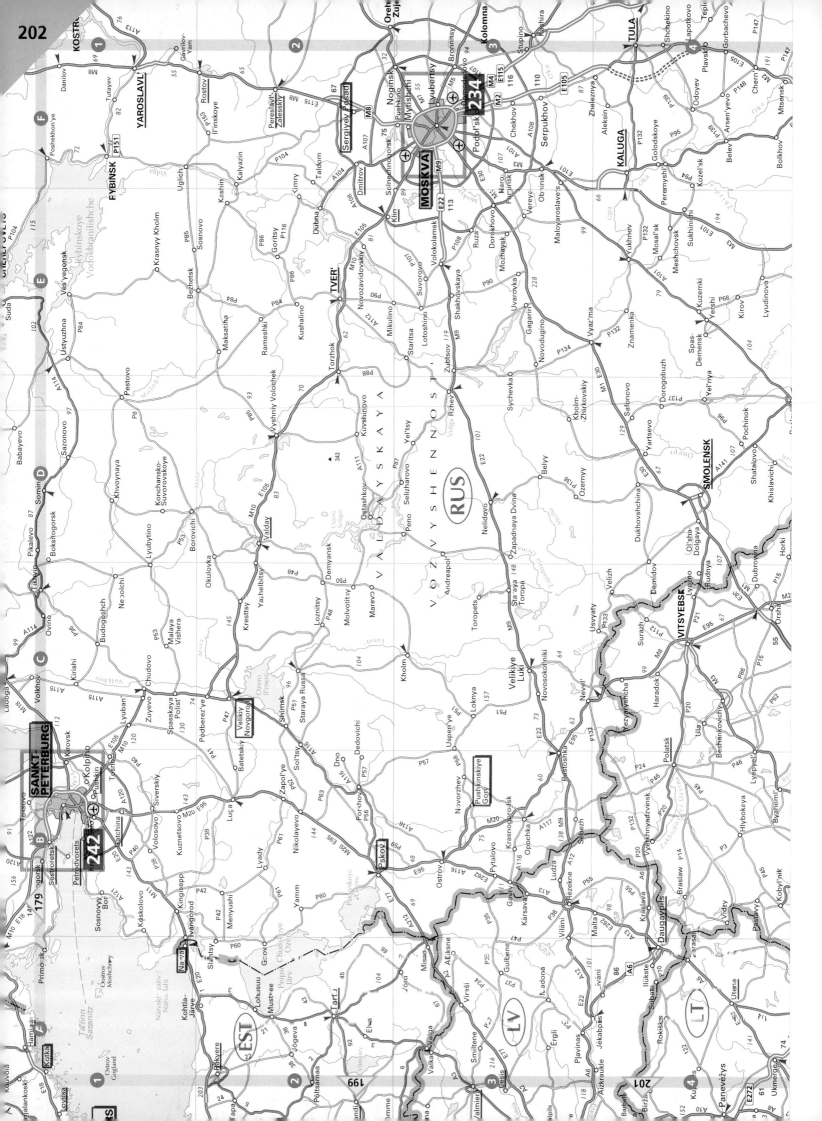

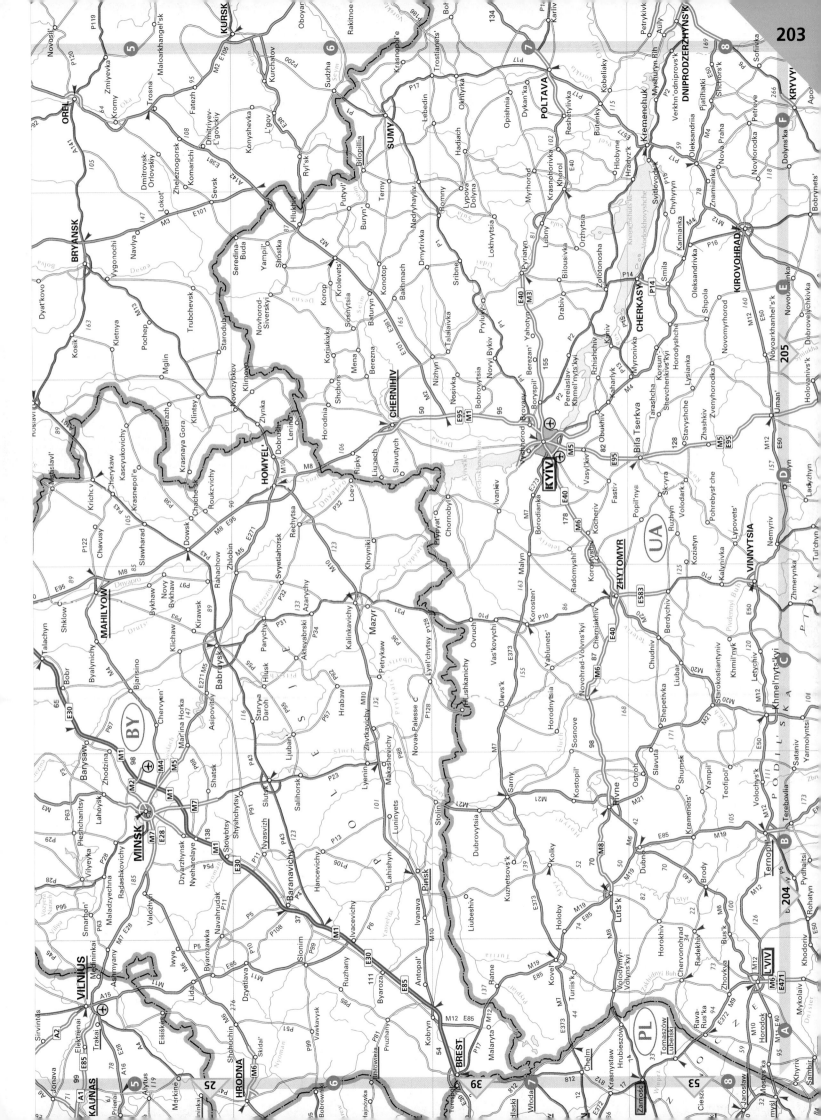

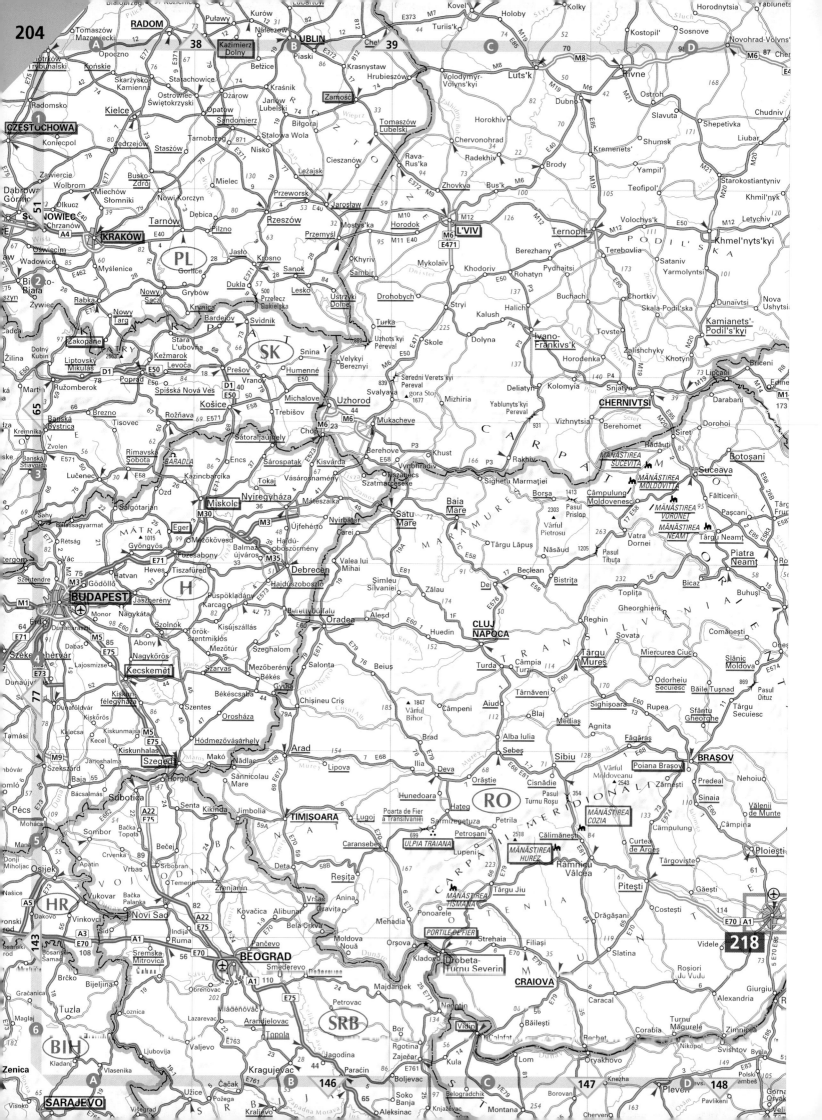

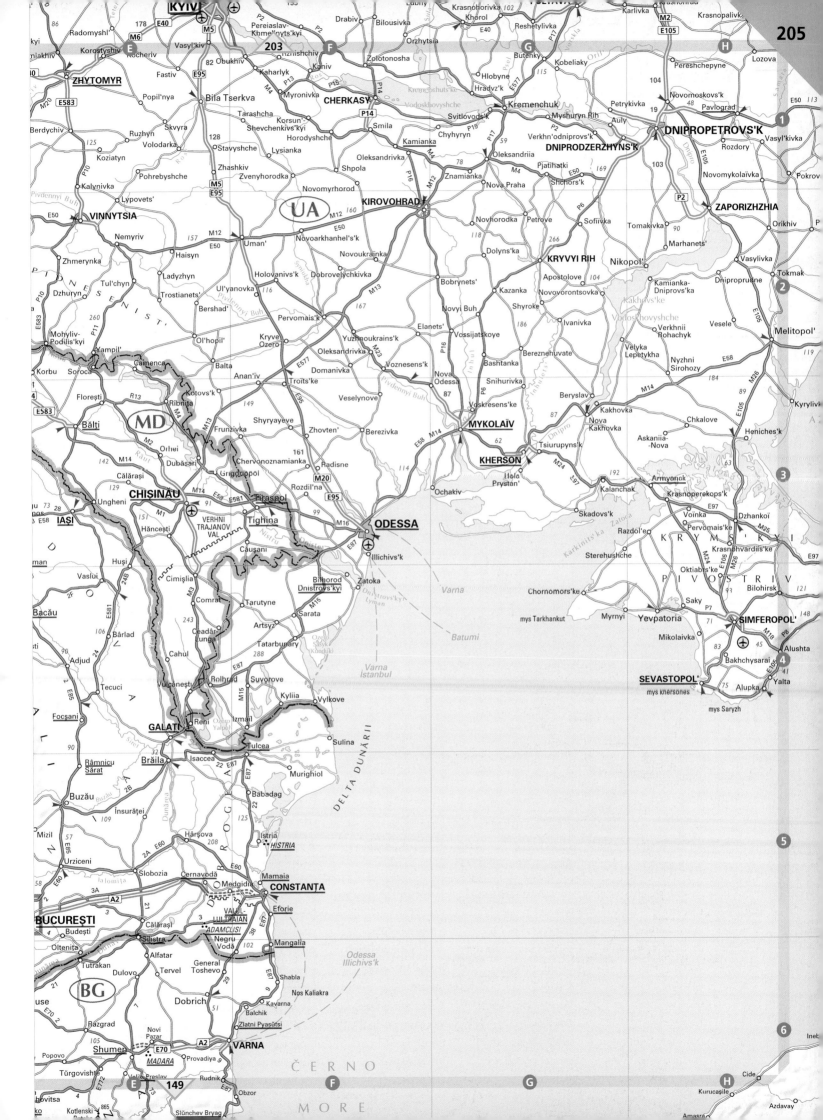

CITY AND URBAN ROUTES
CITTÀ E AREE URBANE
CIUDADES Y ÁREAS URBANAS
VILLES ET AIRES URBAINES
STÄDTE UND ZUFAHRTEN

● City plans
  Piante di città
  Planos de ciudades
  Plans de villes
  Stadtpläne

▢ Urban route maps
  Aree urbane
  Áreas urbanas
  Aires urbaines
  Stadtdurchfahrtspläne

OSLO 235
STOCKHOLM 245
HELSINKI/HELSINGFORS 221
SANKT-PETERBURG 242
TALLINN 246
KØBENHAVN 223
RĪGA 239
MOSKVA 234
VILNIUS 249
LONDON 226-227
AMSTERDAM 207
BERLIN 212-213
WARSZAWA 250
BRUSSEL/BRUXELLES 215
FRANKFURT A.M. 220
PRAHA 238
PARIS 236-237
MÜNCHEN 232-233
BRATISLAVA 214
ZÜRICH 253
WIEN 251
BUDAPEST 216-217
BERN 211
LJUBLJANA 225
ZAGREB 252
MILANO 231
VENÉZIA 248
BUCUREȘTI 218
MARSEILLE 230
FIRENZE 219
BEOGRAD 210
SOFIYA 244
LISBOA 224
MADRID 228-229
BARCELONA 209
ROMA 240-241
SKOPJE 243
İSTANBUL 222
VALENCIA 247
ATIIÍNA 208

	GB Legend	I Legenda	E Leyenda	F Légende	D Zeichenerklärung
	Built-up area	Caseggiati	Zona edificada	Zones bâties	Bebauung
	Building of interest	Edificio d'interesse	Edificio relevante	Édifice remarquable	Bemerkenswertes Gebäude
	Motorway, access points, service area	Autostrada, caselli, stazione di servizio	Autopista, accesos, estación de servicio	Autoroute, accès, aire de service	Autobahn, Anschlüsse, Tankstelle
	Road with motorway characteristics	Superstrada	Autovía	Route-express	Autobahnähnliche Schnellstraße
	Through road	Strada di attraversamento	Travesía	Route de traversée	Hauptdurchfahrtsstraße
	Other road	Altra strada	Otra carretera	Autre route	Sonstige Straße
A9 N202	Numbering of motorway and national roads	Numeri di autostrada e strade nazionali	Números de autopista y carreteras nacionales	Numéros d'autoroute et routes nationales	Autobahnnummer, Staatsstraßennummer
	Road in tunnel	Galleria stradale	Túnel en carretera	Tunnel routier	Straßentunnel
2010	Motorway and road under construction (opening year)	Autostrada e strada in costruzione (anno di apertura)	Autopista y carretera en construcción (año de apertura)	Autoroute et route en construction (année d'ouverture)	Autobahn und straße in Bau (Fertigstellungsjahr)
Utrecht	Destination	Direzione	Direccion	Direction	Richtung
	Railway and station	Ferrovia e stazione	Ferrocarril y estacion	Chemin de fer et gare	Eisenbahn und Bahnhöf
	Garden and park; cemeteries	Giardino e parco; cimiteri	Jardin y parque; cementerios	Jardin et parc; cimetières	Gärten und Park; Friedhöfe
🏥 P	Hospital; Parking	Uspedale; Parcheggio	Hospital; Aparcamiento	Hôpital; Parking	Krankenhaus; Parkplatz
Δ	Camping site	Campeggio	Cámping	Camping	Campingplatz
	Vehicle ferry route	Trasporto auto su traghetto	Transbordador de automóviles	Bac pour autos	Autofähre
	Panoramic view	Punto panoramico	Vista panorámica	Vue panoramique	Aussichtspunkt
M	Underground railway station	Fermata della metropolitana	Estación del metro	Station de métro	U-Bahnhöfe
(i)	Tourist information	Ufficio informazioni	Información turística	Informations touristiques	Touristische Auskünfte
	Pedestrian area	Area pedonali	Área peatonales	Zone réservé aux piétons	Fußgängerzone

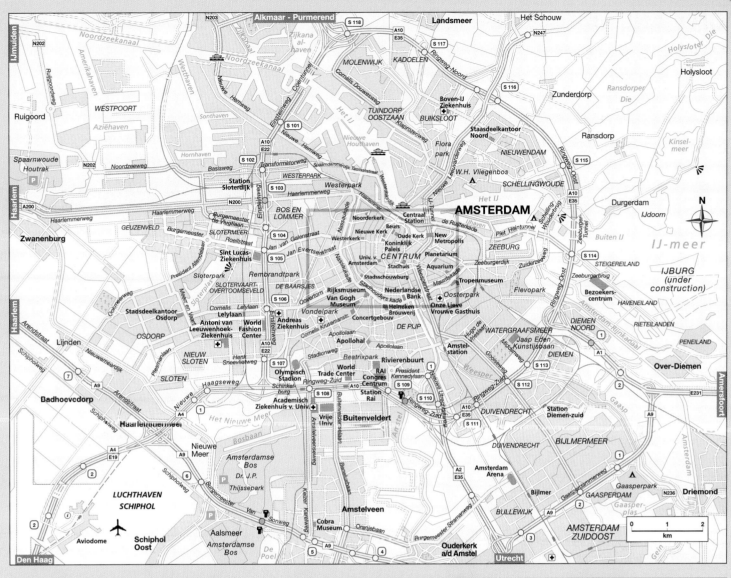

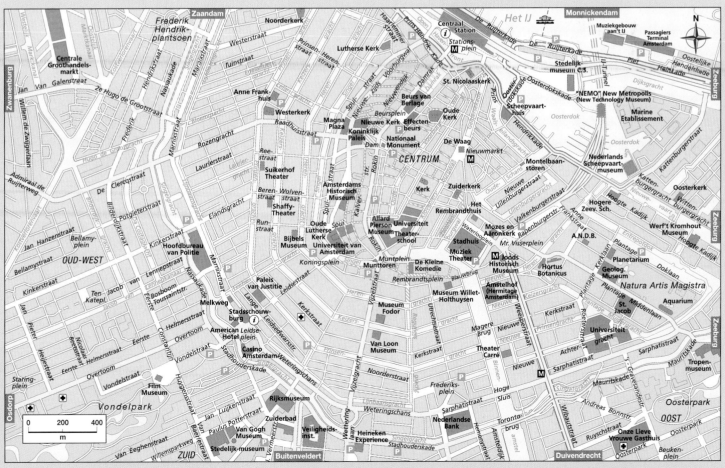

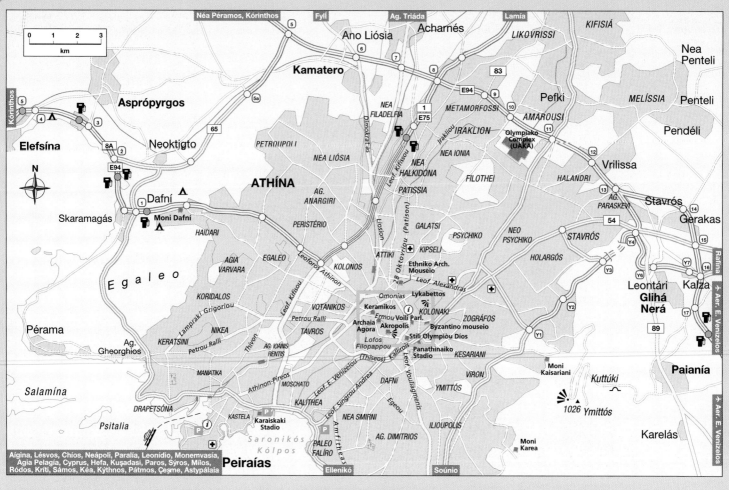

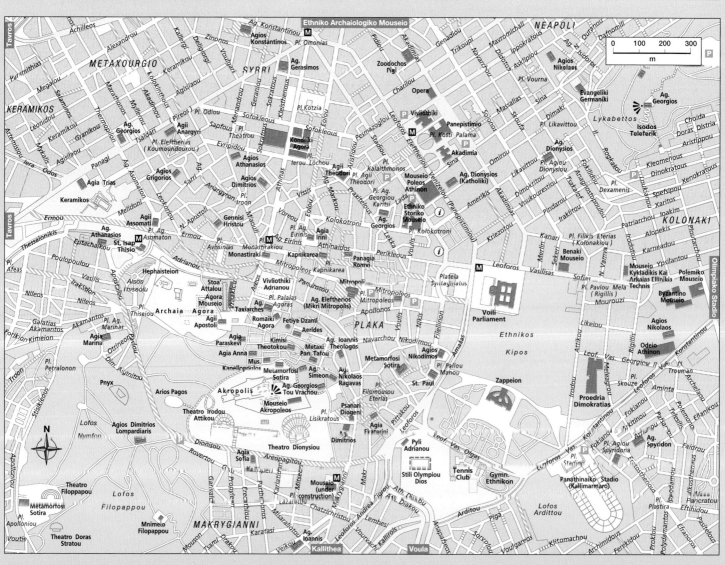

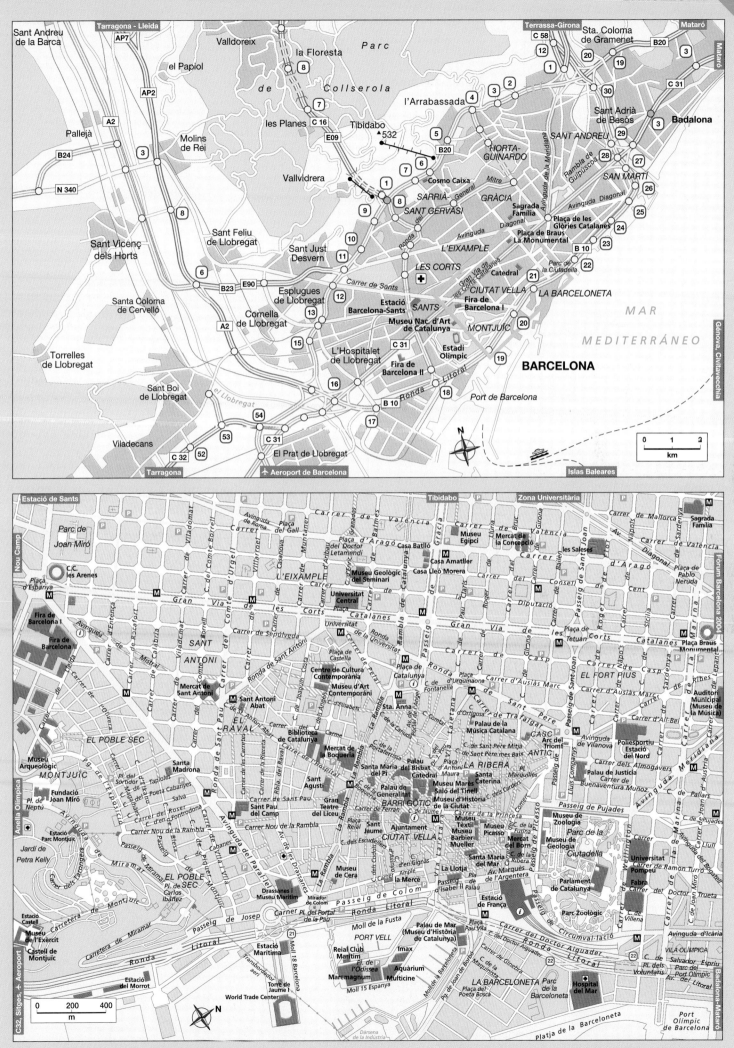

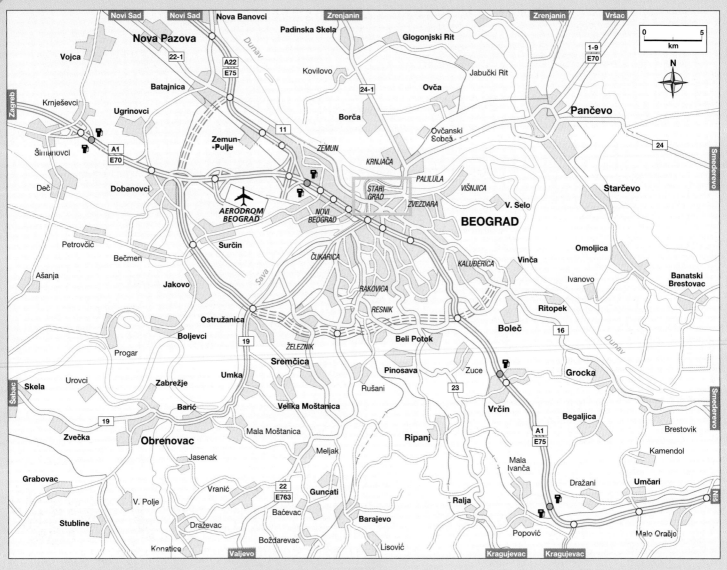

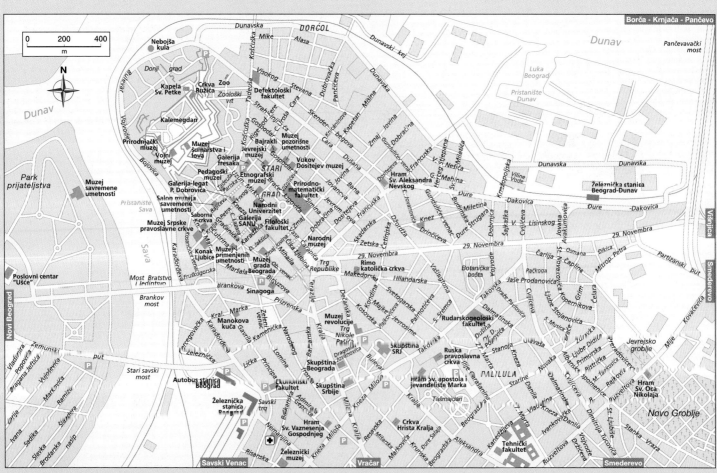

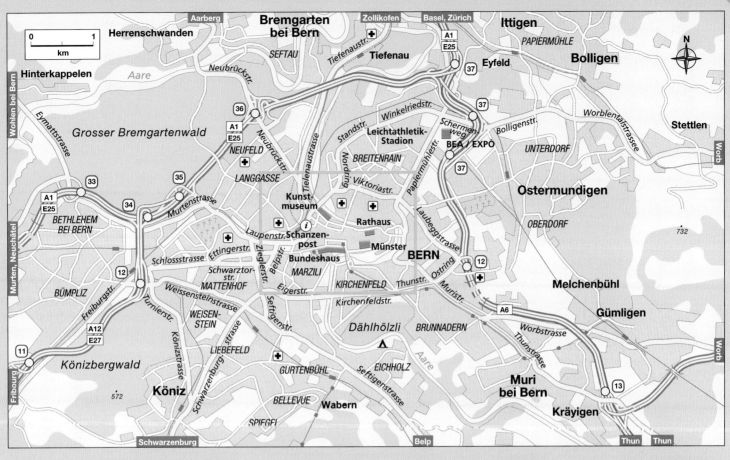

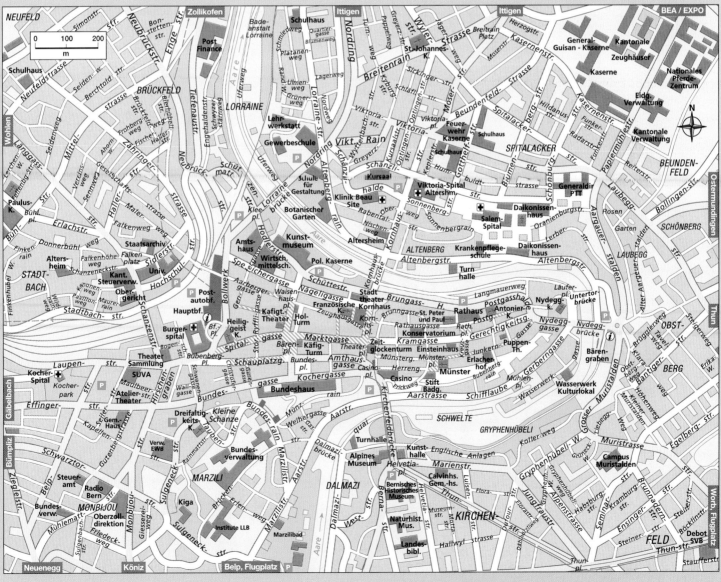

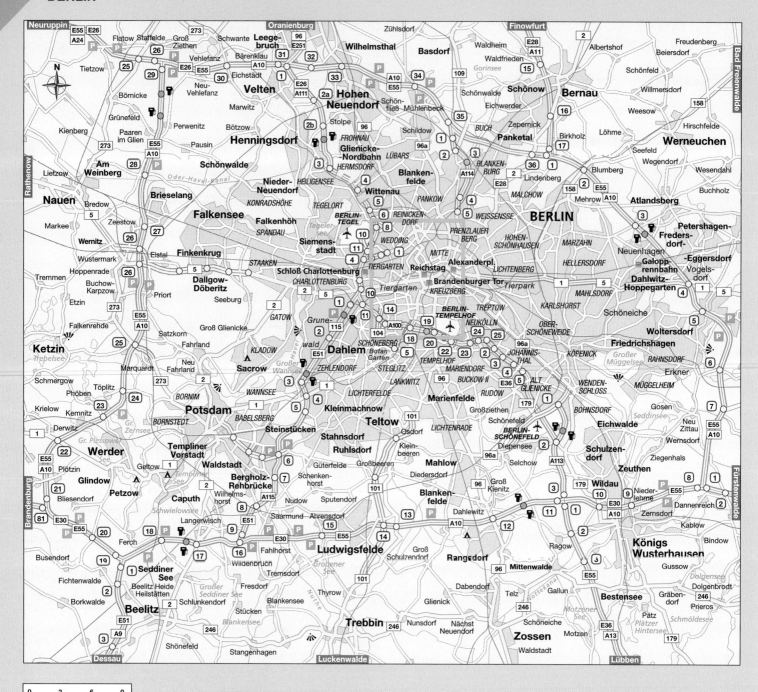

0   3   6   9
km

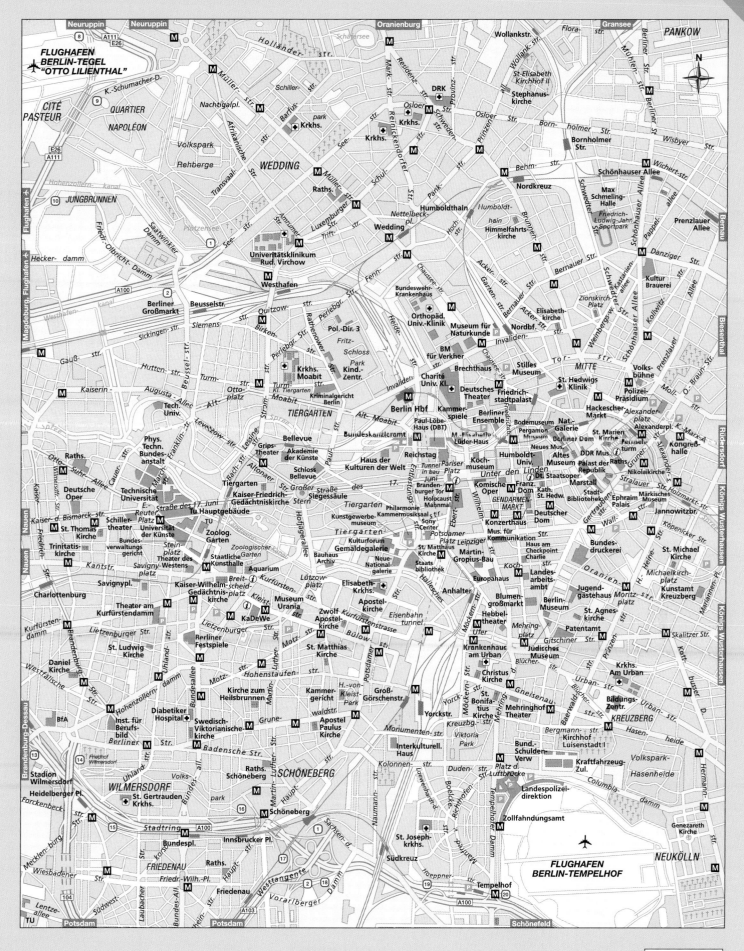

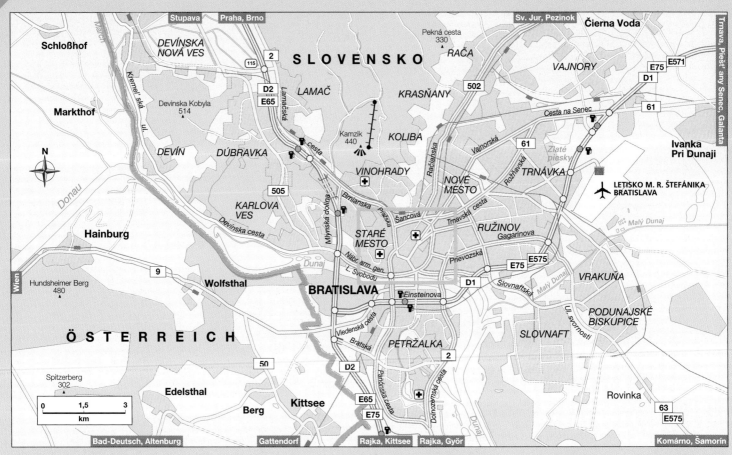

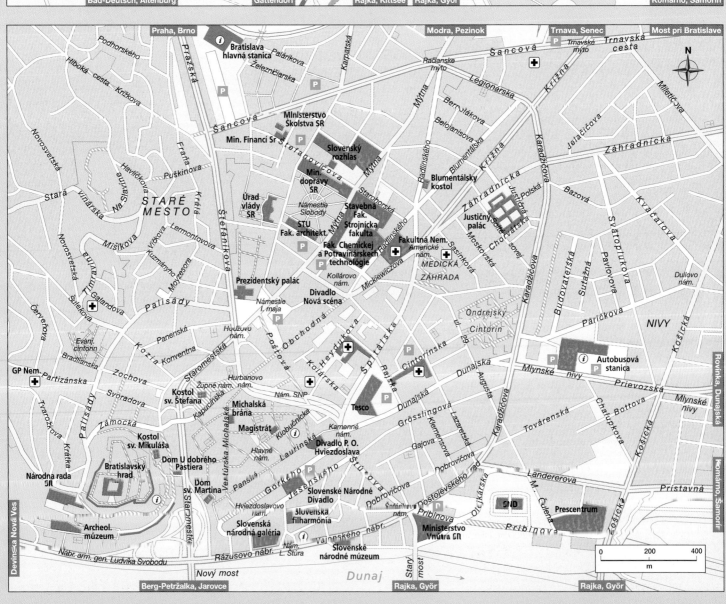

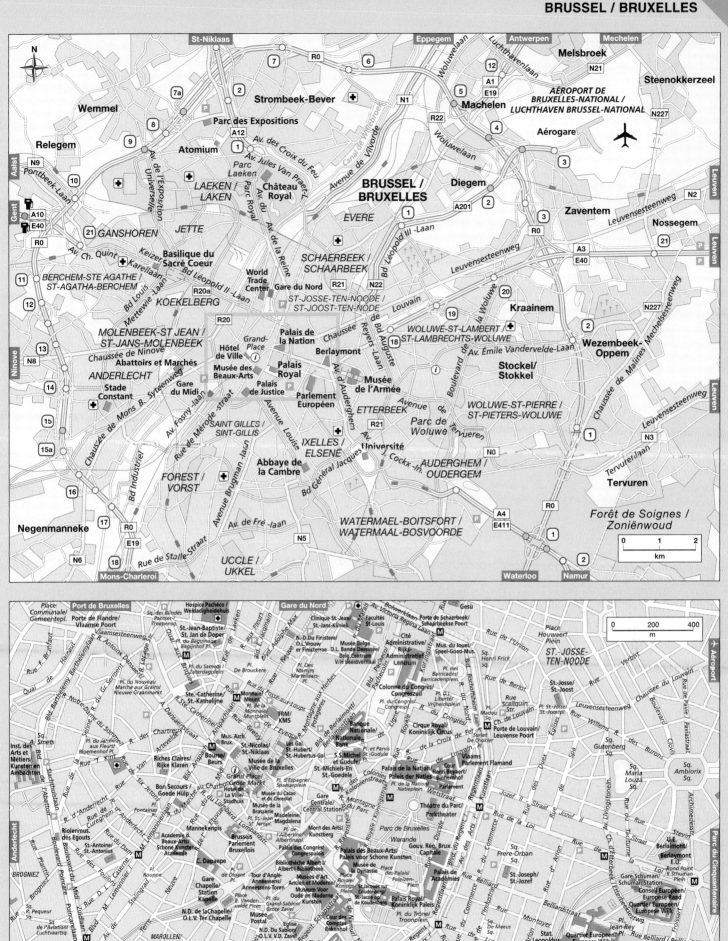

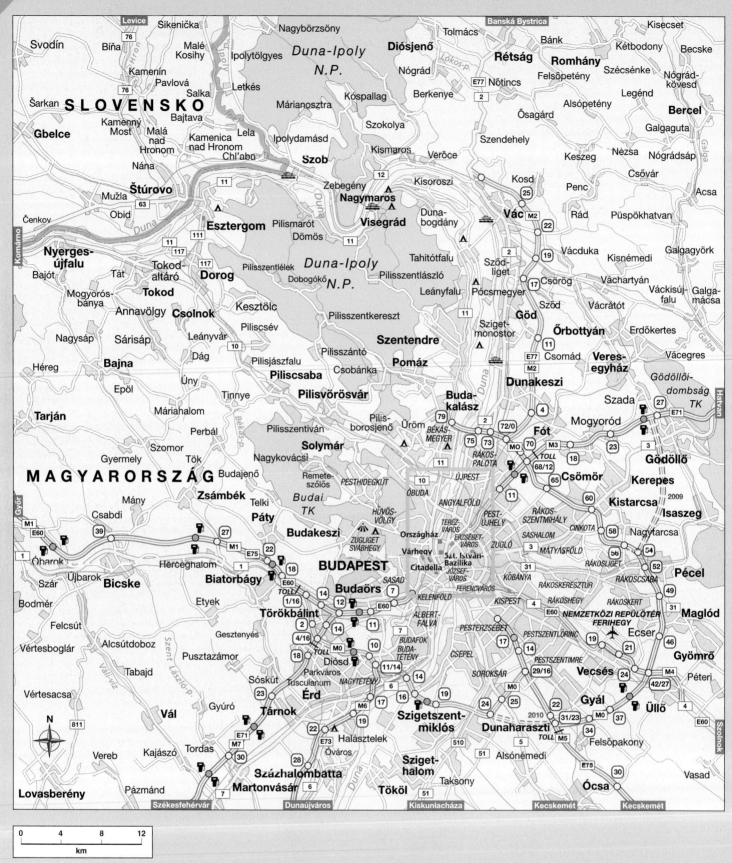

Svodín
Sikenička
Nagybörzsöny
Tolmács
Bánk
Kétbodony
Becske
Kisecset
Bíňa
Malé
Kosihy
Diósjenő
Rétság
Romhány
Szécsénke
Nógrád-
kövesd
Ipolytölgyes
Duna-Ipoly
N.P.
Nógrád
Felsőpetény
Nőtincs
Legénd
Kamenín
Pavlová
Salka
Letkés
Berkenye
Alsópetény
Bercel
Šarkan
SLOVENSKO
Márianosztra
Kóspallag
Ősagárd
Galgaguta
Gbelce
Kamenný
Most
Malá
nad
Hronom
Bajtava
Szokolya
Szendehely
Keszeg
Nézsa
Nógrádsáp
Kamenica
nad Hronom
Chľaba
Lela
Ipolydamásd
Kismaros
Verőce
Szob
Kosd
Penc
Acsa
Nána
Zebegény
Kisoroszi
Vác
Rád
Püspökhatvan
Štúrovo
Nagymaros
Csővár
Mužla
Obid
Visegrád
Duna-
bogdány
Vácduka
Kisnémedi
Galgagyörk
Čenkov
Esztergom
Pilismarót
Vácrátót
Sződ-
liget
Csörög
Váchartyán
Váckisúj-
falu
Galga-
mácsa
Nyerges-
újfalu
Tokod-
altáró
Dorog
Dömös
Pilisszentlélek
Duna-Ipoly
N.P.
Dobogókő
Tahitótfalu
Pilisszentlászló
Pócsmegyer
Sződ
Bajót
Tát
Leányfalu
Mogyorós-
bánya
Tokod
Annavölgy
Csolnok
Kesztölc
Pilisszentkereszt
Szentendre
Sziget-
monostor
Göd
Őrbottyán
Erdőkertes
Nagysáp
Sárisáp
Leányvár
Piliscsév
Pomáz
Csomád
Veres-
egyház
Vácegres
Héreg
Bajna
Dág
Pilisszántó
Dunakeszi
Gödöllői-
dombság
TK
Tarján
Úny
Pilisjászfalu
Csobánka
Buda-
kalász
Szada
Epöl
Pilisszentiván
Pilis-
borosjenő
Üröm
BÉKÁS-
MEGYER
Mogyoród
Fót
Máriahalom
Perbál
Solymár
RÁKOS-
PALOTA
Gödöllő
Szomor
Tinnye
Nagykovácsi
Remete-
szőlős
PESTHIDEGKÚT
ÚJPEST
Csömör
Kerepes
Gyermely
Tök
Budajenő
Budai
TK
Kistarcsa
MAGYARORSZÁG
Mány
Telki
HÜVÖS-
VÖLGY
ÓBUDA
ANGYALFÖLD
RÁKOS-
SZENTMIHÁLY
Isaszeg
Csabdi
Páty
ZUGLIGET
SVÁBHEGY
TERÉZ-
VÁROS
PEST-
ÚJHELY
SASHALOM
CINKOTA
Nagytarcsa
Budakeszi
Zsámbék
Országház
Várhegy
ERZSÉBET-
VÁROS
ZUGLÓ
MÁTYÁSFÖLD
Hércéghalom
BUDAPEST
SASAD
Szt. István-
Bazilika
JÓZSEF-
VÁROS
KŐBÁNYA
RÁKOSLIGET
Pécel
Szár
Újbarok
Bicske
Biatorbágy
Citadella
FERENCVÁROS
RÁKOSKERESZTÚR
RÁKOSCSABA
Óbarok
Etyek
Budaörs
KELENFÖLD
Bodmér
Törökbálint
ALBERT-
FALVA
KISPEST
RÁKOSHEGY
RÁKOSKERT
Maglód
Felcsút
Gesztenyés
NEMZETKÖZI REPÜLŐTÉR
FERIHEGY
Ecser
Alcsútdoboz
BUDAFOK
BUDA-
TÉTÉNY
PESTERZSÉBET
PESTSZENTLŐRINC
Gyömrő
Vértesboglár
Pusztazámor
Diósd
CSEPEL
PESTSZENTIMRE
Vecsés
Tabajd
Parkváros
SOROKSÁR
Vértesacsa
Tusculanum
NAGYTÉTÉNY
Gyál
Üllő
Vál
Gyúró
Érd
Tárnok
Péteri
Lovasberény
Vereb
Kajászó
Tordas
Szigetszent-
miklós
Dunaharaszti
Felsőpakony
Pázmánd
Halásztelek
Óváros
Sziget-
halom
Alsónémedi
Százhalombatta
Martonvásár
Taksony
Ócsa
Vasad
Tököl

0	4	8	12

km

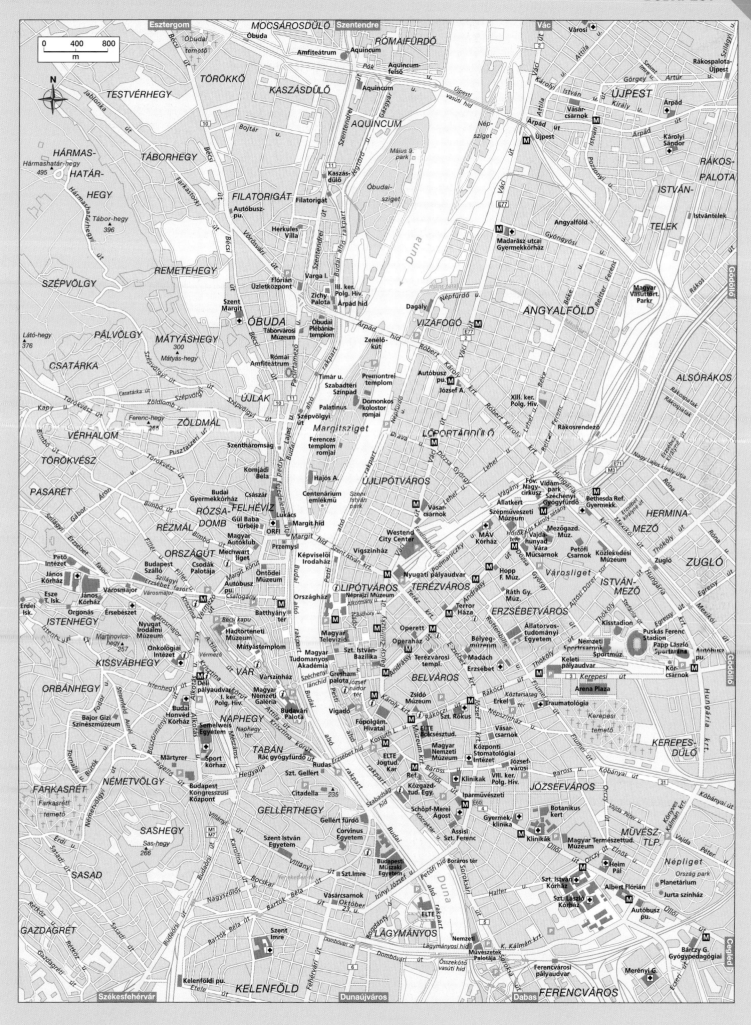

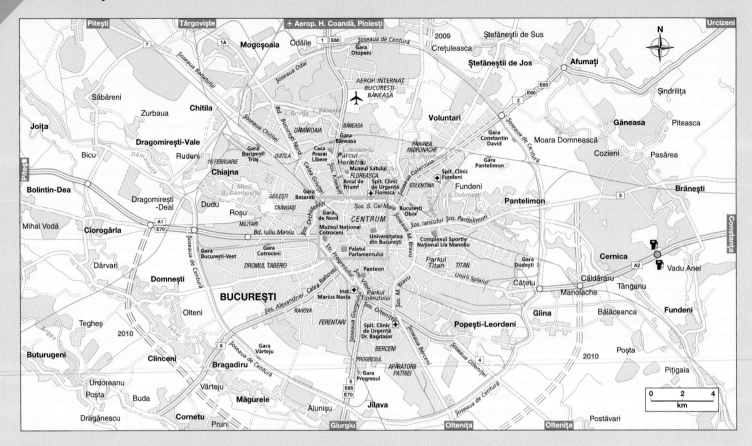

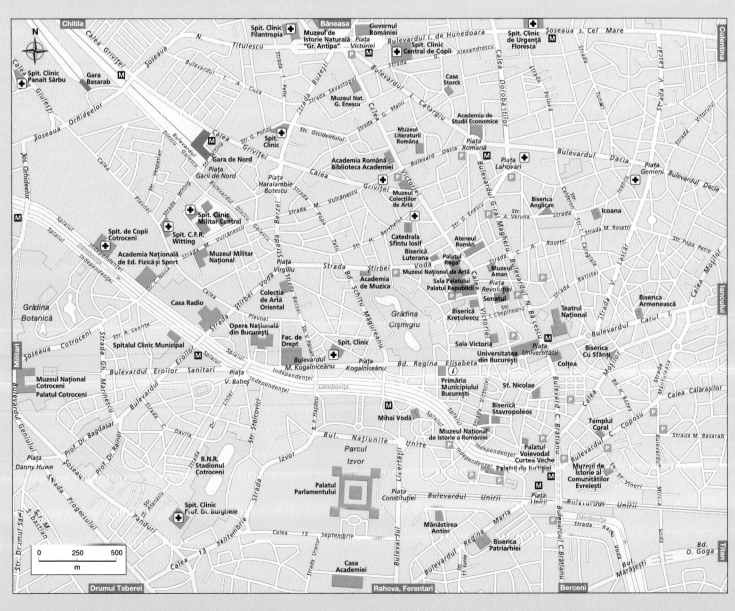

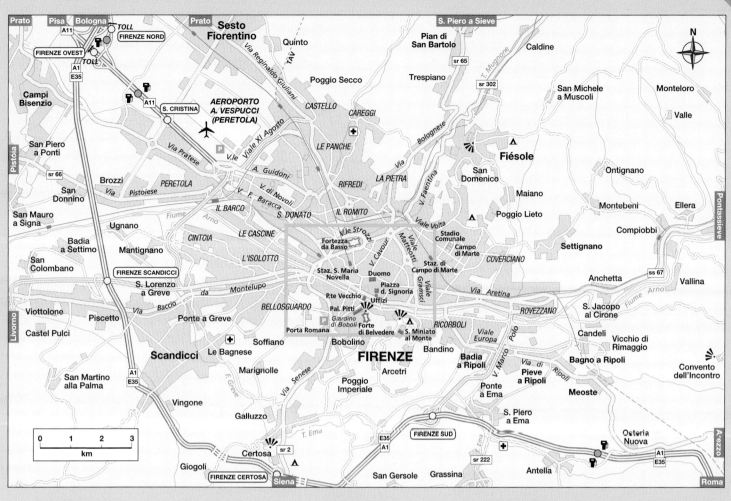

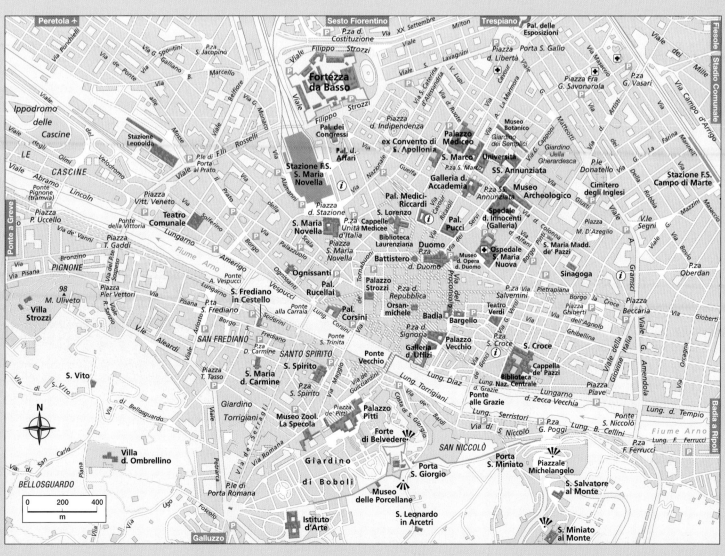

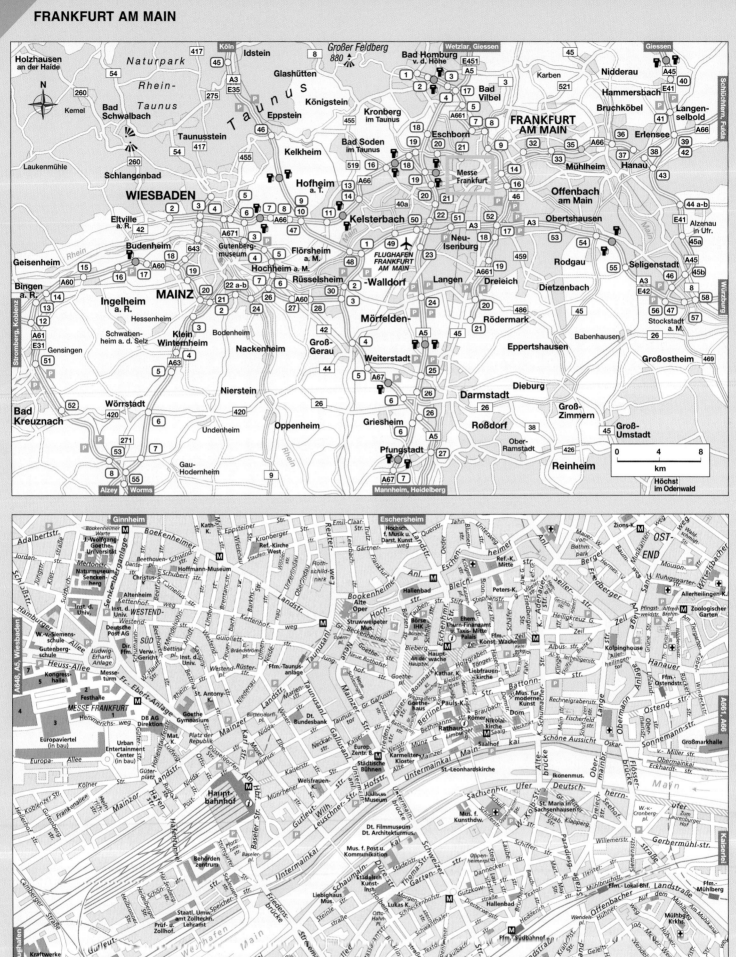

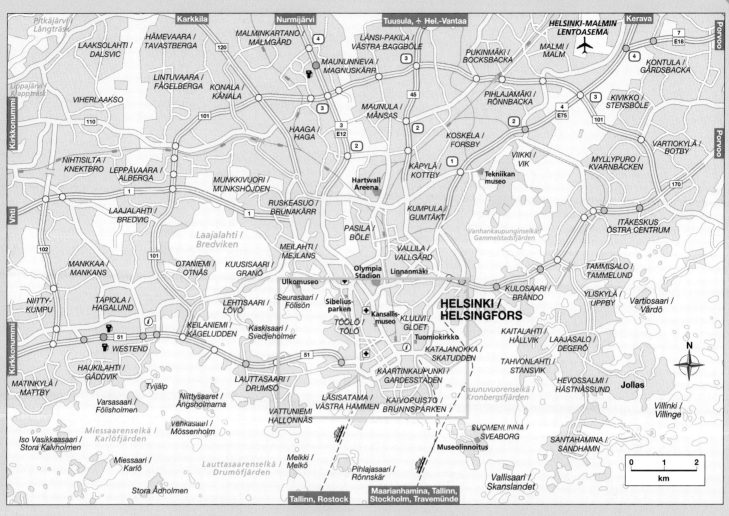

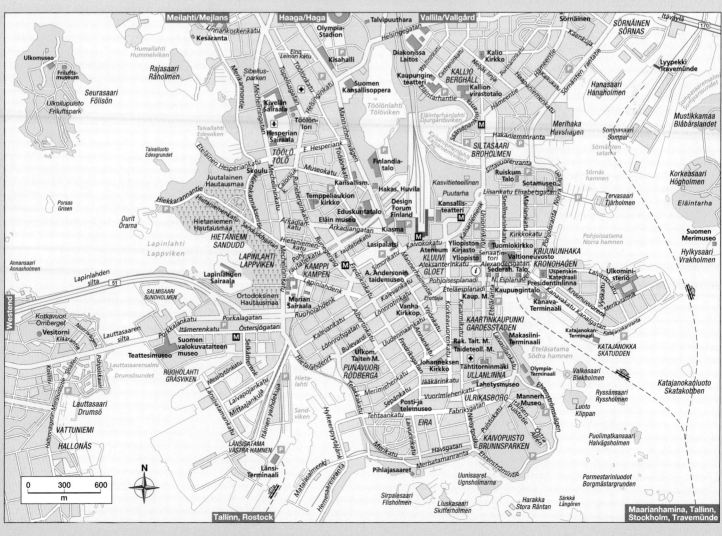

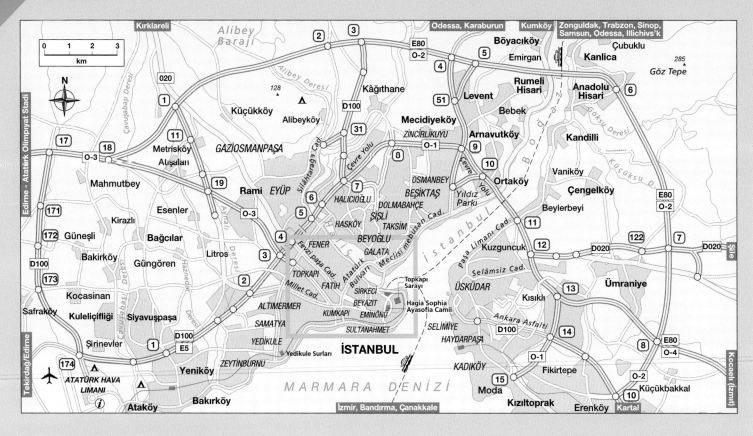

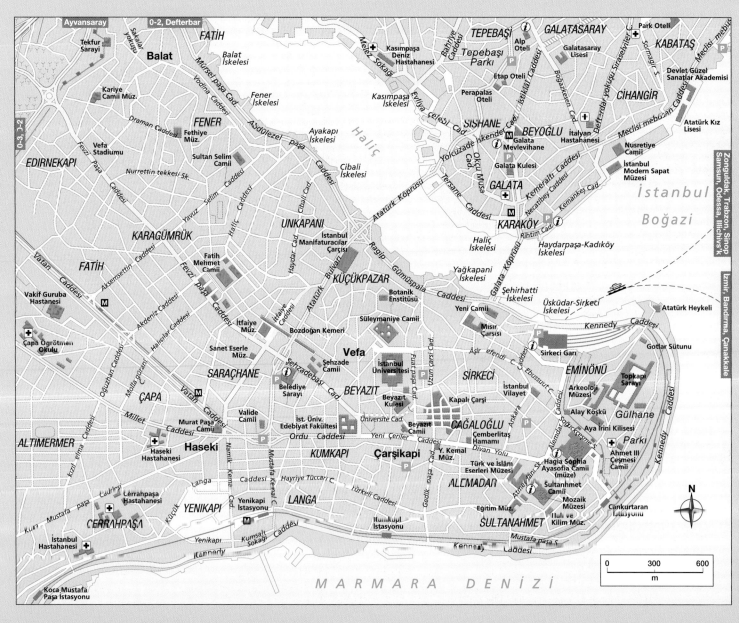

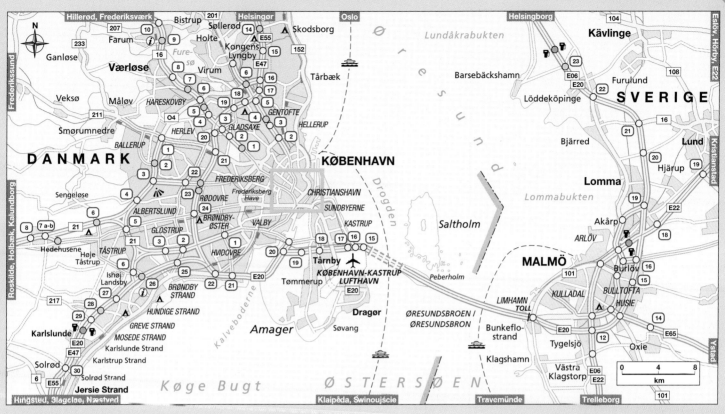

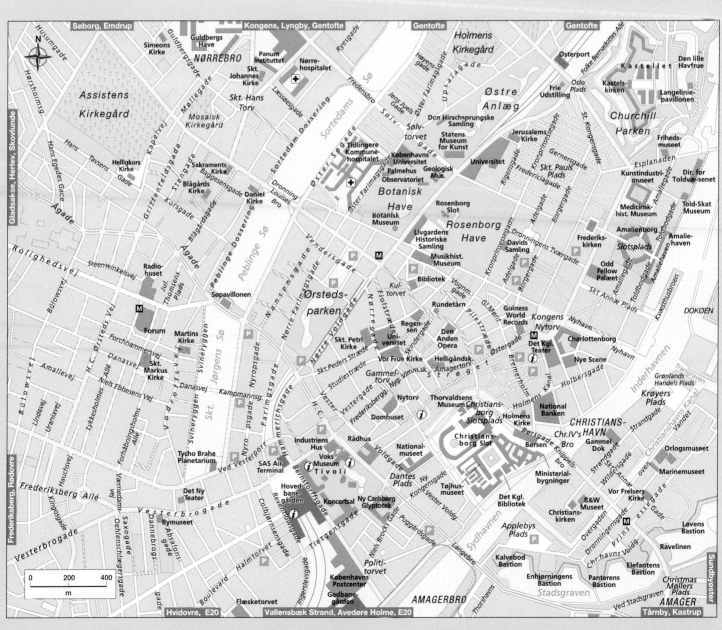

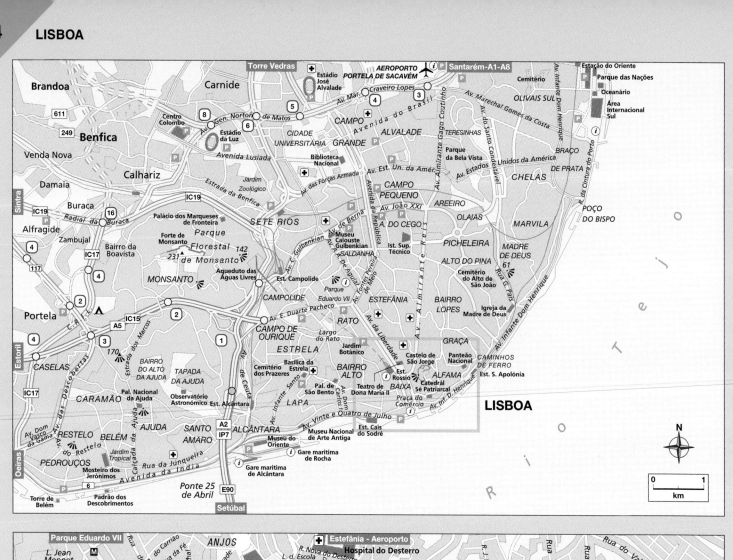

Brandoa
Carnide
Torre Vedras
Estádio José Alvalade
AEROPORTO PORTELA DE SACAVÉM
Santarém-A1-A8
Estação do Oriente
Parque das Nações
611
Av. Mar. Craveiro Lopes
Cemitério
Oceanário
Centro Colombo
8
Av. Gen. Norton de Matos
CAMPO GRANDE
Área Internacional Sul
Benfica
Estádio da Luz
6
CIDADE UNIVERSITÁRIA GRANDE
ALVALADE
Av. Marechal Gomes da Costa
OLIVAIS SUL
BRAÇO DE PRATA
249
Venda Nova
Avenida Lusiada
Avenida do Brasil
Parque da Bela Vista
CHELAS
Calhariz
Biblioteca Nacional
TERESINHAS
Av. Almirante Gago Coutinho
Av. Estados Unidos da América
POÇO DO BISPO
Damaia
Av. das Forças Armadas
Av. Est. Un. da Amér.
CAMPO PEQUENO
Buraca
Jardim Zoológico
AREEIRO
Av. João XXI
MARVILA
IC19
Estrada da Benfica
SETE RIOS
Av. de Berna
A. DO CEGO
OLAIAS
16
Radial da Buraca
Museu Calouste Gulbenkian
SALDANHA
Ist. Sup. Técnico
PICHELEIRA
Alfragide
Palácio dos Marqueses de Fronteira
ALTO DO PINA
MADRE DE DEUS
Zambujal
Forte de Monsanto
Parque Florestal de Monsanto
142
Av. C. Gulbenkian
231
Est. Campolide
Av. de Aguiar Pereira
CAMPOLIDE
Cemitério do Alto de São João
61
MONSANTO
Aqueduto das Águas Livres
Parque Eduardo VII
ESTEFÂNIA
BAIRRO LOPES
Igreja da Madre de Deus
Av. E. Duarte Pacheco
RATO
GRAÇA
CAMINHOS DE FERRO
Av. da Liberdade
Castelo de São Jorge
Panteão Nacional
CAMPO DE OURIQUE
Largo do Rato
ESTRELA
Jardim Botânico
BAIRRO ALTO
Est. Rossio
ALFAMA
Est. S. Apolónia
Cemitério dos Prazeres
Basílica da Estrela
BAIXA
Catedral Sé Patriarcal
LISBOA
Pal. de São Bento
Teatro de Dona Maria II
Observatório Astronómico
LAPA
Pr. do Comércio
Pal. Nacional da Ajuda
CARAMÃO
Est. Alcântara
Av. Vinte e Quatro de Julho
TAPADA DA AJUDA
Av. Inf. D. Henrique
BAIRRO DO ALTO DA AJUDA
Museu do Oriente
Museu Nacional de Arte Antiga
Est. Cais do Sodré
AJUDA
SANTO AMARO
ALCÂNTARA
A2 IP7
RESTELO
BELÉM
Gare marítima de Rocha
Jardim Tropical
Gare marítima de Alcântara
PEDROUÇOS
Rua da Junqueira
Avenida da India
Mosteiro dos Jerónimos
Torre de Belém
Padrão dos Descobrimentos
Ponte 25 de Abril
E90
Setúbal

N

0 — 1 km

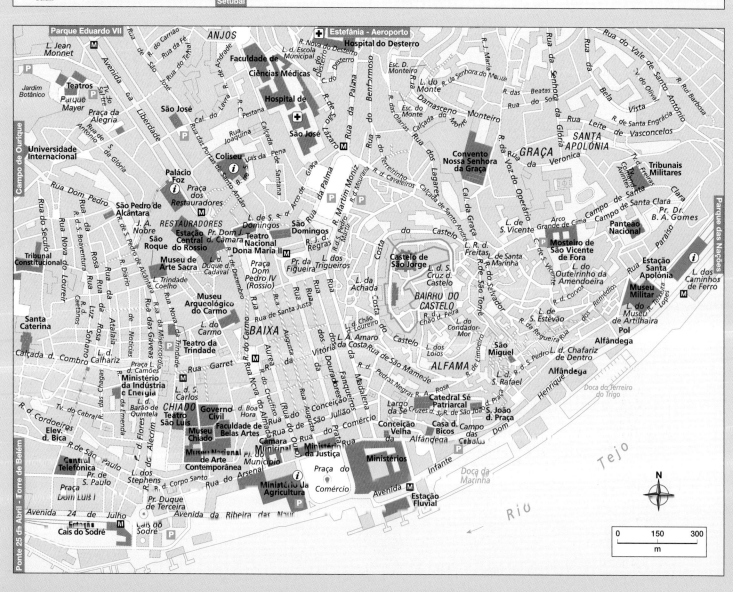

Parque Eduardo VII
ANJOS
Estefânia - Aeroporto
Hospital do Desterro
Rua do Vale de Santo António
L. Jean Monnet
Teatros
Faculdade de Ciências Médicas
Jardim Botânico
Parque Mayer
Praça da Alegria
São José
Hospital de
São José
Coliseu
Convento Nossa Senhora da Graça
SANTA APOLÓNIA
GRAÇA
Universidade Internacional
Palácio Foz
Praça dos Restauradores
Tribunais Militares
São Pedro de Alcântara
RESTAURADORES
J. A. Nobre
Estação Central do Rossio
Teatro Nacional Dona Maria II
São Domingos
Museu de Arte Sacra
São Roque
Praça Dom Pedro IV (Rossio)
Panteão Nacional
Mosteiro de São Vicente de Fora
Museu Arqueológico do Carmo
BAIXA
Castelo de São Jorge
Estação Santa Apolónia
Santa Caterina
BAIRRO DO CASTELO
Museu Militar
Teatro da Trindade
Teatro São Luis
CHIADO
Governo Civil
ALFAMA
Ministério da Indústria e Energia
Museu Chiado
Faculdade de Belas Artes
São Miguel
Alfândega
Central Telefónica
Elev. d. Bica
Museu Nacional de Arte Contemporânea
Catedral Sé Patriarcal
Casa d. Bicos
Conceição Velha
São João d. Praça
Ministério da Justiça
Ministério da Agricultura
Praça do Comércio
Ministérios
Estação Fluvial
Cais do Sodré
Avenida 24 de Julho
Doca da Marinha
Rio Tejo
N

0 — 150 — 300 m

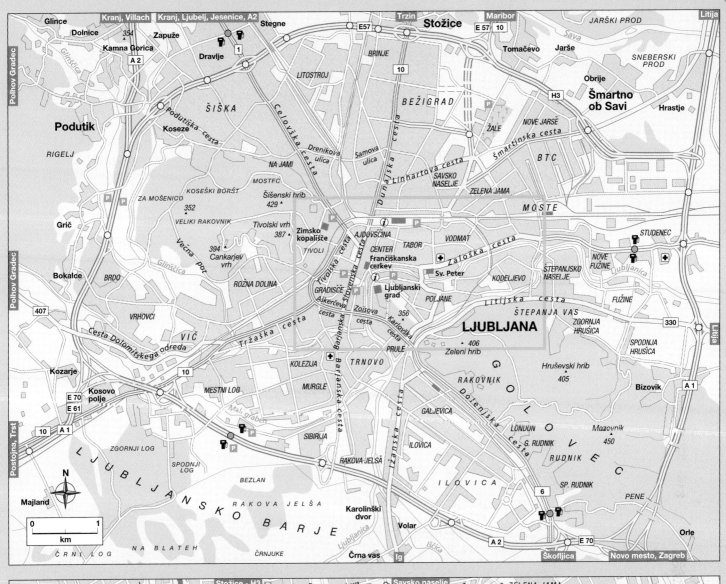

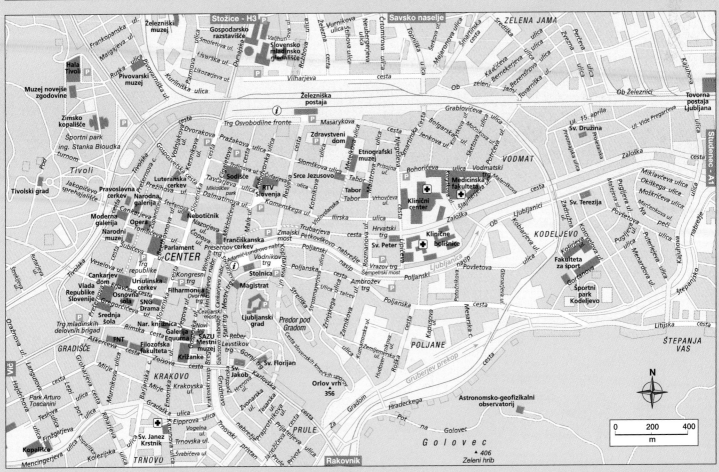

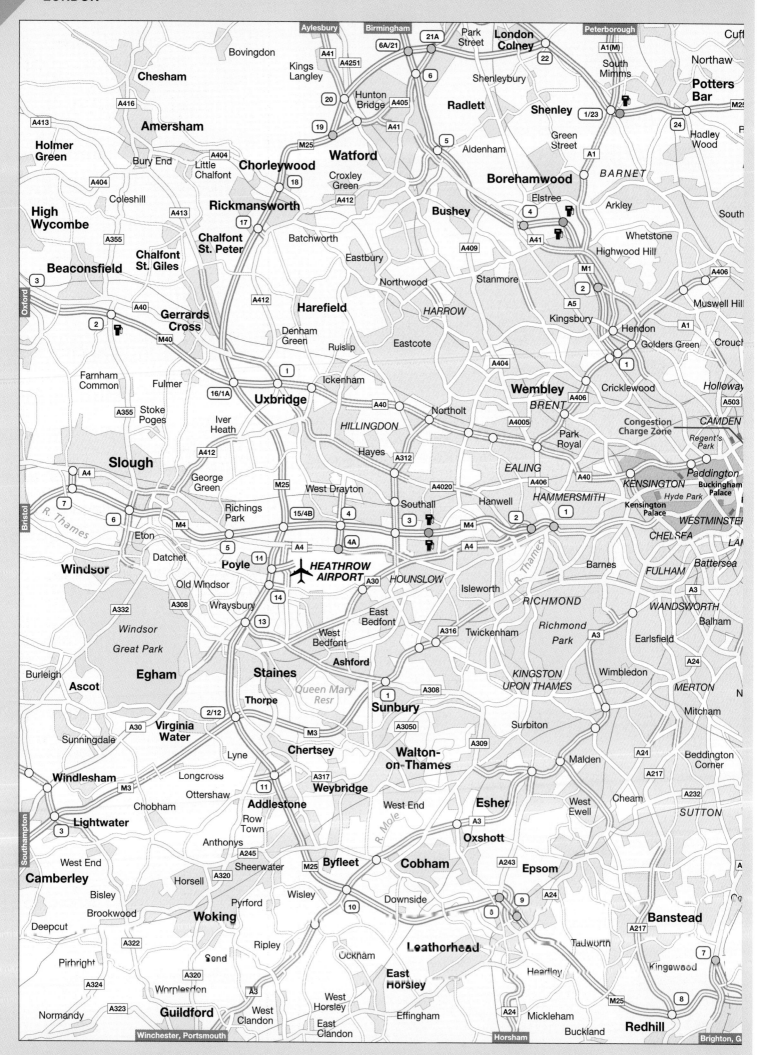

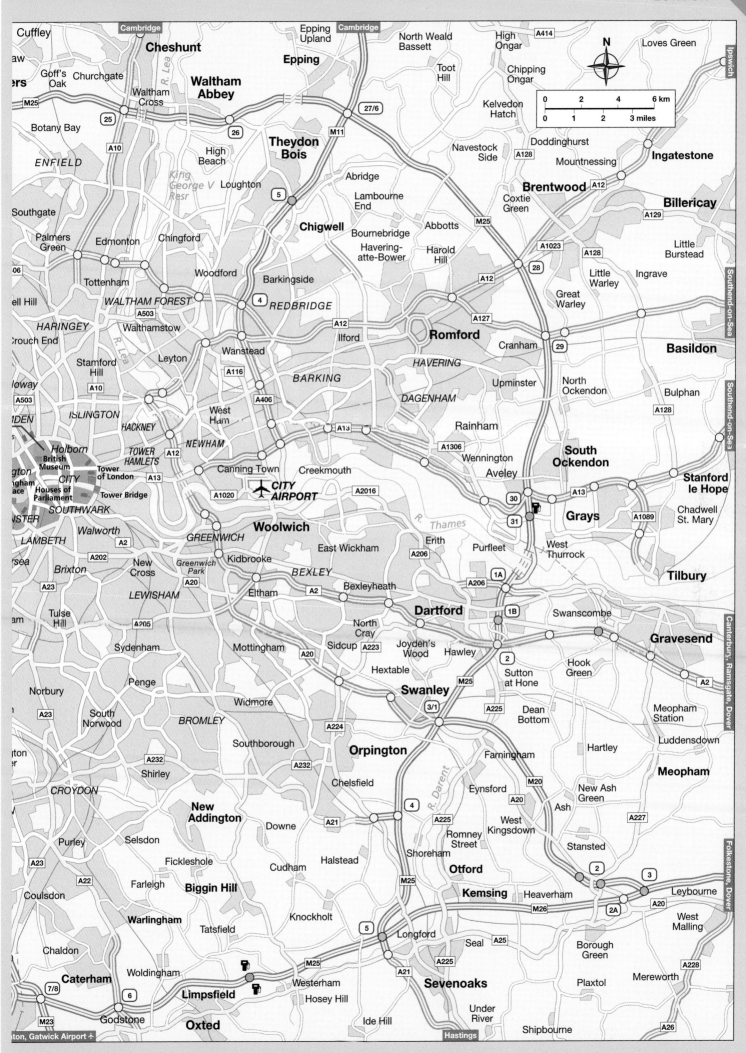

Cuffley
Cheshunt
Epping Upland
North Weald Bassett
Epping
High Ongar
A414
Loves Green
N
Goff's Oak
Churchgate
Waltham Cross
Chipping Ongar
Ipswich
M25
Botany Bay
25
Waltham Abbey
Toot Hill
Kelvedon Hatch
0 2 4 6 km
0 1 2 3 miles
A10
26
ENFIELD
High Beach
27/6
Doddinghurst
A128
Navestock Side
Mountnessing
Ingatestone
Southgate
Theydon Bois
M11
A1023
Brentwood
A12
Billericay
Palmers Green
Edmonton
Chingford
Loughton
Abridge
M25
Coxtie Green
A128
A129
King George V Resr
Lambourne End
Abbotts
28
Little Warley
Little Bursted
Tottenham
Woodford
Chigwell
Bournebridge
Havering-atte-Bower
Harold Hill
A12
Ingrave
ell Hill
WALTHAM FOREST
4
REDBRIDGE
Barkingside
A127
Great Warley
A503
Walthamstow
Ilford
Romford
HARINGEY
Wanstead
Leyton
HAVERING
Cranham
29
Basildon
Crouch End
Stamford Hill
A116
BARKING
DAGENHAM
Upminster
North Ockendon
Bulphan
A10
A406
West Ham
Rainham
A128
loway
ISLINGTON
HACKNEY
NEWHAM
A13
A1306
Wennington
South Ockendon
Holborn
TOWER HAMLETS
A12
Canning Town
Creekmouth
Aveley
30
Stanford le Hope
British Museum
CITY
A13
CITY AIRPORT
A2016
R. Thames
31
Grays
Chadwell St. Mary
Tower of London
A1020
Houses of Parliament
Tower Bridge
SOUTHWARK
Woolwich
Erith
Purfleet
A1089
NSTER
LAMBETH
Walworth
GREENWICH
East Wickham
A206
West Thurrock
Tilbury
Brixton
A2
Greenwich Park
Kidbrooke
BEXLEY
1A
A23
A202
New Cross
A20
Eltham
Bexleyheath
A206
1B
Swanscombe
Gravesend
Tulse Hill
LEWISHAM
Sidcup
Dartford
A2
Sydenham
A205
Mottingham
North Cray
A223
Joyden's Wood
Hawley
2
Hook Green
A2
Norbury
Penge
A20
Hextable
Meopham Station
South Norwood
Sutton at Hone
Luddensdown
A23
BROMLEY
Widmore
Swanley
M25
A225
Dean Bottom
Shirley
A232
Southborough
3/1
Farningham
Hartley
Meopham
CROYDON
A232
Orpington
A224
M20
A227
New Ash Green
Purley
Selsdon
Chelsfield
4
R. Darent
Eynsford
Ash
A23
New Addington
Downe
A21
A20
West Kingsdown
Stansted
Ficklehole
Cudham
Halstead
Romney Street
Farleigh
Biggin Hill
Shoreham
2
Chaldon
Warlingham
Tatsfield
Knockholt
Otford
Heaverham
3
Leybourne
Caterham
Woldingham
M25
Kemsing
M26
A20
7/8
6
Limpsfield
Westerham
5
Longford
Seal
A25
2A
West Malling
M23
Godstone
Oxted
Hosey Hill
Sevenoaks
A21
A225
Borough Green
A228
Gatwick Airport
Hastings
Ide Hill
Under River
Shipbourne
A26
Mereworth
Plaxtol

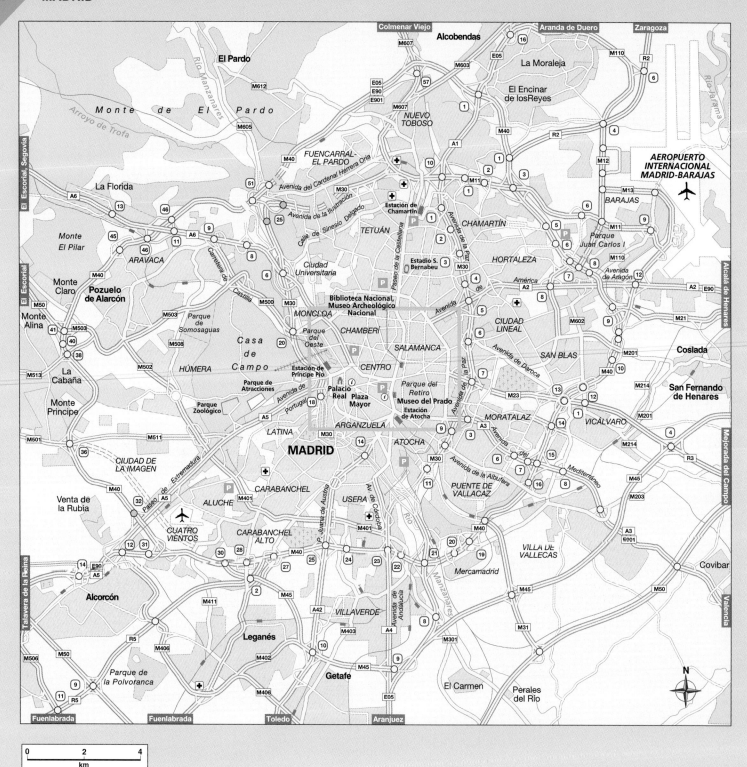

Colmenar Viejo · Alcobendas · Aranda de Duero · Zaragoza

El Pardo

La Moraleja

El Encinar de los Reyes

Monte de El Pardo

Arroyo de Trofa

NUEVO TOBOSO

Río Manzanares

AEROPUERTO INTERNACIONAL MADRID-BARAJAS

La Florida

FUENCARRAL-EL PARDO

Avenida del Cardenal Herrera Oria

BARAJAS

Monte El Pilar

Avenida de la Ilustración

Calle de Sinesio Delgado

Estación de Chamartín

CHAMARTÍN

Parque Juan Carlos I

ARAVACA

TETUÁN

Monte Claro

Pozuelo de Alarcón

Ciudad Universitaria

Estadio S. Bernabeu

HORTALEZA

Monte Alina

MONCLOA

Biblioteca Nacional, Museo Archeológico Nacional

CHAMBERÍ

América

CIUDAD LINEAL

Alcalá de Henares

La Cabaña

Parque de Somosaguas

Parque del Oeste

SALAMANCA

SAN BLAS

Coslada

Monte Principe

Casa de Campo

HÚMERA

CENTRO

Avenida de Daroca

San Fernando de Henares

Estación de Príncipe Pío

Palacio Real Plaza Mayor

Parque del Retiro

MORATALAZ

Parque de Atracciones

Museo del Prado

VICÁLVARO

Parque Zoológico

Avenida de Portugal

Estación de Atocha

ARGANZUELA

LATINA

ATOCHA

Mejorada del Campo

CIUDAD DE LA IMAGEN

Venta de la Rubia

PUENTE DE VALLACAZ

CARABANCHEL

USERA

Mediterráneo

Covibar

ALUCHE

CUATRO VIENTOS

CARABANCHEL ALTO

Av. de Córdoba

Río Manzanares

VILLA DE VALLECAS

Mercamadrid

Alcorcón

Avenida de la Albufera

P. Juana de Austria

VILLAVERDE

Avenida de Andalucía

Leganés

El Carmen

Perales del Río

Parque de la Polvoranca

Getafe

Fuenlabrada · Fuenlabrada · Toledo · Aranjuez

Talavera de la Reina

El Escorial

El Escorial, Segovia

Valencia

N

0 2 4 km

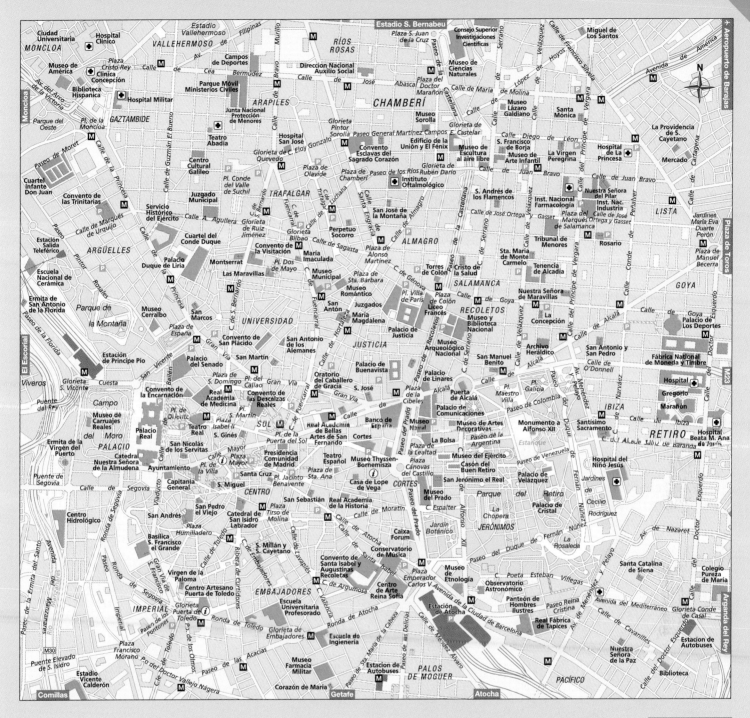

Moncloa
El Escorial
Comillas
Getafe
Atocha

0   200   400
m

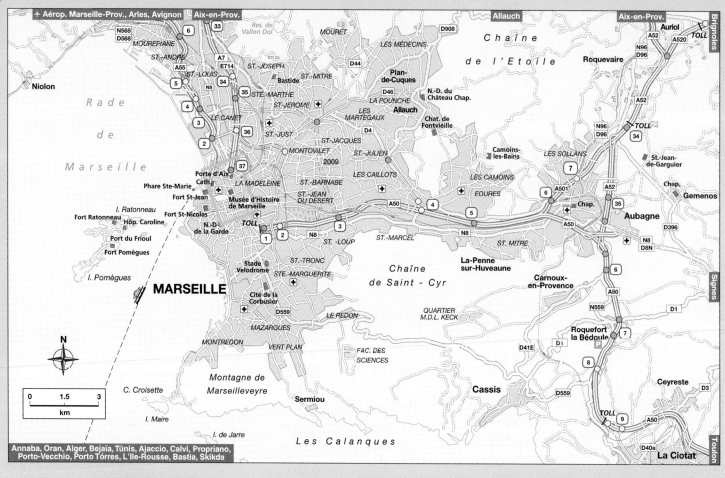

✈ Aérop. Marseille-Prov., Arles, Avignon · Aix-en-Prov. · Allauch · Aix-en-Prov. · Brignoles

N568 · D568 · MOUREPIANE · ST.-ANDRÉ · A7 · E714 · A55 · ST.-LOUIS · N8 · LE CANET · Niolon · Rade · de · Marseille · Res. de Vallon Dol · MOURET · LES MÉDECINS · Chaîne · de l'Etoile · D908 · Auriol · TOLL · A52 · A520 · Roquevaire · N96 · D96 · ST.-JOSEPH · ST.-MARTHE · Bastide · ST.-JÉROME · ST.-JUST · Plan-de-Cuques · LA POUNCHE · N.-D. du Château Chap. · D46 · Chat. de Fontvieille · Allauch · N96 · D96 · TOLL · LES SOLLANS · St.-Jean-de-Garguier · Chap. · Gemenos · ST.-MITRE · ST.-JACQUES · MONTOVILET · 2009 · ST.-JULIEN · LES MARTEGAUX · D4 · LES CAILLOTS · EOURES · LES CAMOINS · Camoins-les-Bains · A501 · A52 · Chap. · Aubagne · D396 · Porte d'Aix Cath. · LA MADELEINE · ST.-BARNABE · ST.-JEAN DU DESERT · A50 · Chap. · A50 · N8 · D8N · Phare Ste-Marie · Fort St-Jean · Musée d'Histoire de Marseille · Fort St-Nicolas · N.-D. de la Garde · TOLL · N8 · ST.-LOUP · ST.-MARCEL · ST.-MITRE · La-Penne sur-Huveaune · Carnoux-en-Provence · N8 · D8N · I. Ratonneau · Fort Ratonneau · Hôp. Caroline · Port du Frioul · Fort Pomègues · I. Pomègues · MARSEILLE · Stade Velodrome · ST.-TRONC · STE.-MARGUERITE · Chaîne de Saint - Cyr · QUARTIER M.D.L. KECK · Roquefort la Bédoule · Cité de la Corbusier · D559 · LE REDON · MAZARGUES · VERT PLAN · FAC. DES SCIENCES · D41E · D1 · N559 · D1 · C. Croisette · MONTREDON · Montagne de Marseilleveyre · Sermiou · Cassis · D559 · Ceyreste · D3 · TOLL · A50 · I. Maire · I. de Jarre · Les Calanques · La Ciotat · D40a

N · 0 · 1.5 · 3 · km

Annaba, Oran, Alger, Bejaïa, Tūnis, Ajaccio, Calvi, Propriano, Porto-Vecchio, Porto Tórres, L'Ile-Rousse, Bastia, Skikda

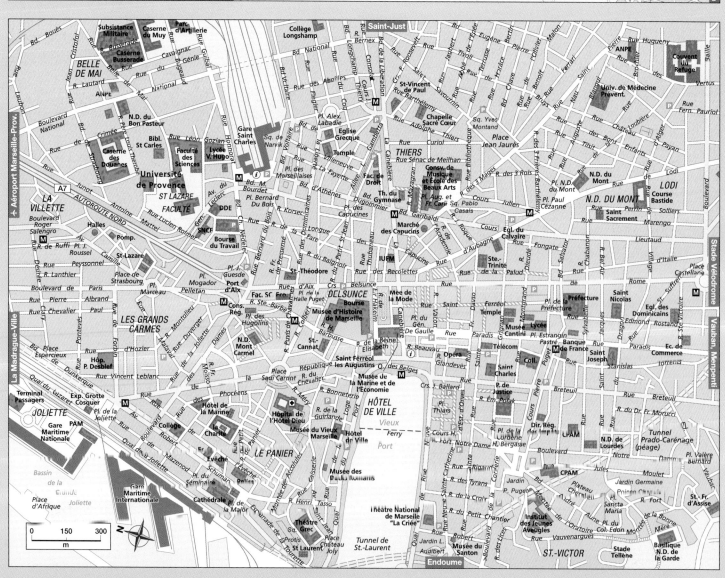

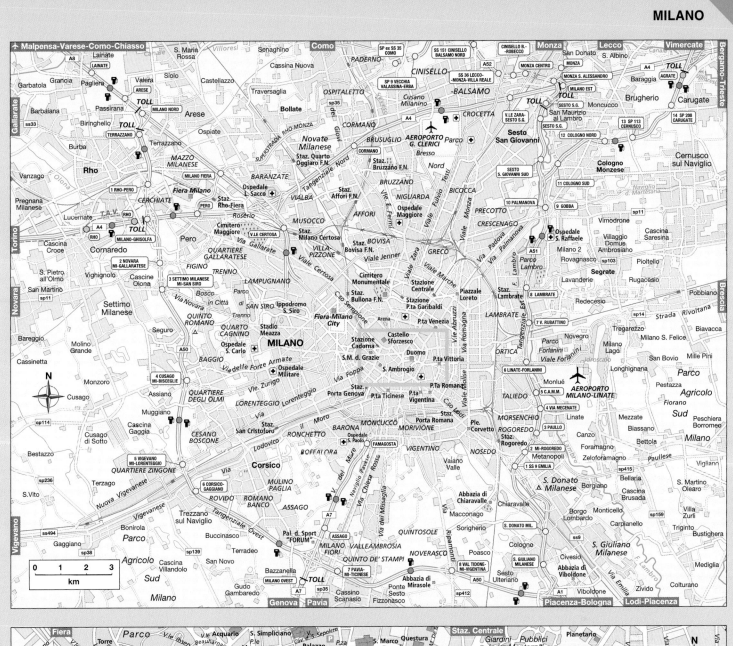

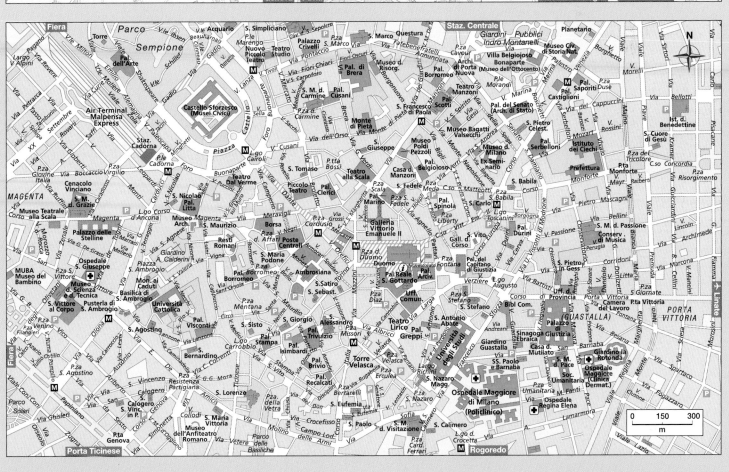

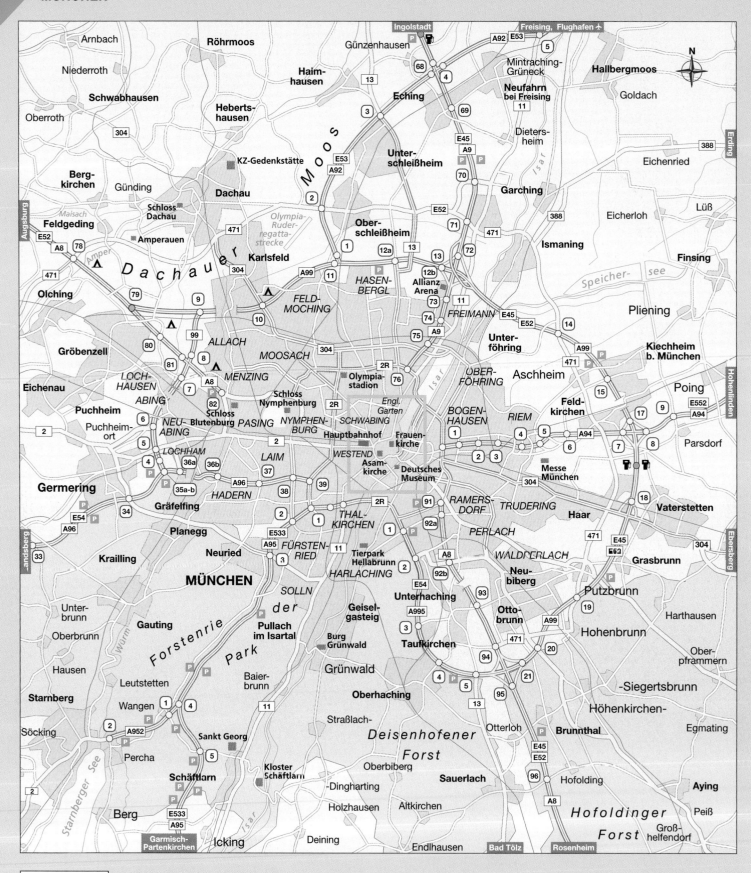

Arnbach
Röhrmoos
Günzenhausen
Ingolstadt
Freising, Flughafen
A92 E53
5
Niederroth
Haim-hausen
68
4
Mintraching-Grüneck
Hallbergmoos
Schwabhausen
Hebertshausen
13
Eching
69
Neufahrn bei Freising
11
Goldach
Oberroth
3
Dietersheim
304
E53
A92
Unter-schleißheim
E45
A9
Eichenried
388
Bergkirchen
Günding
KZ-Gedenkstätte
2
70
Garching
Erding
Schloss Dachau
471
Olympia-Ruderregatta-strecke
Oberschleißheim
71
388
Eicherloh
Lüß
Feldgeding
Amperauen
1
12a
13
72
Ismaning
Maisach
Karlsfeld
A99
11
HASENBERGL
13
Finsing
E52
A8
78
Dachauer
304
Allianz Arena
12b
11
Speicher-see
471
Olching
79
9
FELD-MOCHING
73
FREIMANN
E45
E52
Pliening
Gröbenzell
80
10
ALLACH
74
A9
14
Kiechheim b. München
81
8
MOOSACH
75
Unter-föhring
A99
471
Eichenau
LOCH-HAUSEN
ABING
7
A8
304
2R
OBER-FÖHRING
Aschheim
15
Poing
Puchheim
82
MENZING
Schloss Nymphenburg
76
Olympia-stadion
RIEM
17
9
E552
A94
Puchheim-ort
6
Schloss Blutenburg
NYMPHEN-BURG
2R
Engl. Garten
SCHWABING
BOGEN-HAUSEN
Feld-kirchen
7
8
Parsdorf
2
NEU-ABING
PASING
Hauptbahnhof
Frauen-kirche
1
A94
5
5
LAIM
37
WESTEND
Asam-kirche
6
Messe München
Germering
36a
36b
Asam-kirche
Deutsches Museum
2
3
18
4
35a-b
A96
38
39
2R
91
RAMERS-DORF
TRUDERING
304
Vaterstetten
Gräfelfing
HADERN
2
92a
Haar
471
34
1
THAL-KIRCHEN
PERLACH
E45
E52
E54
A96
E533
92b
WALDPERLACH
304
Planegg
A95
FÜRSTEN-RIED
11
Tierpark Hellabrunn
8
Neu-biberg
Grasbrunn
33
Neuried
HARLACHING
92b
93
Otto-brunn
Putzbrunn
Krailling
SOLLN
E54
A99
19
Harthausen
MÜNCHEN
der
Geisel-gasteig
A995
94
471
20
Hohenbrunn
Gauting
Wald
Unter-brunn
Pullach im Isartal
3
Unterhaching
Ober-pframmern
Oberbrunn
Forstenrie
Park
Burg Grünwald
Taufkirchen
94
21
-Siegertsbrunn
Hausen
Baier-brunn
Grünwald
4
5
95
Höhenkirchen-
Starnberg
Leutstetten
Oberhaching
13
Wangen
1
4
Straßlach-
Otterloh
Brunnthal
Egmating
Söcking
2
A952
Sankt Georg
Deisenhofener
Peiß
Percha
5
Kloster Schäftlarn
Oberbiberg
Sauerlach
96
Hofolding
Aying
Schäftlarn
Forst
-Dingharting
Hofoldinger
Groß-helfendorf
Berg
E533
A95
Holzhausen
Altkirchen
A8
Forst
Garmisch-Partenkirchen
Icking
Deining
Endlhausen
Bad Tölz
Rosenheim

0 2 4
km

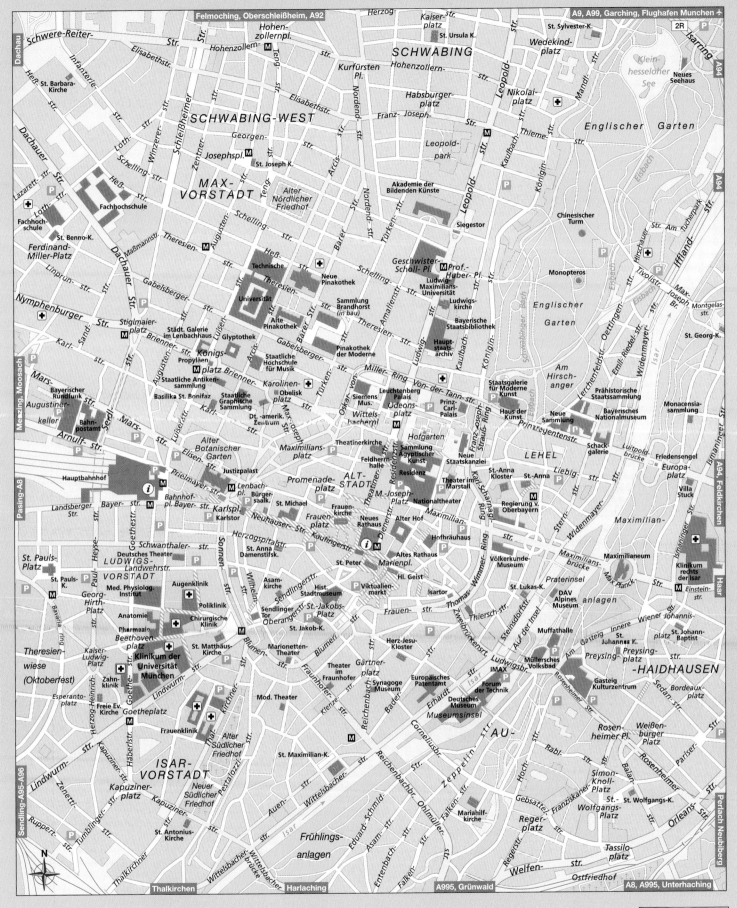

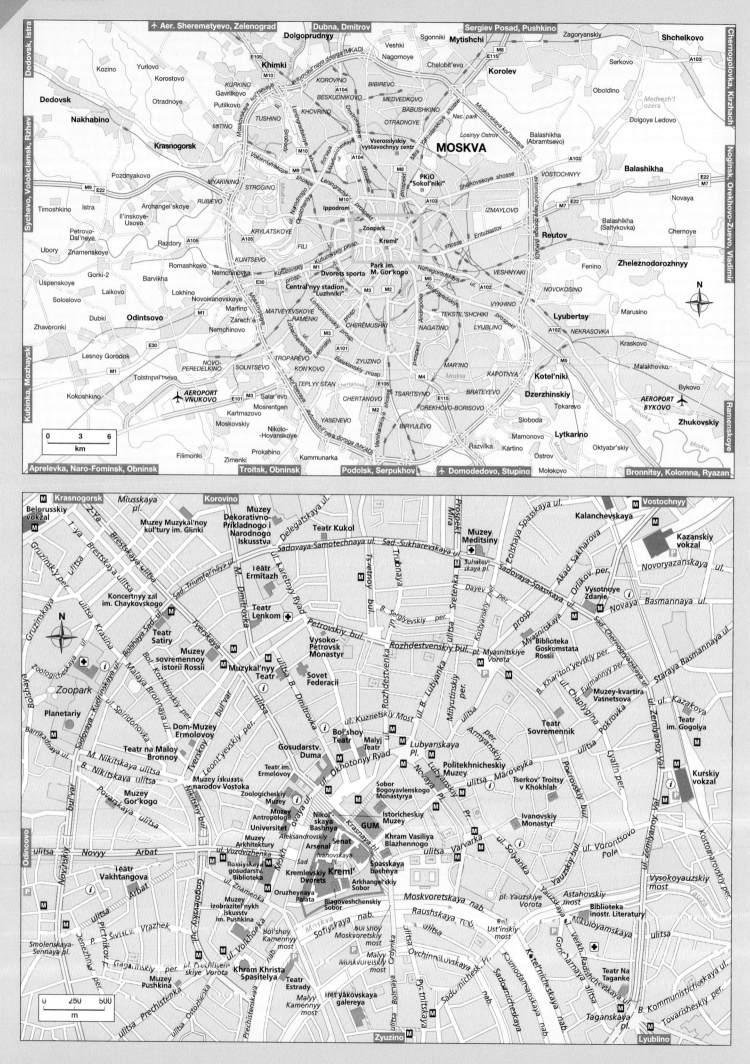

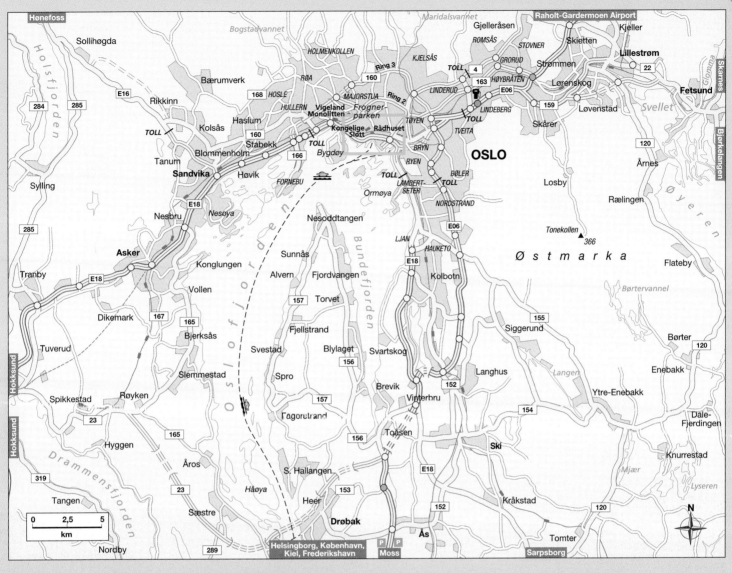

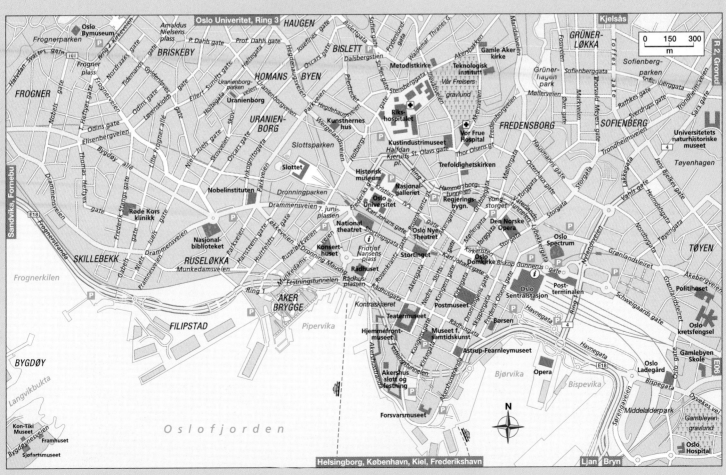

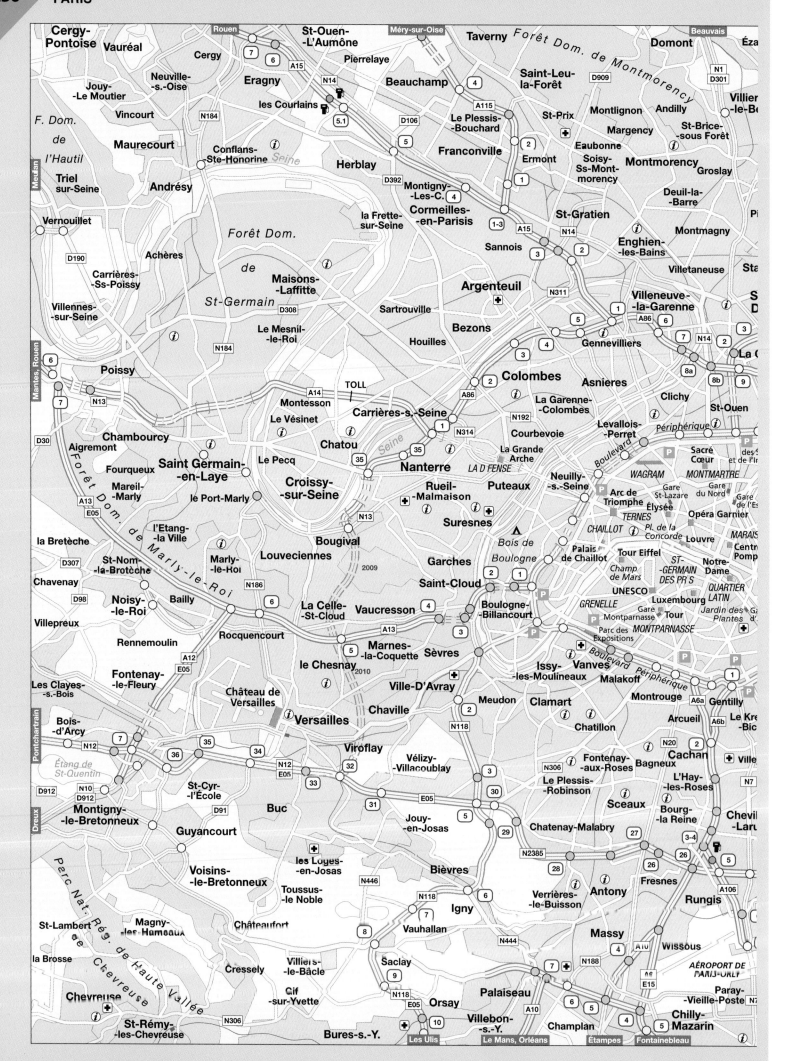

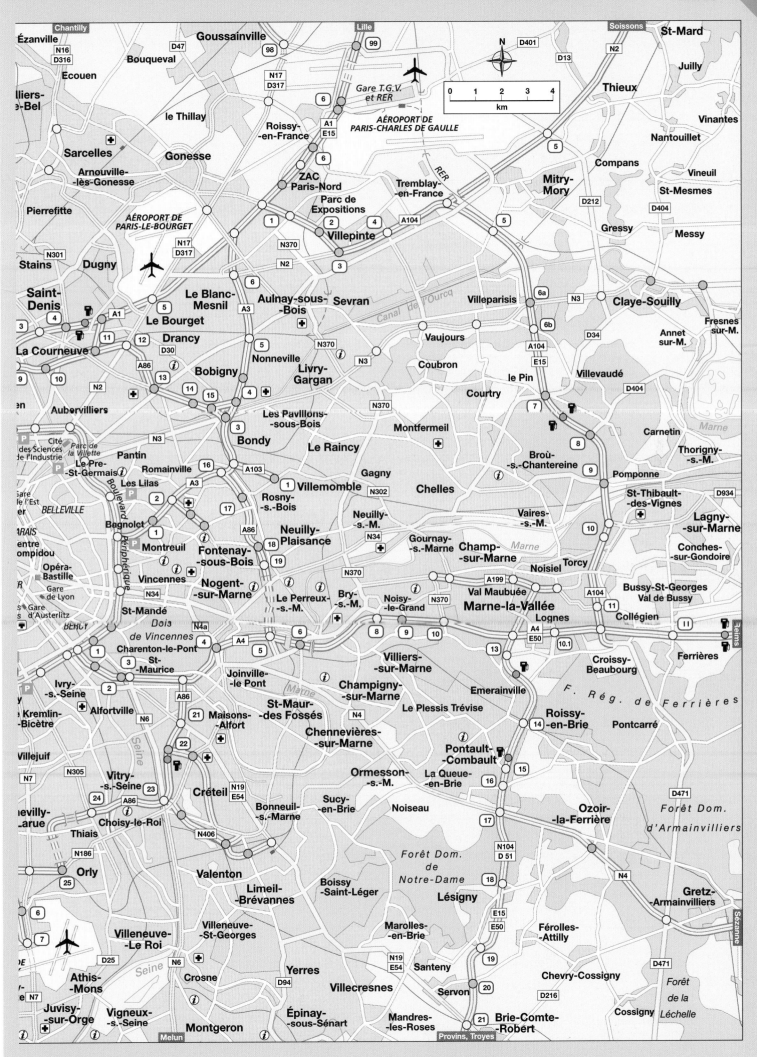

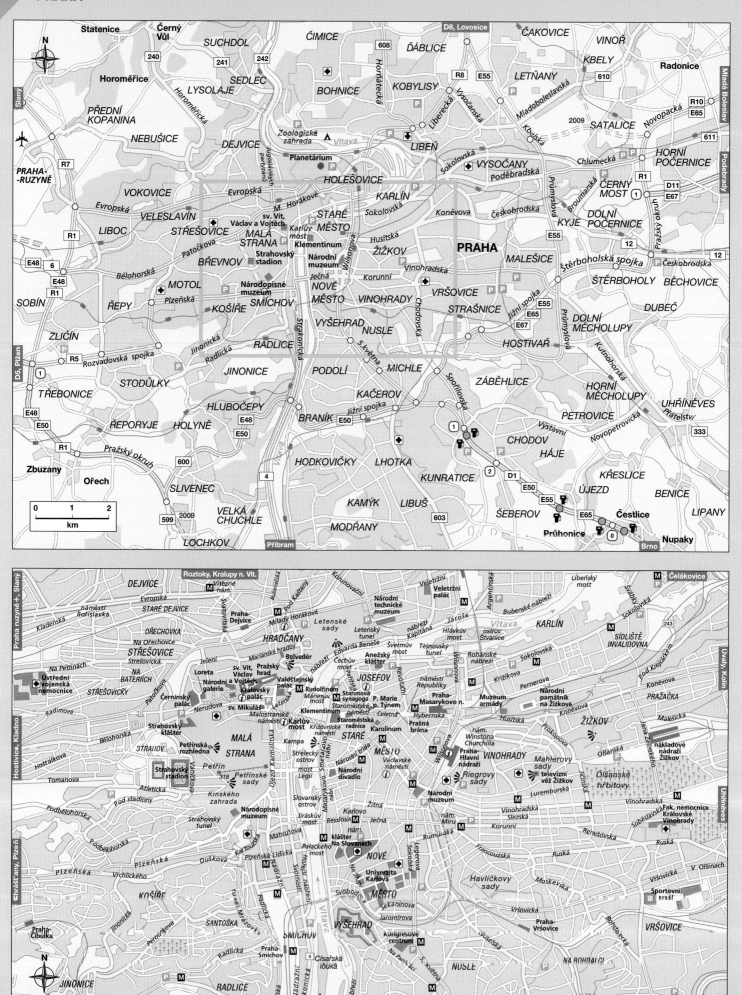

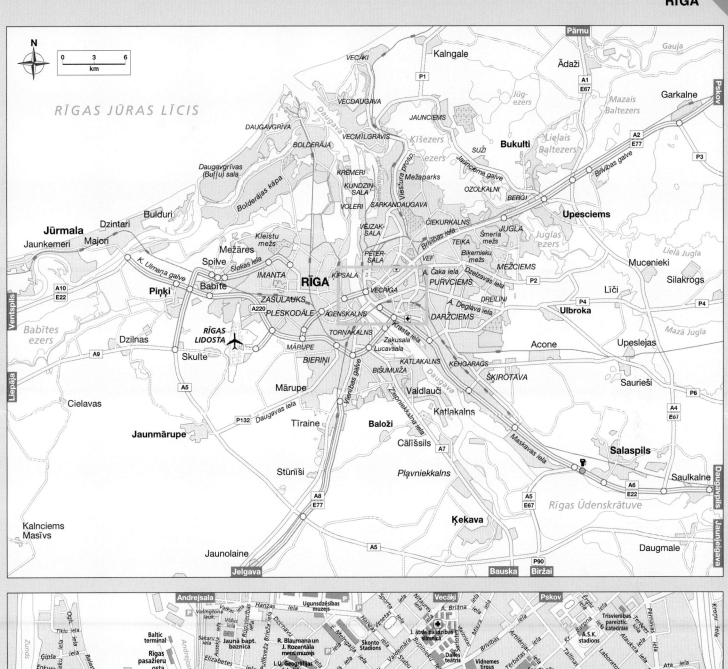

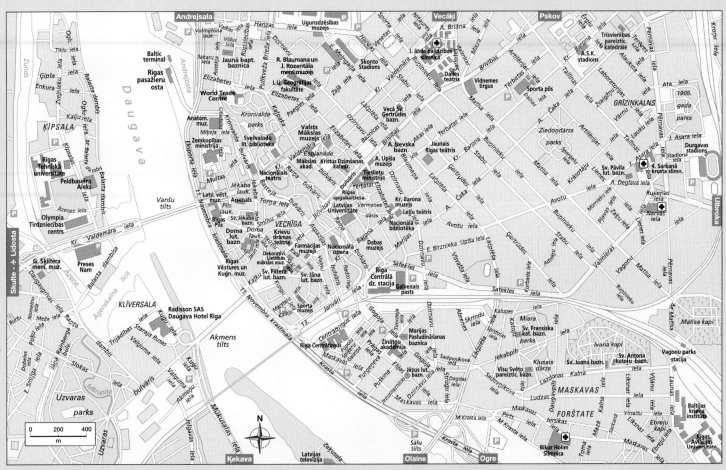

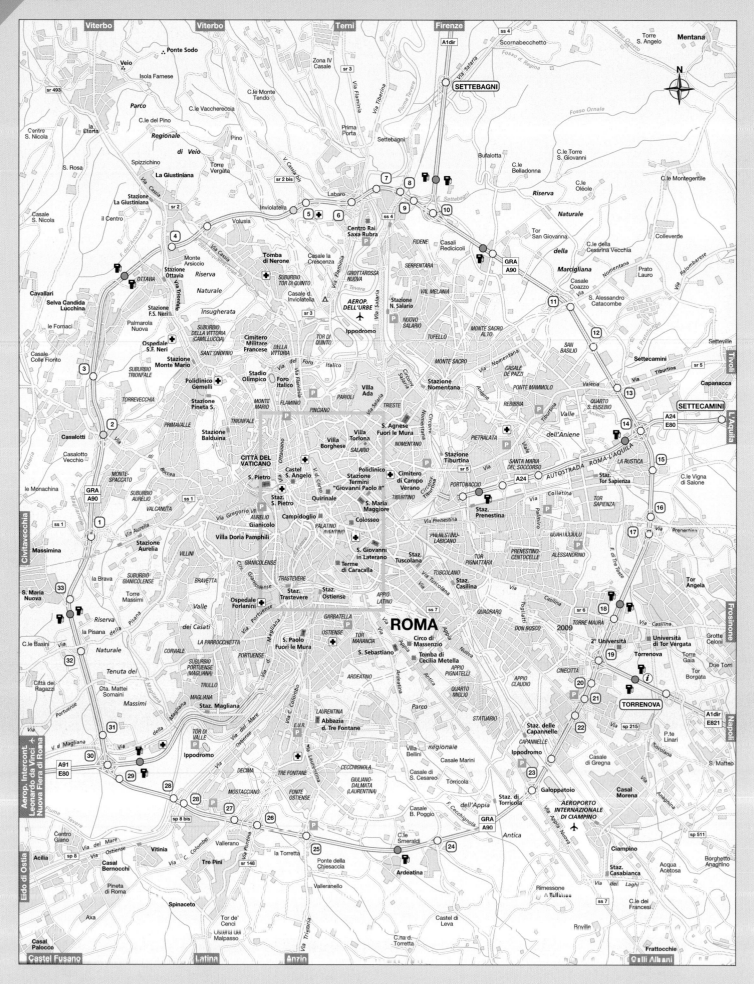

SETTEBAGNI

GRA
A90

SETTECAMINI

ROMA

2009

TORRENOVA

AEROPORTO
INTERNAZIONALE
DI CIAMPINO

CITTÀ DEL
VATICANO

0 1 2 3
km

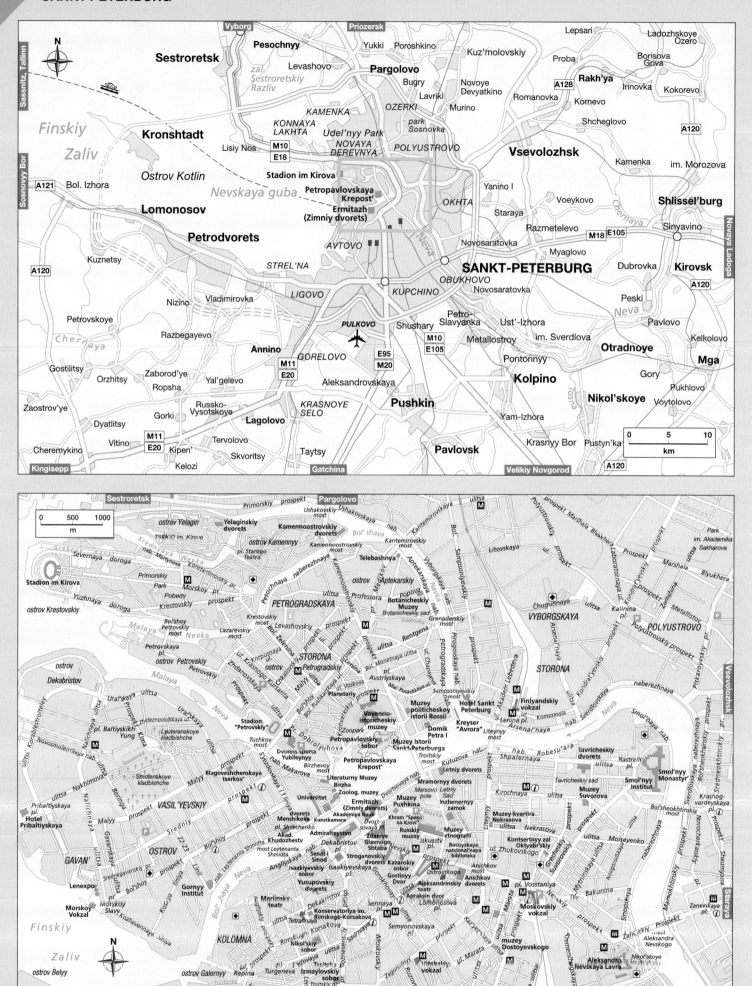

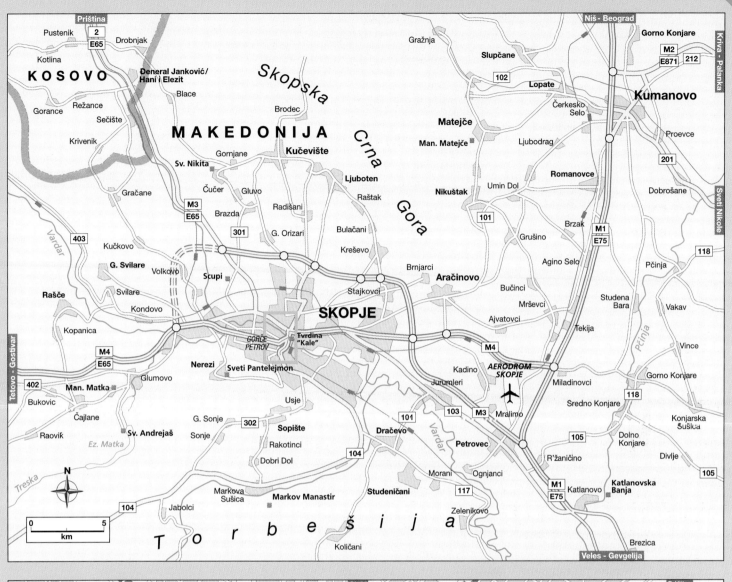

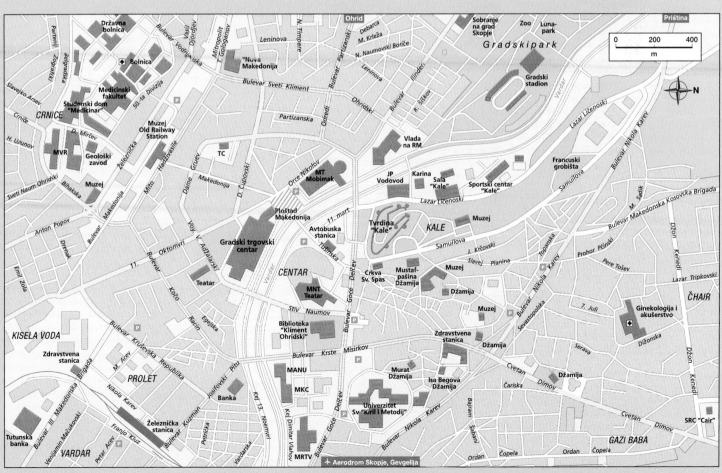

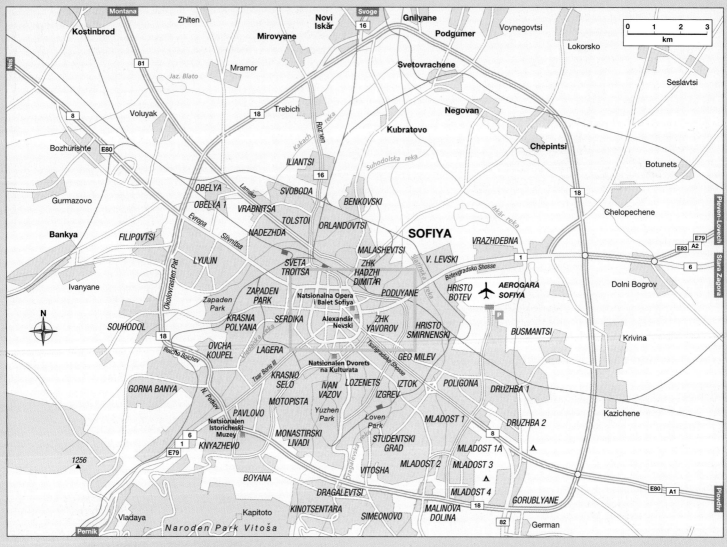

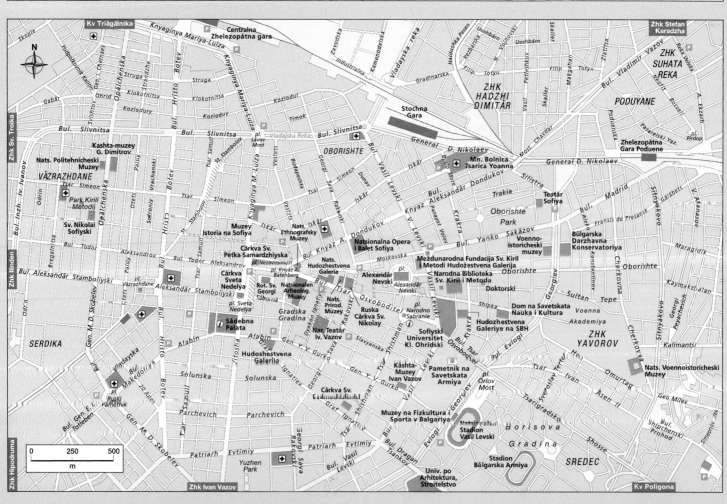

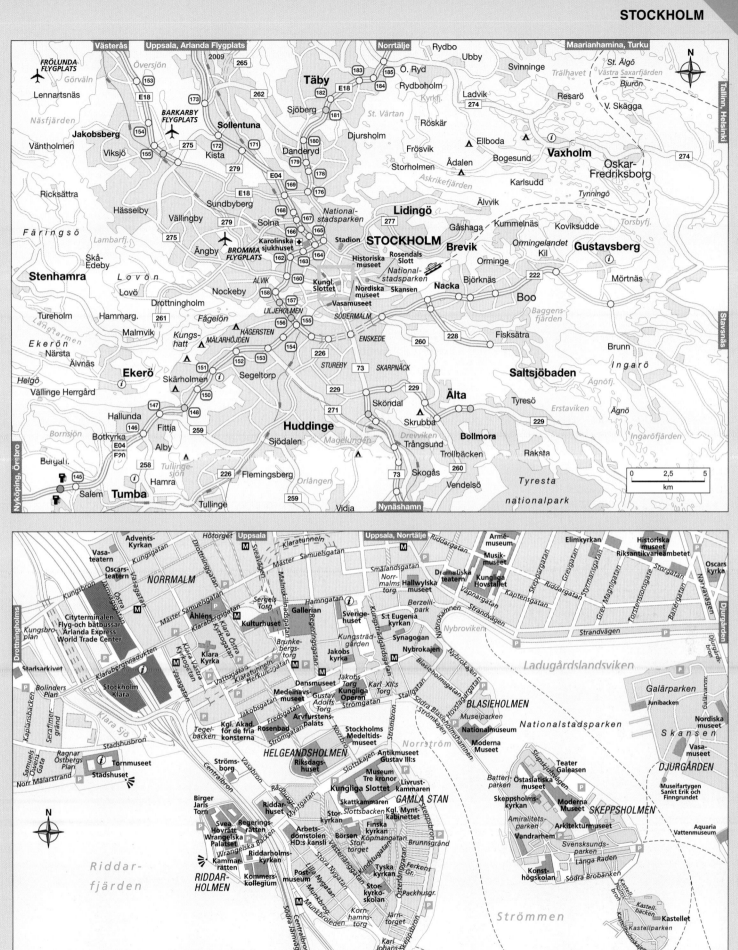

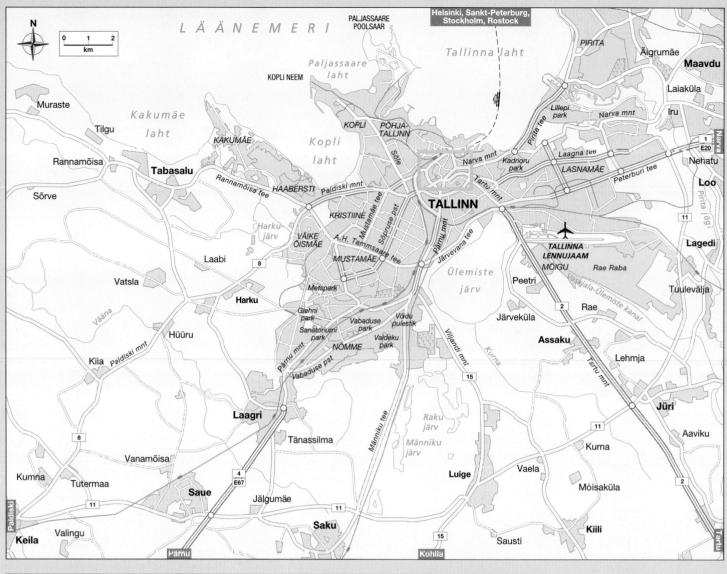

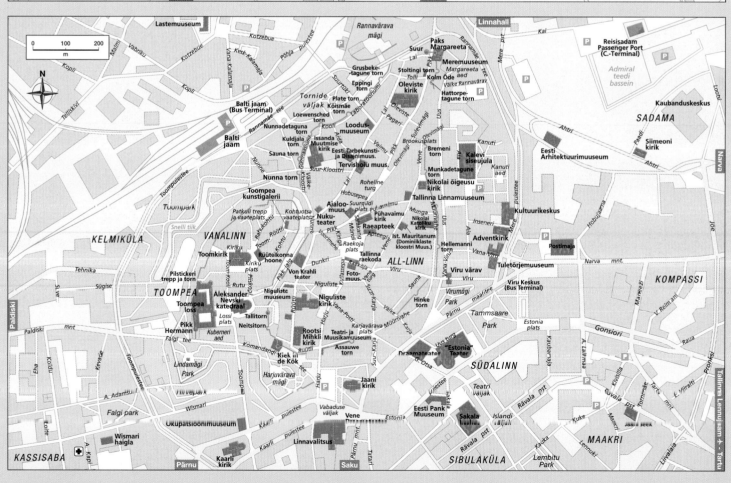

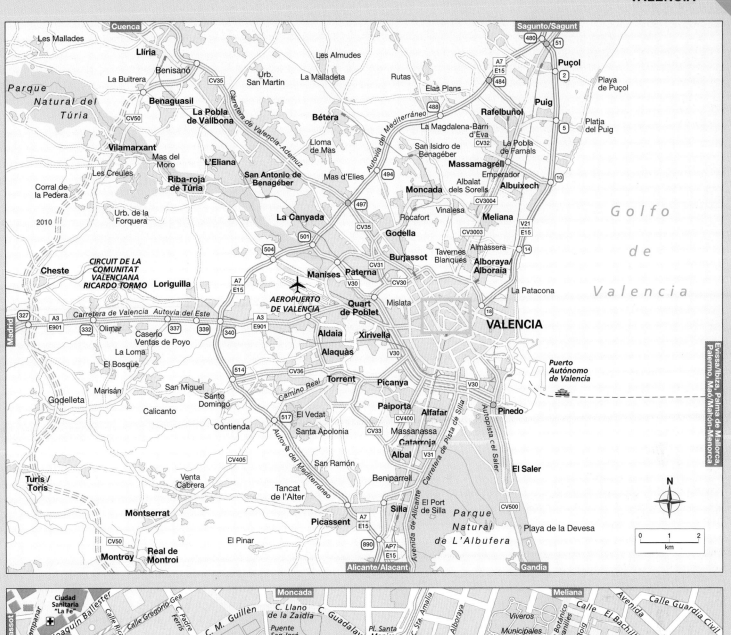

Cuenca
Les Mallades
Llíria
Benisanó
La Buitrera
CV35
Benaguasil
La Pobla de Vallbona
CV50
Vilamarxant
Mas del Moro
L'Eliana
Les Creules
Riba-roja de Túria
San Antonio de Benagéber
Corral de la Pedera
Urb. de la Forquera
2010
Urb. San Martin
La Malladeta
Les Almudes
Rutas
Elas Plans
Bétera
Lloma de Mas
Mas d'Elies
Sagunto/Sagunt
480 51
Puçol
2
Playa de Puçol
A7 E15
484
488
La Magdalena-Barri d'Eva
San Isidro de Benagéber
CV32
Puig
5
Platja del Puig
494
Moncada
La Pobla de Farnals
Massamagrell
Emperador
Albalat dels Sorells
Albuixech
10
497
CV3004
Cheste
CIRCUIT DE LA COMUNITAT VALENCIANA RICARDO TORMO
Loriguilla
La Canyada
501
CV35
Rocafort
Vinalesa
Meliana
CV3003
Godella
Almàssera
V21 E15
Burjassot
Tavernes Blanques
Alboraya/ Alboraia
14
327
A3 E901
Carretera de Valencia
Autovia del Este
A7 E15
Manises
Paterna
CV31
CV30
Mislata
La Patacona
18
VALENCIA
332
Olimar
337
339
340
A3 E901
Quart de Poblet
Aldaia
Xirivella
V30
Golfo de Valencia
Caserío Ventas de Poyo
La Loma
El Bosque
Alaquàs
Puerto Autónomo de Valencia
Godelleta
Marisán
Santo Domingo
Calicanto
514
CV36
Torrent
Picanya
V30
Pinedo
517
El Vedat
Santa Apolonia
Paiporta
CV400
Alfafar
Contienda
CV33
Massanassa
El Saler
San Ramón
Catarroja
Albal
V31
CV405
Venta Cabrera
Beniparrell
Montserrat
Tancat de l'Alter
Picassent
Silla
El Port de Silla
CV500
Parque Natural de L'Albufera
Playa de la Devesa
CV50
El Pinar
890
A7 E15
AP7 E15
Montroy
Real de Montroi
Turis / Toris
Madrid

Evissa/Ibiza, Palma de Mallorca, Palermo, Maó/Mahón-Menorca

N

0 1 2
km

Alicante/Alacant
Gandia

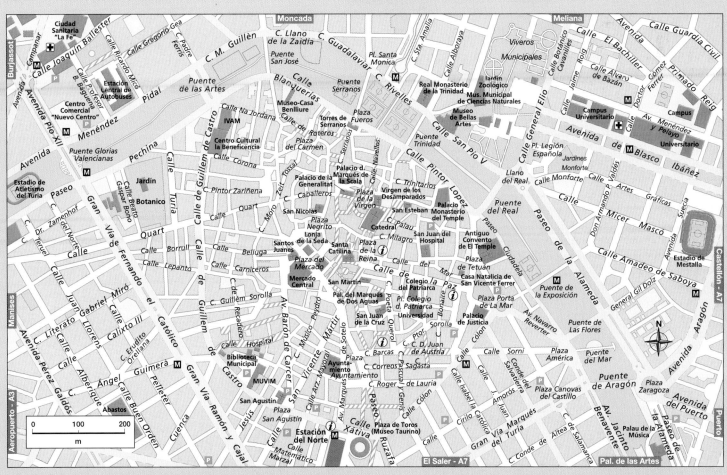

0   100   200
m

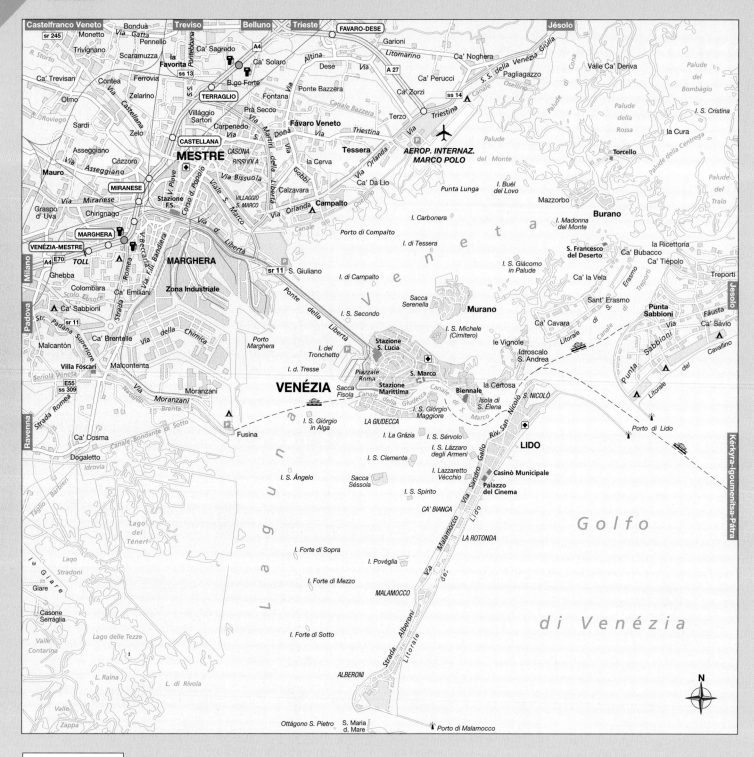

sr 245

Bonduà
Monetto
Via Gatta
Pennello
Pontebbana
Ca' Sagredo
Garioni
Litomarino
Ca' Noghera
Valle Ca' Deríva
Palude del Bombágio

Trivignano
R. Storto
Scaramuzza
la Favorita
ss 13
Ca' Solaro
A4
B.go Forte
Altina
Dese
Via
A 27
Ca' Perucci
S. S. della Venézia Giùlia
Palude di Cona
I. S. Cristina

Ca' Trevisan
Ferrovia
Via Castellana
Via Zelarino
TERRAGLIO
Fontana
Ponte Bazzera
Canale Bazzera
Ca' Zorzi
ss 14
Terzo
Triestina
Pagliagazzo
Osellino
Palude della Rossa
la Cura

Olmo
Contea
Roviego
Sardi
Villággio Sartori
Prà Secco
Fávaro Veneto
Triestina
Terzo
Triestina
AEROP. INTERNAZ. MARCO POLO
del Monte
Palude
Torcello

Mauro
Asseggiano
CASTELLANA
MESTRE
Carpenedo
Via
Donà
CASONA BISSIOLA
Tessera
la Cerva
Via Orlanda
Ca' Da Lio
Punta Lunga
I. Buèl del Lovo
Mazzorbo
I. S. Giácomo in Palude
Palude della Centrega

Asseggiano
Cázzora
MIRANESE
Via Miranese
Chirignago
Via Bissuola
VILLAGGIO S. MARCO
Calzavara
Campalto
Via Orlanda
I. Carbonera
I. di Tessera
Burano
S. Francesco del Deserto
la Ricettoría
Treporti

Graspo d'Uva
Via Miranese
Stazione F.S.
Corso d. Popolo
Viale S. Marco
Via d. Libertà
Porto di Compalto
I. Giácomo in Palude
I. Madonna del Monte
Ca' Bubacco
Ca' Tiépolo

MARGHERA
VENÉZIA-MESTRE
A4 E70
TOLL
Ghebba
Via V. Piave
Romea
V. Beccaría
Fili. Bandiera
sr 11
S. Giuliano
I. di Campalto
Sacca Serenella
Murano
Ca' la Vela
Sant' Erasmo
S. Erasmo
Punta Sabbioni
Fáusta
Ca' Sávio

Milano
Colombara
Ca' Emiliani
Zona Industriale
Ponte della Liberta
I. S. Secondo
I. S. Michele (Cimitero)
Ca' Cavara
le Vignole
Litorale
Canale
Via del Litorale

Padova
Ghebba
Strada Romea
Ca' Brentelle
Via della Chimica
Porto Marghera
I. del Tronchetto
I. d. Tresse
Stazione S. Lucia
S. Marco
Biennale
Idroscalo S. Andrea
Punta Sabbioni
Via del
Cavallino

sr 11
Ca' Sabbioni
Str. Padana superiore
Malcantòn
Seriola Vénta
E55
ss 309
Villa Fóscari
Malcontenta
Piazzale Roma
Stazione Marittima
Sacca Fisola
Canale della Giudecca
la Certosa
Isola di S. Élena
S. NICOLÒ
Porto di Lido

Ravenna
Strada Romea
Moranzani
Moranzani
Brenta
Fusina
I. S. Giórgio in Alga
LA GIUDECCA
I. S. Giórgio Maggiore
Canale di S. Marco
Riv. San. Nicolò
LIDO
Casinò Municipale

Ca' Cosma
Dogaletto
Idrovia
Canale Bondante di Sotto
I. S. Ángelo
I. La Grázia
Sacca Séssola
I. S. Clemente
I. S. Sérvolo
I. S. Lázzaro degli Armeni
I. Lazzaretto Vécchio
I. S. Spirito
Palazzo del Cinema

Laguna
Lago dei Téneri
Lago
Stradoni
Giare
I. Forte di Sopra
I. Povéglia
CA' BIANCA
Via Sandro Gallo
Via Malamocco Lido
LA ROTONDA
Golfo

Ia Giare
Giare
Lago
L. Raína
L. di Rívola
I. Forte di Mezzo
MALAMOCCO
Litorale dei
di Venézia

Casone Serráglia
Valle Contarina
L. delle Tezze
I. Forte di Sotto
Strada Alberoni
Litorale

Valle Zappa
ALBERONI
Ottágono S. Pietro
S. Maria d. Mare
Porto di Malamocco
N

0 1 2 3
km

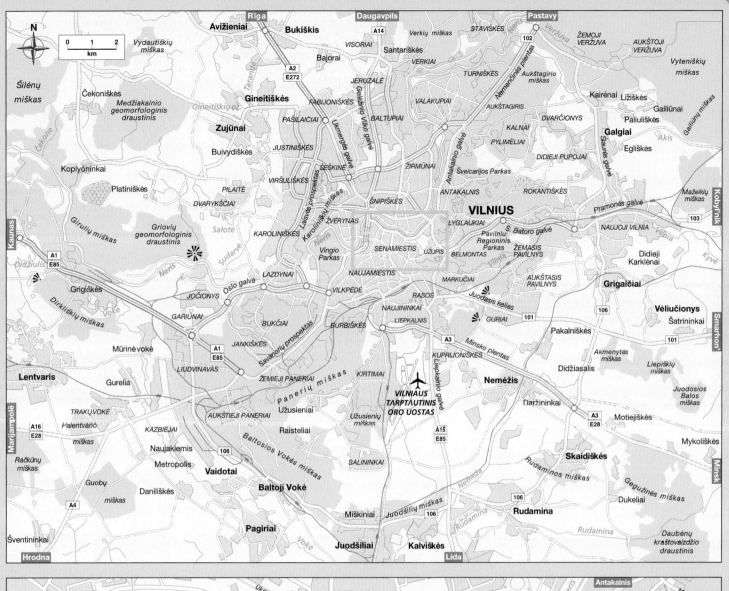

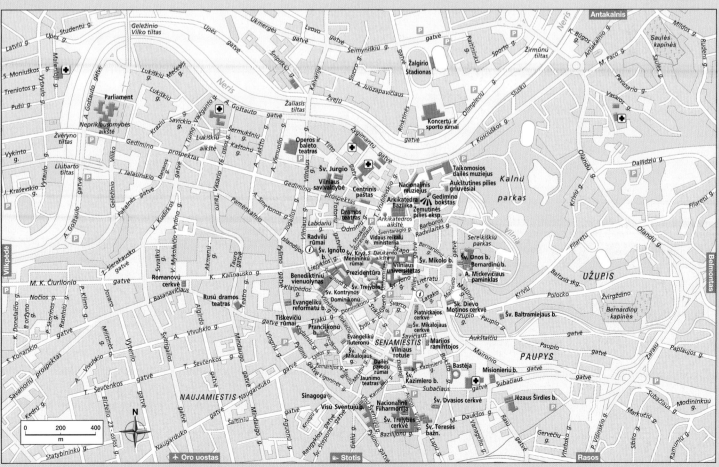

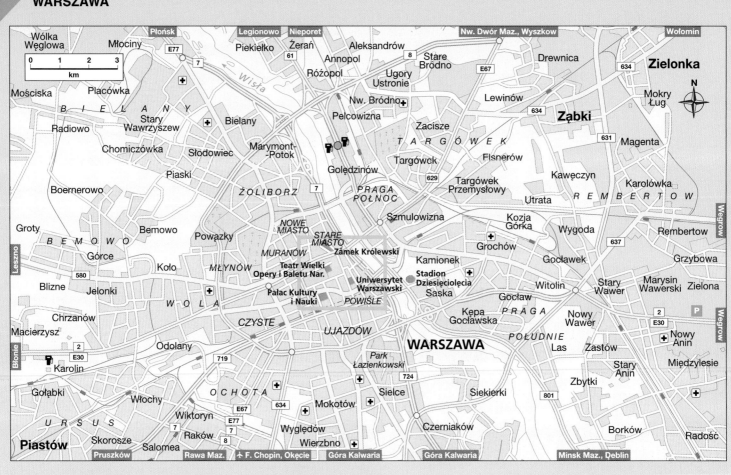

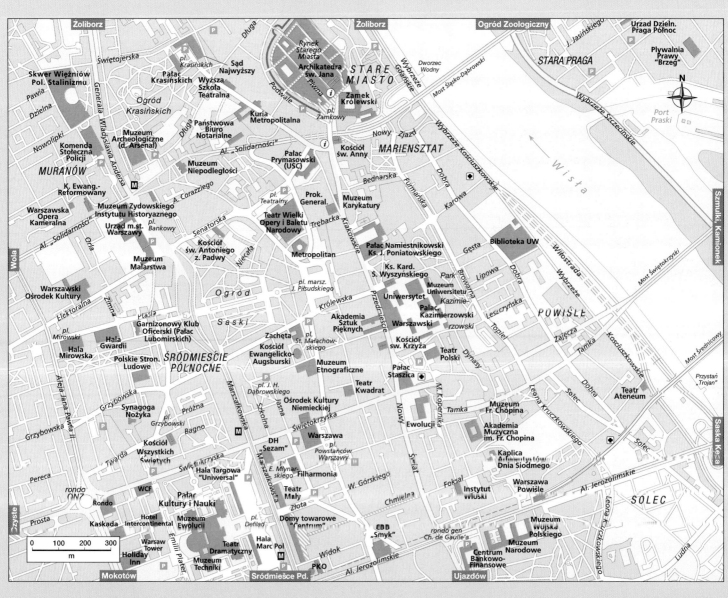

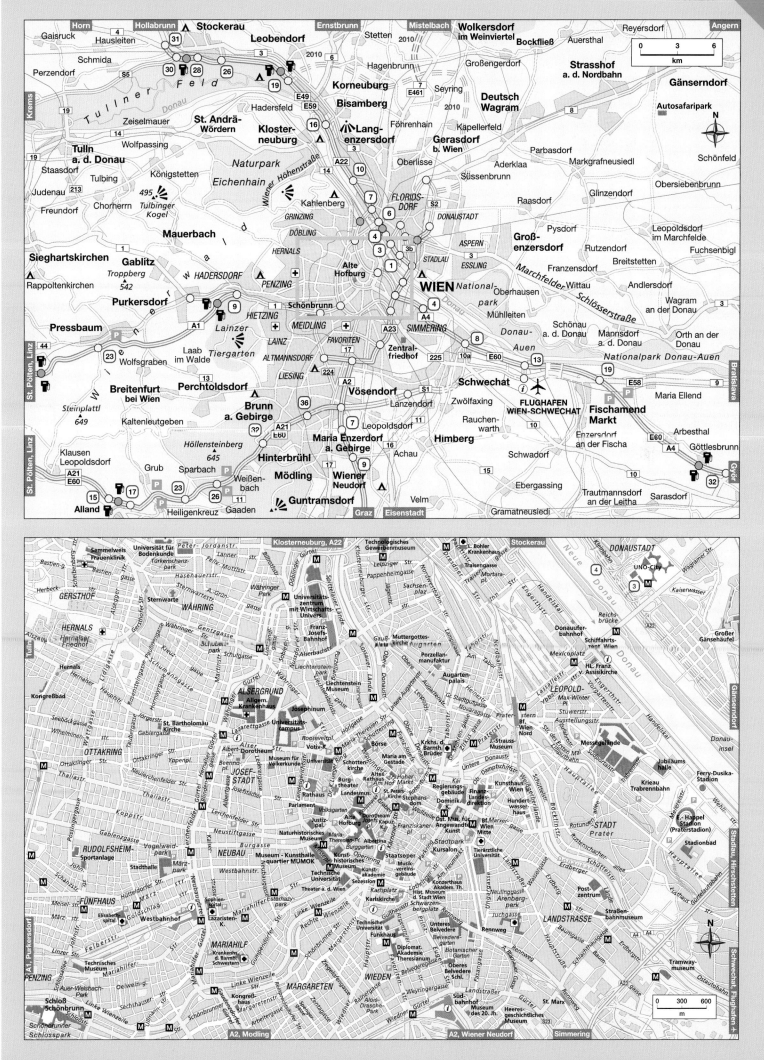

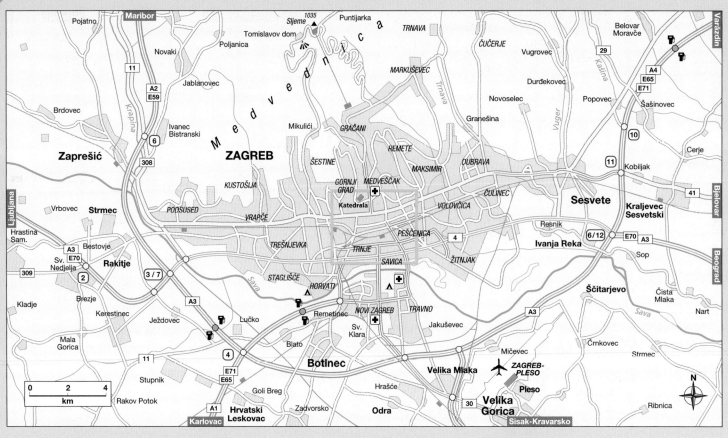

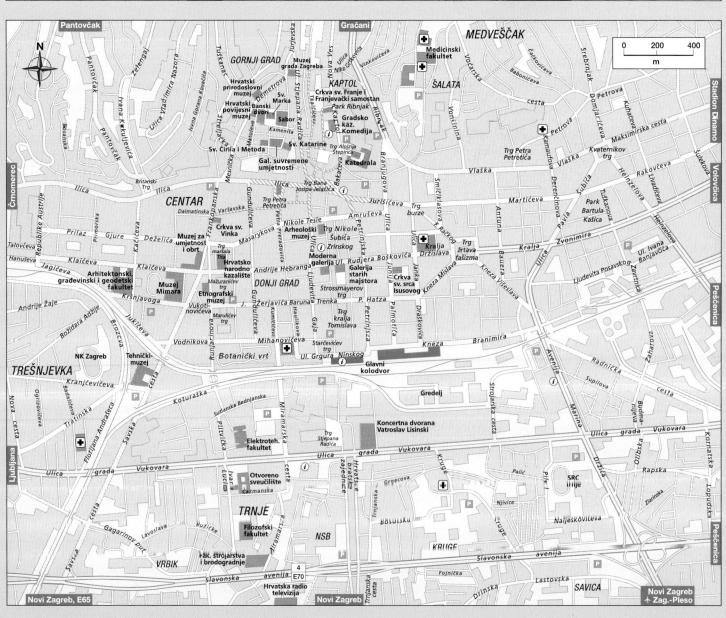

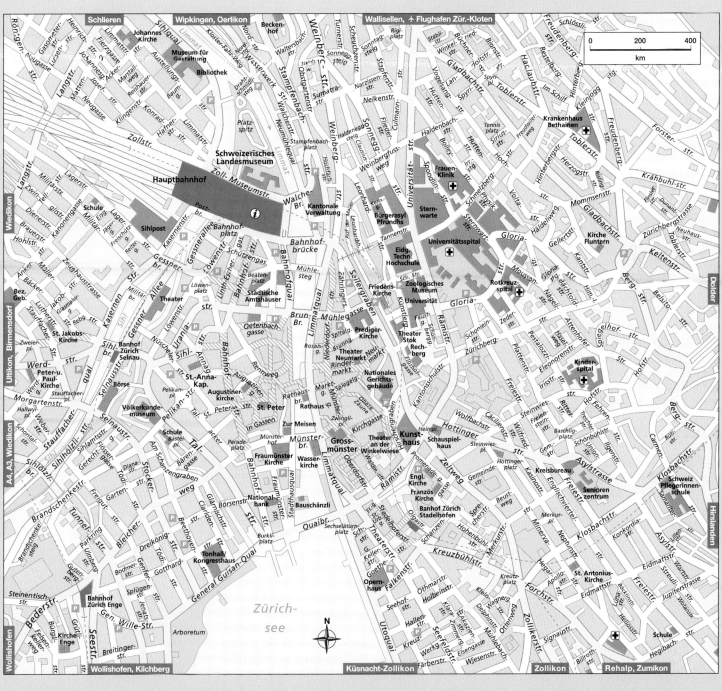

INDEX OF NAMES
INDICE DEI NOMI
ÍNDICE DE TOPÓNIMOS
INDEX DES NOMS
NAMENVERZEICHNIS

How to use the index • Avvertenze per la ricerca
Instrucciones para la consulta • Notices pour la recherche
Erläuterungen des Suchsystems

The index lists the place names, tourist sites, main tunnels and passes contained in the atlas, followed by the abbreviation of the country name to which they belong.
All names contained in two adjoining pages are referenced to the even page number.

L'indice elenca i toponimi dei centri abitati, dei siti turistici, dei principali tunnel e passi presenti nell'atlante, accompagnati dalla sigla della nazione di appartenenza.
Tutti i nomi contenuti in due pagine affiancate sono riferiti alla pagina di numero pari.

El índice presenta los topónimos de localidades, lugares turísticos, principales túneles y puertos de montaña que figuran en el atlas, seguidos de la sigla que indica el País de pertenencia. Todos los nombres contenidos en dos páginas juntas éstan referidos a la página de número par.

L'index récense les noms des localités, sites touristiques, principales tunnels et cols contenus dans l'atlas, suivis par le sigle qui indique le Pays d'appartenance.
Tous les noms contenus dans deux pages l'une à côté de l'autre sont rapportés à la page avec nombre pair.

Der Index enthält die im Atlas vorhandenen Ortsnamen, Sehenswürdigkeiten, wichtigsten Tunnels und Pässe, von dem zugehörigen Staatskennzeichen gefolgt.
Alle in zwei anliegenden Seiten enthaltenen Namen sind auf die Seite mit gerader Zahl bezogen.

A

23 August [RO] 148 G1
Å [N] 180 H2
Å [N] 192 C5
Aabenraa [DK] 156 C4
Aabybro [DK] 160 D3
Aachen [D] 30 F4
Aakirkeby [DK] 158 E4
Aalborg [DK] 160 D3
Aalburg [NL] 16 D6
Aalen [D] 60 B2
Aalestrup [DK] 160 D4
Aalsmane [LV] 198 F4
Aalsmeer [NL] 16 D4
Aalst (Alost) [B] 28 H2
Aalten [NL] 16 G6
Aalter [B] 28 G2
Äänekoski [FIN] 186 G3
Aapajärvi [FIN] 194 D6
Aarau [CH] 58 E5
Aarberg [CH] 58 D5
Aarburg [CH] 58 E5
Aareavaraa [S] 194 B6
Aareschlucht [CH] 70 F1
Aarlen (Arlon) [B] 44 E2
Aars [DK] 160 D4
Aarschot [B] 30 D4
Aarup [DK] 156 D3
Aavasaksa [FIN] 194 B8
Aba [H] 76 B2
Åbacka [S] 190 F3
Abades [E] 88 F4
Abadín [E] 78 E2
Abadino [E] 82 H4
Abádszalók [H] 64 F6
A Baña [E] 78 B2
Abanades [E] 90 B5
Abanilla [E] 104 C2
Abano Terme [I] 110 G1
Abarán [E] 104 C2
Abárzuza [E] 84 A4
Abaújszántó [H] 64 G4
Abbadia [I] 114 G4
Abbadia San Salvatore [I] 114 G2
Abbasanta [I] 118 C4
Abbekås [S] 158 C3
Abbeville [F] 28 D4
Abbeydorney [IRL] 4 B3
Abbeyfeale [IRL] 4 C3
Abbeyleix [IRL] 4 E3
Abbiategrasso [I] 70 F5
Abborrträsk [S] 190 H3
Abdürrahim [TR] 130 H3

Abejar [E] 90 B2
Abela [P] 94 C2
Abéliéra [F] 108 E3
Abélnes [N] 164 C5
Abelvær [N] 190 C4
Abenberg [D] 46 G5
Abengibre [I] 98 E2
Abenójar [E] 96 D4
Abensberg [D] 60 E2
Aberaeron [GB] 10 B6
Aberchirder [GB] 6 F5
Aberdare [GB] 12 F2
Aberdeen [GB] 6 F6
Aberfeldy [GB] 8 E1
Abergavenny [GB] 12 F2
Abergele [GB] 10 C4
Aberlour [GB] 6 E5
Abersee [A] 60 H5
Abersoch [GB] 10 B4
Aberspier [D] 32 H5
Aberystwyth [GB] 10 B6
Abetone [I] 110 E4
Abide [TR] 130 H5
Abide [TR] 152 G2
Abiego [E] 90 G3
Abild [DK] 156 B4
Abild [S] 162 B4
Abingdon [GB] 12 H3
Abington [GB] 8 D4
Abisko [S] 192 F4
Abiul [P] 86 D2
Abja–Paluoja [EST] 198 E3
Abla [E] 102 F4
Ablanitsa [BG] 148 B4
Ablis [F] 42 E4
Åbo [S] 190 C6
Åbo / Turku [FIN] 176 D4
Åboland [S] 166 C5
Abondance [F] 70 C2
Abony [H] 76 E2
Åbosjö [S] 190 G6
Aboyne [GB] 6 F6
Abrantes [P] 86 D4
Abraur [S] 190 G2
Abreschviller [F] 44 G5
Abric d'Ermites [E] 92 A6
Abriès [F] 70 C6
Abrigo de la Peña del Escrito [E] 98 C3
Abrud [RO] 204 C4
Abtei [A] 74 B3
Abtenau [A] 60 H6
Abtsgmünd [D] 60 B2
Abtshagen [D] 20 D3

Åby [N] 164 G3
Åby [S] 162 C4
Åby [S] 168 B5
Abyarowshchyna [BY] 38 F2
Åbyn [S] 196 B4
Accadia [I] 120 G2
Acceglio [I] 108 E2
Accettura [I] 120 H4
Acciaroli [I] 120 F5
Accous [F] 84 D4
Accumoli [I] 116 B3
Acedera [E] 96 B3
Acedo [E] 82 H6
Acehuche [E] 86 G4
Acerenza [I] 120 H3
Acerno [I] 120 F3
Acerra [I] 120 E3
Aceuchal [E] 94 G2
Acharnés [GR] 134 C6
Achenkirch [A] 60 E6
Achensee [A] 60 E6
Achenwald [A] 60 E6
Achern [D] 58 F1
Acheux–en–Amiénois [F] 28 E4
Achílleio [GR] 132 G2
Achilleum [TR] 130 H5
Achim [D] 18 E5
Achinós [GR] 130 C3
Achladochóri [GR] 130 B2
Achladókampos [GR] 136 E2
Achleiten [A] 62 B4
Achnasheen [GB] 6 D4
Achtrup [D] 156 B4
Aci Castello [I] 126 G3
Aci Catena [I] 126 G3
Acinipo [E] 102 A4
Acıpayam [TR] 152 G6
Acireale [I] 126 G3
Aci Trezza [I] 126 G3
Acksi [S] 172 G3
A Coruña / La Coruña [E] 78 C2
Acqua Doria [F] 114 A5
Acquafredda, Castello di– [I] 118 C7
Acqualagna [I] 112 B6
Acquanegra sul Chiese [I] 110 E1
Acquapendente [I] 114 G3
Acquaro [I] 124 D6
Acquasanta Terme [I] 116 C3
Acquasparta [I] 116 A3

Acquaviva delle Fonti [I] 122 D3
Acquedolci [I] 126 F2
Acqui Terme [I] 108 H2
Acri [I] 124 D4
Acropolis Iberica [E] 90 F5
Ács [H] 64 A6
Acsa [H] 64 D5
Acsád [H] 74 F1
Ada [SRB] 76 E5
Adaköy [TR] 154 D2
Adalsbruk [N] 172 C3
Ådalsvollen [N] 190 C6
Adámas [GR] 138 D4
Adamclisi [RO] 204 E5
Adamuz [E] 96 C6
Adanero [E] 88 E3
Adapazarı (Sakarya) [TR] 150 H3
Adare [IRL] 4 C3
Adaševci [SRB] 142 E2
Adelberg [D] 60 B2
Adelboden [CH] 70 D2
Adelebsen [D] 32 F4
Adelfia [I] 122 E3
Adelsheim [D] 46 D5
Adelsö [S] 168 D3
Adelsried [D] 60 C3
Ademuz [E] 98 D2
Adenau [D] 30 G6
Adjud [RO] 204 E4
Admont [A] 62 C6
Ådneram [N] 164 C3
Adolfsström [S] 190 F2
Adony [H] 76 C2
Adorf [D] 48 C3
Adra [E] 102 F5
Adradas [E] 90 B4
Adrall [E] 92 D1
Adramittium Thebe [TR] 152 C1
Adrano [I] 126 F3
Adrigole [IRL] 4 B5
Ádria [I] 110 G2
Adutiškis [LT] 200 H4
Aegviidu [EST] 198 E1
Aerinó [GR] 132 H2
Ærøskøbing [DK] 156 D4
Aerzen [D] 32 F3
A Estrada [E] 78 C3
Aetópetra [GR] 132 C1
Aetós [GR] 128 E4
Aetós [GR] 132 D5
Äetsä [FIN] 176 E2

Afaía [GR] 136 G1
Atántou [GR] 154 D4
Ätärnes [N] 100 C3
Afife [P] 78 A6
Afiónas [GR] 132 A2
Aflenz Kurort [A] 62 D6
A Fonsagrada [E] 78 F3
Afoss [N] 164 G3
Africo [I] 124 D7
Afritz [A] 72 H3
Atşar [TR] 152 H4
Afsluitdijk [NL] 16 E2
Áfysos [GR] 134 A3
Áfytos [GR] 130 B6
Aga [N] 170 C4
Ağaçbeyli [TR] 152 G3
Ağaçlı [TR] 150 E2
Agaete [E] 100 C6
Agalás [GR] 136 A2
Agalatovo [RUS] 178 H4
Ág. Anárgyroi [GR] 132 G2
Ág. Antónios [GR] 130 B5
Ág. Athanásios [GR] 128 H4
Agay [F] 108 E5
Agazzano [I] 110 C2
Áy. Charálampos [GR] 130 F3
Agde [F] 106 E5
Ag. Dimítrios [GR] 132 F4
Ag. Dionýsios [GR] 128 G6
Ag. Dionysíou, Moní– [GR] 130 D5
Agen [F] 66 E5
Agéranos [GR] 136 E5
Agerbæk [DK] 156 B2
Ag. Fotiá [GR] 140 G5
Ág. Geórgios [GR] 132 F4
Agger [DK] 160 B4
Aggersund [DK] 160 D4
Aggsbach–Dorf [A] 62 D4
Aggsbach–Markt [A] 62 D4
Aggtelek [H] 64 E3
Aghadoe [IRL] 4 B4
Aghleam / An Eachléim [IRL] 2 B3
Agía [GR] 132 H1
Agía Ánna [GR] 132 H5
Agía Ánna [GR] 101 D4
Agía Efimía [GR] 132 C6
Agía Galíni [GR] 140 D5
Agia Marina [CY] 154 F5
Agía Marína [GR] 136 G1
Agía Marína [GR] 154 A1
Agía Nápa [CY] 154 G5

Agía Paraskeví [GR] 134 G2
Agia Pelagía [GR] 136 F6
Ag. Marína [GR] 134 C5
Ag. Marína [GR] 140 G3
Agiásos [GR] 134 H2
Agía Triáda [GR] 128 H5
Agía Triáda [GR] 132 D4
Agía Triáda [GR] 136 C1
Ágia Varvára [GR] 140 E5
Ág. Ioánnis [GR] 132 H6
Ág. Ioánnis [GR] 154 A3
Agiófyllo [GR] 132 E1
Ágioi Déka [GR] 140 E5
Agiókampos [GR] 132 H4
Agiókampos [GR] 132 H1
Ágio Pnévma [GR] 130 C3
Ágios Amvrósios (Esentepe) [CY] 154 G5
Ágios Andréas [GR] 136 E3
Ágios Apóstoloi [GR] 136 F5
Agios Athanásios [GR] 128 F4
Agios Dimítrios [GR] 128 G6
Agios Dimítrios [GR] 136 F4
Ágios Efstrátios [GR] 134 E1
Ágios Germanos [GR] 128 E4
Agios Konstantínos [GR] 132 H4
Agios Konstantínos [GR] 152 C5
Ágios Kýrikos [GR] 138 G1
Ágios Léon [GR] 136 A2
Ágios Márkos [GR] 128 H3
Ágios Matthaíos [GR] 132 B2
Ágios Mýron [GR] 140 E5
Ágios Nikitas [GR] 132 C4
Ágios Nikólaos [GR] 132 C2
Ágios Nikólaos [GR] 132 D4
Ágios Nikólaos [GR] 136 E4
Ágios Nikólaos [GR] 136 G2
Ágios Nikólaos [GR] 140 F4
Ágios Pétros [GR] 132 C5
Áyius Petrus [GR] 132 F4
Ágios Theodoros (Çayırova) [CY] 154 G5
Agios Vlásjos [GR] 132 F4
Ágira [I] 126 F3
Ag. Kyriakí [GR] 138 H1
Ağla [TR] 154 E1
Aglasterhausen [D] 46 C5
Ag. Lávra [GR] 136 D1
Aglen [BG] 148 A3
Aglen [N] 190 C4
Agliano [I] 108 H2
Agliate [I] 70 G4
Ag. Loukás [GR] 134 C5

Ag. Marína [GR] 132 G4
Ag. Marína [GR] 134 C5
Ag. Marína [GR] 140 G3
Agnánta [GR] 132 D2
Agnanteró [GR] 132 F2
Agnès [S] 190 H6
Ág. Nikólaos [GR] 130 C6
Agnita [RO] 204 D4
Agno [CH] 70 F3
Agnone [I] 116 E6
Agnone Bagni [I] 126 G4
Agnóntas [GR] 134 B3
Agoitz / Aoiz [E] 84 C4
Agolada [E] 78 C3
Agoncillo [E] 82 H6
Agon–Coutainville [F] 26 D3
Agordo [I] 72 E4
Ágosegyháza [H] 76 D3
Agost [E] 104 D2
Ag. Panteleïmonas [GR] 128 F4
Ag. Pelagía [GR] 140 E4
Ag. Pétros [GR] 132 C5
Ag. Stéfanos [GR] 138 E2
Ag. Theódoroi [GR] 132 H3
Ag. Theódoroi [GR] 136 F1
Ag. Thomás [GR] 140 E5
Ag. Triáda [GR] 134 C6
Ag. Triáda [GR] 140 D5
Águá, Cueva del– [E] 102 F2
Agua Amarga [E] 102 H5
Aguadulce [E] 102 G5
A Guarda / La Guardia [E] 78 A5
A Guarda / La Guardia [E] 96 C2
Aguásmestas [E] 78 G3
Aguas Nuevas [E] 98 B5
Aguda [P] 80 B4
A Gudiña [E] 78 D6
Agudo [E] 96 C3
Águeda [P] 80 B5
Agüero [E] 84 C5

Aguiar [P] 94 D2
Aguiar da Beira [P] 80 D5
Águila, Cuevas del– [E] 88 C5
Aguilafuente [E] 88 F3
Aguilar de Campoo [E] 82 D4
Aguilar de la Frontera [E] 102 C2
Aguilar del Alfambra [E] 98 E1
Águilas [E] 104 B4
Agüimes [E] 100 C6
Agulo [E] 100 B5
Agurain / Salvatierra [E] 82 H5
Aguzadera [E] 100 H3
Ağva / Yeşilçay [TR] 150 G2
Aha [D] 58 F3
Ahascragh [IRL] 2 D5
Ahat [TR] 152 G3
Ahaus [D] 16 G5
Åheim [N] 180 C4
Aheloy [BG] 148 F4
Ahigal [E] 88 A5
Ahíthisar [TR] 152 H3
Ahja [EST] 198 F3
Ahjärvi [FIN] 188 F6
Ahkiolahti [FIN] 188 C1
Ahlainen [FIN] 176 C1
Ahlbeck [D] 20 E3
Ahlbeck [D] 20 E4
Ahlen [D] 32 C3
Ahlerstedt [D] 18 E4
Ahlhorn [D] 18 C6
Ahmetbey [TR] 150 C2
Ahmetbeyler [TR] 152 C2
Ahmetçe [TR] 134 H1
Ahmetler [TR] 152 F3
Ahmetli [TR] 152 D3
Ahmoo [FIN] 176 G4
Ahmovaara [FIN] 188 F1
Ahnsen [D] 32 G2
Ahokylä [FIN] 196 E5
Ahola [FIN] 186 D2
Ahola [FIN] 196 F2
Ahonkylä [FIN] 186 C3
Ahrensbök [D] 18 G3
Ahrensburg [D] 10 O4
Ahrhütte [D] 30 G6
Ahrweiler [D] 30 G5
Ähtäri / Etseri [FIN] 186 F4
Ähtärinranta [FIN] 186 E3
Ähtävä / Esse [FIN] 196 C6
Åhus [S] 158 D2
Ahvela [FIN] 196 F3
Ahveninen [FIN] 186 E5
Ahveninen [FIN] 186 G2
Ahvensalmi [FIN] 188 E4

Ahvenselkä [FIN] 194 E7
Ahverinen [FIN] 188 F2
Aianí [GR] 128 F6
Aibar [E] 84 C4
Aich [D] 60 F3
Aicha [D] 60 H3
Aichach [D] 60 D3
Aichstetten [D] 60 B5
Aidenbach [D] 60 G3
Aidone [I] 126 F4
Aigen [A] 62 B3
Aigiáli [GR] 138 G3
Aigialoúsa (Yenierenköy) [CY] 154 G4
Aígina [GR] 136 G2
Aigínio [GR] 128 G5
Aígio [GR] 132 F6
Aigle [CH] 70 C2
Aiglsbach [D] 60 E3
Aignay-le-Duc [F] 56 G2
Aigósthena [GR] 134 B6
Aigre [F] 54 D6
Aigrefeuille-d'Aunis [F] 54 C5
Aigrefeuille-sur-Maine [F] 54 C2
Aiguablava [E] 92 G3
Aiguebelle [F] 70 B4
Aiguebelle [F] 108 D6
Aigueperse [F] 68 D1
Aigues-Mortes [F] 106 F4
Aigues-Vives [F] 106 C4
Aiguevives [F] 54 G2
Aiguilles [F] 70 B6
Aiguillon [F] 66 E5
Aigurande [F] 54 H5
Äijäjoki [FIN] 194 B5
Äijälä [FIN] 186 G3
Ailefroide [F] 70 B6
Aillant-sur-Tholon [F] 56 E1
Aime [F] 70 B4
Ainaži [LV] 198 D4
Ainet [A] 72 F2
Ainhoa [F] 84 C2
Ainsa [E] 84 E6
Airaines [F] 28 D4
Airan [F] 26 F4
Airasca [I] 70 D6
Aire-sur-l'Adour [F] 84 E2
Aire-sur-la-Lys [F] 28 E3
Airolo [CH] 70 F2
Airvault [F] 54 E3
Aisey-sur-Armançon [F] 56 F2
Aisey-sur-Seine [F] 56 G2
Aïssey [F] 58 B5
Aistaig [D] 58 G2
Aisými [GR] 130 G3
Aiterhofen [D] 60 G2
Aitolikó [GR] 132 E5
Aitrach [D] 60 B4
Aitrang [D] 60 C5
Aittojärvi [FIN] 196 E6
Aittolahti [FIN] 188 F4
Aittoperä [FIN] 196 D5
Aittovaara [FIN] 196 F3
Aiud [RO] 204 C4
Äivo / Uivu [FIN] 196 C6
Aix-en-Othe [F] 42 H6
Aix-en-Provence [F] 108 B4
Aixe-sur-Vienne [F] 66 G1
Aix-les-Bains [F] 68 H3
Aizanoi [TR] 152 G2
Aizenay [F] 54 B3
Aizkraukle [LV] 198 E5
Aizpute [LV] 198 B5
Ajaccio [F] 114 A5
Ajaur [S] 190 H4
Ajaureforsen [S] 190 F3
Ajdovščina [SLO] 74 A5
Ajka [H] 74 H2
Ajnovce [KS] 146 D5
Ajo [E] 82 F3
Ajos [FIN] 196 C3
Akáki [CY] 154 F5
Akalan [TR] 150 D2
Akalen [TR] 152 G6
Akanthoú (Tatlısu) [CY] 154 G5
Akarca [TR] 152 G3
Äkäsjokisuu [FIN] 194 B6
Äkäslompolo [FIN] 194 C6
Akasztó [H] 76 C3
Akbaş [TR] 152 C1
Akbaş [TR] 152 G5
Akbük [TR] 152 D6
Akçakavak [TR] 154 E2
Akçakese [TR] 150 F2
Akçaköy [TR] 152 E5
Akçaköy [TR] 152 H5
Akçaova [TR] 150 G2
Akçaova [TR] 152 E6
Akçay [TR] 152 C1
Akçay [TR] 154 G2
Akdere [TR] 152 G5
Akdoğan (Lysi) [CY] 154 G5
Aken [D] 34 C4
Åker [S] 162 C3
Åkersberga [S] 168 E2
Åkersjön [S] 190 D6
Åkers styckerbruk [S] 168 C3
Akharım [TR] 152 H3
Akhisar [TR] 152 D3
Akhtopol [BG] 148 G5
Akine [TR] 154 F4
Akkarfjord [N] 194 B2
Akkavare [S] 190 H3
Akkaya [TR] 150 H5
Akkent [TR] 152 G4
Akköy [TR] 152 D6
Akköy [TR] 152 F4
Akland [N] 164 F4
Akli [H] 76 A2
Akmeşe [TR] 150 G3
Akmyane [LT] 198 C6
Aknīste [LV] 198 F6
Akonlahti [FIN] 196 G5
Akonpohja [FIN] 188 F5
Akoúmia [GR] 140 D5
Akpınar [TR] 150 H5
Åkra [N] 170 B5
Akrai [I] 126 G5
Akraifia [GR] 134 B5
Akraífnio [GR] 134 B5
Akranes [IS] 192 A2
Akrapol [TR] 152 C2
Åkre [N] 182 C6
Åkrehamn [N] 164 A2
Akr. Évinos [GR] 132 E5
Akrogiáli [GR] 130 C4
Akropótamos [GR] 130 C4
Akrōtíri [CY] 154 F6
Akrotíri [GR] 138 F5
Akrovoúni [GR] 130 D3
Aksakal [TR] 150 D5
Aksakovo [BG] 148 F2
Akşar [TR] 152 G6
Aksaz [TR] 150 C4
Aksaz [TR] 152 F2
Aksaz Kaplica [TR] 152 F4
Aksdal [N] 164 A1
Aksla [N] 180 C6
Aktsyabrski [BY] 202 C6
Åkullsjön [S] 196 A5
Akureyri [IS] 192 C2
Akyaka [TR] 154 F4
Akyazı [TR] 150 H3
Akyazı [TR] 154 G3
Ål [N] 170 F3
Ala [I] 72 C5
Ala [S] 168 G5
Alaattin [TR] 152 G5
Alabanda [TR] 152 E6
Alabodarna [S] 156 H2
Alacadağ [TR] 154 H2
Alacant / Alicante [E] 104 E2
Alacat [TR] 150 E5
Alaçatı [TR] 134 H5
Alà dei Sardi [I] 118 D3
Ala di Stura [I] 70 C5
Aladzha Manastir [BG] 148 G2
Alaejos [E] 88 D2
Alagna-Valsésia [I] 70 E3
A Lagoa / Campo Lameiro [E] 78 B4
Alagón [E] 86 H4
Alagón [E] 90 E3
Alahärmä [FIN] 186 C2
Ala-Honkajoki [FIN] 186 C6
Alajärvi [FIN] 186 D2
Alajärvi [FIN] 196 F3
Alajoki [FIN] 194 D5
Alajoki [FIN] 196 D5
Alakylä [FIN] 194 C7
Alakylä [FIN] 196 D3
Alalampi [RUS] 188 H4
Ala-Livo [FIN] 196 E3
Alamaa [FIN] 186 F2
Alameda [E] 102 C3
Alamedilla [E] 102 F3
Alanäs [S] 190 E5
Alancık [TR] 152 C1
Åland [S] 168 D1
Alandroal [P] 94 E1
Ålandsbro [S] 184 F4
Alange [E] 94 H2
Alanís [E] 94 H4
Alanta [LT] 200 G4
Alap [H] 76 B3
Alapitkä [FIN] 188 C1
Alaquàs [E] 98 E4
Alaraz [E] 88 D4
Alarcón [E] 98 B3
Alaşehir [TR] 152 E4
Ålåsen [S] 190 E6
Alássio [I] 108 G4
Alastaro [FIN] 176 E3
Ala-Temmes [FIN] 196 D4
Alatoz [E] 98 C5
Alatri [I] 116 C6
Alatskivi [EST] 198 F2
Alattu [RUS] 188 H4
Ala-Valli [FIN] 186 C4
Alavattnet [S] 190 E5
Alaveteli / Nedervetil [FIN] 196 C6
Ala-Vieksi [FIN] 196 F5
Alavieska [FIN] 196 C5
Ala-Vuokki [FIN] 196 F4
Alavus [FIN] 186 D4
Alba [I] 108 G2
Alba Adriatica [I] 116 D3
Albacete [E] 98 B5
Albaching [D] 60 F4
Albacken [S] 184 D3
Alba de Tormes [E] 88 C3
Ålbæk [DK] 160 E2
Alba Fucens [I] 116 C5
Albaida [E] 98 E6
Albaina [E] 82 G5
Alba Iulia [RO] 204 C4
Albaladejo [E] 96 G5
Albalate de Cinca [E] 90 G4
Albalate del Arzobispo [E] 90 E5
Albalate de las Nogueras [E] 98 B1
Albalate de Zorita [E] 98 A1
Alban [F] 106 C3
Albánchez [E] 102 H4
Albanella [I] 120 F4
Albano di Lucania [I] 120 H4
Albano Laziale [I] 116 A6
Albaredo d'Adige [I] 110 F1
Albarella [I] 110 H2
Albares [E] 88 H6
Albarracín [E] 98 D1
Albarracín, Cuevas de- [E] 98 D1
Albatana [E] 104 C1
Albena [BG] 148 G2
Albenga [I] 108 G4
Albens [F] 70 A3
Albentosa [E] 98 E3
Alberga [S] 168 B3
Albergaria-a-Velha [P] 80 B5
Alberic [E] 98 E5
Albernoa [P] 94 D3
Albero Alto [E] 90 F3
Alberobello [I] 122 E3
Alberoni [I] 110 H1
Albersdorf [D] 18 E2
Albert [F] 28 E4
Albertacce [F] 114 B3
Albertirsa [H] 76 D1
Albertville [F] 70 B3
Albeşti [RO] 148 G1
Albi [F] 106 B2
Albier Montrond [F] 70 B5
Albignasego [I] 110 G1
Albinea [I] 110 E3
Albissola Marina [I] 108 H3
Albo [F] 114 C2
Albocácer / Albocàsser [E] 98 G2
Albocàsser / Albocácer [E] 98 G2
Alböke [S] 162 G4
Alborala / Alboraya [E] 98 E4
Alboraya / Alboraia [E] 98 E4
Alborea [E] 98 C4
Albox [E] 102 H4
Albrechtice nad Vltavou [CZ] 48 F6
Albrechtsburg [A] 62 D4
Albudeite [E] 104 C3
Albufeira [P] 94 C5
Albujón [E] 104 C4
Albuñol [E] 102 E5
Albuñuelas [E] 102 D4
Alburquerque [E] 86 F5
Alby [S] 162 G6
Alby [S] 184 C4
Alcácer do Sal [P] 94 C1
Alcáçovas [P] 94 D2
Alcadozo [E] 98 B6
Alcafores [P] 86 G3
Alcaide [E] 102 H3
Alcalá de Chivert / Alcalá de Xivert [E] 98 G2
Alcalá de Guadaira [E] 94 G6
Alcalá de Henares [E] 88 G6
Alcalá de la Selva [E] 98 E2
Alcalá del Júcar [E] 98 C5
Alcalá de los Gazules [E] 100 G4
Alcalá del Río [E] 94 G6
Alcalá del Valle [E] 102 A3
Alcalá de Xivert / Alcalá de Chivert [E] 98 G2
Alcalá la Real [E] 102 D3
Álcamo [I] 126 C2
Alcanar [E] 92 A6
Alcanede [P] 86 C4
Alcanena [P] 86 C4
Alcañices [E] 80 G4
Alcañiz [E] 90 F6
Alcántara [E] 86 G4
Alcantara, Gole d'- [I] 124 A8
Alcantarilla [E] 104 C3
Alcantud [E] 90 B6
Alcaracejos [E] 96 C5
Alcaraz [E] 96 H6
Alcaria Ruiva [P] 94 D4
Alcarràs [E] 90 H5
Alçaşehir [TR] 152 G1
Alcaudete [E] 102 D2
Alcaudete de la Jara [E] 96 D1
Alcázar de San Juan [E] 96 G3
Alçitepe [TR] 130 H5
Alcobaça [P] 86 C3
Alcoba de los Montes [E] 96 D3
Alcobendas [E] 88 F5
Alcobertas [P] 86 C3
Alcocèber / Alcossebre [E] 98 G3
Alcocer [E] 90 A6
Alcochete [P] 86 B5
Alcoentre [P] 86 B4
Alcofra [P] 80 C5
Alcoi / Alcoy [E] 104 E1
Alcolea [E] 102 F5
Alcolea del Pinar [E] 90 B4
Alcolea del Río [E] 94 H5
Alconchel [E] 94 F2
Alcora / l'Alcora [E] 98 F3
Alcorcón [E] 88 F6
Alcorisa [E] 90 F6
Alcossebre / Alcocèber [E] 98 G3
Alcoutim [P] 94 D5
Alcover [E] 92 C4
Alcoy / Alcoi [E] 104 E1
Alcubierre [E] 90 F3
Alcubilla de Avellaneda [E] 88 H2
Alcubillas [E] 96 G5
Alcublas [E] 98 E3
Alcúdia [E] 104 F4
Alcudia de Guadix [E] 102 F4
Alcuéscar [E] 86 H6
Alda [E] 82 H5
Aldeacentenera [E] 96 B1
Aldeadávila de la Ribera [E] 80 F5
Aldea del Cano [E] 86 H6
Aldea del Fresno [E] 88 E5
Aldea del Rey [E] 96 E5
Aldea de Trujillo [E] 96 B1
Aldealpozo [E] 90 C3
Aldeanueva de Ebro [E] 84 A5
Aldeaquemada [E] 96 F6
Aldeatejada [E] 88 C3
Aldeavieja [E] 88 E4
Aldeburgh [GB] 14 G3
Aldeia da Ponte [P] 86 G2
Aldeia do Bispo [P] 86 G2
Aldeias das Neves [E] 94 C4
Aldenhoven [D] 30 F4
Aldernäset [S] 190 F5
Aldershot [GB] 14 D4
Aldinci [MK] 128 E1
Aldtsier [NL] 16 F2
Åled [S] 162 B5
Aledo [E] 104 B3
Alegranza [E] 100 E5
Alekovo [BG] 148 C3
Alekovo [BG] 148 E1
Aleksandrovac [SRB] 146 C1
Aleksandrovo [BG] 148 B3
Aleksandrów [PL] 38 A3
Aleksandrów [PL] 38 B6
Aleksandrów [PL] 52 F2
Aleksandrów Kujawski [PL] 36 F1
Aleksandrów Łódzki [PL] 36 G4
Aleksin [RUS] 202 F4
Aleksinac [SRB] 146 D3
Ålem [S] 162 G4
Alemdağ [TR] 150 F2
Ålen [N] 182 C3
Alençon [F] 26 F6
Alenquer [P] 86 B4
Aléria [F] 114 C4
Aléria [F] 114 C4
Alès [F] 106 F3
Áles [I] 118 C5
Aleşd [RO] 204 B4
Alessandria [I] 70 F6
Alessandria del Carretto [I] 122 D6
Alessándria della Rocca [I] 126 D3
Ålesund [N] 180 C3
Alexándreia [GR] 128 G4
Alexandria [RO] 148 B1
Alexandria Troas [TR] 130 H6
Alexandroúpoli [GR] 130 G3
Alf [D] 44 G2
Alfafar [E] 98 E5
Alfaites [P] 86 G2
Alfajarín [E] 90 E4
Alfambra [E] 98 E1
Alfambras [P] 94 B4
Alfândenga da Fé [P] 80 F4
Alfano [I] 120 G5
Alfarela de Jales [P] 80 E4
Alfaro [E] 84 B5
Alfarràs [E] 90 H4
Alfas [E] 104 F2
Alfatar [BG] 148 E1
Alfedena [I] 116 D6
Alfeizerão [P] 86 B3
Alfeld [D] 32 F3
Alfeld [D] 46 H5
Alfena [P] 80 C4
Alfés [E] 90 H5
Alfonsine [I] 110 G3
Alford [GB] 6 F6
Alforja [E] 92 B4
Alfoten [N] 180 C5
Alfoz [E] 78 E2
Alfreton [GB] 10 F5
Alfstad [N] 170 G5
Alfta [S] 174 D2
Algaida [E] 104 E5
Algajola [F] 114 B3
Algar [E] 100 G4
Algar [E] 104 H5
Älgarås [S] 166 F4
Ålgård [N] 164 B5
Ålgård [N] 164 B3
Algarinejo [E] 102 D3
Algarra [E] 98 D3
Algatocín [E] 100 H4
Algeciras [E] 100 G5
Algemesí [E] 98 E5
Älgered [S] 184 E5
Alghero [I] 118 B3
Älghult [S] 162 F4
Alginet [E] 98 E5
Algodonales [E] 100 H3
Algodor [P] 94 D4
Algora [E] 90 A5
Algoso [P] 80 F4
Älgsjö [S] 190 G5
Alguazas [E] 104 C3
Algutsrum [S] 162 G5
Algyő [H] 76 E4
Alhama de Almería [E] 102 G5
Alhama de Aragón [E] 90 C4
Alhama de Granada [E] 102 D4
Alhama de Murcia [E] 104 B3
Alhambra [E] 96 G5
Alhamillo [E] 96 C4
Alhaurín de la Torre [E] 102 B5
Alhaurín el Grande [E] 102 B4
Alhojärvi [FIN] 186 F5
Ålholm Slot [DK] 20 B1
Ålhus [N] 180 C6
Alía [E] 96 C2
Ália [I] 126 D3
Aliaga [E] 98 F1
Aliağa [TR] 152 C3
Alíartos [GR] 134 A5
Alibeyli [TR] 152 D3
Alibunar [SRB] 142 H2
Alibunar [SRB] 204 B5
Aliç [TR] 150 B3
Alicante / Alacant [E] 104 E2
Alicudi Porto [I] 124 A5
Åliden [S] 196 A4
Alife [I] 120 E2
Alifuatpaşa [TR] 150 G3
Alija del Infantado [E] 80 H3
Alijó [P] 80 E4
Alíkampos [GR] 140 C4
Alikanás [GR] 136 A2
Alil Abasi [MK] 128 G1
Alimena [I] 126 E3
Alinci [MK] 128 E3
Alinda [TR] 152 E6
Alingsås [S] 162 B1
Alino [BG] 146 F5
Alinyà [E] 92 D2
Aliseda [E] 86 G5
Alistráti [GR] 130 C3
Ali Terme [I] 124 B7
Alivéri [GR] 134 C6
Aljaraque [E] 94 E5
Aljezur [P] 94 B4
Aljinovići [SRB] 146 A3
Aljubarrota [P] 86 C3
Aljucén [E] 86 G6
Aljustrel [P] 94 C3
Alkmaar [NL] 16 D3
Alkotz [E] 84 B3
Alkoven [A] 62 B4
Alkpınar [TR] 150 C2
Alksniupiai [LT] 200 F4
Alkvettern [S] 166 G2
Állai [I] 118 C5
Allaines [F] 42 E5
Allainville [F] 42 E4
Allan [F] 68 F6
Allanche [F] 68 C3
Alland [A] 62 E5
Allariz [E] 78 C5
Allauch [F] 108 B5
Alleen [N] 164 C5
Alleghe [I] 72 E4
Allejaur [S] 190 G3
Allemont [F] 68 H5
Allenbach [D] 44 G2
Allentsteig [A] 62 D3
Allepuz [E] 98 E1
Aller-Heiligen [D] 58 F1
Allersberg [D] 46 G6
Allershausen [D] 60 E3
Allerum [S] 156 H1
Alleuze, Château d'- [F] 68 C4
Allevard [F] 70 A4
Allgunnen [S] 162 F4
Allihies [IRL] 4 A5
Allingåbro [DK] 160 E5
Allinge [DK] 158 E4
Allo [E] 84 A4
Alloa [GB] 8 E3
Ålloluokta [S] 192 G6
Allonnes [F] 42 E5
Allonnes [F] 54 E2
Allonö [S] 168 B5
Allos [F] 108 D3
Alloue [F] 54 F5
Ållsjön [S] 184 E2
Allstedt [D] 34 B5
Almacelles [E] 90 H4
Almada [P] 86 B5
Almadén [E] 96 C4
Almadén de la Plata [E] 94 G5
Almadenes, Cañón de los- [E] 104 B2
Almadenojos [E] 96 D4
Almadrones [E] 90 A5
Almagreira [P] 100 E4
Almagro [E] 96 F4
Almancil [P] 94 C5
Almandoz [E] 84 B3
Almansa [E] 98 D6
Almanza [E] 82 C4
Almaraz [E] 88 B6
Almargen [E] 102 B3
Almarza [E] 90 B2
Almås [N] 182 C2
Almásfüzitő [H] 64 B6
Almassora / Almazora [E] 98 F3
Almazán [E] 90 B3
Almazora / Almassora [E] 98 F3
Almedina [E] 96 G5
Almeida [P] 80 E6
Almeida de Sayago [E] 80 G5
Almeirim [P] 86 C4
Almelo [NL] 16 G4
Almenar [E] 90 H4
Almenara [E] 98 F4
Almenara [E] 102 B1
Almenara de Tormes [E] 80 G6
Almenar de Soria [E] 90 C3
Almendinilla [E] 102 D3
Almendra [P] 80 E5
Almendral [E] 94 G2
Almendralejo [E] 94 G2
Almenno S. Salvatore [I] 70 H4
Almere [NL] 16 E4
Almería [E] 102 G5
Almerimar [E] 102 F6
Almesåkra [S] 162 D2
Älmestad [S] 162 C1
Älmhult [S] 162 D5
Almodôvar [P] 94 C4
Almodóvar del Campo [E] 96 E4
Almodóvar del Pinar [E] 98 C3
Almodóvar del Río [E] 102 B1
Almogía [E] 102 C4
Almograve [P] 94 B3
Almoharín [E] 86 H6
Almonaster la Real [E] 94 F4
Almonte [E] 94 F6
Almoradí [E] 104 D3
Almoraima [E] 100 G5
Almorox [E] 88 E6
Almourol [P] 86 D4
Almsele [S] 190 F5
Älmsta-Väddö [S] 168 E1
Almudévar [E] 90 F3
Almuñécar [E] 102 D5
Almunge [S] 168 D1
Almuradiel [E] 96 F5
Almvik [S] 162 G2
Almyró [GR] 136 D4
Almyropótamos [GR] 134 D5
Almyrós [GR] 132 H3
Alness [GB] 6 E4
Alnwick [GB] 8 G5
Aloja [LV] 198 E4
Alol' [RUS] 198 H5
Alónnisos [GR] 134 C3
Álora [E] 102 B4
Alosno [E] 94 E5
Alost (Aalst) [B] 28 H2
Alozaina [E] 102 B4
Alp [E] 92 E2
Alpalhão [P] 86 E4
Alpbach [A] 60 E6
Alpedrinha [P] 86 F3
Alpe du Grand Serre [F] 68 H5
Alpen [D] 30 G2
Alpengarten [D] 60 D6
Alpera [E] 98 C5
Alphen-aan den Rijn [NL] 16 D5
Alpiarça [P] 86 C4
Alpirsbach [D] 58 F2
Alportel [P] 94 C5
Alpua [FIN] 196 D5
Alpuente [E] 98 D3
Alpullu [TR] 150 B2
Alqueva [P] 94 E3
Alquézar [E] 90 G3
Als [DK] 160 E4
Alsager [GB] 10 D5
Alsasua / Altsasu [E] 82 H5
Alsen [S] 182 G1
Alsenz [D] 46 B4
Alsfeld [D] 46 D1
Ålshult [S] 162 D5
Alsleben [D] 34 B4
Alsø [DK] 160 F6
Alsóörs [H] 76 A2
Alsótold [H] 64 D5
Alsózsolca [H] 64 F5
Ålstad [N] 192 D5
Ålstad [S] 158 C3
Alstahaug [N] 190 D2
Alstätte [D] 16 G5
Alsterbro [S] 162 F4
Alstermo [S] 162 F4
Alston [GB] 8 F6
Alsunga [LV] 198 B5
Alsvåg [N] 192 D3
Alsvik [N] 192 D6
Alta [N] 194 B3
Altafulla [E] 92 C5
Altamira, Cuevas de- [E] 82 E3
Altamura [I] 122 D3
Altarejos [E] 98 B2
Altaussee [A] 62 A6
Altavilla Silentina [I] 120 F4
Altdahn [D] 44 H4
Altdorf [CH] 58 F6
Altdorf [D] 46 G5
Alt Duvenstedt [D] 18 F2
Altea [E] 104 F2
Altedo [I] 110 F3
Alteidet [N] 192 H1
Altena [D] 32 C5
Altenahr [D] 30 G5
Altenau [D] 32 G4
Altenberg [D] 48 E2
Altenberge [D] 16 H5
Altenberger Dom [D] 30 H4
Altenburg [A] 62 D3
Altenburg [D] 34 C6
Altenfelden [A] 62 B3
Altenglan [D] 44 H3
Altenhundem [D] 32 C5
Altenkirchen [D] 20 D1
Altenkirchen [D] 32 C6
Altenklingen [CH] 58 G4
Altenmarkt [A] 62 C6
Altenmarkt [A] 72 H1
Altenmarkt [D] 60 F5
Altenstadt [D] 60 B4
Altenstadt [D] 60 D5
Altensteig [D] 50 C1
Altentreptow [D] 20 D4
Altenwalde [D] 18 D3
Alter do Chão [P] 86 E5
Alteren [N] 190 E2
Althegnenberg [D] 60 D4
Altheim [A] 60 H4
Althofen [A] 74 B2
Alti [TR] 154 B1
Altimir [BG] 146 G3
Altınoluk [TR] 152 B1
Altınova [TR] 150 F3
Altınova [TR] 152 B2
Altıntaş [TR] 152 H2
Altınyayla [TR] 154 G1
Altipiani di Arcinazzo [I] 116 B6
Altkirch [F] 58 D4
Altlandsberg [D] 34 E2
Altmörbitz [D] 34 C6
Altmünster [A] 62 A5
Altnaharra [GB] 6 E3
Alto de los Leones de Castilla [E] 88 F4
Altomonte [I] 124 D3
Alton [GB] 14 D4
Altopascio [I] 110 E5
Altorricón [E] 90 H4
Altötting [D] 60 G4
Altrier [L] 44 F2
Alt Ruppin [D] 20 C6
Altsasu / Alsasua [E] 82 H5
Alt Schadow [D] 34 F3
Altshausen [D] 58 H3
Altstätten [CH] 58 H5
Alttajärvi [S] 192 G5
Altuna [S] 168 C1
Altura [E] 98 E3
Altwarp [D] 20 E4
Altwindeck [D] 58 F1
Alūksne [LV] 198 F4
Ålum [DK] 160 D5
Ålund [S] 196 A4
Alunda [S] 168 D1
Aluokta [S] 192 F6
Alupka [UA] 204 H4
Aluste [EST] 198 E2
Alvaiázere [P] 86 D3
Alvajärvi [FIN] 186 F1
Alvalade [P] 94 C3
Älvan [S] 166 H5
Älvängen [S] 160 H1
Alvastra [S] 166 G6
Alvdal [N] 182 B5
Älvdalen [S] 172 F2
Alvechurch [GB] 12 H1
Alverca do Ribatejo [P] 86 B5
Alversund [N] 170 B3
Alvesta [S] 162 D4
Alvestad [N] 164 A2
Älvhem [S] 160 H1
Alvignac [F] 66 G4
Alvik [N] 170 C4
Alvik [S] 172 G4
Alvik [S] 196 B3
Alvito [I] 116 C6
Alvito [P] 94 D2
Älvkarleby [S] 174 E4
Alvor [P] 94 B5
Älvros [S] 182 E6
Älvros [S] 182 G5
Älvsbacka [S] 166 F2
Älvsbyn [S] 196 A3
Älvsered [S] 162 B3
Älvsund [S] 184 E5
Ålvundeid [N] 180 F3
Alyekshytsy [BY] 24 G5
Alykí [GR] 130 E4
Alykí [GR] 130 E4
Alykí [GR] 138 E3
Alytus [LT] 24 G2
Alzenall [D] 46 D3
Alzey [D] 46 B4
Alzira [E] 98 E5
Alzon [F] 106 E3
Alzonne [F] 106 B4
Åmådalen [S] 172 G2
Amadora [P] 86 B5
Åmål [S] 166 D4
Amalfi [I] 120 E4
Amaliáda [GR] 136 C2
Amaliápoli [GR] 132 H3
Amalo [GR] 138 G1
Amance [F] 58 B3
Amancey [F] 58 B5
Amandola [I] 116 C2
Amantea [I] 124 D5
Amantia [AL] 128 B5
Amarante [P] 80 C4
Amárantos [GR] 132 F3
Amărăştii de Sus [RO] 146 G2
Amareleja [P] 94 E3
Amári [GR] 140 D5
Amárynthos [GR] 134 C5
Amatrice [I] 116 C3
Amay [B] 30 E5
Ambarès [F] 66 D3
Ambazac [F] 54 G6
Amberg [D] 46 H5
Ambérieu-en-Bugey [F] 68 G2
Ambert [F] 68 D3
Ambiörnarp [S] 162 B3
Ambjörby [S] 172 E4
Ambla [EST] 198 E1
Amble [GB] 8 G5
Ambleside [GB] 10 D2
Amboise [F] 54 G2
Ämbra [EST] 198 E2
Ambrières [F] 26 E5
Åmdal [N] 164 D5
Ameixial [P] 94 C4
Amel [B] 30 F6
Amélia [I] 116 A3
Amélie-les-Bains [F] 92 F2
Amelinghausen [D] 18 F5
Amendolara [I] 122 D6
Amer [E] 92 F3
A Merca [E] 78 C5
Amerongen [NL] 16 E5
Amersfoort [NL] 16 E5
Amersham [GB] 14 E3
Amesbury [GB] 12 G4
A Mezquita [E] 78 E6
Amfiáreio [GR] 134 C5
Amfíkleia [GR] 132 G4
Amfilochía [GR] 132 D4
Amfípoli [GR] 130 C4
Ámfissa [GR] 132 G5
Amiens [F] 28 E5
Åmilden [S] 190 H4
Åminne [S] 168 G4
Amiternum [I] 116 C4
Amlach [A] 72 F2
Åmli [N] 164 E3
Åmli [N] 164 E4
Amlwch [GB] 10 B3
Ammanford [GB] 12 E2
Ämmänsaari [FIN] 196 F4
Ammarnäs [S] 190 F2
Åmmeberg [S] 166 G4
Ammersricht [D] 48 B5
Ammóchostos (Gazimağusa) [CY] 154 G5
Ammótopos [GR] 132 D3
Ammoudára [GR] 140 E4
Ammoudára [GR] 140 F5
Åmnes [N] 164 F2
Amorbach [D] 46 D4
Amoreira, Acueducto de- [P] 86 E6
Amorgós [GR] 138 G4
Amorosi [I] 120 E2
Åmot [N] 164 E1
Åmot [N] 164 G1
Åmot [N] 170 G4
Åmot [N] 170 H3
Åmot [N] 172 C2
Åmot [S] 174 D3
Åmotfors [S] 166 D1
Åmotsdal [N] 164 E1
Amou [F] 84 D2
Ampelákia [GR] 130 H1
Ampelákia [GR] 132 G1
Ampelikó [GR] 134 H2
Ampelónas [GR] 132 G1
Ampezzo [I] 72 F4

Ampfing [D] 60 F4
Amphion [F] 70 B2
Amplepuis [F] 68 F2
Amposta [E] 92 A6
Ampudia [E] 82 C6
Ampuero [E] 82 F3
Ampuis [F] 68 F3
Ampus [F] 108 D4
Amriswil [CH] 58 H4
Am See [A] 72 C2
Amsele [S] 190 H5
Amsteg [CH] 70 F1
Amsterdam [NL] 16 D4
Amstetten [A] 62 C4
Amtoft [DK] 160 C4
Amurrio [E] 82 G4
Amvrosía [GR] 130 F3
Amygdaleónas [GR] 130 D3
Amygdaliá [GR] 132 G5
Amýkles [GR] 136 E4
Amýntaio [GR] 128 F4
Amzacea [RO] 148 G1
Anadia [P] 80 B6
Anáfi [GR] 138 F5
Anafonítria [GR] 136 A2
Anagni [I] 116 B6
Anáktora Néstoros [GR] 136 C4
Análipsi [GR] 138 H4
Anamourion [TR] 154 F4
Anamur [TR] 154 F4
Anan'ïv [UA] 204 G2
Anárgyroi [GR] 128 E5
Anarráchi [GR] 128 E5
Anascaul [IRL] 4 B4
Ånäset [S] 196 A5
Åna-Sira [N] 164 B5
Anastazewo [PL] 36 E2
Änätinpää [FIN] 196 G4
Anatolí [GR] 132 G1
Anatolikó [GR] 128 F5
Anávra [GR] 132 F3
Anávra [GR] 132 G3
Anávyssos [GR] 136 H1
Anaya [E] 88 F4
An Cabhán / Cavan [IRL] 2 E4
Anc. Batterie [F] 108 D2
Ance [LV] 198 C4
Ancenis [F] 40 G6
Ancerville [F] 44 C5
An Charraig / Carrick [IRL] 2 D2
An Cheathrú Rua / Carraroe [IRL] 2 B5
An Chloich Mhór / Cloghmore [IRL] 2 B3
Anchuras [E] 96 D2
An Clochán Liath / Dunglow [IRL] 2 E2
An Coireán / Waterville [IRL] 4 A4
Ancona [I] 112 C6
Ancy-le-Franc [F] 56 F2
Anda [N] 180 C5
An Daingean / Dingle [IRL] 4 A3
Andalo [I] 72 C4
Åndalsnes [N] 180 E3
Andåsen [S] 182 G5
Andau [A] 62 G6
Ändebol [S] 168 B4
Andebu [N] 164 H3
Andechs [D] 60 D5
Andelot [F] 44 D6
Andenes [N] 192 E2
Andenne [B] 30 D5
Andermatt [CH] 70 F1
Andernach [D] 30 H6
Andernos-les-Bains [F] 66 B3
Andersfors [S] 196 A5
Anderslöv [S] 158 C3
Anderstorp [S] 162 C3
Andijk [NL] 16 E3
Andilla [E] 98 E3
Andız [TR] 150 G6
Andocs [H] 76 A3
Andolsheim [F] 58 E3
Andornaktálya [H] 64 E5
Andorno Micca [I] 70 E4
Andorra [E] 90 F6
Andorra la Vella [AND] 84 H6
Andover [GB] 12 H4
Andrade, Castillo de– [E] 78 D2
Andraitx [E] 104 D5
Andravída [GR] 136 B1
Andreapol' [RUS] 202 D3
Andrespol [PL] 36 G4
Andretta [I] 120 G3
Andrézieux-Bouthéon [F] 68 E3
Ándria [I] 122 C2
Andriake [TR] 154 H3
Andrijevica [MNE] 146 A5
Andrítsaina [GR] 136 D3
Ándros [GR] 134 E6
Androússa [GR] 136 D4
Andrychów [PL] 50 G4
Andselv [N] 192 F3
Andújar [E] 102 D1
Anduze [F] 106 F3
An Eachléim / Aghleam [IRL] 2 B3
Ånebjør [N] 164 D3
Åneby [N] 172 B5
Aneby [S] 162 E2
Ånes [N] 180 F1
Anet [F] 42 E3
An Fhairche / Clonbur [IRL] 2 C4
Anfo [I] 72 B5
Anga [S] 168 G4
Änge [S] 182 G1
Ånge [S] 184 C4
Änge [S] 190 G2
Ängebo [S] 184 D6
Angeja [P] 80 B5
Ängelholm [S] 156 H1
Angeli [FIN] 194 C4
Angelókastro [GR] 132 E5
Angelókastro [GR] 136 F2
Angelsberg [S] 168 B1
Ängelsfors [S] 174 D4
Angelstad [S] 162 C5
Angenstein [CH] 58 E4
Anger [A] 74 E1
Angermünde [D] 20 E6
Angern [A] 62 G4
Angers [F] 40 H6
Ängersjö [S] 182 G6
Ängersjö [S] 184 H1
Angerville [F] 42 E5
Ängesan [S] 194 B8
Ängesbyn [S] 196 B3
Anghelo Ruiu, Necropoli– [I] 118 B3
Anghiari [I] 110 G6
Angiari [I] 110 F1
Anglès [E] 92 F3
Angles-sur-l'Anglin [F] 54 F4
Anglet [F] 84 C2
Anglona [LV] 198 G6
Anglure [F] 44 A5
Ango, Manoir d'– [F] 28 C4
Angoulême [F] 66 E1
Angra do Heroísmo [P] 100 D3
Ångskär [S] 174 F4
Ängsö [S] 168 C2
Angueira [P] 80 G4
Angües [E] 90 G3
Anguiano [E] 90 B1
Anguillara Sabazia [I] 114 H5
Anguillara Veneta [I] 110 G2
Angulo [E] 82 G4
Angvika [N] 180 F2
Anholt [DK] 160 G5
Aniane [F] 106 E4
Aniche [F] 28 F4
Anina [RO] 204 B5
Anıtkaya [TR] 152 H2
Anjala [FIN] 178 C3
Anjalankoski [FIN] 178 C3
Anjos [P] 100 E3
Anjum [NL] 16 F1
Ankaran [SLO] 72 H6
Ankarede [S] 190 E4
Ankarsrum [S] 162 G2
Ankarvattnet [S] 190 E4
Ankenesstrand [N] 192 E4
Anklam [D] 20 D4
Ankum [D] 32 D1
Anlezy [F] 56 E4
Ånn [S] 182 E2
Anna [EST] 198 E2
Annaberg [A] 60 H6
Annaberg [A] 62 D5
Annaberg-Buchholz [D] 48 D2
Annadalsvagen [N] 190 D3
Annalong [NIR] 2 G4
Annan [GB] 8 E5
Anna Paulowna [NL] 16 D3
An Nás / Naas [IRL] 2 F6
Anneberg [S] 160 H2
Anneberg [S] 162 E2
Annecy [F] 70 B3
Annefors [S] 174 D2
Annelund [S] 162 B1
Annemasse [F] 70 B2
Annenheim [A] 74 A3
Annerstad [S] 162 C5
Annestown [IRL] 4 E5
Annonay [F] 68 F4
Annopol [PL] 52 D1
Annot [F] 108 D3
Annoux [F] 56 F2
Annweiler [D] 46 B5
Anógeia [GR] 140 E4
Ánoixi [GR] 132 E1
Áno Kalentíni [GR] 132 D3
Áno Kastrítsi [GR] 132 F6
Áno Merá [GR] 138 E2
Anópoli [GR] 140 C5
Áno Sagkri [GR] 138 F3
Áno Sýros [GR] 138 D2
Anould [F] 58 D2
Añover de Tajo [E] 96 F1
Áno Viánnos [GR] 140 F5
Áno Vrontoú [GR] 130 C2
Anquela del Ducado [E] 90 B5
An Rinn / Ringville [IRL] 4 E5
Ans [DK] 160 D6
Ansager [DK] 156 B2
Ansarve [S] 168 F5
Ansbach [D] 46 F5
Anse [F] 68 F2
Ansedónia [I] 114 F4
Anserall [E] 92 D1
Anseremme [B] 30 D6
Ansfelden [A] 62 B4
Ansião [P] 86 D2
Ansó [E] 84 D4
An Spidéal / Spiddal [IRL] 2 B5
Anstad [N] 180 F5
Anstey [GB] 10 F6
Anstruther [GB] 8 F3
Ansvar [S] 194 D8
Antagnod [I] 70 D3
Antanarav [LT] 200 G4
Antandros [TR] 134 H1
Antas [P] 80 D5
Antas, Tempio di– [I] 118 B6
Antas de Ulla [E] 78 D3
Antegnate [I] 70 H5
Anten [S] 160 H1
Antequera [E] 102 C4
Anterselva / Antholz [I] 72 E2
Antey St. André [I] 70 D3
Anthéor [F] 108 E5
Anthí [GR] 130 B3
Antholz / Anterselva [I] 72 E2
Anthótopos [GR] 132 G3
Antibes [F] 108 E5
Antigonea [AL] 128 C6
Antigua [E] 100 E6
Antigua Bilbilis [E] 90 D4
Antigüedad [E] 88 G1
Antíkýra [GR] 132 H5
Antimáchia [GR] 154 B2
An Tinbhear Mór / Arklow [IRL] 4 G4
Antiochia [TR] 152 F5
Antíparos [GR] 138 E3
Antírrio [GR] 132 F5
Ántissa [GR] 134 G2
Ántissa [GR] 134 G2
Antjärn [S] 184 F4
Antnäs [S] 196 B3
Anton [BG] 148 A4
Antonin [PL] 36 E5
Antoniów [PL] 52 D1
Antonovo [BG] 148 D3
Antopal' [BY] 38 H2
Antraigues [F] 68 E5
Antrain [F] 26 D5
Antrim [NIR] 2 G3
Antrodoco [I] 116 B4
Antsla [EST] 198 F3
Anttila [FIN] 196 F5
Anttis [S] 194 B7
Anttola [FIN] 188 D6
Anttola [FIN] 188 F5
Antwerpen (Anvers) [B] 30 C3
An Uaimh / Navan [IRL] 2 F5
Anundshögen [S] 168 C2
Anvers (Antwerpen) [B] 30 C3
Anvin [F] 28 E3
Anykščiai [LT] 200 G4
Anzi [I] 120 H4
Anzio [I] 120 A1
Aoiz / Agoitz [E] 84 C4
Aosta / Aoste [I] 70 D4
Aoste / Aosta [I] 70 D4
Apaj [H] 76 C2
Apamea [TR] 150 E4
Åpåsdal [N] 164 D5
Apátfalva [H] 76 F4
Apatin [MNE] 204 A5
Apatin [SRB] 76 C6
Apchon [F] 68 B3
Ape [LV] 198 F4
Apécchio [I] 110 H6
Apeírathos [GR] 138 F3
Apeldoorn [NL] 16 F5
Apen [D] 18 C5
Apensen [D] 18 F4
Aperlai [TR] 154 H3
Aphrodisias [TR] 152 F5
Apice [I] 120 F2
Apinac [F] 68 E3
Aplared [S] 162 B2
A Pobra de Brollón / Puebla del Brollón [E] 78 D4
A Pobra de Navia [E] 78 E4
A Pobra de Trives [E] 78 D5
Apoíkia [GR] 134 E6
Apolakkiá [GR] 154 C4
Apolda [D] 34 B6
Apollo Aléo, Tempio di– [I] 124 F4
Apóllon [GR] 138 F3
Apollonia [AL] 128 A4
Apollonía [GR] 130 D4
Apollonía [GR] 138 D3
Apollonía [GR] 138 D4
Apollonia [TR] 150 F4
Apollonia [TR] 152 D2
Apollonia [TR] 154 G3
A Pontenova [E] 78 E2
Apostolove [UA] 204 F3
Apothicairerie, Grotte de l'– [F] 40 C5
Äppelbo [S] 172 F4
Appelhülsen [D] 16 H6
Appenweier [D] 44 H6
Appenzell [CH] 58 H5
Appiano / Eppan [I] 72 D3
Appingedam [NL] 16 H2
Appleby-in-Westmorland [GB] 10 E1
Apremont, Gorges d'– [F] 42 F5
Aprica [I] 72 B4
Apricena [I] 116 G6
Aprigliano [I] 124 D4
Aprilia [I] 116 A6
Aprilovo [BG] 148 D3
Apróhomok [H] 64 G4
Ápsalos [GR] 128 F4
Apt [F] 108 B3
Áptera [GR] 140 C4
Àquila [CH] 70 G2
Aquileia [I] 72 G5
Aquilonia [I] 120 G3
Aquino [I] 120 C1
Ar [S] 168 G3
Arabba [I] 72 E3
Araburg [A] 62 E5
Araceli [E] 102 C3
Aracena [E] 94 F4
Aráchova [GR] 132 F4
Aráchova [GR] 132 G5
Aračinovo [MK] 146 D6
Arad [RO] 76 G4
Aradíppou [CY] 154 G5
Aragona [I] 126 D4
Aragonese, Castello– [I] 124 F4
Arahal [E] 100 H2
Arakapas [CY] 154 F6
Åraksbø [N] 164 D3
Åram [N] 180 C4
Aramits [F] 84 D3
Araña, Cueva de la– [E] 98 D5
Aranda de Duero [E] 88 G2
Arandjelovac [SRB] 146 B1
Arandjelovac [SRB] 204 B6
Aranjuez [E] 96 G1
Arantzazu [E] 82 H5
Aras de Alpuente [E] 98 D3
Áratos [GR] 130 F2
Aravaca [E] 88 F5
Aravissós [GR] 128 G4
Arazede [P] 80 B6
Arbanasi [BG] 148 C3
Arbatax [I] 118 E5
Arbesbach [A] 62 C3
Arbetera [E] 90 B6
Arboga [S] 168 B3
Arbois [F] 58 A5
Arbon [CH] 58 H5
Arboréa [I] 118 B5
Arbrå [S] 174 D2
Arbroath [GB] 8 F2
Arbúcies [E] 92 F3
Árbus [I] 118 B6
Arc, Pont d'– [F] 106 G2
Arcachon [F] 66 B3
Arcas [E] 98 B2
Arc de Berà [E] 92 C5
Arce [I] 120 C1
Arcen [NL] 30 F3
Arc-en-Barrois [F] 56 H2
Arcévia [I] 116 B1
Archánes [GR] 140 E5
Archángelos [GR] 132 D3
Archángelos [GR] 154 D4
Archar [BG] 146 F2
Archena [E] 104 C2
Arches [F] 58 C2
Archiac [F] 66 D1
Archidona [E] 102 C3
Archivel [E] 104 A2
Arcidosso [I] 114 G2
Arcille [I] 114 F3
Arcinazzo Romano [I] 116 B5
Arcis-sur-Aube [F] 44 B5
Arco [I] 72 C5
Arco de Baúlhe [P] 80 D3
Arconville [F] 42 F2
Arcos de Jalón [E] 90 B4
Arcos de la Frontera [E] 100 G3
Arcos de la Sierra [E] 98 C1
Arcos de Valdevez [P] 78 B6
Ardagh [IRL] 4 C3
Årdal [N] 180 C6
Ardala [S] 166 E6
Årdala [S] 168 C4
Ardales [E] 102 B4
Årdalsosen [N] 164 B2
Årdalstangen [N] 170 E2
Ardara [IRL] 2 E2
Ardea [I] 116 A6
Ardee [IRL] 2 F5
Arden [DK] 160 D4
Ardenicës [AL] 128 B4
Ardentes [F] 54 H4
Ardez [CH] 72 B2
Ardfert [IRL] 4 B3
Ardfinnan [IRL] 4 D4
Ardglass [NIR] 2 G4
Ardino [BG] 130 E1
Ardisa [E] 84 C6
Ardon [F] 58 A6
Ardore [I] 124 D7
Ardres [F] 14 G6
Ardrossan [GB] 8 C3
Åre [S] 182 E1
Areas [E] 78 B5
Areatza [E] 82 G4
Årebrot [N] 180 B5
Arêches-Beaufort [F] 70 B3
Arèhava [BY] 38 G4
Arén [E] 92 C1
Arenals del Sol / Los Arenales del Sol [E] 104 D3
Arenas [E] 82 D2
Arenas del Rey [E] 102 D4
Arenas de San Pedro [E] 88 D5
Arendal [N] 164 F5
Arendonk [B] 30 D3
Arendsee [D] 20 A6
Arene / Arrankudiaga [E] 82 G4
Arenenberg [CH] 58 G4
Areños [E] 82 D3
Arenys de Mar [E] 92 F4
Arenzano [I] 108 H3
Areópoli [GR] 136 E5
Ares [E] 78 D2
Arès [F] 66 B3
Ares del Maestrat / Ares del Maestre [E] 98 F2
Ares del Maestre / Ares del Maestrat [E] 98 F2
Aréthousa [GR] 130 C4
Aretí [GR] 130 B4
Aretxabaleta [E] 82 H4
Arevalillo [E] 88 C4
Arévalo [E] 88 E3
Arezzo [I] 114 G1
Arfará [GR] 136 D3
Årfora [N] 190 C4
Argalastí [GR] 134 A3
Argállon [E] 96 B5
Argamasilla de Alba [E] 96 G4
Argamasilla de Calatrava [E] 96 E5
Argancy [F] 44 F4
Arganda del Rey [E] 88 G6
Arganil [P] 86 E2
Argási [GR] 136 B2
Argegno [I] 70 G3
Argelès-Gazost [F] 84 E4
Argelès-Plage [F] 92 G1
Argelès-sur-Mer [F] 92 G1
Argenta [I] 110 G3
Argentan [F] 26 F5
Argentat [F] 66 H3
Argentella [F] 114 A3
Argentera [I] 108 E2
Argentiera [I] 118 B3
Argentière [F] 70 C3
Argenton-Château [F] 54 D2
Argenton-sur-Creuse [F] 54 G4
Argentré [F] 26 E6
Argent-sur-Sauldre [F] 56 C2
Argés [E] 96 F2
Arginónta [GR] 154 A2
Argithéa [GR] 132 E3
Argomariz [E] 82 H5
Árgos [GR] 136 E2
Árgos Orestikó [GR] 128 E5
Argostóli [GR] 132 C6
Arguedas [E] 84 B5
Arguís [E] 84 D6
Arguisuelas [E] 98 C3
Argy [F] 54 G3
Argyrádes [GR] 132 B3
Argyroúpoli [GR] 140 C5
Arhéa Olimbía [GR] 136 C2
Århus [DK] 156 D1
Ariano Irpino [I] 120 F2
Ariano nel Polésine [I] 110 H2
Aridaía [GR] 128 F3
Arif [TR] 154 H2
Arilje [SRB] 146 A3
Arinagour [GB] 6 A6
Ariño [E] 90 E5
Arinthod [F] 56 H6
Ariogala [LT] 200 F5
Aristoménis [GR] 136 D4
Aritzo [I] 118 D5
Ariza [E] 90 C4
Årjäng [S] 166 D2
Arjeplog [S] 190 G2
Arjona [E] 102 D1
Arjonilla [E] 102 D1
Arkádi [GR] 140 D4
Arkadia [PL] 36 H3
Arkalochóri [GR] 140 F5
Arkása [GR] 140 H3
Arkesíni [GR] 138 F4
Arkítsa [GR] 132 H4
Arklow / An tInbhear Mór [IRL] 4 G4
Arkösund [S] 168 C5
Arkutino [BG] 148 F5
Ärla [S] 168 C3
Arlanc [F] 68 D3
Arlberg Tunnel [A] 72 B1
Arlempdes [F] 68 D5
Arlena di Castro [I] 114 G4
Arles [F] 106 G4
Arles-sur-Tech [F] 92 F2
Arló [H] 64 E4
Arlon (Aarlen) [B] 44 E2
Arlöv [S] 156 H3
Armadale [GB] 6 B5
Armagh [NIR] 2 F4
Armação de Pera [P] 94 B5
Arméni [GR] 132 G2
Armenioí [GR] 136 C3
Armenistís [GR] 138 G1
Armónoi [GR] 140 D5
Armentières [F] 28 F3
Armilla [E] 102 E4
Armiñon [E] 82 G5
Armólia [GR] 134 G5
Armoy [NIR] 2 G2
Armuña de Tajuña [E] 88 H6
Armutcuk [TR] 152 C1
Armutlu [TR] 150 C5
Armutlu [TR] 150 E4
Armutlu [TR] 152 D4
Armyansk [UA] 204 H3
Árna [GR] 136 E4
Arna [N] 170 B4
Arnac [F] 66 E4
Arnac-Pompadour [F] 66 G2
Arnafjord [N] 170 C2
Arnage [F] 42 B5
Arnager [DK] 158 E4
Arnaía [GR] 130 C5
Årnäs [S] 166 F5
Arnäs [S] 184 G2
Arnavutköy [TR] 150 E2
Arnavutköy [TR] 150 E4
Arnay-le-Duc [F] 56 F4
Arnborg [DK] 156 B1
Arneberg [N] 172 B3
Arneburg [D] 34 C1
Arnedillo [E] 90 C1
Arnedo [E] 84 A5
Arnes [E] 90 G6
Årnes [N] 172 C5
Årnes [N] 190 B5
Årnes [N] 190 C4
Arnhem [NL] 16 F5
Árnissa [GR] 128 F4
Arnoldstein [A] 72 H3
Arnön [S] 174 E1
Arnsberg [D] 32 C4
Arnsburg [D] 46 D2
Arnschwang [D] 48 D6
Arnstadt [D] 46 G1
Arnstein [D] 46 E3
Arnuero [E] 82 F3
Aroanía [GR] 136 D1
Aroche [E] 94 F4
Ároktő [H] 64 F5
Arola [FIN] 194 D3
Arolla [CH] 70 D3
Arolsen [D] 32 E5
Arona [I] 70 F4
Aronkylä [FIN] 186 B4
Åros [N] 164 H1
Arosa [CH] 70 H1
Årosjäkk [S] 192 F5
Årøsund [DK] 156 C3
Arouca [P] 80 C5
Arøysund [N] 164 H3
Arpacık [TR] 154 F2
Arpajon [F] 42 F4
Árpás [H] 62 H6
Arpela [FIN] 196 C2
Arquà Petrarca [I] 110 G1
Arquata del Tronto [I] 116 C3
Arquata Scrivia [I] 110 B2
Arquillinos [E] 102 F1
Arrabal / Oia [E] 78 A5
Arracourt [F] 44 F5
Arraiolos [P] 86 D6
Arrakoski [FIN] 176 H1
Arrankorpi [FIN] 176 H3
Arrankudiaga / Arene [E] 82 G4
Arrans [F] 56 F2
Arras [F] 28 F4
Arrasate o Mondragón [E] 82 H4
Arrate [E] 82 H4
Årre [DK] 156 B2
Arreau [F] 84 F4
Arrecife [E] 100 E6
Arrens-Marsous [F] 84 E4
Arrentela [P] 86 B5
Arriate [E] 102 A4
Arriaundi [E] 82 H4
Arriba Fóssil [P] 86 A5
Arrifana [P] 94 B4
Arriondas [E] 82 C2
Arroba de los Montes [E] 96 D3
Arromanches-les-Bains [F] 26 F3
Arronches [P] 86 F5
Arròs [E] 84 G5
Arròs [F] 84 G5
Arroyo de la Luz [E] 86 G5
Arroyo de la Miel-Benalmádena Costa [E] 102 B5
Arroyo de San Serván [E] 94 G2
Arruda dos Vinhos [P] 86 B4
Årsandøy [N] 190 C4
Ars-en-Ré [F] 54 B4
Arsen'yevo [RUS] 202 F4
Arsiè [I] 72 D5
Arsiero [I] 72 D5
Arslankaya [TR] 152 H1
Årslev [DK] 156 D3
Årsnes [N] 180 D4
Arsoli [I] 116 B5
Ars-sur-Moselle [F] 44 E4
Årsunda [S] 174 E4
Arsvågen [N] 164 A2
Arsy [F] 28 E6
Artà [E] 104 F5
Árta [GR] 132 D3
Artà, Coves d'– [E] 104 F5
Artajona [E] 84 B4
Artana [E] 98 F3
Artánd [H] 76 H2
Arta Terme [I] 72 G3
Arteixo [E] 78 C2
Artemare [F] 68 H3
Artemisía [GR] 136 D4
Artemísio [GR] 134 A3
Artemónas [GR] 138 D3
Artena [I] 116 B6
Artenay [F] 42 E5
Artern [D] 34 A5
Artesa de Segre [E] 92 C3
Artesa de Segre / Montargull [E] 92 C2
Arth [CH] 58 F6
Arth [D] 60 F3
Arthous, Ancient Prieure d'– [F] 84 C2
Arthurstown [IRL] 4 E5
Arties [E] 84 G5
Artix [F] 84 E3
Artjärvi / Artsjö [FIN] 178 B3
Artotína [GR] 132 F4
Artouste-Fabrèges [F] 84 E4
Årtrik [S] 184 E2
Artsjö / Artjärvi [FIN] 178 B3
Artsyz [UA] 204 F4
A Rúa [E] 78 E5
Arucas [E] 100 C6
Arudy [F] 84 D3
Arundel [GB] 14 D5
Arva [E] 94 H6
Årvåg [N] 180 G1
Arvagh [IRL] 2 E4
Arversund [S] 182 G2
Árvi [GR] 140 F5
Arvidsjaur [S] 190 H3
Arvieux [F] 70 B6
Årvik [N] 180 C4
Arvika [S] 166 D2
Årviksand [N] 192 G1
Arvila [EST] 198 F1
Arville [F] 42 C5
Arykanda [TR] 154 H2
Arzachena [I] 118 E2
Arzacq-Arraziguet [F] 84 E2
Aržano [HR] 144 B2
Arzberg [D] 48 C3
Arze-Arce / Uriz [E] 84 C4
Arzignano [I] 72 D6
Arzl [A] 72 C1
Arzúa [E] 78 C3
As [B] 30 E4
Aš [CZ] 48 C3
Ås [N] 166 B2
Ås [N] 182 D2
Ås [S] 182 G2
Ås [S] 184 D2
Aså [DK] 160 E3
Åsa [N] 170 H5
Åsa [S] 160 H3
Asa [S] 162 E4
Aşağıçobanisa [TR] 152 D3
Aşağıgörle [TR] 152 F5
Aşağıinova [TR] 150 C5
Åsan [N] 190 C5
Åsäng [S] 184 E4
Ašanja [SRB] 142 G2
Åsarna [S] 182 G4
Asarum [S] 158 E1
Åsbro [S] 166 H4
Asby [S] 162 E2
Ascain [F] 84 C2
Ascea [I] 120 F5
Ascha [D] 60 G2
Aschach [A] 62 B4
Aschaffenburg [D] 46 D3
Aschau [A] 72 E1
Aschau [D] 60 F5
Aschbach Markt [A] 62 C5
Ascheberg [D] 16 H6
Ascheberg [D] 18 G2
Aschendorf [D] 16 H3
Aschersleben [D] 34 B4
Asciano [I] 114 G1
Ascó [E] 90 H6
Asco [F] 114 B3
Áscoli Piceno [I] 116 C3
Ascoli Satriano [I] 120 G2
Ascona [CH] 70 F3
Ascou Pailhères [F] 106 B6
Åse [N] 192 E3
Åsebyn [S] 166 D3
Åseda [S] 162 E4
Åsele [S] 190 G5
Åseli [N] 192 D6
Asemankylä [FIN] 188 C5
Asemanseutu [FIN] 186 D3
Åsen [N] 190 C6
Åsen [S] 172 F2
Åsen [S] 184 C4
Asendorf [D] 18 E6
Asenovgrad [BG] 148 B6
Asenovo [BG] 148 B2
Åsensbruk [S] 166 D4
Åseral [N] 164 D4
Åserund [N] 166 C1
Asfáka [GR] 132 C1
Asfeld [F] 44 B2
Åsgårdstrand [N] 164 H2
Asha (Pasaköy) [CY] 154 G5
Ashbourne [GB] 10 E5
Ashbourne [IRL] 2 F6
Åsheim [N] 182 C6
Ashford [GB] 14 F5
Ashington [GB] 8 G5
Ashmyany [BY] 200 H6
Ashton-under-Lyne [GB] 10 E4
Asiago [I] 72 D5
Asikkala [FIN] 178 A2
Asila [FIN] 188 D5
Asíni [GR] 136 F2
Asipovitsy [BY] 202 C5
Ask [N] 170 B3
Ask [N] 170 H5
Ask [S] 158 C2
Aska [FIN] 194 D6
Askainen / Villnäs [FIN] 176 D4
Askaniia-Nova [RUS] 204 H3
Askanija Nova [UA] 204 H3
Askeaton [IRL] 4 C3
Askeby [DK] 156 G4
Asker [N] 164 H1
Askersund [S] 166 G4
Askeryd [S] 162 E2
Askim [N] 166 C2
Askim [S] 160 G2
Askland [N] 164 E3
Asklepiyon [TR] 152 C2
Asklipíeio [GR] 154 B2
Asklipíeio [GR] 154 B2
Askola [FIN] 178 B4
Äsköping [S] 168 B3
Askós [GR] 130 B4
Askum [S] 166 B5
Askvoll [N] 170 B1
Askýfou [GR] 140 C5
Aslanapa [TR] 152 G1
Aslestad [N] 164 E2
Åsli [N] 170 G4
Åsljunga [S] 162 B6
Åsmansbo [S] 172 H5
Asmunti [FIN] 196 E2
Asnæs [DK] 156 F2
Åsnes [N] 172 D4
As Nogais [E] 78 E4
Ásola [I] 110 E1
Asolo [I] 72 E5
Asopía [GR] 134 B5
Asopós [GR] 136 F4
Asoru, Nuraghe– [I] 118 D7
Ásos [GR] 132 C5
Ásotthalom [H] 76 D4
Aspa [S] 168 C4
Aspang Markt [A] 62 E6
Asparuhovo [BG] 148 E4
Asparukovo [BG] 148 F3
Aspås [S] 182 G2
Aspe [E] 104 D2
Aspeå [S] 184 F1
Aspet [F] 84 G4
Aspnes [N] 190 D5
Aspö [S] 168 C2
As Pontes de García Rodríguez / Puentes de García Rodríguez [E] 78 D2
Aspres-sur-Buëch [F] 108 C2
Asprópyrgos [GR] 134 B6
Asprόvalta [GR] 130 C4
Aspsele [S] 190 G6
Assamalla [EST] 198 F1
Assel [D] 18 E4
Assé-le-Boisne [F] 26 F6
Assemini [I] 118 C7
Assen [NL] 16 G3
Assens [DK] 156 D3
Assens [DK] 160 E5
Asserbo [DK] 156 G1
Assergi [I] 116 C4
Asseria [HR] 112 G5
Assessos [TR] 152 D6
Ássiros [GR] 128 H4
Assisi [I] 116 A2
Assling [D] 60 F5
Assmannshausen [D] 46 B3

Assoro [I] 126 F3
Assos [TR] 134 H1
Åsta [N] 172 C3
Astaffort [F] 66 E6
Astakós [GR] 132 D5
Åstan [N] 180 H1
Åstan [N] 180 H1
Asten [A] 62 B4
Asten [NL] 30 F3
Asti [I] 70 E6
Astira [TR] 152 C1
Astorga [E] 78 G6
Åstorp [S] 156 H1
Åstrand [S] 172 E5
Astravyets [BY] 200 H5
Ástros [GR] 136 E3
Astrup [DK] 160 D4
Astryna [BY] 24 G3
Astudillo [E] 82 D6
Astura, Torre- [I] 120 B1
Astypálaia [GR] 138 H4
Asvyeya [BY] 198 G6
Ászár [H] 64 A6
Aszód [H] 64 D6
Aszófő [H] 76 A2
Atalaia [P] 86 B5
Atalánti [GR] 132 H4
Atanneus [TR] 152 C2
Atapuerca [E] 82 E6
Atarfe [E] 102 E4
Atašiene [LV] 198 F5
Atburgazi [TR] 152 D6
Atça [TR] 152 E5
Ateca [E] 90 C4
Atella [I] 120 G3
Atessa [I] 116 E5
Ath [B] 28 G3
Athboy [IRL] 2 E5
Athea [IRL] 4 C3
Athenry [IRL] 2 C5
Athéras [GR] 132 C6
Athiénou [CY] 154 G5
Athína [GR] 134 C6
Athleague [IRL] 2 D5
Athlone / Baile Átha Luain [IRL] 2 D5
Athy [IRL] 4 F3
Atienza [E] 90 A4
Atina [I] 116 C6
Atkár [H] 64 E6
Atnbrua [N] 180 H6
Atnosen [N] 182 B6
Atouguia de Baleia [P] 86 B3
A Toxa [E] 78 B4
Ätran [S] 162 B4
Åträsk [S] 190 H5
Atri [I] 116 D3
Atripalda [I] 120 F3
Áttali [GR] 134 C4
Attel [D] 60 F4
Attendorn [D] 32 C5
Attersee [A] 60 H5
Attigny [F] 44 C2
Attleborough [GB] 14 G2
Attmar [S] 184 E5
Attnang-Puchheim [A] 62 A5
Attre [B] 28 G3
Attrup [DK] 160 D3
Åtvidaberg [S] 168 B6
Atzara [I] 118 D5
Atzendorf [D] 34 B4
Atzeneta del Maestrat [E] 98 F3
Au [A] 62 D6
Au [D] 60 E3
Aub [D] 46 E4
Aubagne [F] 108 B5
Aubange [B] 44 E3
Aubenas [F] 68 E6
Aubérive [F] 44 C3
Auberive [F] 56 H2
Aubeterre-sur-Dronne [F] 66 E2
Aubiet [F] 84 G3
Aubigny [F] 54 B3
Aubigny-les-Pothées [F] 28 H6
Aubigny-sur-Nère [F] 56 C2
Auboué [F] 44 E4
Aubrac [F] 68 C5
Aubusson [F] 68 B1
Auce [LV] 198 C6
Aucelon [F] 68 G6
Auch [F] 84 G2
Auchinleck [GB] 8 D4
Auchterarder [GB] 8 E2
Auchtermuchty [GB] 8 E2
Audelange [F] 56 H4
Audenarde (Oudenaarde) [B] 28 G2
Audenge [F] 66 C3
Auderville [F] 26 D1
Audeux [F] 58 B4
Audierne [F] 40 A3
Audincourt [F] 58 C4
Audlem [GB] 10 D5
Audnedal [N] 164 D5
Audressein [F] 84 G5
Audru [EST] 198 D3
Audruicq [F] 14 H6
Audun-le-Roman [F] 44 E3
Aue [D] 48 D2
Auen [CH] 72 F1
Auer / Ora [I] 72 D4
Auerbach [D] 46 H4
Auerbach [D] 48 C2
Auerbacher Schloss [D] 46 C4
Auffach [A] 60 F6
Augher [NIR] 2 F3
Aughnacloy [NIR] 2 F3
Aughrim [IRL] 4 G4
Augsburg [D] 60 D3
Augusta [I] 126 G4
Augustenborg [DK] 156 C4
Augustów [PL] 24 E3
Augustusburg [D] 48 D1
Aukra [N] 180 D2
Aukštadvaris [LT] 24 G1
Auktsjaur [S] 190 H3
Auletta [I] 120 G4
Aulla [I] 110 C4
Aullène [F] 114 B5
Aulnay [F] 54 D5
Aulstad [N] 170 H2
Ault [F] 28 C4
Aulus-les-Bains [F] 84 H5
Auly [RUS] 204 G1
Auma [D] 48 B2
Aumale [F] 28 D5
Aumetz [F] 44 E3
Aumont-Aubrac [F] 68 C5
Aunay-sur-Odon [F] 26 E4
Auneau [F] 42 E4
Aunet [N] 182 D2
Aunet [N] 190 C5
Auneuil [F] 28 D6
Aunfoss [N] 190 D4
Auning [DK] 160 E5
Aups [F] 108 D4
Aura [FIN] 176 E4
Aurach [A] 60 F6
Aurach [D] 46 F5
Auray [F] 40 D4
Aurdal [N] 170 G3
Aure [N] 180 G1
Aurejärvi [FIN] 186 D5
Aurich [D] 18 B4
Aurignac [F] 84 G4
Aurillac [F] 68 B4
Auriol [F] 108 B5
Auris-en-Oisans [F] 70 A5
Auritz / Burguete [E] 84 C3
Aurlandsvangen [N] 170 D2
Auron [F] 108 E3
Auronzo di Cadore [I] 72 F3
Aursjøhytta [N] 180 F4
Aursmoen [N] 166 C1
Aursnes [N] 180 D3
Áusa Corno [I] 72 G5
Ausejo [E] 84 A5
Ausentum [I] 122 G6
Ausserbrünst [D] 60 H3
Austad [N] 164 C6
Austad [N] 164 D3
Austanå [N] 164 E3
Austborg [N] 190 D5
Austhygda [N] 170 F5
Austefjord [N] 180 C4
Austerlitz (Slavkov u Brna) [CZ] 50 C6
Austmarka [N] 172 D5
Austnes [N] 180 D3
Austpollen [N] 192 E4
Austrumdal [N] 164 B4
Auterive [F] 84 H4
Authon [F] 108 D3
Authon-du-Perche [F] 42 C5
Autio [S] 194 B7
Autol [E] 84 A5
Autti [FIN] 194 E8
Auttoinen [FIN] 176 H2
Autun [F] 56 F4
Auve [F] 44 C4
Auvers-s-Oise [F] 42 F3
Auvila [FIN] 188 E6
Auvillers-les-Forges [F] 28 H5
Auxerre [F] 56 E2
Auxi-le-Château [F] 28 D4
Auxonne [F] 56 H4
Auxy [F] 56 F4
Auzances [F] 56 B6
Auzon [F] 68 D3
Avå [FIN] 176 C4
Ava [S] 184 H1
Avafors [S] 196 B2
Availles-Limouzine [F] 54 F5
Aval, Falaise d'- [F] 26 G2
Avala [SRB] 142 G3
Avaldsnes [N] 164 A2
Avallon [F] 56 E3
Ávas [GR] 130 G3
Avaträsk [S] 190 F5
Avaviken [S] 190 G3
Avcılar [TR] 150 E3
Avdímou [CY] 154 F6
Ávdira [GR] 130 E3
Ávdira [GR] 130 E3
Åvedal [N] 164 B5
A Veiga [E] 78 E6
Aveiras de Cima [P] 86 C4
Aveiro [P] 80 B5
Avelengo / Hafling [I] 72 D3
Avellino [I] 120 F3
Aven Armand [F] 106 E2
Avenches [CH] 58 C6
Aven de Marzal [F] 106 G2
Aven d'Orgnac [F] 106 G2
Avène [F] 106 D3
Averbode [B] 30 D3
Aversa [I] 120 D3
Avesnes-le-Comte [F] 28 E4
Avesnes-sur-Helpe [F] 28 G4
Avesta [S] 174 D5
Avetrana [I] 122 F4
Avezzano [I] 116 C5
Avgerinós [GR] 128 E6
Avía [GR] 136 D4
Aviano [I] 72 F5
Aviemore [GB] 6 E5
Avigliana [I] 70 D5
Avigliano [I] 120 G3
Avigna [I] 72 D3
Avignon [F] 106 G3
Ávila [E] 88 E4
Avilés [E] 78 H3
Avinurme [EST] 198 F2
Avinyó [E] 92 E3
Avio [I] 72 C5
Avión [E] 78 C4
Avis [P] 86 D5
Avlákia [GR] 152 C5
Avlémonas [GR] 136 F6
Avlí [GR] 130 D3
Avliótes [GR] 132 A2
Avlóna [GR] 134 C5
Avlonári [GR] 134 C5
Avlum [DK] 160 C6
Avola [I] 126 G5
Avonmouth [GB] 12 F3
Avord [F] 56 C4
Avoriaz [F] 70 C2
Avradsberg [S] 172 F5
Avramov [BG] 148 E4
Avranches [F] 26 D4
Avril [F] 44 E3
Avşar [TR] 152 D6
Avtovac [BIH] 144 D3
Axat [F] 106 B5
Axel [NL] 28 H1
Axioúpoli [GR] 128 G3
Ax-les-Thermes [F] 106 A6
Axmarby [S] 174 E3
Axminster [GB] 12 F4
Axós [GR] 140 E4
Axvall [S] 166 F5
Ay [F] 44 B3
Ayagalip [TR] 130 G5
Ayamonte [E] 94 D5
Ayas [I] 70 D3
Aydın [TR] 152 D5
Aydıncık [TR] 130 G5
Aydıncık [TR] 154 F4
Ayerbe [E] 84 D6
Aykırıkçı [TR] 152 H2
Aylesbury [GB] 14 D3
Ayllón [E] 88 H3
Aylsham [GB] 14 G2
Ayna [E] 98 B6
Ayoó de Vidriales [E] 80 H3
Ayora [E] 98 D5
Ayr [GB] 8 C4
Ayrancı [TR] 152 G2
Ayrancılar [TR] 152 C4
Ay. Seryios (Yenibogaziçi) [CY] 154 G5
Äyskoski [FIN] 186 H2
Äystö [FIN] 186 B4
Aytos [BG] 148 F4
Ayvacık [TR] 134 H1
Ayvalık [TR] 152 B2
Ayvatlar [TR] 152 C2
Azaila [E] 90 F5
Azambuja [P] 86 C4
Azannes-et-Soumazannes [F] 44 D3
Azanúy [E] 90 H3
Azaruja [P] 86 D6
Azath [TR] 150 B2
Azay-le-Ferron [F] 54 G3
Azay-le-Rideau [F] 54 F2
Azeitão [P] 86 B6
Azervadinha [P] 86 C5
Azinheira dos Barros [P] 94 C2
Azıtepe [TR] 152 E4
Aziziye [TR] 150 C1
Aznalcóllar [E] 94 G5
Azpeitia [E] 82 H4
Azuaga [E] 96 A5
Azuara [E] 90 F5
Azuel [E] 96 D5
Azul, Cueva- [E] 104 E6
Azuqueca de Henares [E] 88 G5
Azur [F] 66 A6
Azyory [BY] 24 G4
Azzano Decimo [I] 72 F5
Azzurra, Grotta- [I] 120 D4
Azzurra, Grotta- [I] 120 F5

B

Baad [A] 60 B6
Baal [D] 30 F4
Baamonde [E] 78 D3
Baar [D] 60 D3
Baarle Nassau [NL] 30 D2
Baarn [NL] 16 E4
Babadag [RO] 204 F5
Babadağ [TR] 152 F5
Babaeski [TR] 150 B2
Babaköy [TR] 152 D2
Babek [BG] 148 B5
Babenhausen [D] 46 D3
Babenhausen [D] 60 C4
Babiak [PL] 22 G3
Babiak [PL] 36 F3
Babica [PL] 52 D4
Babice [PL] 50 G4
Băbiciu [RO] 148 A1
Babięta [PL] 24 B4
Babigoszcz [PL] 20 F4
Babimost [PL] 36 A3
Babin Potok [HR] 112 G3
Babjen [AL] 128 C3
BabnoPolje [SLO] 74 B6
Babócsa [H] 74 G5
Bábolna [H] 64 A6
Babriškes [LT] 24 G2
Babruysk [BY] 202 C5
Babušnica [SRB] 146 E4
Babylon [CZ] 48 D5
Babylón [CZ] 62 E2
Bač [MK] 128 E4
Bač [SLO] 74 A6
Bač [SRB] 142 E1
Bača [SLO] 72 H4
Bacău [RO] 204 D4
Baccarat [F] 44 F6
Baceno [I] 70 F2
Bacharach [D] 46 B3
Bachkovo [BG] 148 B6
Bachkovski Manastir [BG] 148 B6
Bachórz [PL] 52 E4
Bačina [SRB] 146 C3
Backåkra [S] 158 D3
Bačka Palanka [MNE] 204 A5
Bačka Palanka [SRB] 142 F1
Bäckaskog [S] 158 D1
Bačka Topola [MNE] 204 A5
Bačka Topola [SRB] 76 D5
Backe [S] 190 F6
Bäckebo [S] 162 F4
Bäckefors [S] 166 D4
Backen [S] 184 D4
Backen [S] 184 E4
Bäckhammar [S] 166 F3
Bački Breg [SRB] 76 C5
Bački Petrovac [SRB] 142 F1
Bački Sokolac [SRB] 76 D5
Backnang [D] 46 D6
Bačko Gradište [SRB] 142 G1
Bačko Novo Selo [SRB] 142 E1
Bačko Petrovo Selo [SRB] 76 E6
Bąćkowice [PL] 52 C1
Bacoli [I] 120 D3
Bacova mahala [BG] 148 B3
Bacqueville-en-Caux [F] 28 B4
Bácsalmás [H] 76 D5
Bácsbokod [H] 76 C5
Bácsborsód [H] 76 C5
Baczyna [PL] 34 H1
Bad Abbach [D] 60 F2
Badacsonytomaj [H] 74 H3
Bad Aibling [D] 60 F5
Badajoz [E] 86 F6
Badalona [E] 92 E4
Badalucco [I] 108 G4
Bad Aussee [A] 62 A6
Bad Bederkesa [D] 18 D4
Bad Bentheim [D] 16 H5
Bad Bergzabern [D] 46 B5
Bad Berka [D] 46 H1
Bad Berleburg [D] 32 D5
Bad Berneck [D] 46 H3
Bad Bertrich [D] 44 G1
Bad Bevensen [D] 18 G5
Bad Bibra [D] 34 B5
Bad Blankenburg [D] 46 H2
Bad Brambach [D] 48 C3
Bad Bramstedt [D] 18 F3
Bad Breisig [D] 30 H5
Bad Brückenau [D] 46 E2
Bad Buchau [D] 60 A4
Badderen [N] 192 H2
Bad Deutsch-Altenburg [A] 62 G5
Bad Doberan [D] 20 B3
Bad Driburg [D] 32 E4
Bad Düben [D] 34 D4
Bad Dürkheim [D] 46 B4
Bad Dürrenberg [D] 34 C5
Bad Dürrheim [D] 58 F3
Bad Elster [D] 48 C3
Bademli [TR] 134 G1
Bademli [TR] 152 C3
Bademli [TR] 152 E5
Bad Ems [D] 46 B2
Baden [A] 62 F5
Baden [CH] 58 F4
Baden (Rheinfelden) [D] 58 E4
Baden-Baden [D] 58 F1
Bad Endorf [D] 60 F5
Badenweiler [D] 58 E3
Baderna [HR] 112 D2
Bädeshte [BG] 148 C5
Bad Essen [D] 32 D2
Bad Frankenhausen [D] 34 A5
Bad Freienwalde [D] 34 F1
Bad Friedrichshall [D] 46 D5
Bad Gandersheim [D] 32 G3
Badgastein [A] 72 G2
Bad Gleichenberg [A] 74 E3
Bad Godesberg [D] 30 H5
Bad Goisern [A] 60 H6
Bad Gottleuba [D] 48 F1
Bad Grund [D] 32 G4
Bad Hall [A] 62 B5
Bad Harzburg [D] 32 H3
Bad Herrenalb [D] 58 F1
Bad Hersfeld [D] 32 F6
Bad Hofgastein [A] 72 G1
Bad Homburg [D] 46 C2
Bad Honnef [D] 30 H5
Bad Hönningen [D] 30 H5
Badia Gran [E] 104 E5
Badia Polésine [I] 110 F2
Badia Tedalda [I] 110 G6
Bad Iburg [D] 32 D2
Bad Ischl [A] 60 H5
Bad Karlshafen [D] 32 F4
Bad Kissingen [D] 46 E3
Bad Kleinen [D] 20 A4
Bad Kleinkirchheim [A] 72 H3
Bad König [D] 46 D4
Bad Königshofen [D] 46 F2
Bad Kösen [D] 34 B6
Bądkowo [PL] 36 F2
Bad Kreuznach [D] 46 B3
Bad Krozingen [D] 58 E3
Bad Laasphe [D] 32 D6
Bad Langensalza [D] 32 H6
Bad Lauchstädt [D] 34 B5
Bad Lausick [D] 34 D6
Bad Lauterberg [D] 32 G4
Bad Leonfelden [A] 62 B3
Bad Liebenstein [D] 46 F1
Bad Liebenwerda [D] 34 E5
Bad Liebenzell [D] 58 G1
Bad Lippspringe [D] 32 E3
Badljevina [HR] 142 C1
Bad Marienberg [D] 46 B1
Bad Meinberg [D] 32 E3
Bad Mergentheim [D] 46 E5
Bad Mitterndorf [A] 62 B6
Bad Münder [D] 32 F2
Bad Münster Ebernburg [D] 46 B3
Bad Münstereifel [D] 30 G5
Bad Muskau [D] 34 G5
Bad Nauheim [D] 46 C2
Bad Nenndorf [D] 32 F2
Bad Neuenahr [D] 30 G5
Bad Neustadt [D] 46 F2
Bad Oeynhausen [D] 32 E2
Badolato [I] 124 E6
Badolato Marina [I] 124 E6
Bad Oldesloe [D] 18 G3
Badonviller [F] 44 F6
Bad Orb [D] 46 D2
Badovinci [SRB] 142 F2
Badow [D] 18 H4
Bad Peterstal [D] 58 F2
Bad Pirawarth [A] 62 F4
Bad Pyrmont [D] 32 E3
Bad Radkersburg [A] 74 E3
Bad Ragaz [CH] 58 H6
Bad Reichenhall [D] 60 G5
Bad Rippoldsau [D] 58 F2
Bad Rothenfelde [D] 32 D2
Bad Saarow-Pieskow [D] 34 F3
Bad Sachsa [D] 32 G4
Bad Säckingen [D] 58 E4
Bad Salzdetfurth [D] 32 G3
Bad Salzuflen [D] 32 E3
Bad Salzungen [D] 46 F1
Bad Schallerbach [A] 62 B4
Bad Schandau [D] 48 F1
Bad Schmiedeberg [D] 34 D4
Bad Schönau [A] 74 F1
Bad Schönborn [D] 46 C5
Bad Schussenried [D] 60 B4
Bad Schwalbach [D] 46 B2
Bad Schwartau [D] 18 G3
Bad Segeberg [D] 18 G3
Bad Sooden-Allendorf [D] 32 F5
Bad St. Leonhard [A] 74 C2
Bad Sülze [D] 20 C3
Bad Tatzmannsdorf [A] 74 F1
Bad Tennstedt [D] 32 H5
Bad Tölz [D] 60 E5
Badu Andria [I] 118 E3
Badules [E] 90 D5
Bad Urach [D] 58 H2
Bad Vöslau [A] 62 F5
Bad Waldsee [D] 60 B4
Bad Wiessee [D] 60 E5
Bad-Wildungen [D] 32 E5
Bad Wilsnack [D] 20 B6
Bad Wimpfen [D] 46 D5
Bad Windsheim [D] 46 F5
Bad Wörishofen [D] 60 C4
Bad Wurzach [D] 60 B5
Bad Zwischenahn [D] 18 C5
Bække [DK] 156 B2
Bækmarksbro [DK] 160 B5
Baelen [B] 30 F5
Baells [E] 90 H3
Baelo Claudia [E] 100 G5
Baena [E] 102 D2
Bæverfjord [N] 180 F2
Baeza [E] 102 F2
Bagà [E] 92 E2
Bagamér [H] 64 H6
Bağarası [TR] 152 D5
Băgarin [BG] 148 D6
Bågede [S] 190 E5
Bagenalstown / Muine Bheag [IRL] 4 F4
Bagenkop [DK] 18 H1
Bagh a Chaisteil / Castlebay [GB] 6 A5
Bagheria [I] 126 D2
Bagn [N] 170 G3
Bagnacavallo [I] 110 G4
Bagnara Calabra [I] 124 C7
Bagnères-de-Bigorre [F] 84 F4
Bagnères-de-Luchon [F] 84 F5
Bagni Contursi [I] 120 F4
Bagni del Másino [I] 70 H3
Bagni di Bormio [I] 72 B3
Bagni di Craveggia [I] 70 F3
Bagni di Lucca [I] 110 E5
Bagni di Rabbi [I] 72 C3
Bagni di Salomone [I] 72 E2
Bagni di Vinadio [I] 108 E3
Bagno a Ripoli [I] 110 F5
Bagno di Romagna [I] 110 G5
Bagnoles-de-l'Orne [F] 26 F5
Bagnoli di Sopra [I] 110 G1
Bagnolo Mella [I] 72 B6
Bagnolo Piemonte [I] 108 F1
Bagnolo San Vito [I] 110 E2
Bagnols-en-Forêt [F] 108 D5
Bagnols-les-Bains [F] 68 D6
Bagnols-sur-Cèze [F] 106 G3
Bagnone [I] 110 D4
Bagnoregio [I] 114 H3
Bagno Vignoni [I] 114 G2
Bagny [PL] 24 E4
Bågø [DK] 156 C3
Bagod [H] 74 F3
Bagolino [I] 72 B5
Bagrationovsk [RUS] 22 H2
Bagsund [N] 190 C5
Báguena [E] 90 D5
Bağyaka [TR] 154 D1
Bağyurdu [TR] 152 D4
Bağyüzü [TR] 152 C2
Bahabón de Esgueva [E] 88 G2
Baharlar [TR] 152 B1
Bahçecik [TR] 150 G3
Bahçeköy [TR] 150 B4
Bahçeköy [TR] 150 D2
Bahillo [E] 82 D5
Baia delle Zagare [I] 116 H6
Bàia Domìzia [I] 120 D2
Baia Mare [RO] 204 C3
Baiano [I] 120 E3
Baião [P] 80 C4
Bàia Sardinia [I] 118 E2
Baiersbronn [D] 58 F2
Baigneux-les-Juifs [F] 56 G3
Baile an Sceilg / Ballinskelligs [IRL] 4 A4
Baile Átha Cliath / Dublin [IRL] 2 F6
Baile Átha Luain / Athlone [IRL] 2 D5
Băile Felix [RO] 76 H2
Bailén [E] 102 E1
Băilești [RO] 146 F2
Băile Tușnad [RO] 204 D4
Baillieborough [IRL] 2 F4
Bailleul [F] 26 H2
Bailleul [F] 28 F2
Bain-de-Bretagne [F] 40 F5
Bains-les-Bains [F] 58 C2
Baio [E] 78 B2
Baiona [E] 78 A5
Bais [F] 26 E6
Baisogala [LT] 200 F4
Baix [F] 68 F5
Baixas [F] 92 G1
Baja [H] 76 C4
Bajánsenye [H] 74 F3
Bajč [SK] 64 B5
Bajina Bašta [SRB] 142 F4
Bajmok [SRB] 76 D5
Bajna [H] 64 B6
Bajram Curri [AL] 146 A6
Bajša [SRB] 76 D6
Bajzë [AL] 144 F4
Bak [H] 74 G3
Bakacak [TR] 150 C5
Bakar [HR] 112 E1
Bakewell [GB] 10 E5
Bakhchysarai [UA] 204 H4
Bakhmach [UA] 202 E6
Bakio [E] 82 G3
Bakırköy [TR] 150 E3
Bakka [N] 164 F1
Bakke [N] 164 F4
Bakke [N] 166 C4
Bakkejord [N] 192 F2
Bakken [N] 182 C1
Bakko [N] 170 F5
Baklan [TR] 152 G4
Bakonszeg [H] 76 G1
Bakonybél [H] 74 H2
Bakonycsernye [H] 76 A1
Bakonygyepes [H] 74 H2
Bakonyjákó [H] 74 H2
Bakonypeterd [H] 76 A1
Bakonysárkány [H] 76 A1
Bakonyszombathely [H] 76 A1
Bakovac [HR] 112 F3
Baks [H] 76 E3
Baksa [H] 76 A5
Baksjöliden [S] 190 G5
Baktakék [H] 64 F4
Baktalórántháza [H] 64 H5
Baktsjaur [S] 190 H3
Bakum [D] 18 C6
Bäl [S] 168 G4
Bala [GB] 10 C5
Balaban [TR] 150 C1
Balabancik [TR] 150 B4
Balaguer [E] 92 B3
Balanegra [E] 102 F5
Bălănești [RO] 148 A1
Balassagyarmat [H] 64 C5
Balástya [H] 76 E4
Balat [TR] 152 D6
Balatonakali [H] 74 H2
Balatonalmádi [H] 76 A2
Balatonbereny [H] 74 G3
Balatonboglár [H] 74 H3
Balatonederics [H] 74 H3
Balatonföldvár [H] 76 A3
Balatonfüred [H] 76 A2
Balatonfűzfő [H] 76 A2
Balatongyörök [H] 74 G3
Balatonkenese [H] 76 A2
Balatonkeresztúr [H] 74 H3
Balatonlelle [H] 74 H3
Balatonszemes [H] 76 A3
Balazote [E] 98 B5
Balbigny [F] 68 E2
Balboa [E] 78 E4
Balbriggan [IRL] 2 F5
Bålby [S] 166 G3
Balchik [BG] 148 G2
Balcılar [TR] 150 B5
Balcon de Europa [E] 102 D5
Baldenstein [CH] 70 H1
Balderschwang [D] 60 B6
Baldock [GB] 14 E3
Baldone [LV] 198 E5
Bale [HR] 112 D2
Baleines, Phare des- [F] 54 B4
Baleira [E] 78 E3
Baleizão [P] 94 D3
Balestrand [N] 170 C1
Balestrate [I] 126 C2
Balewo [PL] 22 F4
Bälgviken [S] 168 B3
Balice [PL] 50 H3
Balıkesir [TR] 152 D1
Balıklıova [TR] 152 B4
Balıköy [TR] 152 F1
Bälinge [S] 158 C1
Bälinge [S] 162 B1
Bälinge [S] 168 D1
Balingen [D] 58 G2
Balinț [RO] 76 H5
Balio Chitarra [I] 126 B2
Baljvine [BIH] 142 B3
Balkanec [BG] 148 B4
Balkanski [BG] 148 D2
Balkány [H] 64 H5
Balkıca [TR] 152 G6
Balla [IRL] 2 C4
Ballaban [AL] 128 C5
Ballachulish [GB] 6 C6
Ballaghaderreen [IRL] 2 D4
Ballangen [N] 192 E4
Ballantrae [GB] 8 C4
Ballao [I] 118 D6
Ballater [GB] 6 E6
Ballebro [DK] 156 C4
Bällefors [S] 166 F5
Ballen [DK] 156 E2
Ballenstedt [D] 34 A4
Balleroy [F] 26 E3
Ballerup [DK] 156 G2
Ballı [TR] 150 B3
Ballina [IRL] 2 C3
Ballina [IRL] 2 C6
Ballinafad [IRL] 2 D4
Ballinagh [IRL] 2 E4
Ballinahinch [NIR] 2 G4
Ballinakill [IRL] 4 E3
Ballinamore [IRL] 2 E4
Ballinascarty [IRL] 4 C5
Ballinasloe [IRL] 2 D5
Ballindine [IRL] 2 C4
Ballindooly Castle [IRL] 2 C5
Ballingarry [IRL] 4 C3
Ballingarry [IRL] 4 E4
Ballinhassig [IRL] 4 C5
Ballinrobe [IRL] 2 C4
Ballinskelligs / Baile an Sceilg [IRL] 4 A4
Ballinspittle [IRL] 4 C5
Ballintober, Abbey- [IRL] 2 C4
Ballintra [IRL] 2 E3
Ballio Zaffarana [I] 126 B2
Ballivor [IRL] 2 E5
Ballobar [E] 90 G4
Ballon [F] 42 B4
Ballon [IRL] 4 F4
Ballsh [AL] 128 B5
Ballshi [AL] 128 B4
Ballstad [N] 192 C4
Ballum [DK] 156 B3
Ballybay [IRL] 2 F4
Ballybofey [IRL] 2 E2
Ballybunion [IRL] 2 B6
Ballycanew [IRL] 4 F4
Ballycastle [IRL] 2 C3
Ballycastle [NIR] 2 G2
Ballyclare [NIR] 2 G3
Ballyconneely [IRL] 2 B4
Ballycotton [IRL] 4 D5
Ballycumber [IRL] 2 D5
Ballydehob [IRL] 4 B5
Ballydesmond [IRL] 4 C4
Ballyduff [IRL] 4 B3
Ballyduff [IRL] 4 D4
Ballyemund [IRL] 4 F4
Ballyfarnan [IRL] 2 D4
Ballygawley [NIR] 2 F3
Ballyglass [IRL] 2 C4
Ballygowan [NIR] 2 G4
Ballyhaunis [IRL] 2 C4
Ballyheige [IRL] 4 B3
Ballyhillin [IRL] 2 F1
Ballyjamesduff [IRL] 2 E4
Ballykeeran [IRL] 2 D5
Ballylanders [IRL] 4 D4
Ballylongford [IRL] 2 B6
Ballylynan [IRL] 4 F3
Ballymacoda [IRL] 4 D5
Ballymahon [IRL] 2 D5
Ballymena [NIR] 2 G3
Ballymoe [IRL] 2 D4
Ballymoney [NIR] 2 G2
Ballymore [IRL] 2 E5
Ballymore Eustace [IRL] 2 F6
Ballymote [IRL] 2 D3
Ballyragget [IRL] 4 E3
Ballyronan [NIR] 2 G3
Ballyroon [IRL] 4 B5
Ballysadare [IRL] 2 D3
Ballyshannon [IRL] 2 E3
Ballyvaughan [IRL] 2 C5
Ballywalter [NIR] 2 H4
Balmaseda [E] 82 G4
Balmazújváros [H] 64 G6
Balme [I] 70 C5
Balmúccia [I] 70 E3
Balogunyom [H] 74 F2
Balş [RO] 146 G1
Balsareny [E] 92 D3
Balsfjord [N] 192 F2
Balsicas [E] 104 C4
Balsorano [I] 116 C6
Bålsta [S] 168 D2
Balsthal [CH] 58 E5
Balta [UA] 204 E2
Baltaköy [TR] 152 E5
Baltanás [E] 88 F1
Baltar [E] 78 C6
Bălţi [MD] 204 E3
Baltimore [IRL] 4 B5
Baltinava [LV] 198 G5
Baltinglass [IRL] 4 F3
Baltiysk [RUS] 22 G1
Baltoji Vokė [LT] 24 H1
Baltrum [D] 18 B3
Balugães [P] 78 A6
Balvan [BG] 148 C3
Balvany [SK] 64 A5
Balvi [LV] 198 G4
Balya [TR] 152 D1
Balzers [FL] 58 H6
Bamberg [D] 46 G4
Bamble [N] 164 G3
Bana [H] 64 A6
Banafjäl [S] 184 G2
Banagher [IRL] 2 D6
Banarlı [TR] 150 C3
Banatski Karlovac [SRB] 142 H2
Banatsko Aranđelovo [SRB] 76 E5
Banatsko Karadjordjevo [SRB] 76 F6

Banatsko Novo Selo [SRB] 142 H2
Banaz [TR] 152 G3
Banbridge [NIR] 2 G4
Banbury [GB] 14 D2
Banchory [GB] 6 F6
Bandaksli [N] 164 E2
Bande [E] 78 C5
Bandholm [DK] 156 F5
Bandırma [TR] 150 D4
Bandol [F] 108 B5
Bandon [IRL] 4 C5
Băneasa [RO] 148 C1
Banff [GB] 6 F5
Bångnäs [S] 190 E4
Bangor [F] 40 C6
Bangor [GB] 10 B4
Bangor [NIR] 2 H3
Bangor Erris [IRL] 2 C3
Bangsbo [DK] 160 E3
Bánhalma [H] 76 F1
Banica [BG] 146 G3
Banie [PL] 20 F6
Banie Mazurskie [PL] 24 D2
Baniska [BG] 148 C2
Banja [SRB] 144 E2
Banja [SRB] 146 B4
Banja Koviljača [SRB] 142 E3
Banjaloka [SLO] 112 F1
Banja Luka [BIH] 142 C3
Banjani [SRB] 146 A1
Banjska [KS] 146 C4
Bánk [H] 64 H6
Banka [SK] 64 A3
Bankeryd [S] 162 D2
Bankháza [H] 76 C2
Bankya [BG] 146 F5
Bannalec [F] 40 C3
Banne [F] 106 F2
Bannesdorf [D] 20 A2
Bañolas / Banyoles [E] 92 F3
Banon [F] 108 C3
Baños de Alicún de las Torres [E] 102 F3
Baños de Cerrato [E] 88 F1
Baños de la Encina [E] 96 E6
Baños de Montemayor [E] 88 B4
Baños de Panticosa [E] 84 E5
Baños de Rio Tobia [E] 82 G6
Bánov [CZ] 62 H2
Bánovce nad Bebravou [SK] 64 B3
Banovići [BIH] 142 D3
Bánréve [H] 64 E4
Bansin [D] 20 E3
Banská Bystrica [SK] 64 C3
Banská Štiavnica [SK] 64 C3
Banské [SK] 64 G2
Bansko [BG] 130 B1
Bansko [MK] 128 H2
Banteer [IRL] 4 C4
Bantheville [F] 44 D3
Ban. Topola [SRB] 76 F6
Bantry [IRL] 4 B5
Bantry House [IRL] 4 B5
Banya [BG] 148 B5
Banya [BG] 148 D4
Banya [BG] 148 F4
Banyalbufar [E] 104 D4
Banyeres de Mariola [E] 104 D1
Banyoles / Bañolas [E] 92 F3
Banyuls-sur-Mer [F] 92 G2
Banz [D] 46 G3
Bapaume [F] 28 F4
Bar [MNE] 144 E5
Bara [RO] 76 H5
Baradla [H] 64 E3
Barajas [E] 88 G5
Barajas de Melo [E] 96 H1
Barakaldo [E] 82 G3
Baralla [E] 78 E4
Baranavichy [BY] 202 B6
Báránd [H] 76 G1
Baranowo [PL] 24 C5
Baranów Sandomierski [PL] 52 D2
Baraona [E] 90 B4
Baraqueville [F] 68 A6
Bårared [S] 162 B5
Barásoain [E] 84 B4
Barbadillo de Herreros [E] 90 A1
Barban [HR] 112 D2
Barbarano Vicentino [I] 72 D6
Barbaros [TR] 150 C3
Barba-Rossahöhle [D] 32 H5
Barbaste [F] 66 E5
Barbastro [E] 90 G3
Barbat [HR] 112 F3
Barbate [E] 100 F6
Bārbele [LV] 198 E6
Barberino Val d'Elsa [I] 110 F6
Barbezieux-St-Hilaire [F] 66 E2
Barbing [D] 60 F2
Barbizon [F] 42 F5
Barbotan-les-Thermes [F] 66 D6
Barby [D] 34 C3
Bårbyborg [S] 162 G6
Bârca [RO] 146 G2
Barcabo [E] 84 E6
Barca de Alva [P] 80 E5
Barcarrota [E] 94 F2
Barcellona-Pozzo di Gotto [I] 124 B7
Barcelona [E] 92 E4
Barcelonnette [F] 108 E2
Barcelos [P] 80 C3
Bárcena de Pie de Concha [E] 82 E3
Barchfeld [D] 46 F1
Barchon [B] 30 E5
Barciany [PL] 24 B3
Barcin [PL] 36 E1
Barcino [PL] 22 B3
Bárcis [I] 72 F4
Barcones [E] 90 A4
Barcs [H] 74 H5
Barczewo [PL] 22 H4
Bardakçi [TR] 152 E2
Bardejov [SK] 52 D6
Bardejovské Kúpele [SK] 52 C5
Bardi [I] 110 C3
Bardo [PL] 50 C2
Bardolino [I] 72 C6
Bardonécchia [I] 70 B5
Bardovo [RUS] 198 H5
Bardowick [D] 18 G5
Bardufoss [N] 192 F3
Bärenalm [A] 62 B6
Barenburg [D] 32 E1
Barendrecht [NL] 16 C5
Barentin [F] 26 H3
Barenton [F] 26 E5
Bärfendal [S] 166 C5
Barfleur [F] 26 E2
Barga [I] 110 D4
Bargas [E] 96 F1
Barge [I] 108 F2
Bargteheide [D] 18 G4
Bari [I] 122 E2
Barič [SRB] 142 G3
Båring [DK] 156 D3
Bari Sardo [I] 118 E5
Barisciano [I] 116 C4
Bariyevo [BG] 148 B4
Barjac [F] 106 G2
Barjas [E] 78 E5
Barjols [F] 108 C4
Barkåker [N] 164 H2
Barkald [N] 182 C5
Barkarö [S] 168 B2
Barkava [LV] 198 F5
Barkowo [PL] 22 C4
Bârlad [RO] 204 E4
Bar-le-Duc [F] 44 D5
Barles [F] 108 D3
Barletta [I] 122 C2
Barlinek [PL] 20 G6
Barlingbo [S] 168 G4
Barmash [AL] 128 D6
Barmouth [GB] 10 B5
Barmstedt [D] 18 F3
Barnard Castle [GB] 10 F2
Bärnau [D] 48 C4
Barneberg [D] 34 A3
Barneveld [NL] 16 E5
Barneville-Carteret [F] 26 D2
Barnewitz [D] 34 D2
Barnówko [PL] 34 G1
Barnsley [GB] 10 F4
Barnstaple [GB] 12 E3
Barnstorf [D] 18 D6
Barntrup [D] 32 E3
Baroña, Castro de- [E] 78 B3
Barovo [MK] 128 F2
Barquilla de Pinares [E] 88 C5
Barr [F] 44 G6
Barracas [E] 98 E3
Barraco [E] 88 E5
Barrafranca [I] 126 E4
Barranco do Velho [P] 94 C5
Barrancos [P] 94 F3
Barrax [E] 98 B5
Barre-des-Cévennes [F] 106 E2
Barreiro [P] 86 B5
Barreiros / San Cosme [E] 78 F2
Barrême [F] 108 D3
Barrosa [E] 100 F4
Barrow-in-Furness [GB] 10 D2
Barruecopardo [E] 80 F5
Barruera [E] 84 F6
Barry [F] 106 G2
Barry [GB] 12 F3
Barryporeen [IRL] 4 D4
Barsunovo [RUS] 198 H5
Barsele [S] 190 G4
Barsinghausen [D] 32 F2
Barssel [D] 18 C5
Barstyciai [LT] 200 D3
Bar-sur-Aube [F] 44 C6
Bar-sur-Seine [F] 44 B6
Barsviken [S] 184 F4
Barth [D] 20 C2
Barton-upon-Humber [GB] 10 G4
Bartoszyce [PL] 22 H2
Barúmini [I] 118 C6
Barussa, Nuraghe- [I] 118 B7
Baruth [D] 34 E3
Barvaux-sur-Ourthe [B] 30 E5
Barver [D] 32 E1
Bårvik [N] 194 A2
Barwice [PL] 22 A4
Barysaw [BY] 202 C5
Baryshevo [RUS] 178 G3
Bârzina [BG] 146 G3
Barzio [I] 70 G3
Bas [E] 92 F2
Bås [N] 164 E4
Bašaid [SRB] 76 F6
Başalan [TR] 152 F5
Basauri [E] 82 G4
Basconcillos del Tozo [E] 82 E5
Basdahl [D] 18 E4
Basel [CH] 58 E4
Baselga di Pinè [I] 72 D4
Båsheim [N] 170 G5
Bashtanka [UA] 202 F8
Basi [LV] 198 B5
Basildon [GB] 14 F4
Basilice [I] 120 F2
Bäsinge [S] 174 D6
Basingstoke [GB] 14 D4
Baška [HR] 112 F2
Baška Voda [HR] 144 B2
Baške Ostarije [HR] 112 G4
Bäsksjö [S] 190 F4
Başlamış [TR] 152 D2
Başmakçı [TR] 152 H4
Bäsna [S] 172 H4
Bassacutena [I] 118 D2
Bassano del Grappa [I] 72 D5
Bassenheim [D] 30 H6
Bassevuovdde [N] 194 C4
Bassoues [F] 84 F2
Bassum [D] 18 D6
Båstad [N] 166 C2
Båstad [S] 162 B6
Bastelica [F] 114 B4
Bastenaken (Bastogne) [B] 44 E1
Baştepe [TR] 152 H3
Bastfallet [S] 174 E5
Bastia [F] 114 C3
Bastia [I] 116 A2
Bastnäs [S] 166 E1
Bastogne (Bastenaken) [B] 44 E1
Bastuträsk [S] 190 H5
Bastuträsk [S] 190 H4
Batajnica [SRB] 142 G2
Batak [BG] 140 A6
Batakiai [LT] 200 E5
Batalha [P] 86 C3
Batanovtsi [BG] 146 F5
Batăr [RO] 76 H3
Bátaszék [H] 76 C4
Baté [H] 76 A4
Batea [E] 90 G6
Batelov [CZ] 48 H6
Batetskiy [RUS] 202 B2
Bath [GB] 12 G3
Batin [BG] 148 C2
Batina [HR] 76 C5
Batlava [KS] 146 C4
Bătmonostor [H] 76 C5
Båtmuseum [N] 180 C4
Batnfjordsøra [N] 180 E2
Batočina [SRB] 146 C2
Bátonyterenye [H] 64 D5
Batorz [PL] 52 E1
Bátovce [SK] 64 B4
Batrina [HR] 142 C2
Båtsfjord [N] 194 E1
Dåtsjaur [S] 190 G2
Battaglia Terme [I] 110 G1
Battenberg [D] 32 D6
Battice [B] 30 E5
Battipáglia [I] 120 F4
Battle [GB] 14 F5
Battonya [H] 76 G4
Batultsi [BG] 146 G4
Baturyn [UA] 202 E6
Bátya [H] 76 C4
Batyk [H] 74 G2
Batz-sur-Mer [F] 40 D6
Baud [F] 26 A6
Baugé [F] 42 A6
Baugy [F] 56 C3
Baume, Cirque de- [F] 56 H5
Baume, Grotte de la [F] 56 D4
Baume-les-Dames [F] 58 B4
Baume-les Messieurs, Abbaye de- [F] 56 H5
Baumholder [D] 44 H3
Baunei [I] 118 E5
Bauska [LV] 198 D6
Bautzen [D] 34 F6
Bavanište [SRB] 142 H2
Bavay [F] 28 G4
Baveno [I] 70 F3
Bavorov [CZ] 48 F6
Bawtry [GB] 10 F4
Bayard [F] 70 A4
Baydakovo [RUS] 198 H6
Bayerisch Eisenstein [D] 48 D6
Bayeux [F] 26 E3
Bayındır [TR] 150 F4
Bayındır [TR] 152 D4
Bayır [TR] 152 E6
Bayırköy [TR] 150 B5
Bayırköy [TR] 150 F4
Baykal [BG] 148 A2
Bayon [F] 44 E6
Bayonne [F] 84 C2
Bayrakçi Mağarasi [TR] 152 D5
Bayramdere [TR] 150 E4
Bayramiç [TR] 152 B1
Bayramşah [TR] 152 G1
Bayreuth [D] 46 H4
Bayrischzell [D] 60 F5
Baza [E] 102 G3
Bazas [F] 66 D4
Bazenheid [CH] 58 G5
Bazoches-sur-Hoëne [F] 26 G5
Bazolles [F] 56 E4
Baztan / Elizondo [E] 82 H4
Bazzano [I] 110 F3
Beaconsfield [GB] 14 D4
Béal an Mhuirthead / Belmullet [IRL] 2 B2
Beariz [E] 78 C4
Beas [E] 94 F5
Beasain [E] 84 A3
Beas de Segura [E] 102 G1
Beateberg [S] 166 F5
Beaucaire [F] 106 G4
Beaufort [IRL] 4 B4
Beaufort-en-Vallée [F] 54 E1
Beaufort-sur-Doron [F] 70 B3
Beaugency [F] 42 D6
Beaujeu [F] 68 F1
Beaulieu-sur-Dordogne [F] 66 H4
Beaulieu-sur-Mer [F] 108 F4
Beaumaris [GB] 10 B4
Beaumes de Venise [F] 106 H3
Beaumesnil [F] 26 H4
Beaumetz [F] 28 E4
Beaumont [B] 28 H4
Beaumont [F] 26 D1
Beaumont [F] 66 F4
Beaumont-de-Lomagne [F] 84 H2
Beaumont-le-Roger [F] 26 H4
Beaumont-sur-Sarthe [F] 26 F6
Beaune [F] 56 G4
Beaune-la-Rolande [F] 42 F6
Beaupréau [F] 54 C2
Beauraing [B] 30 D6
Beauregard, Manoir de- [F] 54 H2
Beaurepaire [F] 68 G4
Beaurepaire-en-Bresse [F] 56 H5
Beausite [F] 44 D4
Beauvais [F] 28 D6
Beauvallon [F] 108 D5
Beauvène [F] 68 E5
Beauvezer [F] 108 D3
Beauville [F] 66 F5
Beauvoir-sur-Mer [F] 54 B2
Beauvoir-sur-Niort [F] 54 D5
Beba Veche [RO] 76 E5
Bebenhausen [D] 58 G2
Bebra [D] 32 F6
Bebrene [LV] 198 F6
Bebrovo [BG] 148 D4
Beccles [GB] 14 H2
Becedas [E] 88 C4
Bečej [SRB] 76 E6
Bečej [SRB] 204 A5
Becerrea [E] 78 E4
Bécherel [F] 26 C5
Bechet [RO] 146 G2
Bechhofen [D] 46 F6
Bechyně [CZ] 48 F6
Becicherecu Mic [RO] 76 G5
Becilla de Valderaduey [E] 82 B5
Beçin Kalesi [TR] 154 C1
Beciu [RO] 148 A2
Beckenried [CH] 58 F6
Beckum [D] 32 C4
Beckum [D] 32 D3
Beclean [RO] 204 C4
Bécon-les-Granits [F] 40 G6
Bečov nad Teplou [CZ] 48 D3
Becsehely [H] 74 G4
Becske [H] 64 D5
Bédarieux [F] 106 D4
Bedburg [D] 30 G4
Beddingestrand [S] 158 C3
Bédée [F] 26 C5
Bedemler [TR] 152 C4
Beden [BG] 130 D1
Bedenac [F] 66 D2
Bedenica [HR] 74 F5
Bedford [GB] 14 E3
Będgoszcz [PL] 20 F5
Będków [PL] 36 H5
Bedlington [GB] 8 G5
Bednarka [PL] 52 D5
Bédole [I] 72 B4
Bedonia [I] 110 C3
Bedous [F] 84 D4
Bedsted [DK] 160 B4
Bedworth [GB] 14 D1
Będzin [PL] 50 G3
Będzino [PL] 20 H3
Beek [NL] 30 E4
Beekbergen [NL] 16 F5
Beek en Donk [NL] 30 E2
Beelitz [D] 34 D3
Beenz [D] 20 D5
Beerfelden [D] 46 D4
Beersel [B] 30 C4
Beeskow [D] 34 F3
Beesten [D] 32 C1
Befreiungshalle [D] 60 E2
Bégard [F] 26 A4
Beglezh [BG] 148 A3
Beg-Meil [F] 40 B3
Begndal [N] 170 G4
Begnecourt [F] 58 B2
Begonte [E] 78 D3
Begov Han [BIH] 142 D3
Begunitsy [RUS] 178 G6
Begur [E] 92 G3
Behramkale [TR] 134 H1
Behramlı [TR] 130 H5
Behringersmühle [D] 46 G4
Beilen [NL] 16 G3
Beilngries [D] 46 H6
Beinwil [CH] 58 E5
Beith [GB] 8 D3
Beitostølen [N] 170 F2
Beiuş [RO] 204 B4
Beja [P] 94 D3
Béjar [E] 88 B4
Bejís [E] 98 E3
Bekçiler [TR] 154 G1
Békés [H] 76 G3
Békéscsaba [H] 76 G3
Békésszentandrás [H] 76 F2
Bekilli [TR] 152 G4
Bekken [N] 172 D1
Bélâbre [F] 54 G4
Bela Crkva [SRB] 204 B5
Bel-Air [F] 26 C6
Bel-Air [F] 54 F5
Bel-Aire [F] 26 C6
Belalcázar [E] 96 C4
Bělá nad Radbuzou [CZ] 48 C5
Bela Palanka [SRB] 146 E4
Bélapátfalva [H] 64 E5
Bělá pod Bezdězem [CZ] 48 G2
Bělá pod Pradědem [CZ] 50 D3
Belava [LV] 198 F5
Belbaşı [TR] 154 H2
Belcaire [F] 106 A5
Bełchatów [PL] 36 G5
Belchin [BG] 146 G5
Belchite [E] 90 E5
Belčišta [MK] 128 D3
Belcoo [NIR] 2 E3
Belecke [D] 32 D4
Beled [H] 74 G1
Belej [HR] 112 E3
Belence [TR] 152 H3
Belene [BG] 148 B2
Belesta [F] 106 B5
Belev [RUS] 202 F4
Belevi [TR] 152 D5
Belevren [BG] 148 F5
Belfast [NIR] 2 G3
Belfir [RO] 76 H3
Belfort [F] 58 C4
Belgern [D] 34 D5
Belgirate [I] 70 F4
Belgodère [F] 114 B3
Belgooly [IRL] 4 C5
Beli [HR] 112 E2
Belianes [E] 92 C3
Belianska Jaskyňa [SK] 52 B6
Belica [BG] 148 D1
Belica [HR] 74 F4
Belica [MK] 128 D2
Belica [MK] 128 E2
Beli Iskăr [BG] 146 G5
Belikij Novgorod [RUS] 202 C2
Belıklıçeşme [TR] 150 C5
Beli Manastir [HR] 76 B6
Belimel [BG] 146 F3
Belin-Béliet [F] 66 C4
Belinchón [E] 96 H1
Belinţ [RO] 76 H5
Belišće [HR] 76 B6
Belitsa [BG] 146 G6
Beljakovci [MK] 146 D6
Beljina [SRB] 142 G3
Belkavak [TR] 152 H1
Bella [I] 120 G3
Bellac [F] 54 F5
Bellaghy [NIR] 2 G3
Bellagio [I] 70 G3
Bellaguarda [E] 90 H5
Bellamont [D] 60 B4
Bellamonte [I] 72 D4
Bellano [I] 70 G3
Bellante [I] 116 D3
Bellapais (Beylerbeyi) [CY] 154 G5
Bellária [I] 110 H4
Bellcaire d'Urgell [E] 92 C3
Belleek [NIR] 2 E3
Bellegarde [F] 42 F6
Bellegarde [F] 106 G4
Bellegarde-en-Marche [F] 68 B1
Bellegarde-sur-Valserine [F] 70 A2
Belle-Isle-en-Terre [F] 40 D2
Bellême [F] 26 G6
Bellenaves [F] 56 D6
Bellencombre [F] 28 C6
Bellengreville [F] 28 C4
Bellevesvre [F] 56 H5
Belleville [F] 68 F2
Belleville-sur-Vie [F] 54 B2
Belley [F] 68 H3
Bellinge [DK] 156 D3
Bellinzona [CH] 70 G3
Bell-lloc d'Urgell [E] 90 H4
Bello [E] 90 D5
Bellö [S] 162 E2
Bellpuig [E] 92 C3
Belluno [I] 72 E4
Bellver, Castell de- [E] 104 E5
Bellver de Cerdanya [E] 92 E2
Bellvik [S] 190 F5
Belmez [E] 96 B5
Belmez de la Moraleda [E] 102 F2
Belmonte [E] 78 G3
Belmonte [E] 96 H3
Belmonte [P] 86 F2
Belmont-sur-Rance [F] 106 D3
Belmullet / Béal an Mhuirthead [IRL] 2 B2
Belœil [B] 28 G3
Belogradchik [BG] 146 E3
Belokamensk [UA] 204 H4
Beloljin [SRB] 146 C4
Belopolci [BG] 130 G1
Belo Pole [BG] 146 F2
Belo Polje [KS] 146 B5
Belopol'ye [UA] 202 F6
Belorado [E] 82 F6
Bělotín [CZ] 50 E5
Belovec [BG] 148 D2
Belovo [BG] 148 A6
Belozem [BG] 148 B5
Belpasso [I] 126 G3
Belsen [D] 18 F6
Belsk Duży [PL] 38 B4
Beltinci [SLO] 74 F3
Belturbet [IRL] 2 E4
Beluša [SK] 64 B2
Belušić [SRB] 146 C2
Belvedere Campomoro [F] 114 A5
Belvedere du Cirque [F] 108 E2
Belvedere Marittimo [I] 124 C3
Belvedere Ostrense [I] 112 C6
Belver [P] 86 E4
Belvès [F] 66 F4
Belvis de la Jara [E] 96 D1
Belyy [RUS] 202 D3
Belz [F] 40 C4
Belz [UA] 52 H2
Bełżec [PL] 52 G2
Belzig [D] 34 D3
Bełżyce [PL] 38 D6
Bembibre [E] 78 F5
Bembirre [E] 78 C2
Bemposta [P] 80 F5
Bemposta [P] 86 D4
Benabarre [E] 90 H3
Benalmádena [E] 102 B5
Benalup [F] 100 G5
Benamaurel [E] 102 G3
Benaojón [E] 100 H4
Benasque [E] 84 F5
Benassal [E] 98 F2
Benassay [F] 54 E4
Benátky nad Jezerou [CZ] 48 G3
Benavente [E] 82 A5
Benavente [P] 86 C5
Benavila [P] 86 D5
Benavites [E] 78 G6
Bencık [TR] 154 C1
Bene [LV] 198 D6
Benediktbeuern [D] 60 D5
Benediktiner-Abtei [D] 60 F4
Benedikt v Slovenskih goricah [SLO] 74 E3
Beneixama / Benejama [E] 104 D1
Benejama / Beneixama [E] 104 D1
Benešov [CZ] 48 G4
Benešov [CZ] 62 C3
Benešov nad Ploučnicí [CZ] 48 F2
Benestad [S] 158 D3
Benetutti [I] 118 D4
Bénévent l'Abbaye [F] 54 G6
Benevento [I] 120 F2
Benfeld [F] 58 E2
Bengtsfors [S] 166 D4
Beničanci [HR] 76 B6
Benicarló [E] 98 H2
Benicasim / Benicàssim [E] 98 G3
Benicàssim / Benicasim [E] 98 G3
Benidorm [E] 104 E2
Beniel [E] 104 C3
Benifaió [E] 98 E5
Benifallet [E] 90 G6
Benifassá, Monestir de- [E] 98 G2
Benigánim [E] 98 E6
Benilloba [E] 104 E1
Benimarfull [E] 104 E1
Benissa [E] 104 F2
Benkovac [HR] 112 G5
Benkovski [BG] 148 F2
Benneckenstein [D] 32 H4
Bennstedt [D] 34 B5
Bénodet [F] 40 B3
Benós [E] 84 F5
Benòs [F] 84 F5
Benquerencia de la Serena [E] 96 B4
Benrath [D] 30 G4
Bensafrim [P] 94 B5
Bensberg [D] 30 H4
Bensersiel [D] 18 C3
Bensheim [D] 46 C4
Bensjö [S] 184 C3
Benzú [MA] 100 G6
Beočin [SRB] 142 F2
Beograd [SRB] 142 G2
Beograd [SRB] 204 B6
Bera / Vera de Bidasoa [E] 84 B2
Berane [MNE] 146 A5
Beranúy [E] 84 F6
Berat [AL] 128 B4
Beratón [E] 90 C3
Berbenno di Valtellina [I] 70 H3
Berberana [E] 82 G4
Bercedo [E] 82 F4
Bercel [H] 64 D5
Berceto [I] 110 D3
Berchem [L] 44 F3
Berching [D] 46 G6
Berchtesgaden [D] 60 G6
Bercinos del Real Camino [E] 82 C5
Berck-Plage [F] 28 D3
Berdalen [N] 164 D2
Berducedo [E] 78 F3
Berducido [E] 78 B4
Berdún [E] 84 C5
Berdychiv [UA] 202 C8
Berechiu [RO] 76 H3
Berehomet [UA] 204 D3
Berehove [UA] 204 B3
Berek [H] 76 F2
Berek [HR] 74 G6
Berest [PL] 52 C5
Berestowitsa [BY] 202 A6
Berettyószentmárton [H] 76 G1
Berettyóújfalu [H] 76 G1
Berezan' [UA] 202 E7
Berezhany [UA] 202 B8
Berezivka [UA] 204 F3
Berezna [UA] 202 D6
Berg [CH] 58 F4
Berg [D] 46 H2
Berg [D] 60 D5
Berg [N] 166 C3
Berg [N] 172 D5
Berg [N] 180 C6
Berg [N] 190 C3
Berg [S] 162 D4
Berg [S] 166 D4
Berga [D] 32 H5
Berga [E] 92 E2
Berga [S] 162 F4
Bergama [TR] 152 C2
Bergamo [I] 70 H4
Bergara [E] 82 H4
Berg bei Neamarkt [D] 46 H5
Bergby [S] 174 E3
Bergdala [S] 162 E5
Berge [N] 164 E1
Berge [S] 182 F1
Bergedorf [D] 18 G4
Bergeforsen [S] 184 E4
Bergen [D] 18 F6
Bergen [D] 18 H6
Bergen [D] 20 D2
Bergen [D] 44 F3
Bergen [D] 48 C3
Bergen [N] 170 B4
Bergen [NL] 16 D3
Bergen (Mons) [B] 28 G4
Bergen aan Zee [NL] 16 D3
Bergen op Zoom [NL] 16 C6
Berger [N] 164 H2
Bergerac [F] 66 E4
Berget [N] 190 E2
Bergfors [S] 192 G4
Bergheim [D] 30 G4
Berghem [S] 160 H3
Bergisch Gladbach [D] 30 H4
Bergkvara [S] 162 F6
Bergland [S] 190 F4
Berglern [D] 60 E3
Berglia [N] 190 D5
Berg-Neustadt [D] 32 C5
Bergö [FIN] 186 A3
Bergö [FIN] 186 A2
Bergondo [E] 78 D2
Bergsäter [S] 190 F4
Bergshamra [S] 168 E2
Bergsjö [S] 166 F3
Bergsjö [S] 184 E6
Bergsjøstøl [N] 170 F4
Berg slussar [S] 166 H5
Bergsmoen [N] 190 C5
Bergstad [FIN] 176 G5
Bergstrøm [N] 166 C3
Bergsviken [S] 196 B3
Bergues [F] 14 H6
Bergum [NL] 16 F2
Bergün [CH] 70 H2
Bergunda [S] 162 D5
Bergundhaugen [N] 172 B2
Bergvik [S] 174 E2
Berhida [H] 76 B2
Beringel [P] 94 D3
Beringen [B] 30 E3
Berini [RO] 76 G6
Bérisal [CH] 70 E2
Berja [E] 102 F5
Berkåk [N] 180 H3
Berkenthin [D] 18 G4
Berkesz [H] 64 H4
Berkheim [D] 60 B4
Berkhof [D] 32 F1
Berkovići [BIH] 144 C3
Berkovitsa [BG] 146 F3
Berkvigen [S] 190 G2
Berlanga [E] 94 H4
Berlanga de Duero [E] 90 A3
Berlevåg [N] 194 E1
Berlin [D] 34 E2
Berlingen [CH] 58 G4
Bermeo [E] 82 H3
Bermillo de Sayago [E] 80 G5
Bern [CH] 58 D6
Bernalda [I] 122 D4
Bernartice [CZ] 48 F5
Bernati [LV] 198 B6
Bernau [D] 34 E2
Bernau [D] 60 F5
Bernaville [F] 28 E4
Bernay [F] 26 G4
Bernburg [D] 34 B4
Berndorf [A] 62 E5
Berne [D] 18 D5
Bernedo [E] 82 H6
Bernek [A] 72 C1
Bernhardsthal [A] 62 G3
Bernkastel-Kues [D] 44 G2
Bernsdorf [D] 34 F5
Bernstein [A] 74 F1
Bernués [E] 84 D5
Beromünster [CH] 58 F5
Beronovo [BG] 148 E4
Beroun [CZ] 48 F4
Berovo [MK] 128 H1
Berre-l'Etang [F] 106 H5
Berrien [F] 40 C2
Berriozar [E] 84 B4
Berrocal [E] 94 F5
Berrocalejo [E] 88 C6
Berroquejo [E] 100 F4
Bersenbrück [D] 32 D1
Beršići [SRB] 146 B2
Bertinoro [I] 110 G4
Bertrix [B] 44 D2
Berwang [A] 60 C6
Berwick-upon-Tweed [GB] 8 F4
Beryslav [UA] 204 G3
Berzaune [LV] 198 F5
Berzeme [F] 68 E6
Berzence [H] 74 G4
Berzosa [E] 88 H2
Besalú [E] 92 F2
Besançon [F] 58 B5
Besande [E] 82 C3
Besenyőtelek [H] 64 E6
Besenyszög [H] 76 E1
Beşevler [TR] 150 G4
Beşevlet [TR] 150 G3
Besigheim [D] 46 D6
Běšiny [CZ] 48 D6
Beška [SRB] 142 G2
Bessan [F] 106 E1
Bessans [F] 70 C5
Bessay-sur-Allier [F] 56 D5
Besse-en-Chandesse [F] 68 C3
Besse-sur-Issole [F] 108 C5
Bessheim [N] 170 F1
Bessines-sur-Gartempe [F] 54 G6
Best [NL] 30 E2
Bestida [P] 80 B5
Bestorp [S] 168 A6
Beszowa [PL] 52 C2
Betancuria [E] 100 E6

Betanzos [E] 78 D2
Betelu [E] 84 B3
Bétera [E] 98 E4
Beteta [E] 90 B6
Bétharram, Grottes de- [F] 84 E4
Bethesda [GB] 10 B4
Béthune [F] 28 E3
Betliar [SK] 64 E3
Betna [N] 180 F2
Betna [N] 180 F2
Betsele [S] 190 G5
Bettenburg [D] 46 F3
Bettna [S] 168 C4
Bettola [I] 110 C2
Bettyhill [GB] 6 E2
Betws-y-Coed [GB] 10 C4
Betz [F] 42 G3
Betzdorf [D] 32 C6
Betzigau [D] 60 C5
Beuel [D] 30 H5
Beuil [F] 108 E3
Beulich [D] 44 H1
Beuron [D] 58 G3
Beuzeville [F] 26 G3
Bevagna [I] 116 A2
Bévercé-Malmedy [B] 30 F5
Beverley [GB] 10 G4
Beverstedt [D] 18 D4
Beverungen [D] 32 F4
Beverwijk [NL] 16 D4
Bevtoft [DK] 156 C3
Bewdley [GB] 12 G1
Bex [CH] 70 C2
Bexhill [GB] 14 E6
Beyağaç [TR] 152 F6
Beyarmudu (Pergamos) [CY] 154 G5
Beyazköy [TR] 150 C2
Beycayırı [TR] 150 B5
Beyce Sultan [TR] 152 G4
Beydağı [TR] 152 E4
Beydilli [TR] 152 H3
Beyel [TR] 152 E1
Beyköy [TR] 152 H6
Beykoz [TR] 150 E2
Beylerbeyi (Bellapaïs) [CY] 154 G5
Beynac-et-Cazenac [F] 66 F4
Beynat [F] 66 H3
Beyobaşı [TR] 154 E1
Bezau [A] 60 B6
Bezdan [SRB] 76 C5
Bezden [BG] 146 F4
Bezděz [CZ] 48 G2
Bezdonys [LT] 200 G5
Bezdružice [CZ] 48 D4
Bezhetë-Makaj [AL] 146 A6
Bezhetsk [RUS] 202 E2
Béziers [F] 106 D4
Béznar [E] 102 E4
Bezzecca [I] 72 C5
B. Hornberg [D] 46 D5
Biała [PL] 50 D3
Białaczów [PL] 38 A5
Biała Piska [PL] 24 D4
Biała Podlaska [PL] 38 F3
Biała Rawska [PL] 38 A4
Białawy Wielkie [PL] 36 C5
Białobrzegi [PL] 38 B4
Białogard [PL] 20 H3
Białogóra [PL] 22 D1
Białowieża [PL] 38 G1
Biały Bór [PL] 22 B4
Białystok [PL] 24 E5
Biancavilla [I] 126 G3
Bianco [I] 124 D7
Biar [E] 104 D1
Biarritz [F] 84 C2
Bias [F] 66 B5
Biasca [CH] 70 G2
Biasteri / Laguardia [E] 82 G6
Biatigala [LT] 200 E4
Biatorbágy [H] 76 C1
Bibaktad [N] 194 C2
Bibbiena [I] 110 G6
Bibbiona [I] 114 E1
Biberach [D] 58 F2
Biberach an der Riss [D] 60 B4
Biberwier [A] 60 D6
Bibione [I] 72 G6
Bibury [GB] 12 H3
Bič [SLO] 74 C5
Bicaj [AL] 128 C1
Bicaz [RO] 204 D4
Bicester [GB] 14 D3
Bichl [D] 60 D5
Bicos [P] 94 C3
Bicske [H] 76 B1
Bidache [F] 84 C2
Bidalite [S] 162 F6
Bidart [F] 84 C2
Biddinghuizen [NL] 16 F4
Biddulph [GB] 10 E5
Bideford [GB] 12 D3
Bidjovagge [N] 192 H2
Bidovce [SK] 64 G3
Bidziny [PL] 52 D1
Bie [S] 168 B4
Bieber [D] 46 D3
Biebersdorf [D] 34 F4
Biecz [PL] 52 C4
Biedenkopf [D] 32 D6
Biegen [D] 34 F3
Biegen [D] 34 F3
Biejkvasslia [N] 190 D2
Biel [E] 84 C5
Biel / Bienne [CH] 58 D5
Bielany Wrocł. [PL] 50 C1
Bielawa [PL] 50 C2
Bielawy [PL] 36 G3
Bielczyny [PL] 22 E5
Bielefeld [D] 32 D3
Bielino [PL] 38 C1
Biella [I] 70 E4
Bielmonte [I] 70 E4
Bielopolje [HR] 112 H3
Bielowy [PL] 52 D4
Bielsa [E] 84 E5
Bielsa, Tunnel de- [E/F] 84 E5
Bielsk [PL] 36 H2
Bielsko-Biała [PL] 50 G4
Bielsk Podlaski [PL] 38 F1
Biely Kameň [SK] 62 G4
Bienenbüttel [D] 18 G5
Bieniów [PL] 34 H4
Bienne / Biel [CH] 58 D5
Bienvenida [E] 94 G3
Bienvenida [E] 96 D4
Bierberchren [D] 46 E5
Bierdzany [PL] 50 E2
Biermé [F] 40 H5
Bierre-Lès-Semur [F] 56 F3
Bierutów [PL] 36 D6
Bierzwnik [PL] 20 G6
Biescas [E] 84 D5
Biesenthal [D] 34 E1
Biesiekierz [PL] 20 H3
Bieskkenjárga [N] 194 C4
Bietigheim [D] 46 D6
Bieżuń [PL] 22 G6
Biga [TR] 150 C5
Bigadiç [TR] 152 D2
Bigastro [E] 104 D3
Biggar [GB] 8 E4
Biggleswade [GB] 14 E3
Bignasco [CH] 70 F2
Bigor [MNE] 144 E4
Bihać [BIH] 112 H3
Biharia [RO] 76 H2
Biharkeresztes [H] 76 H2
Biharnagybajom [H] 76 G1
Bijambarska Pećina [BIH] 142 D4
Bijeljani [BIH] 144 D3
Bijeljina [BIH] 142 E3
Bijelo Brdo [HR] 142 E1
Bijelo Polje [MNE] 146 A4
Bikava [LV] 198 G5
Bikovo [SRB] 76 D5
Bílá [CZ] 50 F5
Bila Tserkva [UA] 202 D8
Bilbao / Bilbo [E] 82 G4
Bilbo / Bilbao [E] 82 G4
Bileća [BIH] 144 D3
Bilecik [TR] 150 G4
Biled [RO] 76 G5
Bílenec [CZ] 48 E3
Biłgoraj [PL] 52 F2
Bilhorod Dnistrovs'kyi [UA] 204 F4
Bílina [CZ] 48 E2
Bilisht [AL] 128 D5
Biljanovac [SRB] 146 B3
Bilje [HR] 76 C6
Bilka [BG] 148 F3
Billdal [S] 160 G2
Billerbeck [D] 16 H6
Billericay [GB] 14 F4
Billesholm [S] 156 H1
Billingen [N] 180 E5
Billingsfors [S] 166 D4
Billom [F] 68 D2
Billsta [S] 184 G4
Billum [DK] 156 A2
Billund [DK] 156 C2
Bilopillia [UA] 202 E7
Bilousivka [UA] 202 E7
Bílovec [CZ] 50 E4
Bilska [LV] 198 F4
Bilsko [PL] 52 B4
Bilto [N] 192 H2
Bíňa [SK] 64 B5
Binas [F] 42 D6
Binasco [I] 70 G5
Binche [B] 28 H4
Bindslev [DK] 160 E2
Binéfar [E] 90 G4
Bingen [D] 46 B3
Bingen [N] 170 G6
Binghöhle [D] 46 G4
Bingsjö [S] 174 C3
Bingsta [S] 182 G3
Binibeca Vell [E] 104 H5
Binic [F] 26 B4
Binkos [BG] 148 D4
Bin Tepeler [TR] 152 E3
Binz [D] 20 D2
Binzen [D] 58 E4
Bioče [MNE] 144 E4
Biograd [HR] 112 G5
Bionaz [I] 70 D3
Bioska [SRB] 144 F1
Bircza [PL] 52 E4
Birgi [TR] 152 E4
Birgittelyst [DK] 160 D5
Biri [N] 172 B3
Birini [EST] 198 E2
Birini [LV] 198 E4
Biristrand [N] 172 B3
Birkala / Pirkkala [FIN] 176 F1
Birkeland [N] 164 C5
Birkeland [N] 164 E5
Birkenfeld [D] 44 G3
Birkenfeld [D] 46 E4
Birkenhead [GB] 10 D4
Birkenwerder [D] 34 E2
Birkerød [DK] 156 G2
Birkfeld [A] 74 E1
Birksdal [N] 180 D6
Birmingham [GB] 10 E6
Birnau [D] 58 H4
Biron, Château de- [F] 66 F4
Birr [IRL] 2 D6
Birstein [D] 46 D2
Birštonas [LT] 24 F1
Biržai [LT] 198 E6
Birżebbuġa [M] 126 C6
Birži [LV] 198 F6
Birzuli [LV] 198 F4
Bisaccia [I] 120 G3
Bisacquino [I] 126 C3
Biscarrosse [F] 66 B4
Biscarrosse-Plage [F] 66 B4
Biscéglie [I] 122 D2
Bischoffen [D] 46 C1
Bischofsgrün [D] 46 H3
Bischofsheim [D] 46 E2
Bischofshofen [A] 72 G1
Bischofswerda [D] 34 F6
Biscoitos [P] 100 D3
Biserci [BG] 148 D1
Bishop Auckland [GB] 10 F2
Bishop's Castle [GB] 10 C6
Bishop's Cleeve [GB] 12 G2
Bishop's Stortford [GB] 14 F3
Bisignano [I] 124 D4
Bisko [HR] 144 A2
Biskupice Oławskie [PL] 50 D1
Biskupice Radłowskice [PL] 52 C3
Biskupiec [PL] 22 F5
Biskupiec [PL] 22 H4
Biskupin [PL] 36 D1
Bisław [PL] 22 D5
Bislev [DK] 160 D4
Bismark [D] 34 B1
Bismo [N] 180 F5
Bispingen [D] 18 F5
Bistrec [BG] 148 E5
Bistreț [RO] 146 F2
Bistrica [MNE] 144 E3
Bistrica [SRB] 146 A3
Bistrica ob S. [SLO] 74 D5
Bistrița [RO] 204 C4
Bistritsa [BG] 146 F5
Bisztynek [PL] 22 H3
Bitburg [D] 44 F2
Bitche [F] 44 G4
Bitetto [I] 122 D3
Bithia [I] 118 C8
Bitola [MK] 128 E3
Bitonto [I] 122 D2
Bítov [CZ] 62 E2
Bitterfeld [D] 34 C4
Bitterstad [N] 192 D4
Bitti [I] 118 D4
Bıvıkalı [TR] 150 C3
Bivio [CH] 70 H2
Bivio Manganaro [I] 126 D2
Bivona [I] 126 D3
Bıyıklı [TR] 152 D5
Bizovac [HR] 76 B6
Bjåen [N] 164 D1
Bjala Cherkva [BG] 148 C3
Bjalizvor [BG] 148 C5
Bjår [N] 164 F1
Bjarisino [BY] 202 C5
Bjärklunda [S] 166 E6
Bjärnå / Perniö [FIN] 176 F5
Bjärnum [S] 158 D1
Bjärred [S] 156 H2
Bjärträ [S] 184 F3
Bjästa [S] 184 G2
Bjelland [N] 164 D5
Bjelovar [HR] 74 G5
Bjerga [N] 164 C1
Bjergby [DK] 160 C5
Bjerkreim [N] 164 B4
Bjerkvik [N] 192 E4
Bjerre [DK] 156 D2
Bjerregård [DK] 156 A1
Bjerringbro [DK] 160 D5
Bjoenstrand [N] 164 B1
Bjølstad [N] 180 G6
Bjoneroa [N] 170 H4
Bjonevika [N] 170 H4
Bjørånes [N] 172 C1
Björbo [S] 172 G5
Bjordal [N] 164 C4
Bjordal [N] 170 B2
Bjørgo [N] 170 G3
Björka [S] 172 G3
Bjørkåsen [N] 192 F3
Björkberg [S] 172 H1
Björkberg [S] 190 G4
Bjørke [N] 180 D4
Bjørkedal [N] 180 C4
Björkefors [S] 162 F1
Bjørkelangen [N] 166 C1
Bjørkflåta [N] 170 F4
Björkfors [S] 190 E3
Björkhöjden [S] 184 D2
Björkliden [S] 192 F4
Björklinge [S] 168 D1
Bjørknes [N] 172 C6
Björkö [FIN] 176 C5
Björkö [S] 162 E3
Björkö [S] 168 F1
Björköby [FIN] 186 A2
Björksele [S] 190 G4
Björksjön [S] 184 F2
Björkvattnet [S] 190 D5
Björkvik [S] 168 B4
Bjørlia [N] 190 C4
Bjørn [N] 190 D2
Björna [S] 184 G1
Björneborg [S] 166 G3
Björneborg / Pori [FIN] 176 D1
Bjørnestad [N] 164 C4
Bjørnevasshytta [N] 164 D2
Bjørnevatn [N] 194 E3
Björnhult [S] 162 G3
Björnlunda [S] 168 C4
Björnrike [S] 182 F4
Björnsholm [S] 162 G1
Björnsjö [S] 184 G1
Bjørnstad [N] 190 D4
Björsäter [S] 166 F5
Björsäter [S] 168 B6
Bjørsvik [N] 170 B3
Bjuråker [S] 184 D6
Bjurberget [S] 172 E4
Bjurfors [S] 196 A5
Bjurholm [S] 190 H6
Bjurholm [S] 190 H6
Bjuröklubb [S] 196 B5
Bjurön [S] 174 G5
Bjursås [S] 172 H4
Bjursele [S] 190 H4
Bjurträsk [S] 190 H4
Bjuv [S] 156 H1
Blace [SRB] 146 C3
Blachownia [PL] 50 F2
Blackburn [GB] 10 E3
Blacklion [IRL] 2 E3
Blackpool [GB] 10 D3
Blackstad [S] 162 G2
Blackwater [IRL] 4 F5
Bladåker [S] 168 E1
Blaenau Ffestiniog [GB] 10 B4
Blagaj [BIH] 144 C2
Blagaj Japra [BIH] 142 A2
Blagoevgrad [BG] 146 F6
Blagoevo [BG] 148 D2
Blagoveštenje, Manastir- [SRB] 146 B2
Blagovica [SLO] 74 C4
Blåhøj [DK] 156 B1
Blaiken [S] 190 F4
Blaikliden [S] 190 F4
Blain [F] 40 F5
Blair Atholl [GB] 8 E1
Blairgowrie [GB] 8 E2
Blaisy-Bas [F] 56 G3
Blaj [RO] 204 C4
Blajan [F] 84 G4
Błąkały [PL] 24 D2
Blakstad [N] 164 E5
Blâmont [F] 44 F6
Blanca [E] 104 C2
Blandford Forum [GB] 12 G4
Blanes [E] 92 F4
Blangy-sur-Bresle [F] 28 D4
Blanických Rytířů, Jeskyně- [CZ] 50 C5
Blankaholm [S] 162 G2
Blankenberge [B] 28 G1
Blankenburg [D] 32 H4
Blankenfelde [D] 34 E2
Blankenhain [D] 46 H1
Blankenheim [D] 30 G6
Blanquefort [F] 66 C3
Blansko [CZ] 50 C6
Blanzac [F] 66 E2
Blarney [IRL] 4 C5
Blarney Castle [IRL] 4 C5
Blascosancho [E] 88 E4
Błaszki [PL] 36 F5
Blatná [CZ] 48 E5
Blatnica [BIH] 142 C3
Blatnica [SK] 64 C2
Blatnice pod Sv. Antonínkem [CZ] 62 H2
Blato [HR] 144 A3
Blato [HR] 144 A2
Blattniksele [S] 190 G3
Blaubeuren [D] 60 B3
Blaufelden [D] 46 E5
Blaustein [D] 60 B3
Blåvand [DK] 156 A2
Blåvik [S] 162 E1
Blaye [F] 66 C2
Błażowa [PL] 52 E4
Blazquez [E] 96 B5
Bleckåsen [S] 182 F1
Bleckede [D] 18 G5
Blecksnäs [FIN] 186 A3
Bled [SLO] 74 B4
Bleiburg [A] 74 C3
Bleicherode [D] 32 G5
Bleik [N] 192 E3
Bleisfjord [N] 192 F4
Blendija [SRB] 146 D3
Bléneau [F] 56 D2
Blentarp [S] 158 C3
Blera [I] 114 H4
Blérancourt [F] 28 F6
Bléré [F] 54 G2
Blériot-Plage [F] 14 G6
Bleskestad [N] 164 C1
Blesle [F] 68 C3
Blessington [IRL] 2 F6
Bletterans [F] 56 H5
Blévy [F] 26 H5
Blexen [D] 18 D4
Bliesbruck-Reinheim, Parc Archéol. de- [F] 44 G4
Blieskastel [D] 44 G4
Bligny-sur-Ouche [F] 56 G4
Blikstorp [S] 166 F6
Blinisht [AL] 128 B1
Blinja [HR] 142 A1
Blintrop [D] 32 C5
Bliznaci [BG] 148 E2
Bliznak [BG] 148 F5
Bliznak [BG] 148 F3
Blizne [PL] 52 E4
Błogoszów [PL] 52 A2
Blois [F] 54 H1
Blokhus [DK] 160 D3
Blokzijl [NL] 16 F3
Blombacka [S] 166 F2
Blomberg [D] 32 E3
Blomsholms-Skeppet [S] 166 C4
Blomstermåla [S] 162 G4
Blönduós [IS] 192 B2
Błonie [PL] 36 C6
Błonie [PL] 38 B3
Błonie [PL] 38 F3
Bloška Polica [SLO] 74 B6
Blötberget [S] 172 H5
Błotnica [PL] 20 G3
Błotnica [PL] 38 B6
Błotno [PL] 20 F4
Blovice [CZ] 48 E5
Bludenz [A] 72 A1
Bludov [CZ] 50 C4
Blumberg [D] 58 F3
Blyth [GB] 8 G5
Bø [N] 164 F2
Bø [N] 164 G2
Bø [N] 170 B3
Bø [N] 170 B1
Bø [N] 192 D4
Bø [N] 192 E2
Bo [S] 166 H4
Boadilla del Monte [E] 88 F5
Boal [E] 78 F2
Boalt [S] 162 D6
Boário Terme [I] 72 B5
Bòbbio [I] 110 C2
Bobbio Pellice [I] 70 C6
Boberg [S] 184 C2
Bobice [PL] 52 E4
Bobin [PL] 52 B3
Bobingen [D] 60 D4
Bobitz [D] 20 A4
Böblingen [D] 58 G1
Bobolice [PL] 22 B3
Boboshevo [BG] 146 F6
Bobovdol [BG] 146 F5
Bobr [BY] 202 C5
Bobrová [CZ] 50 B5
Bobrovytsia [UA] 202 D7
Bobrowice [PL] 34 H4
Bobrowniki [PL] 24 F5
Bobrowniki [PL] 36 F1
Bobrynets' [UA] 204 G2
Bočac [BIH] 142 B3
Boca de Huergano [E] 82 C3
Bocairent [E] 104 E1
Boceguillas [E] 88 G3
Böcen [TR] 150 F5
Bochnia [PL] 52 B4
Bocholt [B] 30 E3
Bocholt [D] 16 G6
Bochov [CZ] 48 D3
Bochum [D] 30 H3
Bocigas [E] 88 E3
Bockara [S] 162 F3
Bockel [D] 18 E5
Bockenem [D] 32 G3
Bocki [PL] 38 E1
Böcksholm [S] 162 E4
Böckstein [A] 72 G2
Bockum Hövel [D] 32 C3
Bocognano [F] 114 B4
Boconád [H] 64 E6
Bócsa [H] 76 D3
Bocsig [RO] 76 H4
Böda [S] 162 H3
Boda [S] 166 E2
Boda [S] 172 H3
Boda [S] 184 E3
Bodaczów [PL] 52 F1
Bodafors [S] 162 D3
Boda glasbruk [S] 162 F5
Bodarsjön [S] 182 G6
Bodegraven [NL] 16 D5
Boden [S] 196 B3
Bodenmais [D] 48 D6
Bodenteich [D] 18 G6
Bodenwerder [D] 32 F3
Bodenwöhr [D] 48 C6
Bodjani [SRB] 142 E1
Bodman [D] 58 G4
Bodmin [GB] 12 C4
Bodø [N] 192 D6
Bodom [N] 190 C5
Bodrogkeresztúr [H] 64 G4
Bodrum [TR] 154 B2
Bodsjö [S] 182 H3
Bodsjöedet [S] 182 E1
Bodträskfors [S] 196 A2
Bodzanów [PL] 36 H2
Bodzanowice [PL] 50 F1
Bodzentyn [PL] 52 C1
Boëge [F] 70 B2
Boën [F] 68 E2
Bogács [H] 64 F5
Bøgard [N] 192 D3
Bogarra [E] 98 A6
Bogatić [SRB] 142 F2
Bogatovo [RUS] 22 G2
Bogatynia [PL] 48 G1
Boğaz (Bogázi) [CY] 154 G5
Boğazcık [TR] 154 G2
Bogázi (Boğaz) [CY] 154 G5
Boğaziçi [TR] 152 D5
Boğazköy [TR] 150 F4
Bogda [RO] 76 H5
Bogdana [RO] 148 D2
Bogdanci [MK] 128 G3
Bogdaniec [PL] 34 H2
Bogë [AL] 146 A6
Boge [S] 168 G4
Bogen [D] 60 G2
Bogen [N] 192 D5
Bogen [N] 192 E4
Bogen [S] 172 D6
Bogense [DK] 156 D2
Bogetići [MNE] 144 E4
Bogge [N] 180 F3
Böglosa [S] 168 C2
Bognanco [I] 70 E3
Bognes [N] 192 E4
Bognor Regis [GB] 14 D5
Bogojevo [SRB] 142 E1
Bogojevo [SRB] 146 D4
Bogoria [PL] 52 C2
Bogorodica [MK] 128 G3
Bogovina [SRB] 146 D2
Bogovinska Pećina [SRB] 146 D2
Bograngen [S] 172 E4
Boguchwałów [PL] 50 E3
Bogumiłowice [PL] 36 G6
Boguszów-Gorce [PL] 50 B2
Bogutovačka Banja [SRB] 146 B3
Bogyiszló [H] 76 C4
Bohain-en-Vermandois [F] 28 F5
Bohal [F] 26 B6
Bohdalov [CZ] 50 A5
Boheeshil [IRL] 4 B4
Bohinjska Bela [SLO] 74 B4
Bohinjska Bistrica [SLO] 74 A4
Böhmenkirch [D] 60 B2
Bohmte [D] 32 D2
Bohonal [E] 96 D2
Bohonal de Ibor [E] 88 B6
Böhönye [H] 74 H4
Bohula [MK] 128 F3
Boialvo [P] 80 B6
Boichinovtsi [BG] 146 F3
Bois-du-Four [F] 68 B6
Boitzenburg [D] 20 D5
Bóixols [E] 92 C2
Boizenburg [D] 18 G5
Böja [S] 166 F5
Bojano [I] 120 E1
Bojanów [PL] 52 D2
Bojanowo [PL] 36 C4
Bøjden [DK] 156 D4
Bojkovice [CZ] 62 H2
Bojnica [BG] 146 E2
Bojnice [SK] 64 B3
Bojnik [SRB] 146 D4
Bojtiken [S] 190 E3
Bokel [D] 18 F3
Bökemåla [S] 162 E6
Bökenäs [S] 166 C6
Bokinić [HR] 112 E3
Böklund [D] 18 F1
Bokod [H] 64 B6
Bokod [H] 64 B6
Bököny [H] 64 H5
Bokros [H] 76 E3
Boksitogorsk [RUS] 202 D1
Boksjok [N] 194 D2
Bol [HR] 144 A2
Bolaños de Calatrava [E] 96 F4
Bolayır [TR] 150 B4
Bolbec [F] 26 H3
Bolca [I] 72 C6
Bölcek [TR] 152 C2
Boldekow [D] 20 D4
Boldogasszonyfa [H] 76 A4
Boldva [H] 64 F4
Bøle [N] 190 B5
Böle [S] 182 G1
Bolekhiv [UA] 52 H6
Bolemin [PL] 34 H2
Bolesławiec [PL] 36 A6
Bolesławiec [PL] 36 E6
Bolesławów [PL] 50 C3
Boleszkowice [PL] 34 G2
Bolfiar [P] 80 B5
Bolfoss [N] 166 C1
Bolgatovo [RUS] 198 H5
Bolgheri [I] 114 E1
Bolhrad [UA] 204 E4
Boliden [S] 196 A4
Bolimów [PL] 38 A3
Bolinglanna / Buaile an Ghleanna [IRL] 2 B3
Boljanići [MNE] 144 E2
Boljevac [SRB] 146 D2
Boljevac [SRB] 204 B6
Boljun [HR] 112 E1
Bolkesjø [N] 164 G1
Bolkhov [RUS] 202 F4
Bolków [PL] 50 B1
Bollebygd [S] 162 B2
Bollène [F] 106 G2
Böllerkirche [D] 46 B3
Bollerup [S] 158 D3
Bollnäs [S] 174 D2
Bollstabruk [S] 184 F3
Bollullos de la Mitación [E] 94 G6
Bollullos Par del Condado [E] 94 F6
Bologna [I] 110 F3
Bologne [F] 44 C6
Bolótana [I] 118 C4
Bolsena [I] 114 H3
Bol'shakovo [RUS] 200 D5
Bol'shaya Izhora [RUS] 178 G5
Bol'shaya Yashchera [RUS] 198 H1
Bol'shie Sabicy [RUS] 198 H2
Bol'shiye Kolpany [RUS] 178 H6
Bol'shoye Zagor'e [RUS] 198 H3
Bol'shoy Sabsk [RUS] 198 G1
Bolstad [S] 166 D5
Bolstadøyri [N] 170 C3
Bolstaholm [FIN] 176 A5
Bolsward [NL] 16 E2
Bolszewo [PL] 22 D2
Boltaña [E] 84 E5
Boltenhagen [D] 18 H3
Boltigen [CH] 70 D1
Bolton [GB] 10 E4
Bolungarvík [IS] 192 A1
Bóly [H] 76 B5
Bolyarovo [BG] 148 E5
Bolyartsi [BG] 148 B6
Bolzano / Bozen [I] 72 D3
Bomarken [S] 166 C3
Bomarsund [FIN] 176 B5
Bomarzo [I] 114 H4
Bombarral [P] 86 B4
Bominago [I] 116 C4
Bom Jesus do Monte [P] 80 C3
Bomsund [S] 184 C2
Bonaduz [CH] 70 H1
Bonaguil, Château de- [F] 66 F5
Bonanza [E] 100 F3
Boñar [E] 82 C3
Bonar Bridge [GB] 6 E4
Bonares [E] 94 F6
Bonäs [S] 166 E2
Bonäs [S] 172 G3
Bonäset [S] 182 F1
Bonåsjøen [N] 192 D5
Bonassola [I] 110 C4
Bonaval [E] 88 G4
Bończa [PL] 38 B4
Bondal [N] 164 F1
Bondemon [S] 166 C4
Bondeno [I] 110 F2
Bondstorp [S] 162 C2
Bonefro [I] 116 F6
Bonete [E] 98 C6
Bonhamn [S] 184 G3
Bonhomme, Col du- [F] 58 D2
Bonifacio [F] 114 B6
Bonifati Marina [I] 124 C4
Bonilla [E] 98 B1
Bönitz [D] 34 E5
Bonlieu [F] 70 A1
Bonn [D] 30 G5
Bonnat [F] 54 H5
Bonndorf [D] 58 F4
Bønnerup Strand [DK] 160 F5
Bonnesvalyn [F] 42 H3
Bonnétable [F] 42 C5
Bonneuil-Matours [F] 54 F4
Bonneval [F] 42 D5
Bonneval-sur-Arc [F] 70 C4
Bonneville [F] 70 B2
Bonnières [F] 42 E3
Bonnieux [F] 106 H4
Bonnigheim [D] 46 D6
Bonny-sur-Loire [F] 56 D2
Bono [I] 118 D4
Bonorva [I] 118 C4
Bonport, Abbaye de- [F] 28 B6
Bonyhád [H] 76 B4
Bonzov [CZ] 50 C5
Boom [B] 30 C3
Boos [D] 30 G6
Boos [D] 60 B4
Boos [F] 28 C5
Booth of Toft [GB] 6 H3
Bootle [GB] 10 D4
Bopfingen [D] 60 C2
Boppard [D] 44 H1
Bor [CZ] 48 D4
Bor [RUS] 198 H2
Bor [S] 162 D4
Bor [SRB] 146 D2
Bor [SRB] 204 C6
Borås [N] 164 F4
Borås [S] 162 B2
Borba [P] 86 E6
Borbona [I] 116 B4
Borchen [D] 32 E4
Borci [BIH] 144 C2
Borculo [NL] 16 G5
Bordány [H] 76 E4
Bordeaux [F] 66 C3
Bordeira [P] 94 A4
Bordères [F] 84 F4
Bordesholm [D] 18 F2
Bordighera [I] 108 F4
Bording [DK] 160 C6
Bore [I] 110 C2
Boreci [SLO] 74 E3
Borek Wielkopolski [PL] 36 D4
Borello [I] 110 G5
Borensberg [S] 166 H5
Borg [N] 192 C4
Borgå / Porvoo [FIN] 178 B4
Borgafjäll [S] 190 E4
Borgarnes [IS] 192 A2
Borgeby [S] 156 H2
Borgen [N] 164 E3
Borgentreich [D] 32 E4
Börger [D] 18 B5
Borger [NL] 16 G3
Börgermoor [D] 18 B5
Borggård [S] 166 H5
Borghamn [S] 166 G6
Borghetto di Borbera [I] 110 B2
Borgholm [S] 162 G4
Borgholzhausen [D] 32 D2
Borghorst [D] 16 H5
Børglumkloster [DK] 160 D3
Borgo Callea [I] 126 D3
Borgoforte [I] 110 E2
Borgomanero [I] 70 F4
Borgönd [H] 76 B2
Borgonovo Val Tidone [I] 70 G6
Borgorose [I] 116 B5
Borgo San Dalmazzo [I] 108 F3
Borgo San Lorenzo [I] 110 F5
Borgosésia [I] 70 E4
Borgo Ticino [I] 70 F4
Borgo Tossignano [I] 110 F4
Borgo Val di Taro [I] 110 C3
Borgo Valsugana [I] 72 D4
Borgo Vercelli [I] 70 F5
Borgsjö [S] 184 D4
Borgsjö [S] 190 G5
Borgstena [S] 162 B1
Borgund [N] 170 E2
Borgund [N] 180 B4
Borgvattnet [S] 184 C1
Borgvik [S] 166 E3
Borielsbyn [S] 196 B2
Borima [BG] 148 B4
Borino [BG] 130 D1
Borislavtsi [BG] 130 G1
Borisoglebskiy [RUS] 194 F3
Borisovo [RUS] 178 G3
Borja [E] 90 D3
Borken [D] 16 G6
Borken [D] 32 E6
Borkenes [N] 192 E3
Borki [RUS] 198 G3
Børkop [DK] 156 C2
Borków [PL] 52 B1
Borkum [D] 16 G1
Borlänge [S] 172 H4
Borlaug [N] 170 E2
Børlia [N] 182 B3
Borlu [TR] 152 E3
Bormes-les-Mimosas [F] 108 D6
Bórmio [I] 72 B3
Borna [D] 34 C6
Borneiro, Castro de- [E] 78 D2

Borne Sulinowo [PL] 22 B5
Bornhöved [D] 18 G3
Börnicke [D] 34 D1
Bornlitz [D] 18 F6
Bornos [E] 100 G3
Bornova [TR] 152 C4
Borodianka [UA] 202 D7
Borodinskoye [RUS] 178 F2
Boronów [PL] 50 F2
Borová Lada [CZ] 62 A2
Borovan [BG] 146 G3
Borovany [CZ] 62 C2
Borovets [BG] 146 G5
Borovica [BG] 146 E3
Borovichi [RUS] 198 H3
Borovik [RUS] 198 G3
Borovo [BG] 148 C2
Borovo [HR] 142 E1
Borovoy [RUS] 196 H4
Borovtsi [BG] 146 F3
Borów [PL] 52 D1
Borowa [PL] 36 D6
Borrby [S] 158 D3
Borre [DK] 156 G4
Borre [N] 164 H2
Borreby [DK] 156 F3
Borredà [E] 92 E2
Borremose [DK] 160 D4
Borriana / Burriana [E] 98 F3
Börringe [S] 158 C3
Borriol [E] 98 F3
Borris [DK] 156 B1
Borris [IRL] 4 F4
Borris-in-Ossory [IRL] 2 D6
Borrisokane [IRL] 2 D6
Borrisoleigh [IRL] 4 E3
Börrum [S] 168 C6
Borş [RO] 76 H2
Borş [RO] 204 B4
Børsa [N] 182 B1
Borşa [RO] 204 C3
Børselv [N] 194 C2
Borsfa [H] 74 F4
Borsh [AL] 132 B1
Borsodiánka [H] 64 F6
Borsodnádasd [H] 64 E4
Börstil [S] 174 G5
Bortholoma [D] 60 B2
Bort-les-Orgues [F] 68 B3
Börtnan [S] 182 F3
Bortnen [N] 180 B5
Borup [DK] 156 G3
Borynia [UA] 52 F6
Boryslav [UA] 52 G5
Boryspil' [UA] 202 D7
Borzechowo [PL] 22 D4
Borzone, Abbazia di- [I] 110 B3
Borzysław [PL] 22 B3
Bosa [I] 118 B4
Bosanci [HR] 112 G1
Bosanska Bojna [BIH] 112 H2
Bosanska Dubica [BIH] 142 B2
Bosanska Gradiška [BIH] 142 C2
Bosanska Kostajnica [BIH] 142 B2
Bosanska Krupa [BIH] 142 A2
Bosanska Rača [BIH] 142 F2
Bosanski Brod [BIH] 142 D2
Bosanski Novi [HR] 142 A2
Bosanski Petrovac [BIH] 142 A3
Bosanski Šamac [BIH] 142 D2
Bosansko Grahovo [BIH] 142 A4
Bošany [SK] 64 B3
Bősárkány [H] 62 G6
Bosc-Mesnil [F] 28 C5
Bosco Chiesanuova [I] 72 C5
Bösel [D] 18 C5
Bosgouet [F] 26 H3
Bosilegrad [SRB] 146 E5
Bosiljevo [HR] 112 G1
Bosjökloster [S] 158 C2
Bosjön [S] 166 F1
Boskoop [NL] 16 D5
Boskovice [CZ] 50 C5
Bosna Klanac [BIH] 142 D4
Bošnjace [SRB] 146 D4
Bošnjaci [HR] 142 E2
Bosruck Tunnel [A] 62 B6
Bössbo [S] 172 F2
Bossbøen [N] 164 E1
Bossea [I] 108 G3
Bossòst [E] 84 F5
Bostandere [TR] 150 C5
Boštanj [SLO] 74 D5
Boste [S] 158 C3
Boston [GB] 10 G6
Bostrak [N] 164 F3
Bosut [SRB] 142 F2
Bőszénfa [H] 76 A4
Boteå [S] 184 F2
Botevgrad [BG] 146 G4
Botevo [BG] 148 F2
Boticas [P] 80 E3
Botinec [HR] 74 E6
Botnen [N] 180 C4
Botngård [N] 190 B6
Bótoa [E] 86 F6
Bötom / Karijoki [FIN] 186 B4
Botoroaga [RO] 148 C1
Botorrita [E] 90 E4
Botoşani [RO] 204 D3
Botricello [I] 124 E5
Botsmark [S] 196 A5
Böttberg [D] 60 E5
Botten [S] 166 D3
Bottheim [N] 180 G5
Bottidda [I] 118 D4
Bottnaryd [S] 162 C2
Bottrop [D] 30 G3
Botun [MK] 128 D3
Botunets [BG] 146 G4
Bouaye [F] 54 B1
Bouchair [F] 28 E5
Bouconville-sur-Madt [F] 44 E5
Boudry [CH] 58 C6
Bouesse [F] 54 H4
Bouges-le-Château [F] 54 H3
Bouguenais [F] 54 B1
Bouillon [B] 44 D2
Bouilly [F] 44 A6
Boulay-Moselle [F] 44 F4
Bouligny [F] 44 E3
Boulogne-sur-Gesse [F] 84 G3
Boulogne-sur-Mer [F] 14 G6
Bouloire [F] 42 C5
Boumois, Château de- [F] 54 E2
Bouniagues [F] 66 E4
Bourbon-Lancy [F] 56 E5
Bourbon-l'Archambault [F] 56 D5
Bourbonne-les-Bains [F] 58 B2
Bourbourg [F] 14 H6
Bourbriac [F] 26 A4
Bourdeaux [F] 68 F6
Bourdeilles [F] 66 F2
Bourg [F] 66 D3
Bourg-Achard [F] 26 H3
Bourganeuf [F] 54 H6
Bourg-Argental [F] 68 F4
Bourg-de-Péage [F] 68 F5
Bourg-en-Bresse [F] 68 G2
Bourges [F] 56 C3
Bourg-et-Comin [F] 44 A2
Bourg-Lastic [F] 68 B2
Bourg-Madame [F] 92 E1
Bourgneuf-en-Retz [F] 54 B2
Bourgogne [F] 44 B3
Bourgoin-Jallieu [F] 68 G3
Bourg-St-Andéol [F] 106 G2
Bourg-St-Maurice [F] 70 C4
Bourgtheroulde-Infreville [F] 26 H4
Bourgueil [F] 54 E2
Bourideys [F] 66 C5
Bourmont [F] 58 B2
Bourne [GB] 10 G6
Bournemouth [GB] 12 G5
Bourneville [F] 26 H3
Bournezeau [F] 54 C3
Boussac [F] 56 B5
Boussens [F] 84 G4
Bouvignes [B] 30 D5
Bouvron [F] 40 F6
Bouxwiller [F] 44 G5
Bouzonville [F] 44 F3
Bova [I] 124 C8
Bovalino [I] 124 D7
Bovallstrand [S] 166 C5
Bova Marina [I] 124 C8
Bovan [SRB] 146 D3
Bovec [SLO] 72 H4
Boveda [E] 78 D4
Bóvegno [I] 72 B5
Bovense [DK] 156 E3
Bøverbru [N] 172 B4
Bøverdal [N] 180 F6
Boves [I] 108 F3
Bović [HR] 112 H1
Bovik [FIN] 176 A5
Bovino [I] 120 G2
Bovolenta [I] 110 G1
Bovolone [I] 110 F1
Bovrup [DK] 156 C4
Boxberg [D] 46 E5
Boxholm [S] 166 G6
Boxmeer [NL] 16 F6
Boxtel [NL] 30 E2
Boyalı [TR] 152 E3
Boyalıca [TR] 150 F4
Boyalıca [TR] 152 F1
Boyalık [TR] 150 E2
Boyle [IRL] 2 D4
Bøylefoss [N] 164 F4
Bøyum [N] 170 D1
Božaj [MNE] 144 E4
Bozalan [TR] 152 F4
Bozan [TR] 152 H4
Božava [HR] 112 F5
Bozburun [TR] 154 D2
Bozcaada [TR] 130 H6
Bozcaatlı [TR] 152 F3
Bozdağ [TR] 152 E4
Bozdoğan [TR] 152 E5
Bozel [F] 70 B4
Bozen / Bolzano [I] 72 D3
Bozhane [TR] 150 F2
Bozhenci [BG] 148 C4
Bozhurishte [BG] 146 F4
Božica [SRB] 146 E5
Boží Dar [CZ] 48 D3
Bozkurt [TR] 152 G5
Bozkuş [TR] 152 G3
Bozkuş [TR] 152 G3
Bozlar [TR] 150 C4
Bozolan [TR] 152 C4
Bozouls [F] 68 B5
Bozouls, Trou de- [F] 68 B5
Bozüyük [TR] 150 G5
Bozveliisko [BG] 148 F3
Bozyaka [TR] 154 F1
Bozyazı [TR] 154 F4
Bózzolo [I] 110 E1
Bra [B] 30 E6
Bra [I] 108 G2
Brå [N] 182 B1
Braås [S] 162 E4
Brabecke [D] 32 D5
Brabova [RO] 146 F1
Bracciano [I] 114 H5
Brachlewo [PL] 22 E4
Bracieux [F] 54 H2
Bracigovo [BG] 148 A6
Bräcke [S] 182 H3
Brackenheim [D] 46 C6
Brackley [GB] 14 D3
Bracknell [GB] 14 D4
Brackwede [D] 32 D3
Brad [RO] 204 C4
Bradford [GB] 10 E3
Bradina [BIH] 144 C1
Bradvari [BG] 148 E1
Brae [GB] 6 G3
Brædstrup [DK] 156 C1
Braemar [GB] 6 E6
Braga [P] 80 C3
Bragança [P] 80 F3
Brahestad / Raahe [FIN] 196 C4
Brahetrolleborg [DK] 156 D4
Brail [CH] 72 B2
Brăila [RO] 204 E5
Braine [F] 44 A2
Braine-le-Comte [B] 28 H3
Braintree [GB] 14 F3
Brake [D] 18 D4
Brakel [B] 28 G3
Brakel [D] 32 E4
Bräkne-Hoby [S] 158 F1
Brålanda [S] 166 D5
Bram [F] 106 B4
Bramberg [A] 72 F1
Bramberg [CH] 72 F1
Brämhult [S] 162 B2
Bramming [DK] 156 B2
Brämön [S] 184 F5
Brampton [GB] 8 E5
Bramsche [D] 32 D2
Branč [SK] 62 H3
Branč [SK] 64 A4
Branca [I] 116 B1
Brancaleone Marina [I] 124 D8
Brancion [F] 56 G6
Brancoli, Pieve di- [I] 110 D5
Brâncoveni [RO] 148 A1
Brand [A] 72 A1
Brandal [N] 180 C3
Brändåsen [S] 182 E5
Brändbo [S] 184 D5
Brandbu [N] 170 H4
Brande [DK] 156 C1
Bränden [S] 182 F6
Brandenberg [A] 60 E6
Brandenburg [D] 34 D2
Brand-Erbisdorf [D] 48 E1
Brandhof [A] 62 D6
Brandis [D] 34 E4
Brändö [FIN] 176 C5
Brandomil [E] 78 B2
Brandon [F] 56 F6
Brandon [GB] 8 F6
Brandstorp [S] 162 D1
Brandval [N] 172 D5
Brandvoll [N] 192 F3
Brandýsek [CZ] 48 F3
Brandýs n Labem [CZ] 48 G3
Branica [BG] 148 D6
Braniewo [PL] 22 F2
Branik [SLO] 72 H5
Branišovice [CZ] 62 F2
Branitz, Schloss- [D] 34 F4
Brankovice [CZ] 50 D6
Brännåker [S] 190 F4
Brännberg [S] 196 A3
Branne [F] 66 D3
Brannenburg [D] 60 F5
Brännland [S] 190 H6
Brañosera [E] 82 D4
Brańsk [PL] 38 E1
Brantôme [F] 66 F2
Branzi [I] 70 H3
Bras-d'Asse [F] 108 C3
Braskereidfoss [N] 172 D4
Braslaw [BY] 200 H4
Braşov [RO] 204 D5
Brassac [F] 106 C3
Brassac-Jumeaux [F] 68 D3
Brasschaat [B] 30 D2
Bras-sur-Meuse [F] 44 D3
Brastad [S] 166 C5
Břasy [CZ] 48 E4
Brąszewice [PL] 36 F5
Brataj [AL] 128 B6
Bråte [N] 166 C1
Bratislava [SK] 62 G4
Bratków Dolny [PL] 36 F4
Bratovoeşti [RO] 146 G1
Brattabø [N] 170 C4
Brattåker [S] 190 F4
Brattbäcken [S] 190 F5
Bratten [S] 190 G5
Brattfors [S] 166 F2
Brattingsborg [DK] 156 E2
Brattjær [N] 190 B5
Brattli [N] 192 F3
Brattsele [S] 190 F6
Brattset [N] 180 G2
Brattvåg [N] 180 D3
Bratunac [BIH] 142 F4
Bråtveit [N] 164 C1
Bratya Daskolovi [BG] 148 C5
Braubach [D] 46 B2
Braunau [A] 60 G4
Braunfels [D] 46 C2
Braunlage [D] 32 H4
Braunschweig [D] 32 H2
Braus, Col de- [F] 108 F4
Bravone [F] 114 C4
Bray / Bré [IRL] 4 G3
Bray-sur-Seine [F] 42 G5
Bray-sur-Somme [F] 28 E5
Brazatortas [E] 96 D5
Brbinj [HR] 112 F5
Brčko [BIH] 142 E2
Brdjani [SRB] 146 B2
Bré / Bray [IRL] 4 G3
Brebina [RO] 148 B1
Brécey [F] 26 D4
Brechin [GB] 8 F2
Brecht [B] 30 D2
Břeclav [CZ] 62 G3
Brecon [GB] 12 F2
Brécy [F] 56 C3
Bred [S] 168 C2
Breda [NL] 16 D6
Bredaryd [S] 162 C4
Bredbyn [S] 184 F1
Breddin [D] 20 B6
Bredebro [DK] 156 B4
Bredelar [D] 32 E4
Bredevad [DK] 156 B4
Bredland [N] 164 D4
Bredsel [S] 196 A3
Bredsjö [S] 166 G1
Bredsjön [S] 184 E4
Bredstedt [D] 18 E1
Bredsten [DK] 156 C2
Bree [B] 30 E3
Breg [SLO] 74 D5
Bregana [HR] 74 E5
Breganze [I] 72 D5
Bregare [BG] 148 A2
Bregenz [A] 60 B6
Bregovo [BG] 146 E1
Bréhal [F] 26 D4
Brehna [D] 34 C5
Breidablik [N] 180 E5
Breidvik [N] 192 D6
Breifonn [N] 170 C5
Breil-sur-Roya [F] 108 F4
Brein [N] 180 C5
Breiðborg [N] 164 C1
Breisach [D] 58 E3
Breisen [D] 34 D1
Breisjøberget [N] 172 D4
Breistein [N] 170 B3
Breitachklamm [D] 60 B6
Breite [CH] 58 F5
Breitenbrunn [D] 60 C4
Breitengussbach Hallstadt [D] 46 G4
Breitenhees [D] 18 G6
Breitungen [D] 46 F1
Breivik [N] 194 A2
Breivikbotn [N] 194 A2
Breivikeidet [N] 192 G2
Brekke [N] 170 B2
Brekken [N] 182 D3
Brekkhus [N] 170 C3
Brekkvasselv [N] 190 D4
Brékovica [BIH] 112 H3
Brekstad [N] 190 B6
Bremen [D] 18 D5
Bremerhaven [D] 18 D4
Bremervörde [D] 18 E4
Bremke [D] 32 D5
Bremke [D] 32 D5
Bremnes [N] 192 D3
Bremsnes [N] 180 E2
Breń [PL] 20 H6
Brenes [E] 94 H6
Brenica [BG] 148 A3
Brenna [N] 182 D5
Brenna [N] 190 D3
Brennero, Passo del- / Brenner Pass [A/I] 72 D2
Brenner Pass / Brennero, Passo del- [A/I] 72 D2
Brennfjell [N] 192 G2
Brennsvik [N] 194 B2
Breno [I] 72 B5
Brénod [F] 68 H2
Brentwood [GB] 14 F4
Brenzone [I] 72 C5
Brescello [I] 110 E2
Bréscia [I] 72 B6
Bresdon [F] 54 D6
Breskens [NL] 28 G1
Bresles [F] 28 D6
Breslovec [BG] 148 B3
Bresnica [SRB] 146 B2
Bressanone / Brixen [I] 72 D3
Bressuire [F] 54 D3
Brest [BG] 148 A2
Brest [BY] 38 F3
Brest [F] 40 B2
Brestova [HR] 112 E2
Brestovac [HR] 142 C1
Brestovac [SRB] 146 D4
Brestovac [SRB] 146 D2
Brestovačka Banja [SRB] 146 D2
Brestovăţ [RO] 76 H5
Brestovik [SRB] 142 H3
Breteau [F] 56 D2
Bretenoux [F] 66 H4
Bretesche, Château de la- [F] 40 E5
Breteuil [F] 26 H5
Breteuil [F] 28 D5
Brétignolles-sur-Mer [F] 54 B3
Bretten [D] 46 C6
Breuberg [D] 46 D4
Breuil-Cervínia [I] 70 D3
Breukelen Ut [NL] 16 D5
Breuna [D] 32 E4
Brevens Bruk [S] 166 H4
Brevik [N] 164 G3
Brevik [S] 166 G5
Brevik [S] 168 E3
Breza [BIH] 142 D4
Breza [SK] 50 G5
Brezičani [BIH] 142 B2
Brežice [SLO] 74 D5
Breziški Grad [SLO] 74 D5
Breznica [BG] 130 C1
Breznica [HR] 74 F5
Breznica Đak. [HR] 142 D1
Březnice [CZ] 48 E5
Breznik [BG] 146 F5
Brezno [SK] 64 D3
Brézolles [F] 26 H5
Brezová [SK] 62 H3
Brezovica [KS] 146 C6
Brezovica [SK] 52 C6
Brezovica [SLO] 74 B5
Brezovo [BG] 148 B5
Brezovo Polje [BIH] 142 E2
Brezovo Polje [HR] 142 A2
Briançon [F] 70 B6
Briare [F] 56 D2
Briatico [I] 124 C6
Bribir [HR] 112 H5
Bribirske Mostine [HR] 112 H5
Briceni [MD] 204 D2
Bricquebec [F] 26 D2
Bridgend [GB] 12 E3
Bridgnorth [GB] 10 D6
Bridgwater [GB] 12 F4
Bridlington [GB] 10 G3
Bridport [GB] 12 F5
Briec [F] 40 B3
Brie-Comte-Robert [F] 42 G4
Brielle [NL] 16 C5
Brienne-le-Château [F] 44 B5
Brienz [CH] 70 E1
Brienza [I] 120 G4
Brieskow-Finkenheerd [D] 34 G3
Brieves [E] 78 G3
Briey [F] 44 E3
Brig [CH] 70 E2
Brigg [GB] 10 G4
Brighouse [GB] 10 E4
Brighton [GB] 14 E5
Brignogan-Plage [F] 40 B1
Brignoles [F] 108 C5
Brignoud [F] 68 H4
Brihuega [E] 88 H5
Brijesta [HR] 144 B3
Brilon [D] 32 D4
Brimnes [N] 170 D4
Brinay [F] 56 B3
Brinches [P] 94 E3
Bríndisi [I] 122 G4
Brinje [HR] 112 G2
Brinkum [D] 18 D5
Brinon [F] 56 E3
Brintbodarna [S] 172 F4
Briones [E] 82 G6
Brione Verzasca [CH] 70 F2
Brionne [F] 26 H4
Brioude [F] 68 D3
Brioux-sur-Boutonne [F] 54 D5
Briouze [F] 26 F5
Brisighella [I] 110 G4
Brissac-Quincé [F] 54 D1
Brissago [CH] 70 F3
Bristol [GB] 12 G3
Bristvica [HR] 116 H1
Brive-la-Gaillarde [F] 66 G3
Briviesca [E] 82 F5
Brixen / Bressanone [I] 72 D3
Brixham [GB] 12 E5
Brixlegg [A] 60 E6
Brka [BIH] 142 E2
Brnaze [HR] 144 A1
Brněnec [CZ] 50 C5
Brno [CZ] 50 C6
Bro [S] 168 D2
Bro [S] 168 G4
Broadford [IRL] 2 C6
Broadstairs [GB] 14 G5
Broager [DK] 156 C4
Brobacken [S] 194 B7
Broby [S] 158 D1
Broby [S] 168 B4
Broćanac [HR] 112 G2
Brocēni [LV] 198 C5
Brock [D] 32 C2
Bröckel [D] 32 G2
Brockenhurst [GB] 12 G5
Brockhöfe [D] 18 G6
Brod [BIH] 144 D2
Brod [KS] 128 D1
Brodarevo [SRB] 146 A4
Brodarica [HR] 112 H6
Broddbo [S] 168 B1
Broddebo [S] 162 F1
Brode [SLO] 74 B5
Brodenbach [D] 44 H1
Broderup [DK] 156 B4
Brodestorf [D] 20 B3
Brodica [SRB] 146 D1
Brodick [GB] 8 C3
Brod na Kupi [HR] 112 F1
Brodnica [PL] 22 F5
Brodowe Łąka [PL] 24 B5
Brody [PL] 34 G4
Brody [PL] 34 H3
Brody [PL] 38 C6
Broglie [F] 26 G4
Brohl [D] 30 H6
Brojce [PL] 20 G3
Brok [PL] 38 C1
Brokind [S] 168 A6
Brolo [I] 124 B6
Bromary [FIN] 176 E6
Brome [D] 32 H2
Bromma [N] 170 G4
Brommat [F] 68 B5
Bromölla [S] 158 E1
Brömsebro [S] 158 G1
Bromsgrove [GB] 12 H1
Bron [F] 68 G3
Brøndby [DK] 156 G3
Brønderslev [DK] 160 E3
Broni [I] 70 G6
Bronice [PL] 34 G4
Bronikowo [PL] 20 H5
Bronisławów [PL] 36 H5
Bronken [N] 172 C4
Bronkow [D] 34 F4
Bronnbach [D] 46 E4
Brønnøysund [N] 190 C3
Brøns [DK] 156 B3
Bronte [I] 126 F3
Broons [F] 26 B5
Brørup [DK] 156 B2
Brösarp [S] 158 D2
Brossac [F] 66 E2
Brossasco [I] 108 F2
Brøstrud [N] 170 F4
Brötjemark [S] 162 D1
Broto [E] 84 E5
Brottby [S] 168 E2
Brøttem [N] 182 B2
Brotterode [D] 46 F1
Brøttum [N] 172 B3
Brou [F] 42 D5
Brouage [F] 54 C5
Brough [GB] 10 E2
Broughshane [NIR] 2 G3
Broughton in Furness [GB] 10 D2
Brouis, Col de- [F] 108 F4
Broumov [CZ] 50 B2
Brouvelieures [F] 58 C2
Brouwershaven [NL] 16 B5
Brovary [UA] 202 D7
Brovst [DK] 160 D3
Brownhills [GB] 10 E6
Brozas [E] 86 G4
Brseč [HR] 112 E2
Brtnice [CZ] 50 A6
Brua [N] 182 C5
Bruchhausen-Vilsen [D] 18 E6
Bruchhauser Steine [D] 32 D5
Bruchsal [D] 46 C5
Bruck [A] 72 F2
Brück [D] 34 D3
Bruck [D] 48 C6
Bruck an der Grossglocknerstrasse [A] 72 G1
Bruck an der Leitha [A] 62 G5
Bruck an der Mur [A] 74 D1
Brückl [A] 74 C3
Brudzeń Duży [PL] 36 G2
Brudzewo [PL] 36 A3
Brüel [D] 20 A4
Bruère-Allichamps [F] 56 C4
Bruff [IRL] 4 D4
Bruflat [N] 170 G3
Bruges (Brugge) [B] 28 G1
Brugg [CH] 58 F4
Brugge (Bruges) [B] 28 G1
Brugnato [I] 110 C4
Bruhagen [N] 180 E2
Brühl [D] 30 G4
Brújula, Puerto de la- [E] 82 F6
Bruksvallarna [S] 182 E3
Brûlon [F] 42 A5
Brumath [F] 44 H5
Brummen [NL] 16 F5
Brumov Bylnice [CZ] 64 A2
Brumunddal [N] 172 B3
Brunau [D] 34 B1
Bruneck / Brunico [I] 72 E2
Brunehamel [F] 28 H5
Brunete [E] 88 F5
Brunflo [S] 182 H2
Brunheda [P] 80 E4
Brunico / Bruneck [I] 72 E2
Bruniquel [F] 66 G6
Brunkeberg [N] 164 E2
Brunlund [DK] 156 C4
Brunna [S] 168 D1
Brunnby [S] 160 H6
Brunnen [CH] 58 F6
Brunnsberg [S] 172 F2
Brunsbüttel [D] 18 E3
Brunskog [S] 166 E2
Brunssum [NL] 30 F4
Bruntál [CZ] 50 D4
Bruravik [N] 170 D4
Brus [SRB] 146 C3
Brusand [N] 164 A4
Brušane [HR] 112 G4
Brusarci [BG] 146 F2
Brusasco [I] 70 E5
Brúsio [CH] 72 B4
Bruška [HR] 112 H5
Brusnichnoye [RUS] 178 E2
Brusník [SK] 64 D4
Brussel / Bruxelles [B] 30 C4
Brüssow [D] 20 E5
Brusy [PL] 22 C4
Bruvno [HR] 112 H4
Bruvoll [N] 172 C4
Bruxelles / Brussel [B] 30 C4
Bruyères [F] 58 C2
Bruzaholm [S] 162 E2
Bruzzano Zeffirio [I] 124 D8
Brvenik [SRB] 146 B3
Brwinów [PL] 38 B3
Bryansk [RUS] 202 E5
Brydal [N] 182 C5
Bryggja [N] 180 B5
Bryne [N] 164 A3
Bryrup [DK] 156 C1
Brza Palanka [SRB] 146 E1
Brzeće [SRB] 146 C4
Brzeg [PL] 50 D1
Brzeg Dolny [PL] 36 C6
Brześć Kujawski [PL] 36 F2
Brzesko [PL] 52 B4
Brzeszcze [PL] 50 G4
Brzezie [PL] 22 B4
Brzezie [PL] 36 E4
Brzeziny [PL] 36 E5
Brzeziny [PL] 36 H4
Brzeźnica [PL] 50 H4
Brzeźnica [PL] 52 D3
Brzeźno [PL] 36 D3
Brzostek [PL] 52 D4
Brzoza [PL] 22 D6
Brzóza [PL] 38 C4
Brzozie Lubawskie [PL] 22 F5
Brzozów [PL] 52 F4
Bua [S] 160 H3
Buaile an Ghleanna / Bolinglanna [IRL] 2 B3
Buavåg [N] 164 A1
Buberget [S] 190 H5
Bubiai [LT] 200 E4
Bubry [F] 40 D3
Buca [TR] 152 C4
Buçaco [P] 80 B6
Bučany [SK] 62 H4
Buccheri [I] 126 F1
Bucchianico [I] 116 D4
Buchach [UA] 204 C2
Bucheben [A] 72 G2
Büchen [D] 18 G4
Buchen [D] 46 D4
Buchenwald [D] 34 A6
Buchholz [D] 18 F5
Buchin Prohod [BG] 146 F4
Buchloe [D] 60 C4
Buchlov [CZ] 62 G2
Büchold [D] 46 E3
Buchs [CH] 58 H6
Buchy [F] 28 C5
Bučin [MK] 128 E3
Búcine [I] 110 F6
Bučište [MK] 128 F1
Bučje [SRB] 144 E2
Bučje [SRB] 146 D2
Bückeburg [D] 32 E2
Bücken [D] 18 E6
Buckfastleigh [GB] 12 E5
Buckie [GB] 6 F5
Buckingham [GB] 14 D3
Bückow [D] 34 F2
Bückwitz [D] 34 D1
Bučovice [CZ] 50 C6
Bucquoy [F] 28 E4
Bucsa [H] 76 F1
Bucureşti [RO] 204 D5
Buczek [PL] 36 G5
Buczyna [PL] 52 F3
Bud [N] 180 E2
Buda [I] 110 G3
Budakeszi [H] 64 C6
Budakovo [MK] 128 E3
Budal [N] 182 B3
Budaörs [H] 64 C6
Budapest [H] 64 C6
Búðardalur [IS] 192 A2
Buddusò [I] 118 D3
Bude [GB] 12 D4
Budeč [CZ] 62 D2
Budeşti [RO] 204 E5
Budilovo [RUS] 198 G2
Budimci [HR] 142 D1
Budimić Japra [BIH] 142 A2
Budimir [HR] 144 A2
Büdingen [D] 46 D2
Budiščina [HR] 74 E5
Budišov nad Budišovkou [CZ] 50 D4
Budjevo [SRB] 146 A4
Budkovce [SK] 64 H3
Budmirici [MK] 128 F3
Budogoshch [RUS] 202 C1
Budomierz [PL] 52 G3
Budoni [I] 118 E3
Budowo [PL] 22 C2
Budoželja [SRB] 146 B3
Budrio [I] 110 F3
Budrovci [HR] 142 D1
Budry [PL] 24 C2
Budva [MNE] 144 D4
Budyně nad Ohří [CZ] 48 F3
Budziszewice [PL] 36 H4
Budzyń [PL] 36 C1
Buo [N] 164 D4
Bue Marino, Grotta del- [I] 118 E4
Bueña [E] 90 D6
Buen Amor, Castillo- [E] 80 H6
Buenavista del Norte [E] 100 B5
Buendia [E] 88 H6
Bufón de Arenillas [E] 82 D2
Bugac [H] 76 D3
Buğdayli [TR] 150 D5
Bugdorf [D] 32 G3
Bugeat [F] 66 H2
Buggerru [I] 118 B6
Bugojno [BIH] 142 C4
Bugøyfjord [N] 194 E3
Bugøynes [N] 194 E2
Bugyi [H] 76 C2
Bühl [D] 58 F1
Buhuşi [RO] 204 D4
Builth Wells [GB] 12 F1
Buis-les-Baronnies [F] 108 B2
Buitenpost [NL] 16 F2
Buitrago [E] 88 G4
Buj [H] 64 G4
Bujalance [E] 102 D1
Bujanovac [SRB] 146 D5
Bujaraloz [E] 90 F4
Buje [HR] 112 D1
Bujoru [RO] 148 C2
Bük [H] 74 F1
Buk [PL] 20 E5
Buk [PL] 36 C3
Bükkábrány [H] 64 F5
Bükkösd [H] 76 A5
Bukonys [LT] 200 F5
Bukovi [SRB] 146 A2
Bukovice [CZ] 50 C4
Bukovo, Manastir- [SRB] 146 E1
Bukowiec [PL] [illegible]
Bukowina Tatrzańska [PL] 52 B6
Bukowo Morskie [PL] 22 A2
Bukowsko [PL] 52 E5
Buksnes [N] 192 E3
Bukta [N] 190 B6
Buktamo [N] [illegible]
Bülach [CH] 58 F4
Bulat-Pestivien [F] 40 D2
Buldan [TR] 152 F4
Bŭlgarene [BG] 148 B4
Bŭlgarene [BG] 148 B3
Bŭlgarevo [BG] 148 G2
Bŭlgarovo [BG] 148 F4

Bülgarska Polyana [BG] 150 A1
Bŭlgarski Izvor [BG] 148 A4
Bulgnéville [F] 58 B2
Bulinac [HR] 74 G6
Bulinovac [SRB] 146 D3
Bulken [N] 170 C3
Bulkowo [PL] 36 H2
Bullarby [S] 166 C4
Bullas [E] 104 B2
Bulle [CH] 70 C1
Bullendorf [A] 62 F3
Bullmark [S] 196 A5
Bulqizë [AL] 128 C2
Bülstringen [D] 34 B2
Bultei [I] 118 D4
Buna [BIH] 144 C2
Bunclody [IRL] 4 F4
Buncrana [IRL] 2 F2
Bunde [D] 16 H2
Bünde [D] 32 E2
Bundoran [IRL] 2 D3
Bungay [GB] 14 G2
Bunge [S] 168 G3
Bunić [HR] 112 G3
Bunkris [S] 172 F2
Bunleix [F] 68 B2
Bunmahon [IRL] 4 E5
Bun na Abhna / Bunnahowen [IRL] 2 B3
Bunnahowen / Bun na Abhna [IRL] 2 B3
Bunnyconnellan [IRL] 2 C3
Buñol [E] 98 E4
Bunratty [IRL] 2 C6
Bunratty Castle [IRL] 2 C6
Buonalbergo [I] 120 F2
Buonconvento [I] 114 G2
Buonfornello [I] 126 D2
Buonvicino [I] 124 C3
Buoux, Fort de- [F] 108 B3
Bur [DK] 160 B5
Burano [I] 72 F6
Burbach [D] 32 C6
Burcei [I] 118 D7
Bureå [S] 190 G3
Bureå [S] 196 A4
Burela [E] 78 E2
Büren [CH] 58 D5
Büren [D] 32 D4
Burfjord [N] 192 H1
Burford [GB] 12 H3
Burg [D] 18 E3
Burg [D] 18 H2
Burg [D] 34 C3
Burg [D] 34 F4
Burgas [BG] 148 F4
Burgau [A] 74 E2
Burgau [D] 60 C3
Burgau [P] 94 B5
Burgbernheim [D] 46 F5
Burgdorf [CH] 58 E5
Burgdorf [D] 32 G2
Burgebrach [D] 46 F4
Bürgel [D] 34 B6
Bürgeln [D] 58 E4
Burgelu / Elburgo [E] 102 B4
Burghaun [D] 46 E1
Burghausen [D] 60 G4
Burg Hessenstein [D] 32 E5
Burgh-Haamstede [NL] 16 B5
Búrgio [I] 126 C3
Burgistein [CH] 58 D6
Burgjoss [D] 46 E3
Burg Klam [A] 62 C4
Burgkunstadt [D] 46 G3
Burglengenfeld [D] 48 B6
Burg Metternich [D] 44 G1
Burgoberbach [D] 46 F5
Burgos [E] 82 E6
Burgsinn [D] 46 E3
Burg Stargard [D] 20 D5
Burgsvik [S] 168 G6
Burguete / Auritz [E] 84 C3
Burgui / Burgi [E] 84 C4
Burguillos [E] 94 G5
Burguillos del Cerro [E] 94 G3
Burhan [TR] 150 F5
Burhaniye [TR] 152 C2
Burharkent [TR] 152 F5
Burie [F] 54 D6
Burila Mare [RO] 146 E1
Burlada [E] 84 B4
Burladingen [D] 58 G2
Burlo [D] 16 G6
Burnham-on-Crouch [GB] 14 F4
Burnham-on-Sea [GB] 12 F3
Burnley [GB] 10 E3
Burón [E] 82 C3
Buron, Château de- [F] 68 D3
Buronzo [I] 70 E4
Burravoe [GB] 6 H3
Burrel [AL] 128 B2
Burriana / Borriana [E] 98 F3
Burs [S] 168 G5
Burs [S] 168 G4
Bursa [TR] 150 F4
Burseryd [S] 162 B3
Bürstadt [D] 46 C4
Burtenbach [D] 60 C3
Burton upon Trent [GB] 10 E6
Burträsk [S] 196 A5
Burvik [S] 196 B5
Burwell [GB] 14 F2
Bury [GB] 10 E4
Buryn' [UA] 202 E6
Bury St Edmunds [GB] 14 F3
Burzenin [PL] 36 F5
Burziya [BG] 146 F3
Busalla [I] 110 B3
Busana [I] 110 D4
Busca [I] 108 F2
Busdorf [D] 18 F1
Buseto Palizzolo [I] 126 B2
Buševec [HR] 74 E6
Bushat [AL] 128 A1
Bushmills [NIR] 2 G2
Bushtricë [AL] 128 C1
Bus'k [UA] 202 B8
Busko-Zdrój [PL] 52 B2
Buśno [PL] 38 G6
Busot [E] 104 E2
Busovača [BIH] 142 D4
Bussang [F] 58 D3
Bussang, Col de- [F] 58 D3
Busseto [I] 110 D2
Bussolengo [I] 72 C6
Bussoleno [I] 70 C5
Bussum [NL] 16 E4
Bustnes [N] 190 E2
Busto Arsízio [I] 70 F4
Busto Garolfo [I] 70 F4
Büsum [D] 18 E2
Butan [BG] 146 G2
Butenky [UA] 202 F7
Butera [I] 126 E4
Bütgenbach [B] 30 F5
Buthrotum [AL] 132 B2
Butler's Bridge [IRL] 2 E4
Butrint [AL] 132 B2
Butryny [PL] 22 H4
Butsyn [UA] 38 H5
Buttapietra [I] 110 F1
Buttelstedt [D] 34 A6
Buttevant [IRL] 4 C4
Buttingsrud [N] 170 H4
Buttlar [D] 46 E1
Buttle [S] 168 G5
Buttstädt [D] 34 B6
Butzbach [D] 46 C2
Bützow [D] 20 B3
Buvarp [N] 190 C5
Buvika [N] 182 B1
Buvika [N] 182 D5
Buxtehude [D] 18 F4
Buxton [GB] 10 E5
Buxu, Cueva del- [E] 82 C2
Buxy [F] 56 F5
Büyükada [TR] 150 F3
Büyükaturak [TR] 152 H2
Büyükbelen [TR] 152 D3
Büyükçekmece [TR] 150 E3
Büyükkaraağaç [TR] 154 E2
Büyükkarıştıran [TR] 150 C2
Büyükkonak [TR] 152 G6
Büyükkonuk (Komi Kebir) [CY] 154 G4
Büyükorhan [TR] 150 F5
Büyüksöğle [TR] 154 H2
Büyükyenice [TR] 152 C2
Büyükyoncalı [TR] 150 D2
Buz [AL] 128 B5
Buzançais [F] 54 G3
Buzancy [F] 44 D3
Buzău [RO] 204 E5
Buzescu [RO] 148 B1
Buzet [HR] 112 D1
Buziaş [RO] 76 H6
Buzyakovtsi [BG] 146 G5
By [S] 166 E1
By [S] 174 D5
Byahoml' [BY] 202 B4
Byala [BG] 148 C2
Byala [BG] 148 F3
Byala Slatina [BG] 146 G3
Byal Izvor [BG] 130 E1
Byalynichy [BY] 202 C5
Byaroza [BY] 202 A6
Byarozawka [BY] 202 A5
Byarum [S] 162 D2
Byberget [S] 182 H4
Bybjerg [DK] 156 F2
Bychawa [PL] 38 E6
Byczki [PL] 36 H4
Byczyna [PL] 36 E6
Bydgoszcz [PL] 22 D6
Bye [S] 182 H2
Bye [S] 184 F4
Byenyakoni [BY] 200 G6
Byershty [BY] 24 G3
Bygdeå [S] 196 A5
Bygdeträsk [S] 196 A5
Bygdin [N] 170 F2
Bygdsiljum [S] 196 A5
Bygland [N] 164 D4
Byglandsfjord [N] 164 D4
Bygstad [N] 170 B1
Bykle [N] 164 D2
Byllis [AL] 128 B5
Byrkjedal [N] 164 B3
Byrkjelo [N] 180 D5
Byrknes [N] 170 A2
Byrness [GB] 8 F5
Byrum [DK] 160 F3
Byrum [S] 162 H3
Byšice [CZ] 48 G3
Byske [S] 196 A4
Bystré [CZ] 50 B5
Bystrianska Jaskyňa [SK] 64 D2
Bystřice [CZ] 48 G4
Bystřice nad Pernštejnem [CZ] 50 B5
Bystřice pod Hostýnem [CZ] 50 D6
Bystřička [CZ] 50 E5
Bystrzyca Kłodzka [PL] 50 C3
Byszki [PL] 22 B5
Byszyno [PL] 20 H4
Bytča [SK] 50 F6
Bytnica [PL] 34 H3
Bytom [PL] 50 F3
Bytom Odrzański [PL] 36 A4
Bytonia [PL] 22 D4
Bytów [PL] 22 C3
Byvattnet [S] 184 F1
Byxelkrok [S] 162 H3
Bzenec [CZ] 62 G2
Bzovík [SK] 64 C4

C

Caaveiro, Monasterio de- [E] 78 D2
Cabação [P] 86 D5
Cabaço [E] 86 D3
Cabaj-Čápor [SK] 64 A4
Cabañaquinta [E] 78 H4
Cabañas [E] 78 D2
Cabanes [E] 98 G3
Čabar [HR] 74 C6
Cabeço de Vide [P] 86 E5
Çabertarla [TR] 152 F4
Cabeza del Buey [E] 96 C4
Cabezamesada [E] 96 G2
Cabezarados [E] 96 E4
Cabezarrubias del Puerto [E] 96 E5
Cabezas Rubias [E] 94 E4
Cabezo de Torres [E] 104 C3
Cabezón de la Sal [E] 82 E3
Cabezuela del Valle [E] 88 B5
Cabo de Gata [E] 102 G6
Cabo de Palos [E] 104 D4
Cabourg [F] 26 F3
Cabra [E] 102 C2
Cabra del Santo Cristo [E] 102 F2
Cabranes [E] 82 C2
Cábras [I] 118 B5
Cabreiros [E] 78 D2
Cabrela [P] 86 C6
Cabrera [E] 104 E6
Cabrerets [F] 66 G5
Cabrillas [E] 88 B3
Cacabelos [E] 78 F5
Čačak [SRB] 146 B2
Čačak [SRB] 204 B6
Cáccamo [I] 126 D2
Cacemes [P] 86 A5
Cáceres [E] 86 H5
Cachivice [CZ] 48 G3
Cachopo [P] 94 D5
Čachtice [SK] 62 H3
Čačini [HR] 76 A6
Cadaqués [E] 92 G2
Cadaval [P] 86 B4
Cadavedo [E] 78 G2
Čađavica [BIH] 142 B3
Čađavica [HR] 76 A6
Čadca [SK] 50 F5
Cadelbosco di Sopra [I] 110 E2
Cadenábbia [I] 70 G3
Cadenberge [D] 18 E3
Cadenet [F] 106 H4
Cadeuil [F] 54 C6
Cadí, Túnel del- [E] 92 E2
Cádiar [E] 102 E5
Cadillac [F] 66 D4
Cadipietra [I] 72 E2
Cádiz [E] 100 F4
Cadrete [E] 90 E4
Caen [F] 26 F3
Caernarfon [GB] 10 B4
Caerphilly [GB] 12 F3
Cafasan [MK] 128 C3
Çağış [TR] 152 D1
Cagli [I] 112 B6
Cágliari [I] 118 C7
Çağman [TR] 154 H3
Cagnano Varano [I] 116 G6
Cagnes-sur-Mer [F] 108 E4
Caherdaniel / Cathair Dónall [IRL] 4 A4
Cahermurphy [IRL] 2 B6
Cahersiveen [IRL] 4 A4
Cahir [IRL] 4 D4
Cahors [F] 66 G5
Cahul [MD] 204 E4
Caiazzo [I] 120 E2
Cairnryan [GB] 8 C5
Cairo Montenotte [I] 108 G3
Cais do Pico [P] 100 C3
Caister-on-Sea [GB] 14 H2
Caivano [I] 120 E3
Cajarc [F] 66 G5
Ćajetina [SRB] 146 A3
Čajniče [BIH] 144 E2
Čakajovce [SK] 64 A4
Çakallar [TR] 152 C1
Çakılı [TR] 150 C2
Çakır [TR] 150 C5
Çakırbeyli [TR] 152 E5
Çakırlı [TR] 150 C4
Çakmak [TR] 154 E1
Čakovec [HR] 74 F4
Çal [TR] 152 G4
Cal [TR] 152 H2
Cala [E] 94 G4
Cala Blanca [E] 104 G4
Cala Blava [E] 104 E5
Calabor [E] 80 F3
Calabritto [I] 120 F3
Calaceite [E] 90 G6
Calacuccia [F] 114 B3
Cala d'Oliva [I] 118 B2
Cala d'Or [E] 104 F6
Calaf [E] 92 D3
Calafat [E] 92 B5
Calafat [RO] 146 F2
Calafell [E] 92 D5
Cala Galdana [E] 104 G4
Cala Gonone [I] 118 E4
Calahonda-Chaparral [E] 102 B5
Calahonda-Chaparral [E] 102 E5
Calahorra [E] 84 A5
Calais [F] 14 G6
Cala Liberotto [I] 118 E4
Cala Mesquida [E] 104 F5
Cala Millor [E] 104 F5
Calamocha [E] 90 D6
Calamonte [E] 94 H2
Cala Moreia-Cala Morlanda [E] 104 F5
Cala Morell [E] 104 G4
Calañas [E] 94 F5
Calanda [E] 90 F6
Calangiánus [I] 118 D3
Cala'n Porter [E] 104 H5
Cala Pi [E] 104 E5
Călăraşi [MD] 204 E3
Călăraşi [RO] 204 E5
Cala Ratjada [E] 104 F5
cala Sa Calobra [E] 104 E4
Cala Santanyí [E] 104 E6
Calascibetta [I] 126 E3
Calasetta [I] 118 B7
Calasparra [E] 104 B2
Calatafimi [I] 126 B2
Calatañazor [E] 90 B3
Cala Tarida [E] 104 B5
Calatayud [E] 90 D4
Calatorao [E] 90 D4
Calatrava, Convento de- [E] 96 E5
Calatrava la Vieja [E] 96 F4
Calau [D] 34 F4
Cala Vadella [E] 104 B5
Calbe [D] 34 B4
Çalca [TR] 152 H3
Caldarola [I] 116 C2
Caldas da Rainha [P] 86 B3
Caldas de Monchique [P] 94 B4
Caldas de Reis [E] 78 B3
Caldas de Vizela [P] 80 C3
Caldelas [P] 78 B6
Caldes de Boí [E] 84 F6
Caldes de Malavella [E] 92 F3
Caldes de Montbui [E] 92 E4
Caldes d'Estrac [E] 92 F4
Caldirola [I] 110 B2
Calella [E] 92 F4
Calella de Palafrugell [E] 92 G3
Calenzana [F] 114 B3
Calera y Chozas [E] 88 C6
Caleruega [E] 88 H2
Cales de Mallorca [E] 104 F5
Calheta [P] 100 A3
Calheta [P] 100 C3
Çali [TR] 150 F5
Càlig [E] 92 A6
Calignac [F] 66 E5
Çalıklı [TR] 152 F3
Călimăneşti [RO] 204 C5
Calimera [I] 122 G5
Calitri [I] 120 G3
Calizzano [I] 108 G3
Callac [F] 40 D2
Callan [IRL] 4 E4
Callander [GB] 8 D2
Callington [GB] 12 D4
Callosa d'en Sarrià [E] 104 E2
Callosa de Segura [E] 104 D3
Čalma [SRB] 142 F2
Călmăţuiu [RO] 148 B2
Calne [GB] 12 G3
Calolziocorte [I] 70 G4
Calonge [E] 92 G3
Calp / Calpe [E] 104 F2
Calpe / Calp [E] 104 F2
Çalpınar [TR] 154 H1
Caltabellotta [I] 126 C3
Caltagirone [I] 126 F4
Caltanissetta [I] 126 E3
Caltavuturo [I] 126 E2
Çaltepe [TR] 152 H5
Çalti [TR] 150 H4
Çaltılıbük [TR] 150 E5
Caltra [IRL] 2 D5
Călugăreni [RO] 148 C1
Caluso [I] 70 D5
Calvello [I] 120 H4
Calvi [F] 114 A3
Calvià [E] 104 D5
Calvörde [D] 34 B2
Calw [D] 58 G1
Calzadilla de la Cueza [E] 82 C5
Camacha [P] 100 B3
Camaiore [I] 110 D5
Camaldoli [I] 110 G5
Camaldoli, Eremo di- [I] 110 G5
Çamaltı [TR] 152 C4
Camarasa [E] 92 C2
Camarena de la Sierra [E] 98 E2
Camarès [F] 106 D3
Camaret-sur-Mer [F] 40 B2
Camarillas [E] 98 E1
Camariñas [E] 78 B2
Camarzana de Tera [E] 80 H3
Camas [E] 94 G6
Cambados [E] 78 B4
Cambeo [E] 78 C5
Camberg [D] 46 C2
Camberley [GB] 14 D4
Cambo-les-Bains [F] 84 C2
Camborne [GB] 12 C5
Cambrai [F] 28 F4
Cambre [E] 78 C2
Cambremer [F] 26 G4
Cambridge [GB] 14 F3
Cambrils [E] 92 C5
Camburg [D] 34 B6
Çamdere [TR] 152 G3
Camelford [GB] 12 C4
Çameli [TR] 154 F1
Camenca [MD] 204 E2
Camerino [I] 116 B2
Çamiçi [TR] 152 D6
Camigliatello [I] 124 D4
Camin [D] 18 H4
Caminha [P] 78 A5
Caminomorisco [E] 88 A4
Caminreal [E] 90 D6
Çamkonak [TR] 150 G2
Çamköy [TR] 154 C1
Çamlıbel (Mýrtou) [CY] 154 F5
Çamlık [TR] 152 F2
Çamlıpınar [TR] 154 F4
Cammarata [I] 126 D3
Camogli [I] 110 B3
Camp [IRL] 4 B3
Campagna [I] 120 F4
Campagnático [I] 114 F2
Campan [F] 84 F4
Campana [I] 124 E4
Campanario [E] 96 B3
Campanas / Kanpaneta [E] 84 B4
Campanet, Coves de- [E] 104 E4
Campaspero [E] 88 F2
Campbeltown [GB] 2 H2
Câmpeni [RO] 204 C4
Câmpia Turzii [RO] 204 C4
Campi Bisenzio [I] 110 E5
Campiglia Marittima [I] 114 E2
Campiglia Soana [I] 70 D4
Campillo de Altobuey [E] 98 C3
Campillo de Arenas [E] 102 E3
Campillo de Llerena [E] 96 A4
Campillos [E] 102 B3
Câmpina [RO] 204 D5
Campione d'Italia [I] 70 G3
Campisábalos [E] 88 H4
Campi Salentina [I] 122 G4
Campo [E] 84 F6
Campo [P] 94 E2
Campobasso [I] 120 E1
Campobecerros [E] 78 D6
Campobello di Licata [I] 126 E4
Campobello di Mazara [I] 126 B3
Campocologno [CH] 72 B4
Campo Coy [E] 104 B3
Campodarsego [I] 72 E6
Campo de Caso / Caso [E] 82 C2
Campo de Criptana [E] 96 G3
Campofelice di Fitalia [I] 126 D2
Campofilone [I] 116 D2
Campofiorito [I] 126 C3
Campoformido [I] 72 G5
Campogalliano [I] 110 E3
Campohermoso [E] 102 G5
Campo Lameiro / A Lagoa [E] 78 B4
Campo Ligure [I] 108 H2
Campo Maior [P] 86 F6
Campomanes [E] 78 H4
Campomarino [I] 116 F5
Campomarino [I] 122 F5
Camponaraya [E] 78 F5
Campora San Giovanni [I] 124 D5
Campo Real [E] 88 G6
Camporeale [I] 126 C2
Camporrobles [E] 98 D3
Campos [E] 104 E5
Camposampiero [I] 72 E6
Camposanto [I] 110 F2
Campotejar [E] 102 E3
Campo Túres / Sand in Taufers [I] 72 E2
Camprodón [E] 92 F2
Câmpulung [RO] 204 D5
Câmpulung Moldovenesc [RO] 204 D3
Çamsu [TR] 152 G2
Çamyayla [TR] 152 F6
Çamyuva [TR] 152 G2
Çan [TR] 150 C5
Cañada de Benatanduz [E] 98 F1
Cañadajuncosa [E] 98 B3
Cañaíca del Calar [E] 102 H2
Čanak [HR] 112 G3
Çanakçı [TR] 152 F1
Çanakkale [TR] 150 B5
Canale [I] 108 G1
Canales de Molina [E] 90 C5
Canal S. Bovo [I] 72 E4
Canaples [F] 28 E4
Canas de Senhorim [P] 80 C6
Cañaveral [E] 86 H4
Cañaveral de León [E] 94 G4
Cañaveras [E] 98 B1
Canazei [I] 72 E3
Cancale [F] 26 C4
Cancon [F] 66 E4
Candamo [E] 78 G3
Candamo, Cueva de- [E] 78 H3
Candanchú [E] 84 D4
Çandarlı [TR] 150 G3
Çandarlı [TR] 152 C3
Candás [E] 78 H3
Candasnos [E] 90 G4
Candé [F] 40 G6
Candela [I] 120 G2
Candelária [P] 100 C3
Candelario [E] 88 B4
Candeleda [E] 88 C5
Candia Lomellina [I] 70 F5
Çandır [TR] 154 E2
Canelli [I] 108 H2
Canelobre, Cueva de- [E] 104 E2
Canero [E] 78 G2
Canet [F] 106 E4
Canet de Mar [E] 92 F4
Cañete [E] 98 C2
Cañete la Real [E] 102 B3
Canet-Plage [F] 92 G1
Canfranc [E] 84 D4
Cangas [E] 78 B4
Cangas [E] 78 E2
Cangas del Narcea [E] 78 F3
Cangas de Onís [E] 82 C2
Canha [P] 86 C5
Caniçada [P] 80 D3
Canicatti [I] 126 D4
Canicattini Bagni [I] 126 G5
Caniles [E] 102 G4
Canillas del Aceituno [E] 102 C4
Canino [I] 114 G4
Cañizal [E] 88 D2
Cañizares [E] 90 B6
Canjáyar [E] 102 F5
Cannai [I] 118 B7
Cannara [I] 116 A2
Canne [I] 120 H2
Cánnero Riviera [I] 70 F3
Cannes [F] 108 E5
Canneto [I] 114 E1
Canneto sull'Óglio [I] 110 D1
Cannich [GB] 6 D5
Cannigione [I] 118 E2
Cannóbio [I] 70 F3
Cannock [GB] 10 E6
Canolo [I] 124 D7
Canosa di Púglia [I] 120 H2
Canossa [I] 110 D3
Canossa, Castello di- [I] 110 D3
Can Pastilla [E] 104 E5
Can Picafort [E] 104 F4
Cansano [I] 116 D5
Cantalapiedra [E] 88 D3
Cantalejo [E] 88 F3
Cantalpino [E] 88 D3
Cantanhede [P] 80 B6
Cantavieja [E] 98 F2
Čantavir [SRB] 76 D5
Canterbury [GB] 14 F5
Cantillana [E] 94 H5
Cantoral de la Peña [E] 82 D4
Cantoria [E] 102 H4
Cantù [I] 70 G4
Canvey Island [GB] 14 F4
Cany-Barville [F] 26 H2
Canyet de Mar [E] 92 G4
Canyon [N] 194 B3
Caoria [I] 72 D4
Cáorle [I] 72 F6
Caorso [I] 70 H6
Capaccio [I] 120 F4
Capaci [I] 126 C1
Capalbio [I] 114 F4
Capannoli [I] 110 E6
Caparde [BIH] 142 E3
Caparra, Ruinas de- [E] 88 B5
Caparroso [E] 84 B5
Capbreton [F] 66 A6
Cap-d'Ail [F] 108 F4
Capdella [E] 84 G6
Capdenac-Gare [F] 66 H5
Cap d'en Font [E] 104 H5
Capdepera [E] 104 F5
Capelas [P] 100 E2
Capellades [E] 92 D4
Capendu [F] 106 C5
Capens [F] 84 H4
Capestang [F] 106 D4
Capestrano [I] 116 C4
Cap Ferret [F] 66 B3
Capinha [P] 86 F2
Capistrello [I] 116 C5
Capizzi [I] 126 F2
Čapljina [BIH] 144 C3
Capmany [E] 92 G2
Capo Cavallo [F] 114 A3
Capodimonte [I] 114 G3
Capo di Ponte [I] 72 B4
Capodiponte [I] 110 D4
Capo d'Orlando [I] 124 B8
Capoferrato [I] 118 E7
Capolíveri [I] 114 E3
Capo Rizzuto [I] 124 F5
Caposile [I] 72 F6
Capoterra [I] 118 C7
Cappamore [IRL] 4 D3
Cappenberg [D] 32 C4
Cappoquin [IRL] 4 D5
Capracotta [I] 116 D6
Capráia [I] 114 D2
Capranica [I] 114 H4
Capri [I] 120 D4
Capriati a Volturno [I] 120 D1
Capriccioli [I] 118 E2
Captieux [F] 66 D5
Capua [I] 120 D2
Capurso [I] 122 E3
Čara [HR] 144 A3
Caracal [RO] 148 A1
Caracenilla [E] 98 B2
Caracovo [BG] 148 B5
Caracuel de Calatrava [E] 96 E4
Caraglio [I] 108 F2
Čarakovo [BIH] 142 B2
Caraman [F] 106 B3
Caramulo [P] 80 C6
Caranga [E] 78 G4
Caransebeş [RO] 204 B5
Carantec [F] 40 C1
Car Asen [BG] 148 D3
Carassai [I] 116 C2
Caraula [RO] 146 F1
Caravaca [E] 104 B2
Caravaggio [I] 70 H5
Carbajales de Alba [E] 80 H4
Carbajo [E] 86 F4
Carballo [E] 78 C2
Carbon-Blanc [F] 66 D3
Carboneras [E] 102 H5
Carboneras de Guadazaón [E] 98 C3
Carbonero el Mayor [E] 88 F3
Carbónia [I] 118 B7
Carbonin / Schluderbach [I] 72 E3
Carbonne [F] 84 H4
Carcaboso [E] 88 A5
Carcabuey [E] 102 C3
Carcaixent [E] 98 E5
Carcans [F] 66 C2
Carcans-Plage [F] 66 B2
Carcar [E] 84 A5
Carcare [I] 108 H3
Carcassonne [F] 106 B4
Carcastillo [E] 84 B5
Carcavelo [P] 86 A5
Carcelén [E] 98 C5
Carceri, Eremo delle- [I] 116 A2
Carcès [F] 108 C5
Carcoforo [I] 70 E3
Çardak [TR] 150 B5
Çardak [TR] 152 G3
Çardak [TR] 152 G5
Çardaklı [TR] 152 F6
Cardedeu [E] 92 E4
Cardejón [E] 90 C3
Cardelleda de Valdeorras [E] 78 E5
Cardeña [E] 96 D6
Cardenete [E] 98 C3
Cardiff [GB] 12 F3
Cardigan [GB] 4 H6
Cardito [I] 120 D1
Cardona [E] 92 D3
Carei [RO] 204 B3
Carene [TR] 152 C3
Carennac [F] 66 H4
Carentan [F] 26 E3
Carevac [BIH] 142 B4
Carev Dvor [MK] 128 D3
Carezza al Lago / Karersee [I] 72 D3
Cargèse [F] 114 A4
Carhaix-Plouguer [F] 40 C2
Caria [P] 86 F2
Cariati [I] 124 E4
Caričin Grad [SRB] 146 D4
Caričino [BG] 148 G2
Carignan [F] 44 D2
Carignano [I] 70 D6
Çarıklar [TR] 154 F4
Cariñena [E] 90 D4
Cariño [E] 78 E1
Carinola [I] 120 D2
Carlantino [I] 120 F1
Carlentini [I] 126 G4
Carlet [E] 98 E5
Carling [F] 44 F4
Carlingford [IRL] 2 G4
Carlisle [GB] 8 E6
Carloforte [I] 118 B7
Carlow [D] 18 H4
Carlow / Ceatharlach [IRL] 4 F4
Carlton [GB] 10 F4
Carmagnola [I] 70 D6
Carmarthen [GB] 12 E2
Carmaux [F] 106 C2
Cármenes [E] 78 H4
Carmona [E] 94 H6
Carnac [F] 40 D5
Carndonagh [IRL] 2 F1
Carnew [IRL] 4 F4
Carnia [I] 72 G4
Carnlough [NIR] 2 G3
Carnota [E] 78 B3
Carnoustie [GB] 8 F2
Caro [F] 26 B6
Carolei [I] 124 D4
Carolinensiel [D] 18 C3
Carona [I] 70 H3
Caronía [I] 126 F2
Carosino [I] 122 F4
Carpaneto Piacentino [I] 110 C2
Carpegna [I] 110 H5
Carpenédolo [I] 72 B6
Carpentras [F] 106 H3
Carpi [I] 110 E2
Carpignano Sesia [I] 70 E4
Carpineti [I] 110 E3
Carpineto Romano [I] 116 B6
Cărpiniş [RO] 76 F5
Carpino [I] 116 G6
Carpinone [I] 120 E1
Carpio [E] 88 D2
Carquefou [F] 40 F6
Carqueiranne [F] 108 C6
Carraig Airt / Carrickart [IRL] 2 F1
Carral [E] 78 C2
Carranza / Karrantza [E] 82 F3
Carrapateira [P] 94 A4
Carrara [I] 110 D4
Carraroe / An Cheathrú Rua [IRL] 2 B5
Carrascalejo [E] 96 C1
Carrascosa del Campo [E] 98 A2
Carrazeda de Ansiães [P] 80 E4
Carrazedo [P] 80 E3
Carrbridge [GB] 6 E5
Carregado [P] 86 B4
Carregal do Sal [P] 80 C6
Carrega Ligure [I] 110 B3
Carregueiro [P] 94 C3
Carrick / An Charraig [IRL] 2 D2
Carrickart / Carraig Airt [IRL] 2 F1
Carrickfergus [NIR] 2 G3
Carrickmacross [IRL] 2 F4
Carrick-on-Shannon [IRL] 2 D4
Carrick-on-Suir [IRL] 4 E4
Carriço [P] 86 C2
Carrigaline [IRL] 4 C5
Carrigallen [IRL] 2 E4
Carriganimmy [IRL] 4 C4
Carrigans [IRL] 2 F2
Carrión de Calatrava [E] 96 F4
Carrión de los Condes [E] 82 C5
Carrizo [E] 78 G5

Carrizosas [E] 96 G5
Carro [F] 106 G5
Carros [F] 108 E4
Carrouges [F] 26 F5
Carrowkeel [IRL] 2 F2
Carrù [I] 108 G2
Carryduff [NIR] 2 G4
Carry-le-Rouet [F] 106 H5
Çarshovë [AL] 128 C6
Carsoli [I] 116 B5
Carsulae [I] 116 A3
Cartagena [E] 104 C4
Cártama [E] 102 B4
Cartaxo [P] 86 C4
Cartaya [E] 94 E5
Cartelle [E] 78 C5
Carteret [F] 26 D2
Cartoixa de Porta Coeli [E] 98 E4
Cartoixa d'Escaldei [E] 90 H6
Cartuja de Aula Dei [E] 90 E3
Carviçais [P] 80 F5
Carvin [F] 28 F3
Carvoeiro [P] 94 B5
Carwitz [D] 20 D5
Casabermeja [E] 102 C4
Casabona [I] 124 E4
Casa Branca [P] 86 D5
Casa Branca [P] 94 C2
Casa Branca [P] 94 D1
Casacalenda [I] 116 E6
Casáccia [CH] 70 H2
Casalabate [I] 122 G4
Casalarreina [E] 82 G6
Casalbordino [I] 116 E5
Casal Borsetti [I] 110 H3
Casalbuono [I] 120 G5
Casalciprano [I] 116 E6
Casale [I] 126 D2
Casalecchio di Reno [I] 110 F3
Casale Monferrato [I] 70 E5
Casalmaggiore [I] 110 D2
Casalpusterlengo [I] 70 H6
Casal Velino [I] 120 F5
Casamáina [I] 116 C4
Casamari, Abbazia di- [I] 116 C6
Casamássima [I] 122 E3
Casamicciola Terme [I] 120 D3
Casamozza [F] 114 C3
Casarabonela [E] 102 B4
Casarano [I] 122 G5
Casar de Cáceres [E] 86 H5
Casar de las Hurdes [E] 88 A4
Casares [E] 100 H5
Casares, Cueva de los- [E] 90 B5
Casariche [E] 102 B3
Casarubios del Monte [E] 88 F6
Casas Cueva [E] 102 F3
Casas de Benítez [E] 98 B4
Casas de Don Pedro [E] 96 C3
Casas de Fernando Alonso [E] 98 B4
Casas de Jorós [E] 100 D6
Casas de Juan Núñez [E] 98 C5
Casas del Puerto [E] 104 C2
Casas de Reina [E] 94 H4
Casas-Ibáñez [E] 98 C4
Casatejada [E] 88 B6
Cascais [P] 86 A5
Cascante [E] 84 B6
Cascia [I] 116 B3
Casciana Terme [I] 110 E6
Càscina [I] 110 D5
Căscioarele [RO] 148 D1
Casekow [D] 20 E5
Caselle [I] 70 D5
Caserta [I] 120 E2
Cashel [IRL] 4 D4
Cashel, Rock of [IRL] 4 D4
Casillas del Ángel [E] 100 E6
Casina [I] 110 E3
Casinina [I] 110 H5
Casino di Terra [I] 114 E1
Casinos [E] 98 E4
Čáslav [CZ] 48 H4
Caso / Campo de Caso [E] 82 C2
Casola Valsenio [I] 110 G4
Casoli [I] 116 D5
Casoria [I] 120 E3
Caspe [E] 90 F5
Cassà de la Selva [E] 92 F3
Cassagnes-Bégonhès [F] 68 B6
Cassano allo Ionio [I] 122 C6
Cassano d'Adda [I] 70 G5
Cassano delle Murge [I] 122 D3
Cassel [F] 28 E2
Cassibile [I] 126 G5
Cassine [I] 108 H2
Cassino [I] 120 D1
Cassis [F] 108 B5
Cassuéjouls [F] 68 B5
Castagneto Carducci [I] 114 E1
Castalla [E] 104 D2
Castañar de Ibor [E] 96 C1
Castanet-Tolosan [F] 106 A3
Castanheira de Pera [P] 86 E2
Castasegna [CH] 70 H2
Casteau [B] 28 H3
Casteggio [I] 70 G6
Castejón de Monegros [E] 90 F4
Castejón de Sos [E] 84 F5
Castejón de Valdejasa [E] 90 E3
Castel Bolognese [I] 110 G4
Castelbouc [F] 68 C6
Castelbuono [I] 126 E2
Casteldelfino [I] 108 E2
Castel del Piano [I] 114 G2
Castel del Rio [I] 110 F4
Castel di Iúdica [I] 126 F3
Castel di Sangro [I] 116 D6
Castel di Tora [I] 116 B4
Castel Doria, Terme di- [I] 118 D3
Castelejo [P] 94 A5
Castelfidardo [I] 116 C1
Castelfiorentino [I] 110 E6
Castelflorite [E] 90 G4
Castelfranco Emilia [I] 110 F3
Castelfranco in Miscano [I] 120 F2
Castelfranco Véneto [I] 72 E6
Castel Goffredo [I] 110 E1
Casteljaloux [F] 66 D5
Castellabate [I] 120 F5
Castellammare del Golfo [I] 126 C2
Castellammare di Stábia [I] 120 E3
Castellamonte [I] 70 D5
Castellana, Grotte di- [I] 122 E3
Castellana Grotte [I] 122 E3
Castellana Sícula [I] 126 E3
Castellane [F] 108 D4
Castellaneta [I] 122 E4
Castellar [E] 102 F1
Castellar de la Frontera [E] 100 G5
Castellar de la Muela [E] 90 C5
Castellar de Santiago [E] 96 F5
Castell'Arquato [I] 110 C2
Castell'Azzara [I] 114 G3
Castellazzo Bormida [I] 108 H2
Castelldans [E] 90 H5
Castell d'aro [E] 92 G3
Castell de Cabres [E] 98 G1
Castelldefels [E] 92 D5
Castell de Ferro [E] 102 E5
Castell de Mur / Cellers [E] 92 C2
Castelleone [I] 70 H5
Castelletto d'Orba [I] 110 A2
Castellfollit de la Roca [E] 92 F2
Castellina in Chianti [I] 110 F6
Castelló de la Plana / Castellón de la Plana [E] 98 F3
Castelló de la Ribera [E] 98 E6
Castelló d'Empúries [E] 92 G2
Castellón de la Plana / Castelló de la Plana [E] 98 F3
Castellote [E] 90 F6
Castello Tesino [I] 72 D4
Castellterçol [E] 92 E3
Castellúccio dei Sáuri [I] 120 G2
Castelluccio Sup. [I] 120 H5
Castelluzzo [I] 126 B2
Castelmagno [I] 108 F2
Castelmassa [I] 110 F2
Castelmauro [I] 116 E6
Castelmoron [F] 66 E5
Castelnau [F] 66 H4
Castelnaudary [F] 106 B4
Castelnau-de-Médoc [F] 66 C2
Castelnau-de-Montmiral [F] 106 B2
Castelnau d'Estretefonds [F] 84 H2
Castelnau-Magnoac [F] 84 F3
Castelnau-Montratier [F] 66 F5
Castelnovo ne' Monti [I] 110 D3
Castelnuovo Berardenga [I] 114 G1
Castelnuovo della Dáunia [I] 120 F1
Castelnuovo di Garfagnana [I] 110 D4
Castelnuovo di Porto [I] 116 A5
Castelnuovo di Val di Cecina [I] 114 F1
Castelnuovo Don Bosco [I] 70 E6
Castelnuovo Monterotaro [I] 116 F6
Castelnuovo Scrívia [I] 70 F6
Castelo [P] 86 D2
Castelo Branco [P] 80 F5
Castelo Branco [P] 86 F3
Castelo Branco [P] 100 C3
Castelo de Paiva [P] 80 C4
Castelo de Vide [P] 86 F4
Castelo do Neiva [P] 78 A6
Castel Porziano [I] 114 H6
Castelraimondo [I] 116 B2
Castel San Giovanni [I] 70 G6
Castel San Lorenzo [I] 120 F4
Castel San Pietro Terme [I] 110 F4
Castelsaraceno [I] 120 H5
Castelsardo [I] 118 C2
Castelsarrasin [F] 66 F6
Castelseprio [I] 70 F4
Castelserás [E] 90 F6
Casteltérmini [I] 126 D3
Castelvecchio Subequo [I] 116 C5
Castelverde [I] 70 H6
Castelvetere in Val Fortore [I] 120 F1
Castelvetrano [I] 126 B3
Castel Volturno [I] 120 D2
Castenaso [I] 110 F3
Castets [F] 66 B5
Castiádas [I] 118 D7
Castiglione d'Orcia [I] 114 G2
Castiglioncello [I] 110 D6
Castiglione dei Pepoli [I] 110 F4
Castiglione del Lago [I] 114 H2
Castiglione della Pescáia [I] 114 E3
Càstiglione delle Stiviere [I] 72 B6
Castiglione Messer Marino [I] 116 E6
Castiglione Olona [I] 70 F4
Castiglion Fibocchi [I] 110 G6
Castiglion Fiorentino [I] 114 H1
Castilblanco [E] 96 C2
Castilblanco de los Arroyos [E] 94 G5
Castillejo de Martín Viejo [E] 86 H2
Castilliscar [E] 84 C5
Castillo de Locubín [E] 102 D3
Castillo de Matajudíos [E] 82 D5
Castillo de Tajarja [E] 102 D4
Castillo de Villamalefa [E] 98 F3
Castillon-la-Bataille [F] 66 D3
Castillonnès [F] 66 E4
Castillo Pasiega las Chimenas, Cuevas el- [E] 82 E3
Castione della Presolana [I] 72 A5
Castlebar [IRL] 2 C4
Castlebay / Bagh a Chaisteil [GB] 6 A5
Castlebellingham [IRL] 2 F5
Castleblayney [IRL] 2 F4
Castlebridge [IRL] 4 F5
Castlecomer [IRL] 4 E3
Castledermot [IRL] 4 F3
Castle Douglas [GB] 8 D5
Castleisland [IRL] 4 B4
Castlemaine [IRL] 4 B4
Castlemartyr [IRL] 4 D5
Castleplunkett [IRL] 2 D4
Castlepollard [IRL] 2 E5
Castlerea [IRL] 2 D4
Castletown [GBM] 10 B2
Castletownbere [IRL] 4 B5
Castletown House [IRL] 2 F6
Castletownroche [IRL] 4 D4
Castletownshend [IRL] 4 B5
Castlewellan [NIR] 2 G4
Castrejón [E] 88 D2
Castres [F] 106 B3
Castricum [NL] 16 D3
Castries [F] 106 F4
Castril [E] 102 G3
Castrillo de Don Juan [E] 88 G2
Castrillo de la Reina [E] 88 H2
Castrillón [E] 78 F3
Castro [I] 114 G3
Castro / Dozón [E] 78 C4
Castrobarto [E] 82 F4
Castrocalbón [E] 80 H3
Castro Caldelas [E] 78 D5
Castrocaro Terme [I] 110 G4
Castrocontrigo [E] 78 F6
Castro da Cola [P] 94 C4
Castro Daire [P] 80 C5
Castro dei Volsci [I] 120 C1
Castro del Río [E] 102 C2
Castro de Rei [E] 78 E3
Castrojeriz [E] 82 D6
Castro Marim [P] 94 D5
Castromil [E] 78 E6
Castromonte [E] 88 E1
Castronuevo [E] 88 D1
Castronuño [E] 88 D2
Castropol [E] 78 F2
Castrop-Rauxal [D] 30 H3
Castroreale [I] 124 B7
Castrotorafe, Ruinas de- [E] 80 H4
Castro-Urdiales [E] 82 G3
Castroverde [E] 78 E3
Castro Verde [P] 94 C4
Castroverde de Cerrato [E] 88 F2
Castrovillari [I] 122 C6
Castuera [E] 96 B4
Cataéggio [I] 70 H3
Çatalca [TR] 150 D2
Çatallar [TR] 154 H2
Catane [RO] 146 F2
Catánia [I] 126 G3
Catanzaro [I] 124 E5
Catanzaro Marina [I] 124 E5
Catarroja [E] 98 E5
Catenanuova [I] 126 F3
Cateraggio [F] 114 C4
Cathair Dónall / Caherdaniel [IRL] 4 A4
Catoira [E] 78 B3
Catterick [GB] 10 F2
Cattolica [I] 112 B5
Cattolica Eraclea [I] 126 C3
Catus [F] 66 G5
Caudebec-en-Caux [F] 26 H3
Caudete [E] 104 D1
Caudeval [F] 106 B5
Caudry [F] 28 F4
Caulonia [I] 124 D7
Caulonia [I] 124 E6
Caumont [F] 26 E3
Caumont [F] 84 G4
Caunes-Minervois [F] 106 C4
Cauro [F] 114 B5
Căuşani [MD] 204 F3
Caussade [F] 66 G6
Cauterets [F] 84 E4
Cauville [F] 26 G2
Cava [E] 92 B6
Cava de' Tirreni [I] 120 E3
Cava d'Ispica [I] 126 F5
Cavagliá [I] 70 E5
Cavaillon [F] 106 H4
Cavalaire-sur-Mer [F] 108 D6
Cavalese [I] 72 D4
Cavalière [F] 108 D6
Cavallino [I] 72 F6
Cavallino [I] 122 G5
Cavalls, Cova dels- [E] 98 G2
Cavan / An Cabhán [IRL] 2 E4
Cavárzere [I] 110 G2
Çavdarhisar [TR] 152 G2
Çavdır [TR] 152 H6
Cave del Predil [I] 72 H4
Cavi [I] 110 B3
Caviaga [I] 70 H5
Cavo [I] 114 E2
Cavour [I] 70 C6
Cavriglia [I] 110 F6
Cavtat [HR] 144 C4
Çayağzi [TR] 150 F2
Çaybaşı [TR] 152 D4
Çayçinge [TR] 152 F2
Çayhisar [TR] 154 E1
Çayırova (Ágios Theodoros) [CY] 154 G5
Caylus [F] 66 G6
Cayrols [F] 68 A4
Çayyaka [TR] 150 F5
Cazalegas [E] 88 D6
Cazalla de la Sierra [E] 94 H5
Cazals [F] 66 F4
Cazaubon [F] 66 D6
Cazeneuve, Château de- [F] 66 D4
Cazères [F] 84 G4
Cazin [BIH] 112 H2
Čazma [HR] 74 F6
Cazorla [E] 102 F2
Cea [E] 78 C4
Cea [E] 82 C5
Ceatharlach / Carlow [IRL] 4 F4
Cebolla [E] 96 E1
Čebovce [SK] 64 C4
Cebreiro [E] 78 E4
Cebreros [E] 88 E5
Cebrones del Rio [E] 78 G6
Ceccano [I] 120 C1
Cece [H] 76 B3
Čečejovce [SK] 64 F3
Čechtice [CZ] 48 G5
Čechtín [CZ] 50 A6
Cécina [I] 114 E1
Ceclavín [E] 86 G4
Cecos [E] 78 F4
Cedeira [E] 78 D1
Cedillo [E] 86 F4
Cedros [P] 100 C2
Cedynia [PL] 34 F1
Cee [E] 78 B2
Cefalù [I] 126 E2
Cegléd [H] 76 D2
Ceglie Messàpica [I] 122 F4
Cegrane [MK] 128 D1
Cehegín [E] 104 B2
Ceillac [F] 108 E2
Ceira [P] 86 D2
Čejč [CZ] 62 G2
Čekiške [LT] 200 F5
Ceków Kolonia [PL] 36 E4
Čelákovice [CZ] 48 G3
Celano [I] 116 C5
Celanova [E] 78 C5
Čelarevo [SRB] 142 F1
Celaru [RO] 146 G1
Celbowo [PL] 22 D1
Celbridge [IRL] 2 F6
Čelebić [BIH] 142 B4
Celerina [CH] 70 H2
Čelić [BIH] 142 E3
Čelinac [BIH] 142 C3
Celico [I] 124 D4
Celjahavi [BY] 202 B6
Celje [SLO] 74 D4
Cella [E] 98 D1
Celldömölk [H] 74 G1
Celle [D] 32 G1
Celle di Bulgheria [I] 120 G5
Celle Ligure [I] 108 H3
Cellers / Castell de Mur [E] 92 C2
Celles [B] 28 G3
Celles-sur-Belle [F] 54 D4
Čelopeci [MK] 128 D3
Celorico da Beira [P] 80 D6
Celorico de Basto [P] 80 D4
Celsoy [F] 58 A3
Çeltek [TR] 152 H5
Çeltikköy [TR] 150 B4
Čemerno [BIH] 144 D2
Cemke [TR] 150 F2
Cenad [RO] 76 F4
Cencenighe [I] 72 E4
Cenei [RO] 76 F6
Ceneköy [TR] 150 C3
Cenicientos [E] 88 E5
Cenicero [E] 82 G6
Cenizzate [E] 98 C4
Čenta [SRB] 142 G2
Centallo [I] 108 F2
Centelles [E] 92 E3
Cento [I] 110 F3
Centuri [F] 114 C2
Centúripe [I] 126 F3
Cepagatti [I] 116 D4
Çepan [AL] 128 C5
Čepin [HR] 142 D1
Cepos [P] 86 E2
Čepovan [SLO] 72 H5
Ceprano [I] 120 C1
Cer [MK] 128 D2
Čeralije [HR] 74 H6
Cerami [I] 126 F2
Ceranów [PL] 38 D2
Ceraso [I] 120 F5
Cerbère [F] 92 G2
Cercal [P] 86 B4
Cercal [P] 94 B3
Cerceda [E] 78 C2
Cerceda [E] 88 F5
Cercedilla [E] 88 F4
Cerchiara di Calábria [I] 122 D6
Cerda [I] 126 D2
Cerdedo [E] 78 C4
Cerdeira [P] 86 G2
Cerdon [F] 56 C2
Cerea [I] 110 F1
Cerecinos de Campos [E] 82 B6
Cered [H] 64 E4
Cereixo [E] 78 B2
Ceremosnja [SRB] 146 D1
Ceres [I] 70 D5
Ceresole Reale [I] 70 C4
Céret [F] 92 F2
Cerfontaine [B] 28 H4
Ceriale [I] 108 G3
Cerignola [I] 120 H2
Cérilly [F] 56 C5
Čerín [SK] 64 C3
Cerisiers [F] 42 H6
Cerizay [F] 54 D3
Çerkezköy [TR] 150 D2
Cerknica [SLO] 74 B6
Cerkno [SLO] 74 B5
Cerkovitsa [BG] 148 B2
Cerkvenjak [SLO] 74 E3
Cerkwica [PL] 20 G3
Çermë [AL] 128 B3
Cermei [RO] 76 H3
Cerna [HR] 142 E2
Cernache do Bom Jardim [P] 86 D3
Černá Hora [CZ] 50 C5
Cernavodă [RO] 204 E5
Černá v Pošumaví [CZ] 62 B3
Cernay [F] 58 D3
Cernégula [E] 82 E5
Černičevo [BG] 148 B5
Cerniébaud [F] 58 D6
Cernik [HR] 142 C1
Cernóbbio [I] 70 G4
Černookovo [BG] 148 G1
Černošín [CZ] 48 D4
Černovice [CZ] 48 G6
Černuc [CZ] 48 F3
Cerósimo [I] 122 C5
Cerovačke Špilje [HR] 112 H4
Cerovica [BIH] 144 C3
Çërravë [AL] 128 D4
Cerreto Laziale [I] 116 B5
Cërrik [AL] 128 B4
Cerro de los Angeles [E] 88 F6
Cerro de los Santos [E] 98 C6
Cerro Muriano [E] 96 C6
Certaldo [I] 110 E6
Cervatos [E] 82 E4
Cervatos de la Cueza [E] 82 C5
Červená [CZ] 48 F5
Červená Lhota [CZ] 48 G6
Červená-Řečice [CZ] 48 H5
Červená Skala [SK] 64 E2
Červená Voda [CZ] 50 C4
Červený Hrádek [CZ] 48 E2
Červený Hrádek [CZ] 48 F5
Červený Kameň [SK] 62 G4
Červený Kameň [SK] 64 A2
Červený Kláštor [SK] 52 B5
Červený Kostelec [CZ] 50 B2
Cervera [E] 92 C3
Cervera de la Cañada [E] 90 C4
Cervera del Llano [E] 98 B3
Cervera del Río Alhama [E] 84 A6
Cervera de Pisuerga [E] 82 D4
Cerveteri [I] 114 H5
Cérvia [I] 110 H4
Cervignano del Friuli [I] 72 G5
Cervinara [I] 120 E3
Cervione [F] 114 C4
Cervo [E] 78 E1
Cervo [I] 108 G4
Cesana Torinese [I] 70 B6
Cesarica [HR] 112 F3
Cesarò [I] 126 F2
Cesarzowice [PL] 36 C6
Cesena [I] 110 H4
Cesenático [I] 110 H4
Ceserhát-Suráni [H] 64 D5
Cēsis [LV] 198 E4
Česká Bělá [CZ] 50 A5
Česká Kamenice [CZ] 48 F2
Česká Lípa [CZ] 48 G2
Česká Skalice [CZ] 50 B3
Česká Třebová [CZ] 50 B4
České Budějovice [CZ] 62 C2
České Libchavy [CZ] 50 B4
České Velenice [CZ] 62 C3
Český Brod [CZ] 48 G4
Český Krumlov [CZ] 62 B2
Český Šternberk [CZ] 48 G4
Český Těšín [CZ] 50 F5
Çeşme [TR] 134 H5
Çeşmealti [TR] 152 C4
Cespedosa [E] 88 C4
Cessalto [I] 72 F5
Cessenon-sur-Orb [F] 106 D4
Čestimensko [BG] 148 E3
Čestobrodica [SRB] 146 A2
Cestona / Zestoa [E] 84 A2
Cesvaine [LV] 198 F5
Cetate [RO] 146 F1
Çetibeli [TR] 154 D1
Cetinje [MNE] 144 E4
Cetóbriga [P] 86 B6
Cetona [I] 114 G2
Cetraro [I] 124 C4
Ceuta [E] 100 G6
Ceutí [E] 104 C3
Ceva [I] 108 G3
Cevico Navero [E] 88 F1
Čevo [MNE] 144 E4
Cewków [PL] 52 F3
Ceylan [TR] 154 G2
Ceyrat [F] 68 C2
Ceyzériat [F] 68 G2
Chaalis, Abbaye de- [F] 42 G3
Chabanais [F] 54 F6
Chabeuil [F] 68 F5
Chablis [F] 56 E2
Chabreloche [F] 68 D2
Chabris [F] 54 H3
Chachersk [BY] 202 D5
Chagny [F] 56 G5
Chailland [F] 26 E6
Chaillé-les-Marais [F] 54 C4
Chailley-Turny [F] 42 H6
Chailluz, Fort de- [F] 58 B4
Chairóneia [GR] 132 H5
Chalabre [F] 106 B5
Chalais [F] 66 E2
Chalamont [F] 68 G2
Chalampé [F] 58 E3
Chalandrítsa [GR] 132 F6
Chálki [GR] 132 G2
Chálki [GR] 154 C4
Chalkiádes [GR] 132 G2
Chalkída [GR] 134 B5
Chalkidóna [GR] 128 G4
Challans [F] 54 B2
Challes-les-Eaux [F] 70 A4
Chalonnes-sur-Loire [F] 54 D1
Châlons-en-Champagne [F] 44 B4
Chalon-sur-Saône [F] 56 G5
Chalupy [PL] 36 H6
Châlus [F] 66 G2
Chalusset, Château de- [F] 66 G1
Cham [CH] 58 F5
Cham [D] 48 C6
Chamberet [F] 66 H2
Chambéry [F] 68 H3
Chambilly [F] 56 E6
Chambley-Bussières [F] 44 E4
Chambon-sur-Lac [F] 68 C2
Chambon-sur-Voueize [F] 56 B6
Chambord [F] 54 H2
Chambord, Parc de- [F] 54 H2
Chamelet [F] 68 F2
Chameregg [D] 48 C6
Chammünster [D] 48 C6
Chamonix-Mont-Blanc [F] 70 C3
Champagnac-le-Vieux [F] 68 D3
Champagne-Mouton [F] 54 E5
Champagnole [F] 58 B6
Champaubert [F] 44 A4
Champdeniers [F] 54 D4
Champ du Bataille, Château du- [F] 26 H4
Champ du Feu [F] 44 G6
Champeix [F] 68 C3
Champéry [CH] 70 C2
Champex [CH] 70 C3
Champier [F] 68 G4
Champigné [F] 40 H6
Champigny-sur-Veude [F] 54 F2
Champillon [F] 44 B3
Champlan [F] 42 F4
Champlitte [F] 58 A3
Champlon [B] 30 E6
Champoluc [I] 70 D3
Champorcher [I] 70 D4
Champrond-en-Gâtine [F] 26 H6
Champtoceaux [F] 40 F6
Champvent [CH] 58 C6
Chamrousse [F] 68 H5
Chamusca [P] 86 C4
Chanaleilles [F] 68 D5
Chanas [F] 68 F4
Chandrinós [GR] 136 C4
Chaniá [GR] 140 C4
Chaniótis [GR] 130 C6
Channel Tunnel / La Manche, Tunnel sous- [F/GB] 14 G5
Chantada [E] 78 D4
Chantelle [F] 56 D6
Chantemerle [F] 70 B6
Chantilly [F] 42 G3
Chantonnay [F] 54 C3
Chão de Codes [P] 86 D4
Chaource [F] 44 B6
Chapelle-Royale [F] 42 D5
Chárakas [GR] 140 E5
Charavgí [GR] 128 F5
Charavines [F] 68 G4
Charbonnières-les-Bains [F] 68 F3
Charbowo [PL] 36 D2
Chard [GB] 12 F4
Charenton-du-Cher [F] 56 C4
Charité, Abbaye de la- [F] 58 B4
Charleroi [B] 30 C5
Charlestown [IRL] 2 D4
Charleville / Rath Luirc [IRL] 4 C4
Charleville-Mézières [F] 44 C2
Charlieu [F] 68 E1
Charlottenberg [S] 166 D1
Charly [F] 42 H3
Charly [F] 56 C4
Charmes [F] 44 E6
Charnawchytsy [BY] 38 G2
Charneca [P] 86 A5
Charny [F] 56 D1
Charnyany [BY] 38 G3
Charolles [F] 56 F6
Chârost [F] 56 B3
Charpentry [F] 44 D3
Charrières [CH] 70 C1
Charron [F] 54 C4
Charroux [F] 54 E5
Chartres [F] 42 E4
Charvarica [BG] 146 F6
Charzykowy [PL] 22 C4
Chassant [F] 42 D4
Chasseneuil-s.-Bonnieure [F] 54 E6
Chasse sur Rhone [F] 68 F3
Chassigny [F] 56 H3
Château-Arnoux [F] 108 C3
Châteaubourg [F] 26 D6
Châteaubriant [F] 40 F5
Château-Chinon [F] 56 E4
Château d'Oex [CH] 70 D1
Château-du-Loir [F] 42 B6
Châteaudun [F] 42 D5
Châteaugiron [F] 26 C6
Château-Gontier [F] 40 H5
Château-Landon [F] 42 F5
Château-la-Vallière [F] 42 B6
Château-l'Évêque [F] 66 F3
Châteaulin [F] 40 B2
Châteaumeillant [F] 56 B5
Châteauneuf [F] 66 E1
Châteauneuf-de-Randon [F] 68 D5
Châteauneuf-du-Faou [F] 40 C3
Châteauneuf-du-Pape [F] 106 G3
Châteauneuf-en-Thymerais [F] 26 H6
Châteauneuf-sur-Cher [F] 56 C4
Châteauneuf-sur-Loire [F] 56 C1
Châteauneuf-sur-Sarthe [F] 40 H6
Châteauponsac [F] 54 G5
Château-Porcien [F] 28 H6
Château-Queyras [F] 70 B6
Château-Regnault [F] 44 C1
Châteaurenard [F] 42 G6
Château-Renault [F] 54 G1
Châteauroux [F] 54 H4
Château-Salins [F] 44 F5
Château-Thierry [F] 42 H3
Châteauvillain [F] 56 G2
Châtel [F] 70 C2
Châtelaillon-Plage [F] 54 C5
Châtelet [B] 30 C5
Châtelguyon [F] 68 C2
Châtellerault [F] 54 F3
Chatêl-Montagne [F] 68 E1
Châtel-St-Denis [CH] 70 C1
Châtelus-Malvaleix [F] 54 H5
Châtenois [F] 44 E6
Chatham [GB] 14 F4
Châtillon [I] 70 D4
Châtillon-Coligny [F] 56 D1
Châtillon-en-Bazois [F] 56 E4
Châtillon-en-Diois [F] 68 G6
Châtillon-sur-Chalaronne [F] 68 G2
Châtillon-sur-Indre [F] 54 G3
Châtillon-sur-Loire [F] 56 D2
Châtillon-sur-Marne [F] 44 A3
Châtillon-sur-Seine [F] 56 G2
Châtre, Église de- [F] 54 D6
Chatteris [GB] 14 F2
Chaudes-Aigues [F] 68 C5
Chauffailles [F] 68 F1
Chaufour-lès-Bonnières [F] 42 E3
Chaumergy [F] 56 H5
Chaumont [F] 56 H1
Chaumont-sur-Aire [F] 44 D4
Chaumont-sur-Loire [F] 54 G2
Chaunay [F] 54 E5
Chauny [F] 28 F6
Chaussin [F] 56 H5
Chauvigny [F] 54 F4
Chaux-Neuve [F] 58 B6
Chavaleč [CZ] 50 B2
Chavdar [BG] 130 D1
Chaves [P] 80 E3
Chavusy [BY] 202 D5
Chayki [RUS] 198 H6
Chazelles-sur-Lyon [F] 68 F3
Cheb [CZ] 48 C3
Chęciny [PL] 52 B1
Cheddar [GB] 12 F3
Chef-Boutonne [F] 54 D5
Cheglevici [RO] 76 F5
Cheimarros [GR] 130 B3
Chekhov [RUS] 202 F3
Chekhovo [RUS] 22 H2
Cheles [E] 94 F2
Chełm [PL] 38 F6
Chełmek [PL] 50 G3
Chełmno [PL] 22 D5
Chełmno [PL] 36 F3
Chelmsford [GB] 14 F4
Chełmża [PL] 22 E6
Chełst [PL] 36 B1
Cheltenham [GB] 12 G2
Chelva [E] 98 D3
Chémery-sur-Bar [F] 44 C2
Chemillé [F] 54 D2
Chemin [F] 56 H5
Chemnitz [D] 48 D1
Chenaux [CH] 58 C6
Chêne-Pignier [F] 54 F6
Chénérailles [F] 56 B6
Chenonceaux [F] 54 G2
Chepelare [BG] 130 E1
Chepstow [GB] 12 G3
Chera [E] 98 D4
Cherasco [I] 108 G2
Cherbourg [F] 26 D2
Cherekha [RUS] 198 G3
Cheremykino [RUS] 178 G5
Cherepovo [BG] 148 D6
Cherkasovo [RUS] 178 F3
Cherkasy [UA] 202 E8
Chern [RUS] 202 F4
Cherna Mesta [BG] 146 G6
Chernevo [RUS] 198 G2
Cherniakhiv [UA] 202 C7
Chernihiv [UA] 202 D6
Cherni rid [BG] 130 G1
Chernivtsi [UA] 204 D3
Cherno [RUS] 198 G1

Dolice [PL] 20 G6
Dolíchi [GR] 128 G6
Doljani [HR] 112 H4
Doljani [MNE] 144 E4
Doljevac [SRB] 146 D4
Döllach [A] 72 G2
Döllbach [D] 46 E2
Dolle [D] 34 B2
Døllii [N] 180 H4
Döllstädt [D] 32 H6
Dolmen de Dombate [E] 78 B2
Dolna Banya [BG] 146 G5
Dolna Dikanya [BG] 146 F5
Dolna Grupa [PL] 22 E5
Dolná Krupá [SK] 62 H4
Dolna Mahala [BG] 148 B5
Dolna Mitropolia [BG] 148 B3
Dolna Mitropoliya [BG] 148 A3
Dolná Strehová [SK] 64 D4
Dolni Chiflik [BG] 148 F3
Dolni Cibăr [BG] 146 F2
Dolni Dŭbnik [BG] 148 A3
Dolní Dvořiště [CZ] 62 C3
Dolní Kounice [CZ] 62 F2
Dolní Krupá [CZ] 48 G2
Dolni Lom [BG] 146 E3
Dolní Ročov [CZ] 48 E3
Dolno Dupeni [MK] 128 E4
Dolno Kamartsi [BG] 146 G4
Dolno Kosovrasti [MK] 128 C2
Dolno Levski [BG] 148 A5
Dolno Novkovo [BG] 148 D3
Dolno Tserovene [BG] 146 F3
Dolno Ujno [BG] 146 E5
Dolný Kubín [SK] 50 G6
Dolo [I] 110 H1
Dolores [E] 104 D3
Doloscy [RUS] 198 H6
Dolovo [SRB] 142 H2
Dolsk [PL] 36 C4
Dołubowo [PL] 38 E1
Dolyna [UA] 52 H6
Dolyns'ka [UA] 202 F8
Dolzhicy [RUS] 198 H2
Dołżyca [PL] 52 E6
Dom [A] 74 B2
Domaháza [H] 64 E4
Domaj-Has [AL] 146 B6
Domaniç [TR] 150 G5
Domanovići [BIH] 144 C3
Domašov [CZ] 50 D3
Domaszowice [PL] 50 E1
Domažlice [CZ] 48 D5
Dombas [N] 180 G5
Dombasle [F] 44 F5
Dombegyház [H] 76 G4
Dombóvár [H] 76 B4
Dombrád [H] 64 H4
Dombrot-le-Sec [F] 58 B2
Domburg [NL] 16 B6
Doméniko [GR] 132 F1
Domèvre-en-Haye [F] 44 E5
Domfront [F] 26 E5
Domingão [P] 86 D4
Dömitz [D] 18 H5
Domme [F] 66 G4
Dommitzsch [D] 34 D4
Domnítsa [GR] 132 F4
Domnovo [RUS] 22 H2
Domodedovo [RUS] 202 F3
Domodóssola [I] 70 E3
Domokós [GR] 132 G3
Domousnice [CZ] 48 G3
Dompaire [F] 58 C2
Dompierre [F] 56 E5
Dompierre-du-Chemin [F] 26 D5
Dompierre-sur-Besbre [F] 56 E5
Dompierre-sur-Mer [F] 54 C4
Domrémy-la-Pucelle [F] 44 D6
Dömsöd [H] 76 C2
Domurcali [TR] 150 B1
Dómus de Maria [I] 118 C8
Domusnóvas [I] 118 B6
Domžale [SLO] 74 C5
Donado [E] 80 G3
Donaghadee [NIR] 2 H3
Donaghmore [IRL] 4 E3
Doña Mencía [E] 102 C2
Donaueschingen [D] 58 F3
Donaustauf [D] 60 F2
Donauwörth [D] 60 D2
Don Benito [E] 96 B3
Doncaster [GB] 10 F4
Dondurma [TR] 150 B5
Donegal / Dún na nGall [IRL] 2 E2
Donja Brela [HR] 144 B2
Donja Brezna [MNE] 144 D3
Donja Bukovica [MNE] 144 E3
Donja Kamenica [SRB] 146 A1
Donja Kamenica [SRB] 146 E3
Donja Ljubata [SRB] 146 E5
Donja Šatornja [SRB] 146 B2
Donja Suvaja [HR] 112 H4
Donja-Vrijeska [HR] 74 G6
Donje Ljupče [KS] 146 C5
Donje Petrčane [HR] 112 F5
Donji Koričani [BIH] 142 C3
Donji Krcin [SRB] 146 C3
Donji Lapac [HR] 112 H4
Donji Lipovik [MK] 128 G2
Donji Miholjac [HR] 76 B6
Donji Milanovac [SRB] 146 D1
Donji Stajevac [SRB] 146 E5
Donji Vakuf [BIH] 142 C4
Donji Zemunik [HR] 112 G5
Don Juan, Cueva de- [E] 98 D5
Donnalucata [I] 126 F5
Donnersbach [A] 62 B6
Donnersbachwald [A] 74 B1
Donostia-San Sebastián [E] 84 B2
Donovaly [SK] 64 C2
Dontilly [F] 42 G5
Donzenac [F] 66 G3
Donzère [F] 68 F5
Donzy [F] 56 D3
Doohooma / Dumha Thuama [IRL] 2 B3
Doonbeg [IRL] 2 B6
Doonloughan [IRL] 2 B4
Doorn [NL] 16 E5
Doornik (Tournai) [B] 28 G3
Dörarp [S] 162 C4
Dorchester [GB] 12 F5
Dordives [F] 42 G5
Dordrecht [NL] 16 D5
Dorëz [AL] 128 C3
Dorfen [D] 60 F4
Dorfmark [D] 18 F6
Dorgali [I] 118 E4
Doria, Castello- [I] 110 A3
Dório [GR] 136 D3
Dorkáda [GR] 130 B4
Dorking [GB] 14 E5
Dorkovo [BG] 148 A6
Dormagen [D] 30 G4
Dormánd [H] 64 E6
Dormans [F] 44 A3
Dornas [F] 68 E5
Dornauberg [A] 72 E2
Dornava [SLO] 74 E4
Dornbirn [A] 60 B6
Dornburg [D] 34 B6
Dorndorf [D] 46 F1
Dornes [F] 56 D5
Dorno [I] 70 F5
Dornoch [GB] 6 E4
Dornstetten [D] 58 G2
Dornum [D] 18 B3
Dorog [H] 64 C6
Dorogobuzh [RUS] 202 D4
Dorohoi [RO] 204 D3
Dorohucza [PL] 38 F6
Dorokhovo [RUS] 202 E3
Dorotea [S] 190 F5
Dörpen [D] 16 H3
Dörpstedt [D] 18 E2
Dorsten [D] 30 H2
Dortan [F] 68 H1
Dortmund [D] 32 C4
Dörtyol (Prastio) [CY] 154 G5
Dorum [D] 18 D3
Dörverden [D] 18 E6
Dörzbach [D] 46 E5
Dosbarrios [E] 96 G2
Döşeme [TR] 154 C3
Dos Hermanas [E] 94 G6
Dospat [BG] 130 D1
Dos Torres [E] 96 C5
Døstrup [DK] 156 B3
Dotnuva [LT] 200 F4
Douai [F] 28 F4
Douamont, Fort du- [F] 44 D3
Douarnenez [F] 40 B3
Douchy [F] 42 G6
Doucier [F] 58 A6
Doudeville [F] 26 H2
Doué-la-Fontaine [F] 54 E2
Douglas [GB] 8 D4
Douglas [GBM] 10 B2
Doulaincourt [F] 44 D6
Doulevant-le-Château [F] 44 C6
Doullens [F] 28 E4
Dourdan [F] 42 F4
Dourgne [F] 106 B4
Doussard [F] 70 B3
Douvaine [F] 70 B2
Douzy [F] 44 D2
Dover [GB] 14 G5
Dovre [N] 180 G5
Downham Market [GB] 14 F2
Downings [IRL] 2 E1
Downpatrick [NIR] 2 G4
Dowra [IRL] 2 E3
Dowsk [BY] 202 D5
Doxáto [GR] 130 D3
Dozón / Castro [E] 78 C4
Dozulé [F] 26 G3
Drabiv [UA] 202 E7
Drac, Coves del- [E] 104 F5
Dračevo [MK] 128 E1
Drachenfels [D] 30 H5
Drachenwand [A] 60 H5
Drachselsried [D] 48 D6
Drachten [NL] 16 F2
Drag [N] 190 C4
Drag Ájluokta [N] 192 E5
Dragalevtsi [BG] 146 F5
Drăgănești de Vede [RO] 148 B1
Drăgănești-Olt [RO] 148 A1
Drăgănești-Vlașca [RO] 148 C1
Draganici [HR] 74 D6
Dragaš [KS] 146 B6
Drăgășani [RO] 204 D5
Dragatuš [SLO] 112 G1
Dragichevo [BG] 146 F5
Draginje [SRB] 146 A1
Draginovo [BG] 148 A6
Dragocvet [SRB] 146 C2
Dragoevo [MK] 128 F1
Dragoman [BG] 146 F4
Dragomir [BG] 148 A5
Dragomirovo [BG] 146 F5
Dragomirovo [BG] 148 B2
Dragomirovo [BG] 148 C3
Dragon, Caverne du- [F] 44 B2
Dragør [DK] 156 H3
Dragotina [HR] 142 A1
Dragov Doll [MK] 128 E2
Dragovishtitsa [BG] 146 E5
Dragsfjärd [FIN] 176 E5
Dragsholm Slot [DK] 156 F2
Draguignan [F] 108 D5
Drahanovice [CZ] 50 C5
Drahonice [CZ] 48 F6
Drahovce [SK] 62 H3
Draka [BG] 148 E5
Drakčići [SRB] 146 B3
Draksenić [BIH] 142 B2
Dráma [GR] 130 D3
Dramče [MK] 146 E6
Drammen [N] 164 H1
Drängsered [S] 162 B4
Drängsmark [S] 196 A4
Drânic [RO] 146 G1
Dransfeld [D] 32 F4
Dranske [D] 20 D1
Drasenhofen [A] 62 F3
Drávafok [H] 74 H5
Drávaszabolcs [H] 76 B6
Draviskos [GR] 130 C3
Dravograd [SLO] 74 C3
Drawno [PL] 20 H6
Drawsko Pomorskie [PL] 20 H5
Drążdżewo [PL] 24 B6
Draženov [CZ] 48 D5
Drażniew [PL] 38 F2
Drebkau [D] 34 F4
Drégelypalánk [H] 64 C5
Drei [D] 46 G1
Dreilingen [D] 18 G6
Dren [KS] 146 B4
Dren [MK] 128 F3
Drenchia [I] 72 H4
Drenovac [SRB] 146 D5
Drenovci [HR] 142 E2
Drenovets [BG] 146 F2
Drensteinfurt [D] 32 C3
Drépano [GR] 128 F5
Dresden [D] 34 E6
Dretyń [PL] 22 B3
Dreux [F] 42 E3
Drevsjø [N] 182 D6
Drewitz [D] 34 C3
Drewitz [D] 34 E2
Drezdenko [PL] 36 B1
Drežnica [HR] 112 F2
Dreznik-Grad [HR] 112 G2
Driebergen [NL] 16 E5
Drienovo [SK] 64 C4
Driffield [GB] 10 G3
Drimoleague [IRL] 4 B5
Drina Kanjon [BIH] 142 E4
Drinjača [BIH] 142 E4
Drinovci [BIH] 144 B2
Driny [SK] 62 G4
Drionville [F] 28 E2
Driva [N] 180 H4
Drivstua [N] 180 H4
Drizë [AL] 128 C4
Drlače [SRB] 142 F4
Drnholec [CZ] 62 F2
Drniš [HR] 142 A5
Drnovo [SLO] 74 D5
Drøbak [N] 166 B2
Drobeta-Turnu Severin [RO] 204 C6
Drobin [PL] 36 H1
Drochtersen [D] 18 E3
Drogheda / Droichead Átha [IRL] 2 F5
Drohiczyn [PL] 38 E2
Drohobych [UA] 52 G5
Droichead Átha / Drogheda [IRL] 2 F5
Droichead Nua / Newbridge [IRL] 2 E6
Droitwich [GB] 12 G1
Drołtowice [PL] 36 D5
Dromahair [IRL] 2 D3
Dromcolliher [IRL] 4 C4
Dromore [NIR] 2 E3
Dromore West [IRL] 2 D3
Dronero [I] 108 F2
Dronninglund [DK] 160 E3
Dronten [NL] 16 F4
Dropla [BG] 148 G2
Drosáto [GR] 128 H3
Drosbacken [S] 182 E6
Drosendorf Stadt [A] 62 E2
Drosiá [GR] 134 B5
Drosopigí [GR] 128 E4
Drosopigí [GR] 132 D3
Drosselbjerg [DK] 156 E3
Drottninghaug [N] 180 D4
Droúseia [CY] 154 F6
Drozdowo [PL] 22 B2
Drugan [BG] 146 F5
Drumconrath [IRL] 2 F5
Drumevo [BG] 148 E3
Drumkeeran [IRL] 2 D3
Drumlish [IRL] 2 E4
Drummore [GB] 8 C5
Drumnadrochit [GB] 6 D5
Drumshanbo [IRL] 2 D4
Drumsna [IRL] 2 D4
Drusenheim [F] 44 H5
Druskininkai [LT] 24 F3
Drusti [LV] 198 F4
Druten [NL] 16 E5
Družetić [SRB] 146 A1
Druzhba [BG] 148 G3
Druzhba [RUS] 24 B2
Druzhnaja Gorka [RUS] 198 H1
Drvar [BIH] 142 A3
Drvenik [HR] 144 B3
Dryanovo [BG] 148 C4
Drygały [PL] 24 D4
Drymós [GR] 128 H4
Dryópi [GR] 136 F2
Dryopída [GR] 138 C2
Dryós [GR] 138 E3
Drzewce [PL] 36 F3
Drzewiany [PL] 22 B3
Drzewica [PL] 38 B5
D. Stupnica [HR] 142 A2
Duagh [IRL] 4 C3
Duas Igrejas [P] 80 G4
Dub [SRB] 146 A2
Dubá [CZ] 48 G2
Dubac [HR] 144 C4
Dubăsari [MD] 204 E3
Dubechne [UA] 38 H4
Duben [D] 34 E4
Dubí [CZ] 48 E2
Dubica [HR] 142 B2
Dubienka [PL] 38 G6
Dubin [PL] 36 D5
Dubinino [RUS] 178 F2
Dubliany [UA] 52 G5
Dublin / Baile Átha Cliath [IRL] 2 F6
Dubna [RUS] 202 E2
Dub nad Moravou [CZ] 50 D5
Dubňany [CZ] 62 G2
Dubnica nad Váhom [SK] 64 A2
Dŭbnitsa [BG] 130 C1
Dubno [UA] 202 B8
Dubovsko [BIH] 112 H3
Dubrava [BIH] 142 C3
Dubrava [HR] 74 F5
Dubrava [HR] 74 G4
Dubrava [RUS] 24 D2
Dubrave [BIH] 142 E2
Dubravica [BIH] 142 C4
Dubravka [HR] 144 D4
Dubrovka [RUS] 198 H5
Dubrovnik [HR] 144 C4
Dubrovno [RUS] 198 H3
Dubrovytsia [UA] 202 B7
Dubrowna [BY] 202 C4
Ducey [F] 26 D4
Duchcov [CZ] 48 E2
Ducherow [D] 20 E4
Duclair [F] 26 H3
Dudar [H] 76 A1
Dudelange [L] 44 E3
Düdenköy [TR] 154 H2
Duderstadt [D] 32 G4
Dudeștii Vechi [RO] 76 F5
Dudince [SK] 64 C4
Düdingen [CH] 58 D6
Dudley [GB] 10 D6
Due Carrare [I] 110 G1
Dueñas [E] 88 F1
Duesund [N] 170 B2
Dueville [I] 72 D6
Dufftown [GB] 6 F5
Duga Poljana [SRB] 146 B4
Duga Resa [HR] 112 G1
Duge Njive [HR] 144 B2
Dugi Rat [HR] 144 A2
Duğla [TR] 152 C2
Dugopolje [HR] 144 A2
Dugo Selo [HR] 74 F6
Duhnen [D] 18 D3
Duingen [D] 32 F3
Duingt [F] 70 B3
Duino [I] 72 H5
Duisburg [D] 30 G3
Duka [H] 74 G2
Dukat [AL] 128 A6
Dukat [SRB] 146 E5
Dukhovshchina [RUS] 202 D4
Dukla [PL] 52 D5
Dukovany [CZ] 62 F2
Dūkštas [LT] 200 H4
Dukštos [LT] 200 G5
Dŭlbok Izvor [BG] 148 C6
Duleek [IRL] 2 F5
Dŭlgopol [BG] 148 F3
Dülken [D] 30 F3
Dülmen [D] 16 H6
Dulnain Bridge [GB] 6 E5
Dulovka [RUS] 198 G4
Dulovo [BG] 148 E1
Dulpetorpet [N] 172 D4
Dumača [SRB] 142 F3
Dumakömlöd [H] 76 C3
Dumanlı [TR] 152 G4
Dumbarton [GB] 8 D3
Dumbrăveni [RO] 148 F1
Dumfries [GB] 8 D5
Dumha Thuama / Doohooma [IRL] 2 B3
Dumlupınar [TR] 152 H2
Dümpelfeld [D] 30 G6
Dun [F] 44 D3
Duna [N] 190 C4
Dunaengus [IRL] 2 B5
Dunaff [IRL] 2 F1
Dunaföldvár [H] 76 C3
Dunaharaszti [H] 76 C1
Dunaïvtsi [UA] 204 D2
Dunajská Streda [SK] 62 H5
Dunakeszi [H] 64 C6
Dunakiliti [H] 62 G5
Dunany [IRL] 2 F5
Dunapataj [H] 76 C3
Dunas de São Jacinto [P] 80 B5
Dunaszeg [H] 62 H5
Dunaszekcső [H] 76 C5
Dunaszentbenedek [H] 76 C3
Dunasziget [H] 62 G5
Dunatetétlen [H] 76 C3
Dunaújváros [H] 76 C2
Dunavecse [H] 76 C2
Dunavtsi [BG] 146 E2
Dunbar [GB] 8 F3
Dunbeath [GB] 6 F3
Dunblane [GB] 8 E2
Dunboy Castle [IRL] 4 A5
Dunboyne [IRL] 2 F6
Dunbrody Abbey [IRL] 4 E5
Duncormick [IRL] 4 F5
Dundaga [LV] 198 C4
Dundalk / Dún Dealgan [IRL] 2 F4
Dún Dealgan / Dundalk [IRL] 2 F4
Dundee [GB] 8 F2
Dunderland [N] 190 E2
Dunfanaghy [IRL] 2 E1
Dunfermline [GB] 8 E3
Dungannon [NIR] 2 F3
Dungarvan [IRL] 4 E5
Dungiven [NIR] 2 F2
Dunglow / An Clochán Liath [IRL] 2 E2
Dungourney [IRL] 4 D5
Dunje [MK] 128 F3
Dunjica [MK] 128 G2
Dunker [S] 168 C3
Dunkerque [F] 14 H6
Dunkerque Ouest [F] 14 H6
Dunkineely [IRL] 2 D2
Duńkowice [PL] 52 F3
Dún Laoghaire [IRL] 2 F6
Dunlavin [IRL] 4 F3
Dunleer [IRL] 2 F5
Dun-le-Palestel [F] 54 H5
Dunloe, Gap of- [IRL] 4 B4
Dunloy [NIR] 2 G2
Dunmanway [IRL] 4 C5
Dunmore [IRL] 2 C4
Dunmore Caves [IRL] 4 E4
Dunmore East [IRL] 4 E5
Dunmurry [NIR] 2 G3
Dún na nGall / Donegal [IRL] 2 E2
Dunoon [GB] 8 C3
Duns [GB] 8 F4
Dunshaughlin [IRL] 2 F5
Dunstable [GB] 14 E3
Dun-sur-Auron [F] 56 C4
Dunure [GB] 8 C4
Dunvegan [GB] 6 B4
Duoddar Sion [N] 194 B2
Dupnitsa [BG] 146 F6
Duquesa, Castillo de la- [E] 100 H5
Durabeyler [TR] 152 E1
Durach [BG] 148 E2
Duran [BG] 148 E2
Durance [F] 66 D5
Durango [E] 84 A3
Durankulak [BG] 148 G1
Duras [F] 66 E4
Durasıllı [TR] 152 E3
Durban-Corbières [F] 106 C5
Durbe [LV] 198 B6
Durbuy [B] 30 E5
Dúrcal [E] 102 E4
Đurđenovac [HR] 142 D1
Đurđevac [HR] 74 G5
Đurđevića Tara [MNE] 144 E2
Đurđevik [BIH] 142 E3
Durdevi Stupovi [SRB] 146 B4
Düren [D] 30 G4
Durham [GB] 8 F6
Durhasan [TR] 152 F3
Durlas / Thurles [IRL] 4 E3
Durness [GB] 6 D2
Dürnkrut [A] 62 G4
Dürnstein [A] 62 D4
Durnstein [A] 74 B2
Durón [E] 90 A5
Durrës [AL] 128 A3
Durrow [IRL] 4 E3
Durrow Abbey [IRL] 2 E5
Durrus [IRL] 4 B5
Dursunbey [TR] 152 E1
Durtal [F] 42 A6
Duruelo de la Sierra [E] 90 A2
Dusetos [LT] 200 G4
Dŭskotna [BG] 148 E3
Dusnok [H] 76 C4
Dusocin [PL] 22 E5
Düsseldorf [D] 30 G3
Duszniki [PL] 36 B2
Duszniki-Zdrój [PL] 50 B3
Dutluca [TR] 150 F6
Dutluca [TR] 152 G5
Dutovlje [SLO] 72 H5
Duved [S] 182 E1
Düvertepe [TR] 152 E2
Düzağac [TR] 152 H2
Duzlarla [TR] 152 C2
Dvärsätt [S] 182 G2
Dve Mogili [BG] 148 C2
Dvor [HR] 142 A2
Dvor [SLO] 74 C6
Dvorce [CZ] 50 D4
Dvory nad Žitavou [SK] 64 B5
Dvůr Králové nad Labem [CZ] 50 A3
Dwingeloo [NL] 16 G3
Dyat'kovo [RUS] 202 E5
Dyatlitsy [RUS] 178 G5
Dybäck [S] 158 C3
Dyblin [PL] 36 G2
Dyce [GB] 6 G6
Dyck [D] 30 G4
Dygowo [PL] 20 H3
Dylewo [PL] 24 C5
Dymchurch [GB] 14 F5
Dymniki [BY] 38 G2
Dynów [PL] 52 E4
Dyranut [N] 170 E4
Dyrnes [N] 180 F1
Dyrráchio [GR] 136 D3
Dysbodarna [S] 172 F3
Dýstos [GR] 134 C5
Dyulino [BG] 148 F3
Dyuni [BG] 148 F4
Dyvik [S] 168 E3
Džepišta [MK] 128 C2
Dzhankoï [UA] 204 H3
Dzhebel [BG] 130 F1
Dzhurovo [BG] 146 G4
Dzhuryn [UA] 204 E2
Dziadkowice [PL] 38 E2
Dziadowa Kłoda [PL] 36 D6
Działdowo [PL] 22 G5
Działoszyce [PL] 52 B3
Działoszyn [PL] 36 F6
Dziemiany [PL] 22 C3
Dzierzgoń [PL] 22 F4
Dzierzki [PL] 22 H4
Dzierżoniów [PL] 50 C2
Dzietrzychowo [PL] 24 B2
Džigolj [SRB] 146 D3
Dzivin [BY] 38 H3
Dziwnów [PL] 20 F3
Dziwnówek [PL] 20 F3
Džul'unica [BG] 148 C3
Džumajlija [MK] 128 F1
Dźwierzuty [PL] 22 H4
Dźwirzyno [PL] 20 G3
Dzyarechyn [BY] 24 H5
Dzyarzhynsk [BY] 202 B5

E

Easingwold [GB] 10 F3
Easky [IRL] 2 D3
Eastbourne [GB] 14 E6
East Grinstead [GB] 14 E5
East Kilbride [GB] 8 D3
Eastleigh [GB] 12 H5
Eaux-Bonnes [F] 84 D4
Eaux-Chaudes [F] 84 D4
Eauze [F] 66 D6
Ebberup [DK] 156 D3
Ebbo / Epoo [FIN] 178 B4
Ebbw Vale [GB] 12 F2
Ebecik [TR] 152 F5
Ebeleben [D] 32 H5
Ebelsbach [D] 46 F3
Ebeltoft [DK] 156 E1
Ebeltoft Færge [DK] 156 E1
Eben [A] 60 E6
Ebenfurth [A] 62 F5
Eben im Pongau [A] 72 H1
Ebensee [A] 62 A5
Eberbach [D] 46 B3
Eberbach [D] 46 D5
Eberdingen [D] 46 C6
Ebergötzen [D] 32 G4
Ebermannstadt [D] 46 G4
Ebern [D] 46 G3
Eberndorf [A] 74 C3
Ebersbach [D] 48 G1
Ebersberg [D] 60 E4
Eberschwang [A] 60 H4
Ebersdorf [D] 18 E4
Ebersdorf [D] 60 H3
Eberstein [A] 74 C3
Eberstein [D] 58 F1
Eberswalde [D] 34 F1
Ebes [H] 64 G6
Ebeylı [TR] 150 G4
Ebingen [D] 58 G3
Éboli [I] 120 F4
Ebrach [D] 46 F4
Ebreichsdorf [A] 62 F5
Ebreuil [F] 56 C6
Ebstorf [D] 18 G6
Eceabat [TR] 130 H5
Echallens [CH] 70 C1
Echallon [F] 68 H2
Echarri / Etxarri [E] 84 A3
Échevennoz [I] 70 D3
Echínos [GR] 130 E2
Échourgnac [F] 66 E3
Echternach [L] 44 F2
Écija [E] 102 B2
Eck [A] 62 A6
Ečka [SRB] 142 G1
Eckartsau [A] 62 F5
Eckartsberga [D] 34 B6
Eckernförde [D] 18 F1
Eckerö [FIN] 176 A5
Eckersholm [S] 162 D2
Eckwarden [D] 18 D4
Ecole Valentine [F] 58 B4
Écommoy [F] 42 B5
Écouis [F] 28 C6
Ecoust-St-Mein [F] 28 F4
Ecsegfalva [H] 76 F2
Echte [D] 32 G4
Écueillé [F] 54 G3
Écury [F] 44 B4
Ed [S] 166 C4
Ed [S] 184 E2
Eda [S] 166 D1
Eda glasbruk [S] 166 D1
Edam [NL] 16 E4
Edane [S] 166 E2
Eddelak [D] 18 E3
Ede [NL] 16 E5
Ede [S] 182 H1
Edebäck [S] 172 F6
Edebo [S] 168 E1
Edeby [S] 168 E1
Edefors [S] 184 C1
Edefors [S] 196 A2
Edelény [H] 64 F4
Edenbridge [GB] 14 E5
Edenderry [IRL] 2 E6
Edenkoben [D] 46 B5
Edersee [D] 32 E5
Édessa [GR] 128 F4
Edevik [S] 190 D5
Edewecht [D] 18 C5
Edgeworthstown [IRL] 2 E5
Edhem [S] 166 F6
Edinburgh [GB] 8 E3
Edincik [TR] 150 D4
Edineț [MD] 204 D3
Edirne [TR] 150 A2
Edland [N] 164 D1
Ēdole [LV] 198 B5
Édolo [I] 72 B4
Édon [F] 66 E2
Edremit [TR] 152 C1
Edsbro [S] 168 E1
Edsbruk [S] 162 G1
Edsbyn [S] 174 C2
Edsele [S] 184 D1
Edsleskog [S] 166 D4
Edsta [S] 184 E6
Edsvalla [S] 166 E2
Eeklo [B] 28 G1
Eelde [NL] 16 G2
Een [NL] 16 G2
Efendiköprüsü [TR] 152 G2
Eferding [A] 62 B4
Effeløt [N] 164 G2
Effelsberg, Radiotelskop [D] 30 G5
Efkarpía [GR] 128 H3
Eforie [RO] 204 F5
Efpálio [GR] 132 F5
Efýra [GR] 136 C2
Éfyras [GR] 132 D3
Egebæk [DK] 156 B3
Egeln [D] 34 B3
Egense [DK] 160 E4
Eger [H] 64 E5
Egerlövő [H] 64 F5
Egernsund [DK] 156 C4
Egersund [N] 164 B4
Egervár [H] 74 G2
Egesheim [D] 58 G3
Egeskov [DK] 156 D4
Egestorf [D] 18 F5
Egg [A] 60 B6
Egg [A] 72 D2
Eggedal [N] 170 G5
Eggenburg [A] 62 E3
Eggenfelden [D] 60 G3
Eggesin [D] 20 E4
Egglham [D] 60 G3
Eggum [N] 192 C4
Eghezée [B] 30 D5
Egiertowo [PL] 22 D3
Egilsstaðir [IS] 192 C3
Egletons [F] 68 A3
Eglinton [NIR] 2 F2
Egmond aan Zee [NL] 16 D3
Egna / Neumarkt [I] 72 D4
Egremont [GB] 8 D6
Egsdorf [D] 34 E3
Egtved [DK] 156 C2
Eguzon [F] 54 G5
Egyek [H] 64 F6
Ehingen [D] 60 B3
Ehnen [L] 44 F3
Ehra-Lessien [D] 32 H2
Ehrenburg [A] 60 C6
Ehrenburg [D] 18 D6
Ehrenhausen [A] 74 D3
Ehrwald [A] 60 D6
Eiane [N] 164 B3
Eibar [E] 82 H4
Eibenstock [D] 48 C2
Eibergen [NL] 16 G5
Eibiswald [A] 74 D3
Eich [D] 46 C4
Eichendorf [D] 60 G3
Eichstätt [D] 60 D2
Eid [N] 180 B6
Eida [N] 164 B4
Eidanger [N] 164 G3
Eide [N] 164 B4
Eide [N] 164 C3
Eide [N] 170 B1
Eide [N] 180 E2
Eide [N] 190 D5
Eidem [N] 190 C3
Eidet [N] 180 H1
Eidfjord [N] 170 D4
Eidi [FR] 160 B1
Eidiet [N] 180 C6
Eidsborg [N] 164 E2
Eidsbugarden [N] 170 F1
Eidsbygda [N] 180 E3
Eidsdal [N] 180 E4
Eidsfoss [N] 164 G2
Eidskog [N] 172 D6
Eidslandet [N] 170 B3
Eidsøra [N] 180 F3
Eidstod [N] 164 E2
Eidsund [N] 164 B2
Eidsvåg [N] 180 F3
Eidsvoll [N] 172 C5
Eidsvoll verk [N] 172 C5
Eifa [D] 32 D6
Eigenrieden [D] 32 G5
Eik [N] 164 B2
Eikefjord [N] 180 B6
Eikelandsosen [N] 170 B4
Eiken [N] 164 C4
Eikenes [N] 170 B1
Eiksund [N] 180 C4
Eilenburg [D] 34 D5
Eilsleben [D] 34 A3
Eimisjärvi [FIN] 188 G3
Eina [N] 172 B4
Einastrand [N] 172 B4
Einavoll [N] 172 B4
Einbeck [D] 32 F3
Eindhoven [NL] 30 E2
Einsiedeln [CH] 58 G6
Einzinger Boden [A] 72 F1
Eisenach [D] 32 G6
Eisenbach [D] 46 D1
Eisenbach [D] 58 F3
Eisenberg [D] 34 B6
Eisenerz [A] 62 C6
Eisenhüttenstadt [D] 34 G3
Eisenkappel [A] 74 C4
Eisenstadt [A] 62 F5
Eisensteinhöhle [A] 62 E5
Eisfeld [D] 46 G2
Eisgarn [A] 62 D2
Eišiškės [LT] 24 H2
Eislingen [D] 60 B2
Eisriesenwelt [A] 60 H6
Eitorf [D] 30 H5
Eivindvik [N] 170 B2
Eivissa / Ibiza [E] 104 C5
Ejby [DK] 156 D3
Ejea de los Caballeros [E] 84 C6
Ejheden [S] 172 H2
Ejstrupholm [DK] 156 C1

Ejulve [E] 90 E6
Ek [S] 166 F5
Ekáli [GR] 134 C6
Ekeby [S] 156 H2
Ekeby [S] 166 G6
Ekeby [S] 168 D3
Ekebyholm [S] 168 E2
Ekedal [S] 174 E6
Ekedalen [S] 166 F6
Ekenäs [S] 166 E4
Ekenäs / Tammisaari [FIN] 176 F6
Ekenässjön [S] 162 E3
Ekerö [S] 168 D3
Ekinhisar [TR] 152 H3
Ekinli [TR] 150 H3
Ekkerøy [N] 194 E2
Ekolsund [S] 168 D2
Ekornavallen [S] 166 F6
Ekorrbäcken [S] 194 B7
Ekorrträsk [S] 190 H5
Ekshärad [S] 172 F5
Eksingedal [N] 170 C3
Eksjö [S] 162 E2
Ekträsk [S] 190 H5
Ekzarh Antimovo [BG] 148 E4
Elaía [GR] 136 F4
Elaiochória [GR] 130 B5
Elaiónas [GR] 132 G5
El Alamo [E] 88 F6
El Alcornocal [E] 96 B5
El Altet [E] 104 D2
Elämäjärvi [FIN] 196 D6
Elanets' [UA] 204 F2
Elantxobe [E] 82 H3
Elassóna [GR] 132 F1
El Astillero [E] 82 F3
Eláteia [GR] 132 H4
Eláti [GR] 128 F6
Eláti [GR] 132 E2
Elatoú [GR] 132 F5
El Ballestero [E] 96 H5
El Barco de Ávila [E] 88 C5
El Barraco [E] 88 E5
Elbasan [AL] 128 B3
El Berrón [E] 78 H3
Elbeuf [F] 26 H4
Elbigenalp [A] 72 B1
Elbingerode [D] 32 H4
Elbląg [PL] 22 F3
El Bodón [E] 86 H2
El Bonillo [E] 96 H5
El Bosque [E] 100 H4
Elburg [NL] 16 F4
Elburgo / Burgelu [E] 102 B4
El Burgo de Ebro [E] 90 E4
El Burgo de Osma [E] 90 A3
El Burgo Ranero [E] 82 B5
El Cabaco [E] 88 B4
el Campello [E] 104 E2
El Canal [E] 104 C6
El Cañavate [E] 98 B3
El Carpio [E] 102 C1
El Carpio de Tajo [E] 96 E1
El Casar de Talamanca [E] 88 G5
El Castillo de las Guardas [E] 94 G5
El Castor [E] 100 H3
El Centenillo [E] 96 E6
El Cerro de Andévalo [E] 94 F4
Elche / Elx [E] 104 D2
Elche de la Sierra [E] 104 B1
Elçili [TR] 150 B2
El Coronil [E] 100 H3
El Cotillo [E] 100 E6
El Cubo de Don Sancho [E] 80 F6
El Cubo de Tierra del Vino [E] 80 H5
El Cuervo [E] 100 G3
El'cy [RUS] 202 D3
Elda [E] 104 D2
Eldalsosen [N] 170 C1
Eldena [D] 20 A5
Eldforsen [S] 172 G5
Eldrehaug [N] 170 E2
Elefsína [GR] 134 B6
Eleftherés [GR] 134 B6
Elefthério [GR] 132 G2
Eleftherochóri [GR] 128 E6
Eleftheroupoli [GR] 130 D3
Eleja [LV] 198 D6
El Ejido [E] 102 F5
Elek [H] 76 G3
Elena [BG] 148 C4
Elenite [BG] 148 F4
Eleousa [GR] 154 D4
El Escorial [E] 88 F5
El Espinar [E] 88 E4
el Fondó dels Frares [E] 104 D2
Elgå [N] 182 D5
El Gargantón [E] 96 E3
El Garrobo [E] 94 G5
Elgg [CH] 58 G5
Elgin [GB] 6 E5
El Grado [E] 90 G3
El Grau [E] 98 F4
el Grau / Grao [E] 98 F6
Elgsnes [N] 192 E3
El Guijo [E] 96 C5
Eliaröd [S] 158 D2
Elimäki [FIN] 178 C3
Eling [S] 166 E6
Elin Pelin [BG] 146 G5
Eliseyna [BG] 146 G4
Elizondo [E] 84 C3
Elizondo / Baztan [E] 82 H4
Ełk [PL] 24 D4
Elkeland [N] 164 C5
Elkhovo [BG] 148 E5
Ellan [S] 174 G5
Elle [N] 164 B3
Ellenberg [D] 46 E6
Ellesmere [GB] 10 D5
Elling [DK] 160 E2
Ellinge [S] 158 C2
Ellingen [D] 46 G6
Ellmau [A] 60 F6
Ellon [GB] 6 G6
Ellös [S] 166 C6
Ellrich [D] 32 H4
Ellwangen [D] 46 E6
Elm [CH] 58 G6
Elmacık [TR] 150 B1
El Madroño [E] 94 F5
Elmalı [TR] 154 H2
El Masnou [E] 92 E4
El Médano [E] 100 B5
Elmen [A] 60 C6
El Minguillo [E] 96 G4
El Molar [E] 88 G5
El Molinillo [E] 96 E2
El Moral [E] 102 H2
Elmpt [D] 30 F3
Elmshorn [D] 18 F3
Elmstein [D] 46 B5
Elne [F] 92 G1
Elnesvågen [N] 180 E2
Elo / Monreal [E] 84 B4
Eloro [I] 126 G5
Elorz / Noain [E] 84 B4
Élos [GR] 140 B5
Előszállás [H] 76 C3
Eloúnta [GR] 140 F4
el Palmar [E] 98 F5
El Palmar de Troya [E] 100 G3
El Palmeral [E] 104 D2
El Palo [E] 102 C4
El Pardo [E] 88 F5
El Paular [E] 88 F4
El Pedernoso [E] 96 H3
El Pedroso [E] 94 H5
El Perelló [E] 92 B5
El Perelló [E] 98 F5
Elphin [IRL] 2 D4
El Pinar [E] 100 A5
El Piñero [E] 80 H5
el Pinós / Pinoso [E] 104 D2
El Pito [E] 78 G3
el Pla de Santa Maria [E] 92 C4
El Pobo de Dueñas [E] 90 C6
el Pont de Suert [E] 84 F6
el Port / Sóller [E] 104 E4
el Port de la Selva [E] 92 G2
El Portil [E] 94 E6
el Prat de Llobregat [E] 92 E5
El Priorato [E] 102 A1
El Puente del Arzobispo [E] 96 D1
El Puerto de Santa Maria [E] 100 F4
El Ramonete [E] 104 B4
El Real de la Jara [E] 94 G4
El Real de San Vicente [E] 88 D6
El Recuenco [E] 90 B6
El Retiro [E] 102 B5
El Robledo [E] 96 E3
El Rocío [E] 94 F6
El Rompido [E] 94 E6
El Ronquillo [E] 94 G6
El Royo [E] 90 B2
El Rubio [E] 102 B2
El Sabinar [E] 102 H2
El Saler [E] 98 E5
El Salobral [E] 98 B5
El Saucejo [E] 102 B3
Elsdorf [D] 30 G4
El Serrat [AND] 84 H6
Elsfleth [D] 18 D5
Elšica [BG] 148 A5
Elst [NL] 16 E5
Elsten [D] 18 C6
Elster [D] 34 D4
Elsterberg [D] 48 C2
Elsterwerda [D] 34 E5
El Tejar [E] 102 C3
Elten [D] 16 F6
El Tiemblo [E] 88 E5
Eltmann [D] 46 F3
El Toboso [E] 96 G3
El Tormillo [E] 90 G3
El Torno [E] 88 B5
El Torno [E] 100 G4
Eltravåg [N] 164 A1
El Tumbalejo [E] 94 F5
Eltville [D] 46 B3
Eltz [D] 44 H1
Elva [EST] 198 F3
Elvas [P] 86 F6
Elvbrua [N] 182 D6
Elvdal [N] 172 D1
Elven, Tour d'- [F] 40 D4
El Vendrell [E] 92 D5
Elverum [N] 172 C3
Elverum [N] 192 F3
Elvestad [N] 166 B2
El Villar de Arnedo [E] 84 A5
Elvira [E] 102 E3
Elviria [E] 102 B5
El Viso [E] 96 C5
El Viso del Alcor [E] 94 H6
Elvran [N] 182 C1
Elx / Elche [E] 104 D2
Ely [GB] 14 F2
Élyros [GR] 140 B5
Elzach [D] 58 F2
Elze [D] 32 F3
Emberménil [F] 44 F5
Embrun [F] 108 D2
Embute [LV] 198 C6
Emden [D] 16 H2
Emecik [TR] 154 C2
Emese [TR] 150 C5
Emet [TR] 152 F1
Emiralem [TR] 152 C3
Emlichheim [D] 16 G4
Emmaboda [S] 162 F5
Emmaljunga [S] 162 C6
Emmaste [EST] 198 C2
Emmeloord [NL] 16 F3
Emmen [NL] 16 G3
Emmendingen [D] 58 E3
Emmerich [D] 16 F6
Emmingen-Liptingen [D] 58 G3
Emőd [H] 64 F5
Emona [BG] 148 G4
Émpa [CY] 154 F6
Empesós [GR] 132 E3
Empfingen [D] 58 G2
Empoli [I] 110 E5
Émponas [GR] 154 D4
Emporeiós [GR] 134 G5
Emporeiós [GR] 154 A2
Emporeiós [GR] 154 B3
Empúriabrava [E] 92 G2
Empúries [E] 92 G3
Emsdetten [D] 16 H5
Emsfors [S] 162 G4
Emskirchen [D] 46 F5
Emstek [D] 18 C6
Emtinghausen [D] 18 D6
Emyvale [IRL] 2 F4
Enafors [S] 182 E2
Enäjärvi [FIN] 178 C3
Enånger [S] 174 E1
Enare / Inari [FIN] 194 D4
Enarsvedjan [S] 182 G1
Encamp [AND] 84 H6
Encarnación, Santuario de la- [E] 98 B6
Encinas de Abajo [E] 88 C3
Encinasola [E] 94 F3
Encinedo [E] 78 F6
Enciso [E] 90 C2
Encs [H] 64 F4
Endelave By [DK] 156 D2
Enden [N] 180 H6
Endingen [D] 58 E2
Endrefalva [H] 64 D4
Endrinal [E] 88 C4
Endrőd [H] 76 F2
Enebakk [N] 166 C1
Enese [H] 62 H6
Enevo [BG] 148 E2
Enez [TR] 130 H3
Enfesta / Pontecesures [E] 78 B3
Enfield [IRL] 2 E6
Engelberg [CH] 70 F1
Engelhartszell [A] 62 A3
Engelia [N] 170 H4
Engeln [D] 18 D6
Engelskirchen [D] 30 H4
Engelsviken [N] 166 B3
Engen [D] 58 G3
Enger [D] 32 D2
Enger [N] 170 H4
Engerdal [N] 182 D6
Engerneset [N] 172 D1
Engesland [N] 164 E4
Engesvang [DK] 160 C6
Enghien [B] 28 H3
Engi [CH] 58 G6
Engjane [N] 180 F2
England [D] 18 E1
Englefontaine [F] 28 G4
Engstingen [D] 58 H2
Énguera [E] 98 E6
Enguídanos [E] 98 C3
Enguri [LV] 198 D5
Enkhuizen [NL] 16 E3
Enklinge [FIN] 176 B5
Enköping [S] 168 C2
Enmo [N] 182 B3
Enna [I] 126 E3
Ennezat [F] 68 D2
Ennis / Inis [IRL] 2 C6
Enniscorthy [IRL] 4 F4
Enniscrone [IRL] 2 C3
Enniskean [IRL] 4 C5
Enniskillen [NIR] 2 E3
Ennistymon [IRL] 2 B5
Enns [A] 62 C4
Eno [FIN] 188 G2
Enokunta [FIN] 186 E6
Enonkoski [FIN] 188 E4
Enonkylä [FIN] 196 E5
Enonteki / Enontekiö [FIN] 194 B5
Enontekiö / Enonteki [FIN] 194 B5
Enschede [NL] 16 G5
Ensisheim [F] 58 D3
Entlebuch [CH] 58 E6
Entradas [P] 94 D3
Entraigues [F] 54 H3
Entranis-sur-Nohain [F] 56 D3
Entraygues-sur-Truyère [F] 68 B5
Entre Ambos-os-Rios [P] 80 C4
Entrevaux [F] 108 E4
Entrèves [I] 70 C3
Entrimo [E] 78 C6
Entroncamento [P] 86 D4
Enviken [S] 174 C4
En Xoroi, Cova d'- [E] 104 H5
Enying [H] 76 B2
Eoux [F] 84 G4
Epannes [F] 54 D4
Epanomi [GR] 128 H5
Epe [D] 16 G5
Epe [NL] 16 F4
Épernay [F] 44 B3
Épernon [F] 42 E4
Ephesos [TR] 152 D5
Epidavros, Arhéa- [GR] 136 F2
Épila [E] 90 D4
Épinal [F] 58 C2
Epiry [F] 56 E3
Episcopia [I] 120 H5
Episkopí [CY] 154 F6
Episkopí [GR] 140 C4
Epitálio [GR] 136 C2
Epléný [H] 76 A2
Epône [F] 42 E3
Epoo / Ebbo [FIN] 178 B4
Eppan / Appiano [I] 72 D3
Eppenstein [A] 74 C2
Eppingen [D] 46 C5
Eptachóri [GR] 128 D6
Eptálofos [GR] 132 G5
Epuisay [F] 42 C5
Eraclea [I] 72 F6
Eraclea [I] 122 D5
Eraclea Mare [I] 72 F6
Eraclea Minoa [I] 126 C4
Eräjärvi [FIN] 176 G1
Eräslahti [FIN] 186 F6
Erateiní [GR] 132 G5
Erátyrá [GR] 128 E5
Erba [I] 70 G4
Erbach [D] 46 D4
Erbach [D] 60 B3
Erbalunga [F] 114 C2
Erbè [I] 110 F1
Erbendorf [D] 48 B4
Ercolano [I] 120 E3
Ercsi [H] 76 C2
Érd [H] 76 C1
Erdal [N] 180 C6
Erdek [TR] 150 D4
Erdevik [SRB] 142 F2
Erding [D] 60 E4
Erdőhorváti [H] 64 G4
Erdut [HR] 142 E1
Eremitage [D] 46 H4
Erenköy (Kókkina) [CY] 154 F5
Eresós [GR] 134 G2
Erétria [GR] 134 C5
Erfde [D] 18 E2
Erfjord [N] 164 B2
Erftstadt [D] 30 G5
Erfurt [D] 32 H6
Ergama [TR] 152 D1
Ergili [TR] 150 D5
Ērgli [LV] 198 E5
Ergoldsbach [D] 60 F3
Erice [I] 126 B2
Erice [TR] 152 G3
Ericeira [P] 86 A4
Ericek [TR] 150 F4
Erikli [TR] 150 B4
Eriksberg [S] 168 B4
Eriksberg [S] 184 C2
Eriksberg [S] 190 F4
Erikslund [S] 184 D4
Eriksmåla [S] 162 E5
Erikstad [S] 166 D6
Eringsboda [S] 162 E6
Erka [N] 180 F5
Erkelenz [D] 30 F4
Erla [E] 84 C6
Erlangen [D] 46 G4
Erlenbach [D] 46 D4
Erlsbach [A] 72 E2
Ermelo [NL] 16 E4
Ermenonville [F] 42 G3
Ermesinde [P] 80 C4
Ermidas-Aldeia [P] 94 C3
Ermióni [GR] 136 F3
Ermitage, Grotte de l'- [F] 56 H4
Ermoúpoli [GR] 138 D2
Ermsleben [D] 34 B4
Erndtebrück [D] 32 D6
Ernée [F] 26 D6
Ernerwald [CH] 70 E2
Ernestinovo [HR] 142 E1
Ernstbrunn [A] 62 F3
Erp [D] 30 G5
Erquy [F] 26 B4
Errazu [E] 84 C3
Errenteria / Rentería [E] 84 B2
Erro [E] 84 C3
Erronkari / Roncal [E] 84 C4
Ersekë [AL] 128 D5
Ersmark [S] 196 A6
Ersnäs [S] 196 B3
Erstein [F] 44 H6
Ertuğrul [TR] 152 D1
Ervasti [FIN] 196 E3
Ervedal [P] 86 D5
Ervedosa [P] 80 D4
Ervenik [HR] 112 H5
Ervidel [P] 94 D3
Ervik [N] 180 B4
Ervy-le-Châtel [F] 44 A6
Erwitte [D] 32 D4
Erxleben [D] 34 B3
Erythrés [GR] 134 B6
Erzsébet [H] 76 B5
Eržvilkas [LT] 200 E5
Esa / Yesa [E] 84 C4
Esatçe [TR] 130 H3
Esatlar [TR] 152 G1
Esbjerg [DK] 156 A2
Esblada [E] 92 C4
Esbo / Espoo [FIN] 176 G5
Escairón [E] 78 D4
Escalada [E] 82 E4
Escalaplano [I] 118 D6
Escalona [E] 84 E5
Escalona [E] 88 E6
Escalonilla [E] 96 E1
Escandón, Puerto de- [E] 98 E2
Escariche [E] 88 G6
Escároz / Ezkaroze [E] 84 C4
Escatrón [E] 90 F5
Eschede [D] 32 G1
Eschenbach [D] 46 H4
Eschenburg-Eibelshausen [D] 32 D6
Eschenlohe [D] 60 D6
Escherndorf [D] 46 F4
Eschershausen [D] 32 F3
Esch-sur-Alzette [L] 44 E3
Esch-sur-Sûre [L] 44 E2
Eschwege [D] 32 G5
Eschweiler [D] 30 F4
Escipions, Torre dels- [E] 92 C5
Escombreras [E] 104 C4
Escornalbou [E] 90 H6
Escos [F] 84 D2
Es Cubells [E] 104 C5
Escucha [E] 90 E6
Escúllar [E] 102 F4
Eşen [TR] 154 F3
Esence [TR] 150 E4
Esenköy [TR] 150 H4
Esens [D] 18 C3
Esentepe (Ágios Amvrósios) [CY] 154 G5
Esenyurt [TR] 150 E3
es Figueral [E] 104 C5
Esgos [E] 78 D5
Esguevillas de Esgueva [E] 88 F1
Eskelhem [S] 168 F4
Eskiçine [TR] 152 E6
Eskifjörður [IS] 192 D3
Eski Gediz [TR] 152 G2
Eskihisar [TR] 152 E6
Eskilstuna [S] 168 B3
Eskin [TR] 152 F3
Eskişehir [TR] 150 H5
Eskiyüregil [TR] 150 G5
Eskola [FIN] 196 C5
Eslared [S] 162 C5
Eslarn [D] 48 C5
Eslohe [D] 32 D5
Eslöv [S] 158 C2
Esmared [S] 162 D6
Eşme [TR] 152 F4
Es Mercadal [E] 104 H4
Esmoritz [P] 80 B4
Esnandes [F] 54 C4
Esnouvenaux [F] 56 H1
Espa [N] 172 C4
Espadilla [E] 98 F3
Espalion [F] 68 B5
Esparreguera [E] 92 D4
Espås [N] 182 B1
Espe [S] 170 C4
Espedal [N] 170 G1
Espejo [E] 102 C2
Espeland [N] 164 B4
Espeland [N] 170 B4
Espelandsfoss [N] 170 C5
Espelette [F] 84 C2
Espeli [N] 164 D4
Espelkamp [D] 32 E2
Espera [E] 100 G3
Esperia [I] 120 C1
Espezel [F] 106 B5
Espiel [E] 96 C5
Espinama [E] 82 D3
Espinheiro, Convento de- [P] 94 D1
Espinho [P] 80 B4
Espinilla [E] 82 E4
Espinosa de los Monteros [E] 82 F4
Espírito Santo [P] 94 D4
Esplantas [F] 68 D5
Esponellà [E] 92 F2
Espoo / Esbo [FIN] 176 G5
Esporles [E] 104 E4
Es Port d'Alcúdia [E] 104 F4
es Port d'Andraitx [E] 104 D5
Esposende [P] 78 A6
Espot [E] 84 G6
Espot Esquí [E] 92 E2
Esprels [F] 58 C4
Esse / Ähtävä [FIN] 196 C6
Essen [D] 18 C6
Essen [D] 30 H3
Essenbach [D] 60 F3
Essertaux [F] 28 D5
Esslingen [D] 58 H1
Essoyes [F] 56 G1
Essuilles [F] 28 D6
Essunga [S] 166 D6
Estada [E] 90 G3
Estagel [F] 106 C6
Estaing [F] 68 B5
Estaires [F] 28 F3
Estang [F] 66 D6
Estanyol [E] 104 E5
Estarreja [P] 80 B5
Estavayer-le-Lac [CH] 58 C6
Este [I] 110 G1
Estela [P] 80 B3
Estella / Lizarra [E] 84 A4
Estellenchs [E] 104 D5
Estepa [E] 102 B3
Estepar [E] 82 E6
Estepona [E] 100 H5
Esteras, Cuestas de- [E] 90 B4
Esternay [F] 42 H4
Esterri d'Àneu [E] 84 G5
Esterwegen [D] 18 C5
Estíbaliz, Santuario de- [E] 82 H5
Estissac [F] 44 A6
Estói [P] 94 C5
Estoril [P] 86 A5
Estrées-St-Denis [F] 28 E6
Estremera [E] 96 H1
Estremoz [P] 86 E6
Esztergom [H] 64 C5
Etables-sur-Mer [F] 26 B4
Etagnac [F] 54 F6
Etain [F] 44 E3
Étalans [F] 58 B5
Etalle [B] 44 E2
Étampes [F] 42 F4
Étang-sur-Arroux [F] 56 F4
Etaples [F] 28 D3
Ete [H] 64 A6
Eteläinen [FIN] 176 G2
Etili [TR] 150 B5
Etne [N] 164 B1
Etoges [F] 44 A4
Éton [F] 44 D3
Etréaupont [F] 28 G5
Etrepagny [F] 28 C6
Etretat [F] 26 G2
Etropole [BG] 146 G4
Etseri / Ähtäri [FIN] 186 E4
Ettelbruck [L] 44 F2
Ettenheim [D] 58 E2
Ettlingen [D] 46 B6
Etxarri / Echarri [E] 84 A3
Eu [F] 28 C4
Eudorf [D] 46 D1
Euerhausen [D] 46 E4
Eugénie-les-Bains [F] 66 C6
Eulate [E] 82 H5
Eumeneia [TR] 152 H3
Eunate [E] 84 B4
Eupen [B] 30 F5
Eura [FIN] 176 D2
Euraåminne / Eurajoki [FIN] 176 C2
Eurajoki / Euraåminne [FIN] 176 C2
Euratsfeld [A] 62 C5
Eurialo, Castello- [I] 126 G5
Euromos [TR] 152 D6
Europa-Brücke [A] 72 D1
Europoort [NL] 16 C5
Euskirchen [D] 30 G5
Eussenhausen [D] 46 F2
Eutin [D] 18 G3
Eutzsch [D] 34 D4
Eväjärvi [FIN] 186 F6
Evangelísmos [GR] 132 G1
Evanger [N] 170 C3
Evaux-les-Bains [F] 56 B6
Evciler [TR] 152 B1
Evciler [TR] 152 H4
Evciler [TR] 154 F4
Évdilos [GR] 138 G1
Evendorf [D] 18 F5
Evenstad [N] 172 C2
Everöd [S] 158 D2
Everswinkel [D] 32 C3
Evertsberg [S] 172 F3
Evesham [GB] 12 H2
Evian [F] 70 C2
Evijärvi [FIN] 186 D1
Evinochóri [GR] 132 E5
Evisa [F] 114 A4
Evitskog [FIN] 176 G5
Evje [N] 164 D4
Evolène [CH] 70 D3
Évora [P] 94 D1
Évora Monte [P] 86 D6
Evran [F] 26 C5
Evrensekiz [TR] 150 C2
Evreux [F] 42 D2
Evron [F] 26 E6
Evry [F] 42 F4
Évzonoi [GR] 128 G3
Exaplátanos [GR] 128 F3
Éxarchos [GR] 132 H5
Excideuil [F] 66 G2
Exeter [GB] 12 E4
Exmes [F] 26 G5
Exmouth [GB] 12 E5
Exochí [GR] 128 G5
Exochí [GR] 130 C2
Exómvourgo [GR] 138 E2
Externsteine [D] 32 E3
Extertal [D] 32 E3
Extremo [P] 78 B5
Eydehavn [N] 164 F5
Eyemouth [GB] 8 F4
Eyguières [F] 106 H4
Eygurande [F] 68 B2
Eylie [F] 84 G5
Eymet [F] 66 E4
Eymoutiers [F] 66 H2
Eyrarbakki [IS] 192 A3
Ézaro [E] 78 B2
Ezcaray [E] 82 F6
Ezere [LV] 198 C6
Ezermuiža [LV] 198 C4
Ezernieki [LV] 198 G6
Ezernijeki [LV] 198 D6
Ezine [TR] 130 H6
Ezkaroze / Escároz [E] 84 C4

F

Faaborg [DK] 156 D4
Faak [A] 74 A3
Fabara, Mausoleo de- [E] 90 G5
Fabbrico [I] 110 E2
Fåberg [N] 172 B2
Fabero [E] 78 F4
Fábiánsebestyén [H] 76 F3
Fabriano [I] 116 B1
Facheca [E] 104 E1
Fačkov [SK] 64 B2
Facture [F] 66 C3
Fadd [H] 76 C4
Faenza [I] 110 G4
Faeto [I] 120 F2
Fafe [P] 80 C3
Făgăraş [RO] 204 D4
Fågelfors [S] 162 F4
Fågelsjö [S] 182 G6
Fågelsundet [S] 174 F4
Fågelvik [S] 162 G1
Fageole, Col de la- [F] 68 C4
Fagerås [S] 166 E2
Fagerhaugen [N] 180 H3
Fagerheim Fjellstue [N] 170 E4
Fagerhult [S] 162 D1
Fagerhult [S] 162 F4
Fagerhult [S] 166 C5
Fagernes [N] 170 G3
Fagernes [N] 192 F2
Fagersanna [S] 166 F5
Fagersta [S] 168 A1
Fagerstrand [N] 166 B1
Fagervika [N] 190 D1
Fäggeby [S] 174 D5
Fåglavik [S] 162 B1
Fagnano Castello [I] 124 D4
Fagurhólsmýri [IS] 192 D3
Faial [P] 100 A3
Fai della Paganella [I] 72 C4
Faido [CH] 70 F2
Fains le Sources [F] 44 D4
Faistós [GR] 140 E5
Fajã do Ouvidor [P] 100 C3
Fajã dos Cubres [P] 100 C3
Faja Grande [P] 100 B3
Fakenham [GB] 14 G1
Fåker [S] 182 G3
Fakija [BG] 148 E5
Fakse [DK] 156 G4
Fakse Ladeplads [DK] 156 G4
Falaise [F] 26 F4
Falásarna [GR] 140 B4
Falatádos [GR] 138 E2
Falcade [I] 72 E4
Falconara, Castello di- [I] 126 E4
Falconara Marittima [I] 112 C6
Falcone [I] 124 A7
Falcsut [H] 76 B1
Faldsled [DK] 156 D4
Falerii Novi [I] 114 H4
Falerna [I] 124 D5
Falerna Marina [I] 124 D5
Falerum [S] 162 G1
Falileevo [RUS] 178 F6
Faliráki [GR] 154 D3
Falkenberg [D] 34 E5
Falkenberg [D] 60 G3
Falkenberg [S] 160 H4
Falkenstein [A] 62 F3
Falkenstein [A] 62 F3
Falkenstein [D] 34 A4
Falkenstein [D] 44 F1
Falkenstein [D] 48 C6
Falkenstein [D] 48 C2
Falkenstein, Château de- [F] 44 H5
Falkirk [GB] 8 E3
Falköping [S] 166 E6
Falków [PL] 36 H6
Falla [S] 168 A5
Fällen [S] 162 D5
Fallersleben [D] 32 H2
Fallet [N] 172 C5
Fallet [N] 180 H5
Fällfors [S] 196 A4
Fallingbostel [D] 18 F6
Falmouth [GB] 12 C5
Falset [E] 90 H6
Falsterbo [S] 156 H3
Fălticeni [RO] 204 D3
Falträsk [S] 190 G4
Faludden [S] 168 G6
Falun [S] 174 C4
Faluszíget [H] 76 G2
Famjin [FR] 160 A3
Fana [N] 170 B4
Fanano [I] 110 E4
Fanári [GR] 130 F3
Fanári [GR] 132 F2
Fanbyn [S] 184 D4
Fáncs [H] 76 B3
Fanefjord [DK] 156 G5
Fångåmon [S] 182 F2
Fanjeaux [F] 106 B4
Fannrem [N] 180 H1
Fano [I] 112 C5
Fanós [GR] 128 G3
Fântânele [RO] 148 B2
Fanthyttan [S] 166 H2
Farad [H] 62 G6
Fara Novarese [I] 70 F4
Fårbo [S] 162 G3
Farcheville, Château de- [F] 42 F5
Farébersviller [F] 44 G4
Fareham [GB] 12 H5
Fårevejle [DK] 156 F2
Farfa, Abbazia di- [I] 116 A4
Färgaryd [S] 162 B4
Färgelanda [S] 166 C5
Färila [S] 184 C6
Faringdon [GB] 12 H3
Faringe [S] 168 E1
Färingtofta [S] 158 C1
Farini [I] 110 C2
Färjestaden [S] 162 G5
Farkadóna [GR] 132 F2
Farkasgyepü [H] 74 H2
Farkaždin [SRB] 142 G1
Farlete [E] 90 F4
Fărliug [RO] 76 H6
Färlöv [S] 158 D1
Färna [S] 168 B2
Färnäs [S] 172 G3
Farnese [I] 114 G3
Farnham [GB] 14 D4
Faro [P] 94 C6
Fårö [S] 168 H3
Fårösund [S] 168 H3
Farranfore [IRL] 4 B4
Farre [DK] 160 D6
Fársala [GR] 132 G3
Farsø [DK] 160 D4
Farstad [N] 180 E2
Farstorp [S] 158 D1
Farsund [N] 164 C5
Farum [DK] 156 G2
Fårvang [DK] 160 D6
Fasanerie, Schloss- [D] 46 E2
Fasano [I] 122 E3
Fåset [N] 182 B4
Fasgar [E] 78 G5
Fasovka [UA] 202 D7
Faster [DK] 156 B1
Fasterholt [DK] 156 C1
Fastov [UA] 202 D7

Fatezh [RUS] 202 F5
Fátima [E] 100 H4
Fátima [P] 86 C3
Fatjas [S] 190 H1
Fatnica [BIH] 144 D3
Fättjaur [S] 190 E3
Faucille, Col de la- [F] 70 B1
Faucogney-et-la-Mer [F] 58 C3
Faulbach [D] 46 D4
Faulensee [CH] 70 E1
Faulquemont [F] 44 F4
Fausa [N] 180 D4
Fauske [N] 192 D6
Fauville [F] 26 H2
Fåvang [N] 170 H1
Favara [E] 98 E5
Favara [I] 126 D4
Faverges [F] 70 B3
Faverney [F] 58 B3
Favignana [I] 126 A2
Favone [F] 114 B5
Favorite [D] 46 B6
Favrholt [DK] 160 C6
Fawley [GB] 12 H5
Fayence [F] 108 D4
Fayet [F] 106 D3
Fayl-Billot [F] 58 A3
Fayón [E] 90 G5
Fay-sur-Lignon [F] 68 E5
Fazendas de Almeirim [P] 86 C4
Feakle [IRL] 2 C6
Fécamp [F] 26 G2
Feda [N] 164 C5
Fedje [N] 170 A2
Fedosino [RUS] 198 G4
Feengrotten [D] 46 H2
Fefor [N] 170 G1
Fegen [S] 162 B4
Feggeklit [DK] 160 C4
Fegyvernek [H] 76 F1
Fehrbellin [D] 34 D1
Fehring [A] 74 E2
Feigumfoss [N] 170 E1
Feios [N] 170 D2
Feiring [N] 172 C4
Feistritz [A] 74 E2
Feitos [P] 78 A6
Feketić [SRB] 76 D6
Felanitx [E] 104 F5
Felben [A] 72 F1
Felber-tauern Tunnel [A] 72 F2
Feld [A] 72 H3
Feldafing [D] 60 D5
Feldbach [A] 74 E2
Feldballe [DK] 160 E6
Feldberg [D] 20 D5
Feldberg [D] 58 F3
Feldkirch [A] 58 H5
Feldkirchen [A] 74 B3
Feldkirchen [D] 60 E5
Feldsted [DK] 156 C4
Felechosa [E] 82 B3
Feletto [I] 70 D5
Felgueiras [P] 80 C3
Felgyö [H] 76 E3
Félix [E] 104 B4
Felixstowe [GB] 14 G3
Felizzano [I] 70 E6
Fellbach [D] 58 H1
Fellern [A] 72 F1
Felletin [F] 68 B1
Fellingsbro [S] 168 A3
Felnac [RO] 76 G4
Felonica [I] 110 F2
Felsengarten [D] 46 G3
Felsőleperd [H] 76 B4
Felsőnyárád [H] 64 F4
Felsőszentiván [H] 76 C4
Felsőtárkány [H] 64 E5
Felsőzsolca [H] 64 F4
Feltre [I] 72 E5
Femsjö [S] 162 B4
Femundsenden [N] 182 D6
Fenagh [IRL] 2 E4
Fenais da Ajuda [P] 100 E3
Fene [E] 78 D2
Fenékpuszta [H] 74 G3
Fener [I] 72 E5
Fenestrelle [I] 70 C5
Fénétrange [F] 44 G5
Feneu [F] 40 H6
Fénis [I] 70 D4
Fenit [IRL] 4 B3
Fenstad [N] 172 C5
Fer a Cheval, Cirque du- [F] 58 A5
Feragen [N] 182 D4
Féraklos [GR] 154 D4
Ferbane [IRL] 2 D5
Ferdinandshof [D] 20 E4
Fére [GR] 132 H2
Fère, Château de- [F] 44 A3
Fère-Champenoise [F] 44 B4
Fère-en-Tardenois [F] 44 A3
Ferentino [I] 116 B6
Ferento [I] 114 H3
Féres [GR] 130 H3
Ferez [E] 104 B1
Feria [E] 94 G3
Feričanci [HR] 142 D1
Ferizli [TR] 150 H2
Ferla [I] 126 G5
Ferlach [A] 74 B3
Ferleiten [A] 72 G1
Fermignano [I] 110 H6
Fermo [I] 116 C2
Fermoselle [E] 80 G5
Fermoy [IRL] 4 D4
Fernancaballero [E] 96 E4
Fernán Núñez [E] 102 C2
Ferns [IRL] 4 F4
Fernstein [A] 60 C6
Ferovac [HR] 142 C1
Ferrandina [I] 122 D4
Ferrara [I] 110 G2
Ferreira [E] 78 E2
Ferreira do Alentejo [P] 94 D3
Ferreira do Zêzere [P] 86 D3
Ferreries [E] 104 G4
Ferreruela de Huerva [E] 90 D5
Ferrette [F] 58 D4
Ferriere [I] 110 C3
Ferrières [F] 42 G6
Ferrières-sur-Sichon [F] 68 D2
Ferring [DK] 160 B5
Ferrol [E] 78 D1
Fertöd [H] 62 G6
Fertőrákos [H] 62 F6
Fertőszentmiklós [H] 62 G6
Festenburg [A] 74 E1
Festøy [N] 180 D4
Festung Königstein [D] 48 F1
Festvåg [N] 192 D5
Fethard [IRL] 4 E4
Fethard [IRL] 4 F5
Fethiye [TR] 154 F2
Fetsund [N] 166 C1
Feu, Roche du- [F] 40 B3
Feucht [D] 46 G5
Feuchtwangen [D] 46 F6
Feurs [F] 68 E2
Fevåg [N] 190 B6
Fevik [N] 164 E5
Fiamignano [I] 116 B4
Fiastra, Abbadia di- [I] 116 C2
Fibiş [RO] 76 G5
Fíchti [GR] 136 E2
Ficulle [I] 114 H3
Fidenza [I] 110 D2
Fidje [N] 164 E4
Fieberbrunn [A] 60 F6
Fiegler [A] 74 B2
Fier [AL] 128 A4
Fier, Gorges du- [F] 70 A3
Fiera di Primiero [I] 72 E4
Fierzë [AL] 146 A6
Fiesch [CH] 70 E2
Fieschi, Basilica dei- [I] 110 B3
Fiésole [I] 110 F5
Fiesso Umbertiano [I] 110 G2
Figáleia [GR] 136 D3
Figari [F] 114 D6
Figeac [F] 66 H5
Figeholm [S] 162 G3
Figgjo [N] 164 B3
Figline Valdarno [I] 110 F6
Figueira da Foz [P] 80 A6
Figueira de Castelo Rodrigo [P] 80 E6
Figueiró dos Vinhos [P] 86 D3
Figueras / Figueres [E] 92 G2
Figueres / Figueras [E] 92 G2
Fiholm [S] 168 C3
Fiksdal [N] 180 D3
Filadélfi [GR] 130 B4
Filadélfia [I] 124 D6
Filaga [I] 126 D3
Fil'akovo [SK] 64 D4
Filatova Gora [RUS] 198 G3
Filevo [BG] 148 C6
Filey [GB] 10 G3
Filia [GR] 134 G2
Filiaşi [RO] 204 C6
Filiátes [GR] 132 C2
Filiatrá [GR] 136 C3
Filipovci [BG] 146 E4
Filipów [PL] 24 D3
Filippiáda [GR] 132 D3
Filippoi [GR] 130 D3
Filipstad [S] 166 F2
Filisur [CH] 70 H2
Filitosa [F] 114 A5
Fillan [N] 190 A6
Fillefjell Pass [N] 170 E2
Fillýra [GR] 130 G2
Filótas [GR] 128 F4
Filóti [GR] 138 F3
Filottrano [I] 116 C1
Filskov [DK] 156 B2
Filyriá [GR] 128 G4
Filzmoos [A] 72 H1
Finale Emilia [I] 110 F2
Finale Lígure [I] 108 H3
Fiñana [E] 102 F4
Finby / Särkisalo [FIN] 176 E5
Finderup [DK] 156 B1
Finestrat [E] 104 E2
Fingerboda [S] 166 H2
Finike [TR] 154 H3
Finiq [AL] 132 B1
Finisterre / Fisterra [E] 78 A2
Finja [S] 158 C1
Finnäs [S] 190 H4
Finnbo [S] 174 C4
Finnböle [S] 174 E5
Finnea [IRL] 2 E5
Finneby [S] 182 H5
Finneid [N] 192 D6
Finneidfjord [N] 190 D2
Finnentrop [D] 32 C5
Finnerödja [S] 166 G4
Finnlia [N] 164 G2
Finnøy [N] 192 D5
Finnsnes [N] 192 F3
Finnstad [N] 182 C5
Finntorp [S] 166 D3
Finnvelta [N] 172 D5
Finow [D] 34 E1
Finsand [N] 170 H4
Finsjö [S] 162 G4
Finspång [S] 168 A5
Finsta [S] 168 E2
Finsterwalde [D] 34 E5
Finström [FIN] 176 A5
Fionnay [CH] 70 D3
Fionnphort [GB] 8 B1
Fiorenzuola d'Arda [I] 110 C2
Firá / Thíra [GR] 138 F5
Firbis Castle [IRL] 2 C3
Firenze [I] 110 F5
Firenzuola [I] 110 F4
Firkeel [IRL] 4 A5
Firlej [PL] 38 E4
Firminy [F] 68 E3
Fiscal [E] 84 E5
Fischamend [A] 62 F5
Fischbach [D] 44 H2
Fischbach [D] 44 H4
Fischbeck [D] 32 F3
Fischbeck [D] 34 C2
Fischen [D] 60 B6
Fischerbócsa [H] 76 D3
Fishguard [GB] 4 H6
Fisíni [GR] 130 F6
Fiska [N] 180 C4
Fiskárdo [GR] 132 C5
Fiskebäckskil [S] 166 C6
Fiskebøl [N] 192 D4
Fiskevollen [N] 182 C5
Fiskö [FIN] 176 C4
Fiskøl [N] 164 F2
Fismes [F] 44 A3
Fiss [A] 72 C1
Fisterra / Finisterre [E] 78 A2
Fıstıklı [TR] 150 E4
Fitero [E] 84 A6
Fitjar [N] 170 A5
Fiuggi [I] 116 B6
Fiumefreddo Bruzio [I] 124 D4
Fiumefreddo di Sicilia [I] 124 B8
Fiumicino [I] 114 H6
Fivemiletown [NIR] 2 F3
Fivizzano [I] 110 D4
Fjæra [N] 170 C5
Fjærland [N] 170 D1
Fjäl [S] 182 H2
Fjälkinge [S] 158 D2
Fjällåsen [S] 192 G5
Fjällbacka [S] 166 C5
Fjällgården [S] 182 G4
Fjällnäs [S] 182 D4
Fjällnäs [S] 190 G3
Fjaltring [DK] 160 B5
Fjand Gårde [DK] 160 B5
Fjärås [S] 160 H3
Fjärdhundra [S] 168 C2
Fjell [N] 170 A4
Fjellbu [N] 192 F4
Fjellerup [DK] 160 E5
Fjellheim [N] 170 F3
Fjellsrud [N] 166 C1
Fjelstrup [DK] 156 C3
Fjenneslev [DK] 156 F3
Fjerestad [N] 170 C2
Fjerritslev [DK] 160 D3
Fjon [N] 170 B2
Fjone [N] 164 E3
Fjordgård [N] 192 F2
Fjugesta [S] 166 G3
Flå [N] 170 G4
Flaçà [E] 92 G3
Fladdabister [GB] 6 G4
Fladungen [D] 46 F2
Flagy [F] 58 B3
Flaine [F] 70 C3
Flaka [FIN] 168 G1
Flakaberg [S] 194 A8
Flakaträsk [S] 190 F3
Flakk [N] 182 B1
Flakkstadvågen [N] 192 E3
Flåm [N] 170 D3
Flampourári [GR] 132 D1
Flaran [F] 66 E6
Flärke [S] 184 G1
Flatabø [N] 170 C4
Flateby [N] 166 C1
Flateland [N] 164 E4
Flåten [N] 192 G1
Flåtestøa [N] 172 C2
Flatmark [N] 180 F4
Flatøydegard [N] 170 G3
Flatråker [N] 170 B5
Flätsbo [S] 174 C3
Flått [N] 190 C4
Flattnitz [A] 74 B2
Flauenskjold [DK] 160 E3
Flaugeac [F] 66 E4
Flavigny-sur-Moselle [F] 44 E5
Fléchin [F] 28 E3
Fleckenberg [D] 32 D5
Fleckenstein, Château de- [F] 44 H4
Fleetwood [GB] 10 D3
Flehingen [D] 46 C6
Flekke [N] 170 B1
Flekkefjord [N] 164 C5
Flemma [N] 180 F2
Flen [S] 168 C4
Flensburg [D] 156 C5
Flerahopp [S] 162 F5
Flers [F] 26 E4
Flesberg [N] 164 G1
Flesje [N] 170 C2
Flesland [N] 170 A4
Flesnes [N] 192 E3
Fleurance [F] 84 G2
Fleuré [F] 54 F4
Fleurier [CH] 58 C6
Fleurus [B] 30 C5
Fleury [F] 28 C6
Flims [CH] 70 G1
Flims Waldhaus [CH] 70 G1
Flins [F] 42 F3
Flirsch [A] 72 B1
Flisa [N] 172 D4
Flisbrua [N] 172 D4
Flisby [S] 162 E2
Fliseryd [S] 162 G4
Flix [E] 90 H5
Flize [F] 44 C2
Floby [S] 162 C1
Floda [S] 160 H2
Floda [S] 172 H5
Floda [S] 190 H5
Flögåsen [S] 172 F2
Flogned [S] 166 D1
Flogny-la-Chapelle [F] 56 F1
Flöha [D] 48 D1
Flon [S] 182 E4
Flor [S] 182 H5
Florac [F] 68 D6
Florange [F] 44 E3
Florennes [B] 30 C5
Florenville [B] 44 D2
Floreşti [MD] 204 E3
Florína [GR] 128 E4
Flornes [N] 182 C1
Florø [N] 180 B5
Florstadt [D] 46 D2
Florvåg [N] 170 A3
Flostrand [N] 190 D2
Flötningen [S] 182 D6
Fluberg [N] 170 H3
Flüelen [CH] 58 F6
Fluglafjørdur [FR] 160 B1
Flühli [CH] 58 E6
Flumeri [I] 120 F2
Flumet [F] 70 B3
Fluminimaggiore [I] 118 B6
Flums [CH] 58 H6
Fluren [S] 174 D1
Flymen [S] 162 F6
Flyn [S] 184 D1
Flystveit [N] 164 D4
Flytåsen [S] 174 C2
Fnideq [MA] 100 G6
Foça [TR] 152 B4
Foča-Srbinje [BIH] 144 D2
Fockbek [D] 18 F2
Focşani [RO] 204 E4
Fódele [GR] 140 E4
Foeni [RO] 76 F6
Fogdö [S] 168 C3
Foggia [I] 120 G1
Föglö [FIN] 168 H1
Fohnsdorf [A] 74 C2
Foiano di Chiana [I] 114 G1
Foinikoúntas [GR] 136 D4
Foix [F] 84 H5
Fojnica [BIH] 142 C4
Fojnica [BIH] 144 D2
Fokstugu [N] 180 G5
Földeák [H] 76 F4
Foldereid [N] 190 C4
Földes [H] 76 G1
Foldingbro [DK] 156 B3
Folégandros [GR] 138 E4
Folelli [F] 114 C3
Folgaria [I] 72 C5
Folgarida [I] 72 C4
Folgoso [E] 78 E4
Foliá [GR] 130 D4
Foligno [I] 116 A2
Folkärna [S] 174 D5
Folkestad [N] 180 C4
Folkestone [GB] 14 F5
Folladal [N] 190 C5
Follafoss [N] 190 C5
Folldal [N] 180 H5
Follina [I] 72 E5
Föllinge [S] 190 E6
Follónica [I] 114 E2
Folmava [CZ] 48 D5
Fölsbyn [S] 166 D2
Folwarki [PL] 36 G6
Folyás [H] 64 G5
Fompedraza [E] 88 F2
Fondamente [F] 106 D3
Fondi [I] 120 C1
Fondo [I] 72 C3
Fönebo [S] 184 E6
Fonfría [E] 80 G4
Fonfría [E] 90 D5
Fonni [I] 118 D5
Fonseca, Castillo de- [E] 88 E3
Fontainebleau [F] 42 G5
Fontaine-de-Vaucluse [F] 106 H3
Fontaine-Française [F] 56 H3
Fontaine Guérard, Abbaye de- [F] 28 C6
Fontaine Henry, Château de- [F] 26 F3
Fontaine-le-Dun [F] 26 H2
Fontaine-sur-Coole [F] 44 B4
Fontanars dels Alforins [E] 98 D6
Fontanella [A] 72 A1
Fontanellato [I] 110 D2
Fontanelle [I] 72 F5
Fontanosas [E] 96 D4
Fonte Avellana, Monastero di- [I] 116 B1
Fontecha [E] 82 G5
Fonte Colombo, Convento di- [I] 116 B4
Fontedias [E] 78 C3
Fontenay, Abbaye de- [F] 56 F2
Fontenay-le-Comte [F] 54 C4
Fontenay-Trésigny [F] 42 G4
Fontevraud-l'Abbaye [F] 54 E2
Fontfroide, Abbaye de- [F] 106 C5
Fontgombault [F] 54 G4
Fontinha [P] 86 C2
Fontioso [E] 88 G1
Fontiveros [E] 88 D3
Font-Romeu [F] 92 E1
Fontstown [IRL] 4 F3
Fontvieille [F] 106 G4
Fonyód [H] 74 H3
Fonzaso [I] 72 E5
Föppolo [I] 70 H3
Föra [S] 162 G4
Forbach [D] 58 F1
Forbach [F] 44 G4
Forbes, Castle- [IRL] 2 D4
Forcall [E] 98 F1
Forcalquier [F] 108 C3
Forcarei [E] 78 C4
Forchach [A] 60 C6
Forchheim [D] 46 G4
Forchtenstein [A] 62 F6
Ford [GB] 8 C2
Førde [N] 164 B1
Førde [N] 180 C6
Fordingbridge [GB] 12 G4
Fordongianus [I] 118 C5
Forenza [I] 120 H3
Forfar [GB] 8 F2
Forges-les-Eaux [F] 28 C5
Forino [I] 120 E3
Forio [I] 120 D3
Førland [N] 164 C5
Forli [I] 110 G4
Forli del Sánnio [I] 116 D6
Forlimpopoli [I] 110 G4
Formazza [I] 70 F2
Formby [GB] 10 D3
Formerie [F] 28 D5
Formia [I] 120 C2
Formigine [I] 110 E3
Formiguères [F] 92 E1
Formofoss [N] 190 C5
Fornace [I] 114 G3
Fornaci di Barga [I] 110 D4
Fornalutx [E] 104 E4
Fornelli [I] 118 B2
Fornells [E] 104 H4
Forni Avoltri [I] 72 F3
Forni di Sopra [I] 72 F4
Forni di Sotto [I] 72 F4
Forno Alpi Graie [I] 70 C5
Forno di Zoldo [I] 72 E4
Fornos de Algodres [P] 80 D6
Fornovo di Taro [I] 110 D3
Foros do Arrão [P] 86 D5
Forøy [N] 190 D1
Forráskút [H] 76 E4
Forres [GB] 6 E5
Fors [S] 166 D6
Fors [S] 174 D5
Fors [S] 184 G1
Forsa [N] 192 E4
Forsbacka [S] 174 E4
Forsby / Koskenkylä [FIN] 178 B4
Forserum [S] 162 D2
Forset [N] 170 H2
Forshaga [S] 166 F2
Forsheda [S] 162 C4
Forshem [S] 166 E5
Förslöv [S] 162 B6
Forsmark [S] 174 F5
Forsmo [S] 184 E2
Forsnacken [S] 190 F3
Forsnäs [S] 190 G3
Forsnäs [S] 190 G2
Forsnes [N] 180 F1
Forsøl [N] 194 B2
Forssa [FIN] 176 F3
Forst [D] 34 G4
Forstinning [D] 60 E4
Forsvik [S] 166 G5
Fort Augustus [GB] 6 D5
Forte dei Marmi [I] 110 D5
Forte di Bibbiona [I] 114 E1
Forth [D] 46 G5
Fort-Mahon-Plage [F] 28 D3
Fortrose [GB] 6 E4
Fortun [N] 170 E1
Fortuna [E] 104 C2
Fortuneswell [GB] 12 F5
Fort William [GB] 6 C6
Forvik [N] 190 D3
Fos [F] 84 F5
Fösked [S] 166 F2
Foskros [S] 182 E5
Foskvallen [S] 182 E6
Fosnavåg [N] 180 C4
Fosnes [N] 190 C4
Fossano [I] 108 G2
Fossanova, Abbazia di- [I] 120 C1
Fossbakken [N] 192 F3
Fossby [N] 166 C3
Fossen [N] 180 D6
Fosser [N] 166 C1
Fosses [B] 30 C5
Fossland [N] 190 C5
Fossombrone [I] 112 B6
Fos-sur-Mer [F] 106 G5
Foteiná [GR] 128 G5
Foucarmont [F] 28 C4
Fouesnant [F] 40 B3
Fougères [F] 26 D5
Fougerolles [F] 58 C3
Foulain [F] 56 H2
Foulum [DK] 160 D5
Fouras [F] 54 C5
Fourcès [F] 66 D6
Fourfourás [GR] 140 D5
Foúrka [GR] 128 D6
Fourmies [F] 28 G5
Fourná [GR] 132 F3
Fourneaux [F] 54 H6
Fournels [F] 68 C5
Fournés [GR] 140 C4
Foúrnoi [GR] 138 H1
Fourquet [F] 66 F6
Fours [F] 56 E4
Foústani [GR] 128 G3
Fowey [GB] 12 C5
Foxford [IRL] 2 C3
Foynes [IRL] 4 C3
Foz [E] 78 E2
Foz do Arelho [P] 86 B3
Foz Giraldo [P] 86 E3
Frabosa Soprana [I] 108 G3
Frącki [PL] 24 E3
Fraga [E] 90 G5
Fragkísta [GR] 132 E4
Fragkokástello [GR] 140 C5
Fraize [F] 58 D2
Framley [DK] 156 D1
Framlingham [GB] 14 G3
Frammersbach [D] 46 D3
Främmestad [S] 166 D6
Framnäs [S] 190 H1
Frampol [PL] 52 F2
Framzelle [F] 14 G6
Francardo [F] 114 B3
Francavilla al Mare [I] 116 D4
Francavilla di Sicilia [I] 124 A8
Francavilla Fontana [I] 122 F4
Francelos [P] 80 B4
Francofonte [I] 126 G4
Frändefors [S] 166 D5
Franeker [NL] 16 F2
Frangy [F] 70 A2
Frankenberg [D] 32 E5
Frankenberg [D] 48 D1
Frankenburg [A] 60 H4
Frankenmarkt [A] 60 H5
Frankenthal [D] 46 B4
Frankfurt (Oder) [D] 34 G3
Frankfurt am Main [D] 46 C3
Frankrike [S] 190 D6
Fränsta [S] 184 D4
Františkovy Lázně [CZ] 48 C3
Franzburg [D] 20 C3
Frasassi, Grotte di- [I] 116 B1
Frascati [I] 116 A6
Frasdorf [D] 60 F5
Fraserburgh [GB] 6 G5
Frashër [AL] 128 C5
Frasne [F] 58 B6
Frasno, Puerto de- [E] 90 D4
Frassino [I] 108 F2
Frassinoro [I] 110 E4
Frasso [I] 120 E2
Fratel [P] 86 E4
Fratte Polesine [I] 110 G2
Frauenau [D] 60 H2
Frauenberg [D] 46 D1
Frauenburg [A] 74 B2
Frauenfeld [CH] 58 G4
Frauenkirch [CH] 72 A2
Frauenkirchen [A] 62 G5
Frauenstein [A] 62 B5
Frauenstein [D] 48 E1
Frauschereck [A] 60 H4
Frayssinet [F] 66 G4
Frechen [D] 30 G4
Frechilla [E] 82 C6
Freckenhorst [D] 32 C3
Fredensborg [DK] 156 G2
Fredericia [DK] 156 C2
Frederiks [DK] 160 C5
Frederiksberg [DK] 156 F3
Frederikshavn [DK] 160 E3
Frederikssund [DK] 156 G2
Frederiksværk [DK] 156 G2
Frednowy [PL] 22 F4
Fredrika [S] 190 G5
Fredriksberg [S] 172 G5
Fredrikshamn / Hamina [FIN] 178 D3
Fredrikstad [N] 166 B3
Fredriksten [N] 166 C3
Freest [D] 20 E3
Fregenal de la Sierra [E] 94 G3
Fregene [I] 114 H5
Frei [N] 100 F2
Freiberg [D] 48 E1
Freiburg [D] 18 E3
Freiburg im Breisgau [D] 58 E3
Freiensteinau [D] 46 D2
Freihung [D] 48 B5
Freila [E] 102 F3
Freilassing [D] 60 G5
Freising [D] 60 E3
Freistadt [A] 62 C3
Freital [D] 48 E1
Freixedas [P] 80 E6
Freixianda [P] 86 D3
Freixo de Espada à Cinta [P] 80 F5
Frejev [DK] 160 D4
Frejlev [DK] 20 B1
Fréjus [F] 108 D5
Fréjus, Tunnel de- [F/I] 70 B5
Frenchpark [IRL] 2 D4
Frenštát pod Radhoštěm [CZ] 50 E5
Freren [D] 32 C1
Freshford [IRL] 4 E4
Fresnay-sur-Sarthe [F] 26 F6
Fresnoy [F] 28 F4
Fresnes [F] 58 B3
Fresnes-en-Woëvre [F] 44 E4
Fresno Alhándiga [E] 88 C4
Fresno de la Ribera [E] 88 D1
Fresno de Sayago [E] 80 G4
Fresno de Sayago [E] 80 G5
Fresvik [N] 170 D2
Fréteval [F] 42 D6
Fretigney-et-Velloreille [F] 58 B4
Fretzdorf [D] 20 C6
Freudenberg [D] 32 C6
Freudenberg [D] 46 D4
Freudenstadt [D] 58 F2
Freundsberg [A] 72 E1
Frévent [F] 28 E3
Freyburg [D] 34 B5
Freyenstein [D] 20 B5
Freyming Merlebach [F] 44 F4
Freystadt [D] 46 G6
Freyung [D] 60 H2
Frías [E] 82 F5
Fribourg [CH] 58 D6
Frick [CH] 58 E4
Fridafors [S] 162 D6
Fridingen [D] 58 G3
Friedberg [A] 74 E1
Friedberg [D] 46 C2
Friedberg [D] 60 D3
Friedburg [A] 60 H5
Friedeburg [D] 18 C4
Friedersdorf [D] 34 F3
Friedewald [D] 32 F6
Friedland [D] 20 D4
Friedland [D] 32 F5
Friedland [D] 34 F3
Friedrichroda [D] 46 F1
Friedrichshafen [D] 58 H4
Friedrichskoog [D] 18 E3
Friedrichsort [D] 18 G2
Friedrichstadt [D] 18 E2
Friedrichswalde [D] 20 D6
Friedstein [A] 62 B6
Friesach [A] 74 B2
Friesack [D] 34 D1
Friesenheim [D] 58 E2
Friesoythe [D] 18 C5
Frifelt [DK] 156 B3
Friggesund [S] 184 D6
Frihetsli [N] 192 G3
Frillesås [S] 160 H3
Frinkenberg [A] 72 E1
Frinnaryd [S] 162 E1
Friol [E] 78 D3
Fristad [S] 162 B2
Fritsla [S] 162 B2
Fritzlar [D] 32 E5
Fröderyd [S] 162 E3
Frödinge [S] 162 F2
Frohburg [D] 34 C6
Frohnleiten [A] 74 D1
Froissy [F] 28 D5
Fröjel [S] 168 F5
Frombork [PL] 22 F2
Frome [GB] 12 G4
Fromental [F] 26 F5
Fromentine [F] 54 A2
Frómista [E] 82 D5
Fromy [F] 44 D2
Fronsac [F] 84 F4
Fronteira [P] 86 E5
Frontenhausen [D] 60 F3
Frontera [E] 100 A5
Frontignan [F] 106 E4
Fronton [F] 84 H2
Fröseke [S] 162 F4
Frosinone [I] 116 C6
Fröskog [S] 166 D4
Frösö [S] 182 G2
Frosolone [I] 120 E1
Frossay [F] 40 E6
Frosta [N] 190 B6
Frostavallen [S] 158 C2
Frösthult [S] 168 C2
Frøstrup [DK] 160 C3
Frösunda [S] 168 E2
Frøvi [S] 166 H2
Frøyrak [N] 164 D4
Fruges [F] 28 E3
Frutigen [CH] 70 D1
Fry [GR] 140 G3
Frýdek-Místek [CZ] 50 F5
Frýdlant [CZ] 48 G1
Frýdlant nad Ostravicí [CZ] 50 F5
Frýdštejn [CZ] 48 H2
Frygnowo [PL] 22 G5
Frymburk [CZ] 62 B3
Fryšták [CZ] 50 D6
Frysztak [PL] 52 D4
Ftéri [GR] 132 F6
Fterrë [AL] 128 B6
Fuans [F] 58 C5
Fubine [I] 70 E6
Fucécchio [I] 110 E5
Fuencalderas [E] 84 C5
Fuencaliente [E] 96 D5
Fuencaliente de la Palma [E] 100 A4
Fuencaliente de Lucio [E] 82 E4
Fuencarral [E] 88 F5
Fuendejalón [E] 90 D3
Fuendetodos [E] 90 E4
Fuengirola [E] 102 B5
Fuenlabrada [E] 88 F6
Fuenlabrada de los Montes [E] 96 C3
Fuenmayor [E] 82 G6
Fuensalida [E] 96 E1
Fuensanta [E] 104 C3
Fuente Álamo [E] 98 C6
Fuente Álamo de Murcia [E] 104 C4
Fuentealbilla [E] 98 C4
Fuentecén [E] 88 G2
Fuente Dé [E] 82 D3
Fuente de Cantos [E] 94 G3
Fuente del Arco [E] 94 H4
Fuente del Maestre [E] 94 G3
Fuente del Obispo [E] 102 E2
Fuente de Pedro Naharro [E] 96 H2
Fuente de Santa Cruz [E] 88 E3
Fuente el Fresno [E] 96 F3
Fuente el Sauz [E] 88 G5
Fuente el Sol [E] 88 D3
Fuenteguinaldo [E] 86 H2
Fuentelapeña [E] 88 D2
Fuentelcésped [E] 88 G2
Fuentelespino de Haro [E] 96 H3
Fuentelespino de Moya [E] 98 D3
Fuentemilanos [E] 88 F4
Fuente Obejuna [E] 96 B5
Fuente Palmera [E] 102 B1
Fuentepinilla [E] 90 B3
Fuenterrabía / Hondarribia [E] 84 B2
Fuentes [E] 98 C2

Fuentesaúco [E] 80 H6
Fuentes de Andalucía [E] 102 A2
Fuentes de Ayódar [E] 98 F3
Fuentes de Ebro [E] 90 E4
Fuentes de Jiloca [E] 90 D4
Fuentes de León [E] 94 G4
Fuentes de Nava [E] 82 C6
Fuentes de Oñoro [E] 86 H2
Fuentes de Ropel [E] 82 A5
Fuentidueña de Tajo [E] 96 H1
Fuerte del Rey [E] 102 E2
Fügen [A] 72 E1
Fuglebjerg [DK] 156 F3
Fuglem [N] 182 C2
Fuhrberg [D] 32 G1
Fulda [D] 46 E2
Fulnek [CZ] 50 E5
Fülöpszállás [H] 76 C3
Fulpmes [A] 72 D1
Fulunäs [S] 172 E2
Fumay [F] 30 C6
Fumel [F] 66 F5
Funäsdalen [S] 182 E4
Funchal [P] 100 A3
Fundão [P] 86 F2
Fundres / Pfundres [I] 72 E2
Furadouro [P] 80 B4
Furculeşti [RO] 148 B2
Fure [N] 170 B1
Furnes (Veurne) [B] 28 F1
Fürnitz [A] 72 H3
Fursest [N] 180 D4
Furset [N] 180 E2
Fürstenau [D] 32 C1
Fürstenberg [D] 20 D5
Fürstenfeld [A] 74 E2
Fürstenfeldbruck [D] 60 D4
Fürstenwalde [D] 34 F2
Fürstenwerder [D] 20 D5
Fürstenzell [D] 60 H3
Furta [H] 76 G2
Furtan [S] 166 E2
Fürth [D] 46 G5
Fürth im Wald [D] 48 D6
Furtwangen [D] 58 F3
Furuby [S] 162 E4
Furudal [S] 172 H2
Furuflaten [N] 192 G2
Furusjö [S] 162 D1
Furusund [S] 168 F2
Furutangvik [N] 190 D4
Furuvik [S] 174 E4
Fusa [N] 170 B4
Fuscaldo [I] 124 D4
Fusch [A] 72 G1
Fushë Arrëz [AL] 128 B1
Fushë-Krujë [AL] 128 B2
Fushë-Kuqe [AL] 128 B2
Fushë Muhurr [AL] 128 C2
Fusio [CH] 70 F2
Füssen [D] 60 C6
Futog [SRB] 142 F1
Futrikelv [N] 192 F2
Füzesabony [H] 64 E5
Füzesgyarmat [H] 76 G2
Fuzeta [P] 94 D6
Fyláki [GR] 132 G3
Fylákio [GR] 130 H1
Fylakopi [GR] 138 D4
Fylí [GR] 134 B6
Fylí [GR] 134 C6
Fyllinge [S] 162 B5
Fynshav [DK] 156 D4
Fyresdal [N] 164 E3
Fyrkat [DK] 160 D5
Fyteíes [GR] 132 E4

G

Gaas [A] 74 F2
Gaasbeek [B] 28 H3
Gabarc [BG] 146 G3
Gabarret [F] 66 D6
Gabčíkovo [SK] 62 H5
Gabela [BIH] 144 C3
Gaber [BG] 146 F4
Gabicce Mare [I] 112 B5
Gąbin [PL] 36 H2
Gąbino [PL] 22 B2
Gaboš [HR] 142 E1
Gabrovica [BG] 146 G5
Gabrovka [SLO] 74 C5
Gabrovo [BG] 148 C4
Gać [PL] 24 D6
Gacé [F] 26 G5
Gacko [BIH] 144 D2
Gåda [S] 184 C5
Gäddede [S] 190 E5
Gäddeholm [S] 168 C3
Gadebusch [D] 18 H4
Gadna [H] 64 F4
Gádor [E] 102 G5
Gádoros [H] 76 F3
Gadžin Han [SRB] 146 D4
Gæidno [N] 194 D2
Gæidnovuoppe [N] 194 B4
Gaël [F] 26 B5
Găeşti [RO] 204 D5
Gaeta [I] 120 C2
Gaflenz [A] 62 C5
Gagarin [RUS] 202 E3
Gaggenau [D] 58 F1
Gagliano Castelferrato [I] 126 F3
Gagliano del Capo [I] 122 G6
Gagnef [S] 172 H4
Gahro [D] 34 E4
Gaildorf [D] 46 E6
Gaillac [F] 106 B2
Gaillimh / Galway [IRL] 2 C5
Gaillon [F] 28 C6
Gainsborough [GB] 10 F5
Galatás [GR] 132 B3
Gairloch [GB] 6 C4
Gairo [I] 118 E5
Gaj [HR] 142 B1
Gaj [SRB] 142 H2
Gajary [SK] 62 G4
Gajdobra [SRB] 142 F1
Gakovo [SRB] 76 C5
Gălă [N] 170 H1
Galăbodarna [S] 182 F3
Galan [F] 84 F4
Galanádo [GR] 138 F3
Galanito [N] 194 B4
Galanta [SK] 62 H4
Galapagar [E] 88 F5
Galashiels [GB] 8 E4
Galata [BG] 148 F3
Galatáki, Moní- [GR] 134 B4
Galatás [GR] 136 G2
Galaţi [RO] 204 E4
Galatia (Mehmetcik) [CY] 154 G4
Galati Marina [I] 124 B7
Galatina [I] 122 G5
Galátista [GR] 130 B5
Galatone [I] 122 G5
Galaxídi [GR] 132 G5
Galbally [IRL] 4 D4
Gålborget [S] 184 F1
Galdakao [E] 82 G4
Gáldar [E] 100 C6
Galeata [I] 110 G5
Galera [E] 102 G3
Galéria [F] 114 A3
Galgaguta [H] 64 D5
Galgagyörk [H] 64 D5
Galgamácsa [H] 64 D6
Galicea Mare [RO] 146 F1
Galinóporni (Kaleburnu) [CY] 154 H4
Galiny [PL] 22 H3
Galipsós [GR] 130 C4
Galissás [GR] 138 D2
Galisteo [E] 86 H4
Galižana [HR] 112 D2
Galizano [E] 82 F3
Gallarate [I] 70 F4
Gällared [S] 162 B4
Gallargues [F] 106 F4
Gallarus Oratory [IRL] 4 A3
Gallegos del Río [E] 80 G4
Gallegos de Solmirón [E] 88 C4
Gallenstein [A] 62 C6
Galliate [I] 70 F5
Gallípoli [I] 122 G5
Gällivare [S] 192 G6
Gallneukirchen [A] 62 B4
Gällö [S] 182 H3
Gällstad [S] 162 C2
Gallur [E] 90 D3
Galovo [BG] 146 G2
Gålsjö bruk [S] 184 F2
Galston [GB] 8 D3
Galtelli [I] 118 E4
Galten [DK] 156 D1
Galten [N] 182 D6
Gåltjärn [S] 184 E4
Galtström [S] 184 F5
Galtür [A] 72 B2
Galveias [P] 86 D5
Gálvez [E] 96 E2
Gałwany [PL] 24 B3
Galway / Gaillimh [IRL] 2 C5
Galyatető [H] 64 E5
Gamachos [F] 20 C4
Gambara [I] 110 D1
Gambárie [I] 124 C7
Gambatesa [I] 120 F1
Gambolò [I] 70 F5
Gaming [A] 62 D5
Gamla Gränome [S] 168 D1
Gamla Uppsala [S] 168 D1
Gamleby [S] 162 G2
Gammalsälen [S] 172 F4
Gammel Estrup [DK] 160 E5
Gammel Skagen [DK] 160 E2
Gammelskolla [N] 172 B2
Gammelstaden [S] 196 B3
Gammertingen [D] 60 H3
Gams [CH] 58 H5
Gamvik [N] 194 D1
Gamzigrad [SRB] 146 D2
Gan [F] 84 E3
Ganacker [D] 60 G3
Ganagobie, Prieuré- [F] 108 C3
Gand (Gent) [B] 28 G2
Gandal [N] 164 B3
Găndara [P] 86 E2
Ganderkesee [D] 18 D5
Gandesa [E] 90 G6
Gandia [E] 98 F6
Gandino [I] 70 H4
Gandrup [DK] 160 E4
Gandvik [N] 194 E2
Ganges [F] 106 E3
Gangi [I] 126 E3
Gângiova [RO] 146 G2
Gangkofen [D] 60 G3
Gannat [F] 68 D1
Gänserndorf [A] 62 F4
Gap [F] 108 D2
Gaperhult [S] 166 E4
Gara [H] 76 C5
Garaballa [E] 98 D3
Garabonc [H] 74 G3
Garafía [E] 100 A4
Garaguso [I] 122 C4
Gara Khitrino [BG] 148 E2
Garani [BY] 202 B5
Garavac [BIH] 142 D2
Garbagna [I] 110 B2
Garbno [PL] 24 B3
Garbów [PL] 38 D5
Garbsen [D] 32 F2
Garching [D] 60 G4
Garcia [E] 90 H6
Garciaz [E] 96 B2
Garčin [HR] 142 D2
Gărcov [RO] 148 A2
Gard, Pont du- [F] 106 G3
Garda [I] 72 C6
Gardanne [F] 108 B5
Gårdby [S] 162 G5
Gardeja [PL] 22 E4
Gardelegen [D] 34 B2
Gardíki [GR] 132 F4
Garding [D] 18 E2
Gärdnäs [S] 190 E5
Gardone Riviera [I] 72 B5
Gardone Val Trómpia [I] 72 B5
Gárdony [H] 76 B2
Gårdsby [S] 162 E4
Gardsjöbäcken [S] 190 F3
Gårdskär [S] 174 F4
Gärdslösa [S] 162 G5
Gardstad [N] 190 C4
Gårdstånga [S] 158 C2
Garein [F] 66 C5
Gårelehöjden [S] 184 E1
Garen [N] 170 D4
Gares / Puente la Reina [E] 84 B4
Garešnica [HR] 74 G6
Garéssio [I] 108 G3
Gargaliánoi [GR] 136 C4
Gargas, Grotte de- [F] 84 F4
Gargaur [S] 190 G3
Gargellen [A] 72 A2
Gargilesse-Dampierre [F] 54 H5
Gargnano [I] 72 C5
Gargnäs [S] 190 G3
Garголes de Abajo [E] 90 A5
Gárgyán [H] 76 D4
Gargždai [LT] 200 D4
Gari [MK] 128 D2
Garibaldi, Tomba di- [I] 118 E2
Garípa [GR] 140 E5
Garkalne [LV] 198 D5
Garlasco [I] 70 F5
Garlin [F] 84 E2
Garlstorf [D] 18 F5
Garmisch Partenkirchen [D] 60 D6
Garmo [N] 180 F5
Garnisch Gardens [IRL] 4 B5
Garoza [LV] 198 D5
Garpenberg [S] 174 D5
Garraf [E] 92 D5
Garrafe de Torío [E] 78 H5
Garray [E] 90 B2
Garrel [D] 18 C5
Garristown [IRL] 2 F5
Garrotxa, Zona Volcànica de la- [E] 92 F3
Garrovillas [E] 86 G4
Garrucha [E] 102 H5
Gars am Kamp [A] 62 E3
Garsås [S] 172 G3
Garsnas [S] 158 D3
Gärten [N] 190 B6
Gartland [N] 190 C5
Gartow [D] 20 A6
Gartringen [D] 58 G1
Gartz [D] 20 E5
Garvão [P] 94 C3
Garwolin [PL] 38 C4
Garz [D] 20 D2
Gåsborn [S] 166 G1
Gåsbue [N] 180 F4
Gaschurn [A] 72 B2
Gascueña [E] 98 B1
Gasen [A] 74 D1
Gaskeluokta [S] 190 F4
Gąski [PL] 24 D3
Gąsocin [PL] 38 B1
Gaspoltshofen [A] 62 A4
Gässåsen [S] 184 D5
Gasteiner Klamm [A] 72 G1
Gastes [F] 66 B4
Gastoúni [GR] 136 B2
Gasztony [H] 74 F2
Gata [N] 172 C4
Gata de Gorgos [E] 104 F1
Gatchina [RUS] 178 H6
Gatehouse of Fleet [GB] 8 D5
Gátér [H] 76 E3
Gateshead [GB] 8 G6
Gátova [E] 98 E4
Gatta [I] 110 D3
Gattendorf [A] 62 G5
Gattinara [I] 70 E4
Gaubert [F] 42 E5
Gaucín [E] 100 H4
Gaukås [N] 164 E3
Gaulstad [N] 190 C5
Gaupne [N] 170 D1
Gaushach [D] 46 E3
Gausvik [N] 192 E4
Gautefall [N] 164 F3
Gautestad [N] 164 D4
Gauville [F] 26 G5
Gavaloú [GR] 132 E5
Gavardo [I] 72 B6
Gavarnie [F] 84 E5
Gavarnie, Cirque de- [F] 84 E5
Gávavencsellő [H] 64 G4
Gaverina Terme [I] 70 H4
Gavi [I] 110 A2
Gavião [P] 86 E4
Gavirate [I] 70 F4
Gävle [S] 174 E4
Gavnø Slot [DK] 156 F4
Gavoi [I] 118 D4
Gavorrano [I] 114 F2
Gavray [F] 26 D4
Gavrilov- Yam [RUS] 202 F1
Gávrio [GR] 134 E6
Gávros [GR] 128 E5
Gavry [RUS] 198 G5
Gåvsta [S] 168 D1
Gävunda [S] 172 G4
Gåxsjö [S] 190 E6
Gaziköy [TR] 150 C4
Gazimağusa (Ammóchostos) [CY] 154 G5
Gazoldo degli Ippoliti [I] 110 E1
Gázoros [GR] 130 C3
Gbelce [SK] 64 B5
Gdańsk [PL] 22 E2
Gdov [RUS] 198 G2
Gdów [PL] 52 B4
Gdynia [PL] 22 E2
Gea de Albarracín [E] 98 D1
Geashill [IRL] 2 E6
Geaune [F] 84 E2
Gebesee [D] 32 H6
Geblar [D] 46 F1
Gebze [TR] 150 F3
Geçitkale (Lefkónikon) [CY] 154 G5
Geçkinli [TR] 150 B2
Gedem [D] 46 D2
Gedesby [DK] 20 B1
Gedinne [B] 44 D1
Gediz [TR] 152 G2
Gedser [DK] 20 B1
Gedsted [DK] 160 D4
Gedved [DK] 156 D1
Geel [B] 30 D3
Geertruidenberg [NL] 16 D6
Geeste [D] 16 H4
Geesthacht [D] 18 G4
Gefell [D] 48 B2
Gefrees [D] 46 H3
Gefýra [GR] 128 H4
Gefýria [GR] 132 F3
Gehren [D] 46 G2
Geijersholm [S] 172 F6
Geilenkirchen [D] 30 F4
Geilo [N] 170 E4
Geiranger [N] 180 E4
Geisa [D] 46 E1
Geiselhöring [D] 60 F2
Geiselwind [D] 46 F4
Geisenfeld [D] 60 E3
Geisenhausen [D] 60 F3
Geisingen [D] 58 G3
Geislingen [D] 60 B2
Geisnes [N] 190 C4
Geithain [D] 34 D6
Geithus [N] 170 G6
Gela [I] 126 E5
Geldern [D] 30 G2
Geldrop [NL] 30 E2
Geleen [NL] 30 E4
Gelej [H] 64 F5
Gelembe [TR] 152 D2
Gelgaudiškis [LT] 200 E5
Gelibolu [TR] 150 B5
Gelibolu [TR] 154 D1
Gelida [E] 92 D4
Gelnhausen [D] 46 D3
Gelnica [SK] 64 F2
Gelsa [E] 90 F4
Gelsenkirchen [D] 30 H3
Gelting [D] 156 C5
Gelu [RO] 76 G5
Gembloux [B] 30 D5
Gémenos [F] 108 B5
Gemerská Poloma [SK] 64 E3
Gemerská Ves [SK] 64 E3
Gemert [NL] 30 F2
Gemikonağı (Karavostasi) [CY] 154 F5
Gemiş [TR] 152 H5
Gemlik [TR] 150 F4
Gemmenich [B] 30 F4
Gemona del Friuli [I] 72 G4
Gémozac [F] 54 C6
Gemünd [D] 30 F5
Gemünden [D] 32 E6
Gemünden [D] 44 H2
Gemunden [D] 46 E3
Genappe [B] 30 C4
Génave [E] 96 G6
Genazzano [I] 116 B5
Gençay [F] 54 E4
Gencsapáti [H] 74 F1
Génelard [F] 56 F5
General Inzovo [BG] 148 D5
Generalski Stol [HR] 112 G1
General Toshevo [BG] 148 F1
Generli [TR] 150 C3
Genevad [S] 162 B5
Genève [CH] 70 B2
Gengenbach [D] 58 F2
Genillé [F] 54 G3
Genk [B] 30 E4
Genlis [F] 56 H4
Gennádio [GR] 154 D4
Genna Maria, Nuraghe- [I] 118 C6
Gennep [NL] 16 F6
Gennes [F] 54 E2
Génolhac [F] 68 D6
Génova [I] 110 B3
Genshagen [D] 34 E3
Gent (Gand) [B] 28 G2
Genthin [D] 34 C2
Gentioux [F] 68 A2
Genzano di Lucánia [I] 120 H3
Genzano di Roma [I] 116 A6
Georgianoí [GR] 128 G5
Georgioúpoli [GR] 140 C4
Georgi Traykov [BG] 148 F3
Georgsheil [D] 18 B4
Geotermia, Museo della- [I] 114 F1
Gera [D] 48 C1
Geraardsbergen [B] 28 H3
Gerabronn [D] 46 E5
Gerace [I] 124 D7
Gerakarou [GR] 130 B4
Gérakas [GR] 136 F4
Geráki [GR] 136 E4
Gerakiní [GR] 130 B5
Gérardmer [F] 58 D2
Geras [A] 62 E3
Gerasdorf bei Wien [A] 62 F4
Gerbéviller [F] 44 F6
Gerbstedt [D] 34 B4
Gerce [H] 74 G2
Gerchsheim [D] 46 E4
Geremeas [I] 118 D7
Gerena [E] 94 G5
Gerês [P] 78 B6
Geretsried [D] 60 E5
Gérgal [E] 102 G4
Gerince [TR] 154 C2
Gerlos [A] 72 E1
Germaringen [D] 60 C5
Germasogeia [CY] 154 F6
Germay [F] 44 D6
Germencik [TR] 152 D5
Germering [D] 60 C4
Germering [D] 60 D4
Germersheim [D] 46 B5
Germigny-des-Pres [F] 42 F6
Gernika-Lumo [E] 82 H4
Gernrode [D] 34 A4
Gernsbach [D] 58 F1
Gernsheim [D] 46 C4
Gerola Alta [I] 70 H3
Geroliménas [GR] 136 E5
Gerolstein [D] 30 G6
Gerolzhofen [D] 46 F4
Gerona / Girona [E] 92 F3
Geroskipou [CY] 154 F6
Gerovo [HR] 112 F1
Gerri de la Sal [E] 92 C1
Gersfeld [D] 46 F2
Gersthofen [D] 60 D3
Gerswalde [D] 20 D6
Gesäter [S] 166 C4
Gesäuse [A] 62 C6
Gescher [D] 16 G6
Geseke [D] 32 D4
Gespunsart [F] 44 C2
Gestelnburg [CH] 70 E2
Gesualdo [I] 120 F3
Gesunda [S] 172 G3
Geta [FIN] 176 A5
Getafe [E] 88 F6
Getaria [E] 84 A2
Gettlinge [S] 162 G6
Gettorf [D] 18 F2
Getxo [E] 82 G3
Gévezé [F] 26 C5
Gevgelija [MK] 128 G3
Gevigney-et-Mercey [F] 58 B3
Gevrey-Chambertin [F] 56 G4
Gevsjön [S] 182 E1
Gex [F] 70 B2
Gey [D] 30 F5
Geyikli [TR] 130 H6
Geyre [TR] 152 F5
Geysir [IS] 192 B3
Geyve [TR] 150 G3
Geziq [AL] 128 B1
Gföhl [A] 62 D3
Ghedi [I] 72 B6
Gheorghieni [RO] 204 D4
Ghilarza [I] 118 C4
Ghimpaţi [RO] 148 C1
Ghisonaccia [F] 114 C4
Ghisoni [F] 114 B4
Giáltra [GR] 132 H4
Giannitsá [GR] 128 G4
Giannoúli [GR] 130 H2
Giardinetto [I] 120 G2
Giardini-Naxos [I] 124 B8
Giarmata [RO] 76 G5
Giarratana [I] 126 F5
Giarre [I] 124 A8
Giat [F] 68 B2
Giba [I] 118 B7
Gibellina [I] 126 B2
Gibellina, Ruderi di- [I] 126 C2
Gibilmanna, Santuario di- [I] 126 E2
Gibostad [N] 192 F2
Gibraleón [E] 94 E5
Gibraltar [GBZ] 100 G5
Gic [H] 74 H1
Gidböle [S] 184 G1
Gideå [S] 184 G1
Gideåkroken [S] 190 G5
Gidle [PL] 50 G1
Gieboldehausen [D] 32 G4
Giedraičiai [LT] 200 G5
Gielas [S] 190 E3
Gielniów [PL] 38 A5
Gien [F] 56 C2
Giengedal [N] 180 C5
Giengen [D] 60 C3
Giens [F] 108 C6
Giera [RO] 142 H1
Gierałtowice [PL] 50 G4
Gieselwerder [D] 32 F4
Giessen [D] 46 C1
Gieten [NL] 16 G3
Giethoorn [NL] 16 F3
Gietrzwałd [PL] 22 G4
Giffoni [I] 120 F3
Gifhorn [D] 32 H2
Gigen [BG] 148 A2
Giglio Porto [I] 114 E4
Gignac [F] 106 E4
Gijón / Xixón [E] 82 B1
Giksi [LV] 198 E4
Gilford [NIR] 2 G4
Gilja [N] 164 B3
Gilleleje [DK] 156 G1
Gillhov [S] 182 G4
Gills [GB] 6 F2
Gillstad [S] 166 E5
Gilserberg [D] 32 E6
Gilze [NL] 30 D2
Gimat [F] 84 G2
Gimdalen [S] 184 C3
Gimel-les-Cascades [F] 66 H3
Gimenells, Castell de- [E] 90 G4
Gimmestad [N] 180 C5
Gimo [S] 174 F5
Gimont [F] 84 G3
Ginci [BG] 146 F4
Gingst [D] 20 D2
Ginosa [I] 122 D4
Ginzling [A] 72 E2
Ginzo de Limia / Xinzo de Limia [E] 78 C6
Giões [P] 94 D4
Gióia del Colle [I] 122 E3
Gióia Táuro [I] 124 C6
Gioiosa Marea [I] 124 A7
Giornico [CH] 70 G2
Giove Anxur, Tempio di- [I] 120 C2
Giovinazzo [I] 122 D2
Giraltovce [SK] 52 D6
Girgantai [LT] 24 E2
Girifalco [I] 124 D5
Girne (Kerýneia) [CY] 154 G5
Girolata [F] 114 A3
Giromagny [F] 58 C3
Girona / Gerona [E] 92 F3
Gironella [E] 92 E2
Girvan [GB] 8 C4
Gisholt [N] 164 F3
Gislaved [S] 162 C3
Gislev [DK] 156 E3
Gisors [F] 28 C6
Gisselås [S] 190 E6
Gisselfeld [DK] 156 F3
Gissi [I] 116 E5
Gisslarbo [S] 168 B2
Gistaín [E] 84 F5
Gistel [B] 28 F1
Gistrup [DK] 160 E4
Gittun [S] 190 G2
Giugliano in Campania [I] 120 D3
Giuliano di Roma [I] 120 C1
Giulianova [I] 116 D3
Giulvăz [RO] 76 G6
Giurgiţa [RO] 146 G2
Giurgiu [RO] 148 C1
Give [DK] 156 C2
Givet [F] 30 D6
Givors [F] 68 F3
Givry [B] 28 H4
Givry [F] 56 E3
Givry [F] 56 G5
Givry-en-Argonne [F] 44 C4
Giżałki [PL] 36 E3
Gizdavac [HR] 144 A1
Gizeux [F] 54 F2
Giżycko [PL] 24 C3
Gizzeria [I] 124 D5
Gjakove / Đakovica [KS] 146 B6
Gjelten [N] 182 B5
Gjemnes [N] 180 F2
Gjerbës [AL] 128 C5
Gjerde [N] 180 D6
Gjermundshamn [N] 170 B5
Gjern [DK] 160 D6
Gjerrild [DK] 160 F5
Gjerstad [N] 164 F4
Gjersvik [N] 190 D4
Gjesvær [N] 194 C1
Gjeving [N] 164 F4
Gjinar [AL] 128 C3
Gjirokastër [AL] 128 C6
Gjølme [N] 180 H1
Gjøra [N] 180 G3
Gjóv [FR] 160 B1
Gjøvag [N] 170 B4
Gjøvik [N] 172 B3
Gjøvik [N] 192 E3
G. Konjare [MK] 128 F1
Gkoritsá [GR] 136 E4
Gkoúra [GR] 136 D1
Gla [GR] 134 A5
Gladbeck [D] 30 H2
Gladenbach [D] 32 D6
Gladhammar [S] 162 G2
Gladstad [N] 190 C3
Glamoč [BIH] 142 B4
Glåmos [N] 182 C3
Glamsbjerg [DK] 156 D3
Glandorf [D] 32 D2
Glanmire [IRL] 4 C5
Glanworth [IRL] 4 D4
Glarus [CH] 58 G6
Glasgow [GB] 8 D3
Glashütte [D] 48 E1
Glashütten [A] 74 C3
Glastonbury [GB] 12 F4
Glauchau [D] 48 C1
Glava [BG] 148 A3
Glava [S] 166 D2
Glavan [BG] 148 D5
Glavanovtsi [BG] 146 E4
Glavičice [BIH] 142 E3
Glavinitsa [BG] 148 E1
Glavnik [KS] 146 C4
Gleann Cholm Cille / Glencolumbkille [IRL] 2 D2
Gleann na Muaidhe / Glenamoy [IRL] 2 C3
Głębock [PL] 22 G2
Glebychevo [RUS] 178 F3
Gleichen [D] 46 G1
Gleina [D] 48 C1
Gleinalm Tunnel [A] 74 D1
Gleisdorf [A] 74 E2
Glenamaddy [IRL] 2 D4
Glenamoy / Gleann na Muaidhe [IRL] 2 C3
Glencoe [GB] 6 C6
Glencolumbkille / Gleann Cholm Cille [IRL] 2 D2
Glendalough [IRL] 4 G3
Glenealy [IRL] 4 G4
Glengarriff [IRL] 4 B5
Glénic [F] 54 H5
Glenmore [IRL] 4 E4
Glenrothes [GB] 8 E3
Glenties [IRL] 2 E2
Glenville [IRL] 4 D5
Glesne [N] 170 G5
Gletsch [CH] 70 F2
Gletscher Garten [D] 60 G5
Glewitz [D] 20 C3
Glimåkra [S] 158 D1
Glimmingehus [S] 158 D3
Glin [IRL] 4 C3
Glina [HR] 112 H1
Glinka [PL] 50 G5
Glinojeck [PL] 38 A1
Glinsce / Glinsk [IRL] 2 B4
Glinsk / Glinsce [IRL] 2 B4
G. Lisina [SRB] 146 E5
Glissjöberg [S] 182 G5
Glitterheim [N] 180 F6
Gliwice [PL] 50 F3
Gllavë [AL] 128 B5
Globitsy [RUS] 178 F5
Globočica [KS] 146 C6
Głodowa [PL] 22 B3
Gloggnitz [A] 62 E6
Głogoczów [PL] 50 H4
Glogovac [HR] 74 G5
Głogów [PL] 36 B5
Głogówek [PL] 50 E3
Głogów Małopolski [PL] 52 E3
Glomfjord [N] 190 E1
Glommen [S] 160 H4
Glommersträsk [S] 190 H4
Glömminge [S] 162 G5
Glorup [DK] 156 E4
Glóssa [GR] 134 B3
Glössbo [S] 174 E2
Glossop [GB] 10 E4
Glostrup [DK] 156 G2
Glöte [S] 182 F5
Gloucester [GB] 12 G2
Głowaczów [PL] 38 C4
Główczyce [PL] 22 C2
Glowe [D] 20 D2
Glöwen [D] 20 B6
Główno [PL] 36 H4
Gložan [SRB] 142 F1
Glozhene [BG] 146 G2
Glozhene [BG] 148 A4
Glozhenski Manastir [BG] 148 A4
Głubczyce [PL] 50 E3
Głuchołazy [PL] 50 D3
Głuchów [PL] 36 H5
Głuchów [PL] 36 H4
Głuchowo [PL] 36 C3
Glücksburg [D] 156 C4
Glückstadt [D] 18 E3
Gluda [LV] 198 D5
Glumsø [DK] 156 F3
Glušci [SRB] 142 F2
Głuszyca [PL] 50 B2
Glýfa [GR] 132 H3
Glyfáda [GR] 132 F5
Glyfáda [GR] 136 G1
Glykí [GR] 132 C3
Glyngøre [DK] 160 C4
Gmünd [A] 62 C3
Gmünd [A] 72 H2
Gmund [D] 60 E5
Gmunden [A] 62 A5
Gnarp [S] 184 E5
Gnarrenburg [D] 18 E4
Gnas [A] 74 E3
Gnesau [A] 74 B3
Gnesta [S] 168 D4
Gneux [F] 44 B3
Gniechowice [PL] 50 C1
Gniew [PL] 22 E4
Gniewkowo [PL] 36 E1
Gniezno [PL] 36 D2
Gnisvärd [S] 168 F4
Gnjilane [KS] 146 D5
Gnocchetta [I] 110 H2
Gnoien [D] 20 C3
Gnojnice [BIH] 144 C2
Gnosjö [S] 162 C3
Göbel [TR] 150 D5
Göçbeyli [TR] 152 C2
Göçek [TR] 154 F2
Goch [D] 16 F6
Göd [H] 64 C6
Godafoss [IS] 192 C2
Godalming [GB] 14 D5
Godby [FIN] 176 A5
Godech [BG] 146 F4
Godegard [S] 166 H5
Godelheim [D] 32 F4
Gödenroth [D] 44 H1
Goderville [F] 26 G2
Godętowo [PL] 22 D2
Godkowo [PL] 22 G3
Gödöllő [H] 64 D6
Godovič [SLO] 74 B5
Godowa [PL] 52 D4
Godøynes [N] 192 D6
Gödre [H] 76 A4
Godziesze Wielkie [PL] 36 F5
Godziszewo [PL] 22 E3
Goes [NL] 16 B6
Góglio [I] 70 E2
Gogolin [PL] 50 E2
Gógolo [I] 72 C3
Göhren [D] 20 E2
Goirle [NL] 30 F2
Góis [P] 86 E2
Góito [I] 110 E1
Goizueta [E] 84 B3
Gojani i Madh [AL] 128 B1
Gojsalići [BIH] 142 E4
Gökçedağ [TR] 152 F1
Gökçek [TR] 152 H4
Gökçen [TR] 152 D4

Gökçeören [TR] 152 E3
Gokels [D] 18 F2
Gökova [TR] 154 D1
Gökpınar [TR] 154 H1
Göksholm [S] 166 H3
Göktepe [TR] 150 H3
Göktepe [TR] 152 F6
Gol [N] 170 F3
Gola [HR] 74 G4
Gołąb [PL] 38 D5
Gołańcz [PL] 36 D1
Gölbent [TR] 154 F3
Gölby [FIN] 176 A5
Golchen [D] 20 D4
Gölcük [TR] 150 C4
Gölcük [TR] 150 G3
Gölcük [TR] 152 D2
Gölcük [TR] 152 E4
Golçük [TR] 154 E1
Golčův Jeníkov [CZ] 48 H4
Golczewo [PL] 20 F4
Gołdap [PL] 24 D2
Goldbach [D] 46 D3
Goldberg [D] 20 B4
Goldelund [D] 156 B5
Golden [IRL] 4 D4
Goldenstedt [D] 18 D6
Gölecik [TR] 150 D4
Goleen [IRL] 4 B5
Golegã [P] 86 D4
Goleim [AL] 128 B6
Golema Crcorija [MK] 146 E6
Golemo Selo [SRB] 146 D5
Goleniów [PL] 20 F5
Goleniowy [PL] 50 H2
Golfe-Juan [F] 108 E5
Golfo Aranci [I] 118 E2
Golfo di Sogno [F] 114 B6
Gölhisar [TR] 152 G6
Golina [PL] 36 E3
Goliševa [LV] 198 G5
Golizyno [RUS] 202 F3
Goljam Dervent [BG] 150 B1
Goljamo Belovo [BG] 148 A6
Goljamo Kamenjane [BG]
130 G2
Goljan Man. [BG] 148 D5
Gollden [N] 194 B4
Göllersdorf [A] 62 E3
Gollhofen [D] 46 F4
Golling [A] 60 G6
Gölmarmara [TR] 152 D3
Golmayo [E] 90 B3
Golnice [PL] 36 A5
Golnik [SLO] 74 B4
Golodskoye [RUS] 202 F4
Gölova [TR] 154 H1
Gölpazarı [TR] 150 H4
Golpejas [E] 80 G6
Golspie [GB] 6 E4
Golssen [D] 34 E4
Göltarla [TR] 154 H2
Golub Dobrzyń [PL] 22 E6
Golubovci [MNE] 144 E4
Gołuchów [PL] 36 E4
Golvesh [BG] 148 F1
Gölyaka [TR] 150 D5
Golyalo Krushevo [BG] 148 E5
Golyam porovec [BG] 148 E2
Gölyazi [TR] 150 E5
Gołymin-Ośrodek [PL] 38 B1
Golzow [D] 34 D3
Gómara [E] 90 C3
Gombasecká Jaskyňa [SK]
64 E3
Gombe [TR] 154 G2
Gombo [I] 110 D5
Gömeç [TR] 152 B2
Gomes Aires [P] 94 C4
Gommern [D] 34 B3
Gomunice [PL] 36 G6
Gönc [H] 64 G3
Goncelin [F] 70 A4
Gondomar [P] 80 C4
Gondrecourt [F] 44 D5
Gondrin [F] 66 D6
Gönen [TR] 150 D5
Goni, Nuraghe- [I] 118 D6
Goniá [GR] 140 B4
Goniądz [PL] 24 E4
Gónnoi [GR] 132 G1
Gonnosfanádiga [I] 118 C6
Gönyű [H] 64 A6
Gonzaga [I] 110 E2
Gooik [B] 28 H3
Goole [GB] 10 F4
Goor [NL] 16 G5
Göpfritz [A] 62 D3
Goppenstein [CH] 70 E2
Göppingen [D] 60 B2
Góra [PL] 36 C5
Góra [PL] 36 H2
Góra Kalwaria [PL] 38 C3
Goransko [MNE] 144 D3
Góra Puławska [PL] 38 D5
Góra Świętej Anny [PL] 50 E3
Goražde [BIH] 144 E1
Gorbachevo [RUS] 202 F4
Gördalen [S] 172 E1
Gordaliza del Pino [E] 82 B5
Gordes [F] 106 H3
Gördes [TR] 152 E3
Goren Chiflik [BG] 148 F3
Gorenja Vas [SLO] 74 B5
Goresbridge [IRL] 4 F4
Gorey [IRL] 4 F4
Görgeteg [H] 74 H5
Gorgier [CH] 58 C6
Gorgonzola [I] 70 G5
Gorica [BG] 148 F4
Gorica [BIH] 144 B2
Gorica [HR] 112 F4
Gorica [SLO] 74 D4
Gorica Jamnička [HR] 74 E6
Goričan [HR] 74 F4
Goricë [AL] 128 D4
Gorinchem [NL] 16 D5
Gorino Veneto [I] 110 H3
Goritsy [RUS] 202 E2
Göritz [D] 20 E5
Gorízia [I] 72 H5
Gorjão [P] 86 D4
Gørlev [DK] 156 F3
Gorlice [PL] 52 C5
Görlitz [D] 34 G6
Gormanston Castle [IRL] 2 F5
Gormund [CH] 58 F5
Gorna Beshovica [BG] 146 G3
Gorna Cerovene [BG] 146 F3
Gorna Dikanja [BG] 146 F5
Gorna Kremena [BG] 146 G3
Gorna Mitropoliya [BG] 148 A3
Gorna Oryakhovitsa [BG]
148 C3
Gorna Studena [BG] 148 C3
Gornij [HR] 112 H4
Gorni Tsibur [BG] 146 F2
Gornja Grabovica [BIH] 144 C2
Gornjak, Manastir- [SRB]
146 C1
Gornja Klina [KS] 146 B5
Gornja Ploča [HR] 112 G4
Gornja Radgona [SLO] 74 E3
Gornja Šabanta [SRB] 146 C2
Gornja Toponica [SRB] 146 D3
Gornja Tuzla [BIH] 142 E3
Gornja-Vrijeska [HR] 74 G6
Gornji Lapac [HR] 112 H4
Gornji Milanovac [SRB] 146 B2
Gornji Podgradci [BIH] 142 B2
Gornji Ravno [BIH] 144 B1
Górno [PL] 52 C1
Gorno Alexandrovo [BG]
148 E4
Gorno Novo Selo [BG] 148 C5
Gorno Yabălkovo [BG] 148 E5
Gorobinci [MK] 128 F1
Gorodets [RUS] 198 H2
Gorodno [RUS] 198 H3
Górowo Iławeckie [PL] 22 G2
Gorreana [P] 100 E3
Gorredijk [NL] 16 F2
Gorron [F] 26 E5
Gørslev [DK] 156 G3
Gort [IRL] 2 C5
Górtys [GR] 136 D2
Górtys [GR] 140 F5
Görükle [TR] 150 E4
Gorv [N] 180 B5
Görvik [S] 184 C1
Gorzanów [PL] 50 C3
Görzke [D] 34 C3
Gorzkowice [PL] 36 G6
Gorzków-Osada [PL] 38 F6
Górzna [PL] 22 B5
Górzno [PL] 22 F6
Górzno [PL] 36 E4
Gorzów Śląski [PL] 50 F1
Gorzów Wielkopolski [PL]
34 H2
Górzyca [PL] 34 G2
Gorzyce [PL] 52 D2
Gorzyń [PL] 36 B2
Goržžam [N] 194 D3
Gosaldo [I] 72 E4
Gosau [A] 60 H6
Göschenen [CH] 70 F1
Gościno [PL] 20 G3
Gosdorf [A] 74 E3
Goslar [D] 32 G3
Goślice [PL] 36 H2
Gósol [E] 92 D2
Gospari [LV] 198 F6
Gospić [HR] 112 G4
Gosport [GB] 12 H5
Gossau [CH] 58 H5
Gosselies [B] 30 C5
Gossensass / Colle Isarco
[I] 72 D2
Gössl [A] 62 B6
Gössweinstein [D] 46 G4
Gostilicy [RUS] 178 G5
Gostitsy [RUS] 198 G1
Gostivar [MK] 128 D1
Gostków [PL] 36 F4
Göstling [A] 62 C5
Gostomia [PL] 22 A5
Gostun [SRB] 146 A4
Gostycyn [PL] 22 C5
Gostyń [PL] 36 C4
Gostynin [PL] 36 G2
Goszcz [PL] 36 D5
Goszczanowo [PL] 36 A2
Göteborg [S] 160 G2
Götene [S] 166 E5
Gotenica [SLO] 74 C6
Gotha [D] 32 H6
Gothem [S] 168 G4
Götlunda [S] 168 A3
Gotse Delchev [BG] 130 C1
Gottböle [FIN] 186 A4
Gottby [FIN] 176 A5
Gotthard Tunnel [CH] 70 F2
Göttingen [D] 32 F4
Gottne [S] 184 G1
Gottolengo [I] 110 D1
Gottröra [S] 168 E2
Göttweig [A] 62 D4
Götzis [A] 58 H5
Gouarec [F] 26 A5
Gouda [NL] 16 D5
Goules, Col des- [F] 68 C2
Goulven [F] 40 B1
Gouménissa [GR] 128 G3
Goumois [CH] 58 C5
Gourdon [F] 66 G4
Gourin [F] 40 C3
Gournay-en-Bray [F] 28 C5
Goúrnes [GR] 140 E4
Gourniá [GR] 140 G5
Gourville [F] 54 D6
Gout-Rossignol [F] 66 E2
Gouveia [P] 80 D6
Goúves [GR] 140 F4
Gouvets [F] 26 E4
Gouviá [GR] 132 B2
Gouzon [F] 56 B6
Govedartsi [BG] 146 G6
Govedjari [HR] 144 B3
Gøvstdal [N] 170 F5
Goworowo [PL] 24 C6
Gowran [IRL] 4 F4
Göynükbelen [TR] 150 F5
Gózd [PL] 38 C5
Gozdnica [PL] 34 H5
Gózd-Zaszosie [PL] 52 B1
Gözler [TR] 152 G4
Graal-Müritz [D] 20 B2
Grab [BIH] 144 D4
Grab [PL] 36 D4
Grabarka [PL] 38 E2
Grabaț [RO] 76 F5
Graberje [HR] 142 A1
Gråbo [S] 160 H2
Gråborg [S] 162 G5
Grabovac [SRB] 146 C1
Grabow [D] 20 A5
Grabów [PL] 36 F3
Grabowiec [PL] 52 G1
Grabówka [PL] 24 F5
Grabów nad Prosną [PL] 36 E5
Grabownica Starzeńska [PL]
52 E4
Grabowskie [PL] 24 D5
Gračac [HR] 112 H4
Gračanica [BIH] 142 D3
Gračanica [KS] 146 C5
Gračanica [SRB] 142 F4
Graçay [F] 54 H3
Grächen [CH] 70 E2
Gračišće [HR] 112 D2
Gradac [BIH] 144 C3
Gradac [HR] 144 B3
Gradac [MNE] 144 E2
Gradac [MNE] 144 E4
Gradac, Manastir- [SRB]
146 B3
Gradačac [BIH] 142 D2
Graddis [N] 190 F1
Gräddö [S] 168 F2
Gradec [BG] 146 E2
Gradec Prokupski [HR] 112 H1
Gradefes [E] 82 C4
Graderas, Cueva de las- [E]
90 E6
Gradešnika [MK] 128 F3
Gradets [BG] 148 D4
Gradignan [F] 66 C3
Gradin [SLO] 112 D1
Gradina [HR] 112 F3
Gradina [SRB] 146 E4
Gradinarovo [BG] 148 E3
Gradisca d'Isonzo [I] 72 H5
Gradishte [BG] 148 B3
Gradište [HR] 142 E2
Gradište [SRB] 146 E3
Gradki [PL] 22 H3
Grado [E] 78 G3
Grado [I] 72 G6
Gradówek [PL] 34 H6
Gradsko [MK] 128 F2
Græsted [DK] 156 G1
Grafenau [D] 60 H2
Gräfenberg [D] 46 G4
Grafenegg [A] 62 E4
Gräfenhainichen [D] 34 C4
Grafenwöhr [D] 48 B4
Grafenwörth [A] 62 E4
Grafing [D] 60 E4
Grafrath [D] 60 D4
Gräfsnäs [S] 160 H1
Graglia, Santuário di- [I] 70 E4
Gragnano [I] 120 E3
Gråhaugen [N] 180 G2
Grahovo [MNE] 144 D4
Grahovo [SLO] 74 B6
Graiguenamanagh [IRL] 4 F4
Grainetière, Abbaye de la- [F]
54 C3
Graja, Cueva de la- [E] 102 E2
Grajewo [PL] 24 D4
Gralhos [P] 80 D3
Gralla [A] 74 D3
Grallagh [IRL] 2 D4
Gram [DK] 156 B3
Gramada [BG] 146 E2
Gramat [F] 66 G4
Gramatikovo [BG] 148 F5
Grambow [D] 20 E5
Grametten [A] 62 D2
Gramkow [D] 20 A3
Grammatikó [GR] 132 G3
Gramméni Oxyá [GR] 132 F4
Gramméno [GR] 132 C2
Grammichele [I] 126 F4
Gramsh [AL] 128 C4
Gram Slot [DK] 156 B3
Gramzda [LV] 198 B6
Gramzow [D] 20 D6
Gramzow [D] 20 E5
Gran [N] 172 B4
Granåbron [S] 172 F5
Granada [E] 102 E4
Granadilla de Abona [E] 100 B5
Granard [IRL] 2 E4
Granarolo dell'Emilia [I] 110 F3
Granåsen [S] 190 F5
Granátula de Calatrava [E]
96 F4
Granberget [S] 190 F5
Granboda [FIN] 176 B6
Grancey-le-Château [F] 56 G3
Grandas de Salime [E] 78 F3
Grandcamp-Maisy [F] 26 E2
Grand-Champ [F] 26 A6
Grand Chartreuse, Couvent de
la- [F] 68 H4
Grande-Fougeray [F] 40 F5
Grandjouan [F] 40 F5
Grândola [P] 94 C2
Grandpré [F] 44 C3
Grandrieu [F] 68 D5
Grand Roc [F] 66 F3
Grand-Rozoy [F] 42 H3
Grandson [CH] 58 C6
Grand-St-Bernard, Col du-
[CH/I] 70 C3
Grand-St-Bernard, Tunnel du-
[CH/I] 70 C3
Grandvilliers [F] 28 D5
Grañén [E] 90 F3
Grangärde [S] 172 H5
Grange [IRL] 2 D3
Grange-Bleneau, Château de
la- [F] 42 G4
Grange-le-Bocage [F] 42 H5
Grängesberg [S] 172 H6
Granges-sur-Vologne [F] 58 D2
Grängsjö [S] 184 E5
Granhult [S] 192 H6
Graninge [S] 184 E2
Granitola Torretta [I] 126 B3
Granitz, Jagdschloss- [D] 20 E2
Granja [P] 80 B4
Granja [P] 94 E3
Granja de Moreruela [E] 80 H4
Granja de Torrehermosa [E]
96 B5
Grankulla / Kauniainen [FIN]
176 H5
Grankullavik [S] 162 H3
Granlunda [S] 168 C1
Gränna [S] 162 D1
Grannäs [S] 190 F3
Granne [PL] 38 E2
Grannes [N] 190 E3
Gränningen [S] 184 C2
Granö [S] 190 H5
Granollers [E] 92 E4
Granowo [PL] 36 C3
Gransee [D] 20 D6
Gränsgård [S] 190 G3
Gransherad [N] 164 F1
Gransjö [S] 196 A2
Granssjön [S] 166 D2
Gran Tarajal [E] 100 E6
Grantham [GB] 10 F6
Grantown-on-Spey [GB] 6 E5
Granträsk [S] 190 G5
Granvik [S] 166 G5
Granvika [N] 182 C5
Granville [F] 26 D4
Granvin [N] 170 C3
Granvollen [N] 172 B4
Grao / el Grau [E] 98 F6
Grasbakken [N] 194 E2
Gräsberg [S] 172 H5
Graševo [BG] 148 A6
Grašišće [SLO] 72 H6
Gräsmark [S] 166 E1
Gräsmyr [S] 190 H6
Gräso [S] 174 F5
Gräsö [S] 174 G5
Grassac [F] 66 F1
Grassano [I] 122 C4
Grassau [D] 60 F5
Grasse [F] 108 E4
Grässjön [S] 184 C3
Gråsten [DK] 156 C4
Grästorp [S] 166 D6
Gratangen [N] 192 F4
Gråtanliden [S] 190 F4
Gratkorn [A] 74 D2
Gråträsk [S] 190 H3
Graulhet [F] 106 B3
Graun im Vinschgau / Curon
Venosta [I] 72 B2
Graus [E] 90 H3
Grava [S] 166 E2
Grávalos [E] 84 A5
Gravberget [N] 172 D3
Gravdal [N] 164 B4
Gravdal [N] 192 C4
Grave [NL] 16 E6
Gravedona [I] 70 G3
Gravelines [F] 14 H6
Gravellona Toce [I] 70 F3
Gravens [DK] 156 C2
Gravesend [GB] 14 F4
Gravhaug [N] 180 C5
Graviá [GR] 132 G4
Gravina in Púglia [I] 122 D3
Gravítsa [GR] 132 E3
Gravmark [S] 196 A5
Gravoúna [GR] 130 E3
Gray [F] 58 A4
Grayan-et-Hôpital [F] 54 B6
Graz [A] 74 D2
Grazalema [E] 100 H4
Gražiškiai [LT] 24 E2
Grazzanise [I] 120 D2
Grazzano Visconti [I] 110 C2
Grčak [SRB] 146 C3
Grčarice [SLO] 74 C6
Grdelica [SRB] 146 D4
Greaca [RO] 148 D1
Greaker [N] 164 H2
Great Dunmow [GB] 14 F3
Great Malvern [GB] 12 G2
Great Torrington [GB] 12 D3
Great Yarmouth [GB] 14 H2
Grebbestad [S] 166 B4
Grebenhain [D] 46 D2
Grebenstein [D] 32 F5
Grębkowo [PL] 38 D3
Grębocin [PL] 22 E6
Greding [D] 46 G6
Greencastle [NIR] 2 F5
Greenock [GB] 8 D3
Greetsiel [D] 16 H1
Gregolímano [GR] 132 H4
Greifenburg [A] 72 G3
Greiffenberg [D] 20 E6
Greifswald [D] 20 D3
Greillenstein [A] 62 D3
Grein [A] 62 C4
Greiz [D] 48 C2
Grenaa [DK] 160 F5
Grenade [F] 66 C6
Grenade [F] 84 H2
Grenchen [CH] 58 D5
Grenctale [LV] 198 E6
Grenoble [F] 68 H4
Grense-Jakobselv [N] 194 F3
Grenzland-Turm [CZ] 48 C4
Gréolierès [F] 108 E4
Gréoux-les-Bains [F] 108 C4
Gressoney-la-Trinité [I] 70 E3
Gressoney-St-Jean [I] 70 E4
Gresten [A] 62 D5
Gretna Green [GB] 8 E5
Grettstadt [D] 46 F3
Greussen [D] 32 H5
Greux [F] 44 D6
Grevbäck [S] 166 G6
Greve in Chianti [I] 110 F6
Greven [D] 32 C2
Grevená [GR] 128 E6
Grevenbroich [D] 30 G4
Grevenbrück [D] 32 C5
Grevenmacher [L] 44 F2
Grevesmühlen [D] 18 H3
Greve Strand [DK] 156 G3
Greyabbey [NIR] 2 H4
Greystones [IRL] 4 G3
Grez-en-Bouère [F] 40 H5
Grezzana [I] 72 C6
Grianan of Aileach [IRL] 2 F2
Gries-am-Brenner [A] 72 D2
Griesbach [D] 60 H3
Gries in Sellrain [A] 72 D1
Grieskirchen [A] 62 A4
Griffen [A] 74 C3
Grignan [F] 106 H2
Grignols [F] 66 D5
Grigoriopol [UA] 204 E3
Grillby [S] 168 C2
Grimaldi [I] 124 D5
Grimaud [F] 108 D5
Grimdalen [N] 164 E2
Grimma [D] 34 D6
Grimmen [D] 20 D3
Grimo [N] 170 C4
Grimsås [S] 162 C3
Grimsbu [N] 180 H5
Grimsby [GB] 10 G4
Grimsdalshytta [N] 180 H5
Grimslöv [S] 162 D5
Grímsstaðir [IS] 192 C2
Grimstad [N] 164 E5
Grindaheim [N] 170 F2
Grindal [N] 180 H2
Grindavík [IS] 192 A3
Grindelwald [CH] 70 E1
Grindjorda [N] 192 E4
Grindsted [DK] 156 B2
Grinkiškis [LT] 200 F4
Griñón [E] 88 F6
Grinzane Cavour [I] 108 G2
Gripenberg [S] 162 E1
Gripenberg [S] 162 E1
Grisignano di Zocco [I] 72 D6
Grisolles [F] 84 H2
Grisslehamn [S] 174 G6
Grisvåg [N] 180 F1
Grivitsa [BG] 148 B3
Grizáno [GR] 132 F2
Grižkabūdis [LT] 200 E5
Grøa [N] 180 G3
Gröbers [D] 34 C5
Grobina [LV] 198 B6
Gröbming [A] 74 B1
Grocka [SRB] 142 H3
Gródek [PL] 24 F5
Gródek [PL] 38 G1
Gródek nad Dunajcem [PL]
52 C4
Gröditz [D] 34 E5
Gródki [PL] 52 F1
Grodków [PL] 50 D2
Grodno [PL] 50 B2
Grodzeń [PL] 36 G1
Grodziec [PL] 36 A6
Grodziec [PL] 50 F4
Grodzisk Mazowiecki [PL] 38 B3
Grodzisk Wielkopolski [PL]
36 B3
Groenlo [NL] 16 G5
Groix [F] 40 C4
Grojdibodu [RO] 148 A2
Grójec [PL] 36 D3
Grójec [PL] 38 B4
Grömitz [D] 18 H3
Gromnik [PL] 52 C4
Gromo [I] 72 A4
Gromovo [RUS] 178 G2
Gromovo [RUS] 200 D5
Grøna [N] 180 F5
Gronau [D] 16 G5
Gronau [D] 32 F3
Grönbo [S] 196 A4
Grønbua [N] 180 F6
Grøndal [N] 180 B5
Grong [N] 190 C5
Grönhögen [S] 158 G1
Grønhøj [DK] 160 C5
Gröningen [D] 34 A3
Groningen [NL] 16 G2
Grønnes [N] 180 E3
Grönskåra [S] 162 F4
Grönsö [S] 168 C2
Gropen [S] 166 G3
Grósio [I] 72 B4
Grossarl [A] 72 G1
Grossbeeren [D] 34 E2
Grossbreitenbach [D] 46 G2
Grossburgwedel [D] 32 G2
Grossenbrode [D] 18 H2
Grossenhain [D] 34 E5
Grossenkneten [D] 18 C6
Grossenzersdorf [A] 62 F4
Grosseto [I] 114 F3
Gross-Gerau [D] 46 C3
Gross-Gerungs [A] 62 C3
Grossglobniz [A] 62 D3
Grosshabersdorf [D] 46 F5
Grossharras [A] 62 F3
Grosshöchstetten [CH] 58 E6
Gross Mohrdorf [D] 20 C2
Gross Oesingen [D] 32 H1
Gross-Pertenschlag [A] 62 C4
Gross-Pertholz [A] 62 C3
Grosspetersdorf [A] 74 F2
Grossraming [A] 62 C5
Gross Räschen [D] 34 F5
Gross Schönebeck [D] 34 E1
Gross-Siegharts [A] 62 D3
Gross-Umstadt [D] 46 D3
Grosswoltersdorf [D] 20 C6
Grostenquin [F] 44 F4
Grosuplje [SLO] 74 C5
Grøtavær [N] 192 E3
Grötholen [S] 182 E6
Grotli [N] 180 E5
Grotnes [S] 170 C4
Grottaglie [I] 122 F4
Grottaminarda [I] 120 F2
Grottammare [I] 116 D2
Grotteria [I] 124 D7
Grouw [NL] 16 F2
Grova [N] 164 F3
Grövelsjön [S] 182 D5
Grovfjord [N] 192 E4
Grozďovo [BG] 148 F3
Grožnjan [HR] 112 D1
Gr. Strömkendorf [D] 20 A3
Grua [N] 172 B5
Grubben [N] 190 E3
Grube [D] 18 H2
Grubišno Polje [HR] 74 G6
Gruda [HR] 144 D4
Grude [BIH] 144 B2
Grude [S] 162 B1
Grudusk [PL] 22 H6
Grudziądz [PL] 22 E5
Gruemirë [AL] 144 E5
Gruia [RO] 146 E1
Gruibingen [D] 60 B3
Gruissan [F] 106 D5
Grumentum [I] 120 H5
Grums [S] 166 E3
Grünau [A] 62 B5
Grünberg [D] 46 D1
Grünburg [A] 62 B5
Grundfors [S] 190 E4
Grundforsen [S] 172 E2
Grundlsee [A] 62 A6
Grundsel [S] 190 H3
Grundsjö [S] 190 F5
Grundsjö [S] 190 F4
Grundsjön [S] 184 C5
Grundsund [S] 166 C6
Grundsunda [S] 184 H2
Grundtjärn [S] 184 E1
Grünenplan [D] 32 F3
Grungedal [N] 164 E1
Grünheide [D] 34 F2
Grünhof [D] 20 E4
Grünstadt [D] 46 B4
Grunwald [PL] 22 G5
Grupčin [MK] 128 D1
Grüsch [CH] 58 H6
Gruškovje [SLO] 74 E4
Gruvberget [S] 174 D3
Gruyères [CH] 70 C1
Gruža [SRB] 146 B2
Gruzdžiai [LT] 200 E3
Grybów [PL] 52 C5
Grycksbo [S] 172 H4
Gryfice [PL] 20 G4
Gryfino [PL] 20 F5
Gryfów Śląski [PL] 48 H1
Grykë [AL] 128 A4
Gryllefjord [N] 192 E2
Grymyr [N] 170 H5
Gryneion [TR] 152 C3
Gryt [S] 168 C4
Gryt [S] 168 C6
Grytgöl [S] 166 H4
Grythyttan [S] 166 G2
Grytsjö [S] 190 E4
Grytstorp [S] 166 H5
Gryzy [PL] 24 D3
Grzmiąca [PL] 22 A4
Grzybno [PL] 22 F5
Gschnitz [A] 72 D2
Gschöder [A] 62 D6
Gschwend [D] 46 E6
Gstaad [CH] 70 D2
Gstadt [D] 60 F5
Guadahortuna [E] 102 E3
Guadajoz [E] 94 H6
Guadalajara [E] 88 G5
Guadalcanal [E] 94 H4
Guadalcázar [E] 102 B1
Guadalerzas [E] 96 F3
Guadalest [E] 104 E2
Guadalmez [E] 96 C4
Guadalmina [E] 102 A5
Guadalupe [E] 96 C2
Guadalupe, Monasterio de- [E]
96 C2
Guadalupe, Santuario de- [E]
102 F1
Guadamur [E] 96 E2
Guadarrama [E] 88 F5
Guadix [E] 102 F4
Guagno [F] 114 B4
Gualdo Cattáneo [I] 116 A2
Gualdo Tadino [I] 116 B2
Guarcino [I] 116 C6
Guarda [CH] 72 B2
Guarda [P] 86 G2
Guardamar del Segura [E]
104 D3
Guardavalle [I] 124 D6
Guardiagrele [I] 116 D5
Guardialfiera [I] 116 E6
Guardia Lombardi [I] 120 F3
Guardia Piemontese [I] 124 C4
Guardia Sanframondi [I] 120 E2
Guardias Viejas [E] 102 F5
Guardo [E] 82 C4
Guareña [E] 94 H2
Guarromán [E] 96 E6
Guasila [I] 118 C6
Guastalla [I] 110 E2
Guazzora [I] 70 F6
Gubanitsy [RUS] 178 G6
Gubbhägen [S] 190 E5
Gúbbio [I] 116 A1
Gubbmyran [S] 172 E2
Gubbträsk [S] 190 G4
Guben [D] 34 G4
Guber [BIH] 144 B1
Guberevac [SRB] 146 B2
Gubin [PL] 34 G4
Guča [SRB] 146 B2
Gücenoluk [TR] 152 H1
Gudavac [BIH] 142 A2
Guddal [N] 170 B1
Guderup [DK] 156 C4
Gudhjem [DK] 158 E4
Gudow [D] 18 G4
Gudvangen [N] 170 D2
Guebwiller [F] 58 D3
Güéjar Sierra [E] 102 E4
Guémené-Penfao [F] 40 F5
Guémené-sur-Scorff [F] 40 D3
Guenange [F] 44 F3
Guer [F] 26 B6
Guérande [F] 40 D6
Guéret [F] 54 H6
Guérigny [F] 56 D4
Guethary [F] 84 C2
Gueugnon [F] 56 E5
Güglingen [D] 46 C6
Guglionesi [I] 116 F5
Gugny [PL] 24 E5
Guía de Isora [E] 100 B5
Guichen [F] 26 C6
Guidonia [I] 116 A5
Guíglia [I] 110 E3
Guignes [F] 42 G4
Guijuelo [E] 88 C4
Guildford [GB] 14 D4
Guillaumes [F] 108 E3
Guillena [E] 94 G5
Guillestre [F] 108 E2
Guils [E] 92 D1
Guilvinec [F] 40 B3
Güimar [E] 100 C5
Guimarães [P] 80 C3
Guimerà [E] 92 C3
Guimiliau [F] 40 C2
Guincho [P] 86 A5
Guînes [F] 14 G6
Guingamp [F] 26 A4
Guipry [F] 40 F4
Guísamo [E] 78 D2
Guisborough [GB] 10 G2
Guise [F] 28 G5
Guissény [F] 40 B1
Guissona [E] 92 C3
Guitalens [F] 106 B3
Guitiriz [E] 78 D2
Guîtres [F] 66 D3
Gujan-Mestras [F] 66 B3
Gükçeyazı [TR] 152 D1
Gulbene [LV] 198 F4
Guldborg [DK] 156 F5
Gülec [TR] 150 C5
Gulgofjorden [N] 194 D1
Gulla [N] 180 G2
Gullabo [S] 162 F6
Gullaskruv [S] 162 F4
Gullbrå [N] 170 C2
Gulleråsen [S] 172 H3
Gullfoss [IS] 192 B3
Gullhaug [N] 164 H2
Gullringen [S] 162 F2
Gullsby [S] 172 E6
Gullspång [S] 166 F4
Gullstein [N] 180 F1
Güllü [TR] 152 F4
Güllüce [TR] 150 E5
Güllük [TR] 154 C1
Gülpınar [TR] 134 G1
Gulsele [S] 190 F6
Gulsrud [N] 170 H5
Gulsvik [N] 170 G4
Gülübintsi [BG] 148 D5
Gülübovo [BG] 148 D5
Gulyantsi [BG] 148 B2
Gumboda [S] 196 A5
Gumhöjden [S] 166 F1
Gumiel de Hizán [E] 88 G2
Gumlösa [S] 158 D1
Gummersbach [D] 32 C5
Gumpoldskirchen [A] 62 F5
Gumtow [D] 20 B6
Gümüldür [TR] 152 C5
Gümüşpınar [TR] 150 D2
Gümüşsu [TR] 152 H4
Gümüşsuyu [TR] 150 D3
Gümüşyeni [TR] 150 G5
Gümzovo [BG] 146 E2
Gundelfingen [D] 60 C3
Gundelsheim [D] 46 D5
Güneşli [TR] 152 E2
Güney [TR] 152 F4
Güney [TR] 152 G5
Güneyköy [TR] 152 F2
Güngör (Koutsovéntis) [CY]
154 G5
Gunja [HR] 142 E2
Günlüce [TR] 152 F1
Gunnarn [S] 190 G4
Gunnarp [S] 162 B4

Gunnarsbyn [S] 196 B2
Gunnarskog [S] 166 D1
Gunnarskulla [FIN] 176 G5
Gunnarvattnet [S] 190 E5
Gunnebo [S] 162 G2
Gunnilbo [S] 168 B2
Gunten [CH] 70 E1
Güntersberge [D] 32 H4
Guntersblum [D] 46 C4
Guntersdorf [A] 62 E3
Guntertshausen [A] 60 G4
Guntín [E] 78 D3
Günzburg [D] 60 C3
Gunzenhausen [D] 46 F6
Gurçeşme [TR] 150 C5
Gurcz [PL] 22 C4
Güre [TR] 152 F3
Güre [TR] 152 H3
Güreci [TR] 150 B5
Gurgazu [F] 114 B6
Gurk [A] 74 B2
Gurkovo [BG] 148 C4
Gurlevo [RUS] 178 F6
Gürpinar [TR] 150 E3
Gurrea de Gállego [E] 90 F3
Gürsu [TR] 150 F4
Gurtnellen [CH] 70 F1
Gušće [HR] 142 B1
Gusev [RUS] 24 D1
Gusinje [MNE] 146 A5
Gusmar [AL] 128 B6
Gúspini [I] 118 C6
Gusselby [S] 166 H2
Güssing [A] 74 F2
Gusswerk [A] 62 D6
Gustavfors [S] 172 F5
Gustavs / Kustavi [FIN] 176 C4
Gustavsberg [S] 168 E3
Gustavsberg [S] 190 H4
Gustavsfors [S] 166 D3
Güstrow [D] 20 B4
Gusum [S] 168 B6
Gusvattnet [S] 190 E5
Guta [BY] 202 D6
Gutcher [GB] 6 H3
Gutenstein [A] 62 E5
Gütersloh [D] 32 D3
Gutštejn [CZ] 48 D4
Guttannen [CH] 70 F1
Guttormsgard [S] 170 F4
Gützkow [D] 20 D3
Güvercinlik [TR] 154 C1
Güzelbahçe [TR] 152 C4
Güzelpinar [TR] 152 G4
Güzelyalı (Vavylás) [CY] 154 F5
Güzelyurt (Mórfou) [CY] 154 F5
Guzet-Neige [F] 84 H5
Gvardeiskoye [RUS] 22 H2
Gvardeysk [RUS] 24 B1
Gvarv [N] 164 F2
Gvozd [HR] 112 H1
Gvozd [MNE] 144 E3
Gwatt [CH] 70 D1
Gwda Wielka [PL] 22 B4
Gy [F] 58 B4
Gya [N] 164 B4
Gyarmat [H] 74 H1
Gyermely [H] 64 B6
Gyl [N] 180 F2
Gylien [S] 194 B8
Gylling [DK] 156 D2
Gýmeš [SK] 64 B4
Gymnó [GR] 134 C5
Gyomaendrőd [H] 76 F2
Gyömrő [H] 76 D1
Gyöngyös [H] 64 E5
Gyöngyöspata [H] 64 D5
Gyönk [H] 76 B3
Győr [H] 62 H6
Gysinge [S] 174 E6
Gýtheio [GR] 136 E4
Gyttorp [S] 166 G2
Gyueshevo [BG] 146 E6
Gyula [H] 76 G3
Gyulaj [H] 76 B4
Gzy [PL] 38 B1

H

Häädemeeste [EST] 198 D3
Haag [A] 62 C4
Haag [D] 60 F4
Haag am Hausruck [A] 62 A4
Haaksbergen [NL] 16 G5
Haapajärvi [FIN] 196 D6
Haapajoki [FIN] 196 C4
Haapa-Kimola [FIN] 178 B3
Haapakylä [FIN] 188 C3
Haapala [FIN] 196 D3
Haapamäki [FIN] 186 E4
Haapamäki [FIN] 188 D1
Haapamäki [FIN] 188 D3
Haapamäki [FIN] 196 E6
Haapasalmi [FIN] 188 F4
Haapavesi [FIN] 196 D5
Haapsalu [EST] 198 D2
Haar [D] 60 E4
Haarajoki [FIN] 176 H4
Haarajoki [FIN] 186 H5
Haarala [FIN] 186 G2
Haaraoja [FIN] 196 D4
Haarby [DK] 156 D3
Haaren [D] 32 E4
Haarlem [NL] 16 D4
Haavisto [FIN] 186 F5
Habartice [CZ] 48 G1
Habas [F] 84 D2
Habay [B] 44 E2
Habernau [A] 62 B5
Hablingbo [S] 168 F5
Habo [S] 162 D2
Håbol [S] 166 D4
Habry [CZ] 48 H4
Håby [S] 166 C5
Hachdorf [D] 58 G2
Hachenburg [D] 46 B1
Hachmühlen [D] 32 F2
Hacıdanişment [TR] 150 B1
Hacısungur [TR] 150 B3
Hackås [S] 182 G3
Häckeberga [S] 158 C3
Hacketstown [IRL] 4 F4
Hacksjö [S] 190 G5
Håcksvik [S] 162 B3
Hadamar [D] 46 B2
Hädanberg [S] 184 F1
Haddington [GB] 8 F3
Haderslev [DK] 156 C3
Haderup [DK] 160 C5
Hadiach [UA] 202 F7
Hadım [TR] 152 G4
Hadleigh [GB] 14 G3
Hadmersleben [D] 34 B3
Hadrian's Wall [GB] 8 F5
Hadsten [DK] 160 D6
Hadsund [DK] 160 E4
Hadzhidimitrovo [BG] 148 C2
Hadzhidimovo [BG] 130 C2
Hadžići [BIH] 144 C1
Hægeland [N] 164 D5
Hærland [N] 166 C2
Hafling / Avelengo [I] 72 D3
Hafsmo [N] 180 G1
Haftorsbygget [S] 172 F1
Haga [N] 172 C5
Hagafoss [N] 170 F3
Hagby [S] 162 F5
Hagby [S] 168 D2
Hagebro [DK] 160 C5
Hagen [D] 18 D4
Hagen [D] 32 C4
Hagenberg [A] 62 C4
Hagenburg [D] 32 F2
Hagenow [D] 18 H5
Hageri [EST] 198 D2
Hagetmau [F] 84 E2
Hagfors [S] 172 F6
Häggås [S] 190 F5
Häggemåla [S] 162 G4
Häggenås [S] 182 H1
Häggsåsen [S] 182 G2
Häggsjöbränna [S] 182 E1
Häggsjömon [S] 190 G5
Häggsjövik [S] 190 E6
Haglebu [N] 170 G4
Hagondange [F] 44 E4
Haguenau [F] 44 H5
Håhellarhytta [N] 164 D3
Hahn [D] 18 C4
Hahnbach [D] 46 H5
Hahót [H] 74 G3
Haibach ob der Donau [A] 62 B4
Haid [A] 62 B4
Haidmuhle [D] 62 A3
Haiger [D] 32 D6
Haigerloch [D] 58 G2
Häijää [FIN] 176 E1
Hailsham [GB] 14 E6
Hailuoto / Karlö [FIN] 196 D4
Haina [D] 32 E6
Hainburg [A] 62 G4
Hainfeld [A] 62 E5
Hainichen [D] 48 D1
Hainsbach [D] 60 F2
Haithabu [D] 18 F1
Hajdúböszörmény [H] 64 G6
Hajdúdorog [H] 64 G5
Hajdúhadház [H] 64 H5
Hajdúnánás [H] 64 G5
Hajdúsámson [H] 64 H6
Hajdúszoboszló [H] 64 G6
Hajdúszovát [H] 76 G1
Hajdúvid [H] 64 G6
Hajerdin [BG] 146 G3
Hajnówka [PL] 38 F1
Hajós [H] 76 C4
Håkafot [S] 190 E5
Håkenby [N] 166 C3
Hakkas [S] 194 A7
Hakkenpää [FIN] 176 D1
Häkkilä [FIN] 186 F3
Häkkiskylä [FIN] 186 F5
Hakkstabben [N] 194 B2
Hakokylä [FIN] 196 F4
Håksberg [S] 172 H5
Hakuni [FIN] 186 C4
Håkvika [N] 192 E4
Halaç [TR] 154 H3
Hålaforsen [S] 184 E1
Halámky [CZ] 62 C2
Hala Sultan Tekkesi [CY] 154 G5
Halásztelek [H] 76 C1
Halberstadt [D] 34 A3
Hald [DK] 160 E5
Halden [N] 166 C3
Haldensee [A] 60 C6
Haldensleben [D] 34 B2
Halenkov [CZ] 50 E6
Halesworth [GB] 14 G3
Håle-Täng [S] 166 D5
Hälgö [S] 168 C4
Halhjem [N] 170 B4
Halič [SK] 64 D4
Halich [UA] 204 C2
Halifax [GB] 10 E4
Halikarnassos [TR] 154 B2
Halikko [FIN] 176 E4
Halitpaşa [TR] 152 D3
Haljala [EST] 198 E1
Halk [DK] 156 C3
Halkivaha [FIN] 176 E2
Halkosaari [FIN] 186 C3
Hälla [S] 190 F6
Hallabro [S] 162 E6
Hallaçli [TR] 150 D2
Hallandsfossen [N] 164 D3
Hallapuro [FIN] 186 E2
Hallaryd [S] 162 C6
Hällbacken [S] 190 F2
Hällbo [S] 174 D2
Halle [B] 28 H3
Halle [D] 32 D3
Halle [D] 34 C5
Hälleberga [S] 162 F5
Hällefors [S] 166 G2
Hälleforsnäs [S] 168 B3
Hallein [A] 60 G6
Hallen [S] 182 G2
Hallenberg [D] 32 D5
Hallerud [S] 166 G4
Hällesjö [S] 184 D3
Hällestad [S] 166 H5
Hällevadsholm [S] 166 C5
Hälleviksstrand [S] 166 C6
Halli [FIN] 186 F5
Hallignicourt [F] 44 C5
Hallila [FIN] 178 B3
Hallingby [N] 170 H5
Hällingsåfallet [S] 190 E5
Hall in Tirol [A] 72 D1
Hällnäs [S] 174 F4
Hällnäs [S] 190 G2
Hällnäs [S] 190 H5
Hällristningar [S] 166 C4
Hallsberg [S] 166 H4
Hallshuk [S] 168 G3
Hällsjö [S] 184 F2
Hällsta [S] 168 B3
Hallstahammar [S] 168 B2
Hallstatt [A] 62 A6
Hallstavik [S] 168 E1
Halltorp [S] 162 F6
Halluin [F] 28 F2
Hällvik [S] 190 G2
Hallviken [S] 190 E6
Halmstad [S] 162 B5
Halna [S] 166 F5
Halne [N] 170 E4
Halne Fjellstue [N] 170 E4
Hals [DK] 160 E4
Hals [N] 180 F2
Halsa [N] 180 F2
Hal'shany [BY] 200 H6
Hålsjö [S] 184 E6
Halsskov [DK] 156 E3
Halstead [GB] 14 F3
Halsteren [NL] 16 C6
Halsua [FIN] 186 E1
Haltdalen [N] 182 C3
Haltern [D] 30 H2
Haltwhistle [GB] 8 F5
Haluna [FIN] 188 D1
Halvarsgårdarna [S] 172 H5
Halver [D] 32 C5
Ham [F] 28 F5
Hamallaj [AL] 128 A2
Hamamdere [TR] 152 F3
Hamamköy [TR] 152 E5
Hamar [N] 172 C3
Hambergen [D] 18 D5
Hamburg [D] 18 F4
Hamburgsund [S] 166 B5
Hambye, Abbaye de- [F] 26 D4
Hamdibey [TR] 150 C6
Hamdorf [D] 18 F2
Hämeenkyrö / Tavastkyro [FIN] 176 E1
Hämeenlinna / Tavastehus [FIN] 176 G3
Hämeler Wald [D] 32 G2
Hameln [D] 32 F3
Hämelschenburg [D] 32 F3
Hamersleben [D] 34 A3
Hamidiye [TR] 150 B3
Hamidiye [TR] 150 D1
Hamilton [GB] 8 D3
Hamina / Fredrikshamn [FIN] 178 D3
Hamingberg [N] 194 F1
Hamitli [TR] 150 B2
Hamlagrøosen [N] 170 C3
Hamm [D] 32 C3
Hammar [S] 166 G4
Hammarland [FIN] 176 A5
Hammarn [S] 166 G2
Hammarnäs [S] 182 G2
Hammarstrand [S] 184 D2
Hammarvika [N] 190 A6
Hammaslahti [FIN] 188 F3
Hammel [DK] 160 D6
Hammelburg [D] 46 E3
Hammer [N] 190 C5
Hammer [N] 190 C5
Hammerbach [D] 46 D2
Hammerdal [S] 182 H1
Hammerfest [N] 194 B2
Hammerhøj [DK] 160 D5
Hammershus [DK] 158 E4
Hamminkeln [D] 16 G6
Hamnbukt [N] 194 C3
Hamnes [N] 192 G2
Hamoir [B] 30 E5
Hampetorp [S] 168 A3
Hampovica [HR] 74 G5
Hamra [S] 172 H1
Hamrångefjärden [S] 174 E3
Hamre [N] 164 E5
Hamre [S] 174 D1
Hamremoen [N] 170 G5
Hams, Coves dels- [E] 104 F5
Hamula [FIN] 186 G2
Hamula [FIN] 188 C2
Hamzabey [TR] 150 C2
Hamzali [MK] 128 H2
Hamzići [BIH] 144 C2
Han [MNE] 144 D4
Hån [S] 166 C2
Hån [S] 172 G5
Hanasand [N] 164 B2
Hanaskog [S] 158 D1
Hanau [D] 46 D3
Hançalar [TR] 152 G4
Hănceşti [MD] 204 E3
Hancevichy [BY] 202 B6
Handegg [CH] 70 F1
Handeland [N] 164 C3
Handen [S] 168 E3
Handlová [SK] 64 B3
Handöl [S] 182 E2
Handsjö [S] 182 G4
Hanerau-Hademarschen [D] 18 E2
Hanestad [N] 182 C6
Hanftal [A] 62 F3
Hangaskylä [FIN] 186 B4
Hangö / Hanko [FIN] 176 E6
Hangvar [S] 168 G3
Hanhimaa [FIN] 194 C6
Han i Hotit [AL] 144 E4
Hank [NL] 16 D6
Hankamäki [FIN] 196 F6
Hankasalmi [FIN] 186 H4
Hanken [S] 166 G5
Hankensbüttel [D] 32 H1
Hanko / Hangö [FIN] 176 E6
Hanna [PL] 38 F4
Hannivirta [FIN] 188 E4
Hann-Münden [D] 32 F5
Hannover [D] 32 F2
Hannuit (Hannut) [B] 30 D4
Hannusranta [FIN] 196 F5
Hannut (Hannuit) [B] 30 D4
Hanoğlu [TR] 152 G3
Han Pijesak [BIH] 142 E4
Hanskühnenburg [D] 32 G4
Hansnes [N] 192 G1
Hanstedt [D] 18 F5
Hanstholm [DK] 160 C3
Han-sur-Lesse [B] 30 D6
Han-sur-Nied [F] 44 F4
Hantháza [H] 76 D2
Hanušovce [SK] 64 G2
Hanušovice [CZ] 50 C4
Haparanda [S] 196 C2
Häppälä [FIN] 186 H4
Hapträsk [S] 196 A2
Hara [EST] 198 D2
Härad [S] 168 C3
Haradok [BY] 202 C4
Harads [S] 196 A2
Häradsbäck [S] 162 D5
Haraneset [N] 190 C4
Haras du Pin [F] 26 F5
Harbergsdalen [S] 190 E4
Harbo [S] 174 E6
Harboøre [DK] 160 B4
Harburg [D] 18 F4
Harburg [D] 60 C2
Hardegg [A] 62 E3
Hardegsen [D] 32 F4
Hardelot-Plage [F] 28 D2
Hardemo [S] 166 H3
Hardenberg [NL] 16 G4
Harderwijk [NL] 16 E4
Hardeshøj [DK] 156 C4
Hardheim [D] 46 D4
Hardom [FIN] 178 B4
Hareid [N] 180 C3
Haren [D] 16 H3
Haren [NL] 16 G2
Harestua [N] 172 B5
Harfleur [F] 26 G3
Harg [S] 174 G5
Hargla [EST] 198 F4
Hargnies [F] 30 D6
Hargshamn [S] 174 G5
Harhala [FIN] 176 G2
Haría [E] 100 E5
Harivaara [FIN] 188 F1
Härjänvaara [FIN] 170 F5
Härjåsjön [S] 182 G6
Harjavalta [FIN] 176 D2
Harju [FIN] 196 E4
Harjula [FIN] 196 D3
Harjunmaa [FIN] 188 C5
Harjunsalmi [FIN] 186 F6
Harkány [H] 76 B5
Härkeberga [S] 168 C2
Härkmeri [FIN] 186 B5
Härkmyran [S] 194 A8
Härlec [BG] 146 G2
Harlech [GB] 10 B5
Härlev [DK] 156 G3
Harlingen [NL] 16 E2
Harlösa [S] 158 C2
Harlow [GB] 14 E4
Harmancık [TR] 150 F6
Harmandallar [TR] 152 F3
Harmanec [SK] 64 C3
Harmanecká Jaskyňa [SK] 64 C3
Harmånger [S] 184 E6
Harmanköy [TR] 150 H4
Härmänkylä [FIN] 196 F4
Härmänmäki [FIN] 196 F4
Harmelen [NL] 16 D5
Harndrup [DK] 156 D3
Härnösand [S] 184 F4
Haro [E] 82 G5
Harodz'ki [BY] 200 H6
Haroldswick [GB] 6 H3
Háromfa [H] 74 G5
Haroué [F] 44 E6
Harpefoss [N] 170 H1
Harpenden [GB] 14 E3
Harplinge [S] 162 B5
Harpstedt [D] 18 D6
Harrå [S] 192 G5
Harrachov [CZ] 48 H2
Harran [N] 190 D5
Harre [DK] 160 C4
Harrogate [GB] 10 F3
Harrsjöhöiden [S] 190 E5
Harrsjön [S] 190 E5
Harrström [FIN] 186 A3
Harsa [S] 174 D1
Härsängen [S] 166 D5
Harsefeld [D] 18 E4
Harsewinkel [D] 32 D3
Hârşova [RO] 204 E5
Harsprånget [S] 190 H1
Harstad [N] 192 E3
Harste [D] 32 F4
Harsum [D] 32 G2
Harsvik [N] 190 B5
Harta [H] 76 C3
Hartberg [A] 74 E1
Hartha [D] 34 D6
Hartland [GB] 12 D3
Hartlepool [GB] 10 G2
Hartmannshain [D] 46 D2
Hartola [FIN] 186 G6
Hårve [S] 184 C6
Harwich [GB] 14 G3
Harzgerode [D] 34 A4
Hasanağa [TR] 150 E6
Hasanbey [TR] 150 D5
Hasanpaşa [TR] 150 G5
Haselund [D] 18 E1
Haselünne [D] 18 B6
Håsjö [S] 184 D3
Hasköy [TR] 130 H3
Hasköy [TR] 150 B2
Hasköy [TR] 152 G3
Haslach [A] 62 B3
Haslach [D] 58 F2
Hasle [DK] 158 E4
Haslemden [N] 172 D4
Haslemere [GB] 14 D5
Haslev [DK] 156 G3
Hasparren [F] 84 C2
Haspe [D] 30 H3
Hasseki [TR] 134 H4
Hassel [D] 18 E6
Hassela [S] 184 E5
Hasselfelde [D] 32 H4
Hasselfors [S] 166 G4
Hasselt [B] 30 E4
Hasselt [NL] 16 F4
Hassfurt [D] 46 F3
Hassi [FIN] 186 F6
Hasslach [D] 46 H3
Hassle [S] 166 F4
Hassleben [D] 20 D5
Hässleholm [S] 158 D1
Hästbo [S] 174 D5
Hästbo [S] 174 E4
Hastersboda [FIN] 168 H1
Hästholmen [S] 166 G6
Hastiere-Lavaux [B] 30 D6
Hastings [GB] 14 F6
Hästveda [S] 158 D1
Hasvik [N] 194 A2
Hatě [CZ] 62 E3
Haţeg [RO] 204 C5
Hatfield [GB] 14 E3
Hatfjelldal [N] 190 E3
Hatıplar [TR] 152 D3
Hatsola [FIN] 188 D5
Hattem [NL] 16 F4
Hattingen [D] 30 H3
Hattonchâtel [F] 44 E4
Håttorp [S] 166 F4
Hattstedt [D] 18 E1
Hattula [FIN] 176 G2
Hattuvaara [FIN] 188 H1
Hattuvaara [FIN] 196 G6
Hatulanmäki [FIN] 196 E5
Hatvan [H] 64 D6
Hatvik [N] 170 B4
Haug [N] 170 E1
Haugan [N] 190 B6
Haugastøl [N] 170 E4
Haugbøen [N] 180 F3
Hauge [N] 164 B5
Haugesund [N] 164 A1
Hauggrend [N] 164 E2
Haughom [N] 164 C4
Haugsdorf [A] 62 E3
Haugsten [N] 170 G1
Hauho [FIN] 176 G2
Haukå [N] 180 B5
Haukedal [N] 170 C1
Haukeland [N] 170 B4
Haukeligrend [N] 164 D1
Haukeliseter [N] 170 D5
Haukilahti [FIN] 196 G4
Haukipudas [FIN] 196 D3
Haukivuori [FIN] 188 D5
Hauklappi [FIN] 188 E6
Haule [NL] 16 G2
Haunersdorf [D] 60 G3
Haunia [FIN] 176 D1
Haurida [S] 162 D2
Hausach [D] 58 F2
Hausen [D] 30 H5
Hausen [D] 46 E3
Hausen [D] 60 C4
Häusern [D] 58 F4
Hausham [D] 60 E5
Hausjärvi [FIN] 176 H3
Häusling [A] 62 D4
Hausmannstatten [A] 74 D2
Hautajärvi [FIN] 194 F7
Haut-Asco [F] 114 B3
Haut-Barr, Château du- [F] 44 G5
Hautecombe, Abbaye de- [F] 68 H3
Hautefort, Château de- [F] 66 G3
Haute-Nendaz [CH] 70 D2
Hauterive, Abbaye de- [CH] 58 D6
Hauteville-Lompnes [F] 68 H2
Hauteville Plage [F] 26 D3
Haut Kœnigsbourg [F] 58 D2
Hautmont [F] 28 G4
Hauzenberg [D] 62 A3
Havaj [SK] 52 D6
Havant [GB] 14 D5
Håvberget [S] 172 G5
Havdhem [S] 168 G5
Håvedalen [S] 166 C4
Havelange [B] 30 D5
Havelberg [D] 34 C1
Haverdal [S] 162 B5
Haverfordwest [GB] 12 D1
Haverhill [GB] 14 F3
Häverö [S] 168 E1
Håverud [S] 166 D4
Havířov [CZ] 50 F4
Hävla [S] 168 B4
Havlíčkův Brod [CZ] 48 H5
Havnäs [S] 190 F5
Havnbjerg [DK] 156 C4
Havneby [DK] 156 A4
Havnebyen [DK] 156 F1
Havnsø [DK] 156 F2
Havøysund [N] 194 B1
Havraň [CZ] 48 E2
Hayran [TR] 152 C1
Havsa [TR] 150 B2
Havstensund [S] 166 B4
Hawick [GB] 8 E4
Hayange [F] 44 E3
Hayle [GB] 12 B5
Haymana [TR] 152 H1
Hay-on-Wye [GB] 12 F2
Hayrabolu [TR] 150 B3
Hayriye [TR] 150 E4
Hayrıye [TR] 152 G5
Haywards Heath [GB] 14 E5
Hazebrouck [F] 28 E2
Hazlov [CZ] 48 C3
Hazmburk [CZ] 48 F3
Hcıkasım [TR] 150 B5
Headford [IRL] 2 C4
Heathfield [GB] 14 E5
Hebnes [N] 164 B2
Heby [S] 168 C1
Hechingen [D] 58 G2
Hecho [E] 84 D4
Hechtel [B] 30 E3
Hechthausen [D] 18 E4
Hed [S] 168 A2
Hedal [N] 170 G4
Hedared [S] 162 B2
Hedås [S] 166 F2
Hédauville [F] 28 E4
Hedburg [D] 46 G3
Hedby [S] 172 H4
Hedbyn [S] 166 H1
Heddal [N] 164 F2
Hedderen [N] 164 D3
Hédé [F] 26 C5
Hede [S] 168 B1
Hedehusene [DK] 156 G2
Hedekas [S] 166 C5
Hedemora [S] 174 D5
Heden [FIN] 188 B5
Heden [S] 172 E1
Heden [S] 172 G2
Hedenäset [S] 194 B8
Hedensted [DK] 156 C2
Hedesunda [S] 174 E5
Hedeviken [S] 182 F4
Hee [DK] 160 B6
Heek [D] 16 H5
Heemstede [NL] 16 D4
Heerde [NL] 16 F4
Heerenveen [NL] 16 F3
Heerlen [NL] 30 F4
Heeze [NL] 30 E3
Hegerum [S] 162 G2
Heggenes [N] 170 G2
Heglibister [GB] 6 G4
Hegra [N] 182 C1
Hegyeshalom [H] 62 G5
Hegyhátsál [H] 74 F2
Hegykő [H] 62 G6
Heia [N] 190 C5
Heia [N] 192 F3
Heidal [N] 180 G6
Heide [D] 18 E2
Heideck [D] 46 G6
Heidelberg [D] 46 C5
Heiden [D] 16 G6
Heidenau [D] 48 E1
Heidenheim [D] 60 C2
Heidenreichstein [A] 62 D2
Heigrestad [N] 164 B4
Heikendorf [D] 18 G2
Heikkurila [FIN] 188 E5
Heiland [N] 164 F3
Heilbad Heiligenstadt [D] 32 G5
Heilbronn [D] 46 D5
Heilevong [N] 180 B6
Heiligenberg [D] 58 H4
Heiligenblut [A] 72 G2
Heiligenbösch-Kirche [D] 44 G2
Heiligenhafen [D] 18 H2
Heiligenkreuz [A] 62 E4
Heiligenkreuz [A] 62 E5
Heiligenkreuz [A] 74 F2
Heiligenroth [D] 46 B2
Heiligkreuztal [D] 58 H3
Heilsbronn [D] 46 F5
Heimaey [IS] 192 A3
Heimdal [N] 182 B1
Heimertingen [D] 60 B4
Heinämaa [FIN] 178 B3
Heinämäki [FIN] 186 H1
Heinävaara [FIN] 188 G2
Heinävesi [FIN] 188 E3
Heinersdorf [D] 34 F2
Heino [NL] 16 F4
Heinola [FIN] 178 B2
Heinoniemi [FIN] 188 F4
Heinrichsruh [D] 20 E4
Heinsberg [D] 30 F4
Heippes [F] 44 D4
Heiterwang [A] 60 C6
Heituinlahti [FIN] 178 D2
Hejde [S] 168 G5
Hejlsminde [DK] 156 C3
Hejnice [CZ] 48 H1
Hejnsvig [DK] 156 B2
Hekal [AL] 128 B5
Hekimdağ [TR] 150 H5
Hel [PL] 22 E2
Heldenberg [A] 62 E4
Heldrungen [D] 34 A5
Helechal [E] 96 B4
Helensburgh [GB] 8 D2
Helfenburk [CZ] 48 F6
Helfštýn [CZ] 50 D5
Helgen [N] 164 F3
Helgum [S] 184 E2
Hell [N] 182 C1
Hella [N] 170 D1
Helland [N] 180 G1
Helle [N] 164 C4
Helle [N] 164 F4
Helleland [N] 164 B4
Hellendoorn [NL] 16 G4
Helleristninger [N] 180 B5
Helleristninger [N] 194 B3
Hellesøy [N] 170 A3
Hellesylt [N] 180 D4
Hellevad [DK] 156 B4
Hellevik [N] 170 B1
Hellevoetsluis [NL] 16 C5
Helligskogen [N] 192 G3
Hellín [E] 104 B1
Hellinge [DK] 156 E5
Hellsö [FIN] 168 H1
Helmond [NL] 30 E2
Helmsdale [GB] 6 E3
Helmsley [GB] 10 F3
Helmstedt [D] 34 A3
Helnessund [N] 192 D5
Helsa [D] 32 F5
Helsingborg [S] 156 H1
Helsinge [DK] 156 G1
Helsingfors / Helsinki [FIN] 176 H5
Helsingør [DK] 156 H1
Helsinki / Helsingfors [FIN] 176 H5
Helstad [N] 190 D4
Helston [GB] 12 B5
Heltermaa [EST] 198 C2
Helvia Recina [I] 116 C1
Hemau [D] 46 H6
Hemel Hempstead [GB] 14 E3
Hemer [D] 32 C4
Hèming [F] 44 G5
Hemling [S] 190 G6
Hemmet [DK] 156 A1
Hemmingen [S] 190 H4
Hemmingsmark [S] 196 A4
Hemmoor [D] 18 E3
Hemnes [N] 166 C2
Hemnesberget [N] 190 D2
Hemse [S] 168 G5
Hemsedal [N] 170 F3
Hemslingen [D] 18 F5
Hen [N] 170 H5
Henån [S] 166 C6
Hencida [H] 76 H1
Hendaye [F] 84 B2
Hendek [TR] 150 H3
Hendrik Ido Ambacht [NL] 16 D5
Hengelo [NL] 16 G5
Hengersberg [D] 60 G2
Heniches'k [UA] 204 H3
Hénin Beaumont [F] 28 F3
Henley-on-Thames [GB] 14 D4
Hennan [S] 184 D5
Henneberg [D] 46 F2
Hennebont [F] 40 C4
Hennef [D] 30 H5
Hennerhöle [A] 60 H6
Henne Strand [DK] 156 A2
Hennezel [F] 58 B2
Henningsvær [N] 192 D4
Hénoville [F] 28 D3
Henrichemont [F] 56 C3
Henriksfjäll [S] 190 E4
Henryków [PL] 50 C2
Henstedt-Ulzburg [D] 18 F3
Hepokongäs [FIN] 196 E4
Hepola [FIN] 196 C3
Heppenheim [D] 46 C4
Heraclea [MK] 128 E3
Herad [N] 164 C5
Herad [N] 170 F3
Heradsbygd [N] 172 C3
Herajoki [FIN] 188 F1
Herakleia [TR] 152 D6
Hera Lacinia, Tempio di- [I] 124 F5
Hérault, Gorges de l'- [F] 106 E3
Herbault [F] 54 G1
Herberstein [A] 74 E2
Herbertingen [D] 58 H3
Herbertstown [IRL] 4 D4
Herbesthal [B] 30 F5
Herbeumont [B] 44 D2
Herbignac [F] 40 E5
Herbolzheim [D] 58 E2
Herborn [D] 46 C1
Herbrechtingen [D] 60 C3
Herby [PL] 50 F2
Herceg Novj [MNE] 144 D4
Hercegovac [HR] 74 G6
Hercegovska Goleša [SRB] 144 E2
Hercegszántó [H] 76 C5
Herdal [N] 180 D4
Herdberg [D] 32 D4
Herdla [N] 170 A3
Herdoniae [I] 120 G2
Hereford [GB] 12 G2
Herefoss [N] 164 E4
Héreg [H] 64 B6
Hereke [TR] 150 F3
Herencia [E] 96 G3
Herend [H] 74 H2

Herentals [B] 30 D3
Herfølge [DK] 156 G3
Herford [D] 32 E2
Hergiswil [CH] 58 F6
Héricourt [F] 58 C4
Heringsdorf [D] 20 E3
Herisau [CH] 58 H5
Hérisson [F] 56 C5
Herl'any [SK] 64 G2
Herleshausen [D] 32 G6
Herlufsholm [DK] 156 F3
Hermagor [A] 72 G3
Hermannsburg [D] 18 F6
Hermanns-Denkmal [D] 32 E3
Heřmanovice [CZ] 50 D3
Hermansverk [N] 170 D2
Heřmanův Městec [CZ] 50 A4
Herment [F] 68 B2
Hermeskeil [D] 44 G3
Hermo [E] 78 F4
Hermsdorf [D] 48 B1
Hernani [E] 84 B2
Herne [D] 30 H3
Herne Bay [GB] 14 G5
Herning [DK] 160 C6
Hernstein [A] 62 E5
Heroldsberg [D] 46 G5
Herøya [N] 164 G3
Herøysund [N] 170 B5
Herråkra [S] 162 E4
Herräng [S] 174 G5
Herraskylä [FIN] 186 D4
Herre [N] 164 G3
Herrenberg [D] 58 G1
Herrenchiemsee [D] 60 F5
Herrera [E] 96 E4
Herrera [F] 102 B2
Herrera del Duque [E] 96 C3
Herrera de los Navarros [E] 90 D5
Herrera de Pisuerga [F] 82 D5
Herrería [E] 90 C5
Herreruela [E] 86 G5
Herrestad [S] 166 C5
Herrgotts Kirche [D] 46 E5
Herrljunga [S] 162 B1
Herrnburg [D] 18 G3
Herrnhut [D] 48 G1
Herröskkatan [FIN] 168 G1
Herrsching [D] 60 D4
Herrskog [S] 184 F3
Herrvik [S] 168 G5
Hersbruck [D] 46 H5
Herselt [B] 30 D3
Hertford [GB] 14 E3
Hertník [SK] 52 C6
Hervás [E] 88 B5
Hervik [N] 164 B2
Herzberg [D] 20 B4
Herzberg [D] 32 G4
Herzberg [D] 34 D1
Herzberg [D] 34 E4
Herzberg [D] 46 E1
Herzfeld [D] 32 D4
Herzfelde [D] 34 F2
Herzlake [D] 18 B6
Herzogenaurach [D] 46 G5
Herzogenburg [A] 62 E4
Herzsprung [D] 20 C6
Hesdin [F] 28 D3
Hesel [D] 18 C4
Heskestad [N] 164 B4
Heskestad [N] 164 C5
Hesnæs [DK] 20 B1
Hessel [DK] 160 C4
Hesselagergård [DK] 156 E4
Hessich-Lichtenau [D] 32 F5
Hess Oldendorf [D] 32 F2
Hessvik [N] 170 C4
Hestad [N] 170 C1
Hestenesøyri [N] 180 C5
Hestra [S] 162 C3
Hestra [S] 162 E1
Hetin [SRB] 76 F6
Het Loo [NL] 16 F5
Hettange-Grande [F] 44 E3
Hettstedt [D] 34 B4
Hetvehely [H] 76 A5
Heustreu [D] 46 F2
Heverlee [B] 30 D4
Heves [H] 64 E6
Hévíz [H] 74 G3
Hevlín [CZ] 62 F3
Hexentanzplatz [D] 34 A4
Hexham [GB] 8 F6
Heyrieux [F] 68 G3
Heysham [GB] 10 D3
Hidas [H] 76 B4
Hidasnémeti [H] 64 G3
Hieflau [A] 62 C6
Hiendelaencina [E] 88 H4
Hierapolis [TR] 152 G5
Hiersac [F] 54 D6
Hietakylä [FIN] 188 C3
Hietanen [FIN] 188 C6
Hietaniemi [FIN] 194 F6
Hietaperä [FIN] 196 F5
High Cross [IRL] 4 F3
High Wycombe [GB] 14 D4
Higuera, Torre de la- [E] 100 F2
Higuera de la Serena [E] 96 B4
Higuera de Vargas [E] 94 F2
Higuera la Real [E] 94 F3
Higueruela [E] 98 C5
Hiihnavaara [FIN] 194 E6
Hiirola [FIN] 188 C5
Hiitinen / Hitis [FIN] 176 E6
Híjar [E] 90 F5
Hilchenbach [D] 32 C5
Hildal [N] 170 C5
Hildburghausen [D] 46 G2
Hilden [D] 30 G4
Hilders [D] 46 E2
Hildesheim [D] 32 G3
Hildre [N] 180 D3
Hilertshausen [D] 60 E3
Hilkerode [D] 32 G4
Hilla [FIN] 176 G5
Hille [S] 174 E4
Hillegom [NL] 16 D4
Hillerød [DK] 156 G2
Hillerstorp [S] 162 C3
Hillesøy [N] 192 F2
Hilliilä [FIN] 196 C5
Hillion [F] 26 B4
Hillsand [S] 190 E5
Hillsborough [NIR] 2 G4
Hillswick [GB] 6 G3
Hilltown [NIR] 2 G4
Hilmo [N] 182 C2
Hilpoltstein [D] 46 G6
Hilterfingen [CH] 70 E1
Hiltulanlahti [FIN] 188 C2
Hilvarenbeek [NL] 30 E2
Hilversum [NL] 16 E4
Himanka [FIN] 196 C5
Himankakylä [FIN] 196 C5
Himarë [AL] 128 B6
Himlštejn [CZ] 48 D3
Himmelkoron [D] 46 H3
Himmelpforten [D] 18 E4
Hinckley [GB] 10 E6
Hindås [S] 160 H2
Hindelang [D] 60 C6
Hinderburg [D] 34 C1
Hindsig [DK] 156 B2
Hinnerjoki [FIN] 176 D3
Hinnerup [DK] 160 D6
Hinneryd [S] 162 C5
Hinojal [E] 86 H4
Hinojos [E] 94 F6
Hinojosa del Duque [E] 96 C4
Hinojosa del Valle [E] 94 H3
Hinterbichl [A] 72 F2
Hinterrhein [CH] 70 G2
Hintersee [D] 20 E4
Hinterstoder [A] 62 B6
Hinterthal [A] 72 G1
Hintertux [A] 72 D1
Hinterweidenthal [D] 44 H4
Hinterzarten [D] 58 F3
Hío [E] 78 B4
Hırkalı [TR] 152 E3
Hirnsdorf [A] 74 E2
Hirnyk [UA] 52 H2
Hirrlingen [D] 58 G2
Hirschaid [D] 46 G4
Hirschau [D] 48 B5
Hirschberg [D] 48 B2
Hirschegg [A] 60 B6
Hirschhorn [D] 46 C5
Hirsch-Stein [D] 48 B3
Hirsilä [FIN] 186 E6
Hirsingue [F] 58 D4
Hirson [F] 28 G5
Hîrşova [RO] 204 E5
Hirtshals [DK] 160 E2
Hirvassalmi [FIN] 194 D5
Hirvasvaara [FIN] 194 E7
Hirvensalmi [FIN] 186 H6
Hirvihaara [FIN] 176 H4
Hirvijärvi [S] 194 B8
Hirvijoki [FIN] 186 D2
Hirvisalo [FIN] 178 B2
Hisarcık [TR] 152 F2
Hisardžik [SRB] 146 A3
Hisarlık [TR] 150 G4
Hisartepe Dascylium [TR] 150 E4
Histria [RO] 204 F5
Hita [E] 88 H5
Hitchin [GB] 14 E3
Hitiaş [RO] 76 H6
Hitis / Hiitinen [FIN] 176 E6
Hitovo [BG] 148 F1
Hittarp [S] 156 H1
Hitterdal [N] 182 D4
Hitzacker [D] 18 H5
Hiukkajoki [FIN] 188 F5
Hjallerup [DK] 160 E3
Hjällstad [S] 172 E4
Hjälmseryd [S] 162 D3
Hjältanstorp [S] 184 D4
Hjärnarp [DK] 162 B6
Hjartåsen [N] 190 E2
Hjärtum [S] 166 C6
Hjelle [N] 180 C5
Hjelle [N] 180 D5
Hjellestad [N] 170 A4
Hjelmeland [N] 164 B2
Hjelset [N] 180 E3
Hjerkinn [N] 180 G4
Hjerpsted [DK] 156 B4
Hjerting [DK] 156 A2
Hjo [S] 166 F6
Hjøllund [DK] 156 C1
Hjørring [DK] 160 E2
Hjorte [DK] 156 D3
Hjorted [S] 162 G2
Hjorteset [N] 180 C5
Hjortkvarn [S] 166 H4
Hjortsberga [S] 158 F1
Hjortsberga [S] 162 D4
Hjulsbro [S] 168 A6
Hjulsjö [S] 166 G2
Hlinsko [CZ] 50 B4
Hlobyne [UA] 202 F7
Hlohovec [SK] 62 H4
Hluboká nad Vltavou [CZ] 62 C2
Hlučín [CZ] 50 E4
Hluk [CZ] 62 H2
Hlukhiv [UA] 202 E6
Hlusk [BY] 202 C6
Hlybokaya [BY] 202 B4
Hlyniany [UA] 52 G4
Hniezdne [SK] 52 B6
Hnilec [SK] 64 E2
Hnúšt'a [SK] 64 D3
Hobermayer-Hofen [A] 74 E2
Hobol [H] 74 H5
Hobro [DK] 160 D5
Hocalar [TR] 152 H3
Hoče [SLO] 74 D4
Hoces del Cabriel [E] 98 C4
Hoces del Duratón [E] 88 G3
Hoces del Riaza [E] 88 G2
Höchberg [D] 46 E4
Hochburg [A] 60 G4
Hochburg [D] 58 E2
Hochdonn [D] 18 E3
Hochdorf [CH] 58 F5
Höchenschwand [D] 58 F4
Hochfelden [F] 44 H5
Hochosterwitz [A] 74 B3
Hochspeyer [D] 46 B4
Höchst [D] 46 D4
Höchstadt [D] 46 G4
Höchstädt [D] 60 C3
Hochstatten [D] 46 B3
Höckendorf [D] 48 E1
Hockenheim [D] 46 C5
Hoczew [PL] 52 E5
Hodal [N] 182 C4
Hodalen [N] 182 C4
Hodejov [SK] 64 E4
Hodenhagen [D] 18 E6
Hodkovice nad Mohelkou [CZ] 48 G2
Hódmezővásárhely [H] 76 E4
Hodøl [N] 182 D4
Hodonín [CZ] 62 G2
Hodoš [SLO] 74 F3
Hodošan [HR] 74 F4
Hoedekenskerke [NL] 28 H1
Hoei (Huy) [B] 30 D5
Hoek van Holland [NL] 16 C5
Hoenzethen [D] 18 G6
Hof [D] 48 B3
Hof [D] 58 F1
Hofgeismar [D] 32 F4
Hofheim [D] 46 F3
Hofles [N] 190 C4
Höfn [IS] 192 C3
Hofors [S] 174 D4
Hofstad [N] 190 B5
Höganäs [S] 156 H1
Hogdal [S] 166 B4
Högé [S] 182 G2
Högerud [S] 166 E2
Högfors [S] 166 H1
Högfors / Karkkila [FIN] 176 G4
Höghult [S] 162 F2
Höglint [S] 168 F4
Höglunda [S] 184 D2
Högnabba [FIN] 186 D1
Högsäter [S] 166 D5
Högsby [S] 162 F4
Høgset [N] 180 E2
Högsjö [S] 184 F3
Høgstadgård [N] 192 G3
Hogstorp [S] 166 C5
Högvålen [S] 182 E5
Hőgyész [H] 76 B4
Hohenau [A] 62 G3
Hohenbachschlucht [A] 72 B1
Hohenberg [A] 62 E5
Hohenbrunn [D] 60 E4
Hohenburg [D] 46 H5
Hoheneck [D] 46 F5
Hohenems [A] 58 H5
Hohenfels [D] 46 B4
Hohenhewen [D] 58 G4
Hohenkirchen [D] 60 E4
Hohenlimburg [D] 32 C4
Hohenlinden [D] 60 F4
Hohenlockstedt [D] 18 F3
Hohenneuffen [D] 58 H2
Hohenpeissenberg [D] 60 D5
Hohenschwangau [D] 60 C6
Hohenstein [D] 46 B2
Hohensyburg [D] 32 C4
Hohentauern [A] 74 C1
Hohentwiel [D] 58 G4
Hohen Wehrda [D] 46 E1
Hohenwerfen [A] 60 G6
Hohenwestedt [D] 18 F2
Hohenzollern [D] 58 G2
Hohne [D] 32 G1
Hohneck [F] 58 D3
Hohrodberg [F] 58 D3
Hohwacht [D] 18 G2
Hoikhankylä [FIN] 186 H3
Hoilola [FIN] 188 H3
Hoisko [FIN] 186 D2
Højby [DK] 156 F2
Højer [DK] 156 B4
Højerup [DK] 156 G4
Højslev Stby [DK] 160 C5
Hojsova Stráž [CZ] 48 D6
Hok [S] 162 D3
Hökåsen [S] 168 B2
Hökhuvud [S] 174 F5
Hokka [FIN] 186 H5
Hokksund [N] 164 G1
Hökön [S] 162 D6
Hoks Herrgård [S] 162 D3
Hokusukoski [FIN] 186 E4
Hol [N] 170 F3
Hol [S] 162 B1
Holand [N] 190 D5
Hola Prystan' [UA] 204 G3
Holašovice [CZ] 62 B2
Holbæk [DK] 156 F2
Holbeach [GB] 10 G6
Holbøl [DK] 156 C4
Holckenhavn [DK] 156 E3
Holdorf [D] 32 D1
Hole [S] 172 F5
Holeby [DK] 20 A1
Holedeč [CZ] 48 E3
Holešov [CZ] 50 D6
Holíč [SK] 62 G3
Holice [CZ] 50 B4
Hölick [S] 174 E1
Holiseva [FIN] 186 F5
Holja [FIN] 176 G2
Höljes [S] 172 E3
Hollabrunn [A] 62 E3
Hollád [H] 74 G3
Høllen [N] 164 D6
Hollenbach [D] 60 D3
Hollenegg [A] 74 D3
Hollenstedt [D] 18 F4
Hollerath [D] 30 F5
Hollestein [A] 62 C5
Hollfeld [D] 46 G4
Hollingsholm [N] 180 E2
Hollola [FIN] 176 H2
Hollolan [FIN] 176 H2
Hollum [NL] 16 F1
Höllviken [S] 156 H3
Holm [DK] 156 C4
Holm [FIN] 196 B6
Holm [N] 166 B3
Holm [N] 190 C4
Holm [S] 184 D4
Hólmavík [IS] 192 B2
Holmec [SLO] 74 C3
Holmedal [S] 166 D2
Holmegil [N] 166 C3
Holmestrand [N] 164 H2
Holmfirth [GB] 10 E4
Holmfors [S] 190 G4
Holmfors [S] 196 A3
Holmön [S] 196 A6
Holmsjö [S] 162 F6
Holmsjö [S] 184 C3
Holmsjö [S] 190 G6
Holmsund [S] 196 A6
Holmsveden [S] 174 E3
Holmudden [S] 168 H3
Holm-Zhirkovskij [RUS] 202 D3
Holoby [UA] 202 B7
Holovanivs'k [UA] 204 F2
Holovne [UA] 38 G5
Holøydal [N] 182 C5
Holsætra [N] 170 H2
Holsbybrunn [S] 162 E3
Holsen [N] 170 C1
Holsljunge [S] 162 B3
Holstebro [DK] 160 B5
Holsted [DK] 156 B2
Holsworthy [GB] 12 D4
Holt [GB] 14 G1
Holt [N] 164 F4
Holt [N] 192 F3
Holten [NL] 16 G5
Holtet [N] 166 C4
Holtet [N] 172 D4
Holtsås [N] 164 F2
Holtsee [D] 18 F2
Holtslåtten [N] 172 C4
Holwerd [NL] 16 F1
Holycross [IRL] 4 E4
Holyhead [GB] 10 B3
Holywell [GB] 10 C4
Holywood [NIR] 2 G3
Holzdorf [D] 34 D4
Holzgau [A] 72 B1
Holzkirchen [D] 60 E5
Holzleitensattel [A] 72 C1
Holzminden [D] 32 F3
Holzschlag [D] 58 F3
Homberg [D] 32 F6
Homberg [D] 46 D1
Homborsund [N] 164 E5
Hombukt [N] 192 H1
Homburg [D] 44 G4
Hommelstø [N] 190 D3
Hommelvik [N] 182 C1
Hommersåk [N] 164 B3
Homokszentgyörgy [H] 74 H5
Homps [F] 106 C4
Homyel' [BY] 202 D6
Honaz [TR] 152 G5
Hondarribia / Fuenterrabía [E] 84 B2
Hönebach [D] 32 F6
Hønefoss [N] 170 H5
Honfleur [F] 26 G3
Høng [DK] 156 F3
Honiton [GB] 12 F4
Honkajoki [FIN] 186 C5
Honkakoski [FIN] 186 B6
Honkola [FIN] 186 G3
Hønning [DK] 156 B3
Honningsvåg [N] 180 B4
Honningsvåg [N] 194 C1
Honrubia [E] 98 B3
Honrubia de la Cuesta [E] 88 G3
Hontalbilla [E] 88 F3
Hontoria de la Cantera [E] 82 E6
Hontoria del Pinar [E] 90 A2
Hoofddorp [NL] 16 D4
Hoogerheide [NL] 30 C2
Hoogeveen [NL] 16 G3
Hoogezand [NL] 16 G2
Hoogkarspel [NL] 16 E3
Hoogstraten [B] 30 D2
Hooksiel [D] 18 C5
Höör [S] 158 C2
Hoorn [NL] 16 E3
Hopfgarten [A] 60 F6
Hoplandsjøen [N] 170 A2
Hopovo, Manastir- [SRB] 142 F2
Hopperstad Stavkirke [N] 170 C2
Hopseidet [N] 194 D1
Hopsten [D] 32 C2
Hoptrup [DK] 156 C3
Hora-Sv-Šebestiána [CZ] 48 E2
Horažďovice [CZ] 48 E6
Horb [D] 58 G2
Horbelev [DK] 20 B1
Hörby [S] 158 C2
Horcajo de los Montes [E] 96 D3
Horcajo de Santiago [E] 96 H2
Horche [E] 88 H5
Hörda [S] 162 D4
Horda [S] 162 D4
Hordain [F] 28 F4
Horgen [CH] 58 F5
Horgevik [N] 164 E2
Horgoš [SRB] 76 E5
Horgoū [MNE] 204 A5
Horia [RO] 76 G4
Hořice [CZ] 50 A3
Horitschon [A] 62 F6
Hörja [S] 158 C1
Horjul [SLO] 74 B5
Hörken [S] 166 G1
Horki [BY] 202 D4
Hormogos [E] 88 E6
Horn [A] 62 E3
Horn [D] 32 E3
Horn [D] 58 G4
Horn [N] 170 H4
Horn [N] 190 D3
Horn [S] 162 F2
Hornachos [E] 94 H3
Hornachuelos [E] 96 B6
Horná Štubňa [SK] 64 C3
Hornbæk [DK] 156 G1
Hornberg [D] 46 D5
Hornberg [D] 58 F2
Hornburg [D] 32 H3
Horncastle [GB] 10 G5
Horndal [S] 174 D5
Hörne [D] 18 E3
Horne [DK] 156 D4
Horneburg [D] 18 F4
Hörnefors [S] 190 H6
Hornesund [N] 164 D5
Horní Benešov [CZ] 50 D4
Horní Cerekev [CZ] 48 H6
Horní Lideč [CZ] 50 E6
Horní Loděnice [CZ] 50 D4
Hornindal [N] 180 D5
Hørning [DK] 156 D1
Horní Planá [CZ] 62 B3
Horní Vltavice [CZ] 62 A2
Hornnes [N] 164 D4
Hornos [E] 102 G1
Hornos de Peal [E] 102 F2
Hornoy [F] 28 D5
Hornsea [GB] 10 G4
Hornslet [DK] 160 E6
Hörnum [D] 156 A4
Hornum [DK] 160 D4
Horný Tisovník [SK] 64 C4
Horodenka [UA] 204 D2
Horodło [PL] 38 G6
Horodnytsia [UA] 202 C7
Horodok [UA] 52 G4
Horodyshche [UA] 202 E8
Horokhiv [UA] 202 B8
Horonkylä [FIN] 186 B4
Hořovice [CZ] 48 E4
Horred [S] 160 H3
Hörröd [S] 158 D2
Horrskog [S] 174 E5
Horsens [DK] 156 D2
Horsham [GB] 14 E5
Hørsholm [DK] 156 G2
Horslunde [DK] 156 E4
Horsmanaho [FIN] 188 E2
Horšovský Týn [CZ] 48 D5
Horst [B] 30 D4
Horst [D] 18 G5
Horst [NL] 30 F3
Hörstel [D] 32 C2
Horstmar [D] 16 H5
Horsunlu [TR] 152 F5
Hort [H] 64 D6
Horta [P] 100 C3
Horten [N] 164 H2
Hortezuela [E] 90 A3
Hortigüela [E] 88 H1
Hortobágy [H] 64 G6
Hörup [D] 156 B5
Hørve [DK] 156 F2
Horven [N] 190 C4
Horw [CH] 58 F6
Hosby [DK] 156 D2
Hoscheld [L] 44 F2
Hosenfeld [D] 46 E2
Hoset [N] 192 D6
Hoshtevë Vithkuq [AL] 128 C6
Hosjö [S] 174 C4
Hoslemo [N] 164 D2
Hospental [CH] 70 F1
Hospice de France [F] 84 F5
Hospital [IRL] 4 D4
Hospital de Orbigo [E] 78 G6
Hossa [FIN] 196 F3
Hossegor [F] 66 A6
Hosszúpályi [H] 76 H1
Hosszú-Pereszteg [H] 74 G2
Hostalric [E] 92 F4
Hoštejn [CZ] 50 C4
Hostens [F] 66 C4
Hosteřadice [CZ] 62 F2
Hostianské Nemce [SK] 64 C4
Hostinné [CZ] 50 A2
Hostomice [CZ] 48 F4
Hoston [N] 180 H2
Hostouň [CZ] 48 D5
Hostovice [SK] 52 E6
Hostýn [CZ] 50 D6
Hotagen [S] 190 E5
Hotarele [RO] 148 D1
Hoting [S] 190 F5
Hotton [B] 30 E6
Hötzelsdorf [A] 62 E3
Hou [DK] 160 E4
Houdain [F] 28 E3
Houdan [F] 42 E3
Houdelaincourt [F] 44 D5
Houeillès [F] 66 D5
Houffalize [B] 30 E6
Houlbjerg [DK] 160 D5
Houlgate [F] 26 F3
Hourtin [F] 66 C2
Hourtin-Plage [F] 66 C2
Houthalen [B] 30 E3
Houtsala [FIN] 176 C5
Houtskär / Houtskari [FIN] 176 C5
Houtskari / Houtskär [FIN] 176 C5
Hov [DK] 156 D1
Hov [N] 170 H3
Hov [S] 166 G6
Hova [S] 166 F4
Hovborg [DK] 156 B2
Hovda [N] 170 G3
Hovdala [S] 158 C1
Hovden [N] 164 D1
Hovden [N] 192 D3
Høve [DK] 156 F2
Hove [DK] 160 B5
Hove [N] 180 C6
Hövelhof [D] 32 E3
Hoven [DK] 156 B1
Hoverberg [S] 182 G3
Hovet [N] 170 E3
Hovi [FIN] 188 C2
Hovin [N] 164 F1
Hovin [N] 182 B2
Hovinsholm [N] 172 C4
Hovland [N] 164 B4
Hovland [N] 170 C4
Hovmantorp [S] 162 E5
Hovsta [S] 166 H3
Howard, Castle- [IRL] 4 G4
Howth [IRL] 2 F6
Höxter [D] 32 F4
Hoya [D] 18 E6
Hoya-Gonzalo [E] 98 C5
Høyanger [N] 170 C1
Høydalen [N] 164 F3
Høydalsmo [N] 164 E2
Høydalsseter [N] 180 E6
Hoyerswerda [D] 34 F5
Høyjord [N] 164 H2
Høylandet [N] 190 C4
Hoym [D] 34 B4
Hoyos [E] 86 G3
Hoyos del Espino [E] 88 C5
Höytiä [FIN] 186 F4
Hozha [BY] 24 F3
Hrabaw [RUS] 202 C6
Hrachovo [SK] 64 D3
Hrad Beckov [SK] 64 A3
Hradec Králové [CZ] 50 A3
Hradec nad Moravicí [CZ] 50 E4
Hradec nad Svitavou [CZ] 50 B5
Hrádek [CZ] 48 F2
Hrádek [CZ] 50 A3
Hrádek [CZ] 62 F3
Hrádek nad Nisou [CZ] 48 G1
Hradhoviště [CZ] 62 C2
Hradyz'k [UA] 202 F8
Hranice [CZ] 50 E5
Hranovnica [SK] 64 E2
Hrastik [SLO] 74 D5
Hrastovlje [SLO] 72 H6
Hrebenne [PL] 52 G3
Hřensko [CZ] 48 F1
Hriňová [SK] 64 D3
Hrob [CZ] 48 E2
Hrochův Týnec [CZ] 50 B4
Hrodna [BY] 24 F4
Hronov [CZ] 50 B2
Hrotovice [CZ] 62 E2
Hrtkovci [SRB] 142 F2
Hrubieszów [PL] 52 G1
Hrubov [SK] 52 E6
Hrubý Rohozec [CZ] 48 H2
Hrud [PL] 38 F3
Hrušov [SK] 64 B4
Hrušovany [CZ] 62 F3
Hrvace [HR] 144 A1
Hrvatska Kostajnica [HR] 142 B2
Huaröd [S] 158 D2
Huarte [E] 84 B4
Huben [A] 72 C2
Huben [A] 72 F2
Hubenov [CZ] 48 E4
Hubertusburg [D] 34 D5
Hubertusstock, Jagdschloss- [D] 20 D6
Hucqueliers [F] 28 D3
Huda Luknja [SLO] 74 D4
Huddersfield [GB] 10 E4
Huddinge [S] 168 D3
Huddunge [S] 174 E6
Hudiksvall [S] 174 E1
Huedin [RO] 204 C4
Huélago [E] 102 F3
Huélamo [E] 98 C2
Huelgoat [F] 40 C2
Huelma [E] 102 E3
Huelva [E] 94 E6
Huércal de Almería [E] 102 G5
Huércal-Overa [E] 102 H4
Huerta del Rey [E] 88 H2
Huerta de Valdecarábanos [E] 96 G2
Huérteles [E] 90 C2
Huerto [E] 90 G3
Huesa [E] 102 F2
Huesca [E] 84 D6
Huéscar [E] 102 G3
Hueselgau [D] 32 G6
Huete [E] 98 A1
Huétor Tájar [E] 102 D3
Hüfingen [D] 58 F3
Hufthamar [N] 170 A4
Hugtinsalmi [FIN] 178 C2
Huhla [BG] 130 G1
Huhtala [FIN] 196 D2
Huhtapuhto [FIN] 196 D5
Huhti [FIN] 176 F2
Huhtilampi [FIN] 188 G3
Huhus [FIN] 188 G2
Huissinkylä [FIN] 186 C3
Huittinen [FIN] 176 E2
Huizen [NL] 16 D3
Huizen [NL] 16 E4
Huizingen [B] 28 H3
Hujakkala [FIN] 178 E3
Hukkala [FIN] 188 E2
Hukvaldy [CZ] 50 E5
Hulderbo [N] 180 G5
Hulín [CZ] 50 D6
Huljen [S] 184 E4
Hulle [N] 180 G1
Hullsjön [S] 184 D4
Hulsing [DK] 160 E2
Hulst [NL] 28 H1
Hult [S] 162 E2
Hult [S] 166 F3
Hultanäs [S] 162 E4
Hultsfred [S] 162 F3
Hultsjö [S] 162 D3
Hum [BIH] 144 D2
Hum [HR] 112 E1
Humada [E] 82 E5
Humanes [E] 88 H5
Humble [DK] 156 E5
Humenné [SK] 64 H2
Humla [S] 162 C1
Humlebæk [DK] 156 G2
Humlum [DK] 160 B5
Hümme [D] 32 F4
Hummelsta [S] 168 C2
Hummelvik [N] 192 H1
Humpolec [CZ] 48 H5
Humppi [FIN] 186 F2
Humppila [FIN] 176 F3
Humprecht [CZ] 48 H2
Hunaudaye, Château de- [F] 26 B4
Hundåla [N] 190 D2
Hunderdorf [D] 60 G2
Hundested [DK] 156 G2
Hundorp [N] 170 H1
Hunedoara [RO] 204 C5
Hünfeld [D] 46 E1
Hunge [S] 182 H3
Hungen [D] 46 D2
Hungerford [GB] 12 H3
Hunnebostrand [S] 166 B5
Hunspach [F] 46 B6
Hunstanton [GB] 10 H6
Huntingdon [GB] 14 E2
Huntly [GB] 6 F5
Huopanankoski [FIN] 186 F2
Hurbanovo [SK] 64 B5
Hurdal [N] 172 B4
Hurdal Verk [N] 172 C4
Hurez, Mănăstirea- [RO] 204 C5
Huriel [F] 56 C5
Hurissalo [FIN] 188 D6
Hurskaala [FIN] 188 C4
Hŭrsovo [BG] 148 E2
Hurtanmaa [FIN] 178 D2
Hurup [DK] 160 B4
Hurva [S] 158 C2
Hus [CZ] 62 B2
Husa [N] 170 B5
Huså [S] 182 F1
Husaby [S] 166 E5
Húsavík [IS] 192 C2
Husbondliden [S] 190 G4
Husby [DK] 160 B5
Husbygård [S] 168 C4
Husby Långhundra [S] 168 D2
Husby-Sjuhundra [S] 168 E2
Huşi [RO] 204 E3
Husinec [CZ] 62 B2
Huskvarna [S] 162 D2
Husnes [N] 170 B5
Husö [FIN] 176 C6
Hustopeče [CZ] 62 F2
Husum [D] 18 E1
Husum [S] 184 G2
Husvika [N] 190 D3
Huta [PL] 52 C5
Huta Zawadzka [PL] 38 A4
Hutovo [BIH] 144 C3
Hüttenberg [A] 74 C2
Hüttschlag [A] 72 G1
Huttwil [CH] 58 E5
Huutijärvi [FIN] 176 F1
Huwniki [PL] 52 F4
Huy (Hoei) [B] 30 D5
Hvalba [FR] 160 A3
Hvalpsund [DK] 160 C4
Hvalvik [FR] 160 B1
Hvam [N] 172 B6
Hvammstangi [IS] 192 B2
Hvar [HR] 144 A2
Hveragerði [IS] 192 A3
Hvidbjerg [DK] 160 B4
Hvide Sande [DK] 156 A1
Hvittingfoss [N] 164 G2
Hvolsvöllur [IS] 192 A3
Hvoznitsa [BY] 38 G4
Hybo [S] 184 D6
Hycklinge [S] 162 F2
Hyde [GB] 10 E4
Hyen [N] 180 C5
Hyères [F] 108 C6
Hyervyaty [BY] 200 H5
Hyggen [N] 164 H1
Hylestad [N] 164 D3
Hyllested Skovgårde [DK] 160 F6
Hyltebruk [S] 162 B4
Hynnekleiv [N] 164 E4
Hyry [FIN] 196 D3
Hyrynsalmi [FIN] 196 F4
Hyssna [S] 160 H2
Hythe [GB] 14 F5
Hyttegrend [N] 192 F3
Hytti [FIN] 178 E2

Jörlanda [S] 160 G1
Jormua [FIN] 196 F5
Jormvattnet [S] 190 E4
Jörn [S] 190 H4
Joroinen / Jorois [FIN] 188 D4
Jorois / Joroinen [FIN] 188 D4
Jørpeland [N] 164 B3
Jorquera [E] 98 C5
Jørstad [N] 190 C5
Jošan [HR] 112 H4
Jošanica [BIH] 144 D1
Jošanica, Manastir- [SRB] 146 C2
Jošanička Banja [SRB] 146 B3
Jošavka [BIH] 142 C3
Josefov [CZ] 50 B3
Jøsenfjorden [N] 164 C2
Joševa [SRB] 142 F3
Josipdol [HR] 112 G2
Josipovac [HR] 76 B6
Jössefors [S] 166 D2
Josselin [F] 26 B6
Jøssund [N] 190 C5
Jostedal [N] 180 D6
Jósvafő [H] 64 F3
Jouarre [F] 42 H4
Jõuga [EST] 198 F1
Jougne [F] 58 B6
Joukio [FIN] 188 F6
Joukokylä [FIN] 196 F3
Joure [NL] 16 F3
Journaankylä [FIN] 178 B4
Joutsa [FIN] 186 G6
Joutseno [FIN] 178 E2
Joutsijärvi [FIN] 194 E7
Jovan [S] 190 G4
Joviac [F] 68 F6
Jøvik [N] 192 G2
Jovsa [SK] 64 H2
Joyeuse [F] 68 E6
Józefów [PL] 38 C3
Józefów [PL] 38 D6
Józefów [PL] 52 F2
Józsa [H] 64 G6
Juankoski [FIN] 188 D1
Juan-les-Pins [F] 108 E5
Judaberg [N] 164 B2
Judenburg [A] 74 C2
Judinsalo [FIN] 186 G6
Juelsminde [DK] 156 D2
Jugendburg [D] 46 C1
Jugon-les-Lacs [F] 26 B5
Jugorje [SLO] 74 D6
Juhtimäki [FIN] 186 D6
Juillac [F] 66 G3
Juist [D] 16 H1
Jukkasjärvi [S] 192 G5
Juknaičiai [LT] 200 D5
Juktån [S] 190 G4
Jule [N] 190 D5
Jülich [D] 30 F4
Julierpass [CH] 70 H2
Julita [S] 168 B3
Joullouville [F] 26 D4
Jumièges [F] 26 H3
Jumilla [E] 104 C1
Juminen [FIN] 196 F6
Jumisko [FIN] 194 E8
Jumkersrott [D] 18 B3
Jumkil [S] 168 D1
Jung [S] 166 E6
Jungsund [FIN] 186 B2
Juniville [F] 44 C3
Junnikkala [FIN] 178 E1
Junosuando [S] 194 B7
Junqueira [P] 80 E4
Junsele [S] 190 F6
Juntusranta [FIN] 196 F3
Juodupė [LT] 198 F6
Juojärvi [FIN] 188 E3
Juoksengi [S] 194 B8
Juoksenki [FIN] 194 C8
Juokslahti [FIN] 186 F5
Juorkuna [FIN] 196 E4
Jupiter [RO] 148 G1
Jurbarkas [LT] 200 E5
Jurignac [F] 66 E1
Jurklošter [SLO] 74 D5
Jurków [PL] 52 B4
Jūrmala [LV] 198 D5
Jurmo [FIN] 176 C4
Jurmo [FIN] 176 D6
Jurovski Brod [HR] 74 D6
Jurowce [PL] 24 E5
Jurva [FIN] 186 B3
Jurvala [FIN] 178 D2
Jurvansalo [FIN] 186 G2
Jushkino [RUS] 198 G2
Jushkozero [RUS] 196 H3
Jussey [F] 58 B3
Juszkowy Gród [PL] 24 F6
Juta [H] 74 H4
Jüterbog [D] 34 D3
Jutis [S] 190 F2
Jutrosin [PL] 36 D5
Jutsajaura [S] 192 G6
Juujärvi [FIN] 194 E8
Juuka [FIN] 188 E1
Juupajoki [FIN] 186 E6
Juurikka [FIN] 188 G4
Juva [FIN] 176 D4
Juva [FIN] 188 D5
Juvanum [I] 116 D5
Juvigny-le-Tertre [F] 26 E4
Juvola [FIN] 188 E4
Juvre [DK] 156 B3
Juzennecourt [F] 44 C6
Južnyj [RUS] 22 H2
Jyderup [DK] 156 F2
Jylhä [FIN] 186 G1
Jyllinge [DK] 156 G2
Jyllinkoski [FIN] 186 C5
Jyrkäntoski [FIN] 194 F8
Jyrkha [FIN] 196 F5
Jyväskylä [FIN] 186 G4

K

Kaalamo [RUS] 188 G4
Kaalasjärvi [S] 192 G5
Kaalinen / Ikalis [FIN] 186 D6
Kaamanen [FIN] 194 D4
Kaanaa [FIN] 186 E6
Kääntöjärvi [S] 192 H5
Kaarela [FIN] 196 D3
Kaaresuvanto [FIN] 192 H4
Kaarina [FIN] 176 D4
Kaarma [EST] 198 C3
Käärmelahti [FIN] 188 F5
Kaarssen [D] 18 H5
Kaartilankoski [FIN] 188 E5
Kaatsheuvel [NL] 16 D6
Kaavi [FIN] 188 D2
Kaba [H] 76 G1
Kabakca [TR] 150 D2
Kabalar [TR] 152 G4
Kabaltepe [TR] 130 H5
Kabböle [FIN] 178 B4
Kåbdalis [S] 190 H2
Kabelvåg [N] 192 D4
Kabile [LV] 198 C5
Kabiešikovo [BG] 148 F4
Kać [SRB] 142 F1
Kačanik [KS] 146 C6
Kacelovo [BG] 148 D2
Kaceřov [CZ] 48 E4
Kachanovo [RUS] 198 G4
Kačikol [KS] 146 C5
Káčina [CZ] 48 H4
Kácov [CZ] 48 G4
Kaczorów [PL] 50 B1
Kadaň [CZ] 48 E3
Kadarkút [H] 74 H4
Kadıkalesi [TR] 152 D5
Kadıköy [TR] 150 B4
Kadıköy [TR] 152 F4
Kadıköy [TR] 154 G2
Kadłubówka [PL] 38 E1
Kadłub Turawski [PL] 50 E2
Kadrifakovo [MK] 128 F1
Kadyanda [TR] 154 F2
Kadzidło [PL] 24 C5
Käenkoski [FIN] 188 G1
Kåfjord [N] 194 C1
Kaga [S] 166 H5
Kåge [S] 196 A4
Kågeröd [S] 158 C2
Kagkádi [GR] 136 C1
Kaharlyk [UA] 202 D7
Kahla [D] 46 H1
Kaiáfas [GR] 136 C2
Kaïméni Chóra [GR] 136 G2
Käina [EST] 198 C2
Kainach bei Voitsberg [A] 74 D2
Kainasto [FIN] 186 B4
Kaindorf [A] 74 E2
Kainu [FIN] 186 D1
Kainulasjärvi [S] 194 B7
Kaipiainen [FIN] 178 C2
Kairahta [FIN] 186 G4
Kairala [FIN] 194 E7
Kairila [FIN] 176 D1
Kaisepakte [S] 192 F4
Kaiserbach [D] 46 D6
Kaisersesch [D] 30 G6
Kaiserslautern [D] 44 H3
Kaiser-Wilhelm-Koog [D] 18 E3
Kaisheim [D] 60 D2
Kaišiadoris [LT] 200 F5
Kaitainsalmi [FIN] 196 F5
Kaitsor [FIN] 186 B2
Kaivanto [FIN] 196 E4
Kaivomäki [FIN] 188 D5
Kajaani / Kajana [FIN] 196 E5
Kajana / Kajaani [FIN] 196 E5
Kajánújfalu [H] 76 E3
Kajetans-Brücke [A] 72 C2
Kajoo [FIN] 188 E1
Kájov [CZ] 62 B2
Kajraly [RUS] 194 F7
Kakanj [BIH] 142 D4
Kakarriq [AL] 128 A1
Kakavi [AL] 132 C1
Kakerbeck [D] 34 B1
Kakhovka [UA] 204 G3
Käkilahti [FIN] 196 E5
Kaklıc [TR] 152 C4
Kaklik [TR] 152 G5
Kaklik [TR] 152 G5
Kakmă [HR] 112 G5
Kąkolewnica Wschodnia [PL] 38 E4
Kakopetriá [CY] 154 F5
Kakóvatos [GR] 136 C3
Kăkrina [BG] 148 B3
Kakslauttanen [FIN] 194 D5
Kaktyni [LV] 198 E5
Kakuåsen [S] 190 E6
Kakushöhle [D] 30 G5
Kál [H] 64 E6
Kälä [FIN] 186 H5
Kalaja [FIN] 196 D6
Kalajoki [FIN] 196 C5
Kalak [N] 194 D2
Kalakoski [FIN] 186 D4
Kalamáki [GR] 132 H2
Kalamáki [GR] 134 A2
Kalamariá [GR] 128 H4
Kalamáta [GR] 136 D4
Kalámi [GR] 140 C4
Kalamítsi [GR] 130 D6
Kálamos [GR] 134 C5
Kalamotí [GR] 134 G5
Kalampáki [GR] 130 D3
Kalampáki [GR] 132 E2
Kalanchak [RUS] 204 G3
Kalándra [GR] 130 B6
Kalá Nerá [GR] 132 H2
Kalanti [FIN] 176 C3
Kälarne [S] 184 D3
Kálathos [GR] 154 D4
Kalavárda [GR] 154 D3
Kalávryta [GR] 136 D1
Kalax [FIN] 186 A4
Kalbe [D] 34 B1
Kalce [SLO] 74 B5
Kalčevo [BG] 148 E5
Káld [H] 74 G2
Kaldfarnes [N] 192 E3
Kaldhussoter [N] 180 E4
Kale [TR] 152 D1
Kale [TR] 152 F6
Kale [TR] 154 H3
Kaleburnu (Galinóporni) [CY] 154 H4
Kalekovets [BG] 148 B5
Kaleköy [TR] 130 G5
Kalela [FIN] 176 D3
Kalenić, Manastir- [SRB] 146 C2
Kálergo [GR] 134 D5
Kalesija [BIH] 142 E3
Kalety [PL] 50 F2
Kalétzi [GR] 132 D2
Kalétzi [GR] 136 C1
Kaleva [FIN] 176 E4
Kalevala [RUS] 196 G3
Kalí [GR] 128 G4
Kaliánoi [GR] 136 E1
Kalidón [GR] 132 E5
Kaliningrad [RUS] 22 G1
Kalinkavichy [BY] 202 C6
Kalinovik [BIH] 144 D2
Kalinovka [RUS] 24 C1
Kalinovo [PL] 24 D3
Kalinovo [SK] 64 D4
Kalirráchi [GR] 128 E6
Kalisty [PL] 22 G3
Kalisz [PL] 36 E4
Kalisz Pomorski [PL] 20 H5
Kalivári [GR] 134 E6
Kalix [S] 196 C2
Kaljord [N] 192 D4
Kalkan [TR] 154 G3
Kalkar [D] 16 F6
Kalkgruber [DK] 160 C5
Kalkım [TR] 152 C1
Kalkkinen [FIN] 178 A2
Kall [D] 30 G5
Kall [S] 182 F1
Källa [S] 162 H4
Kallarat [AL] 128 B6
Källarbo [S] 174 C5
Kallaste [EST] 198 F2
Kallbäck [FIN] 178 A4
Källberget [S] 182 F3
Källered [S] 160 H2
Kalli [EST] 198 D3
Kallimasiá [GR] 134 G5
Kallinge [S] 158 F1
Kallio [FIN] 186 D5
Kallio [FIN] 196 F5
Kalliojoki [FIN] 196 G4
Kallislahti [FIN] 188 E5
Kallithéa [GR] 128 G6
Kallithéa [GR] 130 C3
Kallithéa [GR] 130 C6
Kallithéa [GR] 136 D2
Kallithéa [GR] 154 D3
Kalliuskoski [FIN] 196 E4
Kallmünz [D] 48 B6
Kalló [H] 64 D5
Kallön [S] 190 G3
Kalloní [GR] 134 G2
Kalloní [GR] 136 F2
Kállósemjén [H] 64 H5
Kallsedet [S] 190 D6
Kallträsk [FIN] 186 B5
Källunga [S] 162 B1
Kallunki [FIN] 194 F7
Kalmakattio [FIN] 194 C5
Kálmánháza [H] 64 G5
Kalmar [S] 162 G5
Kalmari [FIN] 186 F3
Kalná [CZ] 48 G4
Kalna [SRB] 146 E3
Kalná nad Hronom [SK] 64 B4
Kalnciems [LV] 198 D5
Kalnik [PL] 22 G3
Kalochóri [GR] 128 E5
Kaló Chorió [GR] 140 F5
Kalocsa [H] 76 C4
Kalofer [BG] 148 B5
Kalogriá [GR] 132 E6
Kaloí Liménes [GR] 140 E5
Kalókastro [GR] 130 B3
Kalonéri [GR] 128 E5
Kaló Nero [GR] 136 C3
Kalopanagiótis [CY] 154 F5
Kaloskopí [GR] 132 G4
Kalotina [BG] 146 F4
Kaloyan [BG] 148 F2
Kaloyanovo [BG] 148 B5
Kálóz [H] 76 B2
Kalpáki [GR] 132 C1
Kalpio [FIN] 196 E4
Kals [A] 72 F2
Kalsdorf [A] 74 D2
Kalsdorf [A] 74 E2
Kalsvik [S] 168 E3
Kaltanenai [LT] 200 G4
Kaltenkirchen [D] 18 F3
Kaltennordheim [D] 46 F2
Kaltinėnai [LT] 200 E4
Kaluga [RUS] 202 F4
Kalugerovo [BG] 148 A5
Kalundborg [DK] 156 E2
Kalush [UA] 204 C2
Kałuszyn [PL] 38 C3
Kalv [S] 162 B3
Kalvåg [N] 180 B5
Kalvarija [LT] 24 E2
Kalvatn [N] 180 D4
Kalvehave [DK] 156 G4
Kalven [N] 194 B1
Kälviä / Kelviå [FIN] 196 C6
Kälvik [S] 162 G2
Kalvitsa [FIN] 188 C5
Kalvola [FIN] 176 G2
Kalwang [A] 74 C1
Kalwaria Zebrzydowska [PL] 50 H4
Kalyazin [RUS] 202 F2
Kálymnos [GR] 154 A2
Kalynivka [UA] 202 C8
Kalývia [GR] 132 E4
Kám [H] 74 G2
Kamanski Vučiak [HR] 142 C1
Kamáres [GR] 138 D3
Kamáres [GR] 138 E3
Kamáres [GR] 140 E5
Kamariótissa [GR] 130 F4
Kamburovo [BG] 148 D3
Kamchiya [BG] 148 F3
Káméiros [GR] 154 D4
Kamen [BG] 148 C3
Kámen [CZ] 48 G5
Kamen [D] 32 C4
Kamenari [MNE] 144 D4
Kaména Voúrla [GR] 132 H4
Kamen Bryag [BG] 148 G2
Kamengrad [BIH] 142 B2
Kamenica [MK] 146 E6
Kamenice nad Lipou [CZ] 48 G6
Kamenichý Hrad [SK] 52 C6
Kameničná [SK] 64 A5
Kamenka [RUS] 178 F3
Kamennogorsk [RUS] 178 F2
Kamenný Újezd [CZ] 62 C2
Kameno [BG] 148 F4
Kamenovo [BG] 148 D2
Kamensko [HR] 142 C1
Kamensko [HR] 144 B2
Kamenz [D] 34 F6
Kamëz [AL] 128 B2
Kamianets'-Podil's'kyi [UA] 204 D2
Kamianka [UA] 202 E8
Kamianka-Dniprovs'ka [UA] 204 H2
Kamičak [BIH] 142 B3
Kamień [PL] 52 E3
Kamienica [PL] 52 B5
Kamieniec Ząbkowicki [PL] 50 C2
Kamienka [SK] 52 B5
Kamień Krajeński [PL] 22 C5
Kamienna Góra [PL] 50 B2
Kamień Pomorski [PL] 20 F3
Kamieńsk [PL] 36 G6
Kamínia [GR] 130 F6
Kamínia [GR] 132 D1
Kamion [PL] 38 A2
Kammerstein [A] 74 C1
Kamnica [SLO] 74 C5
Kamnik [SLO] 74 C4
Kampánis [GR] 128 H4
Kampen [D] 156 A4
Kampen [NL] 16 F4
Kamperland [NL] 16 B6
Kampiá [GR] 134 G4
Kampinos [PL] 38 A3
Kamp Lintfort [D] 30 G3
Kampor [HR] 112 F3
Kámpos [GR] 132 F5
Kámpos [GR] 136 D4
Kámpos [GR] 138 H2
Kámpos [GR] 140 B4
Kamula [FIN] 196 E5
Kamyanyets [BY] 38 G2
Kamyanyuki [BY] 38 G2
Kamýk nad Vltavou [CZ] 48 F5
Kanal [SLO] 72 H5
Kanala [FIN] 186 E1
Kanála [GR] 138 C2
Kanália [GR] 132 H2
Kanalláki [GR] 132 C3
Kanatlarci [MK] 128 E3
Kańczuga [PL] 52 E3
Kandava [LV] 198 C5
Kandel [D] 46 B5
Kandern [D] 58 E4
Kandersteg [CH] 70 D2
Kandestederne [DK] 160 E2
Kandíla [GR] 136 E2
Kandira [TR] 150 G2
Kanepi [EST] 198 F3
Kanestraum [N] 180 F2
Kanfanar [HR] 112 D2
Kangas [FIN] 196 D5
Kangasaho [FIN] 186 E3
Kangasala [FIN] 176 F1
Kangashäkki [FIN] 186 G3
Kangaskylä [FIN] 186 F1
Kangaslampi [FIN] 188 D4
Kangasniemi [FIN] 186 H5
Kanin [PL] 22 B2
Kaninkola [FIN] 176 E4
Kaniv [UA] 202 E7
Kanižarica [SLO] 74 D6
Kanjiža [SRB] 76 E5
Kanjon Cetine [HR] 144 A2
Kanjon Ugar [BIH] 142 C3
Kankaanpää [FIN] 186 C6
Kankainen [FIN] 186 G4
Kankova [SLO] 74 E3
Kånna [S] 162 C5
Kannonkoski [FIN] 186 F2
Kannus [FIN] 196 C5
Kannuskoski [FIN] 178 D2
Kanpaneta / Campanas [E] 84 B4
Kansız [TR] 150 E5
Kanstad [N] 192 E4
Kantala [FIN] 188 C4
Kántanos [GR] 140 B5
Kanteemaa [FIN] 176 E3
Kántia [GR] 136 F2
Kantojoki [FIN] 194 F8
Kantokylä [FIN] 196 D5
Kantomaanpää [FIN] 194 C8
Kantornes [N] 192 F2
Kantorp [S] 168 B4
Kantti [FIN] 186 C5
Kanturk [IRL] 4 C4
Kányavár [H] 74 F3
Kaolinovo [BG] 148 E2
Kaona [SRB] 146 B3
Kaonik [BIH] 142 D4
Kaonik [SRB] 146 C3
Kąp [PL] 24 C3
Kapaklı [TR] 150 E4
Kapaklı [TR] 152 D3
Kapandríti [GR] 134 C5
Kāpas [LV] 198 C5
Kapčiamiestis [LT] 24 F3
Kapelludden [S] 162 G5
Kapfenberg [A] 74 D1
Kapıkaya [TR] 152 F2
Kapıkırı [TR] 152 D6
Kapinci [HR] 74 H6
Kapitan Andreevo [BG] 150 A2
Kaplica (Davlós) [CY] 154 G4
Kaplice [CZ] 62 C3
Kapolcs [H] 74 H2
Kápolna [H] 64 E5
Kaposfüred [H] 74 H4
Kaposvár [H] 76 A4
Kapp [N] 172 B4
Kappel [D] 44 H2
Kappel [D] 58 E2
Kappeln [D] 18 F1
Kappelshamn [S] 168 G3
Kappelskär [S] 168 F2
Kappl [A] 72 B1
Kaprun [A] 72 F1
Kapsáli [GR] 136 F6
Kápsas [GR] 136 E2
Kapušany [SK] 64 G2
Kapuvár [H] 62 G6
Karaağaç [TR] 150 G2
Karabayır [TR] 154 F1
Karabeylı [TR] 152 G3
Karabiga [TR] 150 C4
Karabörtlen [TR] 154 E1
Karaburun [TR] 134 H4
Karaburun [TR] 150 E2
Karacaali [TR] 150 F4
Karacabey [TR] 150 E5
Karacaköy [TR] 150 D2
Karacalar [TR] 152 D2
Karacalar [TR] 152 E2
Karaçalı [TR] 150 G2
Karaçam [TR] 152 D2
Karacaoğlan [TR] 150 B2
Karacaşehir [TR] 150 H5
Karacasu [TR] 152 F5
Karaçulha [TR] 154 F2
Karád [H] 76 A3
Karahallı [TR] 152 G4
Karahisar [TR] 152 F5
Karainebeyli [TR] 150 B5
Karaisen [BG] 148 C3
Karakadağ [TR] 150 C1
Karakagür [TR] 150 B3
Karakamza [TR] 150 B1
Karakaya [TR] 152 D6
Karakiani [GR] 136 G1
Karakoumi (Karakum) [CY] 154 G5
Karaköy [TR] 152 B1
Karaköy [TR] 152 D4
Karaköy [TR] 152 F4
Karakum (Karakoumi) [CY] 154 G5
Karakür [TR] 152 F2
Karakurt [TR] 152 D2
Karakuzu [TR] 152 C3
Karala [EST] 198 C3
Karalaks [N] 194 C3
Karali [RUS] 188 H3
Karalin [BY] 24 H5
Karamanci [BG] 148 C6
Karamandere [TR] 150 D2
Karamanlı [TR] 152 H6
Karamürsel [TR] 150 F3
Karamyshevo [RUS] 198 H3
Karancslapujtő [H] 64 D4
Karaova [TR] 154 C1
Karapazarı [TR] 150 H5
Karapelit [BG] 148 F2
Karapürçek [TR] 150 H3
Karasjok [N] 194 C3
Karasu [TR] 150 H2
Kárász [H] 76 B4
Karataş [TR] 152 E3
Karats [S] 190 G1
Karavanški Predor [A/SLO] 74 B4
Karavás [GR] 136 F6
Karaveliler [TR] 152 C2
Karavelovo [BG] 148 E5
Karavos [GR] 134 C5
Karavostasi (Gemikonağı) [CY] 154 F5
Karavostásis [GR] 138 E4
Karavukovo [SRB] 142 E1
Karayakuplu [TR] 150 G3
Karbasan [TR] 152 G4
Karbenning [S] 168 B1
Kårböle [S] 182 H6
Karby [DK] 160 C4
Karby [S] 168 E2
Karcag [H] 76 F1
Karczowiska [PL] 36 B5
Kardakáta [GR] 132 C6
Kardam [BG] 148 G1
Kardámaina [GR] 154 B2
Kardámyla [GR] 134 G4
Kardamýli [GR] 136 D4
Kardašova-Řečice [CZ] 48 G6
Kardítsa [GR] 132 F2
Kärdla [EST] 198 C2
Kardos [H] 76 F3
Kardoskút [H] 76 F4
Kåremo [S] 162 G5
Karersee / Carezza al Lago [I] 72 D3
Karesuando [S] 192 H4
Kärevere [EST] 198 F2
Kargalı [TR] 150 F2
Kargı [TR] 154 F2
Kargów [PL] 52 C2
Kargowa [PL] 36 B3
Karhujärvi [FIN] 194 E7
Karhukangas [FIN] 196 D5
Karhula [FIN] 178 C4
Kårhus [N] 164 B1
Karhusjärvi [FIN] 178 E2
Kari [FIN] 188 D1
Karianí [GR] 130 C4
Karigasniemi [FIN] 194 C3
Karijoki / Bötom [FIN] 186 B4
Karine [TR] 152 C6
Karinkanta [FIN] 196 D4
Karis / Karjaa [FIN] 176 F5
Karise [DK] 156 G3
Karítaina [GR] 136 D2
Karjaa / Karis [FIN] 176 F5
Karjala [FIN] 176 D3
Karjalohja [FIN] 176 F5
Kärjenkoski [FIN] 186 B5
Kärkäälä [FIN] 186 G3
Karkaloú [GR] 136 D2
Kärki [LV] 198 E4
Karkkila / Högfors [FIN] 176 G4
Karkku [FIN] 176 E1
Karklampi [FIN] 186 F6
Kärkölä [FIN] 176 F4
Kärkölä [FIN] 176 H3
Karksi-Nuia [EST] 198 E3
Karlby [FIN] 168 H1
Karleby / Kokkola [FIN] 196 C6
Karlevistenen [S] 162 G5
Karlewo [PL] 22 F6
Karl Gustav [S] 160 H3
Karlholmsbruk [S] 174 F4
Karlino [PL] 20 H3
Karlö / Hailuoto [FIN] 196 D4
Karlobag [HR] 112 F4
Karlovac [HR] 112 G1
Karlóvasi [GR] 152 C5
Karlova Studánka [CZ] 50 D4
Karlovo [BG] 148 B4
Karlovy Vary [CZ] 48 D3
Karłowice [PL] 50 D1
Karlsberg [D] 44 H2
Karlsberg [S] 162 D1
Karlsberg [S] 172 H1
Karlsborg [S] 166 G5
Karlsborg [S] 196 C3
Karlshamn [S] 158 E1
Karlshöfen [D] 18 E4
Karlskoga [S] 166 G3
Karlskrona [S] 158 F1
Karlslunde Strand [DK] 156 G3
Karlsrud [N] 170 F5
Karlsruhe [D] 46 B6
Karlstad [S] 166 F3
Karlstadt [D] 46 E3
Karlštejn [CZ] 48 F4
Karlštejn [CZ] 50 B5
Karlstift [A] 62 C3
Karlstorp [S] 162 E3
Karmas [S] 192 F6
Kärnä [FIN] 186 D2
Kärnä [FIN] 186 G2
Kärnäsens Hembygdsgärd [S] 166 F1
Karniszyn [PL] 22 G6
Karnobat [BG] 148 E4
Karojba [HR] 112 D1
Karousádes [GR] 132 A2
Karow [D] 20 B4
Karpacz [PL] 50 A2
Karpasolo [FIN] 188 F3
Kárpathos [GR] 140 H3
Karpenísi [GR] 132 F4
Karperó [GR] 132 E1
Karpuzlu [TR] 152 E6
Karrantza / Carranza [E] 82 F3
Kärrbackstrand [S] 172 E3
Kärrbo [S] 168 A1
Karrebæksminde [DK] 156 F4
Kärsämä [FIN] 196 D4
Kärsämäki [FIN] 196 D5
Kärsava [LV] 198 G5
Karsibór [PL] 20 E4
Karşıyaka [TR] 150 D4
Karsjö [S] 174 D1
Karstädt [D] 20 A5
Karst en Yesos [E] 102 H5
Kärstna [EST] 198 E3
Karstø [N] 164 A2
Karstula [FIN] 186 F3
Kartal [TR] 150 F3
Kartala [BG] 146 G6
Kartena [LT] 200 D4
Kartéri [GR] 132 C3
Karteros [GR] 140 E4
Karthaía [GR] 138 C2
Karttula [FIN] 186 H2
Kartuzy [PL] 22 D2
Karungi [S] 196 C2
Karunki [FIN] 196 C2
Karup [DK] 160 C5
Karuse [EST] 198 D2
Karvala [FIN] 186 D2
Kärväskylä [FIN] 186 G1
Kårvatn [N] 180 G3
Karvia [FIN] 186 C5
Karvik [N] 192 H2
Kårvikhamn [N] 192 F2
Karviná [CZ] 50 F4
Karvio [FIN] 188 E3
Karvounári [GR] 132 C3
Karwia [PL] 22 D1
Karwica [PL] 24 C4
Karyá [GR] 128 G6
Karyá [GR] 132 C4
Karyá [GR] 136 E2
Karyés [GR] 130 D5
Karyés [GR] 132 G3
Karyés [GR] 136 E3
Karyótissa [GR] 128 G4
Karyoúpoli [GR] 136 E5
Károstos [GR] 134 D6
Kås [DK] 160 D3
Kaş [TR] 154 G3
Kasaba [TR] 154 G3
Kašalj [SRB] 146 B4
Kascyukovichy [BY] 202 D5
Kåseberga [S] 158 D3
Kasejovice [CZ] 48 E5
Kashin [RUS] 202 E2
Kashirskoye [RUS] 200 C5
Kašina [HR] 74 E5
Kasinka Wielka [PL] 52 B4
Kåskats [S] 190 H2
Kaski [FIN] 176 F5
Kaskii [FIN] 188 D5
Kaskinen / Kaskö [FIN] 186 A4
Kaskö / Kaskinen [FIN] 186 A4
Kas'kovo [RUS] 178 G5
Kaslania Pass [GR] 128 F5
Käsmu [EST] 198 E1
Kasnäs [FIN] 176 E6
Káspakas [GR] 130 F6
Kašperk [CZ] 48 E6
Kašperské Hory [CZ] 48 E6
Kaspichan [BG] 148 E3
Kassa [FIN] 194 B7
Kassándreia [GR] 130 B6
Kassari [EST] 198 C2
Kassel [D] 32 F5
Kassiópi [GR] 132 B2
Kassópi [GR] 132 C3
Kastabos [TR] 154 D2
Kastaniá [GR] 128 G5
Kastaniá [GR] 132 E2
Kastaniá [GR] 132 F3
Kastaniá [GR] 136 E4
Kastaniá [GR] 136 E1
Kastaniá [GR] 136 F5
Kastaniés [GR] 150 A2
Kastelholms [FIN] 176 B5
Kastellaun [D] 44 H2
Kastélli [GR] 140 B4
Kastélli [GR] 140 F5
Kaštel Stari [HR] 142 A5
Kaštel Žegarski [HR] 112 H5
Kasterlee [B] 30 D3
Kastl [D] 46 H5
Kastlösa [S] 162 G6
Kastneshamn [N] 192 E3
Kastorf [D] 18 G4
Kastoriá [GR] 128 E5
Kastráki [GR] 132 E4
Kastre [EST] 198 F3
Kastri [GR] 140 C6
Kástro [GR] 134 A5
Kástro [GR] 134 B3
Kástro [GR] 136 B1
Kastrosykiá [GR] 132 C3
Kastrup [DK] 156 H3
Kaszaper [H] 76 F4
Katáfyto [GR] 130 C2
Katákolo [GR] 136 B2
Kataloinen [FIN] 176 H2
Kätänjoki [FIN] 186 D3
Katápola [GR] 138 G4
Katará Pass [GR] 132 E1
Katastári [GR] 136 A2
Kätaviken [S] 190 E2
Katerbow [D] 20 C6
Kateríni [GR] 128 G5
Kateřinská [CZ] 50 C6
Katerloch [A] 74 D2
Katerma [FIN] 196 F5
Kätkasuvanto [FIN] 194 B6
Kätkesuando [S] 194 B6
Katlanovo [MK] 128 E1
Katlanovska Banja [MK] 128 F1
Katlenburg-Duhm [D] 32 G4
Káto Achaïa [GR] 132 E6
Káto Alepochóri [GR] 134 B6
Káto Aséa [GR] 136 D3
Katochí [GR] 132 E5
Káto Dolianá [GR] 136 E3
Káto Kleitoría [GR] 136 D1
Káto Makrinoú [GR] 132 E5
Káto Nevrokópi [GR] 130 C2
Káto Pýrgos [CY] 154 F5
Káto Samikó [GR] 136 C2
Káto Tithoréa [GR] 132 H5
Katoúna [GR] 132 D4
Káto Velitsés [GR] 136 C1
Káto Vérmio [GR] 128 F5
Katovice [CZ] 48 E6
Káto Vlasía [GR] 136 D1
Káto Vrontoú [GR] 130 C2
Katowice [PL] 50 G3
Káto Zákros [GR] 140 H5
Katrineberg [S] 174 D3
Katrineholm [S] 168 B4
Katschberg Tunnel [A] 72 H2
Kattavía [GR] 154 C5
Katthammarsvik [S] 168 G5
Kattilakoski [FIN] 186 D1
Kättilstad [S] 162 F1
Kattisavan [S] 190 G4
Kattlunds [S] 168 G6
Kattuvuoma [S] 192 G4
Katumäki [FIN] 188 C3
Katundi i Ri [AL] 128 A2
Katuntsi [BG] 130 B2
Katwijk aan Zee [NL] 16 C4
Katy [PL] 20 F4
Kąty [PL] 52 E2
Katyčiai [LT] 200 D5
Katymár [H] 76 C5
Kąty Wrocławskie [PL] 50 C1
Kaub [D] 46 B3
Kaufbeuren [D] 60 C5

274 Kau - Koc

Kaufering [D] 60 D4
Kaufungen [D] 32 F5
Kauhajärvi [FIN] 186 C5
Kauhajärvi [FIN] 186 D2
Kauhajoki [FIN] 186 B4
Kauhava [FIN] 186 C2
Kaukalampi [FIN] 176 H3
Kaukela [FIN] 176 H1
Kaukonen [FIN] 194 C6
Kauksi [EST] 198 F2
Kaukuri [FIN] 176 F5
Kaulbach [D] 44 H3
Kaunas [LT] 200 F5
Kaunata [LV] 198 G5
Kauniainen / Grankulla [FIN] 176 H5
Kaunos [TR] 154 E2
Kauns [A] 72 C1
Kaupanger [N] 170 D2
Kaurajärvi [FIN] 186 C2
Kauria [FIN] 178 D1
Kauša [LV] 198 F6
Kausala [FIN] 178 B3
Kaustby / Kaustinen [FIN] 196 C6
Kaustinen / Kaustby [FIN] 196 C6
Kautokeino [N] 194 B4
Kauttua [FIN] 176 D3
Káva [H] 76 D1
Kavacık [TR] 150 B3
Kavacık [TR] 152 E1
Kavacık [TR] 152 H5
Kavadarci [MK] 128 F2
Kavajë [AL] 128 A3
Kavak [TR] 150 B4
Kavakdere [TR] 150 C2
Kavakköy [TR] 152 E6
Kavakli [TR] 130 H2
Kavaklı [TR] 150 B2
Kavaklı [TR] 150 E3
Kavaklıdere [TR] 152 E6
Kavála [GR] 130 D3
Kavarna [BG] 148 G2
Kavaröskaten [S] 174 G5
Kåvenvallen [S] 182 E4
Kävlinge [S] 158 C2
Kávos [GR] 132 B3
Kavoúsi [GR] 140 G5
Kavşit [TR] 152 E5
Kavýli [GR] 130 H1
Kaxholmen [S] 162 D2
Kayabaşı [TR] 154 G1
Kayaköy [TR] 152 D4
Kayaköy [TR] 154 F2
Kayalar [TR] 150 D6
Kayapa [TR] 150 B1
Kayapa [TR] 152 C1
Käyhtiönmaa [FIN] 176 D2
Kayı [TR] 150 C3
Käylä [FIN] 194 F8
Kaymakçi [TR] 152 E4
Kaymaz [TR] 150 G2
Kaynarca [TR] 150 G2
Käyrämö [FIN] 194 D7
Kayran [TR] 152 F5
Kaysersberg [F] 58 D2
Kazaklar [TR] 152 F4
Kazanci [BIH] 142 B4
Kažani [MK] 128 E3
Kazanka [UA] 204 G2
Kazanlŭk [BG] 148 C4
Kazárma [GR] 136 D4
Kazichene [BG] 146 G5
Kazimierza Wielka [PL] 52 B3
Kazimierz Biskupi [PL] 36 E3
Kazimierz Dolny [PL] 38 D5
Kâzımpaşa [TR] 150 G3
Kazincbarcika [H] 64 F4
Kazlu-Rūda [LT] 24 F1
Kaznějov [CZ] 48 E4
Kaz'yany [BY] 200 H4
Kcynia [PL] 22 C6
Kdyně [CZ] 48 D5
Kéa [GR] 138 C2
Keadue [IRL] 2 D4
Keady [NIR] 2 F4
Kebrene [TR] 152 B1
Kecel [H] 76 C4
Kecskemét [H] 76 D2
Kėdainiai [LT] 200 F5
Kédros [GR] 132 F3
Kędzierzyn–Koźle [PL] 50 E3
Keel [IRL] 2 B3
Keenagh [IRL] 2 D5
Keenová [CZ] 48 D5
Kefalári [GR] 136 E1
Kéfalos [GR] 154 A3
Kefalóvryso [GR] 132 C1
Kefalóvryso [GR] 132 F1
Kefermarkt [A] 62 C4
Kefken [TR] 150 G2
Keflavík [IS] 192 A3
Kehidakustány [H] 74 G3
Kehl [D] 44 H6
Kehra [EST] 198 E1
Kehra [EST] 198 E1
Kehrig [D] 30 H6
Kehtna [EST] 198 E2
Keighley [GB] 10 E3
Keihärinkoski [FIN] 186 F2
Keihäskoski [FIN] 176 E3
Keikyä [FIN] 176 E2
Keila-Joa [EST] 198 D1
Keipene [LV] 198 E5
Keisala [FIN] 186 E2
Keitele [FIN] 186 G1
Keith [GB] 6 F5
Kekava [LV] 198 D5
Kékestető [H] 64 E5
Kelankyla [FIN] 196 E2
Kelberg [D] 30 G6
Kelbra [D] 32 H5
Këlcyrë [AL] 128 C6
Kelebia [H] 76 D4
Kelebija [SRB] 76 D5
Kelefá [GR] 136 E5
Kelekçi [TR] 152 G6
Kelemér [H] 64 E4
Keler [TR] 152 C5
Keles [TR] 150 F5
Kelheim [D] 60 E2
Kell [D] 44 G3
Kélla [GR] 128 F4
Kellemberg [D] 30 F4
Kellenhusen [D] 18 H2
Kellerberg [D] 32 D5
Kellinghusen [D] 18 F3
Kelloselkä [FIN] 194 F7
Kells [IRL] 2 F5
Kells [IRL] 4 B4
Kelmė [LT] 200 E4
Kelottijärvi [FIN] 192 H4
Kelso [GB] 8 F4
Keltaniemi [FIN] 178 B2
Kelujärvi [FIN] 194 D6
Kelvä [FIN] 188 F1
Kelviä / Kälviä [FIN] 196 C6
Kemaliye [TR] 152 E3
Kemalpaşa [TR] 152 D4
Kemberg [D] 34 D4
Kemecse [H] 64 H4
Kemence [H] 64 C5
Kemenesmagasi [H] 74 G1
Kemer [TR] 150 C4
Kemer [TR] 152 F5
Kemer [TR] 154 F2
Kemerburgaz [TR] 150 E2
Kemerköy [TR] 154 G3
Kémes [H] 76 A5
Kemi [FIN] 196 C3
Kemihaara [FIN] 194 E5
Kemijärvi [FIN] 194 E7
Keminmaa [FIN] 196 C2
Kemiö / Kimito [FIN] 176 E5
Kemnath [D] 48 B4
Kemnitz [D] 20 D3
Kemnitz [D] 34 D3
Kempele [FIN] 196 D4
Kempen [D] 30 G3
Kempolovo [RUS] 178 G5
Kempten [D] 60 C5
Kendal [GB] 10 E2
Kenderes [H] 76 F1
Kendice [SK] 64 G2
Kengis [S] 194 B7
Kengyel [H] 76 E2
Kenmare [IRL] 4 B4
Kentrikó [GR] 128 H3
Kéntro [GR] 136 C1
Kenyeri [H] 74 G1
Kenzingen [D] 58 E2
Kepa [RUS] 196 H3
Kepez [TR] 150 B5
Kępice [PL] 22 B3
Kepno [PL] 36 E6
Kepsut [TR] 152 D1
Kerameía [GR] 134 H2
Keramídi [GR] 132 H2
Keramítsa [GR] 132 C2
Keramos [TR] 154 C1
Keramotí [GR] 130 E3
Keräntöjärvi [S] 194 B6
Kerasiá [GR] 134 B4
Kerasochóri [GR] 132 E3
Kerasóna [GR] 132 D3
Keratéa [GR] 136 H1
Keratókampos [GR] 140 F5
Kerava / Kervo [FIN] 176 H4
Kerecsend [H] 64 E5
Kerekegyháza [H] 76 D2
Kerí [GR] 136 A2
Kerien [F] 26 A4
Kerimäki [FIN] 188 F5
Kerisalo [FIN] 188 D4
Kerjean, Château de– [F] 40 B1
Kerken [D] 30 G3
Kerkíni [GR] 128 H3
Kerkonkoski [FIN] 186 H3
Kerkrade [NL] 30 F4
Kérkyra [GR] 132 B2
Kerma [FIN] 188 E3
Kermen [BG] 148 D4
Kernascléden [F] 40 C3
Kerpen [D] 30 G4
Kerpiçlik [TR] 152 F2
Kërrabë [AL] 128 B3
Kersilö [FIN] 194 D6
Kerstimbo [S] 174 E5
Kerteminde [DK] 156 E3
Kertészsziget [H] 76 G2
Kertil [TR] 152 D2
Kervo / Kerava [FIN] 176 H4
Kerýneia (Girne) [CY] 154 G5
Kerzers [CH] 58 D6
Kesälahti [FIN] 188 G5
Keşan [TR] 150 B3
Kesarevo [BG] 148 D3
Kesasjäry [S] 194 B8
Kesh [NIR] 2 E3
Keskastel [F] 44 G5
Keskikylä [FIN] 196 D4
Keskinen [FIN] 196 F4
Kesselfall [A] 72 F1
Kesselsdorf [D] 34 E6
Kesten'ga [RUS] 196 H2
Kesteren [NL] 16 E5
Kesti [FIN] 186 B4
Kestilä [FIN] 196 E5
Keswick [GB] 8 E6
Keszthely [H] 74 G3
Kétegyháza [H] 76 G3
Ketenovo [MK] 146 E6
Ketomella [FIN] 194 B5
Kętrzyn [PL] 24 C3
Kétsoproni [H] 76 F3
Kettering [GB] 14 E2
Kettilsby [S] 166 D3
Kettwig [D] 30 G3
Kęty [PL] 50 G4
Ketzin [D] 34 D2
Keula [D] 32 G5
Keuruu [FIN] 186 F4
Keväjärvi [FIN] 194 E4
Kevelaer [D] 30 F2
Kevo [FIN] 194 D3
Kežmarok [SK] 52 B6
Khaapalampi [RUS] 188 H5
Khadzhiloni [BY] 24 H3
Kharava [BY] 38 H1
Kharmanli [BG] 148 D6
Khaskovo [BG] 148 C6
Khelyulya [RUS] 188 H5
Kherson [UA] 204 G3
Khisariya [BG] 148 B5
Khiytola [RUS] 178 G1
Khlebarovo [BG] 148 D2
Khmel'nyts'kyi [UA] 202 C8
Khmil'nyk [UA] 202 C8
Khodoriv [UA] 204 C2
Kholm [RUS] 202 C3
Kholm–Zhirkovskiy [RUS] 202 D3
Khorol [UA] 202 F7
Khotyn [UA] 204 D2
Khoyniki [BY] 202 D6
Khredino [RUS] 198 H3
Khust [UA] 204 C3
Khvoynaya [RUS] 202 D1
Khyriv [UA] 52 F5
Kiáto [GR] 132 H6
Kiaunoriai [LT] 200 E4
Kibæk [DK] 156 B1
Kiberg [N] 194 F2
Kiburi [LV] 198 B6
Kibyra [TR] 152 G6
Kičevo [MK] 128 D2
Kichenitsa [BG] 148 D2
Kichevo [BG] 148 F2
Kidałowice [PL] 52 F3
Kidderminster [GB] 12 G1
Kidlington [GB] 14 D3
Kidričevo [SLO] 74 E4
Kidsgrove [GB] 10 E5
Kidwelly [GB] 12 E2
Kiefersfelden [D] 60 F6
Kiel [D] 18 G2
Kielajoki [FIN] 194 D4
Kielce [PL] 52 B1
Kienberg [A] 72 F2
Kienborg [CH] 58 E5
Kiental [CH] 70 E1
Kierinki [FIN] 194 C7
Kiernozia [PL] 36 H3
Kiesilä [FIN] 178 D1
Kietävälä [FIN] 188 E6
Kietrz [PL] 50 E4
Kiezmark [PL] 22 E3
Kifisiá [GR] 134 C6
Kifjord [N] 194 D1
Kihelkonna [EST] 198 C3
Kihlanki [FIN] 194 B6
Kihniö [FIN] 186 D5
Kiihtelysvaara [FIN] 188 G3
Kiikala [FIN] 176 F4
Kiikka [FIN] 176 E2
Kiikoinen [FIN] 176 E1
Kiiminki [FIN] 196 D3
Kiiskilä [FIN] 196 D6
Kiistala [FIN] 194 C6
Kije [PL] 52 B2
Kijevo [BIH] 144 D1
Kijevo [HR] 142 A4
Kijevo [KS] 146 B5
Kijmajärvi [FIN] 176 E2
Kikerino [RUS] 178 G6
Kikinda [MNE] 204 B5
Kikinda [SRB] 76 F5
Kikół [PL] 36 G1
Kikut [N] 170 E4
Kil [N] 164 F4
Kil [S] 166 E2
Kil [S] 166 H3
Kila [GR] 128 F5
Kila [S] 166 E3
Kila [S] 168 B1
Kilafors [S] 174 D2
Kılavuzlar [TR] 152 H6
Kilbaha [IRL] 2 A6
Kilbeggan [IRL] 2 E5
Kilberry [IRL] 2 F5
Kilboghamn [N] 190 D2
Kilcar / Cill Charthaigh [IRL] 2 D2
Kilcock [IRL] 2 F6
Kilcolman Castle [IRL] 4 C4
Kilconnell [IRL] 2 D5
Kilcoole [IRL] 4 G3
Kilcooley Abbey [IRL] 4 E4
Kilcormac [IRL] 2 D6
Kilcullen [IRL] 2 E6
Kilcurry [IRL] 2 F4
Kildare [IRL] 2 E6
Kilderss [NIR] 2 F3
Kildorrery [IRL] 4 D4
Kilebygd [N] 164 G3
Kilen [N] 164 F2
Kilfenora [IRL] 2 B5
Kilfinnane [IRL] 4 D4
Kilgarvan [IRL] 4 B4
Kilifarevo [BG] 148 C4
Kilingi–Nõmme [EST] 198 E3
Kilitbahir [TR] 130 H5
Kilkee [IRL] 2 B6
Kilkeel [NIR] 2 G4
Kilkenny / Cill Chainnigh [IRL] 4 E4
Kilkieran / Cill Chiaráin [IRL] 2 B4
Kilkinkylä [FIN] 188 C6
Kilkinlea [IRL] 4 C3
Kilkís [GR] 128 H3
Kill [IRL] 4 E5
Killadysert [IRL] 2 B6
Killala [IRL] 2 C3
Killaloe [IRL] 2 C6
Killarney / Cill Airne [IRL] 4 B4
Killashandra [IRL] 2 E4
Killashee [IRL] 2 D5
Killeberg [S] 162 C6
Killeigh [IRL] 2 E6
Killenaule [IRL] 4 E4
Killimer [IRL] 2 B6
Killimor [IRL] 2 D5
Killin [GB] 8 D2
Killinge [S] 192 G5
Killinkoski [FIN] 186 D4
Killorglin [IRL] 4 B4
Killybegs [IRL] 2 D2
Killyleagh [NIR] 2 G4
Kilmacduagh Cathedral [IRL] 2 C5
Kilmacrenan [IRL] 2 E2
Kilmacthomas [IRL] 4 E5
Kilmaganny [IRL] 4 E4
Kilmaine [IRL] 2 C4
Kilmallock [IRL] 4 D4
Kilmanahan [IRL] 4 E4
Kilmarnock [GB] 8 D3
Kilmartin [GB] 8 C2
Kilmeaden [IRL] 4 E5
Kilmeage [IRL] 2 E6
Kilmeedy [IRL] 4 C4
Kilmelford [GB] 8 C2
Kilmichael [IRL] 4 C5
Kilmore Quay [IRL] 4 F5
Kilnaleck [IRL] 2 E4
Kilpisjärvi [FIN] 192 G3
Kilpola [FIN] 188 D5
Kilrush [IRL] 2 B6
Kilshanny [IRL] 4 B3
Kilsmo [S] 166 H4
Kilsyth [GB] 8 D3
Kiltealy [IRL] 4 F4
Kilternan [IRL] 4 G3
Kiltimagh [IRL] 2 C4
Kilvakkala [FIN] 186 D6
Kilwinning [GB] 8 C3
Kilyos [TR] 150 E2
Kimási [GR] 134 B4
Kimasozero [RUS] 196 H4
Kiminki [FIN] 186 E2
Kimito / Kemiö [FIN] 176 E5
Kimle [H] 62 H5
Kimméria [GR] 130 E2
Kimola [FIN] 178 B2
Kímolos [GR] 138 D4
Kimonkylä [FIN] 178 B3
Kimovaara [RUS] 196 H5
Kimry [RUS] 202 E2
Kincardine [GB] 8 E3
Kindberg [A] 62 D6
Kindelbrück [D] 32 H5
Kinderdijk, Molens van– [NL] 16 D5
Kinding [D] 46 G6
Kindsjön [S] 172 E4
Kinéta [GR] 134 B6
Kingisepp [RUS] 198 G1
Kingsbridge [GB] 12 D5
Kingscourt [IRL] 2 F5
King's Lynn [GB] 14 F1
Kingston upon Hull [GB] 10 G4
Kington [GB] 12 F1
Kınık [TR] 150 F5
Kınık [TR] 152 C2
Kınık [TR] 154 F3
Kınık [TR] 154 G1
Kınıkyeri [TR] 152 G6
Kinlochbervie [GB] 6 D2
Kinlochewe [GB] 6 C4
Kinlochleven [GB] 6 C6
Kinlough [IRL] 2 D3
Kinna [S] 162 B3
Kinnadoohy [IRL] 2 B4
Kinnarp [S] 162 C1
Kinnbäck [S] 196 B4
Kinnegad [IRL] 2 E5
Kinni [FIN] 178 C1
Kinnitty [IRL] 2 D6
Kinnula [FIN] 186 F1
Kinnuranlahti [FIN] 188 C1
Kinrooi [B] 30 E3
Kinross [GB] 8 E2
Kinsale [IRL] 4 C5
Kinsarvik [N] 170 C4
Kintai [LT] 200 D4
Kintaus [FIN] 186 F4
Kinvarra [IRL] 2 C5
Kióni [GR] 132 D5
Kiónia [GR] 138 E2
Kipen' [RUS] 178 G5
Kipi [EST] 198 C3
Kipilahti [FIN] 178 B4
Kipina [FIN] 196 E3
Kipoureío [GR] 132 F1
Kirakkakongäs [FIN] 194 D4
Kiralan [TR] 152 G4
Királyegyháza [H] 76 A5
Kıranköy [TR] 152 F3
Kirawsk [BY] 202 C5
Kiraz [TR] 152 E4
Kirazlı [TR] 150 B5
Kirbla [EST] 198 D2
Kırcasalih [TR] 150 B2
Kirchbach [A] 72 G3
Kirchbach [A] 74 E2
Kirchberg [A] 60 F6
Kirchberg [D] 44 H2
Kirchberg [D] 46 E5
Kirchberg an der Pielach [A] 62 D5
Kirchbichl [A] 60 F6
Kirchdorf [D] 20 A3
Kirchdorf [D] 32 E1
Kirchdorf an der Krems [A] 62 B5
Kirchen [D] 18 C3
Kirchenlamitz [D] 48 B3
Kirchentellinsfurt [D] 58 H2
Kirchenthumbach [D] 46 H4
Kirchhain [D] 32 E6
Kirchheim [D] 32 F6
Kirchheimbolanden [D] 46 B4
Kirchheim unter Teck [D] 58 H1
Kirchhm i.I. [A] 60 H4
Kirchlauter [D] 46 F3
Kirchlinteln [D] 18 E6
Kirchschlag [A] 62 F6
Kirchseeon [D] 60 E4
Kirchundem [D] 32 C5
Kirchzell [D] 46 D4
Kircubbin [NIR] 2 H4
Kireç [TR] 152 E1
Kirikküla [EST] 198 D1
Kırıklar [TR] 152 C1
Kiriou, Roche de– [F] 40 D2
Kiriši [RUS] 202 C1
Kirjaluokta [S] 192 F5
Kir'jamo [RUS] 178 E6
Kirkağaç [TR] 152 D2
Kirkby Lonsdale [GB] 10 E2
Kirkcaldy [GB] 8 E3
Kirkcudbright [GB] 8 D5
Kirkeby [N] 182 D1
Kirkehamn [N] 164 B5
Kirke Hvalsø [DK] 156 F3
Kirkenær [N] 172 D4
Kırkenes [N] 194 E3
Kirkholt [DK] 160 E3
Kírki [GR] 130 G3
Kirkjubæjarklaustur [IS] 192 B3
Kirkjubøur [FR] 160 B2
Kirkkolati [RUS] 188 H4
Kirkkonummi / Kyrkslätt [FIN] 176 G5
Kırklareli [TR] 150 B1
Kirkonkylä [FIN] 176 E4
Kırkpınar [TR] 152 H6
Kirkvollen [N] 182 D2
Kirkwall [GB] 6 G2
Kirn [D] 44 H2
Kirov [RUS] 202 E4
Kirovohrad [UA] 202 E8
Kirovsk [RUS] 202 B1
Kirovskoye [RUS] 178 G3
Kirriemuir [GB] 8 F2
Kirtorf [D] 46 D1
Kiruna [S] 192 G5
Kisa [S] 162 F1
Kisbér [H] 64 A6
Kisdobsza [H] 74 H5
Kiseljak [BIH] 144 C1
Kishartyán [H] 64 D5
Kisielice [PL] 22 F4
Kisielnica [PL] 24 D5
Kisko [FIN] 176 F5
Kisköre [H] 64 F6
Kiskőrös [H] 76 D3
Kiskundorozsma [H] 76 E4
Kiskunfélegyháza [H] 76 E3
Kiskunhalas [H] 76 D4
Kiskunlacháza [H] 76 C2
Kiskunmajsa [H] 76 D4
Kışla [TR] 152 F3
Kisláng [H] 76 B2
Kisslegg [D] 60 B5
Kisszállás [H] 76 D4
Kist [D] 46 E4
Kistanje [HR] 112 H5
Kistelek [H] 76 E4
Kisújszállás [H] 76 F1
Kisvárda [H] 64 H4
Kiszkowo [PL] 36 D2
Kiszombor [H] 76 F4
Kitajaur [S] 190 H2
Kitee [FIN] 188 G4
Kiten [BG] 148 F5
Kition [CY] 154 G5
Kitkiöjärvi [S] 194 B6
Kitkiöjoki [S] 194 B6
Kítros [GR] 128 G5
Kitsi [FIN] 196 H6
Kittelfjäll [S] 190 E4
Kittendorf [D] 20 C4
Kittilä [FIN] 194 C6
Kittsee [A] 62 G5
Kitula [FIN] 176 F4
Kitula [FIN] 186 G5
Kitzbühel [A] 60 F6
Kitzingen [D] 46 F4
Kitzloch–Klamm [A] 72 G1
Kiukainen [FIN] 176 D2
Kiurujärvi [FIN] 194 E6
Kiuruvesi [FIN] 196 E6
Kiutaköngäs [FIN] 194 F8
Kivadár [H] 74 H5
Kivéri [GR] 136 E2
Kivesjärvi [FIN] 196 E4
Kiviapaja [FIN] 188 E5
Kivijärvi [FIN] 186 F2
Kivik [S] 158 D3
Kivikangas [FIN] 186 E1
Kivilahti [FIN] 188 G1
Kivilompolo [FIN] 194 B5
Kivilompolo [FIN] 194 C8
Kivioja [FIN] 194 C8
Kiviõli [EST] 198 F1
Kivisalmi [FIN] 186 H3
Kivisuo [FIN] 186 G5
Kivivaara [FIN] 196 G5
Kivi–Vigala [EST] 198 D2
Kivotós [GR] 128 E6
Kıyıkışlacık [TR] 154 C1
Kıyıköy [TR] 150 D1
Kızılca [TR] 152 G6
Kızılcabölük [TR] 152 F5
Kızılcasöğüt [TR] 152 G3
Kızılinler [TR] 150 H5
Kızılören [TR] 152 H3
Kızılyaka [TR] 154 D1
Kjeeringvika [N] 192 E4
Kjelda [N] 190 C4
Kjeldebotn [N] 192 E4
Kjelfossen [N] 170 D2
Kjellerup [DK] 160 D6
Kjellmyra [N] 172 D4
Kjernmoen [N] 172 D3
Kjerringvoll [N] 182 C3
Kjerret [N] 166 D1
Kjerringvåg [N] 190 A6
Kjerringvik [N] 190 C6
Kjerstad [N] 180 D3
Kjøllefjord [N] 194 D1
Kjølsdal [N] 180 C5
Kjøpsvik [N] 192 E4
Kjøra [N] 180 H1
Kjulo / Köyliö [FIN] 176 D2
K. Kamíla [GR] 130 B3
Klacka–Lerberg [S] 166 G2
Kläckeberga [S] 162 G5
Kladanj [BIH] 142 E4
Kladnica [SRB] 146 A3
Kladnice [HR] 142 A5
Kladno [CZ] 48 F3
Kladovo [SRB] 204 C6
Kladruby [CZ] 48 D4
Klæbu [N] 182 B1
Klaffer [A] 62 D3
Klagenfurt [A] 74 B3
Klaipėda [LT] 200 D4
Klakegg [N] 180 D6
Klaksvík [FR] 160 B1
Klamila [FIN] 178 D3
Klana [HR] 112 E1
Klanac [HR] 112 G3
Klanjec [HR] 74 E5
Klanxbüll [D] 156 B4
Klåpen [N] 192 E3
Kläppen [S] 190 G3
Klarabro [S] 172 E4
Klärke [S] 184 E3
Klarup [DK] 160 E4
Klašnice [BIH] 142 C2
Klässbol [S] 166 E2
Klášterec nad Ohří [CZ] 48 D3
Klášter Teplá [CZ] 48 D4
Kláštor pod Znievom [SK] 64 C2
Klatovy [CZ] 48 D5
Klaukkala [FIN] 176 G4
Klaus an der Pyhrnbahn [A] 62 B5
Klausdorf [D] 20 D2
Klausdorf [D] 34 E3
Klausen / Chiusa [I] 72 D3
Klazienaveen [NL] 16 H3
Klazomenai [TR] 152 C4
Klębowiec [PL] 22 A5
Klecko [PL] 36 D2
Kleczew [PL] 36 E3
Klein Glödniz [A] 74 B3
Kleinhau [D] 30 F5
Kleinhaugsdorf [A] 62 E3
Klein Vielen [D] 20 C5
Kleinzell [A] 62 E5
Kleisoúra [GR] 132 D3
Kleive [N] 180 E3
Kleivegrend [N] 164 E2
Kleivstua [N] 170 H5
Klejniki [PL] 24 F6
Klemensker [DK] 158 E4
Klement [A] 62 F3
Klempenow [D] 20 D4
Klempicz [PL] 36 C1
Klenčí pod Čerchovem [CZ] 48 D5
Klenike [SRB] 146 D5
Klenjë [AL] 128 C2
Klenovica [HR] 112 F2
Kleppe [N] 164 A3
Kleppestø [N] 170 A3
Klerken [B] 28 F2
Kleśno [PL] 36 A1
Kleszczele [PL] 38 F2
Kletnya [RUS] 202 E5
Kleve [D] 16 F6
Klevshult [S] 162 D3
Klezeno [RUS] 198 G4
Klichaw [RUS] 202 C5
Kliczków [PL] 34 H5
Klietz [D] 34 C1
Klimátia [GR] 132 C2
Kliment [BG] 148 E2
Klimontów [PL] 52 B3
Klimontów [PL] 52 D2
Klimovo [RUS] 178 F3
Klimpfjäll [S] 190 E4
Klin [RUS] 202 E2
Klina [KS] 146 B5
Klinča Sela [HR] 74 E6
Klingenbach [A] 62 F6
Klingenmunster [D] 46 B5
Klingenthal [D] 48 C3
Klink [D] 20 C5
Klintehamn [S] 168 F5
Klintfors [S] 196 A4
Klintholm [DK] 156 G4
Klintsy [RUS] 202 D5
Kliplev [DK] 156 C4
Klippan [S] 158 C1
Klippen [S] 190 E3
Klippen [S] 190 G5
Klippinge [DK] 156 G3
Klírou [CY] 154 G5
Klis [HR] 144 A2
Klisino [PL] 50 E3
Klisura [BG] 148 A4
Klisura [SRB] 146 E5
Klisura Sutjeske [BIH] 144 D2
Klitmøller [DK] 160 C3
Klixbüll [D] 156 B4
Kljajićevo [SRB] 76 D6
Ključ [BIH] 142 B3
Klobouky u Brna [CZ] 62 G2
Kłobuck [PL] 50 F1
Klobuczyn [PL] 36 B5
Klobuk [BIH] 144 B2
Klockestrand [S] 184 F3
Kłoczew [PL] 38 D4
Kłodawa [PL] 34 H1
Kłodawa [PL] 36 F3
Kłodzko [PL] 50 C3
Kløfta [N] 172 B5
Klokkarvik [N] 170 A1
Klokkervik [N] 194 C2
Klokočevac [SRB] 146 D1
Klokočevci [HR] 76 B6
Klokotnica [BIH] 142 D3
Klooster [NL] 16 G4
Klos [AL] 128 B2
Klos [AL] 128 B1
Kloštar Ivanić [HR] 74 F6
Kloštar Podravski [HR] 74 G5
Kloster [S] 174 D5
Kloster Arnstein [D] 46 B2
Kloster Chorin [D] 34 F1
Klosterkirche in Altenmarkt [D] 60 G3
Klösterle [A] 72 B1
Klosterneuburg [A] 62 F4
Klosterruiner [N] 180 B4
Klosters [CH] 72 A2
Kloster Schäftlarn [D] 60 E5
Kloster Zella [D] 32 G5
Kloster Zinna [D] 34 D3
Kloten [S] 166 H1
Klötze [D] 34 A1
Klövertäsk [S] 196 B3
Kløvimoen [N] 190 D3
Klövsjö [S] 182 G4
Kl. Plasten [D] 20 C4
Kluczbork [PL] 50 E1
Klucze [PL] 50 G3
Kluczewsko [PL] 50 H1
Kluis [D] 20 D2
Kluki [PL] 22 C1
Kluki [PL] 36 G5
Klukowa Huta [PL] 22 D3
Klupe [BIH] 142 C3
Klusy [PL] 24 D4
Klutsiön [S] 182 E5
Klütz [D] 18 H3
Klyastsitsy [BY] 198 H6
Knaben [N] 164 C4
Knäm [S] 166 B4
Knapphus [N] 164 B1
Knäred [S] 162 B5
Knaresborough [GB] 10 F3
Knarvik [N] 170 B3
Knäsjö [S] 190 G6
Knätten [S] 182 G5
Knebel [DK] 160 E6
Knetzgau [D] 46 F3
Kneža [SLO] 72 H4
Knežak [SLO] 74 B6
Kneževi Vinogradi [HR] 76 C6
Kneževo [HR] 76 B5
Knezha [BG] 146 G3
Knežica [BIH] 142 B2
Knić [SRB] 146 B2
Knídi [GR] 128 F6
Knidos [TR] 154 B3
Kniebis [D] 58 F2
Knighton [GB] 10 C6
Knights Town [IRL] 4 A4
Knin [HR] 142 A4
Knislinge [S] 158 D1
Knittelfeld [A] 74 C2
Knivsta [S] 168 D2
Knjaževac [SRB] 146 E3
Knock [IRL] 2 C4
Knockcroghery [IRL] 2 D5
Knocknalina / Cnocán na Líne [IRL] 2 B2
Knocktopher [IRL] 4 E4
Knokke–Heist [B] 28 G1
Knosós [GR] 140 E4
Knottingley [GB] 10 F4
Knudshoved [DK] 156 E3
Knurów [PL] 50 F3
Knurowiec [PL] 38 C1
Knutby [S] 168 E1
Knutsford [GB] 10 D4
Knyazevo [RUS] 198 H5
Knyazhevo [BG] 148 E5
Knyazhicy [RUS] 198 G3
Knyszyn [PL] 24 E5
Kobarid [SLO] 72 H4
Kobbelveid [N] 192 E5
Kobeliaky [UA] 202 F7
København [DK] 156 H2
Koberg [S] 166 D6
Kobeřice [CZ] 50 E4
Kobiele Wielkie [PL] 36 H6
Kobilyane [BG] 130 F1
Kobišnica [SRB] 146 E1
Koblenz [D] 30 H6
Kobryn [BY] 38 G2
Kobuły [PL] 24 B4
Kobylany [PL] 38 F3
Kobylin [PL] 36 D4
Kobyłka [PL] 38 C2
Kobyl'nik [BY] 200 H5
Kocaali [TR] 150 B4
Kocaali [TR] 150 H2
Kocabaş [TR] 152 G5
Kocaburgaz [TR] 150 D4
Kocaçeşme [TR] 150 B4
Kocaeli (İzmit) [TR] 150 G3
Kocakaymaz [TR] 150 G2
Kočani [MK] 128 G1
Kocapınar [TR] 150 D5
Koçarlı [TR] 152 D5
Kocbeře [CZ] 50 A2
Koceljevo [SRB] 146 A1
Kočerin [BIH] 144 B2
Kočevje [SLO] 74 C6
Kočevska Reka [SLO] 74 C6
Kochel [D] 60 D5
Kocherinovo [BG] 146 F6
Kocherov [UA] 202 D7
Kochmar [BG] 148 F2
Kock [PL] 38 E4
Kocs [H] 64 B6
Kocsér [H] 76 E2
Kocsola [H] 76 B4
Kócsújfalu [H] 64 F6
Koczała [PL] 22 B4

Kodal [N] 164 H3
Koden [PL] 38 F3
Kodersdorf [D] 34 G6
Kodesjärvi [FIN] 186 B5
Kodrąb [PL] 36 H6
Koetschette [L] 44 E2
Kofçaz [TR] 150 B1
Köflach [A] 74 D2
Kögbo [S] 174 E4
Køge [DK] 156 G3
Kogila [MK] 128 E3
Kogula [EST] 198 C3
Kohfidisch [A] 74 F2
Kohila [EST] 198 D2
Kohtla-Järve [EST] 198 F1
Koigi [EST] 198 E2
Koijärvi [FIN] 176 F3
Koikkala [FIN] 188 D5
Koiláda [GR] 136 F3
Koilovtsi [BG] 148 B3
Kõima [EST] 198 D2
Köinge [S] 162 B4
Koirakoski [FIN] 196 F6
Koisjärvi [FIN] 176 G4
Koíta [GR] 136 E5
Koivu [FIN] 194 C8
Koivulahti / Kvevlax [FIN] 186 B2
Koivumäki [FIN] 188 E3
Kojetín [CZ] 50 D6
Kökar [FIN] 168 H1
Kokava nad Rimavicou [SK] 64 D3
Kokemäki / Kumo [FIN] 176 D2
Kokin Brod [SRB] 146 A3
Kokkála [GR] 136 E5
Kokkárlo [GR] 152 C5
Kokkila [FIN] 176 E5
Kókkina (Erenköy) [CY] 154 F5
Kókkino Neró [GR] 132 H1
Kokkola / Karleby [FIN] 198 C6
Kokkolahti [FIN] 188 F4
Koldö [AL] 128 C4
Koklioí [GR] 132 C1
Koknese [LV] 198 E5
Kokonvaara [FIN] 188 E2
Kokorevo [RUS] 198 H3
Kokořin [CZ] 48 G3
Koksijde-Bad [B] 28 F1
Kola [BIH] 142 B3
Köla [S] 166 D1
Kołacz [PL] 20 H4
Kołacze [PL] 38 F5
Koláka [GR] 134 A5
Koláre [SK] 64 C5
Kolari [FIN] 194 B7
Kolari [SRB] 142 H3
Kolárovo [SK] 64 A5
Kolåsen [S] 190 D6
Kolašin [MNE] 144 E3
Kolbäck [S] 168 B2
Kołbacz [PL] 20 F5
Kołbaskowo [PL] 20 F5
Kolbenshån [S] 182 E4
Kolbermoor [D] 60 F5
Kołbiel [PL] 38 C3
Kolbotn [N] 166 B1
Kolbudy Górne [PL] 22 D3
Kolbuszowa [PL] 52 D3
Kolby [DK] 156 E2
Kolby Kås [DK] 156 E2
Kołczewo [PL] 20 F3
Kołczygłowy [PL] 22 C3
Koldby [DK] 160 B4
Kolding [DK] 156 C3
Koleczkowo [PL] 22 D2
Koler [S] 196 A3
Kölesd [H] 76 B4
Kolešino [MK] 128 H2
Kolga-Jaani [EST] 198 E2
Kolho [FIN] 186 E5
Koli [FIN] 188 F1
Kolín [CZ] 48 H4
Kolin [PL] 20 G5
Kolind [DK] 160 E6
Kolindrós [GR] 128 G5
Kolinec [CZ] 48 E6
Kölingared [S] 162 C1
Kõljala [EST] 198 C3
Kolka [LV] 198 C4
Kolkonpää [FIN] 188 E5
Kolkontaipale [FIN] 188 D4
Kolky [UA] 202 B7
Kölleda [D] 34 A5
Kollerud [S] 172 E5
Kollínes [GR] 136 E3
Kollund [DK] 156 C4
Kolmården [S] 168 B5
Kolm-Saigurn [A] 72 G2
Köln [D] 30 G4
Kolnica [PL] 50 D2
Kolno [PL] 24 C5
Kolo [BIH] 144 B1
Koło [PL] 36 F3
Kołobrzeg [PL] 20 G3
Kolodruby [UA] 52 H5
Kolokot [KS] 146 C6
Kolomyia [UA] 204 C3
Kolonia Korytnica [PL] 38 D4
Kolonjë [AL] 128 B4
Kolonowskie [PL] 50 F2
Kolophon [TR] 152 C5
Kolossai [TR] 152 G5
Kolossi [CY] 154 F6
Koloveč [CZ] 48 D5
Kolpino [RUS] 202 B1
Kolsätter [S] 182 G5
Kölsillre [S] 182 H4
Kolsjön [S] 184 D5
Kolsva [S] 168 B2
Kolta [SK] 64 B5
Kolu [FIN] 186 E3
Kolunič [BIH] 142 A3
Koluszki [PL] 36 H4
Kolut [SRB] 76 C5
Koluvere [EST] 198 D2
Kolvereid [N] 190 C4
Kolymvári [GR] 140 B4
Komádi [H] 76 G2
Komagvær [N] 194 F2
Koman [AL] 128 B1
Komańcza [PL] 52 E5
Kómara [GR] 130 H1
Komarevo [BG] 148 A2
Komarino [RUS] 198 H3
Komárno [SK] 64 B5
Komarno [UA] 52 G4
Komárom [H] 64 A6
Komar Prolaz [BIH] 142 C4
Koma tou Yialou (Kumyalı) [CY] 154 G4
Komenda [SLO] 74 C4
Kómi [GR] 134 G5
Kómi [GR] 138 E1
Komi Kebir (Büyükkonuk) [CY] 154 G4
Komin [HR] 74 F5
Komirić [SRB] 142 F3
Kómito [GR] 134 D6
Komiža [HR] 116 H2
Komjáti [H] 64 F3
Kömlő [H] 64 E6
Komló [H] 76 B4
Komméno [GR] 132 D3
Kommerniemi [FIN] 188 E5
Kommunary [RUS] 178 G2
Komnes [N] 164 G2
Komniná [GR] 128 F5
Komniná [GR] 130 E2
Komninádes [GR] 128 D5
Komorane [KS] 146 C5
Komorowo [PL] 36 C5
Komorzno [PL] 36 E6
Komossa [FIN] 186 C2
Komotiní [GR] 130 F2
Kömpöc [H] 76 E4
Kompolje [HR] 112 G3
Kompóti [GR] 132 D3
Komsomol'sk [RUS] 22 H1
Komsomol'skoye [RUS] 178 F2
Komula [FIN] 196 F5
Komunari [BG] 148 F3
Komürköy [TR] 150 C2
Konak [SRB] 142 H1
Konakpınar [TR] 152 D1
Konarevo [SRB] 146 B3
Konarzyny [PL] 22 C4
Končanica [HR] 74 G6
Konče [MK] 128 G2
Konchansko-Suvorovskoye [RUS] 202 D1
Kondolovo [BG] 148 F5
Kondorfa [H] 74 F2
Kondoros [H] 76 F3
Kondrić [HR] 142 D1
Koněpruské Jeskyně [CZ] 48 F4
Køng [DK] 156 F4
Konga [S] 162 E6
Köngäs [FIN] 194 C6
Köngäs [FIN] 194 D6
Kongasmäki [FIN] 196 E4
Kongensgruve [N] 164 G1
Kongensvollen [N] 190 A6
Kongerslev [DK] 160 E4
Kong Humbles Grav [DK] 156 E5
Konginkangas [FIN] 186 G3
Kongsberg [N] 164 G1
Kongselva [N] 192 D4
Kongsfjord [N] 194 E1
Kongshavn [N] 164 F5
Kongsmoen [N] 190 D4
Kongsnes [N] 170 C2
Kongsvinger [N] 172 D5
Konice [CZ] 50 C5
Koniecpol [PL] 50 H2
Konieczna [PL] 52 D5
König-Otto-Höhle [D] 46 H5
Königsbrück [D] 34 F6
Königsbrunn [D] 60 D4
Königsee [D] 46 G2
Königsfeld [D] 58 F3
Königshofen [D] 46 E4
Königslutter [D] 32 H2
Königssee [D] 60 G6
Königsstuhl [D] 20 E2
Königstein [D] 46 C2
Königstein [D] 48 F1
Königswartha [D] 34 F5
Königswiesen [A] 62 C4
Königswinter [D] 30 H5
Königs-Wusterhausen [D] 34 E3
Konin [PL] 36 E3
Koniščina [HR] 74 E5
Koniskós [GR] 132 F1
Konispol [AL] 132 B2
Kónitsa [GR] 128 D6
Köniz [CH] 58 D6
Konjevići [BIH] 142 E4
Konjic [BIH] 144 C1
Konjsko [BIH] 144 D4
Könnern [D] 34 B4
Konnerud [N] 164 H1
Konnevesi [FIN] 186 G3
Könni [FIN] 186 C3
Könnu [EST] 198 E1
Konopiště [CZ] 48 G4
Konopiste [MK] 128 F3
Konotop [PL] 20 H5
Konotop [PL] 36 B4
Końskie [PL] 38 A6
Konsko [MK] 128 G3
Konsmo [N] 164 D5
Konstancin-Jeziorna [PL] 38 B3
Konstantynów [PL] 38 E3
Konstantynów Łodzki [PL] 36 G4
Konstanz [D] 58 G4
Konteenperä [FIN] 194 E8
Kontiainen [FIN] 186 D2
Kontiás [GR] 130 F6
Kontinjoki [FIN] 196 F5
Kontiolahti [FIN] 188 F2
Kontiomäki [FIN] 196 F4
Kontiovaara [FIN] 188 G1
Kontkala [FIN] 188 F2
Kontokáli [GR] 132 B2
Kontopoúli [GR] 130 F6
Konttajärvi [FIN] 194 C7
Konush [BG] 148 C6
Konyavo [BG] 148 F5
Konyshevka [RUS] 202 F6
Konz [D] 44 F2
Koonga [EST] 198 D2
Köörtilä [FIN] 186 B6
Koosa [EST] 198 F2
Koparnes [N] 180 C4
Kópasker [IS] 192 C2
Köpenick [D] 34 E2
Koper [SLO] 72 H6
Köpernitz [D] 20 C6
Kopervik [N] 164 A2
Kópháza [H] 62 F6
Kopidlno [CZ] 48 H3
Köping [S] 168 B2
Köpingsvik [S] 162 G4
Kopisto [FIN] 196 C5
Koplik [AL] 144 E5
Köpmanholmen [S] 184 G2
Köpmannebro [S] 166 D4
Koporin, Manastir- [SRB] 146 C1
Kopor'ye [RUS] 178 F5
Koppang [N] 172 C1
Koppangen [N] 192 G2
Kopparberg [S] 166 H1
Kopperå [N] 182 D1
Kopperby [D] 18 F1
Koppom [S] 166 D2
Koprivets [BG] 148 C3
Koprivlen [BG] 130 C2
Koprivna [HR] 74 G5
Koprivnica [SRB] 146 E2
Kopřivnice [CZ] 50 E5
Koprivshtitsa [BG] 148 A5
Köprübaşı [TR] 152 E3
Köprübaşı [TR] 152 F5
Köprühisar [TR] 150 G4
Köprüören [TR] 152 G1
Koprzywnica [PL] 52 D2
Kopsa [FIN] 196 D4
Kõpu [EST] 198 E3
Korbach [D] 32 E5
Korbevac [SRB] 146 D5
Korbielów [PL] 50 G5
Korbu [MD] 204 E2
Korçë [AL] 128 D5
Korčula [HR] 144 B3
Korczew [PL] 38 E2
Korczyców [PL] 34 G3
Korczyna [PL] 52 D4
Korenica [HR] 112 H3
Korenita [SRB] 142 F3
Korentovaara [FIN] 188 H1
Korespohja [FIN] 186 G5
Körez [TR] 152 F3
Korfantów [PL] 50 D2
Körfez [TR] 150 G3
Kórfos [GR] 136 F2
Korgen [N] 190 D2
Korgene [LV] 198 D4
Koria [FIN] 178 C3
Korinós [GR] 128 G5
Korinth [DK] 156 D4
Kórinthos [GR] 136 F1
Kórinthos, Arhéa- [GR] 136 F1
Korisós [GR] 128 E5
Korissía [GR] 138 C2
Korita [BIH] 144 D3
Korita [HR] 144 C4
Koritata [BG] 130 E2
Koritë [AL] 128 C5
Koriten [BG] 148 F1
Koríthi [GR] 136 A1
Korkea [FIN] 196 G5
Korkeakangas [FIN] 188 G4
Korlátka [SK] 62 H3
Körmend [H] 74 F2
Kormu [FIN] 176 G3
Korne [PL] 22 C3
Korneuburg [A] 62 F4
Kornevo [RUS] 22 G2
Kórnik [PL] 36 C3
Kornsjø [N] 166 C4
Kornwestheim [D] 58 H1
Kőrnye [H] 64 B6
Koromačno [HR] 112 E2
Koróni [GR] 136 D4
Kóronos [GR] 138 F3
Koronoúda [GR] 128 H3
Koronowo [PL] 22 D5
Korop [UA] 202 E6
Koropí [GR] 136 H1
Körösladány [H] 76 G2
Köröstarcsa [H] 76 G2
Korosten' [UA] 202 C7
Korostyshiv [UA] 202 D7
Korpavár [H] 74 G4
Korpi [FIN] 196 C6
Korpijärvi [FIN] 188 C6
Korpikå [S] 196 B2
Korpilahti [FIN] 186 G5
Korpilombolo [S] 194 B7
Korpo / Korppoo [FIN] 176 C5
Korpoström [FIN] 176 C5
Korppinen [FIN] 186 G1
Korppoo / Korpo [FIN] 176 C5
Korrigans [F] 40 D6
Korrö [S] 162 E5
Korsåsen [S] 172 H2
Koruburga [S] 162 F3
Korsberga [S] 166 F6
Korsen [N] 190 C5
Korsholm [S] 158 C2
Korsholm / Mustasaari [FIN] 186 B2
Korskrogen [S] 184 C6
Korsmo [N] 172 C5
Korsnäs [FIN] 186 A3
Korsø [DK] 160 C3
Korsør [DK] 156 E3
Korsun'-Shevchenkivs'kyi [UA] 202 F8
Korsveien [N] 182 B2
Korsvoll [N] 180 F1
Korsze [PL] 24 B3
Körteke [TR] 152 F6
Kortekylä [FIN] 186 E2
Korten [BG] 148 D4
Kortenberg [B] 30 C4
Kortesjärvi [FIN] 186 C1
Kortevaara [FIN] 196 G5
Kórthi [GR] 138 D1
Kortrijk (Courtrai) [B] 20 G2
Korucu [TR] 152 C2
Koruköy [TR] 150 C1
Koruköy [TR] 150 B4
Korup [DK] 156 D3
Korušce [HR] 142 A5
Korva [S] 194 B8
Korvala [FIN] 194 D7
Korvaluoma [FIN] 186 C5
Korvenkylä [FIN] 196 D5
Korvensuu [FIN] 176 D4
Koryčany [CZ] 62 G2
Korycin [PL] 24 E4
Korydallós [GR] 132 E1
Koryfási [GR] 136 C4
Korytnica-Kúpele [SK] 64 C2
Korytno [RUS] 198 G2
Korzeniste [PL] 24 D5
Korzenna [PL] 52 C5
Korzunovo [RUS] 194 F3
Korzybie [PL] 22 B2
Kos [GR] 154 B2
Kosanica [MNE] 144 E2
Košarovce [SK] 52 D6
Kościan [PL] 36 C3
Kościelec [PL] 36 F3
Kościerzyna [PL] 22 D3
Kose [EST] 198 E1
Kösedere [TR] 134 G1
Kosel [MK] 128 D3
Koserow [D] 20 E3
Košetice [CZ] 48 G5
Košice [SK] 64 G3
Kosik [RUS] 202 E5
Kosinë [AL] 128 C6
Kosjerić [SRB] 146 A2
Kösk [TR] 152 E5
Koška [HR] 142 D1
Koskeby [FIN] 186 B2
Koskela [FIN] 186 D2
Koskenkorva [FIN] 186 C3
Koskenkylä [FIN] 188 C2
Koskenkylä / Forsby [FIN] 178 B4
Koskenniska [FIN] 194 C4
Koskenpää [FIN] 186 F5
Koski [FIN] 176 E4
Koski [FIN] 176 H2
Koskimäki [FIN] 186 B3
Kóskina [GR] 134 D5
Koskolovo [RUS] 178 F6
Koškovce [SK] 52 E6
Koskue [FIN] 186 C4
Koskullskulle [S] 192 G6
Kosmás [GR] 136 E3
Kósmio [GR] 130 F2
Kosmo [N] 192 D6
Kosmonosy [CZ] 48 G3
Kosola [FIN] 186 C2
Kosovo Polje [KS] 146 C5
Kosovska Mitrovica [KS] 146 C4
Kosów Lacki [PL] 38 D2
Kössen [A] 60 F5
Kost [CZ] 48 H2
Kósta [GR] 136 F3
Kosta [S] 162 E5
Kostanjevac [HR] 74 D6
Kostanjevica [SLO] 74 D5
Kosta Perchevo [BG] 146 E2
Kostelec [CZ] 48 H6
Kostelec nad Černými [CZ] 48 G4
Kostelec nad Labem [CZ] 48 G3
Kostelec nad Orlicí [CZ] 50 B3
Kostelec na Hané [CZ] 50 C5
Kostenets [BG] 146 G5
Kosti [BG] 148 G5
Kostinbrod [BG] 146 F4
Kostojevići [SRB] 146 A2
Kostomłoty [PL] 36 C6
Kostomuksha [RUS] 196 G4
Kostopil' [UA] 202 B7
Kóstos [GR] 138 E3
Kostów [PL] 36 E6
Kostrzyń [PL] 34 G2
Kostrzyn [PL] 36 D2
Kosturino [MK] 128 G2
Košumberk [CZ] 50 B4
Košutovo [KS] 146 B4
Koszalin [PL] 20 H3
Koszęcin [PL] 50 F2
Kőszeg [H] 74 F1
Kosztowo [PL] 22 C6
Koszuty [PL] 36 D3
Koszyce [PL] 52 B3
Kótaj [H] 64 H4
Kotala [FIN] 186 E4
Kótas [GR] 128 E4
Kotë [AL] 128 B5
Kotel [BG] 148 D4
Kőtelec [H] 76 E1
Köthen [D] 34 C4
Kotila [FIN] 196 F4
Kotka [FIN] 178 C4
Kotlarnia [PL] 50 F3
Kotlice [PL] 52 G1
Kotlin [PL] 36 D4
Kotly [RUS] 178 F6
Kotola [FIN] 194 F7
Kotor [MNE] 144 D4
Kotorsko [BIH] 142 D2
Kotor Varoš [BIH] 142 C3
Kotovs'k [UA] 204 E3
Kotowice [PL] 50 G2
Kótronas [GR] 136 E5
Kötschach-Mauthen [A] 72 G3
Kotten [NL] 16 G6
Köttkulla [S] 162 C2
Kotvala [FIN] 186 F1
Kötzting [D] 48 D6
Koufália [GR] 128 G4
Koufós [GR] 130 C6
Kouhi [FIN] 186 H5
Koúklia [CY] 154 F6
Koukounariés [GR] 134 B3
Koúmanis [GR] 136 C2
Koúndouros [GR] 138 C2
Koúrenta [GR] 132 C2
Kourion [CY] 154 F6
Kournás [GR] 140 C5
Kouroúta [GR] 136 B2
Koutsó [GR] 130 E3
Koutsóchero [GR] 132 G2
Koutsourás [GR] 140 G5
Koutsovéntis (Güngör) [CY] 154 G5
Kouvola [FIN] 178 C3
Kovačevac [SRB] 146 B1
Kovachevo [BG] 130 C1
Kovachevtsi [BG] 146 F5
Kovachica [BG] 146 F2
Kovačica [SRB] 142 G2
Kovačica [SRB] 204 B5
Kovarce [SK] 64 A4
Kovarskas [LT] 200 G4
Kovel' [UA] 202 A7
Kovero [FIN] 188 G2
Kovin [SRB] 142 H2
Kovland [S] 184 E4
Kövra [S] 182 G3
Kowal [PL] 36 G2
Kowale Oleckie [PL] 24 D3
Kowalewo Pomorskie [PL] 22 E6
Kowary [PL] 50 A2
Köyceğiz [TR] 154 E1
Köyliö / Kjulo [FIN] 176 D2
Köysivaara [FIN] 194 D5
Koyunhis [TR] 150 F4
Koyunköy [TR] 150 G4
Koyunoba [TR] 152 F2
Kozağacı [TR] 154 G1
Kozak [TR] 152 C2
Kozan [TR] 150 G4
Kozáni [GR] 128 F5
Kozarac [BIH] 142 B2
Kozarac [HR] 76 B6
Kozar Belene [BG] 148 B3
Kozel [CZ] 48 E5
Kozel'sk [RUS] 202 F4
Koziatyn [UA] 202 C8
Kozica [HR] 144 B2
Koziebrody [PL] 36 H1
Koziegłowy [PL] 50 G2
Kozienice [PL] 38 C4
Kozí Hrádek [CZ] 48 G5
Kozina [SLO] 74 A6
Kozine [LV] 198 G4
Kozjak [MK] 128 D3
Kozlar [TR] 152 G6
Kozlodui [BG] 146 G2
Kozlov Bereg [RUS] 198 G2
Kozłowo [PL] 22 G5
Kozluk [BIH] 142 E3
Kozly [CZ] 48 E2
Kozly [RUS] 198 G4
Koźmin [PL] 36 D4
Kozojedy [CZ] 48 E4
Kozolupy [CZ] 48 D4
Kozpınar [TR] 150 G5
Kożuchów [PL] 36 A4
Kozy [PL] 50 G4
Kozyürük [TR] 150 B3
Krääkkiö [FIN] 176 F2
Krabbesholm [DK] 160 C5
Krabi [EST] 198 F4
Kräckelbäcken [S] 172 D2
Kraddsele [S] 190 F3
Kraftverk Harsprånget [S] 190 H1
Krąg [PL] 22 B3
Kragelund [DK] 160 E3
Kragenæs [DK] 156 F4
Kragerø [N] 164 F4
Kragujevac [SRB] 146 C2
Kragujevac [SRB] 204 B6
Krahës [AL] 128 B5
Kraište [BG] 146 G6
Krajenka [PL] 22 B5
Krajišnik [SRB] 142 H1
Krajn [AL] 128 B1
Krajna [SLO] 74 E3
Krajná Pol'ana [SK] 52 D5
Krajnik Gorny [PL] 20 E6
Krakača [BIH] 112 H2
Kråkan [S] 184 H1
Kråkeland [N] 164 C4
Krakës [LT] 200 F4
Krakhella [N] 170 B1
Kråklingbo [S] 168 G5
Kråklivollen [N] 182 C2
Kråkmo [N] 192 E5
Krakol'ye [RUS] 178 E6
Krakovec [UA] 202 A8
Krakovets' [UA] 52 F3
Kraków [PL] 50 H4
Krakow am See [D] 20 B4
Kråksmåla [S] 162 F4
Králíky [CZ] 50 C4
Kraljeva Sutjesca [BIH] 142 D4
Kraljevica [HR] 112 E2
Kraljevo [SRB] 146 B3
Král'ovany [SK] 50 G6
Kráľov Brod [SK] 64 A5
Králóvec [CZ] 50 B2
Kralovice [CZ] 48 E4
Král'ovský Chlmec [SK] 64 H3
Kralupy nad Vltavou [CZ] 48 F3
Kramfors [S] 184 F3
Kramolin [BG] 148 B3
Krampenes [N] 194 E2
Kramsach [A] 60 E6
Kråmvik [N] 164 E1
Kramvik [N] 194 F2
Kraneá [GR] 132 E2
Kranenburg [D] 16 F6
Kranevo [BG] 148 G2
Krångede [S] 184 D2
Krani [MK] 128 D4
Kraniá [GR] 132 E1
Kraniá Elassónas [GR] 132 F1
Kranichfeld [D] 46 G1
Kranídi [GR] 136 F3
Kranj [SLO] 74 B4
Kranjska Gora [SLO] 72 H3
Krapina [HR] 74 E5
Krapinske Toplice [HR] 74 E5
Krapkowice [PL] 50 E2
Krapperup [S] 156 G1
Krasen [BG] 148 F1
Kraściszyn [PL] 52 F4
Krasikovshchina [RUS] 198 G3
Krāslava [LV] 198 G6
Kraslice [CZ] 48 C3
Krásná Hora nad Vltavou [CZ] 48 F5
Krásna Hôrka [SK] 64 F3
Krásná Lípa [CZ] 48 G1
Krasnasyel'ski [BY] 24 G5
Krasnaya Hora [RUS] 202 D5
Krasne Folwarczne [PL] 24 E5
Kraśniczyn [PL] 38 F6
Kraśnik [PL] 52 E1
Krasnogorodsk [RUS] 198 G5
Krasnogorodskoye [RUS] 202 B3
Krasnogorsk [RUS] 202 F3
Krasnohryvka [UA] 202 D8
Krásno nad Kysucou [SK] 50 F5
Krasnoperekops'k [UA] 204 H3
Krasnopol [PL] 24 E3
Krasnopol'e [BY] 202 D5
Krasnopol'e [UA] 202 F6
Krasnosel'e [RUS] 24 D2
Krasnosielc [PL] 24 B6
Krasnovo [BG] 148 A5
Krasnoye [RUS] 198 H5
Krasnoye Selo [RUS] 178 H5
Krasnoznamensk [RUS] 200 E5
Krasnye Prudy [RUS] 198 G4
Krasnyje Gory [RUS] 198 H1
Krasnystaw [PL] 38 F6
Krasnyy Bor [RUS] 24 B1
Krasnyy Kholm [RUS] 202 E1
Krasocin [PL] 52 A1
Krašov [CZ] 48 E4
Krastë [AL] 128 C2
Krasulje [BIH] 142 B3
Krasznokvajda [H] 64 F3
Krátigos [GR] 134 H2
Kratovo [MK] 146 E6
Kratovska Stena [SRB] 146 A2
Krauchenwies [D] 58 H3
Kraushöhle [A] 62 C6
Krautheim [D] 46 E5
Kravaře [CZ] 48 F2
Kravaře [CZ] 50 F4
Kravarsko [HR] 74 E6
Kravik [N] 170 F5
Kravnsø [DK] 156 A2
Kraymorie [BG] 148 F4
Kražiaai [LT] 200 E4
Kreba-Neudorf [D] 34 G5
Krefeld [D] 30 G3
Kregme [DK] 156 G2
Kreje Lurës [AL] 128 C1
Kremastí [GR] 136 F4
Kremastí [GR] 154 D3
Kremenchuk [UA] 202 F8
Kremenets' [UA] 202 B8
Kremmen [D] 34 D1
Kremna [SRB] 144 E1
Kremnica [SK] 64 C3
Krems [A] 62 E4
Kremsmünster [A] 62 B5
Křemže [CZ] 62 B2
Krenkerup [DK] 20 B1
Křenov [CZ] 50 C5
Krępa [PL] 36 F4
Krepcha [BG] 148 D2
Krepoljin [SRB] 146 D1
Kresna [BG] 130 B1
Kréstena [GR] 136 C2
Kresttsy [RUS] 202 C2
Kretinga [LT] 200 D4
Kreuth [D] 60 E5
Kreuzenstein [A] 62 F4
Kreuzlingen [CH] 58 G4
Kreuztal [D] 32 C6
Kreva [BY] 200 H6
Kriakėnava [LT] 200 F4
Krichim [BG] 148 B6
Kričov [BY] 202 D5
Kriebstein [D] 34 D6
Krieglach [A] 62 D6
Kriezá [GR] 134 C5
Kríkello [GR] 132 F4
Krimml [A] 72 E1
Krimmler Wasserfälle [A] 72 E1
Křinec [CZ] 48 H3
Kringla [N] 170 B2
Krinídes [GR] 130 D3
Kristall-Höhle [D] 46 C2
Kristalopig [GR] 128 E5
Kristberg [S] 166 H5
Kristdala [S] 162 G3
Kristianopel [S] 158 G1
Kristiansand [N] 164 D5
Kristianstad [S] 158 D2
Kristiansund [N] 180 F2
Kristiinankaupunki / Kristinestad [FIN] 186 A5
Kristineberg [S] 172 E1
Kristineberg [S] 190 G4
Kristinefors [S] 172 E5
Kristinehamn [S] 166 F3
Kristinehov [S] 158 D2
Kristinestad / Kristiinankaupunki [FIN] 186 A5
Kristoffervalen [N] 192 G1
Kristóni [GR] 128 H3
Kristvallabrunn [S] 162 F5
Kritinía [GR] 154 C4
Kritsá [GR] 140 F5
Kriva Feja [SRB] 146 E5
Kriváň [SK] 64 D3
Kriva Palanka [MK] 146 E6
Kriva reka [BG] 148 E2
Krivčevo [SLO] 74 C4
Krivelj [SRB] 146 D2
Krivi Dol [MK] 128 F1
Krivodol [BG] 146 F3
Krivogaštani [MK] 128 E3
Křivoklát [CZ] 48 E4
Krivolak [MK] 128 F2
Križ [HR] 74 F6
Křižanov [CZ] 50 B6
Križevci [HR] 74 F5
Krk [HR] 112 E2
Krka [SLO] 74 C5
Krklja [MK] 146 E6
Krnjača [SRB] 142 G2
Krnjak [HR] 112 G1
Krnjeuša [BIH] 142 A3
Krnov [CZ] 50 D4
Krobia [PL] 36 C4
Kroczyce [PL] 50 G2
Krøderen [N] 170 G5
Krogsbølle [DK] 156 D2
Krogsered [S] 162 B4
Krokan [N] 170 E6
Krokebol [N] 166 C1
Krokeés [GR] 136 E4
Krokek [S] 168 B5
Kroken [N] 190 E3
Kroken [N] 192 F2
Kroknes [N] 194 F2
Krokom [S] 182 G2
Krokowa [PL] 22 D1
Kroksjö [S] 190 G5
Kroksjö [S] 196 A5
Krokstad [S] 166 C5
Krokstadelva [N] 164 G1
Krokstadøra [N] 180 H1
Krokstorp [S] 162 G3
Krokstrand [N] 190 E2
Kroksund [N] 166 C2
Kroktorp [S] 172 G5
Krokvåg [S] 184 D2
Krokvik [S] 192 G5
Krolevets' [UA] 202 E6
Królewiec [PL] 38 A6
Królowy Most [PL] 24 F5
Kroměříž [CZ] 50 D6
Kromerowo [PL] 22 H4
Krompachy [SK] 64 F2
Kromy [RUS] 202 F5
Kronach [D] 46 H3
Kronegg [A] 62 C4
Kronoby / Kruunupyy [FIN] 196 C6
Kronsgaard [D] 156 C5
Kronshtadt [RUS] 178 G4
Kropa [SLO] 74 B4
Kröpelin [D] 20 B3
Kropp [D] 18 F2
Kroppenstedt [D] 34 B3
Kropstädt [D] 34 D3
Krościenko [PL] 52 F5
Krościenko nad Dunajcem [PL] 52 B5
Krosna [LT] 24 F2
Krośniewice [PL] 36 G3
Krosno [PL] 22 F3
Krosno [PL] 52 D4
Krosno Odrzańskie [PL] 34 H3
Krossbu [N] 180 E6
Krossen [N] 164 D6
Krostiz [D] 34 C5
Krote [LV] 198 B6
Krotoszyn [PL] 36 D4
Krouna [CZ] 50 B4
Kršan [HR] 112 E2
Kršete [HR] 112 D1
Krško [SLO] 74 D5
Krstac [MNE] 144 D3
Krstac [MNE] 144 E5
Kručov [SK] 52 D6
Krucz [PL] 36 B1
Kruge [HR] 112 H3
Kruglovo [RUS] 22 G1
Kruiningen [NL] 28 H1
Kruisland [NL] 16 C6
Krujë [AL] 128 B2
Kruk [N] 170 G2
Krukowo [PL] 24 B5
Krumbach [A] 62 E6
Krumbach [D] 60 C4
Krumë [AL] 146 B6
Krummendorf [D] 20 B3
Krumovgrad [BG] 130 F1
Krumpendorf [A] 74 B3
Krün [D] 60 D6
Krupá [CZ] 48 E3
Krupac [BIH] 144 C2
Krupac [BIH] 144 D2
Krupaja [SRB] 146 C1
Krupa na Vrbasu [BIH] 142 B3
Krupanj [SRB] 142 F3
Krupe [PL] 38 F6
Krupina [SK] 64 C4

Krupište [MK] 128 F1
Krupnik [BG] 128 H1
Krupp [RUS] 198 G3
Kruså [DK] 156 C4
Kruščić [SRB] 76 D6
Krušedol, Manastir- [SRB] 142 F2
Kruševac [SRB] 146 C3
Kruševo [MK] 128 E2
Krusha [BG] 146 E4
Krushari [BG] 148 F1
Krushevets [BG] 148 F5
Krushovene [BG] 148 A2
Krushovica [BG] 146 G2
Kruszwica [PL] 36 E2
Kruszyna [PL] 50 G1
Krutcy [RUS] 198 H4
Krute [MNE] 128 A1
Krutneset [N] 190 E3
Kruunupyy / Kronoby [FIN] 196 C6
Kruusila [FIN] 176 F4
Krya [TR] 154 E2
Kryakusa [RUS] 198 G3
Krýa Vrýsi [GR] 128 G4
Kryekuq [AL] 128 A4
Krylbo [S] 174 D6
Kryle [DK] 160 B6
Krylovo [RUS] 24 C2
Krymne [UA] 38 H4
Krynica [PL] 52 C5
Krynica Morska [PL] 22 F2
Krynki [PL] 24 F5
Kryopigí [GR] 130 C6
Kryspinów [PL] 50 H4
Kryve Ozero [UA] 204 F2
Kryvyi Rih [UA] 204 G2
Krzęcin [PL] 20 G6
Krzeczów [PL] 36 F6
Krzelów [PL] 36 C5
Krzepice [PL] 50 F1
Krzeszów [PL] 50 B2
Krzeszów [PL] 52 E2
Krzeszowice [PL] 50 H3
Krzeszyce [PL] 34 G2
Krzynowłoga Mała [PL] 22 H6
Krzystkowice [PL] 34 H4
Krzywiń [PL] 36 C4
Krzyżewo [PL] 24 B6
Krzyż Wlkp. [PL] 36 B1
Ksar-es-Seghir [MA] 100 G6
Książ [PL] 50 B1
Książ Wielki [PL] 52 A2
Ktísmata [GR] 132 C1
Kubbe [S] 184 F1
Küblis [CH] 70 H1
Kubrat [BG] 148 D2
Kuç [AL] 128 B6
Kučevo [SRB] 146 D1
Kuchl [A] 60 G6
Kućište [KS] 146 A5
Kucovë [AL] 128 B4
Küçükbahçe [TR] 134 H4
Küçükçekmece [TR] 150 E3
Küçükkuyu [TR] 134 H1
Kuddby [S] 168 B5
Kudever' [RUS] 198 H5
Kudirkos Naumiestis [LT] 24 E1
Kudowa-Zdrój [PL] 50 B3
Kufstein [A] 60 F6
Kuggeboda [S] 158 F1
Kuggerud [N] 172 C5
Kuha [FIN] 196 E2
Kuhanen [FIN] 188 D2
Kühlungsborn [D] 20 B3
Kuhmalahti [FIN] 176 G1
Kuhmo [FIN] 196 G5
Kuhmoinen [FIN] 176 H1
Kühsen [D] 18 G4
Kuhstedt [D] 18 E4
Kühtai [A] 72 C1
Kuimetsa [EST] 198 E2
Kuivajärvi [FIN] 196 G4
Kuivaniemi [FIN] 196 D3
Kuivanto [FIN] 178 B3
Kuivasjärvi [FIN] 186 C5
Kuivasmäki [FIN] 186 F4
Kuivastu [EST] 198 D3
Kukës [AL] 128 C1
Kukinia [PL] 20 H3
Kukko [FIN] 186 E3
Kukko [FIN] 186 E3
Kukkola [FIN] 176 G2
Kukkulankoski [FIN] 196 C2
Kuklin [PL] 22 H5
Kuks [CZ] 50 B3
Kukujevci [SRB] 142 F2
Kükür [TR] 154 F4
Kukurečani [MK] 128 E3
Kula [BG] 146 E2
Kula [BIH] 144 D1
Kula [SRB] 76 D6
Kula [TR] 152 F3
Kulakli [TR] 150 G2
Kula Novinska [HR] 144 C3
Kulaši [BIH] 142 C3
Kulata [BG] 130 B2
Kuldīga [LV] 198 C5
Ku'le [RUS] 198 G3
Kulefall [S] 168 B6
Kuleli [TR] 150 B2
Kulennoinen [FIN] 188 F5
Kulen Vakuf [BIH] 112 H4
Kulhuse [DK] 156 G2
Kuliai [LT] 200 D4
Kullaa [FIN] 176 D1
Kulla Gunnarstorp [S] 156 H1
Kullo / Kulloo [FIN] 178 A4
Kulloo / Kullo [FIN] 178 A4
Küllstedt [D] 32 G5
Kulmain [D] 48 B4
Kulmbach [D] 46 H3
Kuloharju [FIN] 196 E2
Kultaranta [FIN] 176 D4
Kulvemäki [FIN] 196 F5
Kulykiv [UA] 52 H3
Kumafşarı [TR] 152 G6
Kumafşarı [TR] 152 G6
Kumane [SRB] 76 E6
Kumanica [SRB] 146 B3
Kumanovo [MK] 146 D6
Kumarlar [TR] 150 B5
Kumbağ [TR] 150 C3
Kümbet [TR] 150 H5
Kumburk [CZ] 48 H2
Kumburun [TR] 130 H6
Kumkale [TR] 130 H5
Kumköy [TR] 150 E2
Kumla [S] 166 H3
Kumlinge [FIN] 176 B5
Kummavuopio [S] 192 G3
Kummeren [N] 192 D6
Kumo / Kokemäki [FIN] 176 D2
Kumpuvaara [FIN] 196 E2
Kumreut [D] 60 H3
Kumrovec [HR] 74 E5
Kumuu [FIN] 196 G4
Kumyalı (Koma tou Yialou) [CY] 154 G4
Kunadacs [H] 76 D2
Kunágota [H] 76 G4
Kuncsorba [H] 76 F2
Kunda [EST] 198 F1
Kunes [N] 194 C2
Kunfehértó [H] 76 D4
Kungälv [S] 160 G1
Kungsängen [S] 168 D2
Kungsäter [S] 160 H3
Kungsbacka [S] 160 H3
Kungsberg [S] 174 D4
Kungsfors [S] 174 D4
Kungshållet [S] 168 C3
Kungshamn [S] 166 B5
Kungsör [S] 168 B3
Kunhegyes [H] 76 F1
Kunín [CZ] 50 E5
Kunmadaras [H] 76 F1
Kunovice [CZ] 62 H2
Kunow [D] 20 E6
Kunów [PL] 52 C1
Kunowo [PL] 36 C4
Kunpeszér [H] 76 C2
Kunrau [D] 34 A2
Kunštát [CZ] 50 C5
Kunszentmárton [H] 76 E3
Kunszentmiklós [H] 76 C2
Kunžak [CZ] 48 H6
Künzelsau [D] 46 E5
Kuohatti [FIN] 196 G5
Kuohenmaa [FIN] 176 F2
Kuohijoki [FIN] 176 G2
Kuoksu [S] 192 H5
Kuolayarvi [RUS] 194 F7
Kuolio [FIN] 196 F2
Kuona [FIN] 196 D6
Kuopio [FIN] 188 D2
Kuora [FIN] 188 G1
Kuortane [FIN] 186 D3
Kuosku [FIN] 194 E6
Kup [H] 74 H2
Kup [PL] 50 E2
Kupferberg [D] 46 H3
Kupferzell [D] 46 E5
Kupinovo [SRB] 142 G3
Kupirovo [HR] 112 H4
Kupiškis [LT] 200 G4
Kupjak [HR] 112 F1
Kupli [LV] 198 D5
Küplü [TR] 130 H2
Küplü [TR] 150 G4
Kuprava [LV] 198 G4
Kupres [BIH] 142 C4
Kurbinovo [MK] 128 D4
Kurbnesh [AL] 128 B1
Kurchatov [RUS] 202 F6
Kurd [H] 76 B4
Kurdzhali [BG] 130 F1
Kurejoki [FIN] 186 D2
Kuressaare [EST] 198 C3
Kurevere [EST] 198 C3
Kurgolovo [RUS] 178 E5
Kurianka [PL] 24 F4
Kurikka [FIN] 186 C4
Kurilo [BG] 146 F4
Kuřim [CZ] 50 B6
Kurjala [FIN] 188 D3
Kurjenkylä [FIN] 186 D4
Kurkela [FIN] 176 F5
Kurkiyeki [RUS] 188 G6
Kurkkio [FIN] 194 C6
Kurkkio [S] 192 H5
Kürnare [BG] 148 B4
Kürnüç [TR] 150 H4
Kurobası [TR] 134 G1
Kurola [FIN] 188 D4
Kurolanahti [FIN] 188 C2
Kurovitsy [RUS] 178 E6
Kurów [PL] 38 D5
Kurowice [PL] 36 H4
Kurozwęki [PL] 52 C2
Kurravaara [S] 192 G5
Kuršėnai [LT] 200 E4
Kursīši [LV] 198 C6
Kursu [FIN] 194 E7
Kuršumlija [SRB] 146 C4
Kuršumlijska Banja [SRB] 146 C4
Kurşunlu [TR] 150 D4
Kurşunlu [TR] 150 F4
Kurtakko [FIN] 194 C6
Kurtbey [TR] 150 B3
Kurtköy [TR] 150 G3
Kurtköyü [TR] 150 H2
Kurtti [FIN] 196 F3
Kuru [FIN] 176 F1
Kuru [FIN] 186 D6
Kurudere [TR] 152 D4
Kurvinen [FIN] 196 F2
Kurzelów [PL] 50 H1
Kurzeszyn [PL] 38 A4
Kurzętnik [PL] 22 F5
Kuşadası [TR] 152 D5
Kuşçayır [TR] 150 B6
Kuşcenneti [TR] 150 D5
Kusel [D] 44 H3
Kushalino [RUS] 202 E2
Kuside [MNE] 144 D3
Kusmark [S] 196 A4
Küssnacht [CH] 58 F6
Kustavi / Gustavs [FIN] 176 C4
Küstrin-Kietz [D] 34 G2
Kuşu [TR] 152 F2
Kut [HR] 142 A1
Kuta [MNE] 144 E3
Kütahya [TR] 152 G1
Kutemajärvi [FIN] 186 H5
Kutina [HR] 142 B1
Kutjevo [HR] 142 D1
Kutná Hora [CZ] 48 H4
Kutno [PL] 36 G3
Kuttanen [FIN] 194 B5
Kuttura [FIN] 194 D5
Kúty [SK] 62 G3
Kuuksenvaara [FIN] 188 H2
Kuuminainen [FIN] 176 C1
Kuurtola [FIN] 196 F3
Kuusaa [FIN] 186 G4
Kuusaa [FIN] 196 D5
Kuusajoki [FIN] 194 C6
Kuusalu [EST] 198 E1
Kuusamo [FIN] 194 F8
Kuusankoski [FIN] 178 C3
Kuusiniemi [RUS] 196 H3
Kuusjärvi [FIN] 188 E2
Kuusjoki [FIN] 176 F4
Kuuttila [FIN] 186 B2
Kuvaskangas [FIN] 186 B6
Kuvshinovo [RUS] 202 D2
Kuyubaşi [TR] 150 G4
Kuyucak [TR] 150 H5
Kuyucak [TR] 152 E5
Kuyvozi [RUS] 178 H3
Kuzemki [RUS] 202 E4
Kuzma [SLO] 74 E3
Kuzmin [SRB] 142 F2
Kuźmina [PL] 52 E5
Kuznechnoye [RUS] 178 G1
Kuznetsovo [RUS] 198 H1
Kuznetsovs'k [UA] 202 B7
Kuźnia Raciborska [PL] 50 E3
Kuźnica [PL] 24 F4
Kuzovo [RUS] 198 H3
Kuzuluk [TR] 150 H3
Kvačany [SK] 50 H6
Kvænangsbotn [N] 192 H2
Kværndrup [DK] 156 D4
Kvål [N] 182 B2
Kvalsund [N] 194 B2
Kvalsvik [N] 180 C3
Kvalvåg [N] 170 A5
Kvalvåg [N] 180 F2
Kvam [N] 180 H6
Kvam [N] 190 C5
Kvammen [N] 180 G2
Kvamsøy gamle Kirke [N] 170 C2
Kvanndal [N] 170 C4
Kvanne [N] 180 F2
Kvantenburg [S] 166 D5
Kvarnåsen [S] 158 H4
Kvarnberg [S] 172 G2
Kvarnberget [S] 172 G5
Kvarsebo [S] 168 C5
Kvarstadseter [N] 172 B2
Kvås [N] 164 C5
Kvasilov [UA] 202 B7
Kvasowka [BY] 24 G4
Kveaunet [N] 190 D5
Kvėdarna [LT] 200 D4
Kveejdet [N] 190 D5
Kveina [N] 190 C4
Kvelde [N] 164 G3
Kvelia [N] 190 D5
Kvenvær [N] 190 A6
Kvernessetra [N] 172 C1
Kvetkai [LT] 198 E6
Kvevlax / Koivulahti [FIN] 186 B2
Kvicksund [S] 168 B2
Kvigno [N] 170 D2
Kvikkjokk [S] 190 G1
Kvikne [N] 182 B4
Kvilda [CZ] 48 E6
Kvildal [N] 164 C1
Kville [S] 166 C5
Kvillsfors [S] 162 F3
Kvinesdal [N] 164 C5
Kvinlog [N] 164 C4
Kvisler [N] 172 D4
Kvissleby [S] 184 E5
Kvistgård [DK] 156 G2
Kvisvik [N] 180 F2
Kviteseid [N] 164 E2
Kvitnes [N] 180 F2
Kvitten [N] 182 D4
Kwiatkowice [PL] 36 G4
Kwidzyn [PL] 22 E4
Kwilcz [PL] 36 B2
Kybartai [LT] 24 E1
Kyburg [CH] 58 G5
Kycklingvattnet [S] 190 E5
Kyffhäuser-Denkmal [D] 34 A5
Kyïv [UA] 202 D7
Kyjov [CZ] 62 G2
Kyläinpää [FIN] 186 B3
Kylämä [FIN] 186 F6
Kylemore Abbey [IRL] 2 B4
Kyle of Lochalsh [GB] 6 C5
Kyliia [UA] 204 F4
Kyllaj [S] 168 G4
Kylland [N] 164 D4
Kyllburg [D] 44 F1
Kyllíni [GR] 136 B1
Kylmäkoski [FIN] 176 F2
Kylmälä [FIN] 196 E4
Kylmämäki [FIN] 186 H4
Kymbo [S] 162 C1
Kyme [TR] 152 C3
Kými [GR] 134 C4
Kýmina [GR] 128 H4
Kymönkoski [FIN] 186 G2
Kynšperk nad Ohří [CZ] 48 C3
Kypäräjärvi [FIN] 188 E3
Kypärävaara [FIN] 196 F4
Kyparissía [GR] 136 C3
Kypriáki [GR] 132 H5
Kyritz [D] 20 B6
Kyrkhult [S] 162 D6
Kyrkjebygdi [N] 164 E3
Kyrksæterøra [N] 180 G1
Kyrkslätt / Kirkkonummi [FIN] 176 G5
Kyrkstad [S] 196 B5
Kyrksten [S] 166 G2
Kyrö [FIN] 176 E4
Kyrönlahti [FIN] 186 D6
Kyröskoski [FIN] 176 E1
Kyrping [N] 170 B6
Kyšice [CZ] 48 F3
Kysucké Nové Mesto [SK] 50 F6
Kytäjä [FIN] 176 G4
Kýthira [GR] 136 F6
Kýthnos [GR] 138 C2
Kytömäki [FIN] 196 F4
Kyustendil [BG] 146 E6
Kyyjärvi [FIN] 186 E2
Kyynämöinen [FIN] 186 F4
Kyzikos [TR] 150 D4
Kyznecovo [RUS] 202 B1

L

Laa an der Thaya [A] 62 F3
Laage [D] 20 B3
Laage Weitendorf [D] 20 B3
Laaja [FIN] 196 F4
Laajoki [FIN] 176 D3
Laakajärvi [FIN] 196 F5
Laakirchen [A] 62 A5
La Alameda [E] 96 E5
La Alamedilla [E] 88 E4
La Alberca [E] 88 B4
La Alberca de Záncara [E] 98 A3
La Albuera [E] 94 G2
La Aldea del Obispo [E] 96 B1
La Algaba [E] 94 G6
La Almarcha [E] 98 B3
La Almolda [E] 90 F4
La Almudena [E] 104 B2
La Almunia de Doña Godina [E] 90 D4
Laamala [FIN] 188 E6
Laanila [FIN] 194 D5
La Antigua [E] 82 A5
La Antilla [E] 94 E6
Laarbruch [D] 30 F2
Laas [A] 72 G3
Laàs [F] 84 D3
Laasala [FIN] 186 E3
Laatzen [D] 32 F2
La Azohía [E] 104 C4
Labacolla [E] 78 C3
Labajos [E] 88 E4
la Balme [F] 68 G5
La Baña [E] 78 F6
La Bañeza [E] 78 G6
La Barca de la Florida [E] 100 G4
La Barrela [E] 78 D4
La Bassée [F] 28 F3
la Bastide [F] 108 D4
Labastide-d'Armagnac [F] 66 D6
La Bastide de-Sérou [F] 84 H5
Labastide-Murat [F] 66 G4
La Bastide-Puylaurent [F] 68 D6
Labastide-Rouairoux [F] 106 C4
La Bastie d'Urfé [F] 68 E2
La Bâtiaz [CH] 70 C2
La Bâtie-Neuve [F] 108 D2
La Baule [F] 40 E6
La Bazoche-Gouet [F] 42 D5
Läbbyn [S] 166 D3
Łabędzie [PL] 20 H4
la Bégude-de-Mazenc [F] 68 F6
La Belle Etoile [F] 44 A5
Labenne [F] 66 A6
La Bérarde [F] 70 A5
L'Aber-Wrac'h [F] 40 B1
La Bien Aparecida [E] 82 F3
Labin [HR] 112 E2
Labinot Fushë [AL] 128 C3
La Bisbal de Falset [E] 90 H5
la Bisbal d'Empordà [E] 92 G3
Łabiszyn [PL] 36 E1
Labjana [KS] 146 C5
Lábod [H] 74 H4
Laboe [D] 18 G2
Laborel [F] 108 C2
Labouheyre [F] 66 B5
La Bourboule [F] 68 C2
La Bóveda de Toro [E] 88 D2
Łabowa [PL] 52 C5
Labrags [LV] 198 B5
Labraunda [TR] 152 E6
Labrède [F] 66 C3
La Bresse [F] 58 D3
La Brillanne [F] 108 C3
Labrit [F] 66 C5
Łabunie [PL] 52 G1
Läby [S] 174 F6
Laç [AL] 128 B2
Laç [AL] 128 B2
La Cabrera [E] 88 G4
La Caillere-St-Hilaire [F] 54 C3
La Cala del Moral [E] 102 C5
La Calahorra [E] 102 F4
La Calera [E] 100 B5
La Caleta [E] 100 E5
La Caletta [I] 118 E3
Lacalm [F] 68 C5
La Calzada de Calatrava [E] 96 E5
La Calzada de Oropesa [E] 88 C6
La Campana [E] 102 A2
La Campana [E] 104 B4
La Cañada de Cañepla [E] 102 H3
La Cañada de Verich [F] 90 F6
Lacanau [F] 66 C2
Lacanau-Océan [F] 66 B2
La Canonica [F] 114 C3
La Canonja [E] 92 C5
La Canourgue [F] 68 C6
La Capelle [F] 28 G5
Lacapelle-Marival [F] 66 H4
La Capte [F] 108 C6
Laćarak [SRB] 142 F2
La Caridad [E] 78 F2
La Carlota [E] 102 B2
La Carolina [E] 96 E6
La Cartuja [E] 100 F3
Lacaune [F] 106 C3
La Cavalerie [F] 106 D3
Lacave [F] 66 G4
Lacco Ameno [I] 120 D3
Lacedonia [I] 120 G2
La Celle-Dunoise [F] 54 H5
Láceni [RO] 148 B1
La Cerca [E] 82 F4
Láces [I] 72 C3
La Chaise-Dieu [F] 68 D3
La Chambre [F] 70 B4
Lachamp [F] 68 C5
Lachanás [GR] 130 B3
Lachaniá [GR] 154 D4
La Chapelle [F] 68 F1
La Chapelle-d'Angillon [F] 56 C3
la Chapelle-en-Valgaudemar [F] 70 A6
La Chapelle-en-Vercors [F] 68 G5
La Chapelle-Glain [F] 40 G5
la-Chapelle-Laurent [F] 68 C4
La Charité-sur-Loire [F] 56 D3
La Chartre-sur-le-Loir [F] 42 C6
La Châtaigneraie [F] 54 D3
La Châtre [F] 54 H5
La Chaux-de-Fonds [CH] 58 C5
Lachendorf [D] 32 G1
la-Chevignerie [F] 40 E6
la Chèze [F] 26 B5
Lachowo [PL] 24 D4
La Ciotat [F] 108 B5
La Ciudad Encantada [E] 98 C2
Łąck [PL] 36 G2
Läckeby [S] 162 G5
Läckö [S] 166 E5
La Clayette [F] 56 F6
la Clisse [F] 54 C6
La Clusaz [F] 70 B3
La Cluse [F] 68 H2
La Cluse-et-Mijoux [F] 58 B6
La Codosera [E] 86 F5
La Colle Noire [F] 108 E5
La Colle St. Michel [F] 108 D3
Lacona [I] 114 D3
La Concepción [E] 102 C4
Láconi [I] 118 D5
La Coquille [F] 66 G2
La Coronada [E] 96 B3
La Corrèze [F] 66 H3
La Corte [I] 118 B3
La Coruña / A Coruña [E] 78 C2
La Côte-St-André [F] 68 G4
Lacourt [F] 84 G5
La Courtine [F] 68 B2
la Couvertoirade [F] 106 E3
Lacq [F] 84 D3
La Croisière [F] 54 G5
La Croix Ferrée [F] 66 H1
La Croixille [F] 26 D6
La Croix-Valmer [F] 108 D6
La Cueva Santa [E] 98 E3
La Cumbre [E] 96 B1
La Cure [F] 70 B1
Lad [H] 74 H5
Ląd [PL] 36 E3
Ladapeyre [F] 54 H5
Ladbergen [D] 32 C2
Ladby [DK] 156 E3
Lądek-Zdrój [PL] 50 C3
Ládi [GR] 130 H1
Ladíspoli [I] 114 H5
Ladoeiro [P] 86 F3
Ladon [F] 42 F6
Ladoye, Cirque de- [F] 58 A6
Ladushkin [RUS] 22 G2
Ladyzhyn [UA] 204 E2
La Encinilla y El Rubio [E] 100 G3
Lærdalsøyri [N] 170 E2
Laerma [GR] 154 D4
La Espina [E] 78 G3
La Estrella [E] 96 D1
La Felipa [E] 98 C5
La Fère [F] 28 F6
la Ferrière [F] 42 C6
la Ferrière [F] 70 A4
La Ferrière-en-Parthenay [F] 54 E3
Laferté [F] 58 B3
La Ferté-Bernard [F] 42 C5
La-Ferté-Chevresis [F] 28 G5
La Ferté Gaucher [F] 42 H4
la-Ferté-Loupière [F] 56 E1
La Ferté-Macé [F] 26 F5
La Ferté-Milon [F] 42 H3
La Ferté-sous-Jouarre [F] 42 H3
La Ferté-St-Aubin [F] 56 B1
La Ferté-Vidame [F] 26 H5
La-Feuille [F] 28 C5
Laffrey [F] 68 H5
Láfka [GR] 136 E1
La Flèche [F] 42 B6
La Florida [E] 78 G3
La Flotte [F] 54 B4
La Font de la Figuera [E] 98 D6
la Foresta, Convento- [I] 116 B4
Laforsen [S] 182 H6
Lafortunada [E] 84 E5
La Franca [E] 82 D2
Lafrançaise [F] 66 F6
La Fregeneda [E] 80 E5
La Fresneda [E] 90 F6
La Frua [I] 70 F2
La Fuente de San Esteban [E] 80 F6
Lăga [BG] 148 A4
La Gacilly [F] 40 E5
La Gallega [E] 88 H2
Lagan [S] 162 C4
Laganás [GR] 136 B2
Lagarde [F] 44 F5
La Garde-Freinet [F] 108 D5
La Garriga [E] 92 E4
La Garrovilla [E] 94 G1
Lage [D] 32 E3
Łagiewniki [PL] 50 C2
Laginá [GR] 130 B4
La Gineta [E] 98 B5
L'Agiot Élancourt [F] 42 F3
Lagkáda [GR] 134 G4
Lagkáda [GR] 136 E4
Lagkadás [GR] 130 B4
Lagkádia [GR] 136 D2
Lagkadíkia [GR] 130 B4
Lagnieu [F] 68 G2
Lagnö [S] 168 C6
Lagny [F] 42 G3
Lagoa [P] 94 B5
Lagodaž [BG] 146 F6
Lagonegro [I] 120 G5
Lagonísi [GR] 136 H1
Lágos [GR] 130 F3
Lagos [P] 94 B5
Lagosanto [I] 110 H3
Łagów [PL] 34 H3
Łagów [PL] 52 C1
Łagówek [PL] 34 H3
La Granada de Rio Tinto [E] 94 F4
la Granadella [E] 90 H5
La Grand-Combe [F] 106 F2
La Grande-Motte [F] 106 F4
La Granja [E] 88 F4
La Granjuela [E] 96 B5
Lagrasse [F] 106 C5
La Grave [F] 70 B5
Lägsta [S] 190 G6
La Guardia / A Guarda [E] 78 A5
La Guardia / A Guarda [E] 96 G2
Laguardia / Biasteri [E] 82 G6
La Guardia de Jaén [E] 102 E2
Laguarres [E] 90 H3
Laguarta [E] 84 E5
Laguépie [F] 66 H6
La Guerche-de-Bretagne [F] 40 G4
La Guerche-sur-l'Aubois [F] 56 D4
Laguiole [F] 68 B5
Laguna de Duero [E] 88 E2
Laguna del Marquesado [E] 98 C2
Laguna de Negrillos [E] 82 B5
Laguna de Santiago [E] 100 B5
Laguna Negra [E] 90 B2
Lagunas de Villafáfila [E] 82 A6
Lagýna [GR] 128 H4
La Haba [E] 96 B3
Lahane [F] 66 B5
la Haye [F] 28 C5
La Haye-du-Puits [F] 26 D2
Lahdenperä [FIN] 186 F2
Lahemmaa [EST] 198 D1
La Hermida [E] 82 D3
Laheycourt [F] 44 C4
La Higuera [E] 98 C6
Lahinch [IRL] 2 B5
La Hinojosa [E] 98 B3
Lahishyn [UA] 202 B6
Lahnajärvi [S] 194 B7
Lahnalahti [FIN] 188 D4
Lahnasjärvi [FIN] 196 F5
Lahnberg [A] 72 F2
Lahnsattel [A] 62 D5
Lahnstein [D] 30 H6
Laholm [S] 162 B5
Laholuoma [FIN] 186 C5
La Horra [E] 88 G2
Lahoysk [BY] 202 B5
La Hoz de la Vieja [E] 90 E6
Lahr [D] 58 E2
Lähteenkylä [FIN] 176 D2
Lahti [FIN] 176 C3
Lahti / Lahtis [FIN] 178 B2
Lahtis / Lahti [FIN] 178 B2
La Hutte [F] 26 F6
Laibgaliai [LT] 200 G3
Laichingen [D] 60 B3
Laifour, Roches de- [F] 44 C1
L'Aigle [F] 26 G5
La Iglesuela del Cid [E] 98 F2
Laignes [F] 56 F2
Laiguéglia [I] 108 G4
L'Aiguillon [F] 54 B4
Laihela / Laihia [FIN] 186 B3
Laihia / Laihela [FIN] 186 B3
Laillio [FIN] 188 F6
Laïliás [GR] 130 C2
Laimbach [A] 62 D4
Laimoluokta [S] 192 G4
Lainate [I] 70 G4
Lainbach [A] 62 C6
Lainijaur [S] 190 G4
Lainio [S] 192 H5
Lairg [GB] 6 E3
Laisbäck [S] 190 F4
La Isla [E] 82 C2
Laissac [F] 68 B6
Laïsta [GR] 132 D1
Laisvall [S] 190 F2
Laitikkala [FIN] 176 G2
Laitila [FIN] 176 D3
Laitineva [FIN] 196 D4
Laize-la-Ville [F] 26 F4
la-Jaille-Yvon [F] 40 H5
La Jana [E] 98 G2
Lajares [E] 100 E6
La Javie [F] 108 D3
Lajes [P] 100 D3
Lajes das Flores [P] 100 B4
Lajes do Pico [P] 100 C3
Lajkovac [SRB] 146 A1
La Jonchère-St-Maurice [F] 54 G6
la Jonquera [E] 92 G2
Lajoskomárom [H] 76 B3
Lajosmizse [H] 76 D2
Lak [H] 64 F4
Łaka [PL] 50 F4
Lakaluoma [FIN] 186 D3
Lakaniemi [FIN] 186 D2
Łaka Prudnicka [PL] 50 D3
Lakatnik [BG] 146 F4
Lakaträsk [S] 194 A8
Lakavica [MK] 128 G2
Lakfors [N] 190 D3
Lakhdenpokh'ya [RUS] 188 G6
Laki [MK] 128 G1
Lakitelek [H] 76 E3
Lákka [GR] 132 B3
Lakkí [GR] 154 A2
Lákkoi [GR] 140 C4
Lákkoma [GR] 130 G4
Lakkópetra [GR] 132 E6
Lakócsa [H] 74 H5
Lakolk [DK] 156 A3
Lakselv [N] 194 C3
Laktaši [BIH] 142 C2
La Lantejuela [E] 102 B2
Lalapaşa [TR] 150 B1
Lálas [GR] 136 C2
l'Albagés [E] 90 H5
L'Albi [E] 92 B4
l'Alcora / Alcora [E] 98 F3
L'Alcúdia [E] 98 E5
L'Alcúdia (Ilice) [E] 104 D2
L'Alcúdia de Crespins [E] 98 E6
L'Aldea [E] 92 B5
l'Alguenya [E] 104 D2
La Lima [I] 110 E4
Lalín [E] 78 C4
Lalinde [F] 66 F4
La Línea de la Concepción [E] 100 H5
Lalkovo [BG] 150 B1
Lalm [AL] 128 B3
Lalm [N] 180 G6
La Loupe [F] 26 H6
Lalouvesc [F] 68 F4
La Louvière [B] 28 H4
L'Alpe-d'Huez [F] 70 A5
Lalueza [E] 90 F3
La Luisiana [E] 102 B2
Lam [D] 48 D6
La Machine [F] 56 D4
La Maddalena [I] 118 E2
Lama dei Peligni [I] 116 D5
La Magdalena [E] 78 G5
La Malène [F] 68 C6
Lamalou-les-Bains [F] 106 D4
La Manche, Tunnel sous-/ Channel Tunnel [F/GB] 14 G5
La Manga del Mar Menor [E] 104 D4
Lamarche [F] 58 B2
Lamargelle [F] 56 G3
La Marina [E] 104 D3
Lamarosa [P] 86 C5
Lamarque [F] 66 C2
Lamas do Vouga [P] 80 B5
Lamastre [F] 68 F5
La Mata [E] 104 D3
La Matanza [E] 82 B5
La Maucarrière [F] 54 E3
Lambach [A] 62 B4
Lamballe [F] 26 B4
Lambesc [F] 106 H4
Lamborn [S] 174 C3
Lambrecht [D] 46 B5
Lamego [P] 80 D4
la-Melleraye-de-Bretagne [F] 40 F5
L'Ametlla de Mar [E] 92 B5
Lamezia Terme [I] 124 D5
Lamía [GR] 132 G4
Lammhult [S] 162 D4
Lammi [FIN] 176 H2
Lammi [FIN] 186 D1
Lamminkylä [FIN] 188 G2
Lamminkylä [FIN] 196 F4
Lamminkyulya [RUS] 188 F6
Lamminmaa [FIN] 186 C4
La Molina [E] 92 E2
La Mongie [F] 84 F4
La Mota [E] 102 D3
La Mothe-Achard [F] 54 B3
La-Mothe-St-Héray [F] 54 D4
Lamotte-Beuvron [F] 56 B2
La Motte-Chalancon [F] 108 B2

Medemblik [NL] 16 E3
Medena Selišta [BIH] 142 B4
Meden Rudnik [BG] 148 F4
Medenychi [UA] 52 H5
Medet [TR] 152 G6
Medetli [TR] 150 G4
Medevi [S] 166 G5
Medgidia [RO] 204 E5
Medgyesegyháza [H] 76 G3
Medhamn [S] 166 F3
Mediaş [RO] 204 C4
Medicina [I] 110 G3
Medina [H] 76 B4
Medina Azahara [E] 102 C1
Medinaceli [E] 90 B4
Medina del Campo [E] 88 E2
Medina de Pomar [E] 82 F4
Medina de Rioseco [E] 82 B6
Medina-Sidonia [E] 100 G4
Medininkai [LT] 200 G5
Medle [S] 196 A4
Médole [I] 110 E1
Médous, Grotte de- [F] 84 F4
Médousa [GR] 130 E2
Medovina [BG] 146 E2
Medskogen [S] 172 D4
Medstugan [S] 182 E1
Medugorje [BIH] 144 C2
Medulin [HR] 112 D3
Medvedja [SRB] 146 D4
Medved'ov [SK] 62 H5
Medvida [HR] 112 H5
Medvode [SLO] 74 B5
Medyka [PL] 52 F4
Medze [LV] 198 B6
Medzev [SK] 64 F3
Medzilaborce [SK] 52 E6
Medžitlija [MK] 128 E4
Meerane [D] 48 C1
Meerkerk [NL] 16 D5
Meersburg [D] 58 H4
Meeuwen [B] 30 E3
Mefjordvær [N] 192 E2
Méga Chorió [GR] 132 F4
Méga Déreio [GR] 130 G2
Méga Doukáto [GR] 130 F3
Megáli Vólvi [GR] 130 B4
Megalochóri [GR] 132 F2
Megálo Chorió [GR] 154 B3
Megálo Livádi [GR] 138 C3
Megalópoli [GR] 136 D3
Mégara [GR] 134 B6
Megara Hyblaea [I] 126 G4
Méga Spílaio [GR] 132 G6
Megève [F] 70 B3
Megísti [GR] 154 G3
Megístis Lávras, Moní- [GR] 130 D5
Megorjelo [BIH] 144 C3
Meg. Panagía [GR] 130 C5
Megyaszó [H] 64 F4
Mehadia [RO] 204 C5
Mehamn [N] 194 D1
Mehikoorma [EST] 198 G3
Mehmetcik (Galatia) [CY] 154 G4
Mehov Krš [SRB] 146 B4
Mehring [D] 44 G2
Mehtäkylä [FIN] 196 C5
Mehun-sur-Yèvre [F] 56 B3
Meiåvollen [N] 182 C3
Meijel [NL] 30 F3
Meilen [CH] 58 F5
Meillant, Château de- [F] 56 C4
Meilleraye, Abbaye de- [F] 40 F5
Meina [I] 70 F4
Meine [D] 32 H2
Meinerzhagen [D] 32 C5
Meiningen [D] 46 F2
Meira [E] 78 E3
Meirāni [LV] 198 F5
Meiringen [CH] 70 E1
Meisenheim [D] 44 H3
Meisingset [N] 180 F2
Meissen [D] 34 E6
Meitingen [D] 60 D3
Męka [PL] 36 F5
Mekece [TR] 150 G4
Mekinje [SLO] 74 C4
Mekrijärvi [FIN] 188 H2
Meksa Šantić [SRB] 76 D5
Mel [I] 72 E4
Mélampes [GR] 140 D5
Melaniós [GR] 134 G4
Meláтes [GR] 132 D3
Melbeck [D] 18 G5
Melbu [N] 192 D4
Meldal [N] 180 H2
Meldola [I] 110 G4
Meldorf [D] 18 E2
Melegnano [I] 70 G5
Melenci [SRB] 76 E6
Melene [TR] 152 B2
Melfi [I] 120 G3
Melgaço [P] 78 C5
Melgar de Arriba [E] 82 C5
Melgar de Fernamental [E] 82 D5
Melgarejo [E] 100 G3
Melholt [DK] 160 E3
Melhus [N] 180 F2
Melhus [N] 182 B1
Melide [E] 78 D3
Melides [P] 94 B2
Meligalás [GR] 136 D3
Meliki [GR] 128 G5
Melilli [I] 126 G4
Melisenda [I] 118 E6
Mélisey [F] 58 C3
Mélissa [GR] 130 E3
Melissáni [GR] 132 C6
Melíssi [GR] 132 E1
Melissópetra [GR] 128 D6
Melissourgós [GR] 130 B4
Melito di Porto Salvo [I] 124 C8
Melitopol' [UA] 204 H2
Melívoia [GR] 130 E2
Melk [A] 62 D4
Melksham [GB] 12 G3
Mellakoski [FIN] 194 C8
Mellansel [S] 184 F1
Mellansjö [S] 184 C5
Mellanström [S] 190 G3
Mellau [A] 60 B6
Mellby [S] 162 E3
Mellbystrand [S] 162 B5
Melle [D] 32 D2
Melle [F] 54 D5
Mellendorf [D] 32 F1
Mellerud [S] 166 D5
Mellieħa [M] 126 C6
Mellilä [FIN] 176 E3
Mellin [D] 34 A1
Melloussa [MA] 100 G6
Mellrichstadt [D] 46 F2
Mellstaby [S] 158 G1
Melnica [SRB] 146 C1
Melnik [BG] 130 B2
Mělník [CZ] 48 F3
Mel'nikovo [RUS] 178 G2
Mel'nitsy [RUS] 198 G3
Mélrand [F] 26 A5
Melrose [GB] 8 F4
Melsomvik [N] 164 H3
Melsungen [D] 32 F5
Meltaus [FIN] 194 C7
Melton Mowbray [GB] 10 F6
Meltosjärvi [FIN] 194 C8
Melun [F] 42 G4
Melvich [GB] 6 E2
Mélykút [H] 76 D4
Melzo [I] 70 G5
Membrilla [E] 96 F4
Membrío [E] 86 F4
Memer [F] 66 H6
Mem Martins [P] 86 A5
Memmingen [D] 60 B4
Mémorial du Omaha Beach [F] 26 E3
Mena [UA] 202 E6
Menággio [I] 70 G3
Menai Bridge [GB] 10 B4
Menasalbas [E] 96 E2
Menat [F] 56 C6
Mencshely [H] 74 H2
Mendavia [E] 82 H6
Mende [F] 68 C6
Menden [D] 32 C4
Menderes [TR] 152 C4
Mendig [D] 30 H6
Mending [A] 62 C6
Mendrisio [CH] 70 G4
Ménéac [F] 26 B5
Menec [F] 40 D5
Menemen [TR] 152 C4
Menen [B] 28 F2
Menesjärvi [FIN] 194 D4
Ménez Hom [F] 40 B2
Menfi [I] 126 C3
Ménfőcsanak [H] 62 H6
Menga, Cueva de- [E] 102 C4
Mengamuñoz [E] 88 D4
Mengen [D] 58 H3
Mengeš [SLO] 74 C4
Mengíbar [E] 102 E1
Mengishevo [BG] 148 E3
Menídi [GR] 132 D3
Ménigoute [F] 54 E4
Ménina [GR] 132 C2
Menonen [FIN] 176 F3
Mens [F] 68 H6
Menstrup [DK] 156 F4
Menthon [F] 70 B3
Menton [F] 108 F4
Méntrida [E] 88 E6
Menyushi [RUS] 202 B2
Menz [D] 20 C6
Meppel [NL] 16 F3
Meppen [D] 16 H4
Mequinenza [E] 90 G5
Mequinenza, Castillo de- [E] 90 G5
Mer [F] 54 H1
Mera de Boixo [E] 78 D1
Meråker [N] 182 D1
Meran / Merano [I] 72 D3
Merano / Meran [I] 72 D3
Merate [I] 70 G4
Mercatale [I] 114 H1
Mercatino Conca [I] 110 H5
Mercato San Severino [I] 120 F3
Mercato Saraceno [I] 110 G5
Merćez [SRB] 146 C4
Merdrignac [F] 26 B5
Méréville [F] 42 F5
Merges [H] 62 H6
Mergozzo [I] 70 F3
Méribel-les-Allues [F] 70 B4
Meriç [TR] 130 H2
Mérichas [GR] 138 C2
Merichleri [BG] 148 C5
Meriçler [TR] 152 D6
Mérida [E] 94 H2
Merijärvi [FIN] 196 C5
Merikarvia / Sastmola [FIN] 186 B6
Merimasku [FIN] 176 D4
Měřín [CZ] 50 A5
Mering [D] 60 D4
Merkendorf [D] 46 F6
Merkine [LT] 24 G2
Merklingen [D] 60 B3
Merlara [I] 110 F1
Merle, Tours de- [F] 66 H4
Merlevenez [F] 40 C4
Merligen [CH] 70 E1
Mern [DK] 156 G4
Mernye [H] 76 A4
Merošina [SRB] 146 D3
Merrahalsen [N] 170 G1
Mersch [D] 30 F4
Mersch [L] 44 F2
Merseburg [D] 34 C5
Mersinbeleni [TR] 152 D6
Mērsrags [LV] 198 C4
Merthyr Tydfil [GB] 12 F2
Mértola [P] 94 D4
Méru [F] 42 F2
Mervans [F] 56 G5
Merville [F] 28 E3
Méry [F] 44 A5
Meryemana [TR] 152 D5
Merzig [D] 44 F3
Mesagne [I] 122 F4
Mesão Frio [P] 80 D4
Mesariá [GR] 138 D1
Meschede [D] 32 D5
Meschers-sur-Gironde [F] 54 C6
Mešeišta [MK] 128 D3
Mesenikólas [GR] 132 F3
Meshchovsk [RUS] 202 E4
Mési [GR] 130 F3
Mesillas [E] 88 B5
Mesimvría [GR] 130 G3
Mesinge [DK] 156 E3
Meškasalis [LT] 24 G2
Mesklá [GR] 140 C4
Meslay [F] 40 H5
Mesnalien [N] 172 B2
Mesnil-Val [F] 28 C4
Mesocco [CH] 70 G2
Mesochóra [GR] 132 E2
Mesochóri [GR] 132 F1
Mesochóri [GR] 140 G2
Mésola [I] 110 H2
Mesolóngi [GR] 132 E5
Mesón do Vento [E] 78 C2
Mesopótamo [GR] 132 C3
Mespelbrunn [D] 46 D3
Messancy [B] 44 E2
Messas [F] 42 E6
Messdorf [D] 34 B1
Messelt [N] 172 C1
Messina [I] 124 B7
Messines de Baixo [P] 94 C5
Messíni [GR] 136 D4
Messkirch [D] 58 G3
Messlingen [S] 182 E3
Messtetten [D] 58 G3
Mesta [BG] 130 C1
Mestá [GR] 134 G5
Mestanza [E] 96 E5
Městec Králové [CZ] 48 H3
Mestervik [N] 192 F2
Mésti [GR] 130 G3
Mestilä [FIN] 176 D3
Mestlin [D] 20 B4
Město Albrechtice [CZ] 50 D3
Město Libavá [CZ] 50 D5
Mestre [I] 72 E6
Mesvres [F] 56 F5
Mesztegnyő [H] 74 H4
Metabief [F] 58 B6
Metagkítsi [GR] 130 C5
Metaljka [BIH] 144 E2
Metamórfosi [GR] 130 C5
Metanjac [MNE] 146 A4
Metapontium [I] 122 D4
Metaxádes [GR] 130 H1
Metaxás [GR] 128 F6
Metéora [GR] 132 E1
Méteren [F] 28 F2
Méthana [GR] 136 G2
Methóni [GR] 128 G5
Methóni [GR] 136 C4
Metković [HR] 144 C3
Metličina [BG] 148 F2
Metlika [SLO] 74 D6
Metnitz [A] 74 B2
Metóchi [GR] 132 E6
Metóchi [GR] 134 A3
Metsäkylä [FIN] 178 C3
Metsäkylä [FIN] 196 F3
Metsälä / Ömossa [FIN] 186 B5
Metsküla [EST] 198 C3
Métsovo [GR] 132 D1
Metten [D] 60 G2
Mettet [B] 30 C5
Mettingen [D] 32 C2
Mettlach [D] 44 F3
Mettmann [D] 30 G3
Metz [F] 44 E4
Metzervisse [F] 44 F3
Metzingen [D] 58 H2
Meulan [F] 42 F3
Meung-sur-Loire [F] 42 E6
Meuselwitz [D] 34 C6
Meux [B] 30 D5
Mexilhoeira Grande [P] 94 B5
Meximieux [F] 68 G2
Meyenburg [D] 20 B5
Meylan [F] 68 H4
Meymac [F] 68 B2
Meyrargues [F] 108 B4
Meyrueis [F] 106 E2
Meyzieu [F] 68 G3
Mézapos [GR] 136 E5
Mezdra [BG] 146 G4
Mèze [F] 106 E4
Mézel [F] 108 D3
Mežgenin [PL] 24 D6
Mežica [SLO] 74 C4
Mézières [F] 54 F5
Mézières-en-Brenne [F] 54 G4
Mézilhac [F] 68 E5
Mézin [F] 66 D6
Mezőberény [H] 76 G3
Mezőcsát [H] 64 F5
Mezőfalva [H] 76 C2
Mezőhegyes [H] 76 F4
Mezőhék [H] 76 E2
Mezőkeresztes [H] 64 F5
Mezőkovácsháza [H] 76 F4
Mezőkövesd [H] 64 F5
Mezőlak [H] 74 H1
Mezőnyárád [H] 64 F5
Mezőörs [H] 64 A6
Mèzos [F] 66 B5
Mezősas [H] 76 G2
Mezőszilas [H] 76 B3
Mezőtúr [H] 76 F2
Mezquita de Jarque [E] 90 E6
Mezzojuso [I] 126 D2
Mezzolombardo [I] 72 C4
Mgarr [M] 126 C5
Miączyn [PL] 52 G1
Miami Platja [E] 90 H6
Mianowice [PL] 22 C2
Miasteczko Śląskie [PL] 50 F2
Miastko [PL] 22 B3
Miastkowo [PL] 24 C5
Michałkowo [PL] 24 B2
Michalovce [SK] 64 H2
Michałów [PL] 38 C6
Michałów [PL] 52 B2
Michałowo [PL] 24 F6
Micheldorf [A] 62 B5
Michelstadt [D] 46 D4
Michendorf [D] 34 D3
Michów [PL] 38 D5
Michurinskoye [RUS] 178 G3
Middelburg [NL] 16 B6
Middelfart [DK] 156 C3
Middelharnis [NL] 16 C5
Middelkerke-Bad [B] 28 F1
Middlesbrough [GB] 10 F2
Middlewich [GB] 10 D4
Midéa [GR] 136 F2
Midhurst [GB] 14 D5
Midleton [IRL] 4 D5
Midlum [D] 18 D3
Midsland [NL] 16 E1
Midsund [N] 180 D3
Midtgulen [N] 180 B5
Midtskogberget [N] 172 D2
Miechów [PL] 50 H3
Mieders [A] 72 D1
Miedes [E] 90 D4
Międzdroje [PL] 20 F3
Miedźno [PL] 50 G1
Międzybórz [PL] 36 D5
Międzybrodzie Bialskie [PL] 50 G4
Międzychód [PL] 36 B2
Międzygórze [PL] 50 C3
Międzylesie [PL] 50 C3
Międzyrzec Podlaski [PL] 38 E3
Międzyrzecz [PL] 36 A2
Miehikkälä [FIN] 178 D3
Miejsce Piastowe [PL] 52 D5
Miejska Górka [PL] 36 C5
Miélan [F] 84 F3
Mielec [PL] 52 D3
Mielno [PL] 20 H3
Mielno [PL] 34 G5
Mieluskylä [FIN] 196 D5
Mieraslompolo [FIN] 194 D3
Miercurea Ciuc [RO] 204 D4
Mieres [E] 78 H4
Mierkenis [S] 190 F1
Mieron [N] 194 B4
Mieroszów [PL] 50 B2
Miersig [RO] 76 H2
Mierzyno [PL] 22 D1
Miesbach [D] 60 E5
Mieścisko [PL] 36 D2
Mieste [D] 34 B2
Miesterhorst [D] 34 A2
Mieszkowice [PL] 34 G1
Mietoinen [FIN] 176 D4
Mieussy [F] 70 B2
Mifol [AL] 128 A5
Migennes [F] 42 H6
Migliacciaro [F] 114 C4
Migliarino [I] 110 D5
Migliarino [I] 110 G3
Migliónico [I] 122 D4
Mignano Monte Lungo [I] 120 D1
Migne [F] 54 G4
Miguel Esteban [E] 96 G3
Miguelturra [E] 96 E4
Mihăeşti [RO] 148 B1
Mihai Bravu [RO] 148 C1
Mihajlovac [SRB] 146 E1
Mihalgazi [TR] 150 H4
Mihályi [H] 62 G6
Mihla [D] 32 G6
Miiluranta [FIN] 196 E5
Mijares [E] 88 D5
Mijares [E] 98 D4
Mijas [E] 102 B5
Mijoux [F] 70 A1
Mikaelshulen [N] 164 G3
Mikalavas [LT] 24 G2
Mike [H] 74 H4
Mikhaylovo [BG] 146 G3
Mikkelbostad [N] 192 E3
Mikkeli / St Michel [FIN] 188 C6
Mikkelvika [N] 192 F1
Mikleuš [HR] 76 A6
Mikóháza [H] 64 G3
Mikolaivka [UA] 204 H4
Mikołajki [PL] 24 C4
Mikołajki Pomorskie [PL] 22 F4
Mikolin [PL] 50 D2
Mikołów [PL] 50 F3
Mikoszewo [PL] 22 E2
Mikre [BG] 148 A4
Mikrevo [BG] 130 B1
Mikró Chorió [GR] 132 F4
Mikró Déreio [GR] 130 G2
Mikrókampos [GR] 128 H4
Mikrópoli [GR] 130 C3
Mikrothíves [GR] 132 H3
Mikstat [PL] 36 E5
Mikulčice [CZ] 62 G3
Mikulov [CZ] 62 F3
Mikulovice [CZ] 50 D3
Mikulovice [CZ] 62 E2
Miłakowo [PL] 22 G3
Miland [N] 170 F5
Milano [I] 70 G5
Milano Marittima [I] 110 H4
Milanovac [HR] 76 A6
Milanówek [PL] 38 B3
Milatos [GR] 140 F4
Milazzo [I] 124 B7
Mildenhall [GB] 14 F2
Milejczyce [PL] 38 F2
Milejewo [PL] 22 F3
Milena [I] 126 D3
Mileševa, Manastir- [SRB] 146 A3
Mileševo [SRB] 76 E6
Milet [TR] 152 D6
Miletići [HR] 112 G4
Mileto [I] 124 D6
Miletopolis [TR] 150 E4
Milevsko [CZ] 48 F5
Milford [IRL] 2 F2
Milford Haven [GB] 12 D2
Milharadas [P] 94 B4
Milići [BIH] 142 E4
Milicz [PL] 36 D5
Miliés [GR] 134 A2
Milín [CZ] 48 F5
Milína [GR] 134 A3
Milino [MK] 128 F1
Militello in Val di Catania [I] 126 F4
Miljevina [BIH] 144 D2
Millares [E] 98 E5
Millas [F] 92 F1
Millau [F] 106 D2
Millesimo [I] 108 G3
Millesvik [S] 166 E4
Millevaches [F] 68 B2
Millinge [DK] 156 D4
Millom [GB] 10 D2
Millstatt [A] 72 H3
Millstreet [IRL] 4 C4
Milltown [IRL] 4 B4
Milltown Malbay [IRL] 2 B6
Milmarcos [E] 90 C5
Milmersdorf [D] 20 D6
Milna [HR] 144 A2
Miločer [MNE] 144 D4
Miłocin [PL] 38 D5
Miłomłyn [PL] 22 G4
Milos [GR] 138 D4
Milosavci [BIH] 142 C2
Miloševa Kula [SRB] 146 D1
Miłosław [PL] 36 D3
Milovice u Hořic [CZ] 50 A3
Milow [D] 20 A5
Milówka [PL] 50 G5
Milreu [P] 94 C5
Milseburg [D] 46 E2
Milštejn [CZ] 48 G1
Miltach [D] 48 D6
Miltenberg [D] 46 D4
Milton Keynes [GB] 14 E3
Mimizan [F] 66 B4
Mimizan-Plage [F] 66 B4
Mimoň [CZ] 48 G2
Mina de São Domingos [P] 94 D4
Minas de Oro (Romanas) [E] 78 G3
Minas de Riotinto [E] 94 F5
Minateda, Cuevas de- [E] 104 B1
Minateda-Horca [E] 104 B1
Minaya [E] 98 B4
Minde [N] 164 C5
Mindelheim [D] 60 C4
Minden [D] 32 E2
Mindin [F] 40 E6
Mindszent [H] 76 E3
Minehead [GB] 12 E3
Mineo [I] 126 F4
Mineralni Bani [BG] 148 C6
Minerbio [I] 110 F3
Minervino di Lecce [I] 122 H5
Minervino Murge [I] 120 H2
Minervio [F] 114 C2
Minglanilla [E] 98 C4
Mingorria [E] 88 E4
Minićevo [SRB] 146 E3
Minne [S] 182 H5
Minnesund [N] 172 C4
Minnetler [TR] 152 D1
Miño [E] 78 D2
Mínoa [GR] 138 G4
Minot [F] 56 G2
Minsen [D] 18 C3
Minsk [BY] 202 B5
Mińsk Mazowiecki [PL] 38 C3
Minturnae [I] 120 D2
Minturno [I] 120 D2
Miočić [HR] 142 A5
Miočinovići [HR] 142 A1
Mioković́evo [HR] 74 H6
Mionica [SRB] 146 A1
Mira [E] 98 D3
Mira [I] 72 E6
Mira [P] 80 B6
Mirabel [E] 88 H4
Mirabella Imbáccari [I] 126 F4
Mirabello [I] 110 F2
Miradolo Terme [I] 70 G6
Mirador del Fito [E] 82 C2
Miraflores [E] 82 E6
Miraflores [E] 96 E4
Miraflores de la Sierra [E] 88 F4
Miramar [F] 108 E5
Miramare [I] 112 B5
Miramare, Castello di- [I] 72 H6
Miramas [F] 106 G4
Mirambeau [F] 66 D2
Miramont-de-Guyenne [F] 66 E4
Miranda [E] 84 B4
Miranda de Ebro [E] 82 G5
Miranda do Corvo [P] 86 D2
Miranda do Douro [P] 80 G4
Mirande [F] 84 F3
Mirandela [P] 80 E4
Mirándola [I] 110 F2
Mirano [I] 72 E6
Mirantes [E] 78 G5
Miravci [MK] 128 G2
Miravet [E] 90 H6
Mirebeau [F] 54 E3
Mirebeau [F] 56 H3
Mirecourt [F] 44 E6
Mirepoix [F] 106 B5
Miřkov [CZ] 48 D5
Mirna [SLO] 74 C5
Mirna Peč [SLO] 74 C5
Mirnice [HR] 144 A2
Miróbriga [P] 94 B2
Mirocin Średni [PL] 34 H4
Miroslav [CZ] 62 F2
Mirosławiec [PL] 20 H5
Mirošov [CZ] 48 E5
Mirovice [CZ] 48 F5
Mirovo [BG] 146 G5
Mirow [D] 20 C5
Mirów [PL] 50 G2
Mirsk [PL] 48 H1
Mirto [I] 124 E3
Mirueña [E] 88 D4
Mişca [RO] 76 H3
Misi [FIN] 194 D7
Mišičevo [SRB] 76 D5
Misilmeri [I] 126 D2
Miskolc [H] 64 F4
Miskolctapolca [H] 64 F5
Mislata [E] 98 E4
Mislinja [SLO] 74 D4
Missanello [I] 120 H5
Misso [EST] 198 F4
Mistelbach [A] 62 F3
Misten [N] 192 D5
Misterbianco [I] 126 G3
Misterhult [S] 162 G3
Mistretta [I] 126 F2
Misurina [I] 72 E3
Miszewo [PL] 22 D2
Mitchelstown [IRL] 4 D4
Mitchelstown Caves [IRL] 4 D4
Míthymna [GR] 134 G2
Mitrašinci [MK] 128 G1
Mitrópoli [GR] 132 F3
Mitrova Reka [SRB] 146 B4
Mitrovo [SRB] 146 C3
Mitseh [A] 74 C2
Mittådalen [S] 182 E3
Mittelberg [A] 60 B6
Mittelberg [A] 72 C2
Mittelberg [D] 60 C5
Mittelsaida [D] 48 E2
Mittelstenahe [D] 18 E4
Mittenwald [D] 60 D6
Mittenwalde [D] 20 D5
Mittenwalde [D] 34 E3
Mittersill [A] 72 F1
Mitterteich [D] 48 C4
Mittet [N] 180 E3
Mittewald [A] 72 F3
Mittweida [D] 34 D6
Mitwitz [D] 46 G3
Mizhiria [UA] 204 C3
Mizil [RO] 204 E5
Miziya [BG] 146 G2
Mjåland [N] 164 E4
Mjällby [S] 158 E2
Mjällom [S] 184 G3
Mjåvatn [N] 164 E4
Mjell [N] 170 C1
Mjöbäck [S] 162 B3
Mjölby [S] 166 H6
Mjølfjell [N] 170 D3
Mjölkbäcken [S] 190 E2
Mjönäs [S] 166 F1
Mjøndalen [N] 164 G1
Mjønes [N] 180 H1
Mjørlund [N] 172 B4
Mjösebo [S] 162 F4
Mjösjöby [S] 190 G6
M. Kalývia [GR] 132 F2
Mladá Boleslav [CZ] 48 G3
Mladá Vožice [CZ] 48 G5
Mladé Buky [CZ] 50 A2
[illegible] [CZ] 60 C5
Mladenovac [SRB] 146 B1
Mladenovac [SRB] 204 B6
Mlado Nagoričane [MK] 146 D6
Mlamolovo [BG] 146 F5
Mława [PL] 22 G6
Mleczno [PL] 36 B5
Mlekarevo [BG] 148 D5
Mlini [HR] 144 C4
Mliniště [BIH] 142 B4
Młodasko [PL] 36 B2
Mlogoszyn [PL] 36 G3
Młynary [PL] 22 F3
Młynarze [PL] 24 C6
Mnich [CZ] 48 G6
Mnichovice [CZ] 48 G4
Mnichovo Hradiště [CZ] 48 G2
Mnichów [PL] 52 B2
Mniów [PL] 38 B6
Mníšek nad Hnilcom [SK] 64 F2
Mníšek pod Brdy [CZ] 48 F4
Mniszek [PL] 38 B5
Mo [N] 164 E2
Mo [N] 170 B2
Mo [N] 172 C4
Mo [N] 180 D4
Mo [S] 166 C4
Mo [S] 166 D3
Mo [S] 166 G3
Mo [S] 174 E2
Mo [S] 184 E2
Moan [N] 182 B5
Moaña [E] 78 B4
Moate [IRL] 2 D5
Moča [SK] 64 B5
Mocejón [E] 96 F1
Móchlos [GR] 140 G4
Mochós [GR] 140 F4
Mochowo [PL] 36 G1
Mochy [PL] 36 B4
Möckern [D] 34 C3
Mockfjärd [S] 172 H4
Möckmühl [D] 46 D5
Möckow [D] 20 D3
Moclín [E] 102 D3
Modane [F] 70 B5
Modave [B] 30 D5
Módena [I] 110 E3
Módi [GR] 132 H4
Módica [I] 126 F5
Modigliana [I] 110 G4
Modlęcin [PL] 34 H2
Modliborzyce [PL] 52 E1
Mödling [A] 62 F5
Modliszewko [PL] 36 D2
Modra [SK] 62 G4
Modra Špilja [HR] 116 H3
Modrava [CZ] 60 H2
Modriča [BIH] 142 D2
Modriště [MK] 128 E2
Modron [BIH] 142 D2
Modruš [HR] 112 G2
Modrý Kameň [SK] 64 C4
Modugno [I] 122 D2
Moeche, Castillo de- [E] 78 D1
Moelv [N] 172 B3
Moen [N] 192 F3
Moena [I] 72 D4
Moers [D] 30 G3
Moesgård [DK] 156 D1
Mofalla [S] 166 F6
Moffat [GB] 8 E4
Mofjell [N] 164 E4
Mogadouro [P] 80 F5
Mogán [E] 100 C6
Mogielnica [PL] 38 B4
Mogilica [BG] 130 E2
Mogilište [BG] 148 G2
Mogilno [PL] 36 E2
Móglia [I] 110 E2
Mogliano Veneto [I] 72 E6
Moglicë [AL] 128 C4
Mogno [CH] 70 F2
Mogno [CH] 70 F2
Mogón [E] 102 F2
Mogorella [I] 118 C5
Mogorić [HR] 112 G4
Mogoro [I] 118 C6
Moguer [E] 94 E6
Moha [H] 76 B1
Mohács [H] 76 B5
Mohärad [S] 162 C2
Moharras [E] 98 A4
Moheda [S] 162 D4
Mohelnice [CZ] 50 C4
Moher, Cliffs of- [IRL] 2 B5
Mohill [IRL] 2 E4
Möhkö [FIN] 188 H2
Moholm [S] 166 F5
Mohora [H] 64 D5
Mohyliv-Podilis'kyi [UA] 204 E2
Moi [N] 164 C4
Moià [E] 92 E3
Moikipää / Molpe [FIN] 186 A3
Moimenta da Beira [P] 80 D5
Mo-i-Rana [N] 190 E2
Moirans [F] 68 G4
Moirans-en-Montagne [F] 56 H6
Moíres [GR] 140 E5
Mõisaküla [EST] 198 E3
Moissac [F] 66 F6
Moita [P] 86 B5
Moitas [P] 86 E3
Moixent [E] 98 D6
Mojácar [E] 102 H5
Mojados [E] 88 E2
Mojęcice [PL] 36 C6
Mojkovac [MNE] 144 E3
Mojonera [E] 102 F5
Mojstrana [SLO] 74 B4
Mokliště [MK] 128 F2
Mokobody [PL] 38 D3
Mokra Gora [SRB] 144 E1
Mokren [BG] 148 E4
Mokresh [BG] 146 F2
Mokrin [SRB] 76 F5
Mokronog [SLO] 74 D5
Mokrzyska [PL] 52 B4
Möksy [FIN] 186 E2
Mol [B] 30 D3
Mol [SRB] 76 E6
Mola [I] 72 A4
Mola di Bari [I] 122 E3
Moland [N] 164 E1
Moláoi [GR] 136 F4
Molare [I] 108 H2
Mold [GB] 10 C4
Moldava n. Bodvou [SK] 64 F3
Molde [N] 170 B2
Molde [N] 180 E3
Moldova Nouă [RO] 204 B6
Moldoviţa, Mănăstirea- [RO] 204 D3
Møldrup [DK] 160 D5
Moldusen [N] 172 D5
Moledo [P] 78 A5
Molenheide [B] 30 E3

Murati [EST] 198 F4
Muratlar [TR] 150 B6
Muratlar [TR] 152 F6
Muratlı [TR] 150 C3
Murato [F] 114 C3
Murat-sur-Vèbre [F] 106 D3
Murau [A] 74 B2
Muravera [I] 118 E6
Murazzano [I] 108 G2
Murça [P] 80 E4
Mŭrchevo [BG] 146 F3
Murchin [D] 20 E3
Murcia [E] 104 C3
Murciélagos, Cueva de los- [E] 102 C2
Murcielagos, Cueva de los- [E] 102 E5
Murczyn [PL] 36 E1
Mur-de-Barrez [F] 68 B4
Mur-de-Bretagne [F] 26 A5
Mureck [A] 74 E3
Mürefte [TR] 150 C4
Muret [F] 84 H3
Murga [H] 76 B4
Murgados [E] 78 D1
Murgaševo [MK] 128 E3
Murgia / Murguía [E] 82 G5
Murg-Kraftwerk [D] 58 F1
Murguía / Murgia [E] 82 G5
Muri [CH] 58 F5
Murias de Paredes [E] 78 G4
Murieta [E] 82 H6
Murighiol [RO] 204 F5
Murino [MNE] 146 A5
Muriquan [AL] 128 A1
Murjek [S] 196 A2
Murlo [I] 114 F2
Murnau [D] 60 D5
Muro [E] 104 E4
Muro [F] 114 B3
Muro de Alcoy / Muro del Comtat [E] 104 E1
Muro del Comtat / Muro de Alcoy [E] 104 E1
Murole [FIN] 186 E6
Muro Lucano [I] 120 G3
Murony [H] 76 G3
Muros [E] 78 B3
Murowana Goślina [PL] 36 C2
Mürren [CH] 70 E2
Murrhardt [D] 46 D6
Murrisk Abbey [IRL] 2 B4
Murru [EST] 198 D3
Murska Sobota [SLO] 74 E3
Mursko Središće [HR] 74 F4
Murta [RO] 146 G2
Murtas [E] 102 E5
Murten [CH] 58 D6
Murter [HR] 112 G6
Murtinheira [P] 80 A6
Murtolahti [FIN] 188 D1
Murtosa [P] 80 B5
Murtovaara [FIN] 196 F2
Murvica [HR] 112 G5
Mürzsteg [A] 62 D6
Mürzzuschlag [A] 62 E6
Musamaa [FIN] 186 C2
Musasău de Tinca [RO] 76 H2
Musetrene [N] 180 G6
Mussalo [FIN] 178 C4
Musselkanaal [NL] 16 H3
Mussidan [F] 66 E3
Mussomeli [I] 126 D3
Mussy [F] 56 G2
Mustafa Kemal Paşa [TR] 150 E5
Müstair [CH] 72 B3
Mustajärvi [FIN] 186 E5
Mustajõe [EST] 198 G1
Mustalahti [FIN] 186 F5
Mustasaari / Korsholm [FIN] 186 B2
Mustér / Disentis [CH] 70 G1
Mustikkaperä [FIN] 186 F2
Mustinmäki [FIN] 188 D3
Mustinsalo [FIN] 188 D3
Mustjala [EST] 198 C3
Mustla [EST] 198 E3
Mustola [FIN] 194 E4
Mustvee [EST] 198 F2
Muszaki [PL] 22 H5
Muszyna [PL] 52 C5
Muszynka [PL] 52 C5
Muta [SLO] 74 D3
Mutalahti [FIN] 188 H3
Mutanj [SRB] 146 B2
Mutilva [E] 84 B4
Mutlangen [D] 60 B2
Mutriku [E] 82 H4
Muttalip [TR] 150 H5
Mutterstadt [D] 46 B5
Muurame [FIN] 186 G5
Muurasjärvi [FIN] 196 D6
Muurikkala [FIN] 178 D3
Muurla [FIN] 176 F5
Muurola [FIN] 178 D3
Muurola [FIN] 194 C8
Muuruvesi [FIN] 188 D2
Muxía [E] 78 B2
Múzeum Oravskej Dediny [SK] 50 H6
Muzillac [F] 40 E5
Mužla [SK] 64 B5
Mužlja [SRB] 142 G1
Myakishevo [RUS] 198 H5
Mybotn [N] 192 E3
Myckelgensjö [S] 184 F1
Myczków [PL] 52 E5
Myggenäs [S] 160 G1
Myhinpää [FIN] 186 H3
Myjava [SK] 62 H3
Mykínes [GR] 136 E2
Myking [N] 170 F4
Myklebust [N] 180 B5
Myklebust [N] 180 D3
Myklestøyl [N] 164 D3
Mykolaïv [UA] 52 H5
Mykolaïv [UA] 204 G3
Mýkonos [GR] 138 E2
Myllyaho [FIN] 186 F1
Myllykoski [FIN] 178 C3
Myllykselä [FIN] 176 H2
Myllymaa [FIN] 176 E2
Myllymäki [FIN] 186 E4
Mýloi [GR] 136 E2
Mylopótamos [GR] 136 F6
Mylund [DK] 160 E3
Mynämäki [FIN] 176 D4
Myndos [TR] 154 B2
Myonnesos [TR] 152 C5
Myos [TR] 152 D6
Myra [TR] 154 H3
Myrane [N] 164 B4
Myrås [S] 190 G3
Myrdal [N] 170 D3
Myre [N] 192 D3
Myre [N] 192 E3
Myren [S] 172 E5
Myrhorod [UA] 202 F7
Mýrina [GR] 130 F6
Myrina [TR] 152 C3
Myrkky [FIN] 186 B4
Myrmoen [N] 182 D3
Myrnes [N] 192 H1
Myrnyi [UA] 204 G4
Myronivka [UA] 202 E8
Myrskylä / Mörskom [FIN] 178 B3
Myrtiés [GR] 154 A2
Mýrtos [GR] 140 F5
Mýrtou (Çamlıbel) [CY] 154 F5
Myrvika [N] 190 C4
Myrviken [S] 182 G3
Mysen [N] 166 C2
Myšenec [CZ] 48 F6
Myshall [IRL] 4 F4
Myshuryn Rih [UA] 202 F8
Myślenice [PL] 50 H4
Myślibórz [PL] 34 G1
Myślice [PL] 22 F4
Mysłowice [PL] 50 G3
Mysovka [RUS] 200 D5
Mystegná [GR] 134 H2
Mystrás [GR] 136 E4
Mysubyttseter [N] 180 E5
Myszków [PL] 50 G2
Myszyniec [PL] 24 C5
Mýtikas [GR] 132 D5
Mytilíni [GR] 134 H2
Mytishchi [RUS] 202 F3
Mýtna [SK] 64 D3
Myto [BY] 24 H3
Mýto [CZ] 48 E4
Mzdowo [PL] 22 B3
Mzurki [PL] 36 G5

N

Nå [N] 170 C4
Naamijoki [FIN] 194 B7
Naantali / Nådend [FIN] 176 D4
Naarajärvi [FIN] 188 C4
Naarden [NL] 16 E4
Naarva [FIN] 188 G1
Nääs [S] 160 H2
Naas / An Nás [IRL] 2 F6
Nabaskoze / Navascués [E] 84 C4
Nabbelund [S] 162 H3
Nabburg [D] 48 C5
Náchod [CZ] 50 B3
Nacıvelioba [TR] 150 D5
Nacka [S] 168 E3
Nădab [RO] 76 G3
Nadarzyn [PL] 38 B3
Nadăş [RO] 76 H4
Naddvik [N] 170 E2
Nadela [E] 78 E3
Nådend / Naantali [FIN] 176 D4
Nădlac [RO] 76 F4
Nădlac [RO] 204 B5
Nadrin [B] 30 E6
Nádudvar [H] 76 G1
Nærbø [N] 164 A4
Næstved [DK] 156 F4
Näfels [CH] 58 G6
Náfpaktos [GR] 132 F5
Náfplio [GR] 136 F2
Naggen [S] 184 D5
Naglarby [S] 174 C5
Nagłowice [PL] 52 A2
Nagold [D] 58 G2
Nagu / Nauvo [FIN] 176 D5
Nagyatád [H] 74 H4
Nagybajom [H] 74 H4
Nagybaracska [H] 76 C5
Nagycenk [H] 62 F6
Nagycserkesz [H] 64 G5
Nagydorog [H] 76 B3
Nagyér [H] 76 F4
Nagyfüged [H] 64 E6
Nagygyanté [H] 76 G2
Nagygyimót [H] 74 H1
Nagyhalász [H] 64 H4
Nagyhegyes [H] 64 G6
Nagyhomok [H] 64 H4
Nagyigmánd [H] 64 A6
Nagyiván [H] 64 F6
Nagykálló [H] 64 H5
Nagykanizsa [H] 74 G4
Nagykáta [H] 76 D1
Nagykereki [H] 76 H1
Nagykőlked [H] 74 F2
Nagykónyi [H] 76 B3
Nagykőrös [H] 76 D2
Naglak [H] 76 F4
Nagylóc [H] 64 D5
Nagymágocs [H] 76 F3
Nagymaros [H] 64 C5
Nagyoroszi [H] 64 C5
Nagypuszta [H] 74 H4
Nagyrábé [H] 76 G1
Nagyszénás [H] 76 F3
Nagyvázsony [H] 74 H2
Naharros [E] 90 A4
Naharros [E] 98 B2
Nahe [D] 18 F3
Nahkiaisoja [FIN] 194 C8
Naila [D] 46 H3
Nailloux [F] 106 A4
Nailsworth [GB] 12 G3
Naipu [RO] 148 C1
Nairn [GB] 6 E5
Najac [F] 66 H6
Nájera [E] 82 G6
Näkkälä [FIN] 194 B5
Nakkesletta [N] 192 G1
Nakkila [FIN] 176 D2
Naklik [PL] 52 E2
Naklo [SLO] 74 B4
Nakło nad Notecią [PL] 22 C6
Nakovo [SRB] 76 F5
Nakskov [DK] 156 E5
Nälden [S] 182 G2
Nałęczów [PL] 38 D5
Nálepkovo [SK] 64 F2
Näljänkä [FIN] 196 F3
Nalkki [FIN] 196 E4
Nalzen [F] 106 A5
Nalžovké Hory [CZ] 48 E6
Nalžovské Hory [CZ] 48 E6
Nambroca [E] 96 F2
Namdalseid [N] 190 C5
Namen (Namur) [B] 30 D6
Náměšť nad Oslavou [CZ] 50 B6
Námestovo [SK] 50 G5
Namlos [A] 60 C6
Namma [N] 172 D4
Nämpnäs [FIN] 186 A4
Namsos [N] 190 C5
Namsskogan [N] 190 D4
Namsvassgardån [N] 190 D4
Namur (Namen) [B] 30 D5
Namysłów [PL] 36 D6
Nanclares de la Oca / Langraiz Oka [E] 82 G5
Nancy [F] 44 E5
Nangis [F] 42 G4
Nannestad [N] 172 B5
Nans-les-Pins [F] 108 C5
Nant [F] 106 E3
Nantes [F] 40 F6
Nanteuil-le-Haudouin [F] 42 G3
Nantiat [F] 54 G6
Nantua [F] 68 H2
Nantwich [GB] 10 D5
Naours, Grottes de- [F] 28 E4
Náousa [GR] 128 F4
Náousa [GR] 138 E3
Nåpagård [N] 170 F6
Napi [EST] 198 C2
Naples [TR] 150 C3
Nápoli [I] 120 E3
Na Pomezí [CZ] 50 C3
Naposenaho [FIN] 186 E2
När [S] 168 G5
Nåra [N] 170 A2
Narach [BY] 200 H5
Naraio, Castelo de- [E] 78 D2
Narberth [GB] 12 D1
Narbolía [I] 118 C5
Narbonne [F] 106 D5
Narbonne Plage [F] 106 D5
Narbuvollen [N] 182 C4
Narcao [I] 118 B7
Nardis, Cascata di- [I] 72 C4
Nardò [I] 122 G5
Narechenski Bani [BG] 148 B6
Narew [PL] 24 F6
Narewka [PL] 24 F6
Närhilä [FIN] 186 G3
Narila [FIN] 188 D5
Narjordet [N] 182 C4
Narkaus [FIN] 194 D8
Narlıca [TR] 150 F4
Narni [I] 116 A4
Naro [I] 126 D4
Naro-Fominsk [RUS] 202 F3
Narol [PL] 52 G2
Narón [E] 78 D4
Närpes / Närpiö [FIN] 186 A4
Närpiö / Närpes [FIN] 186 A4
Narta [HR] 74 G6
Nartháki [GR] 132 G3
Nartkowo [PL] 20 G3
Närtuna [S] 168 E2
Naruska [FIN] 194 F6
Narva [EST] 198 G1
Narva [FIN] 176 G2
Närvä [FIN] 186 G6
Närvä [S] 192 H4
Narva-Jõesuu [EST] 198 G1
Närvijoki [FIN] 186 B3
Narvik [N] 192 E4
Näs [S] 162 D1
Näs [S] 166 G2
Näs [S] 168 F6
Näs [S] 172 G5
Naşa [TR] 152 F2
Näsåker [S] 184 E1
N. Åsarp [S] 162 C1
Năsăud [RO] 204 C3
Nasbinals [F] 68 C5
Näsby [S] 158 G1
Näsbyholm [S] 162 D3
Nascimiento del Río Cuervo [E] 98 C1
Näset [S] 184 D4
Näshulta [S] 168 B3
Našice [HR] 142 D1
Nasielsk [PL] 38 B2
Näsinge [S] 166 C4
Nåsland [S] 190 H5
Následovice [CZ] 62 G2
Naso [I] 124 B6
Na Špičáku [CZ] 50 D3
Nassau [D] 46 B2
Nassereith [A] 72 C1
Nässja [S] 166 G5
Nässjö [S] 162 D2
Nässjö [S] 184 D1
Nässvallen [S] 182 F4
Nasswald [A] 62 E6
Nastan [BG] 130 D1
Nästansjö [S] 190 F4
Nastazin [PL] 20 G5
Nästeln [S] 182 G4
Nästi [FIN] 176 D3
Nastola [FIN] 178 B3
Nasüm [S] 158 E1
Näsviken [S] 174 E1
Näsviken [S] 190 F6
Nata [CY] 154 F6
Natalinci [SRB] 146 B1
Nätra Fjällskog [S] 184 G2
Nattavaara [S] 196 A1
Nättraby [S] 158 F1
Nattvatn [N] 194 C3
Naturno / Naturns [I] 72 C3
Naturns / Naturno [I] 72 C3
Naucelle [F] 66 H6
Nauders [A] 72 B2
Nauen [D] 34 D2
Naujoji Akmenė [LT] 198 C6
Naul [IRL] 2 F5
Naumburg [D] 34 B6
Naumestis [LT] 200 F4
Naunhof [D] 34 D5
Nausta [S] 190 H2
Naustbukta [N] 190 C4
Naustdal [N] 180 C6
Nauste [N] 180 F3
Naustvika [N] 180 F4
Nautijaure [S] 190 H1
Nautsung [N] 170 B1
Nauvo / Nagu [FIN] 176 D5
Nava [E] 82 C2
Navacelles, Cirque de- [F] 106 E3
Navacerrada [E] 88 F4
Nava de la Asunción [E] 88 E3
Nava del Rey [E] 88 D2
Navahermosa [E] 96 E2
Navahrudak [BY] 202 B5
Naval [E] 90 G3
Navalagamella [E] 88 E5
Navalcán [E] 88 C6
Navalcarnero [E] 88 F6
Navaleno [E] 90 A2
Navalguijo [E] 88 C5
Navalmanzano [E] 88 F3
Navalmoral [E] 88 D5
Navalmoral de la Mata [F] 88 B6
Navalón [E] 98 D6
Navalperal de Pinares [E] 88 E5
Navalpino [E] 96 D3
Navalvillar de Ibor [E] 96 C1
Navalvillar de Pela [E] 96 B3
Navan / An Uaimh [IRL] 2 F5
Nåvårdalen [N] 182 B3
Navarredonda de Gredos [E] 88 C5
Navarrenx [F] 84 D3
Navarrés [E] 98 E5
Navarrete [E] 82 G6
Navàs [E] 92 E3
Navascués / Nabaskoze [E] 84 C4
Navas de Estena [E] 96 E2
Navas del Madroño [E] 86 G4
Navas del Rey [E] 88 E5
Navas de Oro [E] 88 E3
Navas de San Juan [E] 102 F1
Navata [E] 92 G2
Navatalgordo [E] 88 D5
Nävekvarn [S] 168 C5
Navelli [I] 116 C4
Navelsaker [N] 180 C5
Nave Redonda [P] 94 B4
Näverkärret [S] 166 H2
Naverstad [S] 166 C4
Naveta des Tudons [E] 104 G4
Navia [E] 78 F2
Navilly [F] 56 G5
Navit [N] 192 H2
Navlya [RUS] 202 E5
Navruz [TR] 150 C5
Naxås [S] 182 F1
Náxos [GR] 138 E3
Naxos [I] 124 B8
Nazaré [P] 86 C3
Nazifoaşa [TR] 150 G5
Nazıllı [TR] 152 E5
Nazimovo [RUS] 198 H4
N. Bukovica [HR] 74 H6
N.-D. de Clausis [F] 108 E2
N.-D. de Kerdevot [F] 40 B3
N.D. de la Salette [F] 68 H5
N.-D. de Lure [F] 108 C3
N.-D. de Miracles [F] 108 E4
N.-D.-du-Haut [F] 58 C3
N.-D. du Mai [F] 108 C6
Ndroq [AL] 128 B3
Néa Anchíalos [GR] 132 H3
Néa Artáki [GR] 134 B5
Néa Epídavros [GR] 136 F2
Néa Fókaia [GR] 130 B6
Néa Kallikráteia [GR] 130 B5
Néa Karváli [GR] 130 D3
Néa Kerdýllia [GR] 130 C4
Néa Koróni [GR] 136 D4
Neale [IRL] 2 C4
Néa Liosia [GR] 134 C6
Néa Mádytos [GR] 130 C4
Néa Mákri [GR] 134 C6
Néa Michanióna [GR] 128 H5
Néa Moní [GR] 134 G4
Néa Moudaniá [GR] 130 B5
Neamţ, Mănăstirea- [RO] 204 D3
Neandria [TR] 130 H6
Néa Péramos [GR] 130 D3
Néa Péramos [GR] 134 B6
Néa Plágia [GR] 130 B5
Neápoli [GR] 128 E5
Neápoli [GR] 136 F5
Neápoli [GR] 140 F4
Neapolis [TR] 152 E5
Néa Poteídaia [GR] 130 B5
Néa Róda [GR] 130 C5
Néa Roúmata [GR] 140 B4
Néa Sánta [GR] 130 G2
Néa Stýra [GR] 134 D5
Neath [GB] 12 E2
Néa Tríglia [GR] 130 B5
Néa Výssa [GR] 130 H1
Néa Zíchni [GR] 130 C3
Nebiler [TR] 152 C2
Nebolchi [RUS] 202 C1
Nebra [D] 34 B5
Nechanice [CZ] 50 A3
Neckarelz [D] 46 D5
Neckargemünd [D] 46 C5
Neckargerach [D] 46 D5
Neckarsteinach [D] 46 C5
Neckarsulm [D] 46 D5
Neckenmarkt [A] 62 F6
Necşeşti [RO] 148 B1
Nečtiny [CZ] 48 D4
Neda [E] 78 D1
Nedansjö [S] 184 E4
Nedde [F] 66 H2
Neddemin [D] 20 D4
Neded [SK] 64 A5
Nedelišće [HR] 74 F4
Nederhögen [S] 182 G4
Nedervetil / Alaveteli [FIN] 196 C6
Neder Vindinge [DK] 156 F4
Nedre Eggedal [N] 170 G5
Nedre Gärdsjö [S] 172 H3
Nedre Soppero [S] 192 H4
Nedstrand [N] 164 B2
Nedvědice [CZ] 50 B5
Nędza [PL] 50 E3
Neede [NL] 16 G5
Neermoor [D] 18 B4
Neeroeteren [B] 30 E3
Nefyn [GB] 10 B4
Negorci [MK] 128 G3
Negoslavci [HR] 142 E1
Negotin [SRB] 146 E1
Negotin [SRB] 204 C6
Negotino [MK] 128 F2
Negovanovci [BG] 146 E2
Negrar [I] 72 C6
Negreira [E] 78 B3
Negren-Tino [CH] 70 G2
Négrondes [F] 66 F2
Negru Vodă [RO] 148 G1
Neheim-Hüsten [D] 32 C4
Nehoiu [RO] 204 D5
Neiden [N] 194 E3
Neitisuanto [S] 192 G5
Neittävä [FIN] 196 E4
Nejdek [CZ] 48 D3
Nekromanteío [GR] 132 C3
Neksø [DK] 158 E4
Nelas [P] 80 C6
Nelidovo [RUS] 202 D3
Nellim [FIN] 194 E4
Nellingen [D] 60 B3
Neltaa [FIN] 176 G4
Neman [RUS] 200 D5
Nembro [I] 70 H4
Neméa [GR] 136 E1
Neméa [GR] 136 E1
Nemenčinė [LT] 200 G5
Nemesnádudvar [H] 76 C4
Nemesszalók [H] 74 G1
Németkér [H] 76 C3
Nemila [BIH] 142 D4
Nemours [F] 42 G5
Nemrutkale [TR] 152 C3
Nemška Loka [SLO] 74 C6
Nemšová [SK] 64 A2
Nemti [H] 64 D5
Nemyriv [UA] 52 G3
Nenagh [IRL] 2 D6
Nendeln [FL] 58 H5
Neochóri [GR] 132 E5
Neochóri [GR] 132 F3
Neochóri [GR] 132 F2
Neochóri [GR] 134 A2
Neochóri [GR] 134 C5
Neochóri [GR] 136 B1
Néo Monastíri [GR] 132 G3
Néos Marmarás [GR] 130 C6
Nepi [I] 114 H4
Nepomuk [CZ] 48 E5
Neptun [RO] 148 G1
Nérac [F] 66 E5
Neratovice [CZ] 48 G3
Néré [F] 54 D5
Neresheim [D] 60 C2
Nereta [LV] 198 E6
Nereto [I] 116 D3
Neretva Kanjon [BIH] 144 C2
Nerezine [HR] 112 E3
Nerežišća [HR] 144 A2
Neringa [LT] 200 D5
Neringa-Nida [LT] 200 D5
Néris-les-Bains [F] 56 C6
Nerja [E] 102 D5
Nerja, Cueva de- [E] 102 D5
Nérondes [F] 56 C4
Nerpio [E] 102 H2
Nerpio, Cuevas de- [E] 102 H2
Nersingen [D] 60 B3
Nerskogen [N] 180 H3
Nerva [E] 94 F5
Nervesa della Battaglia [I] 72 E5
Nervi [I] 110 B3
Nerviano [I] 70 G4
Nes [N] 164 F2
Nes [N] 170 D1
Nes [N] 170 H4
Nes [N] 180 C6
Nes [NL] 16 F1
Nesactium [HR] 112 D2
Nesaseter [N] 190 D4
Nesbyen [N] 170 G4
Nesebŭr [BG] 148 F4
Neset [N] 190 E2
Nesflaten [N] 164 C1
Nesheim [N] 170 C3
Neskaupstaður [IS] 192 D3
Neslandsvatn [N] 164 F3
Nesle [F] 28 F5
Nesna [N] 190 D2
Nesoddtangen [N] 166 B1
Nespereira [P] 80 C3
Nesseby [N] 194 E2
Nesselwang [D] 60 C5
Nestáni [GR] 136 E2
Nestavoll [N] 180 H4
Nesterov [RUS] 24 D1
Nestório [GR] 128 D5
Nesttun [N] 170 B4
Nesvik [N] 164 B2
Neszmély [H] 64 B6
Netolice [CZ] 62 B2
Netretić [HR] 112 G1
Nettancourt [F] 44 C4
Netta Pierwsza [PL] 24 E4
Nettetal [D] 30 F3
Nettuno [I] 120 B1
Nettuno, Grotta di- [I] 118 B3
Neubeckum [D] 32 D3
Neuberg [A] 74 E1
Neuberg an der Mürz [A] 62 D6
Neubrandenburg [D] 20 D4
Neubukow [D] 20 A3
Neubulach [D] 58 G1
Neuburg [D] 60 D2
Neuburg [D] 60 H3
Neuchâtel [CH] 58 C5
Neu Darchau [D] 18 G5
Neudorf [D] 34 A4
Neudorf [D] 46 C5
Neudorf-Platendorf [D] 32 H2
Neuenburg [D] 18 C4
Neuenbürg [D] 46 C6
Neuenburg [D] 58 E3
Neuenhaus [D] 16 G4
Neuenkirchen [D] 18 F5
Neuenstein [D] 32 F6
Neuenstein [D] 46 D5
Neuenstein [D] 46 D5
Neuenwalde [D] 18 D3
Neuer Weg [D] 18 C4
Neufahrn [D] 60 F3
Neuf-Brisach [F] 58 E3
Neufchâteau [B] 44 D2
Neufchâteau [F] 44 D6
Neufchâtel-en-Bray [F] 28 C5
Neufchâtel-sur-Aisne [F] 44 B2
Neufeld [D] 18 E3
Neufelden [A] 62 B3
Neuffen [D] 58 H2
Neugersdorf [D] 48 G1
Neuhaus [D] 18 E3
Neuhaus [D] 18 H5
Neuhaus [D] 32 F4
Neuhaus [D] 46 G2
Neuhaus [D] 46 H4
Neuhaus [D] 60 H3
Neuhausen am Rheinfall [CH] 58 F4
Neuhof [D] 34 E3
Neuhofen an der Krems [A] 62 B4
Neuillé Port-Pierre [F] 54 F1
Neuilly-l'Évêque [F] 58 A3
Neuilly-St-Front [F] 42 H3
Neu-Isenburg [D] 46 C3
Neukalen [D] 20 C4
Neukirch [D] 34 F6
Neukirchen [A] 60 G4
Neukirchen [A] 72 F1
Neukirchen [D] 32 E6
Neukirchen [D] 156 B4
Neukloster [D] 20 A3
Neuland [D] 18 E3
Neulengbach [A] 62 E4
Neulingen [D] 46 C6
Neu Lübbennau [D] 34 F3
Neum [BIH] 144 C3
Neumarkt [A] 60 H5
Neumarkt [A] 74 B2
Neumarkt [D] 46 H5
Neumarkt / Egna [I] 72 D4
Neumarkt-St Veit [D] 60 F4
Neu-Moresnet [B] 30 F5
Neumorschen [D] 32 F6
Neu Mukran [D] 20 D2
Neumünster [D] 18 F3
Neunagelberg [A] 62 C3
Neunburg [D] 48 C5
Neung-sur-Beuvron [F] 56 B2
Neunkirchen [A] 62 E6
Neunkirchen [D] 44 G3
Neunkirchen-Seelscheid [D] 30 H4
Neuötting [D] 60 G4
Neupölla [A] 62 D3
Neuruppin [D] 20 C6
Neu Schrepkow [D] 20 B6
Neuschwanstein [D] 60 C6
Neusiedl am See [A] 62 G5
Neuss [D] 30 G3
Neustadt [D] 18 H3
Neustadt [D] 32 E6
Neustadt [D] 34 C1
Neustadt [D] 34 F6
Neustadt [D] 46 E3
Neustadt [D] 46 G2
Neustadt [D] 48 B1
Neustadt [D] 58 F3
Neustadt [D] 60 E2
Neustadt am Rübenberge [D] 32 F2
Neustadt an der Aisch [D] 46 F5
Neustadt an der Waldnaab [D] 48 C4
Neustadt an der Weinstrasse [D] 46 B5
Neustadt-Glewe [D] 20 A5
Neustift [A] 72 D1
Neustift / Novacella [I] 72 D2
Neustrelitz [D] 20 C5
Neu-Ulm [D] 60 B3
Neuvéglise [F] 68 C4
Neuves-Maisons [F] 44 E5
Neuvic [F] 66 E3
Neuvic [F] 68 B3
Neuville [F] 54 E3
Neuville [F] 68 F2
Neuville-aux-Bois [F] 42 E5
Neuvilly-en-Argonne [F] 44 D3
Neuvola [FIN] 186 H4
Neuvy [F] 54 H4
Neuvy-Bouin [F] 54 D3
Neuvy-sur-Barangeon [F] 56 C3
Neuwied [D] 30 H6
Neuzelle [D] 34 G3
Neveklov [CZ] 48 G4
Nevel' [RUS] 202 C3
Neverfjord [N] 194 B2
Nevers [F] 56 D4
Nevès [E] 92 D2
Nevesinje [BIH] 144 C2
Nevlunghavn [N] 164 G3
Nevossuo [FIN] 178 C3
New Alresford [GB] 12 H4
Newark-on-Trent [GB] 10 F5
Newbiggin-by-the-Sea [GB] 8 G5
Newbliss [IRL] 2 F4
Newbridge / Droichead Nua [IRL] 2 E6
Newburgh [GB] 8 E2
Newbury [GB] 12 H4
Newcastle [NIR] 2 G4
Newcastle Emlyn [GB] 10 A6
Newcastle-under-Lyme [GB] 10 D5
Newcastle upon Tyne [GB] 8 G6
Newcastle West [IRL] 4 C3
New Galloway [GB] 8 D5
Newgrange [IRL] 2 F5
Newhaven [GB] 14 E6
Newinn [IRL] 4 D4
Newmarket [GB] 14 F3
Newmarket [IRL] 4 C4
Newmarket-on-Fergus [IRL] 2 C6
Newport [GB] 10 D5
Newport [GB] 12 F3
Newport [GB] 12 H5
Newport [IRL] 2 C3
Newport [IRL] 4 D3
Newport-on-Tay [GB] 8 F2
Newport Pagnell [GB] 14 E3
New Quay [GB] 10 B6
Newquay [GB] 12 C4
New Romney [GB] 14 F5
New Ross / Ros Mhic Thriúin [IRL] 4 F4
Newry [NIR] 2 F4
Newton Abbot [GB] 12 E5
Newton Le Willows [GB] 10 D4
Newtonmore [GB] 6 D6
Newton Stewart [GB] 8 C5
Newtown [GB] 10 C6
Newtownabbey [NIR] 2 G3
Newtownards [NIR] 2 G3
Newtown Butler [NIR] 2 E4
Newtownhamilton [NIR] 2 F4
Newtown Mount Kennedy [IRL] 4 G3
Newtownstewart [NIR] 2 F3
Nexon [F] 66 G2
Nežilovo [MK] 128 E2
Niadinge [LT] 24 G2
Niana [I] 70 E4
Nianfors [S] 174 E1
Niaux, Grotte de- [F] 84 H5
Nibe [DK] 160 D4
Nicaj-Shalë [AL] 146 A6
Nicaj Shoshë [AL] 146 A6
Nicastro [I] 124 D5
Nice [F] 108 E4
Nickelsdorf [A] 62 G5
Nicknoret [S] 190 H4
Nicolosi [I] 126 G3
Nicopolis ad Istrum [BG] 148 C3
Nicosia [I] 126 F3
Nicotera [I] 124 C6
Nidda [D] 46 D2
Nidderau [D] 46 D2
Nideck, Château du- [F] 44 G6
Nideggen [D] 30 F5
Nidzica [PL] 22 G5
Niebla [E] 94 F5
Nieborow [PL] 36 H3
Niebüll [D] 156 B4
Nieby [D] 156 C5
Niechanowo [PL] 36 D2
Niechorze [PL] 20 G3
Niedalino [PL] 20 H3
Niederalben [D] 44 H3
Niederalteich [D] 60 G3
Niederau [A] 60 F6
Niederaula [D] 46 E1
Niederbronn-les-Bains [F] 44 H5

Odensvi [S] 162 F2
Odensvi [S] 168 B2
Oderberg [D] 34 F1
Oderljunga [S] 158 C1
Oderzo [I] 72 F5
Ödeshög [S] 166 G6
Odessa [UA] 204 F3
Ödestugu [S] 162 D2
Odivelas [P] 86 B5
Odivelas [P] 94 D2
Odnes [N] 170 H3
Odolanów [PL] 36 D5
Odoorn [NL] 16 G3
Odorheiu Secuiesc [RO] 204 D4
Odoyev [RUS] 202 F4
Odranci [SLO] 74 F3
Odry [CZ] 50 E5
Odrzywół [PL] 38 B5
Ødsted [DK] 156 C2
Odum [DK] 160 E6
Odžaci [SRB] 142 E1
Odžak [BIH] 142 D2
Odžak [MNE] 144 E2
Ödzemirci [TR] 152 H4
Odziena [LV] 198 E5
Oebisfelde [D] 34 A2
Oederan [D] 48 D1
Oeding [D] 16 G6
Oeijenbraak [B] 30 D3
Oelde [D] 32 D3
Oelsnitz [D] 48 C2
Oensinger Klus [CH] 58 E5
Oersberg [D] 18 F1
Oetmannshausen [D] 32 F5
Oëtre, Roche d'- [F] 26 F4
Oettingen [D] 46 F6
Oetz [A] 72 C1
Öféhértó [H] 64 H5
Offenbach [D] 46 C3
Offenburg [D] 44 H6
Offenheim [D] 46 B4
Offida [I] 116 C2
Ofir [P] 80 B3
Oforsen [S] 172 F6
Ofte [N] 164 E2
Ogenbargen [D] 18 C4
Oğlansini [TR] 154 F1
Ogliastro Cilento [I] 120 F4
Ognica [PL] 20 E6
Ognjanovo [BG] 130 C1
Ogre [LV] 198 E5
Ogrodzieniec [PL] 50 G2
Ogrosen [D] 34 F4
O Grove [E] 78 B4
Ogulin [HR] 112 G2
Ohat [H] 64 F6
Oheb [CZ] 50 A4
Ohlava [FIN] 196 D3
Ohordorf [D] 32 H1
Ohrdruf [D] 46 G1
Ohrid [MK] 128 D3
Öhringen [D] 46 D5
Ohtanajärvi [S] 194 B7
Ohtola [FIN] 186 D4
Öhuta [H] 64 G4
Oía [GR] 138 F5
Oiã [P] 80 B5
Oia / Arrabal [E] 78 A5
Oijärvi [FIN] 196 D3
Oikarainen [FIN] 194 D8
Oimbra [E] 78 D6
Oinasjärvi [FIN] 176 F4
O Incio [E] 78 E4
Oinoanda [TR] 154 G2
Oinói [GR] 134 B6
Oinoskylä [FIN] 186 F2
Oiron [F] 54 E3
Oirschot [NL] 30 E2
Oisemont [F] 28 D4
Oissel [F] 28 B6
Oisterwijk [NL] 16 D6
Oitti [FIN] 176 H3
Oitylo [GR] 136 E5
Oivu / Äivo [FIN] 196 C6
Öja [FIN] 196 C6
Öjaby [S] 162 D4
Ojakylä [FIN] 196 D5
Ojakylä [FIN] 196 E4
Ojala [FIN] 186 D2
Öjarn [S] 190 E6
Ojców [PL] 50 H3
Öje [S] 172 F3
Öjebyn [S] 196 B3
Ojén [E] 102 B5
Ojo Guareña [E] 82 F4
Ojós [E] 104 C2
Ojos Negros [E] 90 C6
Ojrzeń [PL] 38 A1
Öjung [S] 174 C1
Öjvasslan [S] 182 F6
Okalewo [PL] 22 F6
Okalewo [PL] 22 F6
Okány [H] 76 G2
Økdal [N] 182 B3
Okehampton [GB] 12 D4
Oker [D] 32 G3
Okhtyrka [UA] 202 F7
Okkelberg [N] 182 C1
Oklaj [HR] 112 H5
Oklubalı [TR] 150 H5
Okol [AL] 146 A6
Okonek [PL] 22 B5
Okonin [PL] 22 E5
Okopy [PL] 38 G5
Okoř [CZ] 48 F3
Okors [BG] 148 E2
Okrug [HR] 116 H1
Oksajärvi [S] 192 H5
Oksakoski [FIN] 186 E1
Oksava [FIN] 196 D6
Oksböl [DK] 156 A2
Oksdøl [N] 190 C5
Øksendalen [N] 170 H1
Øksendrup [DK] 156 E4
Øksfjord [N] 192 H1
Oksfjordhamn [N] 192 G1
Øksna [N] 172 C3
Øksnes [N] 192 D4
Okstad [N] 182 C2
Oktiabrs'ke [UA] 204 H4
Oktoniá [GR] 134 C4
Okučani [HR] 142 C1
Okulovka [RUS] 202 D2
Okuninka [PL] 38 F4
Ólafsfjördur [IS] 192 C2
Ólafsvík [IS] 192 A2
Ö. Lagnö [S] 168 E2
Olaine [LV] 198 D5
Olargues [F] 106 D4
Olaszfalu [H] 76 A2
Oława [PL] 50 D1
Olazagutia / Olazti [E] 82 H5
Olazti / Olazagutia [E] 82 H5
Olba [E] 98 E3
Olbasa [TR] 152 H6
Olbernhau [D] 48 E2
Ólbia [I] 118 C3
Olbięcin [PL] 52 E1
Oldcastle [IRL] 2 E5
Oldeberkoop [NL] 16 F3
Oldelde [N] 180 B5
Olden [N] 180 D5
Oldenburg [D] 18 C5
Oldenburg [D] 18 H2
Oldenzaal [NL] 16 G5
Olderdalen [N] 192 G2
Olderfjord [N] 194 C2
Oldervik [N] 192 G2
Oldham [GB] 10 E4
Oldmeldrum [GB] 6 F6
Old Mellifont Abbey [IRL] 2 F5
Oldřichovice [CZ] 50 F5
Oleby [S] 172 E5
Olecko [PL] 24 D3
Oléggio [I] 70 F4
Oleiros [E] 78 B3
Oleiros [E] 78 C2
Oleiros [P] 86 E3
Oleksandriia [UA] 202 F8
Oleksandrivka [UA] 202 E8
Oleksandrivka [UA] 204 G2
Olen [B] 30 D3
Ølen [N] 164 B1
Olèrdola [E] 92 D4
Olesa de Montserrat [E] 92 D4
Oleśnica [PL] 36 D6
Olešnice [CZ] 50 B5
Olesno [PL] 50 F1
Oleszno [PL] 50 H1
Oleszyce [PL] 52 F3
Oletta [F] 114 C3
Olette [F] 92 F1
Olevs'k [UA] 202 C7
Ølgod [DK] 156 B2
Olhain, Château Féodal d'- [F] 28 E3
Olhão [P] 94 C6
Ol'hopil' [UA] 204 E2
Oliana [E] 92 D2
Olia Speciosa [I] 118 D7
Olíena [I] 118 D4
Olingdal [S] 182 G6
Olingsjövallen [S] 182 G6
Olite [E] 84 B5
Oliva [E] 98 F6
Oliva de la Frontera [E] 94 F3
Oliva de Mérida [E] 94 H2
Olivadi [I] 124 D6
Olivares [E] 94 G6
Olivares de Júcar [E] 98 B3
Oliveira de Azeméis [P] 80 B5
Oliveira de Frades [P] 80 C5
Oliveira do Bairro [P] 80 B5
Oliveira do Hospital [P] 86 E2
Olivenza [E] 94 F2
Olivet [F] 42 E6
Olivone [CH] 70 G2
Ol'ka [SK] 52 D6
Olkkala [FIN] 176 G4
Olkusz [PL] 50 G3
Ollerup [DK] 156 D4
Olliergues [F] 68 D2
Ollikkala [FIN] 178 C1
Olliia [FIN] 176 E4
Öllölä [FIN] 188 G3
Ölmbrotorp [S] 166 H3
Ölme [S] 166 F3
Olmedilla de Alarcón [E] 98 B3
Olmedillo de Roa [E] 88 G2
Olmedo [E] 88 E3
Olmedo [I] 118 B3
Olmeto [F] 114 B5
Ölmhult [S] 166 F2
Olmillos de Sasamón [E] 82 E5
Olocau del Rey [E] 98 F1
Olofsfors [S] 184 H1
Olofström [S] 158 E1
Olombrada [E] 88 F3
Olomouc [CZ] 50 D5
Olon / Oyon [E] 82 H6
Olonzac [F] 106 C4
Oloron-Ste-Marie [F] 84 D3
Olos Fthiotidos [GR] 132 G4
Olost [E] 92 E3
Olot [E] 92 F2
Olovo [BIH] 142 E4
Ołownik [PL] 24 C2
Olpe [D] 32 C5
Øls [DK] 160 D5
Olsätter [S] 166 F2
Olsberg [D] 32 D5
Olsborg [N] 192 F3
Olseröd [S] 158 D2
Ölserud [S] 166 E4
Ol'sha-Dolgaya [RUS] 202 D4
Olshammar [S] 166 G4
Olší [CZ] 50 B5
Ölsremma [S] 162 C2
Olst [NL] 16 F4
Ølstykke [DK] 156 G2
Olszowa Wola [PL] 38 B4
Olsztyn [PL] 22 H4
Olsztyn [PL] 50 G2
Olsztynek [PL] 22 G4
Olszyna [PL] 34 G4
Olszyna [PL] 34 H6
Oltedal [N] 164 B3
Olten [CH] 58 E5
Olteni [RO] 148 B1
Oltenița [RO] 148 D1
Olteren [N] 192 G3
Oltre il Colle [I] 70 H4
Ölüdeniz [TR] 154 F2
Oluklu [TR] 150 H5
Olula del Río [E] 102 H4
Ólvega [E] 90 C3
Olvera [E] 102 A3
Olympía [GR] 136 C2
Olympiáda [GR] 130 C4
Ólympos [GR] 140 H2
Ólynthos [GR] 130 B5
Olza [PL] 50 E4
Oma, Bosque de- [E] 82 H4
Omagh [NIR] 2 F3
Omalí [GR] 128 E6
Omalós [GR] 140 C5
Oman [BG] 148 E5
Omarska [BIH] 142 B2
Ombygget Stavkirke [N] 170 D2
Omegna [I] 70 F3
Ömerköy [TR] 150 D5
Ömerli [TR] 150 F2
Omiš [HR] 144 A2
Omišalj [HR] 112 E2
Ommen [NL] 16 G4
Ommunddallen [N] 190 B5
Omodos [CY] 154 F6
Omoljica [SRB] 142 H2
Ömossa / Metsälä [FIN] 186 B5
Omsjö [S] 184 F1
Omurtag [BG] 148 D3
Øn [N] 170 B1
Oña [E] 82 F5
Oñati [E] 82 H4
Onda [E] 98 F3
Ondara [E] 104 F1
Ondarroa [E] 82 H4
Ondić [HR] 112 H4
Ö Näsberg [S] 172 F5
Onești [RO] 204 D4
Onguera [E] 82 D2
Onil [E] 104 D1
Onkamo [FIN] 188 G3
Onkamo [FIN] 194 F7
Onkiniemi [FIN] 178 B1
Onnaing [F] 28 G4
Önneköp [S] 158 D2
Onoranza [I] 120 G1
Onsaker [N] 170 H4
Onsevig [DK] 156 E4
Ontiñena [E] 90 G4
Ontinyent [E] 98 E6
Ontojoki Porokylä [FIN] 196 F5
Ontur [E] 98 C6
Önusberg [S] 196 A3
Onuškis [LT] 24 G1
Onzonilla [E] 78 H6
Ooidonk [B] 28 G2
Oola [IRL] 4 D4
Oostburg [NL] 28 G1
Oostduinkerke [B] 28 F1
Oostende (Ostende) [B] 28 F1
Oosterbeek [NL] 16 F5
Oostérend [NL] 16 E1
Oosterhout [NL] 16 D6
Oosterwolde [NL] 16 G3
Oostmalle [B] 30 D3
Ootmarsum [NL] 16 G4
Opaka [BG] 148 D2
Opalenica [PL] 36 B3
Opařany [CZ] 48 F5
Oparić [SRB] 146 C3
Opatija [HR] 112 E1
Opatów [PL] 36 E6
Opatów [PL] 52 D1
Opatówek [PL] 36 E4
Opatowiec [PL] 52 B3
Opava [CZ] 50 E4
Ope [S] 182 G2
Opglabbek [B] 30 E4
Opi [I] 116 C6
O Pino [E] 78 C3
Opinogóra Górna [PL] 38 B1
Opishnia [UA] 202 F7
Opladen [D] 30 G4
Oplenac, Manastir- [SRB] 146 B1
Opletnya [BG] 146 F4
Oploo [NL] 30 F2
Oplotnica [SLO] 74 D4
Opochka [RUS] 198 H5
Opočno [CZ] 50 B3
Opoczno [PL] 38 A5
Opole [PL] 50 E2
Opole Lubelskie [PL] 38 D6
Opol'ye [RUS] 178 F6
Oporów [PL] 36 G3
O Porriño [E] 78 B5
Opovo [SRB] 142 G2
Oppach [D] 34 G6
Oppaker [N] 172 C5
Oppdal [N] 180 H3
Oppdøl [N] 180 F3
Oppeby [S] 162 F1
Oppedal [N] 170 B2
Oppegård [N] 166 B1
Oppenau [D] 58 F2
Oppenheim [D] 46 C3
Oppheim [N] 170 C3
Opphus [N] 172 C2
Oppido Lucano [I] 120 H3
Oppido Mamertina [I] 124 C7
Oppidum d'Ensérune [F] 106 D4
Oppola [RUS] 188 G5
Opponitz [A] 62 C5
Oppsal [N] 164 B3
Opsa [BY] 200 H4
Ópusztaszer [H] 76 E4
Opuzen [HR] 144 B3
Orá [CY] 154 G6
Öra [S] 162 C1
Ora / Auer [I] 72 D4
Oradea [RO] 76 H2
Orahovac [KS] 146 B6
Orahov Do [BIH] 144 C3
Orahovica [HR] 142 D1
Orahovlje [BIH] 144 B2
Oraison [F] 108 C3
Orajärvi [FIN] 194 C7
Orange [F] 106 G3
Orani [I] 118 D4
Oranienbaum [D] 34 C4
Oranienburg [D] 34 E1
Oranmore [IRL] 2 C5
Oraovica [SRB] 146 D4
Öras [N] 182 C2
Orašac [BIH] 112 H3
Orašac [MK] 146 D6
Orašac [SRB] 146 D4
Orasi [F] 114 B6
Orašje [BIH] 142 E2
Orăștie [RO] 204 C5
Oravainen / Oravais [FIN] 186 C2
Oravais / Oravainen [FIN] 186 C2
Öravan [S] 190 G5
Oravasaari [FIN] 186 G4
Oravi [FIN] 188 E4
Oravijoki [FIN] 196 E5
Oravikoski [FIN] 188 D3
Oravisalo [FIN] 188 F3
Oravița [RO] 204 B5
Oravská Lesná [SK] 50 G5
Oravská Polhora [SK] 50 G5
Oravský Podzámok [SK] 50 G6
Orba [E] 104 F1
Ørbæk [DK] 156 E3
Orbassano [I] 70 D6
Orbe [CH] 58 C6
Orbeasca [RO] 148 B1
Orbec [F] 26 G4
Orbetello [I] 114 F4
Orbey [F] 58 D2
Ørby [DK] 156 E1
Örbyhus [S] 174 F5
Örbyhus [S] 174 F5
Orca [P] 86 F3
Orcera [E] 102 G1
Orches [F] 54 F3
Orchies [F] 28 F3
Orchomenós [GR] 132 H5
Orchomenós [GR] 132 H5
Orchomenós [GR] 136 D2
Orcières [F] 70 A6
Orderud [N] 166 C2
Ordes [E] 78 C2
Ordino [AND] 84 H6
Orduña [E] 82 G4
Ore [S] 184 H1
Orebić [HR] 144 B3
Örebro [S] 166 H3
Öregrund [S] 174 G5
Orehova vas Rače [SLO] 74 E4
Orehoved [DK] 156 F4
Orehovica [BG] 148 A2
Orehovno [RUS] 198 H2
Oreiní [GR] 130 C3
Orel [RUS] 202 F5
Ören [TR] 152 C2
Ören [TR] 152 G2
Ören [TR] 154 C1
Ören [TR] 154 F2
Örencık [TR] 150 C6
Örencik [TR] 152 G1
Örenkaya [TR] 152 H3
Orense / Ourense [E] 78 C5
Oreoí [GR] 134 A3
Oresak [BG] 148 B4
Oreshari [BG] 130 G1
Orestiáda [GR] 130 H1
Öreström [S] 190 H5
Oresvika [N] 190 D2
Öreyd [S] 162 C3
Orgáni [GR] 130 G2
Organyà [E] 92 D2
Orgaz [E] 96 F2
Orgelet [F] 56 H6
Orgenvika [N] 170 G5
Orgeval [F] 42 F3
Orgjost [AL] 128 C1
Orgnac-l'Aven [F] 106 G2
Orgon [F] 106 H4
Orgosolo [I] 118 D4
Orgovány [H] 76 D3
Orhaneli [TR] 150 F5
Orhangazi [TR] 150 F4
Orhaniye [TR] 130 H3
Orhanlar [TR] 150 D5
Orhanli [TR] 152 C4
Orhei [MD] 204 E3
Ør. Hvidbjerg [DK] 160 C4
Oria [E] 102 H4
Oria [I] 122 F4
Orihuela [E] 104 D3
Orihuela del Tremedal [E] 98 D1
Orikhiv [UA] 204 H2
Orikum [AL] 128 A6
Orimattila [FIN] 178 B3
Orio [E] 84 B2
Oriolo [I] 122 D5
Oripää [FIN] 176 E3
Orismala [FIN] 186 C3
Orissaare [EST] 198 C3
Oristano [I] 118 C5
Öriszentpéter [H] 74 F3
Orivesi [FIN] 186 E6
Orizare [BG] 148 F4
Ørjarvik [N] 180 E2
Ørje [N] 166 C2
Örjiva [E] 102 E5
Orkanger [N] 180 H1
Örkelljunga [S] 158 C1
Örkény [H] 76 D2
Orléans [F] 42 E6
Orlík nad Vltavou [CZ] 48 F5
Orlovat [SRB] 142 G1
Orly [F] 42 F4
Orly [RUS] 178 E6
Orlya [BY] 24 H4
Orlyak [BG] 148 F2
Orlyane [BG] 148 A3
Ormanlı [TR] 150 D2
Ormea [I] 108 G3
Ormemyr [N] 164 F1
Örménykút [H] 76 F2
Ormestad [N] 164 D6
Órmos [GR] 128 H5
Órmos [GR] 138 D1
Órmos Panagías [GR] 130 C5
Órmos Prínou [GR] 130 E4
Ormož [SLO] 74 E4
Ormsjö [S] 190 F5
Ormskirk [GB] 10 D4
Ornans [F] 58 B5
Ornäs [S] 174 C4
Ornavasso [I] 70 F3
Örnberg [FIN] 186 B2
Ornes [N] 190 D4
Ørnes [N] 190 D1
Orneta [PL] 22 G3
Ørnhøj [DK] 160 B6
Ornö [S] 168 E4
Örnsköldsvik [S] 184 G2
Orolik [HR] 142 E1
Oron-la-Ville [CH] 70 C1
Oropa, Santuário d'- [I] 70 E4
Oropesa [E] 88 C6
Oropesa del Mar / Orpesa [E] 98 G3
Orošac [HR] 144 C4
Orosei [I] 118 E4
Orosháza [H] 76 F3
Oroso [E] 78 C3
Oroszlány [H] 64 B6
Oroszló [H] 76 B4
Ørpen [N] 170 G5
Orpesa / Oropesa del Mar [E] 98 G3
Orpington [GB] 14 E4
Orre [N] 164 A3
Orrefors [S] 162 F5
Orrfors [S] 194 B8
Orrliden [S] 172 E2
Orroli [I] 118 D6
Orrviken [S] 182 G2
Orsa [S] 172 G3
Orsala [S] 172 G5
Orsara di Púglia [I] 120 G2
Örsås [S] 162 B3
Orscholz [D] 44 F3
Örsebo [S] 162 E1
Örserum [S] 162 D1
Orsha [BY] 202 C4
Orsières [CH] 70 C3
Örsjö [S] 162 F5
Ørskog [N] 180 D3
Ørslev [DK] 156 G4
Örslösa [S] 166 E5
Ørsnes [N] 180 D3
Orsogna [I] 116 D5
Orsomarso [I] 120 H6
Orșova [RO] 204 C6
Orsoya [BG] 146 F2
Ørsta [N] 180 C4
Orsta [S] 168 A2
Ørsted [DK] 160 E5
Örsundsbro [S] 168 D2
Ort [A] 60 H4
Ortaca [TR] 150 B5
Ortaca [TR] 154 E2
Ortakent [TR] 154 B2
Ortaklar [TR] 152 D5
Ortaköy [TR] 150 H3
Ortaköy [TR] 152 E6
Orta Nova [I] 120 G2
Ortaoba [TR] 150 C5
Orta San Giúlio [I] 70 F4
Orte [I] 116 A4
Ortenberg [D] 46 D2
Ortenburg [D] 60 H3
Orth [A] 62 F4
Orthez [F] 84 D2
Orthovoúni [GR] 132 E1
Ortigueira [E] 78 E1
Ørting [DK] 156 D1
Ortisei / St Ulrich [I] 72 D3
Orțișoara [RO] 76 G5
Ortnevik [N] 170 C2
Orto [F] 114 B4
Örtomta [S] 168 B5
Ortona [I] 116 E4
Ortona dei Marsi [I] 116 C5
Ortrand [D] 34 E5
Örträsk [S] 190 H5
Ortu [I] 118 C6
Ortueri [I] 118 C5
Öru [EST] 198 F3
Oruçoğlu [TR] 150 F2
Ørum [DK] 160 D5
Ørum [DK] 160 E5
Orume [I] 118 D4
Örup [S] 158 D3
Orval, Abbaye d'- [B] 44 D2
Orvalho [P] 86 E3
Ørvella [N] 164 F2
Orvieto [I] 114 H3
Örviken [S] 196 A4
Orvinio [I] 116 B5
Oryahovec [BG] 130 E1
Oryakhovo [BG] 146 G2
Ö. Ryd [S] 168 B5
Orzechowo [PL] 22 E6
Orzesze [PL] 50 F3
Orzhytsia [UA] 202 E7
Orzinuovi [I] 70 H5
Orzola [E] 100 E5
Orzysz [PL] 24 C4
Os [N] 182 C4
Os [S] 162 D4
Osa [N] 170 D3
Osby [S] 162 C6
Oschatz [D] 34 D5
Oschersleben [D] 34 B3
Öschiri [I] 118 D3
Ościłowo [PL] 38 A1
Ose [N] 164 D3
Øse [N] 192 F4
Osečina [SRB] 142 F3
Oseja de Sajambre [E] 82 C3
Osen [N] 190 B5
Osenets [BG] 148 D2
Osera de Ebro [E] 90 F4
Osidda [I] 118 D4
Osie [PL] 22 D4
Osieczna [PL] 22 D4
Osieczna [PL] 36 C4
Osiecznica [PL] 34 H3
Osiek [PL] 22 E4
Osiek [PL] 52 D2
Osijek [HR] 76 C6
Osikovitsa [BG] 146 G4
Ósilo [I] 118 C3
Osimo [I] 116 C1
Ošinja [BIH] 142 C2
Osinów [PL] 34 F1
Osíou Louká, Moní- [GR] 132 H5
Osipaonica [SRB] 142 H3
Osjaków [PL] 36 F6
Osječenica [MNE] 144 D4
Oskal [N] 194 B4
Oskar [S] 162 F5
Oskar-Fredriksborg [S] 168 E3
Oskarshamn [S] 162 G3
Oskarström [S] 162 B5
Øskendalsøra [N] 180 F3
Oskowo [PL] 22 C2
Osl'any [SK] 64 B3
Osli [H] 62 G6
Oslo [N] 166 B1
Øsløs [DK] 160 C3
Osma [FIN] 194 D3
Osmancalı [TR] 152 C3
Osmaneli [TR] 150 G4
Osmankalfalar [TR] 152 H6
Osmanlar [TR] 152 C1
Osmanli [TR] 150 B2
Os'mino [RUS] 198 H1
Osmjany [BY] 202 A5
Ösmo [S] 168 D4
Osmoy-St-Valery [F] 28 C4
Osnabrück [D] 32 D2
Osnäs [FIN] 176 C4
Ośno Lubuskie [PL] 34 G2
Osoblaha [CZ] 50 D3
Osor [E] 92 F3
Osor [HR] 112 E3
Osorno la Mayor [E] 82 D5
Osowiec [PL] 24 E4
Osowo Lęborskie [PL] 22 C2
Osowo Leśne [PL] 22 D4
Osøyro [N] 170 B4
Os Peares [E] 78 D5
Ospedaletti [I] 108 F4
Ospitaletto [I] 72 A6
Oss [NL] 16 E6
Óssa [GR] 130 B4
Ossa de Montiel [E] 96 H5
Ossiach [A] 74 B3
Ossjøen [N] 170 E1
Östansjö [S] 166 G4
Östansjö [S] 182 G6
Östansjö [S] 190 G3
Östanvik [S] 172 H3
Oštarije [HR] 112 G2
Ostashkov [RUS] 202 D2
Ostaszewo [PL] 22 E3
Östavall [S] 184 C4
Ostbevern [D] 32 C3
Østbirk [DK] 156 C1
Østby [N] 172 E2
Osted [DK] 156 G3
Ostellato [I] 110 G3
Østenå [N] 164 F2
Ostende (Oostende) [B] 28 F1
Østerbo [N] 166 C3
Østerbø [N] 170 E3
Osterburg [D] 34 B1
Osterburken [D] 46 D5
Österbybruk [S] 174 F5
Østerby Havn [DK] 160 F3
Österbymo [S] 162 E2
Österede [S] 184 D3
Österfärnebo [S] 174 E5
Österforse [S] 184 E2
Östergraninge [S] 184 E3
Osterhever [D] 18 E2
Osterhofen [D] 60 G3
Osterholz-Scharmbeck [D] 18 D5
Øster Hurup [DK] 160 E4
Østerild [DK] 160 C3
Østerlars [DK] 158 E4
Österlövsta [S] 174 F5
Østermarie [DK] 158 E4
Östermark / Teuva [FIN] 186 B4
Ostermiething [A] 60 G4
Osterncappeln [D] 32 D2
Österørnet [S] 190 F5
Österö [FIN] 186 B1
Osterode [D] 32 G4
Österreichisches Freilichtmuseum [A] 74 D2
Östersund [S] 182 G2
Östersundom [FIN] 176 H5
Østerud [N] 164 G1
Øster Ulslev [DK] 20 B1
Östervåla [S] 174 E5
Östervallskog [S] 166 C2
Øster Vrå [DK] 160 E3
Ostfildern [D] 58 H1
Östfora [S] 168 C1
Östhammar [S] 174 G5
Ostheim [D] 46 F2
Osthofen [D] 46 B4
Ostia [I] 114 H6
Ostíglia [I] 110 F2
Ostiz [E] 84 B3
Ostland [D] 16 G1
Östloning [S] 184 E4
Östmark [S] 172 E5
Östnäs [S] 196 A6
Östomsjön [S] 172 E1
Ostra [I] 112 C6
Östraby [S] 158 C2
Ostrach [D] 58 H3
Östra Ed [S] 162 G1
Östra Frölunda [S] 162 B3
Östra Husby [S] 168 B5
Östra Kärne [S] 166 G2
Oštra Luka [BIH] 142 B2
Ostrava [CZ] 50 E4
Östra Yttermark [FIN] 186 A4
Østre Kile [N] 164 E3
Oštrelj [BIH] 142 A3
Ostritz [D] 48 G1
Ostróda [PL] 22 G4
Ostrog, Manastir- [MNE] 144 E4
Ostroh [UA] 202 B8
Ostrołęka [PL] 24 C6
Ostromecko [PL] 22 D6
Ostroróg [PL] 36 B2
Ostros [MNE] 128 A1
Ostrov [CZ] 48 D3
Ostrov [RUS] 178 F2
Ostrov [RUS] 198 G4
Ostrovcy [RUS] 198 G2
Ostrov nad Oslavou [CZ] 50 B5
Ostrovo [BG] 148 D2
Ostrowice [PL] 20 H4
Ostrowiec [PL] 22 B3
Ostrowiec Świętokrzyski [PL] 52 C1
Ostrowite [PL] 22 D5
Ostrowite [PL] 36 E2
Ostrów Lubelski [PL] 38 E5
Ostrów Mazowiecka [PL] 38 D1
Ostrów Wielkopolski [PL] 36 E5
Ostrožac [BIH] 112 H3
Ostrožac [BIH] 144 C1
Ostrożany [PL] 38 E2
Ostrzeszów [PL] 36 E5
Ostuni [I] 122 F3
Ostvik [S] 196 A4
Østvika [N] 190 D4
Ostwald [F] 44 H6
Osuna [E] 102 B3
Oswestry [GB] 10 C5
Oświęcim [PL] 50 G4
Osztopán [H] 74 H3
Otalampi [FIN] 176 G4
Otanmäki [FIN] 196 E5
Otanów [PL] 20 F6
Otava [FIN] 188 C6
Otelec [RO] 76 F6
Otepää [EST] 198 F3
Oteren [N] 192 G2
Oterma [FIN] 196 E4
Otero de Bodas [E] 80 H3
Oteševo [MK] 128 D4
Otivar [E] 102 D5
Otley [GB] 10 F3
Otmuchów [PL] 50 D3
Otnes [N] 182 C6
Otočac [HR] 112 G3
Otočec [SLO] 74 D5
Otok [HR] 142 E2
Otok [SLO] 74 B6
Otoka [BIH] 142 A2
Otorowo [PL] 36 C2
Otradnoye [RUS] 178 G2
Otranto [I] 122 H5
Otrić [HR] 112 H4
Otrokovice [CZ] 50 D6
Otsa [EST] 198 F3
Otsagi / Ochagavía [E] 84 C4
Otta [N] 180 G6
Ottana [I] 118 D4
Ottaviano [I] 120 E3
Ottenby [S] 162 G6
Ottenschlag [A] 62 D4
Ottensheim [A] 62 B4
Ottenstein [A] 62 D3
Otterbach [D] 44 H3
Otterbäcken [S] 166 F4
Otterlo [NL] 16 E5
Otterndorf [D] 18 E3
Ottersberg [D] 18 E5
Otterup [DK] 156 D3
Öttevény [H] 62 H6
Ottnang [A] 62 A4
Ottobeuren [D] 60 C4
Ottobiano [I] 70 F5
Ottone [I] 110 B3
Ottsjö [S] 182 E2
Ottweiler [D] 44 G3
Ö. Tväråsel [S] 196 A3
Otwock [PL] 38 C3
Ouanne [F] 56 E2
Oucques [F] 42 D6
Oud Beijerland [NL] 16 C5
Ouddorp [NL] 16 B5
Oudenaarde (Audenarde) [B] 28 G2
Oude-Pekela [NL] 16 H2
Oudewater [NL] 16 D5
Oughterard [IRL] 2 C4
Ouistreham [F] 26 F3
Oulainen [FIN] 196 D5
Oullins [F] 68 F3
Oulu / Uleåborg [FIN] 196 D4
Oulunsalo [FIN] 196 D4

Retuneri [FIN] 188 E2
Retz [A] 62 E3
Reuilly [F] 56 B3
Reus [E] 92 C5
Reusel [NL] 30 E3
Reuterstadt Stavenhagen [D] 20 C4
Reutlingen [D] 58 H2
Reutte [A] 60 C6
Revel [F] 106 B4
Révfülöp [H] 74 H3
Révigny-sur-Ornain [F] 44 C4
Revin [F] 44 C1
Revište [SK] 64 B3
Řevničov [CZ] 48 E3
Revò [I] 72 C3
Revonkylä [FIN] 188 G2
Revonlahti [FIN] 196 D4
Revsnes [N] 170 D2
Revsnes [N] 190 B5
Revsund [S] 182 H3
Revúca [SK] 64 E3
Rewal [PL] 20 F3
Rexbo [S] 172 H4
Rexnin [AL] 128 B6
Reykjalíð [IS] 192 C2
Reykjavík [IS] 192 A3
Rey Moro, Cueva del- [E] 98 D6
Rēzekne [LV] 198 G5
Rezovo [BG] 148 G5
Rgotina [SRB] 146 E2
Rgotina [SRB] 204 C6
Rhade [D] 18 E5
Rhayader [GB] 10 C6
Rheda [D] 32 D3
Rhede [D] 16 G6
Rheinau [D] 44 H6
Rheinbach [D] 30 G5
Rheinberg [D] 30 G2
Rheinböllen [D] 44 H2
Rheindahlen [D] 30 F3
Rheine [D] 16 H5
Rheinfall [D] 58 F4
Rheinfelden [CH] 58 E4
Rheinfelden (Baden) [D] 58 E4
Rheinsberg [D] 20 C6
Rhein-Weser-Turm [D] 32 D5
Rheinzabern [D] 46 B5
Rhêmes-Notre-Dame [I] 70 C4
Rhenen [NL] 16 E5
Rhens [D] 30 H6
Rheydt [D] 30 G3
Rhinau [F] 58 E2
Rhinow [D] 34 C1
Rho [I] 70 G5
Rhoon [NL] 16 C5
Rhosneigr [GB] 10 B4
Rhyl [GB] 10 C4
Rhynern [D] 32 C4
Ría Formosa [P] 94 C6
Riaillé [F] 40 G6
Rialp [E] 84 G6
Riaño [E] 82 C3
Rians [F] 108 C4
Rianxo [E] 78 B3
Riaza [E] 88 G3
Ribabellosa [E] 82 G5
Ribadavia [E] 78 C5
Ribadelago [E] 78 E6
Ribadeo [E] 78 F2
Ribadesella [E] 82 C2
Ribaflecha [E] 90 C1
Ribaforada [E] 84 B6
Ribarci [SRB] 146 E5
Ribariće [SRB] 146 B4
Ribaritsa [BG] 148 A4
Riba-roja de Túria [E] 98 E4
Ribarska Banja [SRB] 146 D3
Ribas de Sil [E] 78 E5
Ribas do Miño, Monasterio de- [E] 78 D4
Ribčev Laz [SLO] 74 A4
Ribe [DK] 156 B3
Ribeauville [F] 58 D2
Ribécourt [F] 28 E6
Ribeira Brava [P] 100 A3
Ribeira de Pena [P] 80 D3
Ribeira Grande [P] 100 E3
Ribeiras [P] 100 C3
Ribeirinha [P] 100 C3
Ribemont [F] 28 F5
Ribera [I] 126 C3
Ribérac [F] 66 E2
Ribera de Cardós [E] 84 G6
Ribera del Fresno [E] 94 H3
Ribes de Freser [E] 92 E2
Ribnica [BIH] 142 D3
Ribnica [SLO] 74 B6
Ribnica [SLO] 74 C6
Rîbniţa [MD] 204 E3
Ribnitz-Damgarten [D] 20 C2
Ribolla [I] 114 F2
Ricadi [I] 124 C6
Říčany [CZ] 48 G4
Riccia [I] 120 F1
Riccione [I] 112 B5
Richelieu [F] 54 F3
Richky [UA] 52 G3
Richmond [GB] 10 F2
Richtenberg [D] 20 C3
Rickarum [S] 158 D2
Rickling [D] 18 G3
Ricla [E] 90 D4
Ricse [H] 64 H4
Riddarhyttan [S] 166 H2
Ridderkerk [NL] 16 D5
Ridjica [SRB] 76 C5
Ridzewo [PL] 24 C3
Riebini [LV] 198 F6
Ried [A] 72 C2
Ried [CH] 72 C1
Riedbach [D] 46 E5
Riedenburg [D] 60 E2
Rieder [D] 60 C5
Riedern [D] 58 F4
Ried im Innkreis [A] 60 H4
Riedlingen [D] 58 H3
Riegel [D] 34 F5
Riegel [D] 58 E2
Riegersburg [A] 74 E2
Riego de Ambrós [E] 78 F5
Riekki [FIN] 196 F2
Riello [E] 78 G5
Rieneck [D] 46 E3
Riesa [D] 34 E5
Riesi [I] 126 E4
Riestedt [D] 34 B5
Rietavas [LT] 200 D4
Rietberg [D] 32 D3
Rieth [D] 20 E4
Rieti [I] 116 B4
Rietschen [D] 34 G5
Rieumes [F] 84 H3
Rieupeyroux [F] 66 H6
Rieussec [F] 106 C4
Rieux [F] 84 H4
Riez [F] 108 C4
Riezlern [A] 60 B6
Rīga [LV] 198 D5
Rígaio [GR] 132 G2
Rigáni [GR] 132 F5
Riglos [E] 84 D5
Rignac [F] 68 A5
Rignano Flaminio [I] 116 A4
Riihimäki [FIN] 176 G3
Riihivaara [FIN] 196 G5
Riihivalkama [FIN] 176 F3
Riiho [FIN] 186 E4
Riipi [FIN] 194 D6
Riispyy [FIN] 186 B5
Riistavesi [FIN] 188 D2
Rijeka [BIH] 142 D4
Rijeka [HR] 112 E1
Rijeka Crnojevića [MNE] 144 E4
Rijssen [NL] 16 G5
Říkonín [CZ] 50 B6
Riksgränsen [S] 192 F4
Rila [BG] 146 F6
Rilci [BG] 148 F2
Rillé [F] 54 F1
Rillo [E] 90 D6
Rilski Man. [BG] 146 F6
Rima [I] 70 E3
Rimaucourt [F] 44 D6
Rimavská Baňa [SK] 64 D3
Rimavská Sobota [SK] 64 E4
Rimbach [D] 60 G3
Rimbo [S] 168 E2
Rimella [I] 70 E3
Rimforsa [S] 162 F1
Rímini [I] 110 H5
Rimito / Rymättylä [FIN] 176 D5
Rimske Toplice [SLO] 74 D5
Rincón de la Victoria [E] 102 C5
Rincón de Soto [E] 84 A5
Rindal [N] 180 G2
Rindown Castle [IRL] 2 D5
Ringamåla [S] 162 E6
Ringarum [S] 168 B6
Ringaskiddy [IRL] 4 D5
Ringe [DK] 156 D3
Ringebu [N] 170 H1
Ringkøbing [DK] 160 B6
Ringnäs [S] 172 F2
Ringnes [N] 170 G5
Ringøy [N] 170 D4
Ringsheim [D] 58 E2
Ringstad [S] 168 B5
Ringsted [DK] 156 F3
Ringville / An Rinn [IRL] 4 E5
Ringwood [GB] 12 G5
Rinkilä [FIN] 188 E5
Rinna [S] 166 G6
Ringøya [N] 192 F4
Rinteln [D] 32 E2
Río [GR] 132 F5
Riobianco / Weissenbach [I] 72 D2
Río de Losa [E] 82 F4
Ríofrio [E] 78 G5
Riofrío de Llano [E] 90 A4
Riola Sardo [I] 118 B5
Riolobos [E] 86 H4
Río Lobos, Cañón del- [E] 88 H2
Riolo Terme [I] 110 G4
Riom [F] 68 C2
Riomaggiore [I] 110 C4
Rio Maior [P] 86 C4
Riomar [E] 92 B6
Rio Marina [I] 114 E2
Rio Mau [P] 80 B3
Riom-ès-Montagnes [F] 68 B3
Rion-des-Landes [F] 66 B5
Rionegro del Puente [E] 80 G3
Rionero in Vúlture [I] 120 G3
Riópar [E] 96 H6
Riós [E] 78 D6
Riosa [E] 78 H4
Rio Saliceto [I] 110 E2
Rioseco de Tapia [E] 78 G5
Rio Torto [P] 80 D6
Rioz [F] 58 B4
Ripač [BIH] 112 H3
Ripacandida [I] 120 G3
Ripanj [SRB] 142 G3
Riparbella [I] 114 E1
Ripatransone [I] 116 C2
Ripats [S] 192 G6
Ripky [UA] 202 D6
Ripley [GB] 10 E5
Ripoll [E] 92 E2
Ripon [GB] 10 F3
Riposto [I] 124 B8
Ripsa [S] 168 C4
Riquewihr [F] 58 D2
Risan [MNE] 144 D4
Risasvallen [S] 182 E4
Risbäck [S] 190 E4
Risberg [S] 172 F3
Riscle [F] 84 E2
Riseberga [S] 158 C1
Riseberga Kloster [S] 166 G3
Risede [S] 190 E5
Rish [BG] 148 E3
Risinge [S] 168 B5
Risliden [S] 190 H4
Risnes [N] 164 C4
Risnes [N] 170 B2
Rišňovce [SK] 64 A4
Risør [N] 164 F4
Risøyhamn [N] 192 E3
Rissa [N] 190 B6
Rissna [S] 182 H2
Risti [EST] 198 D2
Ristiina [FIN] 188 C6
Ristijärvi [FIN] 196 F4
Ristilä [FIN] 186 H4
Ristinge [DK] 156 E5
Ristinkylä [FIN] 188 E3
Ristna [EST] 198 C2
Ristovac [SRB] 146 D5
Risträsk [S] 190 G4
Risulahti [FIN] 188 D6
Risum-Lindholm [D] 156 B5
Risuperä [FIN] 186 E2
Ritíni [GR] 128 G5
Ritola [FIN] 186 D3
Ritsem [S] 192 F5
Ritten / Renon [I] 72 D3
Rittmanshausen [D] 32 G6
Riuttala [FIN] 176 D1
Riva-Bella [F] 26 F3
Riva dei Tarquini [I] 114 G4
Riva del Garda [I] 72 C5
Riva di Solto [I] 72 A5
Rivanazzano [I] 70 F6
Rivarolo Canavese [I] 70 D5
Rivarolo Mantovano [I] 110 E2
Riva Valdobbia [I] 70 E3
Rive-de-Gier [F] 68 F3
Rivello [I] 120 G5
Rivergaro [I] 110 C2
Rivesaltes [F] 92 G1
Rivinperä [FIN] 196 E5
Rivne [UA] 202 B7
Rivoli [I] 70 D5
Rizári [GR] 128 F4
Rízia [GR] 150 A2
Rizokárpasox (Dipkarpaz) [CY] 154 H4
Rízoma [GR] 132 E2
Rizómata [GR] 128 G5
Rizómylos [GR] 132 H2
Rizómylos [GR] 136 D4
Rjånes [N] 180 C4
Rjukan [N] 170 F6
Ro [I] 110 G2
Roa [E] 88 G2
Roa [N] 172 B5
Roald [N] 180 C3
Røan [N] 180 G2
Roana [I] 72 D5
Roanne [F] 66 E2
Roasjö [S] 162 B2
Roavvegieddi [N] 194 D3
Robăneştii de Jos [RO] 146 G1
Robbio [I] 70 F5
Röbel [D] 20 C5
Robella [I] 70 E5
Røberg [N] 182 D1
Robertingue [F] 14 G6
Robertsfors [S] 196 A5
Robleda [E] 86 H2
Robledillo de Gata [E] 86 H3
Robledo [E] 96 H5
Robledo de Chavela [E] 88 E5
Robledo del Buey [E] 96 D2
Robles de la Valcueva [E] 78 H5
Robliza de Cojos [E] 88 B3
Robres [E] 90 F3
Robres del Castillo [E] 90 C1
Robru [N] 170 F3
Rocamadour [F] 66 G4
Roccabianca [I] 110 D2
Roccadáspide [I] 120 F4
Rocca di Cambio [I] 116 C4
Rocca di Mezzo [I] 116 C4
Rocca di Neto [I] 124 F5
Rocca Imperiale [I] 122 D5
Roccalbegna [I] 114 G3
Roccalumera [I] 124 B8
Rocca Malatina, Sassi di- [I] 110 E4
Roccamonfina [I] 120 D2
Roccanova [I] 122 C5
Roccapalumba [I] 126 D2
Rocca Pia [I] 116 D5
Roccaraso [I] 116 D6
Rocca San Casciano [I] 110 G5
Rocca Sinibalda [I] 116 B4
Roccastrada [I] 114 F2
Rocca Vecchia [I] 122 H5
Roccaverano [I] 108 H2
Roccella Iónica [I] 124 D7
Roccelletta del Vescovo di Squillace [I] 124 E5
Rocche di Cusa [I] 126 B3
Rocchetta Belbo [I] 108 G2
Rocella Valdemonte [I] 124 A8
Rochdale [GB] 10 E4
Roche [E] 100 F4
Rochebloine, Château de- [F] 68 E5
Rochechouart [F] 54 F6
Rochecourbière, Grotte de- [F] 106 H2
Rochefort [B] 30 D6
Rochefort [F] 54 C5
Rochefort, Grotte de- [F] 40 H5
Rochefort-en-Terre [F] 40 E5
Rochefort-s-Nenon [F] 56 H4
Rochehaut [B] 44 D2
Rochemaure [F] 68 F6
Rocher, Château du- [F] 26 E6
Rocherolle, Château de la- [F] 54 G4
Rochers, Château des- [F] 26 D6
Rocheservière [F] 54 B2
Rochester [GB] 14 F4
Rochlitz [D] 34 D6
Rochsburg [D] 48 D1
Rociana del Condado [E] 94 F6
Rockcorry [IRL] 2 F4
Rockenhausen [D] 46 B4
Rockhammar [S] 166 H2
Rockneby [S] 162 G5
Rocroi [F] 28 H5
Rød [N] 166 B3
Róda [GR] 132 B1
Rodach [D] 46 G2
Roda de Eresma [E] 88 F4
Roda de Isábena [E] 84 F6
Rødal [N] 180 E4
Rodaljice [HR] 112 H5
Ródanas, Sant. de- [E] 90 D4
Rodange [L] 44 E3
Ródão, Portas de- [P] 86 E4
Rødberg [N] 170 F5
Rødby [DK] 20 A1
Rödby [S] 158 F1
Rødbyhavn [DK] 20 A1
Rødding [DK] 156 B3
Rødding [DK] 160 C5
Rödeby [S] 158 F1
Rodeiro [E] 78 D4
Rødekro [DK] 156 C4
Rodellar [E] 84 E6
Roden [NL] 16 G2
Rodenkirchen [D] 18 D4
Rodewald [D] 32 F1
Rodewisch [D] 48 C2
Rodez [F] 68 B6
Rodgau [D] 46 C3
Rødhus Klit [DK] 160 D3
Rodiá [GR] 132 G1
Rodi Gargánico [I] 116 G5
Roding [D] 48 C6
Rødkærsbro [DK] 160 D5
Rodolívos [GR] 130 C3
Rodópoli [GR] 128 H2
Ródos [GR] 154 D3
Rodovoye [RUS] 198 G4
Rodrigatos de la Obispalía [E] 78 G5
Rodrigo, Castelo- [P] 80 E6
Rødsjøen [N] 190 B6
Rødven [N] 180 E3
Rødvig [DK] 156 G4
Roela [EST] 198 F1
Roermond [NL] 30 F3
Roeselare (Roulers) [B] 28 F2
Roeulx [B] 28 H3
Roffiac [F] 68 C4
Roflaschlucht [CH] 70 G2
Röfors [S] 166 G4
Rofrano [I] 120 G5
Rogač [HR] 142 A6
Rogačica [SRB] 142 F4
Rogalice [PL] 50 D1
Rogalin [PL] 36 C3
Rogaška Slatina [SLO] 74 D4
Rogatec [SLO] 74 E4
Rogatica [BIH] 144 E1
Rogätz [D] 34 B2
Roggenburg [D] 60 C4
Rogil [P] 94 B4
Røgind [DK] 160 B6
Rögla [S] 158 C3
Rogliano [F] 114 C2
Rogliano [I] 124 D5
Rognac [F] 106 H5
Rognan [N] 192 D6
Rogne [N] 170 G2
Rognes [N] 182 B2
Rogovka [LV] 198 G5
Rogovo [RUS] 198 G4
Rogowo [PL] 36 D2
Rogozhinë [AL] 128 B3
Rogoznica [HR] 116 H1
Rogoźno [PL] 36 C2
Rogoźno [PL] 36 F5
Roguszyn [PL] 38 D2
Rohan [F] 26 A5
Rohatec [CZ] 62 G2
Rohatyn [UA] 204 C2
Rohožník [SK] 62 G4
Rohr [A] 72 E1
Rohrbach [A] 62 B3
Rohrbach-lès-Bitche [F] 44 G4
Rohrberg [D] 34 A1
Rohrenfels [D] 60 D3
Rohr in Niederbayern [D] 60 F2
Rohuküla [EST] 198 D2
Rohuneeme [EST] 198 D1
Roisel [F] 28 F5
Roja [LV] 198 C4
Rojales [E] 104 D3
Röjan [S] 182 G4
Rojão Grande [P] 80 C6
Röjdåfors [S] 172 E5
Rojiştea [RO] 146 G1
Rök [S] 166 G6
Röka [S] 190 G4
Röke [S] 158 C1
Rokiciny [PL] 36 H4
Rokietnica [PL] 52 F4
Rokiškis [LT] 200 G3
Rokity [PL] 22 C2
Rökkum [N] 180 F2
Røkland [N] 190 E1
Roknäs [S] 196 A3
Rokua [FIN] 196 E4
Rokycany [CZ] 48 E4
Rokytnice [CZ] 50 B3
Rolandstorp [S] 190 E4
Rold [DK] 160 D4
Røldal [N] 170 C5
Rolfstorp [S] 160 H4
Rolle [CH] 70 B1
Rølvåg [N] 190 D2
Rolvsøy [N] 166 B3
Roma [I] 116 A5
Romagnano Sésia [I] 70 E4
Romakkajärvi [FIN] 194 C7
Romakloster [S] 168 G4
Roman [BG] 146 G3
Roman [RO] 204 D3
Romangordo [E] 88 B6
Romanija [BIH] 144 D1
Romanshorn [CH] 58 H4
Romans-sur-Isère [F] 68 F5
Romashiki [RUS] 178 G2
Rombas [F] 44 E4
Rom By [DK] 160 B5
Romena, Castello di- [I] 110 G5
Romena, Pieve di- [I] 110 G5
Romeral [E] 96 G2
Romfartuna [S] 168 B2
Romilly-sur-Seine [F] 44 A5
Romny [UA] 202 E7
Romont [CH] 70 C1
Romorantin-Lanthenay [F] 54 H2
Romppala [FIN] 188 F1
Romsey [GB] 12 H4
Romtemplom [H] 64 C6
Røn [N] 170 G2
Roncade [I] 72 E6
Roncadelle [I] 72 A6
Roncal / Erronkari [E] 84 C4
Roncegno [I] 72 D4
Roncesvalles [E] 84 C3
Ronchamp [F] 58 C3
Ronchi dei Legionari [I] 72 H5
Ronciglione [I] 114 H4
Ronco Canavese [I] 70 D4
Roncofreddo [I] 110 H5
Ronco Scrivia [I] 110 B3
Ronda [E] 102 A4
Rønde [DK] 160 E6
Ronehamn [S] 168 G5
Rong [N] 170 C3
Rõngu [EST] 198 F3
Ronkeli [FIN] 196 G5
Rönnäng [S] 160 G1
Rönnäs [FIN] 178 B4
Rønne [DK] 158 E4
Ronneburg [D] 48 C1
Ronneby [S] 158 F1
Rønnede [DK] 156 G4
Rönnigsåsen [S] 182 F4
Rönnliden [S] 190 H3
Rönnöfors [S] 190 D6
Rönnskär [S] 196 A4
Rönnynkylä [FIN] 186 F1
Rönö [S] 168 C5
Ronsberg [D] 60 C5
Ronse (Renaix) [B] 28 G3
Roodeschool [NL] 16 G1
Roonah Quay [IRL] 2 B3
Roosendaal [NL] 16 C6
Roosky [IRL] 2 D4
Ropa [PL] 52 C5
Ropaži [LV] 198 E5
Ropczyce [PL] 52 D3
Ropeid [N] 164 B1
Ropinsalmi [FIN] 192 H3
Ropotovo [MK] 128 E2
Ropsha [RUS] 178 E6
Ropsha [RUS] 178 G5
Roque, Pointe de la- [F] 26 G3
Roquebillière [F] 108 F4
Roquebrune-Cap-Martin [F] 108 F4
Roquefort [F] 66 C5
Roquefort-sur-Soulzon [F] 106 D3
Roquemaure [F] 106 G3
Roquesteron [F] 108 E4
Roquetaillade, Château de- [F] 66 D4
Roquetas de Mar [E] 102 F5
Roquetes [E] 92 A5
Rörbäcksnäs [S] 172 E3
Rore [BIH] 142 B4
Rörön [S] 182 G3
Røros [N] 182 C4
Rorschach [CH] 58 H5
Rörum [S] 158 D3
Rørvig [DK] 156 F2
Rørvik [N] 164 C5
Rørvik [N] 182 B1
Rørvik [N] 190 C4
Rörvik [S] 168 F1
Ros' [BY] 24 G5
Rosais [P] 100 C3
Rosala [FIN] 176 E6
Rosal de la Frontera [E] 94 E3
Rosa Marina [I] 122 F3
Rosans [F] 108 B2
Rosarno [I] 124 C6
Rosas / Roses [E] 92 G2
Rosbach [D] 46 C2
Rosche [D] 18 G6
Rościszewo [PL] 36 H1
Roscoff [F] 40 C1
Roscommon [IRL] 2 D5
Roscrea [IRL] 2 D6
Rosdorf [D] 32 F4
Rosegg [A] 74 B3
Roselle [I] 114 F2
Roselle Módica [I] 126 G6
Rosen [BG] 148 F4
Rosenberg [D] 46 E6
Rosenburg [A] 62 E3
Rosendal [N] 170 B5
Rosendal [S] 156 H1
Rosendal [S] 162 E1
Rosenheim [D] 60 F5
Rosenhof [A] 62 C3
Rosenholm [DK] 160 E6
Rosentorp [S] 172 H2
Rosepenna / Machair Loiscthe [IRL] 2 E1
Rosersberg [S] 168 D2
Roses / Rosas [E] 92 G2
Roseto Capo Spúlico [I] 122 D6
Roseto degli Abruzzi [I] 116 D3
Roseto Valfortore [I] 120 F2
Roshchino [RUS] 178 G4
Rosica [BG] 148 F1
Rosice [CZ] 50 B6
Rosignano-Marittimo [I] 110 D6
Rosignano Solvay [I] 114 E1
Rosino [BG] 148 B4
Roşiori [RO] 76 H1
Roşiori de Vede [RO] 148 B1
Roskilde [DK] 156 G2
Rosko [PL] 36 B1
Roskovec [AL] 128 B4
Roslags-Bro [S] 168 E1
Roslags-kulla [S] 168 E2
Roslavl' [RUS] 202 D5
Roslev [DK] 160 C4
Rosli [N] 180 G5
Rosmaninhal [P] 86 F4
Ros Mhic Thriúin / New Ross [IRL] 4 F4
Rosnowo [PL] 22 A3
Rosny sur Seine [F] 42 E3
Rosolina Mare [I] 110 H2
Rosolini [I] 126 G5
Rosoman [MK] 128 F2
Rosporden [F] 40 C3
Ross Abbey [IRL] 2 C4
Rossano [I] 124 E4
Rossas [P] 80 C5
Ross Carbery [IRL] 4 C5
Rosscor [NIR] 2 E3
Rosserk Abbey [IRL] 2 C3
Rosses Point [IRL] 2 D3
Rossfjord [N] 192 F2
Rosshaupten [D] 60 C5
Rossiglione [I] 108 H2
Rossio [P] 86 D4
Rossla [D] 34 A5
Rossland [N] 170 A3
Rosslare Harbour [IRL] 4 F5
Rosslau [D] 34 C4
Rosslea [NIR] 2 F4
Rossnes [N] 170 A3
Rossön [S] 190 F6
Ross-on-Wye [GB] 12 G2
Rossosz [PL] 38 F4
Rossoszyca [PL] 36 F4
Røssvassbukt [N] 190 E3
Röstånga [S] 158 C2
Rostassac [F] 66 F5
Roštejn [CZ] 48 H6
Roštejn [CZ] 48 H6
Röster [S] 168 B6
Rostock [D] 20 B3
Rostov [RUS] 202 F2
Rostrenen [F] 40 D3
Rostrevor [NIR] 2 G4
Röström [S] 190 F5
Røstvollen [N] 182 D5
Rosvik [N] 192 D5
Rosvik [S] 196 B3
Rosyth [GB] 8 E3
Röszke [H] 76 E4
Roszki-Wodźki [PL] 24 E6
Rot [S] 172 F2
Rota [E] 100 F3
Rotberget [N] 172 D4
Roteberg [S] 168 C1
Rotemo [N] 164 D2
Rotenburg [D] 18 E5
Rotenburg [D] 32 F6
Rotenfels [D] 46 B3
Rotgülden [A] 72 H2
Roth [D] 46 G5
Rötha [D] 34 C6
Rothaus [D] 58 F4
Rothemühl [D] 20 E4
Rothenburg [D] 34 G5
Rothenburg, Ruine- [D] 46 G5
Rothenburg ob der Tauber [D] 46 E5
Rothéneuf [F] 26 C4
Rothenstein [D] 60 D2
Rotherham [GB] 10 F4
Rothes [GB] 6 E5
Rothesay [GB] 8 C3
Rotondella [I] 122 D5
Rótova [E] 98 E6
Rotsjö [S] 184 D3
Rott [D] 60 D5
Rott [D] 60 F5
Rottach [D] 60 E5
Rötteln [D] 58 E4
Rottenbach [D] 46 G2
Rottenbuch [D] 60 D5
Rottenburg [D] 58 G2
Rottenburg [D] 60 F3
Rottenmann [A] 62 B6
Rotterdam [NL] 16 C5
Rotthalmünster [D] 60 H4
Röttingen [D] 46 E5
Rottne [S] 162 E4
Rottneros [S] 166 E1
Rottweil [D] 58 G3
Rotvoll [N] 182 D2
Rötz [D] 48 C5
Roubaix [F] 28 F3
Rouchovany [CZ] 62 E2
Roudnice nad Labem [CZ] 48 F3
Rouen [F] 28 B5
Rouffach [F] 58 D3
Rouffignac, Grotte de- [F] 66 F3
Rougé [F] 40 F5
Rougemont [F] 58 C4
Rougemont [F] 58 D3
Rouillac [F] 54 D6
Roujan [F] 106 D4
Roukavichy [BY] 202 D5
Roulers (Roeselare) [B] 28 F2
Roundstone [IRL] 2 B4
Roundwood [IRL] 4 G3
Roússa [GR] 130 G2
Roussillon [F] 68 F4
Roussillon [F] 106 H4
Rouvres-en-Xaintois [F] 44 E6
Rovakka [S] 194 B7
Rovaniemi [FIN] 194 D8
Rovanjska [HR] 112 G4
Rovastinaho [FIN] 196 D2
Rovato [I] 72 A6
Roverbella [I] 110 E1
Rovereto [I] 72 C5
Rövershagen [D] 20 B3
Roverud [N] 172 D5
Roviés [GR] 134 B4
Rovigo [I] 110 G2
Rovinj [HR] 112 D2
Rovišće [HR] 74 F5
Rovjok [N] 192 G3
Rovte [SLO] 74 B5
Rów [PL] 20 F6
Rowy [PL] 22 B1
Ruwy [PL] 36 F5
Royan [F] 54 B6
Royat [F] 68 C2
Royaumont, Abbaye de- [F] 42 F3
Roybon [F] 68 G4
Roye [F] 28 E5
Royère-de-Vassivière [F] 68 A1
Røyken [N] 164 H1
Röykkä [FIN] 176 G4
Røyrvik [N] 190 D4
Røyse [N] 170 H5
Røysheim [N] 180 F6
Royston [GB] 14 E3
Roza [BG] 148 D5
Rožaj [MNE] 146 B5
Różan [PL] 24 C6
Różanki [PL] 34 H1
Rožanstvo [SRB] 146 A3
Rozay-en-Brie [F] 42 G4
Rozdil [UA] 52 H5
Rozdory [RUS] 204 H1
Rozhenski Manastir [BG] 130 B2
Rožmberk nad Vltavou [CZ] 62 B3
Rožmitál pod Třemšínem [CZ] 48 E5
Rožňava [SK] 64 E3
Rožnov pod Radhoštěm [CZ] 50 E5
Rożnów [PL] 52 B4
Rozogi [PL] 24 C5
Rozoy [F] 28 G6
Rozprza [PL] 36 H5
Roztoky [CZ] 48 F3
Rožupe [LV] 198 F6
Rozvadov [CZ] 48 C4
Rozzano [I] 70 G5
Rrëshen [AL] 128 B1
Rtanj [SRB] 146 D2
Ru [E] 78 D3
Ruba [LV] 198 C6
Rubbestadneset [N] 170 A5
Rubena [E] 82 E6
Rubielos de Mora [E] 98 E2
Rubiera [I] 110 E3
Rucava [LV] 200 D3
Ruciane-Nida [PL] 24 C4
Rud [N] 164 H1
Rud [N] 170 G4
Rud [N] 170 H5
Rud [S] 166 F3
Ruda [PL] 24 D4
Ruda [S] 162 F4
Ruda Maleniecka [PL] 38 A6
Rudare [SRB] 146 C4
Rudawica [PL] 34 H5
Rudawka [PL] 24 F3
Ruda Wolińska [PL] 38 D3
Rudelsburg [D] 34 B6
Rudenica [SRB] 146 C3
Rüdersdorf [D] 34 F2
Rüdesheim [D] 46 B3
Rūdiškės [LT] 24 H1
Rudka [PL] 38 E1
Rudka [PL] 38 G5
Rudkøbing [DK] 156 E4
Rudky [UA] 52 G4
Rudna [PL] 22 C5
Rudna [PL] 36 B5
Rudna Glava [SRB] 146 D1
Rudnica [MNE] 144 E2
Rudnica [SRB] 146 B4
Rudnik [BG] 148 F3
Rudnik [KS] 146 B5
Rudnik [PL] 50 E3
Rudnik [PL] 52 E2
Rudnik [SRB] 146 B2
Rudniki [PL] 50 F1
Rudnik Szlachecki-Kol. [PL] 38 D6
Rudno [PL] 38 E1
Rudno [PL] 38 E4
Rudno [SLO] 74 B4
Rudnya [RUS] 202 C4
Rudo [BIH] 144 E1
Rudolphstein [D] 46 H2
Rudolstadt [D] 46 H1
Rudozem [BG] 100 E1
Rudsgrendi [N] 164 F1
Rudsjön [S] 190 F6
Rudskoga [S] 166 G4
Ruds-Vedby [DK] 156 F3
Rudy [PL] 50 F3
Rudy-Rysie [PL] 52 B3
Rudzāti [LV] 198 F5

Rue [F] 28 D3
Rueda [E] 88 E2
Rueda, Monasterio de- [E] 90 F5
Rueda de Jalón [E] 90 D3
Ruelle-sur-Touvre [F] 66 E1
Ruen [BG] 148 F4
Ruffano [I] 122 G6
Ruffec [F] 54 E5
Ruffieux [F] 68 H3
Rugāji [LV] 198 G5
Rugby [GB] 14 D2
Rugeley [GB] 10 E6
Rugldalen [N] 182 C3
Rugles [F] 26 H5
Rugvica [HR] 74 F6
Ruha [FIN] 186 C3
Ruhala [FIN] 186 E5
Ruhällen [S] 168 C1
Rühen [D] 32 H2
Ruhland [D] 34 F5
Ruhmannsfelden [D] 60 G2
Ruhpolding [D] 60 G5
Ruidera [E] 96 G4
Ruínas [I] 118 C5
Ruinas Romanas [E] 88 H3
Ruinas Romanas [E] 96 D1
Ruinas Romanas [E] 98 B3
Ruínas Romanas [P] 94 D2
Rūjiena [LV] 198 E3
Rujište [SRB] 146 D2
Rujište [SRB] 146 D2
Ruju, Nuraghe- [I] 118 D3
Ruka [FIN] 194 F8
Rukke [S] 170 F4
Rullbo [S] 182 H6
Rülzheim [D] 46 B5
Rum [H] 74 G2
Ruma [SRB] 142 F2
Ruma [SRB] 204 A6
Rumboci [BIH] 144 B1
Rumburk [CZ] 48 G1
Rumelifeneri [TR] 150 F2
Rumia [PL] 22 D2
Rumigny [F] 28 H5
Rumilly [F] 70 A3
Rummen [B] 30 D4
Rummukkala [FIN] 188 E3
Rumo [FIN] 196 F5
Rumont [F] 44 D4
Rumpani [LV] 198 F4
Runcorn [GB] 10 D4
Runde [N] 180 C3
Rundfloen [N] 172 E3
Rundvik [S] 184 H1
Runni [FIN] 196 E6
Runović [HR] 144 B2
Ruokojärvi [FIN] 194 C7
Ruokojärvi [S] 194 B8
Ruokolahti [FIN] 178 E1
Ruokto [S] 192 F6
Ruona [FIN] 186 D3
Ruopsa [FIN] 194 E7
Ruorasmäki [FIN] 186 H6
Ruotaanmäki [FIN] 196 E6
Ruoti [I] 120 G3
Ruotsinkylä Svenskby [FIN] 178 C3
Ruotsinpyhtää Strömfors [FIN] 178 C4
Ruovesi [FIN] 186 E5
Rupa [HR] 112 E1
Rupea [RO] 204 D4
Rupt [F] 58 C3
Rus [E] 102 F1
Rusalka [BG] 148 G2
Rusanivka [UA] 202 F7
Rúscio [I] 116 B3
Rusdal [N] 164 B4
Ruse [BG] 148 C2
Ruše [SLO] 74 D4
Rusele [S] 190 G4
Ruševo [HR] 142 D1
Rusfors [S] 190 G4
Rush [IRL] 2 F6
Rushden [GB] 14 E2
Rusiec [PL] 36 F5
Rusinowo [PL] 20 G4
Rusinowo [PL] 22 A6
Rusjasi [MK] 128 D2
Ruskeala [RUS] 188 G4
Ruski Krstur [SRB] 76 D6
Ruskila [FIN] 188 D2
Rusksele [S] 190 G4
Ruskträsk [S] 190 G4
Rusnė [LT] 200 D5
Rusokastro [BG] 148 F4
Rüsselsheim [D] 46 C3
Russi [I] 110 G4
Russliseter [N] 180 G6
Rust [A] 62 F5
Rust [D] 58 E2
Rustad [N] 172 B5
Rustefjelbma [N] 194 D2
Rusvekk [N] 172 D4
Ruswil [CH] 58 E6
Ruszów [PL] 34 H5
Rutalahti [FIN] 186 G5
Rute [E] 102 C3
Rutenbrock [D] 16 H3
Rüthen [D] 32 D4
Ruthin [GB] 10 C4
Rüthnick [D] 34 D1
Rüti [CH] 58 G6
Rüti [CH] 58 G5
Rutigliano [I] 122 E3
Rutka-Tartak [PL] 24 E2
Rutki-Kossaki [PL] 24 D6
Rutledal [N] 170 B2
Rutvik [S] 196 B3
Ruukki [FIN] 196 D4
Ruunaa [FIN] 196 G6
Ruurlo [NL] 16 F5
Ruutana [FIN] 176 F1
Ruuvaoja [FIN] 194 E6
Ruvallen [S] 182 E3
Ruvanaho [FIN] 194 F7
Ruvasiahtio [FIN] 188 F2
Ruvo di Púglia [I] 122 D2
Ruwer [D] 44 G2
Ruza [RUS] 202 E3
Ruzhany [BY] 24 H6
Ruzhintsi [BG] 146 E3
Ruzhyn [UA] 202 D8
Růžkovy Lhotice [CZ] 48 G5
Ružomberok [SK] 64 C2
Ry [DK] 156 D1
Ryå [DK] 160 D3
Ryabovo [RUS] 178 F4
Ryakhovo [BG] 148 D1
Ryákia [GR] 128 G5
Rybachiy [RUS] 200 C5
Rybarzowice [PL] 50 G5
Rybinsk [RUS] 202 F1
Rybnica [PL] 50 A1
Rybnik [PL] 50 F4
Rybník [SK] 64 E3
Rybno [PL] 22 G5
Ryboły [PL] 24 F6
Rychliki [PL] 22 F3
Rychnburk [CZ] 50 B4
Rychnov nad Kněžnou [CZ] 50 B3
Rychnowo [PL] 22 G4
Rychtal [PL] 36 E6
Rychwał [PL] 36 E3
Ryczywół [PL] 38 C4
Ryd [S] 162 D6
Rydaholm [S] 162 D4
Ryde [GB] 12 H5
Rydet [S] 160 G3
Rydland [N] 182 B6
Rydsnäs [S] 162 E2
Rydułtowy [PL] 50 F4
Rydzyna [PL] 36 C4
Rye [GB] 14 F5
Ryen [N] 164 E5
Ryfoss [N] 170 F2
Rygge [N] 166 B2
Rygozy [RUS] 198 H5
Ryhälä [FIN] 188 E5
Ryhäntä [FIN] 196 F4
Rykene [N] 164 E5
Ryki [PL] 38 D4
Ryl'sk [RUS] 202 F6
Rymań [PL] 20 G3
Rymanów [PL] 52 D5
Rýmařov [CZ] 50 D4
Rymättylä / Rimito [FIN] 176 D5
Rýmnio [GR] 128 F6
Ryn [PL] 24 C3
Rynarzewo [PL] 22 D6
Ryomgård [DK] 160 E5
Rypefjord [N] 194 B2
Rypin [PL] 22 F6
Ryslinge [DK] 156 D3
Ryssby [S] 162 D4
Rysum [D] 16 H2
Rytel [PL] 22 C4
Rytinki [FIN] 196 E2
Rytkynkylä [FIN] 196 D5
Rytro [PL] 52 B5
Ryuttyu [RUS] 188 H4
Rýzmberk [CZ] 48 D5
Rząśnik [PL] 38 C1
Rzecin [PL] 36 B1
Rzeczenica [PL] 22 B4
Rzeczyca [PL] 38 A5
Rzęgnowo [PL] 22 H6
Rzemień [PL] 52 D3
Rzepin [PL] 34 G3
Rzesznikowo [PL] 20 G4
Rzeszów [PL] 52 E3
Rzewnowo [PL] 20 F3
Rzgów [PL] 36 G4
Rzhev [RUS] 202 D3
Rzhishchiv [UA] 202 E7

S

Sääksjärvi [FIN] 186 D2
Sääksmäki [FIN] 176 F2
Saal [D] 60 F2
Saalbach [A] 72 F1
Saalburg [D] 46 C2
Saales [F] 44 G6
Saalfeld [D] 46 H2
Saalfelden [A] 60 G6
Saamatti [FIN] 176 F5
Saanannaja [FIN] 192 G3
Saanen [CH] 70 D1
Saaramaa [FIN] 178 D3
Saarbrücken [D] 44 G4
Saarburg [D] 44 F3
Sääre [EST] 198 C4
Saare [EST] 198 F2
Saarela [FIN] 186 G1
Saarenkylä [FIN] 194 D8
Saarenmaa [FIN] 176 D2
Saaresmäki [FIN] 196 E5
Saari [FIN] 188 F5
Saarijärvi [FIN] 186 F3
Saarikko [FIN] 176 F3
Saarikoski [FIN] 192 H3
Saarinen [FIN] 196 F4
Saario [FIN] 188 G3
Saarivaara [FIN] 188 G3
Saariväara [FIN] 196 G4
Saarlouis [D] 44 F3
Saas Almagell [CH] 70 E3
Saas-Fee [CH] 70 E3
Saas Grund [CH] 70 E3
Sääskijärvi [FIN] 196 E2
Sääskjärvi [FIN] 178 B3
Sababurg [D] 32 F4
Šabac [MNE] 204 A6
Šabac [SRB] 142 F2
Sabadell [E] 92 E4
Sabaro [E] 82 C4
Sabáudia [I] 120 B2
Sabbioneta [I] 110 E2
Sabbucina [I] 126 E3
Sabile [LV] 198 C5
Sabiñánigo [E] 84 D5
Sabinarde Calatañazor [E] 90 A2
Sabinosa [E] 100 A5
Sabinov [SK] 52 C6
Sabiote [E] 102 F2
Sables-d'Or-les-Pins [F] 26 B4
Sablé-sur-Sarthe [F] 42 A5
Såbole [S] 182 F1
Saborsko [HR] 112 G2
Sabres [F] 66 C5
Sabrosa [P] 80 D4
Sabugal [P] 86 G2
Sabuncu [TR] 150 H6
Saby [S] 162 E1
Šaca [SK] 64 G3
Săcălaz [RO] 76 G5
Sacavém [P] 86 B5
Sacecorbo [E] 90 B5
Sacedón [E] 88 H6
Saceruela [E] 96 D4
Sacile [I] 72 F5
Sacra di San Michele [I] 70 C5
Sada [E] 78 D2
Sádaba [E] 84 B5
Sadala [EST] 198 F2
Sadikkiri [TR] 152 H1
Sadikov Bunar [SRB] 146 E4
Sadina [BG] 148 D2
Sadki [PL] 22 C6
Sadova [RO] 146 G2
Sadovets [BG] 148 A3
Sadovo [BG] 148 B6
Sadovo [BG] 148 F3
Sądów [PL] 34 G3
Sadowne [PL] 38 C2
Sadrazamköy (Livera) [CY] 154 F5
S. Adriano [I] 110 G4
Sadská [CZ] 48 G3
Sädvaluspen [S] 190 F2
Sæbø [N] 170 D4
Sæbø [N] 180 D4
Sæbøvik [N] 170 B5
Sæby [DK] 160 E3
Sæd [DK] 156 B4
Sædinenie [BG] 148 B5
Sædinenie [BG] 148 C5
Saelices [E] 96 H2
Sælvig [DK] 156 E2
Saepinum [I] 120 E1
Saerbeck [D] 32 C2
Sætra [N] 192 E2
Sætre [N] 164 H2
Sætre [N] 172 C2
Saeul [L] 44 E2
Sævareid [N] 170 B4
Sævråsvåg [N] 170 B3
Safa [TR] 150 G5
Safara [P] 94 E3
Safary-Park [A] 62 F4
Säffle [S] 166 E3
Saffron Walden [GB] 14 F3
Safonovo [RUS] 202 D4
Şag [RO] 76 G6
Sagard [D] 20 D2
S'Agaró [E] 92 G4
S. Agata di Esaro [I] 124 C3
Saggrenda [N] 164 G2
Sagiáda [GR] 132 B2
Sågmyra [S] 172 H4
Sagone [F] 114 A4
Sagres [P] 94 A5
Şagu [RO] 76 G5
Sagu / Sauvo [FIN] 176 E5
Sagunt / Sagunto [E] 98 F4
Sagunto / Sagunt [E] 98 F4
Sagvåg [N] 170 A5
Ságvár [H] 76 A3
Sahagún [E] 82 C5
Sahalahti [FIN] 176 G1
Sahankylä [FIN] 186 C4
Sahavaara [S] 194 B7
Sahilköy [TR] 150 F2
Şahin [TR] 150 B3
Sahinburgaz [TR] 150 D4
Sahrajärvi [FIN] 186 F4
Šahy [SK] 64 C5
Saignelégier [CH] 58 D5
Saija [FIN] 194 E7
Saikari [FIN] 186 H3
Saillagouse [F] 92 E1
Saillans [F] 68 G6
Sailly Flibeaucourt [F] 28 D4
Säimen [FIN] 188 F4
Sains [F] 28 G5
Saint Albain [F] 56 G6
Sainte-Lucie-de-Tallano [F] 114 B5
Sainte-Marie-Siché [F] 114 B5
Saintes [F] 54 C6
Saintfield [NIR] 2 G4
Saint-Ghislain [B] 28 G4
Saint Hilaire de la Côte [F] 68 G4
Saint-Jacques [I] 70 D3
Sairinen [FIN] 176 D4
Saissac [F] 106 B4
Saittarova [S] 192 H6
Saivomuotka [S] 194 B5
Sajaniemi [FIN] 176 G3
Sajenek [PL] 24 E3
Šajkaš [SRB] 142 G1
Sajószentpéter [H] 64 F4
Sakar [TR] 150 H4
Sakaravaara [FIN] 196 F4
Sakarya (Adapazari) [TR] 150 H3
Šakiai [LT] 200 E5
Säkinmäki [FIN] 186 H3
Sakıremer [TR] 152 D6
Sakızlık [TR] 150 G5
Sakowczyk [PL] 52 E5
Sakskøbing [DK] 156 F5
Saky [UA] 204 H4
Säkylä [FIN] 176 D3
Sala [S] 168 C1
Šal'a [SK] 64 A4
Salaberg [A] 62 C5
Salacgrīva [LV] 198 D4
Sala Consilina [I] 120 G4
Saladamm [S] 168 C1
Salahmi [FIN] 196 E5
Salamajärvi [FIN] 186 E1
Salamanca [E] 80 H6
Salamína [GR] 134 B6
Salamis [CY] 154 G5
Salantai [LT] 200 D4
Salaóra [GR] 132 D4
Salar [E] 102 D4
Salard [RO] 76 H1
Salardú [E] 84 G5
Salas [E] 78 G3
Salaš [SRB] 146 E2
Salas de los Infantes [E] 88 H1
Salaspils [LV] 198 E5
Salau [F] 84 G5
Salbohed [S] 168 B1
Salbris [F] 56 B2
Salcia [RO] 146 E1
Šalčininkai [LT] 200 G6
Salcombe [GB] 12 D5
Sălcuța [RO] 146 F1
Saldaña [E] 82 C5
Salduba [E] 90 E3
Saldus [LV] 198 C5
Sale [I] 70 F6
Saleby [S] 166 E5
Salem [D] 58 H4
Salema [P] 94 A5
Salemi [I] 126 B2
Sälen [S] 172 E2
Salernes [F] 108 D4
Salerno [I] 120 F4
Salers [F] 68 B4
S. Alessio Siculo [I] 124 B8
Saletta [I] 70 C5
Salgótarján [H] 64 D4
Šalgovík [SK] 64 G2
Salhus [N] 170 B3
Sali [HR] 112 F5
Salice [F] 114 B4
Salice Terme [I] 70 F6
Salies-de-Béarn [F] 84 D2
Salies-du-Salat [F] 84 G4
Salignac-Eyvigues [F] 66 G4
Salihli [TR] 152 E3
Salihorsk [BY] 202 B6
Salinas [E] 78 H3
Salinas [E] 104 D2
Salinas de Pinilla [E] 96 H5
Salinas de Pisuerga [E] 82 D4
Salin-de-Giraud [F] 106 G5
Saline di Volterra [I] 114 F1
Sälinkää [FIN] 176 H3
Salins-les-Bains [F] 58 B5
Salir [P] 94 C5
Salisbury [GB] 12 G4
Salka [SK] 64 C5
Salla [FIN] 194 E7
Sallanches [F] 70 B3
Sallent de Gállego [E] 84 D4
Sälleryd [S] 158 G1
Salles [F] 66 C4
Salles-Curan [F] 68 B6
Salles-s.-l'Hers [F] 106 A4
Sällinge [S] 166 H2
Sallmunds [S] 168 G6
Salme [EST] 198 C3
Salmenkylä [FIN] 186 E4
Salmenniemi [FIN] 186 F2
Salmerón [E] 90 A6
Salmi [FIN] 186 D3
Salmi [S] 194 B7
Salmivaara [FIN] 194 E7
Sal'miyarvi [RUS] 194 F3
Salmoral [E] 88 D4
Salo [FIN] 176 E4
Salò [I] 72 B6
Salobreña [E] 102 D5
Saločiai [LT] 198 E6
Salon [F] 44 B5
Salona [HR] 144 A2
Salon-de-Provence [F] 106 H4
Salonta [RO] 76 H3
Salorino [E] 86 F5
Salou [E] 92 C5
Salovci [SLO] 74 F3
Salsåker [S] 184 F3
Salsbruket [N] 190 C4
Salse di Nirano [I] 110 E3
Salses-le-Château [F] 106 C6
Salsnes [N] 190 C4
Salsomaggiore Terme [I] 110 D2
Salsta [S] 168 D1
Salt [E] 92 F3
Saltash [GB] 12 D5
Saltbæk [DK] 156 E2
Saltoluokta [S] 192 F6
Saltrød [N] 164 F5
Saltsjöbaden [S] 168 E3
Saltum [DK] 160 D3
Saltvik [FIN] 176 B5
Saltvik [S] 162 G3
Saluböle [S] 184 H1
Saluzzo [I] 108 F2
Salvacañete [E] 98 D2
Salvada [P] 94 D3
Salvagnac [F] 106 B2
Salvarola, Terme di- [I] 110 E3
Salvaterra de Magos [P] 86 C5
Salvaterra de Miño [E] 78 B5
Salvatierra [E] 96 E5
Salvatierra / Agurain [E] 82 H5
Salvatierra de los Barros [E] 94 G2
Salviac [F] 66 G4
Salzburg [A] 60 G5
Salzburg [D] 46 F2
Salzgitter-Bad [D] 32 G3
Salzgitter-Lebenstedt [D] 32 G3
Salzhausen [D] 18 F5
Salzkotten [D] 32 D4
Salzwedel [D] 18 H6
Salzweg [D] 60 H3
Sama de Langreo [E] 78 H4
Samadet [F] 66 C6
Samadet [F] 84 E2
Samailli [TR] 152 E5
Samandıra [TR] 150 F3
Samarína [GR] 128 D6
Samassi [I] 118 C6
Samatan [F] 84 G3
Sambiase [I] 124 D5
Sambir [UA] 52 G5
Sambuca di Sicília [I] 126 C3
Sambucheto [I] 116 B3
Sambuci [I] 116 B5
Sambucina, Abbazia della- [I] 124 D4
Samedan [CH] 72 A3
Samer [F] 28 D2
Sámi [GR] 132 C6
Samitier [E] 84 E6
Şamlı [TR] 150 D6
Sammakkovaara [FIN] 188 E2
Sammatti [FIN] 186 D4
Sammi [FIN] 186 B6
Samnaun [CH] 72 B2
Samo [I] 124 C7
Samobor [HR] 74 E6
Samoëns [F] 70 C3
Samoklęski [PL] 38 E5
Samokov [BG] 146 G5
Samokov [MK] 128 D2
Samolva [RUS] 198 G3
Samoranovo [BG] 146 F6
Šamorín [SK] 62 G5
Samos [E] 78 E4
Sámos [GR] 152 C5
Samoš [SRB] 142 H1
Samos, Monasterio de- [E] 78 E4
Samostan Pleterje [SLO] 74 D6
Samothráki [GR] 130 F4
Samovodene [BG] 148 C3
Sampatikí [GR] 136 F3
Samper [E] 84 E6
Samper de Calanda [E] 90 F5
Sampéyre [I] 108 F2
Sampo [RUS] 198 G1
Samtens [D] 20 D2
Samugheo [I] 118 C5
Saná [GR] 130 B5
Sanad [SRB] 76 E5
San Adrián [E] 84 A5
San Agustín [E] 98 C3
San Agustín [E] 100 C6
San Andrés [E] 78 D1
San Anton Leitza [E] 84 B3
Sanary-sur-Mer [F] 108 C6
San Asensio [E] 82 G6
Sanat Eufemia [E] 82 D4
Sanaüja [E] 92 C3
San Bartolomé de las Abiertas [E] 96 D1
San Bartolomé de la Torre [E] 94 E5
San Bartolomeo in Galdo [I] 120 F1
San Benedetto dei Marsi [I] 116 C5
San Benedetto del Tronto [I] 116 D2
San Benedetto in Alpe [I] 110 G5
San Benedetto Po [I] 110 E2
San Benito [E] 96 D5
San Bernardino [CH] 70 G2
San Bernardino, Tunnel del- [CH] 70 G2
San Biagio di Callalta [I] 72 F6
San Biágio Plátani [I] 126 D3
San Bonifácio [I] 72 C6
San Bruzio [I] 114 F3
San Calogero [I] 126 C3
San Cándido / Innichen [I] 72 E3
San Carlos del Valle [E] 96 G5
San Casciano dei Bagni [I] 114 G2
San Casciano in Val di Pesa [I] 110 F6
San Cataldo [I] 122 G4
San Cataldo [I] 126 E3
Sancergues [F] 56 D3
Sancerre [F] 56 D3
Sancey-le-Grand [F] 58 C5
Sanchidrián [E] 88 E4
San Chírico Raparo [I] 120 H5
San Cipirello [I] 126 C2
San Claudio al Chienti [I] 116 C1
San Clemente [E] 98 A4
San Clemente a Casuria [I] 116 D4
San Clemente al Vomano [I] 116 D3
San Clodio, Monasterio de- [E] 78 C4
Sancoins [F] 56 D4
San Cosme / Barreiros [E] 78 F2
San Cristóbal de la Laguna [E] 100 C5
San Cristóbal de la Vega [E] 88 E3
Sancti Petri [E] 100 F4
Sancti-Spíritus [E] 88 A3
Sancti-Spíritus [E] 96 C3
Sancti Spiritus, Convent del- [E] 98 F4
Sancy-sur-Nied [F] 44 F4
Sand [N] 164 B1
Sand [N] 172 C4
Sånda [N] 164 E4
Sanda [N] 164 F2
Sanda [S] 174 G6
San Damiano d'Asti [I] 70 E6
Sandane [N] 180 C5
San Daniele del Friuli [I] 72 G4
San Daniele Po [I] 110 D2
Sandanski [BG] 130 B2
Sandared [S] 162 B2
Sandarne [S] 174 E2
Sandau [D] 34 C1
Sandaucourt [F] 44 E6
Sandbach [GB] 10 D5
Sande [D] 18 C4
Sande [N] 164 H2
Sande [N] 170 C1
Sandefjord [N] 164 H3
Sandeid [N] 164 B1
Sandem [N] 166 C2
San Demetrio Corone [I] 124 D4
Sanden [N] 164 F2
Sander [N] 172 C5
Sandhem [S] 162 C1
Sandias [E] 78 C5
Sandıklı [TR] 152 H3
Sand in Taufers / Campo Túres [I] 72 E2
Sandizell [D] 60 D3
Sandl [A] 62 C3
Sandla [EST] 198 C3
Sandnäset [S] 184 D4
Sandnes [N] 164 B3
Sandnes [N] 164 F3
Sandnes [N] 194 D2
Sandness [GB] 6 G3
Sandnessjøen [N] 190 D2
Sando [E] 80 G6
Sandö Bro [S] 184 F3
Sandomierz [PL] 52 D2
San Dónaci [I] 122 G4
San Donà di Piave [I] 72 F6
San Donato Milanese [I] 70 G5
Sandøreng [N] 190 E3
Sándorfalva [H] 76 E4
Sandown [GB] 12 H5
S. Andrea [I] 72 C6
S. Andrea [I] 120 D2
S. Andrea Apostolo dello Iónio [I] 124 E6
S. Andrés del Rabanedo [E] 78 H5
Sandrigo [I] 72 D6
Šandrovac [HR] 74 G5
Sandsbraten [N] 170 G5
Sandsjö [S] 172 G1
Sandsjö [S] 190 G5
Sandsjön [S] 166 F1
Sandsjönäs [S] 190 G4
Sandslån [S] 184 F3
Sandsletta [N] 192 D4
Sandsøy [N] 192 E3
Sandstad [N] 172 D4
Sandstad [N] 190 A6
Sandstedt [D] 18 D4
Sandur [FR] 160 A2
Sandvatn [N] 164 C4
Sandve [N] 164 A2
Sandvig [DK] 158 E4
Sandvik [N] 172 D2
Sandvik [S] 162 G4
Sandvika [N] 164 H1
Sandvika [N] 190 C6
Sandvika [N] 190 D2
Sandvikal [N] 164 C5
Sandviken [S] 174 E4
Sandvikvåg [N] 170 A5
Sandwich [GB] 14 G5
San Emiliano [E] 78 G4
San Esteban [E] 84 B3
San Esteban de Gormaz [E] 88 H3
San Fele [I] 120 G3
San Felice Circeo [I] 120 B2
San Felice in Balsignano [I] 122 D2
San Felice sul Panaro [I] 110 F2
San Ferdinando di Púglia [I] 120 H2
San Fernando [E] 100 F4
San Francisco [E] 82 B6
San Fratello [I] 126 F2
San Fruttuoso [I] 110 B3
Sånga [S] 184 F2
San Galgano, Abbazia di- [I] 114 F2
Sangarcía [E] 88 E4
San Gavino Monreale [I] 118 C6
Sangazi [TR] 150 F3
San Gemini [I] 116 A3
San Gemini Fonte [I] 116 A3
Sangerhausen [D] 34 B5
San Germano [I] 70 E5
San Gimignano [I] 110 E6
San Ginesio [I] 116 C2
Sanginkylä [FIN] 196 E4
San Giorgio [I] 118 D6
San Giorgio di Livenza [I] 72 F6
San Giórgio di Nogaro [I] 72 G5
San Giorgio Iónico [I] 122 F4
San Giovanni, Grotta- [I] 122 F4
San Giovanni, Grotta di- [I] 118 B6
San Giovanni al Mavone [I] 116 C4
San Giovanni a Piro [I] 120 G5
San Giovanni di Sínis [I] 118 B5
San Giovanni in Croce [I] 110 D2
San Giovanni in Fiore [I] 124 E4
San Giovanni in Persiceto [I] 110 F3
San Giovanni in Venere [I] 116 E4
San Giovanni Lupatoto [I] 72 C6
San Giovanni Rotondo [I] 116 G6
San Giovanni Suergiu [I] 118 B7
San Giovanni Valdarno [I] 110 F6
San Giovenale [I] 114 H4
Sangis [S] 196 C2
San Giuliano Terme [I] 110 D5
San Giuseppe Jato [I] 126 C2
San Giustino [I] 110 G6
San Giusto [I] 116 B2
Sangla [EST] 198 F3
San Godenzo [I] 110 F5
Sangonera la Verde [E] 104 C3
Sangüesa / Zangoza [E] 84 C5
Sanguinet [F] 66 B4
Sáni [GR] 130 B6
San Ignacio de Loiola [E] 82 H4
Sanitz [D] 20 C3
San Javier [E] 104 D4
San José [E] 102 G6
San José / Sant Josep [E] 104 C5
San José del Valle [E] 100 G4
San Juan de Alicante / Sant Joan d'Alacant [E] 104 E2
San Juan del Olmo [E] 88 D4
San Juan de los Terreros [E] 104 B4
San Juan del Puerto [E] 94 E6
San Juan de Muskiz [E] 82 G3
San Juan de Ortega [E] 82 F6
Sankovo [RUS] 202 E1
Sankt Andrä [A] 62 G5
Sankt Gertraud / Santa Gertrude [I] 72 C3
Sankt Kathrein am Hauenstein [A] 62 E6
Sankt Leonhard [A] 72 C2
Sankt Leonhard in Passeier / San Leonardo in Passiria [I] 72 D2
Sankt Magdalena / Santa Maddalena Vallalta [I] 72 E2
Sankt Margareten [A] 74 B3
Sankt Martin [A] 60 G6
Sankt-Michaelisdonn [D] 18 E3
Sankt-Peterburg [RUS] 178 H4
Sankt Valentin auf der Haide / San Valentino alla Muta [I] 72 B2
San Lazzaro di Savena [I] 110 F3
San Leo [I] 110 H5
San Leonardo [I] 120 H1
San Leonardo, Monasterio de- [E] 88 C3
San Leonardo de Yagüe [E] 90 A2
San Leonardo in Passíria / Sankt Leonhard in Passeier [I] 72 D2
San Lorenzo [I] 124 C8
San Lorenzo de Calatrava [E] 96 E5
San Lorenzo de El Escorial [E] 88 F5
San Lorenzo de la Parrilla [E] 98 B2
San Lorenzo in Campo [I] 112 B6
San Lorenzo Nuovo [I] 114 G3
San Luca [I] 124 C7
Sanlúcar de Barrameda [E] 100 F3
Sanlúcar la Mayor [E] 94 G6
San Lúcido [I] 124 D4
Sanluri [I] 118 C6
San Marcello Pistoiese [I] 110 E4
San Marco Argentano [I] 124 D4
San Marco dei Cavoti [I] 120 F2
San Marco in Lamis [I] 116 G6
San Marino [RSM] 110 H5
Sânmartin [RO] 76 H2
San Martín de la Vega [E] 88 F6
San Martín del Pedroso [E] 80 G4
San Martín del Rey Aurelio / Sotrondio [E] 78 H4
San Martín de Pusa [E] 96 E1
San Martín de Unx [E] 84 B5
San Martín de Valdeiglesias [E] 88 E5
San Martino Buon Albergo [I] 72 C6
San Martino dei Colli [I] 114 H2
San Martino della Battaglia [I] 72 C6
San Martino delle Scale [I] 126 C2

Soragna [I] 110 D2
Söråker [S] 184 F4
Sorano [I] 114 G3
Sorbas [E] 102 H5
Sorbie [GB] 8 C5
Sørbø [N] 164 B2
Sörbo [S] 166 C5
Sørbotn [N] 192 F2
Sörbygden [S] 184 D3
Sørbymagle [DK] 156 F3
Sørdal [N] 190 E1
Sore [F] 66 C4
Söréd [H] 76 B1
Søre Herefoss [N] 164 E5
Soreide [N] 170 C2
Søre Moen [N] 190 C6
Sørenget [N] 190 C5
Soresina [I] 70 H5
Sörfjärden [S] 184 E5
Sør-Flatanger [N] 190 B5
Sörfors [S] 190 H6
Sörforsa [S] 174 E1
Sórgono [I] 118 D5
Sorgues [F] 106 G3
Sörgutvik [N] 190 C4
Sørhella [N] 180 G4
Soria [E] 90 B3
Soriano Calabro [I] 124 D6
Soriano nel Cimino [I] 114 H4
Sorica [SLO] 74 B4
Sorihuela del Guadalimar [E] 102 G1
Sorita [E] 98 G1
Sørkjosen [N] 192 G2
Sorkun [TR] 152 H3
Sorkwity [PL] 24 B4
Sørli [N] 190 D5
Sörmjöle [S] 190 H6
Sørmo [N] 192 F3
Sorø [DK] 156 F3
Soroca [MD] 204 E2
Soroní [GR] 154 D3
Sorpe [E] 84 G5
Sørreisa [N] 192 F3
Sorrento [I] 120 E4
Sorsakoski [FIN] 188 D3
Sorsele [S] 190 G3
Sörsjön [S] 172 E2
Sorso [I] 118 C3
Sort [E] 84 G6
Sortavala [RUS] 188 H5
Sortino [I] 126 G4
Sörtjärn [S] 182 G4
Sortland [N] 192 D3
Sør-Tverrfjord [N] 192 H1
Sørumsand [N] 166 C1
Sorunda [S] 168 D4
Sörup [D] 156 C5
Sørup [DK] 160 D4
Sørvær [N] 194 A2
Sørværøy [N] 192 C5
Sørvågen [N] 192 C5
Sørvágur [FR] 160 A1
Sörvattnet [S] 182 E5
Sørvik [N] 190 B6
Sørvik [N] 192 E3
Sörviken [S] 184 D1
Sørvollen [N] 182 C5
Sösdala [S] 158 C2
Sos del Rey Católico [E] 84 C5
Soses [E] 90 H5
Sošice [HR] 74 D6
Sośnica [PL] 20 H5
Sośnica [PL] 50 G2
Sośnicowice [PL] 50 F3
Sosnicy [RUS] 198 H1
Sosnivka [UA] 52 H2
Sosnove [UA] 202 B7
Sosnovo [RUS] 178 G3
Sosnovo [RUS] 198 H1
Sosnovyy [RUS] 196 H1
Sosnovyy Bor [RUS] 178 F5
Sosnowica [PL] 38 F5
Sosnowiec [PL] 50 G3
Sospel [F] 108 F4
Sossano [I] 110 F1
Šoštanj [SLO] 74 D4
Sóstis [GR] 130 F2
Søstrefoss [N] 180 D4
Sostrup [DK] 160 F5
Sot [SRB] 142 F2
Sotaseter [N] 180 E5
Soteska [SLO] 74 C6
Søtholmen [N] 166 C4
Sotillo de la Adrada [E] 88 E5
Sotillo de las Palomas [E] 88 D6
Sotin [HR] 142 E1
Sotkamo [FIN] 196 F5
Sotkuma [FIN] 188 F2
Sotobañado y Priorato [E] 82 D5
Soto del Barco [E] 78 H3
Soto de los Infantes [E] 78 G3
Soto del Real [E] 88 F5
Sotos [E] 98 C2
Sotresgudo [E] 82 D5
Sotrondio / San Martín del Rey Aurelio [E] 78 H4
Sotta [F] 114 B6
Sotteville les Rouen [F] 28 B5
Sottomarina [I] 110 H1
Sottrum [D] 18 E5
Sottunga [FIN] 176 B5
Sotuélamos [E] 96 H4
Soual [F] 106 B3
Soúda [GR] 140 C4
Souesmes [F] 56 C2
Soufflenheim [F] 46 B6
Souflí [GR] 130 H2
Soúgia [GR] 140 B5
Souillac [F] 66 G4
Souilly [F] 44 D4
Soulac-sur-Mere [F] 54 B6
Soulaines-Dhuys [F] 44 C6
Soulópoulo [GR] 132 C2
Soultz [F] 44 H5
Soultz [F] 58 D3
Soumoulou [F] 84 E3
Soúnio [GR] 130 E2
Soúnio [GR] 136 H2
Souppes-sur-Loing [F] 42 G5
Sourdeval [F] 26 E4
Sourdon [F] 28 E5
Soure [P] 86 D2
Sournia [F] 92 F1
Sourotí [GR] 130 B5
Soúrpi [GR] 132 H3
Sousceyrac [F] 66 H4
Sousel [P] 86 E6
Soustons [F] 66 A6
Soutelo [E] 78 C4
Southampton [GB] 12 H5
Southend-on-Sea [GB] 14 F4
South Molton [GB] 12 E4
Southport [GB] 10 D3
South Shields [GB] 8 G6
Southwold [GB] 14 H3
Soutomaior, Castillo de- [E] 78 B4
Souvála [GR] 136 G1
Souvigny [F] 56 D5
Søvang [DK] 156 B4
Søvassli [N] 180 H1
Sovata [RO] 204 D4
Sövdeborg [S] 158 C3
Söve [TR] 150 D5
Sover [I] 72 D4
Soverato [I] 124 E6
Soveria Mannelli [I] 124 D5
Sövestad [S] 158 D3
Sovetsk [RUS] 200 D5
Sovetskiy [RUS] 178 F3
Søvik [N] 180 D3
Sovinec [CZ] 50 D4
Sovjan [AL] 128 D4
Sowia Góra [PL] 36 B2
Sowiniec [PL] 20 G6
Soyen [D] 60 F4
Søyland [N] 164 A4
Sozaro [TR] 150 C1
Sozopol [BG] 148 F4
Spa [B] 30 E5
Spacco della Regina [I] 114 F4
Spaichingen [D] 58 G3
Spakenburg [NL] 16 E4
Spalding [GB] 10 G6
Spálené Poříčí [CZ] 48 E5
Spalt [D] 46 G6
Spanchevci [BG] 146 F3
S. Pancrázio [I] 72 C3
Spandau [D] 34 E2
Spånga [S] 168 C3
Spangenberg [D] 32 F5
Spangereid [N] 164 C6
Spannberg [A] 62 F4
Španovica [HR] 142 C1
S. Pantaleón de Losa [E] 82 F4
Sparanise [I] 120 D2
Spare [LV] 198 C5
Sparreholm [S] 168 C4
Sparresholm [DK] 156 F4
Spárta [GR] 134 B6
Spartà [I] 124 B7
Spárti [GR] 136 E4
Spárto [GR] 132 D4
Spas [AL] 146 B6
Spasovo [BG] 148 G1
Spasskaya Polist' [RUS] 202 C1
Spáta [GR] 134 C6
Spatharaíoi [GR] 138 H1
Spean Bridge [GB] 6 C6
Specke [S] 166 D2
S. Pedro [P] 94 E2
S. Pedro de Cardeña [E] 82 E6
S. Pedro de Teverga [E] 78 G4
Speinshart [D] 48 B4
Spekedalssetra [N] 182 C5
Spello [I] 116 A2
Spenge [D] 32 D2
Spennymoor [GB] 10 F1
Spenshult [S] 162 B4
Spentrup [DK] 160 E5
Spercheiáda [GR] 132 F4
S. Pere de Ribes [E] 92 D4
Sperlonga [I] 120 C2
Spétses [GR] 136 F3
Speyer [D] 46 C5
Spezzano Albanese [I] 124 D3
Spicino [RUS] 198 G2
Spickendorf [D] 34 C5
Spiddal / An Spidéal [IRL] 2 B5
Spiegelau [D] 60 H2
Spiekeroog [D] 18 C3
Spielbg [D] 46 F5
Spielfeld [A] 74 D3
S. Pietro al Natisone [I] 72 H4
Spiez [CH] 70 E1
Spijkenisse [NL] 16 C5
Spílaia Diroú [GR] 136 E5
Spíli [GR] 140 D5
Spilimbergo [I] 72 F4
Spilja Hrustovača [BIH] 142 B3
Spillum [N] 190 C5
Spina, Necropoli di- [I] 110 G3
Spinalógka [GR] 140 F4
Spinazzola [I] 120 H3
Spincourt [F] 44 E3
Spind [N] 164 C5
Špindlerův-Mlýn [CZ] 50 A2
Spineta Nuova [I] 120 F4
Špionica Donja [BIH] 142 D3
Špišić Bukovica [HR] 74 G5
Spiss [A] 72 B2
Spišská Belá [SK] 52 B6
Spišská Nová Ves [SK] 64 E2
Spišské Podhradie [SK] 64 F2
Spišský Hrad [SK] 64 F2
Spišský Štvrtok [SK] 64 E2
Spital am Pyhrn [A] 62 B6
Spittal an der Drau [A] 72 H3
Spitz [A] 62 D4
Spjærøy [N] 166 B3
Spjald [DK] 160 B6
Spjelkavik [N] 180 D3
Spjutsund [FIN] 178 B4
Split [HR] 144 A2
Splügen [CH] 70 G2
Spodnja Idrija [SLO] 74 B5
Spodsbjerg [DK] 156 E4
Špogi [LV] 198 F6
Spohle [D] 18 C4
Spoleto [I] 116 B3
Spoltore [I] 116 D4
Spotorno [I] 108 H3
Spøttrup [DK] 160 C4
Sprakensehl [D] 32 H1
Spręcowo [PL] 22 G4
Spreenhagen [D] 34 F3
Spremberg [D] 34 F5
Spresiano [I] 72 E5
Springe [D] 32 F2
Sproge [S] 168 F5
Spy [B] 30 D5
Spychowo [PL] 24 C4
Spydeberg [N] 166 B2
Spytkowice [PL] 50 H5
Squillace [I] 124 E6
Squinzano [I] 122 G4
Srahmore [IRL] 2 C3
Srbac [BIH] 142 C2
Srbica [KS] 146 C5
Srbobran [MNE] 204 A5
Srbobran [SRB] 76 E6
Srdevići [BIH] 144 B1
Srdiečko [SK] 64 D2
Srebărna [BG] 148 E1
Srebrenica [BIH] 142 F4
Srebrenik [BIH] 142 D3
Sredets [BG] 148 C5
Sredets [BG] 148 F5
Središče ob Dravi [SLO] 74 F4
Sredishte [BG] 148 F1
Srednje [BIH] 142 D4
Srednogortsi [BG] 130 E1
Sredno Gradishte [BG] 148 C5
Sredogriv [BG] 146 E3
Śrem [PL] 36 C3
Sremska Kamenica [SRB] 142 F1
Sremska Mitrovica [MNE] 204 A6
Sremska Mitrovica [SRB] 142 F2
Sremska Rača [SRB] 142 F2
Sremski Karlovci [SRB] 142 F2
Sribne [UA] 202 E7
Srní [CZ] 62 A2
Środa Śląska [PL] 36 C6
Środa Wielkopolska [PL] 36 D3
Srokowo [PL] 24 C3
S. Roque do Pico [P] 100 C3
Srpci [MK] 128 E3
Srp. Itebej [SRB] 76 F6
Srpska Crnja [SRB] 76 F6
Srpski Miletić [SRB] 76 C6
S. Salvador de Leyre [E] 84 C4
S. Silvestre de Guzmán [E] 94 E5
S. Stefano d'Aveto [I] 110 C3
Sta [S] 182 E1
Staaken [D] 34 E2
Sta. Ana, Monasterio de- [E] 104 C2
Staatz [A] 62 F3
Stabbestad [N] 164 F4
Stabbursnes [N] 194 C2
Stabekk [N] 166 B1
Sta. Casilda [E] 82 F5
Stachy [CZ] 48 E6
Sta. Coloma [AND] 84 H6
Sta. Coloma de G. [E] 92 E4
Sta. Cristina de Lena [E] 78 H4
Stade [D] 18 E4
Stadl a. d. Mur [A] 74 B2
Stadra [S] 166 G2
Stadskanaal [NL] 16 H3
Stadt Allendorf [D] 32 E6
Stadthagen [D] 32 F2
Stadtilm [D] 46 G1
Stadtkyll [D] 30 F6
Stadtlauringen [D] 46 F3
Stadtlohn [D] 16 G5
Stadtoldendorf [D] 32 F3
Stadtroda [D] 48 B1
Stadtsteinach [D] 46 H3
St Aegyd [A] 62 D5
Sta. Elena [E] 84 E5
Sta. Espina, Monasterio de- [E] 88 E1
Stäfa [CH] 58 G5
Staffanstorp [DK] 158 C3
Staffarda, Abbazia di- [I] 108 F2
Staffelstein [D] 46 G3
Stafford [GB] 10 E5
St-Affrique [F] 106 D3
Stágeira [GR] 130 C4
St-Agnant [F] 54 C5
St-Agrève [F] 68 E5
Stahle [D] 32 F3
Stai [N] 172 C1
Staicele [LV] 198 E4
St-Aignan [F] 40 G5
St-Aignan [F] 54 H2
Staigue Fort [IRL] 4 B4
Stainach [A] 62 B6
Staines [GB] 14 E4
Stainsland [N] 164 D4
Stainville [F] 44 D5
Stainz [A] 74 D2
Stakčín [SK] 64 H2
Stakenjokk [S] 190 E4
Stakkvik [N] 192 G1
Stalać [SRB] 146 C3
St-Alban [F] 68 C5
St Albans [GB] 14 E3
Stalden [CH] 70 E2
Stalheim [N] 170 D3
Stalheims-Kleivene Museum [N] 170 C3
Stalída [GR] 140 F4
Stall [A] 72 G2
Stallarholmen [S] 168 C3
Stallberg [D] 20 E4
Ställberg [S] 166 G1
Ställdalen [S] 166 G1
Stalon [S] 190 F4
Stalowa Wola [PL] 52 E2
St-Amand-en-Puisaye [F] 56 D2
St-Amand-les-Eaux [F] 28 G3
St-Amand-Longpré [F] 42 C6
St-Amand-Montrond [F] 56 C4
St-Amans [F] 68 C5
St-Amant-Roche-Savine [F] 68 D3
Sta. Maria da Real [E] 78 C4
Sta. Maria de Conxo [E] 78 C3
Sta. Maria de la Vega [E] 88 D2
Sta. María de Lebeña [E] 82 D3
Sta. Maria de Melque [E] 96 E2
Sta. Maria de Mezonzo [E] 78 D3
Sta. Maria la Real [E] 82 D4
Sta. Maria la Real [E] 84 A6
Stambolovo [BG] 148 C3
St-Ambroix [F] 106 F2
Sta. Maria de Bellpuig de les Avellanes [E] 92 B2
St-Amé [F] 58 C3
Stameriena [LV] 198 F4
Stamford [GB] 14 E1
Stamná [GR] 132 E5
St-Amour [F] 56 H6
Stampfen [A] 72 G2
Stams [A] 72 C1
Stamsund [N] 192 D4
St Andrä [A] 74 C3
St-André [F] 42 D3
St Andreasberg [D] 32 G4
St-André-de-Cubzac [F] 66 D3
St-André-les-Alpes [F] 108 D3
St Andrews [GB] 8 F2
Stånga [S] 168 G5
Stange [N] 172 C4
Stangerum [DK] 160 E5
Stanghelle [N] 170 B3
Staniewice [PL] 22 B2
Stanišić [SRB] 76 C5
Stanisławów [PL] 38 C3
Štanjel [SLO] 72 H5
Stanjevci [MK] 128 F1
Staňkov [CZ] 48 D5
St Annaparochie [NL] 16 F2
Stanós [GR] 130 C4
Stans [CH] 58 F6
Stansstad [CH] 58 F6
St-Anthème [F] 68 E3
St-Antoine [F] 68 G4
St.-Antoine, Chapelle- [F] 84 D3
St Anton [A] 72 B1
St-Antonin-Noble-Val [F] 66 G6
St. Antonino [F] 114 B3
Stany [PL] 52 D2
Stanzach [A] 60 C6
St-Août [F] 54 H4
Stapar [SRB] 76 C6
Staphorst [NL] 16 F3
Stapnes [N] 164 B4
Stąporków [PL] 38 B6
Stara [PL] 36 H6
Stará Bystrica [SK] 50 G6
Stara Cerlev [SLO] 74 C6
Starachowice [PL] 38 B6
Stara Gradiška [HR] 142 C2
Stara Krašnica [PL] 50 B1
Stará L'ubovňa [SK] 52 C6
Stara Moravica [SRB] 76 D5
Stara Novalja [HR] 112 F3
Stara Pazova [SRB] 142 G2
Stara Reka [BG] 148 D4
Stará Turá [SK] 62 H3
Stará Voda [CZ] 48 C4
Staravolya [BY] 38 G1
Stara Wrona [PL] 38 B2
Staraya Russa [RUS] 202 C2
Staraya Toropa [RUS] 202 C3
Stara Zagora [BG] 148 C5
Starcevo [BG] 130 E2
Stare Czarnowo [PL] 20 F5
Stare Dębno [PL] 20 H4
Stare Hory [SK] 64 C2
Stare Jeżewo [PL] 24 E5
Staré Město [CZ] 50 C3
Staré Město [CZ] 50 C4
Staré Město [CZ] 62 H2
Stare Osieczno [PL] 20 H6
Stargard-Szczeciński [PL] 20 F5
Stårheim [N] 180 C5
Stari Bar [MNE] 144 E5
Stari Dojran [MK] 128 H3
Starigrad [HR] 112 F3
Stari Grad [HR] 144 A2
Stari Gradac [HR] 74 G5
Starigrad Paklenica [HR] 112 G4
Stari Mikanovci [HR] 142 D1
Stari Slankamen [SRB] 142 G2
Staritsa [RUS] 202 E3
Starjak [HR] 74 E6
Starkov [CZ] 50 B5
Starnberg [D] 60 D4
Starod [SLO] 112 E1
Starodub [RUS] 202 E5
Starogard [PL] 20 G4
Starogard Gdański [PL] 22 E3
Starokostiantyniv [UA] 202 C8
Staromieście [PL] 50 H2
Staro Nagoričane, Manastir- [MK] 146 D6
Staro Oryakhovo [BG] 148 F3
Staropol'ye [RUS] 198 G1
Starosel [BG] 148 B5
Staroselci [BG] 148 A3
Staro selo [BG] 148 A4
Staro Selo [BG] 148 D1
Starożreby [PL] 36 H2
Starup [DK] 156 B2
Starup [DK] 156 C3
Starý Bernštejn [CZ] 48 G2
Stary Borek [PL] 52 E4
Starychi [UA] 52 G3
Stary Dzierzgoń [PL] 22 F4
Stary Gózd [PL] 38 B5
Starý Hrozenkov [CZ] 64 A2
Staryi Sambir [UA] 52 F5
Stary Plzenec [CZ] 48 E5
Stary Sącz [PL] 52 B5
Starý Smokovec [SK] 52 B6
Stary Szelków [PL] 38 B1
Starý Vestec [CZ] 48 G3
Stary Wieś [PL] 38 E6
Staryya Darohi [BY] 202 C6
Starzyny [PL] 50 H2
St-Astier [F] 66 F3
Staszów [PL] 52 C2
Stat. Angístis [GR] 130 C3
Stathelle [N] 164 G3
Statland [N] 190 C5
Statte [I] 122 E4
St-Aubane [F] 108 E4
St-Auban-sur-l'Ouvèze [F] 108 B2
St-Aubin-d'Aubigné [F] 26 C5
St-Aubin-du-Cormier [F] 26 D5
St-Aubin-sur-Mer [F] 26 F3
St.-Augustin, Château de- [F] 56 D4
St-Aulaye [F] 66 E2
Staume [N] 180 C5
Staupitz [D] 34 E5
St Austell [GB] 12 C5
Stava [S] 162 D1
Stavang [N] 180 B6
Stavanger [N] 164 B3
Stavaträsk [S] 196 A4
Stave [N] 192 E3
Staveley [GB] 10 F5
Stavelot [B] 30 E5
Stavenisse [NL] 16 C6
Staveren [NL] 16 E3
Stavern [D] 16 H3
Stavern [N] 164 G3
Stavertsi [BG] 148 A3
Stavkirke [N] 164 F2
Stavkirke [N] 170 E1
St-Avold [F] 44 F4
Stavre [S] 182 H3
Stavreviken [S] 184 E4
Stavrochóri [GR] 140 G5
Stavrodrómi [GR] 136 D2
Stavrós [GR] 128 G4
Stavrós [GR] 130 C4
Stavrós [GR] 132 C5
Stavrós [GR] 132 G3
Stavrós [GR] 134 B4
Stavrós [GR] 134 C6
Stavrós [GR] 140 C4
Stavrós tis Psókas [CY] 154 F5
Stavroúpoli [GR] 130 E2
Stavsjø [N] 172 B3
Stavsnäs [S] 168 E3
Stawiguda [PL] 22 G4
Stawiski [PL] 24 D5
Stawiszyn [PL] 36 E4
St-Aygulf [F] 108 D5
St-Bard [F] 68 B1
St. Barthélemy [CH] 70 C1
St.-Barthélemy [F] 26 E4
St. Bartholomä [D] 60 G6
St-Béat [F] 84 F5
St-Beauzély [F] 106 D2
St-Benin [F] 56 D4
St-Benoît-du-Sault [F] 54 G5
St-Benoît-sur-Loire [F] 42 F6
St-Bertrand-de-Comminges [F] 84 F4
St.-Blaise [F] 106 G5
St Blasien [D] 58 F4
St-Blin [F] 44 D6
St-Bonnet-de-Joux [F] 56 F6
St-Bonnet-en-Champsaur [F] 68 H6
St-Bonnet-le-Château [F] 68 E3
St-Brevin-les-Pins [F] 40 E6
St-Brice-en-Coglès [F] 26 D5
St-Brieuc [F] 26 B4
St-Calais [F] 42 C5
St-Cast-le-Guildo [F] 26 B4
St-Céré [F] 66 H4
St-Cergue [CH] 70 B1
St-Cernin [F] 68 B4
St-Chamas [F] 106 H4
St-Chamond [F] 68 F3
St-Chély-d'Apcher [F] 68 C5
St-Chély-d'Aubrac [F] 68 B5
St-Chinian [F] 106 D4
St Christina / Santa Cristina [I] 72 D3
St Christoph [A] 72 B1
St. Christophe-en-Oisans [F] 70 A5
St-Ciers-sur-Gironde [F] 66 D2
St-Cirq-Lapopie [F] 66 G5
St.-Clair [F] 26 F3
St-Clar [F] 66 E6
St-Claud [F] 54 E6
St-Claude [F] 70 A1
St Clears [GB] 12 D2
St-Clément [F] 44 F6
St-Clément-sur-Durance [F] 108 E2
St-Côme-d'Olt [F] 68 B5
St.-Cosme-en-Vairais [F] 26 G6
St-Cyprien [F] 66 F4
St-Cyprien-Plage [F] 92 G1
St. David's [GB] 12 D1
St-Denis [F] 42 F3
St-Denis-d'Oléron [F] 54 B5
St-Denis d'Orques [F] 42 A5
St-Didier-en-Velay [F] 68 E4
St-Dié [F] 58 D2
St-Dizier [F] 44 C5
St-Donat-sur-l'Herbasse [F] 68 F4
St. Doulagh's Church [IRL] 2 F6
Steane [N] 164 E2
Ste-Anne-d'Auray [F] 26 A6
Ste-Anne-la-Palud [F] 40 B2
Ste.-Barbe [F] 40 C3
Stechelberg [CH] 70 E2
Štěchovice [CZ] 48 F4
Steckborn [CH] 58 G4
Ste-Croix [CH] 58 C6
Ste-Croix-Volvestre [F] 84 G4
Steeg [A] 72 B1
Steenbergen [NL] 16 C6
Ste.-Engrâce [F] 84 D4
Ste-Enimie [F] 68 C6
Steenvoorde [F] 28 E2
Steenwijk [NL] 16 F3
Stefáni [GR] 132 D3
Štefanikova Mohyla [SK] 62 H3
Stefaniná [GR] 130 C4
Stefanovo [BG] 148 F2
Ste-Foy-la-Grande [F] 66 E3
Stegaros [N] 170 E5
Ste-Gauburge-Ste-Colombe [F] 26 G5
Stege [DK] 156 G4
Stegeborg [S] 168 B5
Stegersbach [A] 74 E2
Stegna [PL] 22 E2
St-Egrève [F] 68 H4
Ste-Hélène [F] 66 C3
Ste-Hermine [F] 54 C3
Stehnovo [RUS] 198 H4
Steigen [N] 192 D5
Steilwände [D] 60 B5
Stein [A] 62 D4
Stein [D] 46 G5
Stein [N] 170 H5
Stein [N] 190 B5
Steinaberg bru [N] 170 C5
Steinach [A] 72 D2
Stein am Rhein [CH] 58 G4
Steinau [D] 46 E2
Steinbach [D] 46 H2
Steinberg [A] 74 F1
Steinberg [D] 156 C5
Steinberg am Rofan [A] 60 E6
Steine [N] 170 B2
Steinestø [N] 170 B3
Steinfeld [A] 72 G3
Steinfeld [D] 30 G5
Steinfeld [D] 32 D1
Steinfurt [D] 16 H5
Steingaden [D] 60 D5
Steinhagen [D] 20 C3
Steinhausen [D] 60 B4
Steinheim [D] 32 E3
Steinhorst [D] 32 G1
Steinibach [CH] 58 G6
Steinkjer [N] 190 C5
Steinløysa [N] 180 E2
Stein Pass [A/D] 60 G6
Steinsåsen [N] 182 D4
Steinsberg [D] 46 C5
Steinsbøle [S] 170 F5
Steinsburg [D] 46 F2
Steinsdal [N] 190 B6
Steinsholt [N] 164 G2
Steinsøynes [N] 180 F1
Steinsvik [N] 180 C4
Ste.- Jalle [F] 108 B2
Steknica [PL] 22 C1
Ste-Livrade-sur-Lot [F] 66 E5
Stellendam [NL] 16 C5
St-Eloy-les-Mines [F] 56 C6
Ste-Marie-aux-Mines [F] 58 D2
Ste-Marie-de-Campan [F] 84 F4
Ste-Marie-du-Mont [F] 26 E2
Ste-Maure-de-Touraine [F] 54 F3
Ste-Maxime [F] 108 D5
Ste-Menehould [F] 44 C4
Ste-Mère-Eglise [F] 26 E2
St-Emilion [F] 66 D3
Sten [S] 162 D1
Stenay [F] 44 D3
Stenbjerg [DK] 160 B4
Stenbo [S] 162 G3
Stendal [D] 34 C2
Stende [LV] 198 C5
Steneby [S] 166 D4
Stengelsrud [N] 164 G1
St Englmar [D] 60 G2
Stenhammar [S] 168 B4
Stenhamra [S] 168 D3
Stení [GR] 134 C4
Steninge [S] 160 H5
Steninge [S] 168 D2
Stenlille [DK] 156 F3
Stenløse [DK] 156 G2
Stennäs [S] 190 G6
Stenó [GR] 136 E2
Stenoma [GR] 132 F4
Stensele [S] 190 F4
Stensjö [S] 162 G3
Stensjön [S] 162 E2
Stenstorp [S] 166 F6
Stensträsk [S] 190 H4
Stenstrup [DK] 156 D4
Stensund [S] 190 G2
Stensund [S] 190 G3
Stensunda [S] 168 E1
Stenträsk [S] 190 H2
Stenudden [S] 190 G2
Stenungsund [S] 160 G1
Steornabhagh / Stornoway [GB] 6 C2
Stepanci [MK] 128 E2
Stepnica [PL] 20 F4
Stepojevac [SRB] 146 B1
Sterdyń-Osada [PL] 38 D2
Sterehushche [UA] 204 G3
Sterlawki Wielkie [PL] 24 C3
Stern, Manastir- [BIH] 142 C2
Stern / la Villa [I] 72 E3
Stérna [GR] 130 D2
Sternberg [D] 20 B4
Šternberk [CZ] 48 H6
Šternberk [CZ] 50 D5
Stérnes [GR] 140 C4
Stérnia [GR] 138 E1
Sterringi [N] 180 F5
Sterzing / Vipiteno [I] 72 D2
Ste-Sévère [F] 56 B5
Stes-Maries-de-la-Mer [F] 106 F5
St. Estèphe [F] 66 C2
Ste-Suzanne [F] 42 A4
Stęszew [PL] 36 C3
Štětí [CZ] 48 F2
St-Étienne [F] 68 E3
St-Étienne [F] 108 C3
St-Étienne-de-Baïgorry [F] 84 C3
St-Etienne-de-St-Geoirs [F] 68 G4
St-Etienne-de-Tinée [F] 108 E3
Ste-Tulle [F] 108 C4
Stevenage [GB] 14 E3
Stevrek [BG] 148 D3
Stewarton [GB] 8 D3
Steyerberg [D] 32 E1
Steyersberg [A] 62 E6
Steyr [A] 62 B5
Steyr-Durchbruch [A] 62 B5
Stezherovo [BG] 148 B2
St-Fargeau [F] 56 D2
St.-Fiacre [F] 40 C3
St-Firmin [F] 68 H6
St-Florent [F] 40 G6
St-Florent [F] 56 B3
St-Florent [F] 114 C3
St.-Florent-des-Bois [F] 54 C3
St-Florentin [F] 42 H6
St. Florian [A] 60 H4
St-Flour [F] 68 C4
St-Fort-sur-Gironde [F] 66 D1
St.-Fort-sur-le-Né [F] 66 D1
St-Fulgent [F] 54 C2
St Gallen [A] 62 C6
St Gallen [CH] 58 H5
St Gallenkirch [A] 72 B1
St-Galmier [F] 68 E3
St. Gangolf [D] 44 F3
St-Gaudens [F] 84 G4
St-Gaultier [F] 54 G4
St-Geniez-d'Olt [F] 68 B6
St-Genis-de-Saintonge [F] 66 D1
St-Genix-sur-Guiers [F] 68 H3
St. George [CH] 70 B1
St Georgen [A] 60 H5
St Georgen [A] 74 C2
St Georgen [D] 58 F3
St-Georges [F] 40 G6
St-Georges-de-Didonne [F] 54 C6
St. Georges-on-Couzan [F] 68 E2
St-Geours-de-Maremne [F] 66 B6
St-Germain [F] 42 F3
St-Germain [F] 66 G2
St-Germain-de-Calberte [F] 106 F2
St-Germain-de-Joux [F] 68 H2
St-Germain-des-Fossés [F] 56 D6
St-Germain-des-Vaux [F] 26 D1
St-Germain-du-Bois [F] 56 G5
St-Germain-du-Plain [F] 56 G5
St-Germain-Laval [F] 68 E2
St-Germain-Lembron [F] 68 C3
St-Germain-l'Herm [F] 68 D3
St-Germain-Plage [F] 26 D3
St-Germer-de-Fly [F] 28 D6
St-Gervais [F] 106 D3
St-Gervais-d'Auvergne [F] 68 C1
St-Gervais-les-Bains [F] 70 C3
St-Géry [F] 66 G5
St-Gildas-des-Bois [F] 40 E5
St Gilgen [A] 60 H5
St-Gilles [F] 106 G4
St-Gilles-Croix-de-Vie [F] 54 B2
St-Gilles-Pligeaux [F] 26 A4
St-Gingolph [CH] 70 C2
St-Girons [F] 84 G5
St-Girons-en-Marensin [F] 66 B5
St-Girons-Plage [F] 66 A5

St Goar [D] 46 B2
St Goarshausen [D] 46 B2
St-Gobain [F] 28 F6
St-Gorgon-Main [F] 58 B5
St-Guénolé [F] 40 B3
St-Guilhem-le-Desert [F] 106 E3
St Helens [GB] 10 D4
St Helier [GBJ] 26 C3
St. Hilaire Cottes [F] 28 E3
St-Hilaire-de-Villefranche [F] 54 C5
St-Hilaire-du-Harcouët [F] 26 D5
St-Hippolyte [F] 58 C5
St-Hippolyte-du-Fort [F] 106 F3
St. Höga [S] 160 G1
St-Honoré les-Bains [F] 56 E4
St-Hubert [B] 44 D1
Stia [I] 110 G5
Sticciano Scalo [I] 114 F2
Stiefern [A] 62 E3
Stiens [NL] 16 F2
Stift Zwettl [A] 62 D3
Stigen [N] 172 E2
Stigen [S] 166 D5
Stigfoss [N] 180 E3
Stigliano [I] 122 C4
Stigliano, Bagni di- [I] 114 H5
Stignano [I] 124 D7
Stigsjö [S] 184 F4
Stigtomta [S] 168 C4
Stiklestad [N] 190 C6
Stilla [N] 194 B3
Stilo [I] 124 D6
St-Imier [CH] 58 D5
Stimlje [KS] 146 C5
St Ingbert [D] 44 G4
Stintino [I] 118 B2
Štip [MK] 128 F1
Stirling [GB] 8 E3
Štirovača [HR] 112 F3
Štítary [CZ] 62 E2
Štítnik [SK] 64 E3
Štíty [CZ] 50 C4
St Ives [GB] 12 B5
St Ives [GB] 14 F2
Stixenstein [A] 62 E6
St-Jacut [F] 26 C4
St. Jakob [A] 72 F2
St Jakob im Rosental [A] 74 B3
St-James [F] 26 D5
Stjärnsund [S] 166 G4
Stjärnsund [S] 174 D5
St. Jaume d'Enveja [E] 92 B6
St-Jean-Brévelay [F] 26 A6
St-Jean-Cap-Ferrat [F] 108 F4
St. Jean d'Angély [F] 54 D5
St-Jean-de-Bournay [F] 68 G3
St-Jean-de-Losne [F] 56 H4
St-Jean-de-Luz [F] 84 B2
St-Jean-de-Maurienne [F] 70 B5
St-Jean-de-Monts [F] 54 A2
St-Jean-du-Bruel [F] 106 E3
St-Jean-du-Gard [F] 106 F2
St-Jean-du-Liget, Chapelle- [F] 54 G3
St-Jean-en-Royans [F] 68 G5
St-Jean-le-Thomas [F] 26 D4
St-Jean-Pied-de-Port [F] 84 C3
St. Jeans-d'Arves [F] 70 B5
St-Jeoire [F] 70 B2
St. Joan de Penyagolosa [E] 98 F2
St Johann am Tauern [A] 74 C1
St Johann im Pongau [A] 72 G1
St Johann in Tirol [A] 60 F6
St Johnstown [IRL] 2 F2
Stjørdal [N] 182 C1
St.-Jores [F] 26 D3
St-Jorioz [F] 70 B3
St-Jory [F] 84 H3
St-Jouan-de-l'Isle [F] 26 B5
St-Jouin-de-Marnes [F] 54 E3
St-Juéry [F] 106 C2
St-Julien [F] 56 H6
St-Julien [F] 84 G4
St-Julien-Chapteuil [F] 68 E4
St-Julien-de-Vouvantes [F] 40 G5
St. Julien-du-Verdon [F] 108 D4
St-Julien-en-Beauchêne [F] 68 G6
St.-Julien-en-Born [F] 66 B5
St-Julien-en-Genevois [F] 70 B2
St-Julien-l'Ars [F] 54 F4
St-Junien [F] 54 F6
St Just [GB] 12 B5
St-Just-en-Chaussée [F] 28 E6
St-Just-en-Chevalet [F] 68 E2
St-Justin [F] 66 D5
St. Kanzian [A] 74 C3
St Lambrecht [A] 74 B2
St-Lary-Soulan [F] 84 F5
St-Laurent [F] 26 E3
St-Laurent [F] 66 G1
St.-Laurent-de-la-Cabrerisse [F] 106 C5
St.-Laurent-de-la-Salanque [F] 92 G1
St-Laurent-des-Autels [F] 54 C1
St.-Laurent-en-Gâtines [F] 54 G1
St-Laurent-en-Grandvaux [F] 70 B1
St-Laurent-les-Bains [F] 68 D6
St-Laurent-Médoc [F] 66 C2
St-Leger [F] 56 F4
St.-Léon, Chapelle- [F] 44 G5
St-Léonard-de-Noblat [F] 66 H1
St Leonhard [A] 62 D4
St-Leu-d'Esserent [F] 42 F2
St-Lizier [F] 84 G4
St-Lô [F] 26 E3
St Lorenzen [A] 72 F3
St-Louis [F] 58 E4
St-Loup-sur-Semouse [F] 58 C3
St-Luc [CH] 70 D2
St-Lunaire [F] 26 C4
St-Lys [F] 84 H3
St-Macaire [F] 66 D4
St-Maclou [F] 26 G3
St-Maixent-l'Ecole [F] 54 D4
St. Malm [S] 168 B4
St-Malo [F] 26 C4
St-Mamest [F] 66 F3
St. Marcel [F] 70 B4
St-Marcellin [F] 68 G4
St. Marcellin-en-Forez [F] 68 E3
St. Marein [A] 74 E2
St Margaret's Hope [GB] 6 G2
St. Märgen [D] 58 F3
St. Maria [D] 46 E6
St. Maria zu den Engeln [CH] 58 G5
St-Mars-la-Jaille [F] 40 G6
St. Martin [A] 62 C3
St. Martin [F] 40 E5
St-Martin-d'Auxigny [F] 56 C3
St-Martín-de-Crau [F] 106 G4
St-Martin-de-Londres [F] 106 E3
St. Martin-d'Entraunes [F] 108 E3
St-Martin-de-Ré [F] 54 B4
St-Martin-du-Canigou [F] 92 F1
St-Martin-Lestra [F] 68 F3
St-Martin-l'Heureux [F] 44 C3
St. Martin Tennengebirge [A] 60 H6
St-Martin-Vésubie [F] 108 F3
St-Martory [F] 84 G4
St-Mathieu [F] 66 F1
St-Mathieu, Pointe de- [F] 40 A2
St-Mathieu-de-Tréviers [F] 106 E3
St-Maurice [CH] 70 C2
St-Maurice-la-Clouère [F] 54 E4
St. Maurice la Sotterraine [F] 54 G5
St-Maurice-Navacelles [F] 106 E3
St Maurice-sur-Moselle [F] 58 C3
St Mawes [GB] 12 C5
St. Maximin-la-Ste-Baume [F] 108 C5
St-Méen [F] 26 B5
St. Meinrad [CH] 58 G5
St. Mellösa [S] 166 H3
St Michael [A] 74 C1
St. Michael [A] 74 F2
St Michael i. Lungau [A] 72 H2
St Michel / Mikkeli [FIN] 188 C6
St.-Michel-de Cuxa [F] 92 F1
St-Michel-de-Maurienne [F] 70 B5
St. Michel de Rieufret [F] 66 C4
St-Michel-en-Grève [F] 40 D1
St-Michel-en-l'Herm [F] 54 C4
St-Michel-Mont-Mercure [F] 54 C3
St-Mihiel [F] 44 D4
St. Miquel del Fai [E] 92 E3
St-Morand [F] 58 D4
St Moritz [CH] 70 H2
St-Nazaire [F] 40 E6
St. Nazaire les Eymes [F] 68 H4
St-Nectaire [F] 68 C2
St Neots [GB] 14 E2
St.-Nicodème [F] 26 A5
St-Nicolas [F] 40 E5
St.-Nicolas (St-Niklaas) [B] 28 H2
St Nicolas-de-Port [F] 44 E5
St-Nicolas-de-Redon [F] 40 E5
St-Nicolas-du-Pélem [F] 26 A4
St-Niklaas (St.-Nicolas) [B] 28 H2
St Niklaus [CH] 70 E2
St Nikolai [A] 74 B1
Støa [N] 172 E2
Stobeč [HR] 144 A2
Stobi [MK] 128 F2
Stoby [S] 158 D1
Stocka [S] 184 E6
Stockach [D] 58 G4
Stockaryd [S] 162 D3
Stockbridge [GB] 12 H4
Stockelsdorf [D] 18 G3
Stockenboy [A] 72 H3
Stockerau [A] 62 F4
Stockheim [D] 46 G3
Stockholm [S] 168 D3
Stockport [GB] 10 E4
Stocksbo [S] 174 C1
Stocksbo [S] 174 D4
Stockton on Tees [GB] 10 F2
Stoczek Klasztorny [PL] 22 H3
Stoczek Łukowski [PL] 38 D3
Stod [CZ] 48 D5
Stod [N] 190 C5
Stöde [S] 184 D4
Stødi [N] 190 E1
St Oedenrode [NL] 30 E2
Stojan Mikhaylovski [BG] 148 E2
Stojmirovo [MK] 128 H1
Stoke-on-Trent [GB] 10 E5
Stokite [BG] 148 B4
Stokkasjøen [N] 190 D3
Stokke [N] 164 H3
Stokkemarke [DK] 156 F5
Stokkland [N] 164 F2
Stokkvågen [N] 190 D2
Stokmarknes [N] 192 D4
Štoky [CZ] 48 H5
Stola [S] 166 E5
Stolac [BIH] 144 C3
Stolberg [D] 30 F4
Stolbovo [RUS] 198 G5
Stolbzy [BY] 202 B5
Stolin [BY] 202 B7
Stollberg [D] 48 C2
Stollberg [D] 48 D2
Stöllet [S] 172 E5
Stolno [PL] 22 F5
St Olof [S] 158 D3
Stolpe [D] 20 E6
Stolpe [D] 34 E2
Stolpen [D] 34 F6
Stołpie [PL] 38 F5
Stolzenau [D] 32 E1
St-Omer [F] 28 E2
Stómio [GR] 132 G1
Stömne [S] 166 E2
Stomorska [HR] 142 A6
Ston [HR] 144 C3
Stonařov [CZ] 48 H6
Stone [GB] 10 E5
Stonehaven [GB] 8 G1
Stongfjorden [N] 180 B6
Stonglandseidet [N] 192 E3
Stønjyumfoss [N] 170 E2
Stopanja [SRB] 146 C3
Stopnica [PL] 52 C2
Storå [S] 166 H2
Storå / Isojoki [FIN] 186 B5
Stora Blåsjön [S] 190 E4
Storås [N] 180 H2
Stora Sjöfallet [S] 192 F5
Storbäck [S] 190 F4
Storborgaren [S] 190 G6
Storby [FIN] 174 H5
Stord [N] 170 B5
Stordal [N] 180 D4
Stordalen [S] 192 F4
Storebro [S] 162 F2
Storebru [N] 180 B6
Store Darum [DK] 156 B3
Storehaug [N] 170 C1
Store Heddinge [DK] 156 G3
Storekorsnes [N] 194 B2
Storelv [N] 194 A2
Storelvavoll [N] 182 D3
Store Merløse [DK] 156 F3
Store Molvik [N] 194 D1
Støren [N] 182 B2
Storestandal [N] 180 D4
Storestølen [N] 170 E3
Stor-Evdal [N] 172 C1
Storfjellseter [N] 182 B6
Storfjord [N] 192 G3
Storfors [S] 166 G2
Storforshei [N] 190 E2
Storfosna [N] 190 B6
Storfossen [N] 194 C4
Storhögen [S] 182 H2
Storholmsjö [S] 190 E6
Storjola [S] 190 E4
Storjord [N] 190 E1
Storjord [N] 190 E1
Storjorda [N] 190 E1
Storkow [D] 34 F3
Storkyro / Isokyrö [FIN] 186 B2
Storlægda [N] 182 C5
Storli [N] 180 G3
Storlien [S] 182 D2
Stormi [FIN] 176 E2
Stornara [I] 120 G2
Stornaset [S] 190 F5
Stornes [N] 192 G2
Stornorrfors [S] 190 H6
Stornoway / Steornabhagh [GB] 6 C2
Storo [I] 72 B5
Storoddan [N] 180 G1
Storsätern [S] 182 D5
Storsävarträsk [S] 190 H5
Storseterfossen [N] 180 E4
Storsjö [S] 182 E3
Storslett [N] 192 G2
Størstein [N] 192 G1
Storsteinnes [N] 192 F3
Storsund [S] 196 A3
Stortinden [N] 194 B2
Storuman [S] 190 F4
Storvallen [S] 182 D2
Storvik [S] 174 D4
Storvika [N] 190 B5
Storvollen [N] 180 H4
Storvorde [DK] 160 E4
Storvreta [S] 168 D1
Stössen [D] 34 B6
St Oswald [A] 62 C3
St. Oswald [A] 74 D3
St.-Oswald [F] 44 F3
Stotel [D] 18 D4
Sto. Toribio de Liébana [E] 82 D3
Stotternheim [D] 32 H6
St. Ottilien [D] 60 D4
Stouby [DK] 156 C2
St-Ouen [F] 28 D4
Stourbridge [GB] 10 D6
Stournaraíika [GR] 132 E2
Støvring [DK] 160 D4
Støvringgård [DK] 160 E5
Stowbtsy [BY] 202 B5
Stowmarket [GB] 14 G3
Stow-on-the-Wold [GB] 12 H2
Stožec [CZ] 62 B2
Stozher [BG] 148 F2
St-Palais [F] 84 D3
St-Palais-sur-Mer [F] 54 B6
St. Pankraz [A] 62 B5
St-Pardoux-la-Rivière [F] 66 F2
St Paul [A] 74 C3
St-Paul [F] 108 E2
St-Paul [F] 108 E4
St-Paul-Cap-de-Joux [F] 106 B3
St-Paul-de-Fenouillet [F] 106 C6
St-Paulien [F] 68 D4
St-Paul-lès-Dax [F] 66 B6
St-Pé [F] 84 E4
St-Péray [F] 68 F5
St-Père [F] 56 E3
St-Père-en-Retz [F] 40 E6
St. Peter [A] 74 B3
St. Peter [CH] 70 H1
St Peter-Ording [D] 18 D2
St Peter Port [GBG] 26 C2
St-Péver [F] 26 A4
St-Philbert [F] 54 B2
St-Pierre-d'Albigny [F] 70 A4
St-Pierre-de-Chartreuse [F] 68 H4
St-Pierre-de-Chignac [F] 66 F3
St. Pierre d'Extravache [F] 70 C5
St-Pierre-d'Oléron [F] 54 B5
St-Pierre-Église [F] 26 E2
St-Pierre-en-Port [F] 26 H2
St-Pierre-le-Moûtier [F] 56 D4
St-Pierre-Quiberon [F] 40 C5
St-Pierre-sur-Dives [F] 26 F4
St-Pois [F] 26 E4
St-Pol-de-Léon [F] 40 C1
St-Pol-sur-Ternoise [F] 28 E3
St Pölten [A] 62 E4
St-Pons-de-Thomieres [F] 106 C4
St-Porchaire [F] 54 C5
St-Pourçain-sur-Sioule [F] 56 D6
St. Priest [F] 68 G3
St-Privat [F] 68 A3
St-Quay-Portrieux [F] 26 B4
St.-Quen-en-Belin [F] 42 B5
St-Quentin [F] 28 F5
St. Quirin [D] 48 C4
Strà [I] 110 G1
Straach [D] 34 D3
Strabane [NIR] 2 F2
Strachówka [PL] 38 C2
Stracia [I] 124 C8
Stracin [MK] 146 D6
Strådalen [S] 182 E5
Stradalovo [BG] 146 F6
Stradbally [IRL] 4 B3
Stradbally [IRL] 4 F3
Stradella [I] 70 G6
Stradone [IRL] 2 E4
Strádov [CZ] 50 A4
Straduny [PL] 24 D3
Straelen [D] 30 F3
Strakonice [CZ] 48 E6
Straldzha [BG] 148 E4
Stralki [BY] 198 G6
Strålsnäs [S] 166 H6
Stralsund [D] 20 D2
St-Rambert [F] 68 E3
St-Rambert-d'Albon [F] 68 F4
St-Rambert-en-Bugey [F] 68 G2
Stramnes [N] 170 B3
Strand [N] 172 C2
Strand [N] 192 D3
Strand [S] 190 E6
Stranda [N] 180 D4
Stranda [N] 194 C2
Strandby [DK] 160 C4
Strandby [DK] 160 E2
Strandcally Castle [IRL] 4 D5
Strande [D] 18 G2
Strandebarm [N] 170 B4
Strandhill [IRL] 2 D3
Strandlykkja [N] 172 C4
Strangford [NIR] 2 G4
Strängnäs [S] 168 C3
Strängsered [S] 162 C2
Strångsjö [S] 168 B4
Stráni [CZ] 62 H2
Stranice [SLO] 74 D4
Stranorlar [IRL] 2 E2
Stránov [CZ] 48 G3
Stranraer [GB] 8 C5
St-Raphaël [F] 108 D5
Strasbourg [F] 44 H6
Strasburg [D] 20 E5
Straševina [MNE] 144 E3
Stråsjö [S] 174 D1
Strassburg [A] 74 B2
Strassengel [A] 74 D2
Strassfurt [D] 34 B4
Strasswalchen [A] 60 H5
Stratford-upon-Avon [GB] 12 H2
Strathaven [GB] 8 D3
Stratinska [BIH] 142 B2
Stratóni [GR] 130 C4
Stratoníki [GR] 130 C4
Strátos [GR] 132 E5
Straubenhardt [D] 46 C6
Straubing [D] 60 G2
Straum [N] 190 D2
Straume [N] 164 E1
Straume [N] 164 F3
Straume [N] 170 A4
Straumen [N] 180 F1
Straumen [N] 190 C4
Straumen [N] 190 C6
Straumen [N] 190 D2
Straumen [N] 192 D6
Straumfjorden [N] 192 D5
Straumsjøen [N] 192 D3
Straumsnes [N] 192 D4
Straumsnes [N] 192 E2
Straupitz [D] 34 F4
Strausberg [D] 34 F2
Straussfurt [D] 32 H5
Stravaj [AL] 128 C4
Straža [SRB] 146 D2
Strazh [RUS] 202 D5
Stražica [BG] 148 D3
Strážky [SK] 52 B6
Strážnice [CZ] 62 G2
Strážný [CZ] 62 A2
Strážske [SK] 64 H2
Štrba [SK] 64 E2
Štrbské Pleso [SK] 52 A6
Street [GB] 12 F4
Strehaia [RO] 204 C6
Strehla [D] 34 E5
Streitberg [D] 46 G4
Strękowa Góra [PL] 24 E5
Strelcha [BG] 148 A5
Strelci [BG] 148 B5
Střeliště [CZ] 50 A6
Strel'na [RUS] 178 H5
Strem [A] 74 F2
St-Rémy-de-Provence [F] 106 G4
St. Ronan [F] 40 B2
Strenči [LV] 198 E4
Strendene [N] 190 D3
Strengberg [A] 62 C4
Stresa [I] 70 F3
S. Tresund [S] 190 F4
Streufdorf [D] 46 F2
St.-Révérien [F] 56 E3
Strezimirovci [SRB] 146 E4
Strezovce [SRB] 146 D6
Strib [DK] 156 C2
Stříbro [CZ] 48 D4
Štrigova [HR] 74 F4
Strilky [UA] 52 F5
Strimasund [S] 190 E2
St-Riquier [F] 28 D4
Strittjomvare [S] 190 G3
Strittmat [D] 58 E4
Striževac [SRB] 146 E4
Strmica [HR] 142 A4
Strmilov [CZ] 48 H6
Strobl [A] 60 H5
Strøby Egede [DK] 156 G3
Stroevo [BG] 148 B5
Strofyliá [GR] 134 B4
Ströhem [D] 32 E1
Strokestown [IRL] 2 D4
Strøm [N] 190 A6
Ström [S] 166 D2
Strömåker [S] 190 F5
St.-Roman, Abbaye de- [F] 106 G3
Strömbacka [S] 184 E6
Stromberg [D] 46 B3
Strómboli [I] 124 C5
St-Rome-de-Tarn [F] 106 D2
Strömfors [S] 196 A4
Strömholm [S] 190 G3
Strømmen [N] 166 B1
Strömmen [S] 182 E5
Strömnäs [S] 190 F4
Stromness [GB] 6 F2
Strompdalen [N] 190 D4
Strömsbruk [S] 184 E6
Stromsfors [S] 168 B5
Strömsholm [S] 168 B2
Strömsillret [S] 172 E1
Strömsnäs [S] 184 D2
Strömsnäsbruk [S] 162 C5
Strømsood [N] 170 G4
Strömsrum [S] 162 G4
Strömstad [S] 166 B4
Strömsund [S] 190 E6
Strömsund [S] 190 F3
Strond [N] 164 E3
Strongoli [I] 124 F4
Stronie Śląskie [PL] 50 C3
Stroove [IRL] 2 F2
Stropkov [SK] 52 D6
Stroppo [I] 108 E2
Stroud [GB] 12 G3
Stróvles [GR] 140 B5
Stróża [PL] 50 H4
Str. Pole [PL] 22 F3
Strub Pass [A] 60 G6
Strücklingen [D] 18 C5
Struer [DK] 160 B5
Struga [MK] 128 D3
Strugi-Krasnyye [RUS] 198 H2
Strugovo [MK] 128 E3
Struha [BY] 24 G4
Struhařov [CZ] 48 G4
Struino [BG] 148 E2
Strumica [MK] 128 G2
Strumień [PL] 50 F4
Strupina [PL] 36 C5
Stružec [HR] 142 B1
Stryama [BG] 148 B5
Strycksele [S] 190 H5
Stryi [UA] 204 C2
Stryj [UA] 52 H5
Stryjów [PL] 52 F1
Strykow [PL] 36 G4
Strymonikó [GR] 130 B3
Stryn [N] 180 D5
Strzałkowo [PL] 36 E3
Strzegocin [PL] 38 B2
Strzegom [PL] 50 B1
Strzegowo [PL] 38 A1
Strzelce [PL] 34 H1
Strzelce [PL] 36 G3
Strzelce Krajeńskie [PL] 36 A1
Strzelce Małe [PL] 36 H6
Strzelce Opolskie [PL] 50 E2
Strzelin [PL] 50 C2
Strzelno [PL] 36 E2
Strzyżów [PL] 38 G6
Strzyżów [PL] 52 D4
St.-Sabin, Chapelle- [F] 66 D5
St-Saëns [F] 28 C5
St. Salvator [A] 74 B2
St.-Samson-la-Poterie [F] 28 D5
St-Satur [F] 56 D3
St-Saturnin-lès-Apt [F] 108 B3
St-Saulge [F] 56 E4
St-Sauvant [F] 54 E4
St-Sauveur-en-Puisaye [F] 56 D2
St-Sauveur-le-Vicomte [F] 26 D2
St-Sauveur-sur-Tinée [F] 108 E3
St-Savin [F] 66 D2
St-Savin-sur-Gartempe [F] 54 F4
St-Seine-l'Abbaye [F] 56 G3
St-Sernin-sur-Rance [F] 106 C3
St-Sever [F] 26 E4
St-Sever [F] 66 C6
St. Slatnik [HR] 142 C2
St-Sulpice [F] 106 B3
St. Sulpice-les-Feuilles [F] 54 G5
St. Sundby [S] 168 B3
St. Susanna [E] 92 D3
St-Symphorien [F] 66 C4
St-Symphorien-de-Lay [F] 68 E2
St-Symphorien-d'Ozon [F] 68 F3
St-Symphorien-sur-Coise [F] 68 F3
St-Thégonnec [F] 40 C2
St-Thiébault [F] 58 A2
St-Trivier-de-Courtes [F] 56 G6
St.-Trond (St.-Truiden) [B] 30 D4
St-Tropez [F] 108 D5
St.-Truiden (St.-Trond) [B] 30 D4
Stubalj [HR] 142 B1
Stubbekøbing [DK] 156 G5
Stubbergård [DK] 160 C5
Stuben [A] 72 B1
Štubik [SRB] 146 E1
Stubline [SRB] 142 G3
Studánky [CZ] 62 B3
Studena [BG] 146 F5
Studená [CZ] 48 H6
Studenec [CZ] 48 H2
Studenica [SRB] 146 B3
Studénka [CZ] 50 E5
Studenzen [A] 74 E2
Studina [RO] 148 A2
Studzienice [PL] 22 C3
Studzienki [PL] 22 C6
Stugudal [N] 182 D3
Stuguflåten [N] 180 F4
Stugun [S] 184 C2
Stuguvollmoen [N] 182 D3
Stühlingen [D] 58 F4
Stuibenfall [A] 72 C1
Stukenbrock [D] 32 E3
Stülpe [D] 34 E3
St.-Ulrich, Château- [F] 58 D2
St Ulrich / Ortisei [I] 72 D3
Stupari [BIH] 142 E3
Stupava [SK] 62 G4
Stupinigi [I] 70 D6
Stupnik [HR] 74 E6
Stuposiany [PL] 52 F6
Sturehov [S] 168 D3
Štúrovo [SK] 64 B5
St-Ursanne [CH] 58 D4
Stuttgart [D] 58 H1
St-Vaast-la-Hougue [F] 26 E2
St Valentin [A] 62 C4
St-Valery-en-Caux [F] 26 H2
St-Valery-sur-Somme [F] 28 D4
St-Vallier-de-Thiey [F] 108 E4
St-Vallier-sur-Rhône [F] 68 F4
St-Vaury [F] 54 H5
St. Veit [A] 72 F2
St Veit [A] 74 B3
St-Véran [F] 108 E1
St Vigil / Marebbe [I] 72 E3
St-Vincent [I] 70 D4
St-Vincent, Grotte de- [F] 108 D3
St-Vincent-de-Tyrosse [F] 66 A6
St. Vincent-du-Lorouër [F] 42 C6
St-Vincent-les-Forts [F] 108 D2
St Vith [B] 30 F6
St-Vivien-de-Médoc [F] 66 C1
St-Wandrille [F] 26 H3
St Wendel [D] 44 G3
St Wolfgang [A] 60 H5
St-Yan [F] 56 E6
Stykkishólmur [IS] 192 A2
Stylída [GR] 132 G4
Stymfalía [GR] 136 E1
St-Yorre [F] 68 D1
Stýpsi [GR] 134 G2
Stýra [GR] 134 D5
Styri [N] 172 C5
St-Yrieix-la-Perche [F] 66 G2
Styrnäs [S] 184 F2
Styrsö [S] 160 G2
Suadiye [TR] 150 G3
Suances [E] 82 E3
Suaredda [I] 118 E3
Subačius [LT] 200 F4
Subaşi [TR] 150 D2
Subaşı [TR] 152 D5
Subate [LV] 198 F6
Subbiano [I] 110 G6
Suben [A] 60 H4
Subiaco [I] 116 B5
Subkowy [PL] 22 E3
Subotica [MNE] 204 A5
Subotica [SRB] 76 D5
Subotište [SRB] 142 G2
Sučany [SK] 64 C2
Suceava [RO] 204 D3
Sucevița, Mănăstirea- [RO] 204 D3
Sucha [PL] 48 H1
Sucha Beskidzka [PL] 50 H4
Suchá Hora [SK] 50 H6
Suchań [PL] 20 G5
Suchdol nad Lužnicí [CZ] 62 C2
Suchedniów [PL] 38 B6
Suchorze [PL] 22 B3
Suchowola [PL] 24 E4
Suchożebry [PL] 38 D3
Süchteln [D] 30 G3
Sucina [E] 104 C3
Sućuraj [HR] 144 B3
Sudbø [N] 164 E1
Sudbury [GB] 14 F3
Suddesjaur [S] 190 H2
Süden [D] 18 E1
Süderbrarup [D] 18 F1
Süderende [D] 156 A4
Süderlügum [D] 156 B4
Sudok [S] 196 A2
Sudova Vyshnia [UA] 52 G4
Sudzha [UA] 202 F6
Sueca [E] 98 E5
Suelli [I] 118 D6
Sugères [F] 68 D3
Süğütlü [TR] 150 H2
Suhindol [BG] 148 B3
Suhinichi [RUS] 202 E4
Suhl [D] 46 G2
Suho Polje [BIH] 142 E3
Suhopolje [HR] 74 H6
Šuica [BIH] 144 B1
Suijavaara [S] 194 B5
Suikka [FIN] 178 E1
Suinula [FIN] 176 F1
Suinula [FIN] 186 F5
Suio, Terme di- [I] 120 D2
Suippes [F] 44 C3
Sukeva [FIN] 196 E5
Sukhinichi [RUS] 202 E4
Sukobin [MNE] 128 A1
Sukošan [HR] 112 G5
Sükösd [H] 76 C4
Sukovo [SRB] 146 E4
Sul [N] 190 C6
Šula [MNE] 144 E2
Sulåmo [N] 182 D1
Suldal [N] 164 C1
Suldalseid [N] 164 C1
Suldalsosen [N] 164 C1
Sulden / Solda [I] 72 C3
Suldrup [DK] 160 D4
Sulechów [PL] 36 A3
Sulęcin [PL] 34 H2
Sulęczyno [PL] 22 C3
Sulejów [PL] 36 H5
Sulejówek [PL] 38 C3
Sulesund [N] 180 C3
Süleymaniye [TR] 150 B3
Süleymanlı [TR] 152 D3
Sulina [RO] 204 F4
Sulingen [D] 32 E1
Suliszewo [PL] 20 G6
Sulitjelma [N] 192 D6
Sulkava [FIN] 188 E5
Sulkava [FIN] 196 E6
Sulkavanjärvi [FIN] 186 G1
Sulkavankylä [FIN] 186 D4
Sułkowice [PL] 50 H4
Süller [TR] 152 E2
Süller [TR] 152 G4
Sully [F] 56 F4
Sully-sur-Loire [F] 56 C1
Sulmierzyce [PL] 36 D5
Sulmierzyce [PL] 36 G6
Sulmona [I] 116 D5
Süloğlu [TR] 150 B1
Sul'Ovské Skaly [SK] 50 F6
Sułów [PL] 36 D5
Sultançayırı [TR] 150 D5
Sultanhisar [TR] 152 E5
Sultanica [TR] 130 H4
Sultanköy [TR] 130 H2
Sultanköy [TR] 150 D3
Sülümenli [TR] 152 G4
Sulva / Solf [FIN] 186 B2
Sulviken [S] 190 D6
Sülysáp [H] 76 D1
Sulz [D] 58 G2
Sulzbach [A] 74 E3
Sulzbach [D] 46 D6
Sulzbach [D] 46 E6
Sulzbach-Rosenberg [D] 46 H5
Sumacarcer [E] 98 E5
Sumartin [HR] 144 A2
Sumba [FR] 160 A3
Sümeg [H] 74 G2
Sumer [BG] 148 F3
Sumiainem [FIN] 186 G3
Sumiswald [CH] 58 E6
Summa [FIN] 178 C3
Šumperk [CZ] 50 C4

Usvaty [RUS] 202 C4
Usvyaty [RUS] 202 C4
Utajärvi [FIN] 196 E4
Utåker [N] 170 B5
Utansjö [S] 184 F3
Utbjoa [N] 164 B1
Utebo [E] 90 E3
Utena [LT] 200 G4
Utersum [D] 156 A5
Úterý [CZ] 48 D4
Uthlede [D] 18 D4
Utiel [E] 98 D4
Utne [N] 170 C4
Utrecht [NL] 16 D5
Utrera [E] 100 G2
Utrillas [E] 90 E6
Utrine [SRB] 76 E5
Utsjö [S] 172 F4
Utsjoki [FIN] 194 D3
Utstein [N] 164 A2
Uttendorf [A] 60 G4
Uttendorf [A] 72 F1
Uttermossa [FIN] 186 B5
Uttersberg [S] 168 A2
Utti [FIN] 178 C3
Utting [D] 60 D4
Uttoxeter [GB] 10 E5
Utula [FIN] 178 E1
Utvalnäs [S] 174 E4
Utvängstorp [S] 162 C1
Utvik [N] 180 D5
Utvorda [N] 190 C4
Uukuniemen Kk. [FIN] 188 G5
Uukuniemi [FIN] 188 G5
Uurainen [FIN] 186 F4
Uuro [FIN] 186 B5
Uuro [FIN] 188 F2
Uusijoki [FIN] 194 F5
Uusikaarlepyy / Nykarleby [FIN] 186 C1
Uusikartano [FIN] 176 E3
Uusikaupunki / Nystad [FIN] 176 C3
Uusikylä [FIN] 178 B3
Uusi-Värtsilä [FIN] 188 G3
Uutela [FIN] 194 D6
Uva [FIN] 196 F4
Uvac [BIH] 144 E1
Úvaly [CZ] 48 G4
Uvanå [S] 172 F5
Uvarovka [RUS] 202 E3
Uvdal [N] 170 F4
Uvernet-Fours [F] 108 D2
Uyeasound [GB] 6 H3
Uzdowo [PL] 22 G5
Uzel [F] 26 A5
Uzerche [F] 66 G2
Uzès [F] 106 G3
Uzeste [F] 66 D4
Uzhorod [UA] 204 B3
Uzhots'kyi, Pereval- [UA] 52 F6
Užice [SRB] 146 A2
Uzlovoye [RUS] 200 E5
Užpaliai [LT] 200 G4
Üzümlü [TR] 154 F2
Uzunköprü [TR] 150 B3
Uzunkuyu [TR] 152 B4
Uzunpinar [TR] 152 G4
Uzuntarla [TR] 150 G3
Užventis [LT] 200 E4

V

Vå [N] 164 E1
Vä [S] 158 D2
Vaajakoski [FIN] 186 G4
Vaajasalmi [FIN] 186 H3
Vääkiö [FIN] 196 F3
Vääksy [FIN] 178 A2
Vaala [FIN] 196 E4
Vaalajärvi [FIN] 194 D6
Vaalimaa [FIN] 178 D3
Vaaljoki [FIN] 176 D3
Vaarakylä [FIN] 196 F5
Vaaraniva [FIN] 196 F3
Väärinmaja [FIN] 186 E5
Vaas [F] 42 B6
Vaasa / Vasa [FIN] 186 B2
Vaassen [NL] 16 F4
Väätäiskylä [FIN] 186 E3
Vabalninkas [LT] 200 F3
Vabres-l'Abbaye [F] 106 D3
Vác [H] 64 C5
Vacha [D] 46 F1
Vachartyán [H] 64 C6
Väckelsång [S] 162 E5
Vad [S] 168 A1
Vădastra [RO] 148 A2
Vadépuszta [H] 76 A3
Väderstad [S] 166 G6
Vadheim [N] 170 C1
Vadili (Vatili) [CY] 154 G5
Vadna [H] 64 F4
Vado Ligure [I] 108 H3
Vadsø [N] 194 E2
Vadstena [S] 166 G5
Vaduz [FL] 58 H6
Væggerløse [DK] 20 B1
Vafaïka [GR] 130 E3
Vafiochóri [GR] 128 G3
Vág [H] 74 G1
Våga [N] 164 A2
Vågåmo [N] 180 G5
Vagan [BIH] 142 B4
Våge [N] 164 A1
Våge [N] 164 C6
Våge [N] 170 B5
Vage [N] 180 E3
Vågen [N] 190 A6
Vägeva [EST] 198 F2
Vaggeryd [S] 162 D3
Vaggsvik [N] 192 F3
Vágia [GR] 134 B5
Vagiónia [GR] 140 E5
Vaglio Basilicata [I] 120 H4
Vagnhärad [S] 168 D4
Vagos [P] 80 B5
Vågsbygd [N] 164 D6
Vägsele [S] 190 G5
Vägsjöfors [S] 172 E5
Vågslid [N] 164 D1
Vágur [FR] 160 A3
Vähäkyro / Lillkyro [FIN] 186 B2
Vahanka [FIN] 186 E3
Vahastu [EST] 198 E2
Vaheri [FIN] 186 G5
Väï [GR] 140 H4
Vaiano [I] 110 F5
Vaiges [F] 40 H5
Vaiguva [LT] 200 E4
Vaihingen [D] 46 C6
Väike-Maarja [EST] 198 F1
Väike Rakke [EST] 198 F3
Vailly [F] 44 A2
Vailly [F] 56 C2
Vainikkala [FIN] 178 E2
Vainupea [EST] 198 E1
Vainutas [LT] 200 D5
Vaison-la-Romaine [F] 106 H3
Vaite [F] 58 A3
Vajmat [S] 190 H2
Vajnede [LV] 198 C6
Vajont [I] 72 F4
Vajszló [H] 76 A5
Vajzë [AL] 128 B5
Vakarel [BG] 146 G5
Vakern [S] 172 F5
Vakiflar [TR] 150 C2
Vaksdal [N] 170 B3
Vaksevo [BG] 146 F6
Vakumonë [AL] 128 B3
Välådalen [S] 182 E2
Valajanaapa [FIN] 196 D2
Valajaskoski [FIN] 194 D8
Valandovo [MK] 128 G2
Valanhamn [N] 192 G1
Valareña [E] 84 B6
Valaská Belá [SK] 64 B2
Valašská Polanka [CZ] 50 E6
Valašské Klobouky [CZ] 50 E6
Valašské Meziříčí [CZ] 50 E5
Valbella [CH] 70 H1
Valberg [F] 108 E3
Vålberg [S] 166 E3
Valbiska [HR] 112 E2
Valbo [S] 174 E4
Valbondione [I] 72 A4
Valbonë [AL] 146 A5
Valbonnais [F] 68 H5
Vâlcani [RO] 76 F5
Valcarlos / Luzaide [E] 84 C3
Val-Claret [F] 70 C4
Valcum [H] 74 G3
Valdagno [I] 72 D6
Valdahon [F] 58 B5
Valdaj [RUS] 202 D2
Valdalen [N] 182 D5
Valday [RUS] 202 D2
Valdeazores [E] 96 D2
Valdecaballeros [E] 96 C2
Valdecabras [E] 98 C2
Valdecarros [E] 88 C3
Valdedios [E] 82 C2
Valdeganga [E] 98 C5
Valdeinfierno [E] 96 B5
Valdelacas de Tajo [E] 96 C1
Val del Charco del Agua Amarga, Cueva de la- [E] 90 F6
Valdeltormo [E] 90 G6
Valdemadera [E] 84 A6
Valdemārpils [LV] 198 C4
Valdemarsvik [S] 168 C6
Valdemorillo [E] 88 F5
Valdemoro [E] 88 F6
Valdemoro Sierra [E] 98 C2
Valdenoceda [E] 82 F4
Valdepeñas [E] 96 F5
Valdepeñas de Jaén [E] 102 E3
Valdepolo [E] 82 C4
Valderas [E] 82 B5
Valderice [I] 126 B2
Valderoure [F] 108 D4
Valderöy [N] 180 C3
Valderrobres [E] 98 G1
Valdesalor [E] 86 H5
Val d'Esquières [F] 108 D5
Valdeverdeja [E] 96 C1
Valdieri [I] 108 F3
Val d'Isère [F] 70 C4
Val-d'Izé [F] 26 D6
Valdobbiádene [I] 72 E5
Valdoviño [E] 78 D1
Valdštejn [CZ] 48 H2
Valdunquillo [E] 82 B6
Valea lui Mihai [RO] 204 B3
Valea Rea [RO] 148 F1
Valebø [N] 164 F2
Valečov [CZ] 48 G2
Vale da Rosa [P] 94 C5
Vale de Açor [P] 94 D3
Vale de Cambra [P] 80 C5
Vale de Lobos [P] 94 C5
Vale de Santarém [P] 86 C4
Vale do Arco [P] 86 D4
Vale do Côa, Parque Arqueológico do- [P] 80 E5
Vale do Poço [P] 94 D4
Vålega [P] 80 B5
Valéggio sul Míncio [I] 110 E1
Valen [N] 170 B5
Valença do Minho [P] 78 B5
Valençay [F] 54 H3
Valence [F] 66 F6
Valence [F] 68 F5
Valence d'Albigeois [F] 106 C2
Valence-sur-Baïse [F] 66 E6
València [E] 98 E4
Valencia de Alcántara [E] 86 F5
Valencia de Don Juan [E] 82 B5
Valencia de las Torres [E] 94 H3
Valencia del Ventoso [E] 94 G3
Valencia de Mombuey [E] 94 F3
Valenciennes [F] 28 G4
Văleni [RO] 148 B1
Vălenii de Munte [RO] 204 D5
Valensole [F] 108 C4
Valentano [I] 114 G3
Valentigney [F] 58 C4
Valenza [I] 70 F6
Våler [N] 166 B2
Våler [N] 172 D4
Valeria [E] 98 B3
Vales Mortos [P] 94 E4
Valevåg [N] 170 B6
Valfábbrica [I] 116 A2
Valga [EST] 198 F4
Valgeristi [EST] 198 D2
Valgrisenche [I] 70 C4
Valguarnera Caropepe [I] 126 F3
Valijoki [FIN] 178 D2
Välijoki [FIN] 194 D8
Valimítika [GR] 132 G6
Välivaara [FIN] 196 G6
Valjevo [SRB] 146 A1
Valjevo [SRB] 204 A6
Valjimena [E] 88 C4
Valjok [N] 194 C3
Valka [LV] 198 F4
Valkeajärvi [FIN] 186 E4
Valkeakoski [FIN] 176 F2
Valkeala [FIN] 178 C2
Valkeavaara [FIN] 188 G4
Valkenburg [NL] 30 F4
Valkenswaard [NL] 30 E3
Valkiamäki [FIN] 188 E6
Valkininkai [LT] 24 H2
Valko / Valkom [FIN] 178 B4
Valkom / Valko [FIN] 178 B4
Valla [S] 182 F1
Valla [S] 184 D3
Vallada [E] 78 F4
Valladolid [E] 88 E2
Vallåkra [S] 156 H2
Vallargärdet [S] 166 F2
Vallata [I] 120 F3
Vallbona de les Monges [E] 92 C4
Valldal [N] 180 E4
Valldemossa [E] 104 E4
Valle [LV] 198 E6
Valle [N] 164 D2
Valle de Abdalajís [E] 102 B4
Valle de Cabuérniga [E] 82 E3
Valle dei Templi [I] 126 D4
Valle de la Serena [E] 96 A3
Valle de los Caídos [E] 88 F5
Valle de Matamoros [E] 94 F3
Valledoria [I] 118 C2
Vallehermoso [E] 100 B5
Vallelunga Pratameno [I] 126 D3
Vallen [S] 184 D1
Vallentuna [S] 168 E2
Valleraugue [F] 106 E2
Vallet [F] 54 C2
Valletta [M] 126 C6
Vallfogona de Ripollès [E] 92 E2
Vallheim [N] 190 D4
Vallivana [E] 98 G2
Vallo di Lucania [I] 120 F5
Valloire [F] 70 B5
Valloires, Abbaye de- [F] 28 D3
Vallombrosa [I] 110 F5
Vallon-en-Sully [F] 56 C5
Vallon-Pont-d'Arc [F] 68 E6
Vallorbe [CH] 58 B6
Vallorcine [F] 70 C3
Vallø Slot [DK] 156 G3
Vallouise [F] 70 B6
Valls [E] 92 C4
Vallsbo [S] 174 D3
Vallset [N] 172 C4
Vallsta [S] 174 D1
Vallter 2000 [E] 92 E2
Vallvik [S] 174 E2
Valmadrid [E] 90 E4
Valmiera [LV] 198 E4
Valmigère [F] 106 C5
Valmojado [E] 88 E6
Valmontone [I] 116 B6
Valmorel [F] 70 B4
Val Moutier [CH] 58 D5
Valö [S] 174 F5
Valognes [F] 26 D2
Valongo [P] 80 C4
Valoria la Buena [E] 88 F1
Valøy [N] 190 C4
Valøya [N] 190 C5
Valozhyn [BY] 200 H6
Valpaços [P] 80 E3
Valpelline [I] 70 D3
Valporquero de Torío [E] 78 H5
Valpovo [HR] 76 B6
Valras-Plage [F] 106 D5
Valréas [F] 106 H2
Vals [CH] 70 G2
Valsamónero [GR] 140 E5
Valsavaranche [I] 70 C4
Valsebo [S] 166 C3
Valset [N] 190 B6
Valsinni [I] 122 D5
Valsjöbyn [S] 190 E5
Valsjön [S] 184 D5
Valskog [S] 168 B3
Vals-les-Bains [F] 68 E6
Valsøybotn [N] 180 G2
Välsta [S] 184 E6
Val-Suzon [F] 56 G3
Valtesíniko [GR] 136 D2
Val Thorens [F] 70 B5
Valtiendas [E] 88 G3
Valtierra [E] 84 B5
Valtimo [FIN] 196 F5
Valtola [FIN] 178 C2
Váltos [GR] 130 H1
Valtournenche [I] 70 D3
Valvanera, Monasterio de- [E] 90 B1
Valverde [E] 100 A5
Valverde, Santuario di- [I] 118 B3
Valverde de Cervera [E] 84 A6
Valverde de Júcar [E] 98 B3
Valverde del Camino [E] 94 F5
Valverde de Leganés [E] 94 F2
Valverde del Fresno [E] 86 G3
Valzul [A] 72 B2
Vama Veche [RO] 148 G1
Vamberk [CZ] 50 B3
Vamdrup [DK] 156 C3
Våmhus [S] 172 G3
Vamlingbo [S] 168 F6
Vammala [FIN] 176 E2
Vámos [GR] 140 C4
Vámosmikola [H] 64 C5
Vámospércs [H] 64 H6
Vámosszabadi [H] 62 H6
Vampula [FIN] 176 E3
V. Ämtervik [S] 166 E2
Vamvakoú [GR] 132 G2
Vanås [S] 158 D1
Vana-Vigala [EST] 198 D2
Vanda / Vantaa [FIN] 176 H5
Vandel [DK] 156 C2
Vandellós [E] 90 H6
Vandenesse [F] 56 E4
Vandoies / Vintl [I] 72 E2
Vändra [EST] 198 E2
Vandžegala [LT] 200 F5
Väne [LV] 198 C5
Vanebu [N] 164 G2
Vänersborg [S] 166 D5
Väne-Ryr [S] 166 D6
Vaneskoski [FIN] 186 C6
Vånga [S] 158 D1
Vangaži [LV] 198 E5
Vängel [S] 190 F6
Vangsnes [N] 170 D2
Vanha-Kihlanki [S] 194 B6
Vanhakylä [FIN] 186 B5
Vanhamäki [FIN] 188 C5
Vänjaurbäck [S] 190 G5
Vänjaurträsk [S] 190 G5
Vânju Mare [RO] 146 E1
Vankiva [S] 158 D1
Vännacka [S] 166 D2
Vännäs [S] 190 H6
Vännäsberget [S] 194 B8
Vännäsby [S] 190 H6
Vannes [F] 40 D5
Vansbro [S] 172 G4
Vanse [N] 164 C5
Vansjö [S] 168 B1
Vänsjö [S] 182 H6
Vanstad [S] 158 D3
Vantaa / Vanda [FIN] 176 H5
Vanttauskoski [FIN] 194 D8
Vanvik [N] 164 C1
Vanvikan [N] 190 B6
Vanyarc [H] 64 D5
Vaplan [S] 182 G2
Vara [S] 166 E6
Varabla [EST] 198 D3
Varades [F] 40 G6
Varages [F] 108 C4
Varakļāni [LV] 198 F5
Varaldsøy [S] 170 B5
Varallo [I] 70 E4
Varanava [BY] 200 G6
Varangerbotn [N] 194 E2
Varano de' Melegari [I] 110 D3
Varaždin [HR] 74 F4
Varaždinske Toplice [HR] 74 F4
Varazze [I] 108 H3
Varberg [S] 160 H4
Varbola [EST] 198 D2
Vărbovo [BG] 148 D6
Varbyane [BG] 148 E2
Varces [F] 68 H5
Várda [GR] 136 B1
Varde [DK] 156 B2
Vardim [BG] 148 C2
Vardište [BIH] 144 E1
Vårdö [FIN] 176 B5
Vardø [N] 194 F2
Várdomb [H] 76 C4
Vårdsberg [S] 168 A5
Varduva [LT] 200 D3
Varekil [S] 166 C6
Varel [D] 18 C4
Varellaíoi [GR] 134 D5
Varena [LT] 24 G2
Varengeville-sur-Mer [F] 28 C4
Varenna [I] 70 G3
Varennes-en-Argonne [F] 44 D3
Varennes-sur-Allier [F] 56 D6
Vareš [BIH] 142 D4
Varese [I] 70 F4
Varese Ligure [I] 110 C3
Vårgårda [S] 162 B1
Vargön [S] 166 D5
Vargträsk [S] 190 G5
Varhaug [N] 164 A4
Várhus [N] 182 C3
Vári [GR] 138 D2
Variaș [RO] 76 G5
Varilhes [F] 84 H5
Varín [SK] 50 F6
Väring [S] 166 F5
Váris [GR] 128 F6
Varjakka [FIN] 196 D4
Varjisträsk [S] 190 H2
Varkaus [FIN] 188 D4
Várkiza [GR] 136 H1
Varland [N] 164 E1
Värmdö [S] 168 E3
Värmlandsbro [S] 166 E3
Varmo [I] 72 G5
Värmskog [S] 166 E2
Varna [BG] 148 F3
Varna [SRB] 142 F3
Varna (Vahrn) [I] 72 D2
Värnamo [S] 162 D4
Varnany [BY] 200 H5
Varnhem [S] 166 F5
Varniai [LT] 200 E4
Varnja [EST] 198 F2
Varnsdorf [CZ] 48 G1
Varntresk [N] 190 E3
Väröbacka [S] 160 H3
Városerdő [H] 76 G3
Városföld [H] 76 D3
Varoška Rijeka [BIH] 112 H2
Városlőd [H] 74 H2
Varovnik [BG] 148 F5
Varp [S] 166 C4
Varpaisjärvi [FIN] 196 F6
Várpalota [H] 76 B2
Varpanen [FIN] 178 C1
Varparanta [FIN] 188 E4
Varparanta [FIN] 188 F2
Varpsjö [S] 190 F5
Värriö [FIN] 194 E6
Vars [F] 108 E2
Vârșand [RO] 76 G3
Vårsås [S] 166 F6
Varshko [RUS] 178 G3
Varsi [I] 110 C3
Varsseveld [NL] 16 F6
Vartdal [N] 180 C4
Vartemyagi [RUS] 178 H4
Vartius [FIN] 196 G4
Vârtoapele [RO] 148 B1
Vârtopu [RO] 146 F1
Värtsilä [FIN] 188 G3
Varv [S] 166 H5
Varvara [BG] 148 A6
Varvara [BG] 148 G5
Varvára [GR] 130 C4
Varzi [I] 110 B2
Varzy [F] 56 E3
Vasa / Vaasa [FIN] 186 B2
Vasalemma [EST] 198 D1
Vasankari [FIN] 196 C5
Vasarapera [FIN] 194 F8
Vasarás [GR] 136 E3
Vasbotna [N] 190 C5
Väse [S] 166 F3
Vasiláki [GR] 136 C2
Vasilevo [BG] 148 G2
Vasil'evskoye [RUS] 198 H4
Vasiliká [GR] 130 B5
Vasiliká [GR] 134 B3
Vasiliká [GR] 134 C2
Vasilikí [GR] 132 C5
Vasilikó [GR] 134 B5
Vasilikós [GR] 136 B2
Vasilishki [BY] 24 H3
Vasilítsi [GR] 136 D5
Vasil Levski [BG] 148 D5
Vasil'yevo [RUS] 198 G4
Vaškai [LT] 198 D6
Vaskelovo [RUS] 178 H3
Vaskio [FIN] 176 E4
Vaskivesi [FIN] 186 D5
Vasknarva [EST] 198 G2
Vaskút [H] 76 C5
Vasles [F] 54 E4
Vaslui [RO] 204 E4
Vassbø [N] 164 B4
Vassbotten [S] 166 C4
Vassenden [N] 170 G1
Vassenden [N] 180 C6
Vässes [GR] 136 D3
Vassli [N] 180 G1
Vassmolösa [S] 162 F5
Vassnäs [S] 182 E1
Vasstrand [N] 192 F2
Vassurány [H] 74 F1
Vassy [F] 26 E4
Västan [S] 184 E5
Västansfors [S] 168 A1
Västansjö [S] 184 F3
Västansjö [S] 190 E3
Västansjö [S] 190 F4
Västansjön [S] 184 E5
Västbacka [S] 172 G1
Västbacken [S] 182 F1
Västeräker [S] 168 D2
Väster-Arådalen [S] 182 F3
Västerås [S] 168 B2
Västerby [S] 168 D4
Västerfärnebo [S] 168 B1
Västergarn [S] 168 F5
Västerhaninge [S] 168 E3
Västerhus [S] 184 G2
Västermyckeläng [S] 172 F2
Västermyrriset [S] 190 G5
Västerrottna [S] 166 E1
Västersel [S] 184 G2
Västervik [S] 162 G2
Vastila [FIN] 178 C3
Västillä [FIN] 186 F6
Västland [S] 174 F5
Vasto [I] 116 E5
Västra Yttermark [FIN] 186 A4
Västrum [S] 162 G2
Vasvár [H] 74 G2
Vasylivka [UA] 204 H2
Vasyl'kiv [UA] 202 D7
Vasyl'kivka [UA] 204 F3
Vát [H] 74 G1
Vatan [F] 54 H3
Vaterá [GR] 134 G3
Váthi [GR] 128 H3
Vathý [GR] 134 B5
Vathý [GR] 138 H4
Vathý [GR] 152 C6
Vathýlakkos [GR] 128 F5
Vathýlakkos [GR] 130 D2
Vathýpetro [GR] 140 E5
Vatili (Vadili) [CY] 154 G5
Vatne [N] 164 B3
Vatne [N] 164 D4
Vatne [N] 180 C4
Vatne [N] 180 D3
Vatnstraum [N] 164 E5
Vatólakkos [GR] 128 E6
Vatopedíou, Moní- [GR] 130 D5
Vatoúsa [GR] 134 G2
Vatra Dornei [RO] 204 D3
Vatta [H] 64 F5
Vättershus [S] 162 D1
Vattjom [S] 184 E4
Vattlång [S] 184 F6
Vattnäs [S] 172 G3
Vatvet [N] 166 C3
Vau [P] 94 B5
Vaucelles, Abbaye de- [F] 28 F4
Vauclaix [F] 56 E3
Vaucluse [F] 58 C5
Vaucouleurs [F] 44 D5
Vaudoy en Brie [F] 42 G4
Vau i Dejës [AL] 128 B1
Vauldalen [N] 182 D3
Vauvenargues [F] 108 B4
Vauvert [F] 106 F4
Vauville [F] 26 D1
Vauvillers [F] 58 B3
Vaux-Le Vicomte [F] 42 G4
Vavylás (Güzelyalı) [CY] 154 F5
Vawkavysk [BY] 24 G5
Vaxholm [S] 168 E3
Växjö [S] 162 E4
Våxtorp [S] 162 B6
Vayrac [F] 66 H4
Vaysal [TR] 150 B1
Važecká Jaskyňa [SK] 64 D2
V. Bodarna [S] 160 H1
Vean [N] 180 G1
Vebbestrup [DK] 160 D4
Veberöd [S] 158 C3
Veblungsnes [N] 180 E3
Vebomark [S] 196 A5
Vecbebri [LV] 198 E5
Večelkov [SK] 64 E4
Vechta [D] 18 C6
Vecilla de Valderaduey [E] 82 C4
Vecinos [E] 88 B3
Veckholm [S] 168 D2
Vecpiebalga [LV] 198 F5
Vecsés [H] 76 C1
Vecumnieki [LV] 198 E5
Veda [S] 184 F3
Vedavågen [N] 164 A2
Vedbæk [DK] 156 G2
Veddelev [DK] 156 G2
Veddige [S] 160 H3
Vedea [RO] 148 C2
Vedelago [I] 72 E5
Vedersø Klit [DK] 160 B5
Vedevåg [S] 166 H2
Vedjeön [S] 190 E5
Vedum [S] 166 E6
Veendam [NL] 16 H2
Veenendaal [NL] 16 E5
Veere [NL] 16 B6
Vegacervera [E] 78 H5
Vega de Espinareda [E] 78 F4
Vega de los Árboles [E] 96 G4
Vegadeo [E] 78 F2
Vega de Pas [E] 82 F3
Vega de Valcarce [E] 78 E4
Vegårshei [N] 164 F4
Vegas de Coria [E] 88 B4
Vegas del Condado [E] 78 H5
Vegger [DK] 160 D4
Veggli [N] 170 F5
Veghel [NL] 16 E6
Veglie [I] 122 G5
Vegset [N] 190 C5
Vegusdal [N] 164 E4
Vehkajärvi [FIN] 176 G1
Vehkalahti [FIN] 178 B1
Vehkaperä [FIN] 186 E3
Vehmaa [FIN] 176 D4
Vehmaa [FIN] 188 D5
Vehmasmäki [FIN] 188 C3
Vehmersalmi [FIN] 188 D2
Vehniä [FIN] 186 G4
Vehu [FIN] 186 E3
Vehuvarpee [FIN] 186 C6
Veidnesklubben [N] 194 C2
Veikkola [FIN] 176 G5
Veinge [S] 162 B5
Veio [I] 114 H5
Veiros [P] 86 E6
Veisiejai [LT] 24 F3
Veitshöchheim [D] 46 E4
Veivirženai [LT] 200 D4
Vejano [I] 114 H4
Vejby [DK] 156 G1
Vejbystrand [S] 162 B6
Vejen [DK] 156 B2
Vejer de la Frontera [E] 100 F5
Vejers Strand [DK] 156 A2
Vejinac [BIH] 112 H2
Vejle [DK] 156 C2
Vejprty [CZ] 48 D2
Vekilski [BG] 148 F2
Velada [E] 88 D6
Velagići [BIH] 142 B3
Vela Luka [HR] 144 A3
Velanídia [GR] 136 F5
Velas [P] 100 C3
Velbert [D] 30 H3
Velburg [D] 46 H6
Velbuzhdki Pateka (Velbuzhdki Prolaz) [BG/MK] 146 E6
Velbuzhdki Prolaz (Velbuzhdki Pateka) [BG/MK] 146 E6
Velchevo [BG] 148 B4
Veldelen [N] 190 C5
Velden [A] 74 B3
Velden [D] 46 H4
Velden [D] 60 F4
Veldhoven [NL] 30 E2
Velebit [SRB] 76 E5
Velefique [E] 102 G4
Velehrad [CZ] 62 G2
Velēna [LV] 198 F4
Velence [H] 76 B2
Velenje [SLO] 74 D4
Velešín [CZ] 62 C2
Velešta [MK] 128 D3
Velestíno [GR] 132 H2
Vélez-Blanco [E] 102 H3
Vélez-Málaga [E] 102 C5
Vélez-Rubio [E] 102 H3
Velgošti [MK] 128 D3
Vel. Grđevac [HR] 74 G6
Velhartice [CZ] 48 E6
Vel. Horozhanka [UA] 52 H4
Veličani [BIH] 144 C3
Velika [HR] 142 C1
Velika Brusnica [BIH] 142 D2
Velika Dapčevica [HR] 74 G6
Velika Drenova [SRB] 146 C3
Velika Gorica [HR] 74 E6
Velika Kladuša [HR] 112 H2
Velika Kopanica [HR] 142 D2
Velika Kruša [KS] 146 B6
Velika Plana [SRB] 146 C1
Velika Remeta, Manastir- [SRB] 142 F2
Velika Slatina [KS] 146 C5
Velike Lašče [SLO] 74 C5
Veliki Preslav [BG] 148 E3
Veliki Šiljegovac [SRB] 146 D3
Veliki Tabor [HR] 74 D5
Velikiye Luki [RUS] 202 C3
Veliki Zdenci [HR] 74 G6
Veliko Orašje [SRB] 146 C1
Veliko Tŭrnovo [BG] 148 C3
Veli Lošinj [HR] 112 E4
Velimlje [MNE] 144 D3
Velingrad [BG] 148 A6
Velipojë [AL] 128 A1
Veliternë [AL] 128 D4
Velizh [RUS] 202 C4
Veljun [HR] 112 G2
Velká Bíteš [CZ] 50 B6
Velká Hleďsebe [CZ] 48 C4
Velká nad Veličkou [CZ] 62 H2
Velké Bílovice [CZ] 62 G3
Velké Brezno [CZ] 48 F2
Velké Heraltice [CZ] 50 D4
Velké Kapušany [SK] 64 H3
Velké Karlovice [CZ] 50 E6
Veľké Leváre [SK] 62 G3
Velké Losiny [CZ] 50 C4
Velké Meziříčí [CZ] 50 B6
Velké Němčice [CZ] 62 F2
Velké Opatovice [CZ] 50 C5
Veľké Raškovce [SK] 64 H3
Veľke Ripňany [SK] 64 A3
Veľké Uherce [SK] 64 B3
Velkua [FIN] 176 D4
Velkuanmaa [FIN] 176 D5
Velký Beranov [CZ] 50 A5
Velký Bor [CZ] 48 E5
Velký Folkmar [SK] 64 F2
Veľký Krtíš [SK] 64 D4
Veľký Meder [SK] 62 H5
Veľký Šariš [SK] 64 G2
Velký Újezd [CZ] 50 D5
Velle [N] 180 D4
Velleclaire [F] 58 B4
Velleia [I] 110 C2
Velles [F] 54 H4
Velletri [I] 116 A6
Vellinge [S] 156 H3
Vel. Ljubin [UA] 52 G4
Velp [NL] 16 F5
Velpke [D] 32 H2
Velta [N] 172 D4
Vel. Trnovac [SRB] 146 D5
Veltrusy [CZ] 48 F3
Veluće [SRB] 146 C3
Velušina [MK] 128 E4
Velvary [CZ] 48 F3
Velventós [GR] 128 F5
Vel'ye [RUS] 198 H4
Velyka Lepetykha [UA] 204 G2
Velyki Mosty [UA] 52 H3
Velykyi Bereznyi [UA] 204 B2
Vemb [DK] 160 B5
Vemdalen [S] 182 F4
Vemhån [S] 182 G5
Vemmelv [DK] 156 F3
Vemmenæs [DK] 156 E4
Ven [N] 164 B3
Vena [S] 162 F3
Venabu [N] 170 H1
Venaco [F] 114 B4
Venafro [I] 120 D1
Venäjä [FIN] 176 F3
Venaria Reale [I] 70 D5
Venåsen [N] 180 H6
Venčane [SRB] 146 B1
Vence [F] 108 E4
Venda Nova [P] 80 D3
Vendargues [F] 106 F4
Vendas de Galizes [P] 86 E2
Vendas Novas [P] 86 C6
Vendays-Montalivet [F] 66 C1
Vendel [S] 174 F5
Vendelsö [S] 168 E3
Vendeuvre [F] 44 B6
Vendinha [E] 94 E2
Vendôme [F] 42 D6
Vendranges [F] 68 E2
Veneheitto [FIN] 196 E4

Veneskoski [FIN] 186 C3
Venets [BG] 148 C5
Venets [BG] 148 E4
Venets [BG] 148 E2
Venevere [EST] 198 F2
Venézia [I] 72 E6
Venialbo [E] 80 H5
Venjan [S] 172 F3
Venlo [NL] 30 F3
Venn [N] 182 B2
Vénna [GR] 130 F3
Vennesla [N] 164 D5
Vennesund [N] 190 C4
Venngarn [S] 168 D2
Venosa [I] 120 H3
Venoy [F] 56 E2
Venray [NL] 30 F2
Vent [A] 72 C2
Venta de Arraco [E] 84 D4
Venta de Baños [E] 88 F1
Venta del Moro [E] 98 D4
Venta de los Santos [E] 96 G6
Venta del Pobre [E] 102 H5
Ventadour, Château de- [F] 68 A3
Venta el Alto [E] 94 G5
Venta Nueva [E] 78 F4
Ventas de Huelma [E] 102 D4
Ventas de Zefarraya [E] 102 C4
Venté [LT] 200 D5
Ventimíglia [I] 108 F4
Ventiseri [F] 114 B5
Ventnor [GB] 12 H5
Vento, Grotta del- [I] 110 D5
Ventosa de Pisuerga [E] 82 D5
Ventspils [LV] 198 B4
Venus [RO] 148 G1
Venzone [I] 72 G4
Vepsä [FIN] 196 D4
Vera [E] 102 H5
Vera [N] 190 C6
Vera de Bidasoa / Bera [E] 84 B2
Vera de Moncayo [E] 90 D3
Verba [UA] 38 H6
Verbania [I] 70 F3
Verberie [F] 42 G2
Verbicaro [I] 120 H6
Verbier [CH] 70 D3
Vercelli [I] 70 E5
Verch. Syn'ovydne [UA] 52 G6
Verdalsøra [N] 190 C6
Verdelles, Château de- [F] 42 A5
Verden [D] 18 E6
Verdenberg [CH] 58 H6
Verdens Ende [N] 164 H3
Verdikoússa [GR] 132 F1
Verdun [F] 44 D4
Verea [E] 78 C5
Vereja [RUS] 202 E3
Veresegyház [H] 64 C6
Vereya [RUS] 202 E3
Verfeil [F] 106 A3
Vergato [I] 110 F4
Vergeletto [CH] 70 F2
Verghia [F] 114 A5
Vergi [EST] 198 E1
Vérgi [GR] 130 B3
Vergiate [I] 70 F4
Vergína [GR] 128 G5
Vergt [F] 66 F3
Verh. Osel'ki [RUS] 178 H4
Verín [E] 78 D6
Verinsko [BG] 146 G5
Verket [N] 164 H2
Verkhn'odniprovs'k [UA] 204 G1
Verl [D] 32 D3
Verma [N] 180 F4
Vermafoss [N] 180 F4
Vermenton [F] 56 E2
Vermeş [RO] 76 H6
Vermiglio [I] 72 C4
Vermosh [AL] 146 A5
Vermuntila [FIN] 176 C3
Vernazza [I] 110 C4
Vern-d'anjou [F] 40 G6
Vernet [F] 84 H3
Vernet-les-Bains [F] 92 F1
Verneuil-sur-Avre [F] 26 H5
Verningen [N] 164 G3
Vernio [I] 110 F5
Vernon [F] 42 E2
Vernoux-en-Gâtine [F] 54 D3
Verny [F] 44 E4
Verőce [H] 64 C5
Véroia [GR] 128 G5
Verolanuova [I] 72 A6
Veroli [I] 116 C6
Verona [I] 72 C6
Verpelét [H] 64 E5
Verrabotn [N] 190 B6
Verrès [I] 70 D4
Verrières-de-Joux [F] 58 B6
Versailles [F] 42 F3
Verseg [H] 64 D6
Versmold [D] 32 D3
Versoix [CH] 70 B2
Versols-et-Lapeyre [F] 106 D3
Vertaala [FIN] 186 G4
Verteillac [F] 66 E2
Vertop [AL] 128 B5
Vertou [F] 54 C1
Vertus [F] 44 B4
Verucchio [I] 110 H5
Veruela, Monasterio de- [E] 90 D3
Verum [S] 162 C6
Verviers [B] 30 E5
Vervins [F] 28 G5
Vervnäs [S] 172 E2
Verwood [GB] 12 G5
Verzej [SLO] 74 E3
Verzuolo [I] 108 F2
Verzy [F] 44 B3
Vesala [FIN] 196 F2
Vesamäki [FIN] 186 H2
Vesanka [FIN] 186 G4
Vesanto [FIN] 186 G2
Vescovato [F] 114 C3
Vescovato [I] 110 D1
Vése [H] 74 G4
Veselec [BG] 148 E2
Veselie [BG] 148 F5
Veselí nad Lužnicí [CZ] 48 G6
Veselí nad Moravou [CZ] 62 H2
Veselinovo [BG] 148 E3
Veselynove [UA] 204 F3
Veshchevo [RUS] 178 F3
Veshtica [BG] 146 E2
Vesivehmaa [FIN] 178 A2
Veskoniemi [FIN] 194 D4
Vesnovo [RUS] 24 D1
Vesoul [F] 58 B3
Véssa [GR] 134 G5
Vessingebro [S] 160 H4
Vestbjerg [DK] 160 E3
Vestby [N] 166 B2
Vestbygd [N] 164 B5
Vester Åby [DK] 156 D4
Vesterby [DK] 156 D2
Vesterby [DK] 156 F4
Vester Egense [DK] 156 D2
Vester Egesborg [DK] 156 F4
Vesterli [N] 192 D6
Vesterø Havn [DK] 160 F3
Veste Rosenberg [D] 46 H3
Vestervig [DK] 160 B4
Vestfossen [N] 164 G1
Vestmanna [FR] 160 A1
Vestmarka [N] 166 D1
Vestnes [N] 180 E3
Vestone [I] 72 B5
Vestpollen [N] 192 D4
Vestre Jakobselv [N] 194 E2
Ves'yegonsk [RUS] 202 E1
Veszprém [H] 76 A2
Veszprémvarsány [H] 76 A1
Vésztő [H] 76 G2
Veteli / Vetil [FIN] 186 D1
Vetil / Veteli [FIN] 186 D1
Vetlanda [S] 162 E3
Vetlefjorden [N] 170 D1
Vetovo [BG] 148 D2
Vetovo [HR] 142 C1
Vetralla [I] 114 H4
Vetren [BG] 148 C4
Vetren [BG] 148 F4
Vetrino [BG] 148 F2
Větrný Jeníkov [CZ] 48 H5
Vetschau [D] 34 F4
Vettasjärvi [S] 192 H6
Vetti [N] 170 E1
Vettisfossen [N] 170 E1
Vetulónia [I] 114 F2
Vetunica [MK] 146 E6
Veules-les-Roses [F] 26 H2
Veulettes-sur-Mer [F] 26 H2
Veurne (Furnes) [B] 28 F1
Vevang [N] 180 E2
Vevey [CH] 70 C1
Vévi [GR] 128 E4
Vevring [N] 180 B6
Veynes [F] 108 C2
Veyrier [F] 70 B3
Vezdemarbán [E] 88 D1
Vézelay [F] 56 E3
Vézelise [F] 44 E6
Vézénobres [F] 106 F3
Vezin le Coquet [F] 26 C6
Vezirhan [TR] 150 G4
Vezzano [I] 72 C4
Vezzolano, Abbazia di- [I] 70 E6
V. Gafsele [S] 190 F5
V. Husby [S] 168 B5
Viadana [I] 110 E2
Viaduct du Millau [F] 106 D2
Viais [F] 54 B2
Vial. Berestavica [BY] 24 G5
Via Mala [CH] 70 H2
Viana [E] 82 H6
Viana de Duero [E] 90 B3
Viana do Alentejo [P] 94 D2
Viana do Bolo [E] 78 E6
Viana do Castelo [P] 78 A6
Vianden [L] 44 F2
Viane [F] 106 C3
Vianen [NL] 16 D5
Vianne [F] 66 E5
Vianos [E] 96 H6
Viaréggio [I] 110 D5
Vias [F] 106 E4
Viator [E] 102 G5
Viborg [DK] 160 D5
Vibo Valentia [I] 124 D6
Vibraye [F] 42 C5
Viby [DK] 156 G3
Viby [S] 166 G4
Vic [E] 92 E3
Vič [SLO] 74 C3
Viča [SRB] 146 B3
Vicarello [I] 114 H4
Vicchio [I] 110 F5
Vicdessos [F] 84 H5
Vicedo [E] 78 E1
Vic-en-Bigorre [F] 84 F3
Vicenza [I] 72 D6
Vic-Fezensac [F] 84 F2
Vichtis / Vihti [FIN] 176 G4
Vichy [F] 68 D1
Vickan [S] 160 G3
Vic-le-Comte [F] 68 D2
Vico [E] 84 A5
Vico [F] 114 A4
Vico del Gargano [I] 116 H6
Vico Equense [I] 120 E4
Vicoforte, Santuario di- [I] 108 G3
Vicovaro [I] 116 B5
Vic-sur-Aisne [F] 28 F6
Vic-sur-Cère [F] 68 B4
Victoire, Abbaye de la- [F] 42 G3
Victoria [M] 126 C5
Vidaga [LV] 198 F4
Vidago [P] 80 E3
Vidamlya [BY] 38 G2
Viðareiði [FR] 160 B1
Vidauban [F] 108 D5
Viddal [N] 180 D4
Viddalba [I] 118 D2
Vide [P] 86 F2
Videbæk [DK] 156 B1
Videle [RO] 204 D6
Videseter [N] 180 E5
Vidhas [AL] 128 B3
Vidigueira [P] 94 D2
Vidin [BG] 146 E2
Vidlin [GB] 6 H3
Vidnava [CZ] 50 D3
Vidsel [S] 196 A3
Vidzy [BY] 200 H4
Viechtach [D] 48 D6
Vieira [P] 86 C2
Vieja, Cueva de la- [E] 98 D5
Vieki [FIN] 196 G6
Viekšniai [LT] 198 C6
Vielikie Lazy [UA] 204 B3
Viella [E] 84 G5
Viella, Túnel de- [E] 84 F5
Vielsalm [B] 30 E6
Vienenburg [D] 32 H3
Vienne [F] 68 F3
Vieremä [FIN] 196 E6
Viernheim [D] 46 C4
Viersen [D] 30 G3
Vieru [RO] 148 C2
Vierumäki [FIN] 178 B2
Vierville [F] 26 E3
Vierzehnheiligen [D] 46 G3
Vierzon [F] 56 B3
Viesimo [FIN] 188 G3
Viešintos [LT] 200 G4
Viesīte [LV] 198 E6
Viesites [LV] 198 E6
Vieste [I] 116 H6
Vietas [S] 192 F5
Vietri di Potenza [I] 120 G4
Vietri sul Mare [I] 120 E4
Vieux-Boucau-les-Bains [F] 66 A6
Vievis [LT] 200 G5
Vif [F] 68 H5
Vig [DK] 156 F2
Vigeland [N] 164 C6
Vigévano [I] 70 F5
Vigge [S] 182 G3
Viggianello [I] 120 H6
Viggiano [I] 120 H5
Vígla [GR] 132 D3
Vígľaš [SK] 64 C3
Vigmostad [N] 164 D5
Vignale Monferrato [I] 70 E6
Vignanello [I] 114 H4
Vigneulles [F] 44 E4
Vignola [I] 110 E3
Vignola Mare [I] 118 D2
Vignory [F] 44 C6
Vigo [E] 78 B4
Vigo di Fassa [I] 72 D3
Vigrestad [N] 164 A4
Viguera [E] 90 B1
Vihantasalmi [FIN] 178 C1
Vihanti [FIN] 196 D4
Vihasjärvi [FIN] 176 G1
Vihiers [F] 54 D2
Vihren [BG] 130 B1
Vihtari [FIN] 188 E3
Vihtasuo [FIN] 196 G6
Vihti / Vichtis [FIN] 176 G4
Vihtijärvi [FIN] 176 G4
Vihtiläjärvi [FIN] 186 C6
Viiala [FIN] 176 F2
Viiksimo [FIN] 196 G4
Viinijärvi [FIN] 188 E2
Viinikoski [FIN] 196 E3
Viinistu [EST] 178 B6
Viisarimäki [FIN] 186 G5
Viitaila [FIN] 176 H2
Viitajärvi [FIN] 186 F2
Viitaniemi [FIN] 188 D1
Viitasaari [FIN] 186 G2
Viitavaara [FIN] 196 F4
Viitna [EST] 198 E1
Viiciems [LV] 198 F4
Vijenac [MNE] 144 E2
Vik [IS] 192 B3
Vik [N] 164 E5
Vik [N] 170 C2
Vik [N] 180 C4
Vik [N] 180 G1
Vik [N] 190 C3
Vik [S] 158 D3
Vik [S] 168 D2
Vika [N] 164 D3
Vika [S] 172 G3
Vika [S] 174 C4
Vikajärvi [FIN] 194 D7
Vikan [N] 180 F1
Vikane [N] 166 B3
Vikanes [N] 170 B3
Vikarbyn [S] 172 H3
Vikby [FIN] 186 B2
Vike [N] 180 F3
Vikebukt [N] 180 E3
Vikedal [N] 164 B1
Viken [S] 156 H1
Viken [S] 182 H4
Viker [N] 170 H4
Viker [S] 166 G2
Vikersund [N] 170 G5
Vikesá [N] 164 B4
Vikmanshyttan [S] 174 C5
Vikoč [BIH] 144 E2
Vikran [N] 192 F2
Viksjö [S] 184 E3
Viksøyri [N] 170 C2
Vikštejn [CZ] 50 E4
Viksvatn [N] 190 B5
Viktring [A] 74 B3
Vikvallen [S] 190 H3
Vikvarvet [N] 182 C2
Vila Baleira [P] 100 B3
Viladamat [E] 92 G3
Viladecans [E] 92 E4
Vila de Rei [P] 86 D3
Vila do Bispo [P] 94 A5
Vila do Conde [P] 80 B3
Vila do Porto [P] 100 E4
Vilafamés [E] 98 F3
Vila Fernando [P] 86 G2
Vila Flor [P] 80 E4
Vilafranca de Bonany [E] 104 E5
Vilafranca del Maestrat / Villafranca del Cid [E] 98 F2
Vilafranca del Penedès [E] 92 D4
Vila Franca de Xira [P] 86 B5
Vila Franca do Campo [P] 100 E3
Vila Fresca de Azeitão [P] 86 B6
Vilagarcía de Arousa [E] 78 B3
Vilaka [LV] 198 G4
Vilaller [E] 84 F6
Vila Mea [P] 80 E3
Vilameán [E] 78 B5
Vilamor [E] 84 G6
Vilamoura [P] 94 C5
Vilāni [LV] 198 F5
Vilanova d'Alcolea [E] 98 G3
Vilanova de Arousa [E] 78 B3
Vila Nova de Cerveira [P] 78 A5
Vila Nova de Famalicão [P] 80 C3
Vila Nova de Foz Côa [P] 80 E5
Vila Nova de Gaia [P] 80 B4
Vilanova de la Barca [E] 90 H4
Vila Nova de Milfontes [P] 94 B3
Vila Nova de Ourém [P] 86 D3
Vila Nova de Paiva [P] 80 D5
Vila Nova de S. André [P] 94 B2
Vila Nova de São Bento [P] 94 E3
Vila Nova do Corvo [P] 100 C3
Vilanova i la Geltrú [E] 92 D5
Vila Pouca de Aguiar [P] 80 D3
Vila Praia de Âncora [P] 78 A5
Vilarandelo [P] 80 E3
Vilar de Barrio [E] 78 D5
Vilardevós [E] 78 D6
Vila Real [P] 80 D4
Vila Real de Santo António [P] 94 D5
Vilar Formoso [P] 86 H2
Vila-rodona [E] 92 C4
Vilarouco [P] 80 E5
Vilars, Cova dels- [E] 90 H4
Vila-seca [E] 92 C5
Vilassar de Mar [E] 92 E4
Vila Velha de Ródão [P] 86 E4
Vila Verde [P] 78 B6
Vila Verde [P] 80 F3
Vila Verde da Raia [P] 80 E3
Vila Verde de Ficalho [P] 94 E3
Vila Viçosa [P] 86 E6
Vilches [E] 102 F1
Vildbjerg [DK] 160 C6
Vilémov [CZ] 48 H4
Vilhelmina [S] 190 F5
Vília [GR] 134 B6
Vilinska Jama [HR] 74 D6
Viljakkala [FIN] 186 D6
Viljandi [EST] 198 E3
Viljolahti [FIN] 188 E4
Vilkaviškis [LT] 24 E1
Vilkija [LT] 200 F5
Villa Adriana [I] 116 B5
Villaba del Rey [E] 98 B1
Villa Bartolomea [I] 110 F2
Villablanca [E] 94 D5
Villablino [E] 78 G4
Villabona [E] 84 B2
Villacañas [E] 96 G2
Villa Cancellieri [I] 126 F5
Villacarrillo [E] 102 F1
Villa Castelli [I] 122 F4
Villacastín [E] 88 E4
Villach [A] 72 H3
Villacidro [I] 118 C6
Villada [E] 82 C5
Villadangos del Páramo [E] 78 G6
Villa del Prado [E] 88 E6
Villa del Río [E] 102 D1
Villa de Ves [E] 98 D5
Villadiego [E] 82 E5
Villadoro [I] 126 E3
Villadossola [I] 70 E3
Villaeles de Valdavia [E] 82 D5
Villaescusa de Haro [E] 96 H3
Villa Estense [I] 110 G2
Villa Formosa [E] 86 E5
Villafranca del Bierzo [E] 78 F5
Villafranca del Cid / Vilafranca del Maestrat [E] 98 F2
Villafranca de los Barros [E] 94 G3
Villafranca de los Caballeros [E] 96 G3
Villafranca di Verona [I] 110 E1
Villafranca Montes de Oca [E] 82 F6
Villafranca Piemonte [I] 70 D6
Villafranca Tirrena [I] 124 B7
Villafrati [I] 126 D2
Villafrechós [E] 82 B6
Villafruela [E] 88 G1
Villafuerte [E] 88 F2
Villagarcia de la Torre [E] 94 H3
Village, Roche aux- [F] 44 C1
Villaggio Apulo [I] 122 E3
Villaggio Mancuso [I] 124 E5
Villagonzalo Pedernales [E] 82 E6
Villagordo [E] 102 E2
Villagrains [F] 66 C4
Villagrande Strisaili [I] 118 E5
Villaharta [E] 96 C6
Villahermosa [E] 96 G5
Villahoz [E] 88 G1
Villaines la Gonais [F] 42 C5
Villaines-la-Juhel [F] 26 F6
Villajos, Ermita de- [E] 96 G3
Villajoyosa / la Vila Joiosa [E] 104 E2
Villala [FIN] 188 F4
Villalba Alta [E] 78 E2
Villalba de Duero [E] 88 G2
Villalba de Guardo [E] 82 C4
Villalba del Alcor [E] 94 F6
Villalba de la Sierra [E] 98 C2
Villalba de los Alcores [E] 88 E1
Villalba de los Barros [E] 94 G2
Villalcázar de Sirga [E] 82 D5
Villalgordo del Marquesado [E] 98 A3
Villa Literno [I] 120 D3
Villalón de Campos [E] 82 C6
Villalpando [E] 82 B6
Villalpardo [E] 98 C4
Villaluenga [E] 96 F1
Villamalea [E] 98 C4
Villamañán [E] 78 H6
Villamanín de la Tercia [E] 78 H5
Villamanrique [E] 96 G6
Villamanrique de la Condesa [E] 94 F6
Villamar [I] 118 C6
Villamartín [E] 100 G3
Villamartín de Campos [E] 82 C6
Villamartín de Don Sancho [E] 82 C4
Villamassargia [I] 118 B7
Villamayor [E] 80 H6
Villamayor de Santiago [E] 96 H2
Villamediana de Iregua [E] 82 H6
Villamesias [E] 96 B2
Villa Minozzo [I] 110 D4
Villamuelas [E] 96 F2
Villandraut [F] 66 D4
Villandry [F] 54 F2
Villanova [I] 122 F3
Villanova d'Asti [I] 70 D6
Villanova Monteleone [I] 118 B3
Villanova Tulo [I] 118 D5
Villanúa [E] 84 D5
Villanubla [E] 88 E1
Villanueva de Alcardete [E] 96 H3
Villanueva de Algaidas [E] 102 C3
Villanueva de Argaño [E] 82 E5
Villanueva de Cameros [E] 90 B1
Villanueva de Cañedo [E] 80 H6
Villanueva de Córdoba [E] 96 C5
Villanueva de Gállego [E] 90 E3
Villanueva de Huerva [E] 90 E4
Villanueva del Aceral [E] 88 E3
Villanueva de la Fuente [E] 96 H5
Villanueva de la Jara [E] 98 B4
Villanueva de la Reina [E] 102 E1
Villanueva del Arzobispo [E] 102 G1
Villanueva de las Cruces [E] 94 E5
Villanueva de la Serena [E] 96 B3
Villanueva de la Sierra [E] 86 H3
Villanueva de las Torres [E] 102 F3
Villanueva de la Vera [E] 88 C5
Villanueva del Campo [E] 82 B6
Villanueva del Duque [E] 96 C5
Villanueva del Fresno [E] 94 F2
Villanueva de los Castillejos [E] 94 E5
Villanueva de los Infantes [E] 96 G5
Villanueva del Rey [E] 96 B5
Villanueva del Río Segura [E] 104 C2
Villanueva del Río y Minas [E] 94 H5
Villanueva del Trabuco [E] 102 C4
Villanueva de San Carlos [E] 104 H5
Villanueva de Sigena [E] 90 G4
Villanueva de Tapia [E] 102 C3
Villanuño de Valdavia [E] 82 D5
Villány [H] 76 B5
Villa Opicina [I] 72 H6
Villapalacios [E] 96 H6
Villapiana Scalo [I] 122 D6
Villaplana [I] 122 D6
Villa Potenza [I] 116 C1
Villapriolo [I] 126 E3
Villaputzu [I] 118 E6
Villaquejida [E] 82 B5
Villaquilambre [E] 78 H5
Villarcayo [E] 82 F4
Villard-de-Lans [F] 68 G5
Villardebelle [F] 106 B5
Villar de Cantos [E] 98 B3
Villar de Ciervo [E] 80 E6
Villardeciervos [E] 80 G3
Villar de Domingo García [E] 98 B1
Villardefrades [E] 88 D1
Villar del Arzobispo [E] 98 E3
Villar del Pedroso [E] 96 C1
Villar del Pozo [E] 98 B5
Villar del Rey [E] 86 F6
Villar de Olalla [E] 98 B2
Villar de Peralonso [E] 80 G6
Villar de Rena [E] 96 B3
Villar de Río [E] 90 C2
Villarejo de Fuentes [E] 96 H2
Villarejo de Salvanés [E] 96 G1
Villares de la Reina [E] 80 H6
Villares del Saz [E] 98 B2
Villargordo del Cabriel [E] 98 C4
Villaricos [E] 104 A5
Villarino [E] 80 F5
Villariño de Conso [E] 78 D6
Villarluengo [E] 98 F1
Villarmayor [E] 80 G6
Villa Romana del Casale [I] 126 E4
Villarosa [I] 126 E3
Villar Perosa [I] 70 C6
Villarquemado [E] 98 D1
Villarramiel [E] 82 C6
Villarreal de San Carlos [E] 88 A6
Villarreal- la Vila Reial [E] 98 F3
Villarrobledo [E] 96 H4
Villarroga de los Pinares [E] 98 F1
Villarroja [E] 84 A5
Villarroya de la Sierra [E] 90 C4
Villarrubia de los Ojos [E] 96 F3
Villars [CH] 70 C2
Villars-les-Dombes [F] 68 G2
Villars-sur-Var [F] 108 E4
Villarta [E] 98 C4
Villarta de los Montes [E] 96 D3
Villarta de San Juan [E] 96 F3
Villarubia de Santiago [E] 96 G1
Villasadino [E] 82 D5
Villasalto [I] 118 D6
Villasana de Mena [E] 82 F4
Villa San Giovanni [I] 124 C7
Villa Santa Maria [I] 116 D5
Villasante [E] 82 F4
Villa Santina [I] 72 G4
Villaseco de los Gamitos [E] 80 G6
Villaseco de los Reyes [E] 80 G5
Villasequilla [E] 96 F2
Villasimíus [I] 118 D7
Villa S. Lucia degli Abruzzi [I] 116 D4
Villasor [I] 118 C6
Villasrubias [E] 86 H3
Villastar [E] 98 D2
Villatobas [E] 96 G2
Villatoro [E] 82 E6
Villatoya [E] 98 C4
Villava [E] 84 B4
Villavelayo [E] 90 A1
Villaverde del Río [E] 94 H5
Villaverde de Trucios [E] 82 G3
Villaviciosa [E] 82 C2
Villaviciosa [E] 96 C6
Villavieja [E] 80 F6
Villa Vomano [I] 116 C3
Villé [F] 58 D2
Villebois-Lavalette [F] 66 E2
Ville-Devant-Chaumont [F] 44 D3
Villedieu-les-Poêles [F] 26 D4
Villedomain [F] 54 G3
Ville-en-Tardenois [F] 44 B3
Villefagnan [F] 54 E5
Villefontaine [F] 68 G3
Villefort [F] 68 D6
Villefranche [F] 108 F4
Villefranche-d'Albigeois [F] 106 C2
Villefranche-de-Conflent [F] 92 F1
Villefranche-de-Lauragais [F] 106 A4
Villefranche-de-Lonchat [F] 66 E3
Villefranche-de-Panat [F] 106 D2
Villefranche-de-Rouergue [F] 66 H5
Villefranche-du-Périgord [F] 66 F4
Villefranche-sur-Cher [F] 54 H2
Villefranche-sur-Saône [F] 68 F2
Villegats [F] 54 E5
Villel [E] 98 D2
Villemur [F] 106 A2
Villena [E] 104 D1
Villenauxe-la-Grande [F] 42 H5
Villeneuve [F] 66 H5
Villeneuve [F] 106 G3
Villeneuve d'Ascq [F] 28 F3
Villeneuve-de-Berg [F] 68 E6
Villeneuve-de-Marsan [F] 66 C6
Villeneuve-l'Archevêque [F] 42 H6
Villeneuve-Loubet [F] 108 E4
Villeneuve-sur-Allier [F] 56 D5
Villeneuve-sur-Lot [F] 66 E5
Villeneuve-sur-Yonne [F] 42 G6
Villerbon [F] 42 D6
Villeréal [F] 66 F4
Villeromaine [F] 42 D6
Villers [B] 30 C5
Villers [F] 26 G3
Villers-Bocage [F] 26 E3
Villers-Bretonneux [F] 28 E5
Villers-Cotterêts [F] 42 H3
Villersexel [F] 58 C4
Villers-le-Lac [F] 58 C5
Villerville [F] 26 G3
Villeseque [F] 66 G5
Ville-sur-Illon [F] 58 C2
Villetta Barrea [I] 116 D6
Villiers-St-Georges [F] 42 H4
Villingen [D] 58 F3
Villingsberg [S] 166 G3
Villmanstrand / Lappeenranta [FIN] 178 E2
Villnäs / Askainen [FIN] 176 D4
Villoldo [E] 82 C5
Villon [F] 56 F2
Villorba [I] 72 E5
Villoria [E] 88 D3
Villoslada de Cameros [E] 90 B1
Villstad [S] 162 C3
Villvattnet [S] 190 H5
Vilmajor [H] 76 F3
Vilmány [H] 64 G3
Vilnius [LT] 200 G5
Vilobacka [FIN] 186 C1
Vilovo [SRB] 142 G1
Vilppula [FIN] 186 E5
Vils [DK] 160 C4
Vilsbiburg [D] 60 F3
Vilseck [D] 46 H5
Vilshofen [D] 60 H3
Vilshult [S] 162 D6
Vilsund [DK] 160 C4
Vilunai [LT] 24 G1
Vilusi [MNE] 144 D3
Viluste [EST] 198 F3
Vilyeyka [BY] 202 B5
Vimianzo [E] 78 B2
Vimieiro [P] 86 D6
Vimioso [P] 80 G4
Vimmerby [S] 162 F2
Vimoutiers [F] 26 G4
Vimpeli [FIN] 186 D2
Vimperk [CZ] 62 A2
Vina [SRB] 146 D4
Vinac [BIH] 142 C4
Vinádio [I] 108 E3
Vinaixa [E] 92 C4
Vinaròs [E] 92 A6
Vinarsko [BG] 148 F4
Vinay [F] 68 G4
Vinça [F] 92 F1
Vinchiaturo [I] 120 E1
Vinci [I] 110 E5
Vindbyholt [DK] 156 G4
Vindelgransele [S] 190 G4
Vindeln [S] 190 H5
Vinderslev [DK] 160 D6
Vinderup [DK] 160 C5
Vindsvik [N] 164 C2
Vinebre [E] 90 H6
Vinga [RO] 76 G5
Vinga [RO] 76 H4
Vingåker [S] 168 B4
Vingelen [N] 182 C4
Vingnes [N] 172 B2
Vingrau [F] 106 C6
Vingrom [N] 170 H2
Vingstad [N] 192 G3
Vinhais [P] 80 F3
Vinica [BG] 148 E3
Vinica [MK] 128 G1
Vinica [SK] 64 C4
Vinica [SLO] 112 G1
Viničani [MK] 128 F2
Viniegra de Abajo [E] 90 B1
Vinishte [BG] 146 F3
Vinjani [HR] 144 B2
Vinje [N] 164 E1
Vinje [N] 170 C3
Vinjeøra [N] 180 G2
Vinkovci [HR] 142 E1
Vinliden [S] 190 G5
Vinnytsia [UA] 202 C8
Vinon-sur-Verdon [F] 108 C4
Vinslöv [S] 158 D1
Vinsnes [N] 164 E3
Vinsternes [N] 180 F1
Vinstra [N] 170 H1
Vintgar [SLO] 74 B4
Vintjärn [S] 174 D3
Vintl / Vandoies [I] 72 E2
Vintrosa [S] 166 G3
Viñuela de Sayago [E] 80 G5
Viñuelas [E] 88 G5
Vinuesa [E] 90 B2
Vinzelberg [D] 34 B2
Violès [F] 106 H3
Viozene [I] 108 G3
Vipava [SLO] 74 A5
Vipiteno / Sterzing [I] 72 D2
Vira [HR] 144 A2
Virdois / Virrat [FIN] 186 D4
Vire [F] 26 E4
Viré [F] 56 G6
Vire Court [F] 40 B3

ROAD DISTANCES
DISTANZE STRADALI
DISTANCIAS KILOMÉTRICAS
DISTANCES ROUTIÈRES
STRASSENENTFERNUNGEN

Frankfurt am Main-Ljubljana = 803 km

Column headers (diagonal), left to right:
Amsterdam, Athina, Barcelona, Belfast, Beograd, Berlin, Bern, Birmingham, Bordeaux, Bratislava, Brussel / Bruxelles, București, Budapest, Dublin, Edinburgh, Frankfurt am Main, Genève, Göteborg, Hamburg, Helsinki / Helsingfors, istanbul, København, Köln, Kyïv, Lisboa, Ljubljana, London, Luxembourg, Madrid

```
2885
1549 2224
1213 3025 2229
1779 1044 1981 2712
655 2362 1863 1768 1257
835 1674 944 1687 1363 922
372 2730 1691 525 2290 1297 1166
1081 2365 552 1702 2007 1634 852 1161
1225 1618 1866 2226 571 671 938 1704 1854
206 2783 1344 1032 1673 763 637 514 883 1181
2181 1106 2597 3209 619 1646 1893 2692 2613 977 2136
1398 1429 1897 2390 377 864 1111 1873 2020 194 1353 826
641 3027 1944 164 2587 1594 1466 304 1483 2015 814 2989 2181
1190 3243 2160 250 2802 1810 1571 460 1698 2231 1030 3205 2396 416
445 2396 1323 1434 1281 550 423 917 1150 788 400 1744 961 1207 1429
908 1635 778 1653 1331 1119 165 1136 687 1088 706 1946 1261 1426 1648 573
1178 2924 2602 1381 1810 535 1684 905 2252 1248 1307 2258 1440 1056 1050 1270 1837
463 2776 1763 1592 1547 294 910 1074 1489 985 591 1961 1178 1364 697 487 1059 503
1839 3347 3203 1520 2226 1046 2195 1599 2728 1631 1870 2070 1760 1535 1458 1781 2348 636 1014
2747 1092 2913 3680 935 2179 2294 3212 2929 1509 2605 681 1320 3452 3675 2213 2261 2778 2493 3208
920 2767 2220 2053 1664 390 1378 1535 1927 1100 1048 2110 1292 1686 2048 955 1528 316 355 827 2630
265 2578 1342 1251 1464 575 585 734 1062 972 208 1928 1145 1024 1258 192 735 1141 425 1696 2396 882
2111 1994 3093 3224 1322 1378 2190 2707 2988 1251 2123 888 1123 2996 3219 1874 2340 2037 1675 1338 1569 1883 1935
2244 3399 1237 2869 3188 2797 2074 2352 1198 3067 2082 3804 3103 2641 2864 2340 1915 3442 2670 3899 4119 3117 2250 4187
1241 1572 1455 2223 530 999 836 1706 1471 435 1153 1146 443 1996 2218 803 802 1490 1202 2119 1462 1346 987 1565 2628
442 2910 1450 708 2039 1090 947 193 989 1521 320 2495 1687 480 645 720 905 743 898 1723 2964 1338 539 2369 2153 1496
363 2355 1149 1246 1469 762 431 728 946 1010 213 2086 1183 1018 1233 240 500 1432 610 1928 2483 1130 188 2072 2102 956 529
1773 3369 614 2397 2573 2343 1535 1879 706 2458 1591 3206 2489 2169 2392 1849 1374 2901 2134 3425 3556 2631 1735 3598 619 2046 1509 1615
661 3415 1794 406 2374 1425 1282 138 1333 1865 664 2837 2031 214 339 1064 1240 1053 1242 1501 3309 1677 876 2706 2497 1838 323 888 206
1236 2306 505 1906 1526 1541 623 1388 647 1419 1034 2141 1441 1678 1881 1003 422 2243 1442 2797 2500 1965 1025 2542 1662 999 1172 832 109
1077 656 977 1928 1026 1033 350 1391 985 919 876 1642 942 1700 1891 662 318 1925 1112 2442 1990 1574 823 2037 2134 499 1178 669 156
1742 2448 2878 2856 1513 1124 1938 2338 2714 1178 1850 1341 1125 2628 2833 1620 2205 1654 1408 783 1997 1510 1662 557 3927 1593 2163 1817 357
2449 2864 3584 3559 2084 1830 2644 3042 3420 1885 2556 1809 1854 3331 3539 2326 2933 1503 2114 1089 2471 1694 2368 871 4489 2300 2874 2523 427
827 1990 1370 3426 947 585 437 1297 1278 466 739 1564 639 1588 1792 390 591 1083 789 2058 1909 1242 573 1718 2452 407 1074 521 196
1852 592 1555 2704 1161 1693 1132 2166 1698 1376 1628 1240 1399 2477 2666 1444 1085 2664 1908 3174 1414 2370 1600 2492 2712 935 1953 1442 214
1532 3221 2790 823 2109 834 1981 902 2514 1547 1618 2557 1739 838 753 1567 2134 298 802 700 3077 613 1446 2336 3686 1789 1026 1714 321
508 2895 1039 1128 1800 1068 565 610 583 1324 312 2396 1489 900 1113 573 529 1626 887 2178 2778 1365 488 2428 1736 1240 410 373 129
2087 3242 1076 2712 2986 2637 1916 2195 1000 2889 1893 3602 2902 2484 2696 2153 1758 3249 2450 3752 3971 2908 2072 3997 300 2459 1824 1930 531
887 1946 1709 1952 900 341 769 1435 1601 328 902 1304 522 1725 1923 510 965 912 645 1865 1860 764 693 1362 2687 664 1222 731 221
1618 2807 2825 2849 1917 996 1971 2257 2704 1333 1704 1760 1408 2621 2763 1527 2137 779 1273 309 2402 1276 1537 1029 3803 1748 2050 1799 339
1654 895 1354 2516 985 1493 932 1968 1503 1175 1457 1433 1198 2288 2468 1243 884 2466 1710 2977 1603 2181 1405 2294 2514 755 1755 1244 194
2180 3190 3388 3507 2241 1558 2546 2831 3279 1809 2360 2116 1842 3279 3339 2127 2712 827 1848 380 2748 1018 2157 1196 4164 2223 2619 2375 422
1727 1121 1990 2763 303 1523 1372 2245 2007 849 1737 824 577 2535 2704 1290 1350 2079 1691 2568 1173 1881 1554 1601 3160 539 2006 1478 260
2236 3340 998 2863 2957 2838 1922 2343 1183 2842 2057 3573 2935 2636 2858 2345 1759 3469 2662 3980 4073 3119 2255 3991 403 2430 1974 2128 510
2139 654 2402 3136 424 1668 1783 2619 2418 998 2143 598 800 2908 3115 1702 1750 2210 2098 2648 781 2062 1961 1530 3567 951 2413 1890 299
2159 735 2358 3092 380 1624 1739 2615 2375 954 2099 372 756 2864 3071 1714 1707 2166 2054 2604 582 2018 1917 1310 3523 907 2369 1846 294
1580 3246 2935 1354 2155 879 2029 1433 2562 1593 1704 2603 1785 1369 1292 1615 2182 470 848 166 3123 661 1530 1338 3733 1835 1557 1762 325
1920 3347 3127 3175 2226 1310 2284 2568 3017 1631 2097 2070 1760 2947 3036 1829 2450 470 1585 0 3208 661 1895 1338 4105 2119 2380 2076 374
2333 516 2597 3336 619 1862 1978 2854 2613 1193 2338 696 1001 3100 3310 1955 1945 2434 2293 2848 646 2286 2156 1608 3499 1145 2608 2085 318
2103 735 1805 3244 566 1888 1748 2702 2383 1211 2058 886 1014 3016 3210 1842 1715 2484 2182 2963 1053 2336 2045 1755 3572 915 2497 1979 295
3004 4692 4371 2199 3914 2663 3619 3772 4153 3264 3330 4280 3460 2479 2199 3206 3772 1014 2710 1381 4074 2247 3121 2719 5324 3530 3567 3352 485
1897 2565 351 2501 2322 2202 1283 1983 803 2206 1681 2937 2285 2273 2482 1663 1123 2908 2151 3449 3299 2630 1721 3341 894 1795 1629 1492 342
1636 2550 2776 2841 1487 1018 1948 2263 2654 1077 1756 1401 1121 2613 2727 1510 2114 1039 1280 596 2044 1491 1555 738 3821 1492 2023 1803 332
1202 2097 2342 2317 1158 584 1519 1799 2225 643 1309 1240 788 2089 2293 1084 1685 1115 868 970 2119 967 1121 774 3387 1057 1594 1320 291
1148 1664 1789 2162 614 676 861 1644 1777 77 1104 1022 240 1938 2154 711 1011 1318 936 1697 1576 1166 895 1328 2990 378 1444 933 238
1326 1435 1586 2326 405 1101 968 1843 1603 417 1328 1014 347 2098 2302 943 936 1592 1279 2131 1358 1444 1145 1403 2751 135 1594 1074 219
```